BLOOD AND BROKEN GLASS

I wish to dedicate this book to the memory of Gerard 'Soggy' O'Hara, an 18-year-old innocent Catholic, gunned down by Stephen 'Top Gun' McKeag and another thug from the UFF on 27 September1992.

'Gerard was a quiet, loveable, innocent little fella who loved nothing more than playing with his young nephews, listening to music and watching television. The nearest he got to the Troubles and violence was watching through a window.'

Gerard's family priest at the innocent boy's funeral.

BLOOD AND BROKEN GLASS

Northern Ireland's Violent Countdown Towards Peace, 1991–93

Ken M. Wharton

Helion & Company

Helion & Company Limited
Unit 8, Amherst Business Centre
Budbrooke Road
Warwick
CV34 5WE
England
Tel. 01926 499 619
Email: info@helion.co.uk
Website: www.helion.co.uk
Twitter: @helionbooks
Visit our blog http://blog.helion.co.uk/

Published by Helion & Company 2019. Reprinted in paperback 2022
Designed and typeset by Donald Sommerville, Montacute, Somerset
Cover designed by Paul Hewitt, Battlefield Design (www.battlefield-design.co.uk)

The opinions expressed in this book are those of the individuals quoted and do not necessarily accord with views held by the author or publisher.

ISBN 978-1-804510-52-0

British Library Cataloguing-in-Publication Data.
A catalogue record for this book is available from the British Library.

Dedications

To every man and woman who served in Northern Ireland, irrespective of your corps or regiment, irrespective of your roles; you are my comrades and the honour of knowing you is all mine.

To the innocent civilians on both sides of the sectarian divide who only wanted to lead a peaceful life, my empathy and my respect, especially Michelle Williamson, Elaine Hsellhoff and Tanya Austin.

To the late Ken 'B' and Colour Sergeant Ken Ambrose, Tim Marsh, Rob McGough and Dave Parkinson. Your passing has left a void in all our lives.

To the 1,300+ who never returned to their loved ones.

To Steven McLaughlin, Darren Ware, Dave Hallam, Ken Pettengale, Gren Wilson, Dave Judge, Dave Pomfret, John Corr, Len Chappell, Les Welling, John Hollis: to the Royal Green Jackets, *Celer et Audax.*

To Mike Sangster, Tim Francis, John & Bernie Swaine, Mick Potter, Royal Artillery, *Ubique.*

To Mike Day, for your inspiration and tireless help. Mark Denton, for your tireless enthusiasm.

To Mick 'Benny' Hill, Steve 'Foxy' Norman, Andy Thomas, Royal Anglians. Dougie Durrant, ADU.

To Mark 'C', James Henderson, B. R., Haydn Williams, Glen Espie, Michael and Emma Forde, Mary Gilbride, Elle Mac, Maureen Herron and the men and Greenfinches of the Ulster Defence Regiment.

To Mark and Allison Overson who started me on a long road.

To Kenny Donaldson and the staff at SEFF.
Lee McDowell at the Ely Centre, Enniskillen.

To J. B., ATO.

To Kenneth Anderson, Kev Wright, Tommy Clarke, Nick Sword, Royal Corps of Transport.

To Dave 'Slops' Langston, Army Catering Corps.

To Eddie Atkinson & Mick Brooks, Green Howards.

My cousin John Leighton, a Royal Artillery TA soldier.

To the children and loved ones of our fallen: Tammy Card, Ann Travers, Tracey Abraham, Stevie Karen Rumble, Carol Richards, Eddie Haughey, Stephen Gault, Anita and Martin Haughey, Craig Agar, Rita Martin, Ruth Forrest, Brian Johnston, Kate Carroll, Donna Munro and Mark Olphert.

To my children: Anne-Marie, Anna-Martina, Jonathan, Jenny, Robbie, Alex and Nathan; love you all, and always will.

To my grandchildren: Sherriden, Kelsy, William, Sammy, Layla-Mae, Megan, Clara and Lydia; and to Ezra and to my adopted and very loved grandchildren: Morgan Addy, Charlie and Ralf Pearson.

Finally, to Adam Griffiths, Narelle Pearson, Andy Thomas, Fiona Addy, Alice Binbay and Dean Holmes: ever-patient, ever-persevering partners of my children. And to Lily Flaskas and Layla Fowle in Queensland.

To my Canadian friend Sandie Blair.

'This senseless act of barbarity, carried out in such a cowardly fashion by faceless criminals is in sharp contrast to the dedicated and caring attitude exemplified by these two officers.'

RUC Chief Constable Hugh Annesley following the murder of two RUC officers, Drew Beacom and Ernest Smith, at Fivemiletown on 12 December, 1993.

'When you have to scrape up the remains of your family and friends and put them into black bin bags after an explosion, you don't easily forget. This sounds so clinical, but it is a fact of life here: you never get all the remains. For days afterwards, you see the grey crows feasting on the bits you could not find. That is very, very hard for anyone to take.'

Leslie Finlay on the deaths of over 20 of his friends, all killed by the IRA.

'Catholics and Protestants drink in the pub together. They enjoyed their drink together, but it is so sad it had to end up like this.'

Jim Moore, landlord of the Rising Sun at Greysteel after the UFF slaughtered seven people in the 'trick or treat' massacre.

Contents

List of Plates		xi
Foreword *by Mark Urban*		xiii
My Thoughts		xv
Introduction		17
Part One: 1991		
1.	January	21
2.	February	26
3.	March	36
4.	April	45
5.	May	52
6.	June	65
7.	July	74
8.	August	80
9.	September	90
10.	October	99
11.	'You Evil Cowards'	106
12.	December	121
Part Two: 1992		
13.	January	131
14.	February	144
15.	March	157
16.	April	161
17.	May	170
18.	June	176
19.	July	183
20.	August	188
21.	September	197
22.	October	204
23.	November	210
24.	December	218
Part Three: 1993		
25.	January	227
26.	February	235
27.	March	243

28. April 255
29. May 263
30. June 269
31. July 274
32. August 283
33. September 291
34. October 300
35. November 325
36. December 332

Select Bibliography 342
Index 345

Plates

Solicitor Pat Finucane, killed by a Loyalist murder gang in Belfast. (*Pacemaker Press*)
Sinn Féin's Gerry Adams and Martin McGuinness at the funeral of PIRA man Patrick Kelly in 1987. (*Pacemaker Press*)
Memorial to the UDR soldiers killed in the PIRA attack at Glenanne Barracks, 31 May 1991.
Evidence of the desecration of the memorial at Teebane.
Monument to the workmen murdered at Teebane crossroads on 17 January 1992.
Alleged site of the Teebane bomb's trigger point.
The approximate site of the Teebane blast.
The signpost which one of the Teebane survivors saw when he recovered consciousness.
David Harkness, one of the victims of the Teebane bomb blast. (*Courtesy of Ruth Forrest*)
Site of the UFF murder of five Catholics at a betting shop on the Lower Ormeau Road in Belfast, 5 February 1992, and the memorial that now stands nearby.
The scene outside the Brian Graham bookmaker's shop, North Queen Street, after a shooting when five men were injured, 29 April 1993. (*Belfast Telegraph*)
Michelle Baird (aged seven), Evelyn Baird (27), Sharon McBride (29) and Leanne Murray (13), all murdered by the IRA in the Shankill bomb blast. (*Belfast Telegraph*)
The scene of the UFF attack on Catholic workmen at the Andersonstown Cleansing Depot, October 1993.
The modern-day site of the Rising Sun pub at Greysteel where the UVF murdered eight drinkers on 30 October 1993.
A UDA mural in the Rathcoole/Rathfern area.
The 'temporary' peace lines still divide Belfast. This one is on Cupar Way, separating the Catholic Springfield Road and Falls Road from the Protestant Shankill.

Foreword

Mark Urban

There's no easy way to tell the story of the British Army's campaign in Northern Ireland. In the form of Operation Banner, its Ministry of Defence codename, it went on for 38 years. These years of conflict involved thousands of lives lost, hundreds of battalion 'emergency tours', and dozens of long-established bases whose names became engraved in the Army's collective consciousness.

It was not a conflict of major military offensives or battles, Operation Motorman, the move against paramilitary 'no go areas' in 1972 being the exception that proves the rule. So how do you chart its ups and downs, its many tragic losses, and the overall shape of the conflict?

Ken Wharton's answer has been to break down nearly four decades of Operation Banner into multiple volumes. The emphasis, since he started producing his books in 2008, has been on voices from the British military. His focus is unashamedly that of the Parachute Regiment Tom in Newry or the bombardier 'stagging on' for hours in his sangar overlooking the Bogside. These are not intended to be balanced accounts of the 'there were bad men on all sides' variety but relay the views of the men and women in khaki. They use words that I wouldn't, but then that's sort of the point of these books. The voices of the ordinary soldier were surprisingly rarely heard during the Troubles themselves.

As a newspaper reporter trying to cover the upcoming 20th anniversary of Operation Banner in the late 1980s, I had to apply repeatedly to be allowed to accompany soldiers on the streets and write about their experiences. In the end it was only by pointing out that I had just returned from Afghanistan, where I had been allowed to embed with Soviet Army soldiers on operations, that I was able to overcome the MoD's absurd position that reporting on the Army in Northern Ireland by British national newspaper correspondents was, in their words, 'unhelpful'. For many years then, the ordinary soldier, experiencing operations in rural Fermanagh or the Divis Street flats, was effectively silenced by his or her own political masters.

When some spike in violence or tragedy occasionally brought the issue centre stage there were various phrases used to describe the military role in Northern Ireland, from being piggy in the middle, to holding the ring, buying time, or reducing violence to 'acceptable levels'. Doing this involved a great deal of difficult, dangerous, and unglamorous work. Often mundane, or mind-numbingly boring, sometimes terrifying, the foot patrols or OP stags went on year after year, rain or shine, on a scale that almost defies any chronicler.

Ken's mission, though, has been to tell this untellable story. And you only need to read some of the many five-star reviews of his books of Amazon to see that he has touched a chord with readers. There are many from those who served, who thank him for conveying what it was like, and many others who did not and are simply grateful that these experiences have been related.

This latest volume, *Blood and Broken Glass*, focuses on the years 1991–3. By this point the Provisional IRA campaign had reduced in intensity as the protagonists inched towards a political endgame, and as the secret war succeeded in penetrating, in order to undermine them, many of its active service units. At this time, though, their sectarian enemies, notably the UFF and UVF, stepped up their own campaign of murder and intimidation. The view that emerges in *Blood and Broken Glass* is very much an attitude of a plague on both their houses, as far as the perpetrators of Loyalist and Republican violence were concerned. While some in military intelligence colluded with the sectarian killers, the view of the ordinary soldier emerges from these pages as neutral – or rather one of contempt for the men of violence in both communities.

With this latest book, Ken's series inches closer to its finale. What he's done, like so many of those who patrolled the streets during those decades of operations, is perform a necessary task that others were unwilling to take on.

Mark Urban is a writer and broadcaster,
the author of several bestselling works of military history,
including *Big Boys' Rules*, *Rifles* and *Task Force Black.*

My Thoughts

I have often been asked about my thoughts on Northern Ireland and the Troubles, not just about my own tours, but of the 1,400 plus soldiers' deaths of which I have written. By the time I have finished my 11th book, I will have covered every single Operation Banner military death, honouring those who fell in or as a consequence of the Troubles. I will brook no argument from those who maintain that the MoD's figure of *circa* 750 is correct. The real toll was twice that, and until I breathe my last, I will fight to uphold their memories thanks to the good offices of Mark Campbell and Michael Sangster.

Although this is of no relevance to my chronicling of the Troubles, I am currently reading a book about the life and murders of paedophile killer, Robert Black. This superb book by Robert Giles and Chris Clark contains the following quote: '*His little victims, like all children who die young, were angels.*' I would like to echo his poignant words and further dedicate this book and all those that I have written or will write, to the angels of Northern Ireland who died during the Troubles.

As I write of each individual, I cannot pretend that there are not tears in my eyes. I think that the ones who will remain in my heart and who will re-visit my final moments on earth are:

Sergeant John Haughey, Royal Artillery,
mortally wounded, yet still concerned enough as to ask after
the safety of his lads.

Trooper James Nowasad, Royal Tank Regiment,
unknowingly smiling at the IRA assassin sent to kill him.

Rifleman Dave Walker, Royal Green Jackets,
alone with his thoughts on the roof of North Howard Street Mill on a hot July night.

Lance Corporal Alfie Johnston, Ulster Defence Regiment,
father of four young children, who was killed whilst inspecting a suspect vehicle
at Cherrymount, Enniskillen.

Private Gary Barlow, Queen's Lancashire Regiment,
terrified and alone and surrounded by female predators from the Falls Road.

Lance Corporal Davie Card, Royal Green Jackets,
as his comrades desperately tried to reach him after he was mortally wounded
at Bernagh Drive in Andersonstown.

Private Tommy Stoker, Light Infantry,
fatally wounded on his first day in Belfast, lying there, uncomprehending
in a derelict house in the Ardoyne.

To every single one of our fallen, it is my absolute honour, but sad privilege to remember you all.

Ken Wharton

Introduction

I am not afraid to judge the recent past and whilst I come down largely on the side of the Security Forces (SF), I am not afraid to include the 'lumps and bumps' of that history, even where this is critical of the parts played by the British Army and the Royal Ulster Constabulary (RUC).

So, I would ask all those members of Sinn Féin, their 'armchair warrior' supporters and the UK Labour left: if the North was absorbed into the Republic and places such as Belfast, Londonderry – which they would re-name 'Derry' – and Lisburn became part of Ireland, what changes would result? What differences would the new Irish citizens see on the streets? Apart from road signs and speed limits in kilometres rather than miles, and an almost overnight proliferation of Irish language signs, what would the differences really be? An Garda Síochána uniforms instead of Police Service of Northern Ireland (PSNI) ones; An Post instead of the Royal Mail, but what else?

Would the air become freer, easier to breathe, would it feel like 'liberty'? Or would the new citizenship still have to pay income tax and VAT? Would they still have to pay parking fees and fines, would they still have to obey government and local council rules? Of course, they would, and there would be few discernible distinctions or differences. So, for all that violence, those 4,000+ deaths, all those billions of pounds wasted, all those grieving families and entrenched hatred and division over nearly four decades, the only difference would be that they would pay their income tax to a suited man in an office sitting in front of the tricolour instead of the Union flag.

Part One

1991

The war dragged on into its 23rd year, another year of violence and seemingly interminable struggle, as both sets of paramilitaries continued killing in the same nihilistic manner. It was a year in which 27 soldiers would lose their lives, 13 of them in non-terrorist incidents; two of the deaths would be former Ulster Defence Regiment (UDR) soldiers, killed because of past association as the Regiment lost 11 more members. The Royal Green Jackets lost five men, all killed in non-combat situations. It was a year in which the IRA proved that when it came to the 'unthinkable' they could do the unthinkable, when they actually bombed a hospital! In all, 119 people died in or as a consequence of the Troubles as the Republicans struggled on, taking lives in their pursuit of an impossible victory, and the Loyalists continued doing what they were best at: killing innocent Catholics. A total of 55 civilians would die this year, the highest number since 1976.

1

January

Four people died during this month; there were no military deaths, but an RUC Reserve (RUCR) member was killed, as were two innocent Catholics in clearly sectarian attacks. Additionally, a member of the Provisional IRA killed himself in unusual circumstances.

Shortly before midnight on New Year's Day, Patrick Sheehy (31), a gunman in the Provisional IRA, was found dead at a shop in Nenagh, Co. Tipperary, in the Irish Republic. Sheehy and another PIRA man, John Conaghty, were linked to an IRA bomb factory in north London which the police had stumbled on in December 1988, whilst in pursuit of a stolen car. A search turned up automatic and semi-automatic weapons, ammunition, 150 pounds of Semtex high explosive and a hit list of almost 100 British political figures and other officials headed by Prime Minister Margaret Thatcher. It is also alleged that Sheehy was the bomber who killed 11 Royal Marine bandsmen in a huge explosion at Deal Barracks in Kent in September 1989 and he was also linked to an IRA bombing attack on an Army barracks at Mill Hill in August 1988, which killed REME soldier Michael Robbins.

Sheehy, also known as the 'Jackal' – no doubt competing with the leader of the UVF's mid-Ulster brigade, Robin Jackson, for the epithet – was buried at Ballysteen in a cemetery on a hilltop there; some six years later, Sinn Féin activist Coireall McCurtain referred to the mass murderer as 'a dedicated and brave Volunteer'. I doubt if the bereaved families from Deal or Mill Hill would agree with that eulogy. Various press agencies reported that Patrick Sheehy had evaded arrest for some time and had been pursued from West Germany to the Irish republic; his death in Tipperary was noted to be as a result of a gunshot wound.

On the 2nd, in a gesture of conciliation with the southern Irish, an invitation to Mary Robinson, President of the Irish Republic, to visit Belfast, was mooted by both Loyalists and Nationalists. However, when this was put to a vote, it was overwhelmingly defeated by Loyalist councillors on Belfast City Council and the invite was withdrawn.

The following Saturday – the 5th – after a period of relative quiet, the Provisionals launched a series of incendiary attacks in districts outside the secured area of Belfast city centre. In the resulting explosions, although there were no deaths, a factory and six Protestant-owned shops were destroyed. The 'economic war' went on, although the Republicans must have instinctively realised that their terror campaign was failing, though this was never publicly acknowledged. The British were not going to be 'driven into the sea' and nor was there an appetite amongst the Ulster Scots to be 'resettled' in Scotland. On the Monday, in the wake of the weekend attacks, Richard Needham, a senior man at the Northern Ireland Office (NIO), was very outspoken in his criticisms of Gerry Adams, who, in his capacity as

President of Sinn Féin – and *not* as leader of the Provisional IRA – had failed to criticise his terrorist comrades. Given that Adams was strangely quiet following atrocities such as La Mon, the Droppin' Well, Claudy, Kingsmills and the Abercorn, it was hardly a shock that he would fail to condemn the fire-bombings. Needham told the media that 'Mr Adams demands jobs for West Belfast; would these jobs also be fire-bombed by the IRA?' This stirred the bearded one and former barman into accusing Mr Needham of 'theatrical hysterics'.

On the same day, that the IRA were wrecking businesses in Belfast, the UVF killed another Catholic, this time in a remote area near Lurgan, in Co. Armagh, as the mid-Ulster brigade struck yet again. Sometime during Friday 4th, just as their Republican rivals were preparing to send their matchbox and cassette-style incendiary devices into Belfast, the UVF hijacked a car in Lurgan. A three-man murder squad drove into the rural area of Magheralin, between Moira and Lurgan, parked, and entered the home of the Lynch family in Acres Road, through an unlocked door. They surprised Gervais Lynch (26), who was helping look after the house whilst his parents and sister were at Saturday night Mass. The gang shot him three times with an AK-47 automatic rifle, and left him mortally wounded in the porch of the house. His lifeless body was discovered by his shocked family later that evening. He had no known connections with the Republican movement and was simply the victim of a random sectarian killing.

The killing was almost certainly the handiwork of Robin 'the Jackal' Jackson, a man described by Anne Cadwallader, as 'one of the most prolific killers of the Troubles'. In her book *Lethal Allies* she writes: 'The number of people he killed ranges from a conservative estimate of fifty up to a hundred, and even more. Certainly, if he did not pull the trigger himself, he is estimated to have been involved in the murders of scores of ordinary Catholics.' He was a former member of 11 UDR.

On the 17th, Northern Ireland Secretary Peter Brooke met senior representatives of Northern Ireland's Social and Democratic Labour Party (SDLP) who had been voicing their disagreement about the logistics and timing of talks on a possible future united Ireland. SDLP leader John Hume's main concerns lay in the fact that the British government had reserved the right to determine the exact moment at which the government of the Irish Republic would be invited to have its say. The Loyalists were still, naturally, deeply suspicious of the ill-fated and deeply controversial Anglo-Irish Agreement (AIA) and were also putting pressure on Brooke and the NIO, as well as the new Prime Minister, John Major. The 'Grey Man' had only been in power since late November 1990 and was still very much finding his feet. Suddenly Brooke and Major found themselves in the same position as the British soldier on the streets of Northern Ireland, as 'piggy in the middle'. I shall deal with Hume's efforts in making proposals for peace – the Hume–Adams Initiative – in the later chapters of this book.

Four days after this meeting, the Provisionals, with their perverted logic and sickening eagerness to kill because of past associations, shot dead a former RUCR officer. In doing so, they left five grown-up children fatherless as they continued their bloody policy of border genocide against the Co. Fermanagh Protestants, and gave Loyalists an excuse, albeit, unneeded, to retaliate. Cullen Stephenson (65) worked at a dairy at Fivemiletown, and had been a member of the police reserve until April 1989, when he retired to concentrate on his family and his full-time job. On the evening of the 21st, he returned to his house in Church

Street, Brookeborough, a journey of some five miles, and only a 20-minute drive from the Republican stronghold of Rosslea. As he parked, several masked men who had been hiding in nearby bushes opened fire on him with automatic weapons, hitting him several times; he died instantly. Stray rounds entered the window of his house, narrowly missing his wife and one of his daughters. Using the grounds of a nearby Catholic Church through which to escape, the IRA killers then raced away in a stolen car towards Rosslea and the nearby Irish border. The unit then slipped into Ireland, but it has been made clear to me that the killers, four or possibly five IRA men, lived in Rosslea and would soon have returned to their homes in the Republican village to melt into the background. They would have lain low, that is until it was 'Brew Day' when they could collect their Income Support, courtesy of the British taxpayer and the British government which they purported to despise.

The dead man's daughter spoke poignantly of her father at his funeral. She said: 'Daddy isn't the first and he won't be the last. If his death would stop the killing at least that would be something, but it won't. He is dead and it won't change anything. There will still be families like us who will have to suffer. Daddy was a very popular man and hadn't an enemy in the world apart from these people who disliked him simply because he wore a uniform, but that was two years ago.' The following is from a friend who still lives in the border area and requested anonymity, as he has several Catholic neighbours who have made it clear that they want to be a part of the Irish Republic and despise all things British.

Border Murders
County Fermanagh Resident

I knew the murdered man and although he was not a particular pal of mine, we were on nodding terms. We knew that he had been a police reservist, but he had retired some time ago, and worked over at Fivemiletown and was well known in the area. The Republican filth who killed him and became instant heroes to their filthy supporters, were real brave men. Five of them, all armed with automatic weapons, lay in wait for him when he came back from the creamery, because they knew that he would be tired from a hard day's work and that he was unarmed. These cowardly dogs shot him down in such cowardly fashion and they knew that they were safe. I am told that they ran through the grounds of a nearby Taig church and were laughing and shouting, and cheering the killing of an unarmed man. I was also told that, a few days later, they were drinking in the Rosslea Arms, with the local Nationalist shit buying them round after round of drinks.

Just three days after the killing of the former police reservist, the MoD announced that the additional infantry battalion – approximately 600 soldiers – which had been sent over to bolster security in the Province just before Christmas, was being withdrawn. It is not recorded how the Stephenson family, in the wake of their tragedy, reacted to the reduction in security, given that the IRA had a seemingly free hand in the border region anyway.

On the 26th, the RUC, flanked by soldiers, carried out an early morning raid on the Belfast offices of *An Phoblacht* ('The Republic') in Andersonstown. They seized computer equipment and vast quantities of documents and Republican publications, much to the chagrin of Mr Adams, who protested vociferously about the raid. During this year, a Loyalist splinter group, using the imaginative title the Loyalist Retaliation and Defence Group (LRDG), attacked *An Phoblacht* specifically. They launched firebomb attacks against newsagents who sold the magazine, against street sellers and even killed those who sold or distributed it. In August of this year, they shot Jim Carson dead for selling it in his paper shop (*see* Chapter 8) and the following month they shot dead another newsagent, Lawrence Murchan (*see* Chapter 9). On 12 December 1992, *An Phoblacht* worker Malachy Carey was shot dead by the LRDG in Ballymoney (*see* Chapter 24).

Although strictly speaking, the following piece about the Irish Republican village/township of Rosslea relates to the final stages of this author's 1988–90 book, it is worth including as, brief though it is, it demonstrates the courage of minorities who lived their entire lives in fear. In 2016, the final surviving Protestant-owned business in Rosslea closed down.

Mark 'C', UDR & Royal Artillery

On 29 November 1990, a 50-year-old man called Thomas Kerr passed away from a heart attack in Enniskillen; so what you may say? Well Thomas Kerr was in fact, a quiet, single, shy man, a Protestant living in the Republican stronghold of Rosslea, Fermanagh. What made him special was that he was serving with the RUC as a full-time Reservist, stationed first in Belcoo, and then Enniskillen RUC Barracks as they were then known. For me this made him a hero; imagine coming and going on and off duty, having to go back to the same house, knowing full well you could be attacked at any time by your so-called neighbours. No wonder at the early age of 50, Thomas died from a heart attack on duty in Enniskillen RUC Barracks, I have to wonder, did the stress of his job, on and off duty contribute to his early demise; we will never know, but it cannot have helped.

The day after the Belfast raid, the 27th, the UFF carried out a 'retaliatory' murder when they killed a Catholic father, claiming that they had purposely left five children fatherless, because the IRA had done the same to the five children of the dead RUCR officer. Sean Rafferty (44) lived in the Nationalist Oldpark Road enclave in North Belfast; he was an innocent Catholic – as was Gervais Lynch before him – who was simply in the wrong place at the wrong time, no matter how much of a cliché that might appear to be. He was at his home in Rosapenna Court, close to the Ardoyne, but conversely, only a stone's throw from the Loyalist Cliftonville Road. UFF gunmen, including Stephen 'Top Gun' McKeag, arrived at the house in a car stolen from the Shankill and burst in as Mr Rafferty was washing the dishes with his wife and daughter. They shot him down, in front of his shocked family, fatally wounding him. As he lay dying, with his children screaming in horror, one of the gunmen stood over the defenceless man and fired several more rounds into his body.

David Lister and Hugh Jordan in their excellent book *Mad Dog* about Johnny Adair refer to the killing being carried out by Adair and his so-called 'Dream Team', as a bet: 'One shocking example of Adair's capacity for ruthlessness was made known to Special Branch following a sectarian murder in North Belfast. It emerged that the "C" Company team were present on a Sunday evening in a Shankill Road club with the intention of engaging in a session of drinking. Upon the arrival of the first round of drinks the mood of the party was jovial when one of the assembled dozen or so members shouted: "Let's bang a Taig," which was slang for let's shoot a Catholic. Although this comment was intended in jest, Adair picked up on the suggestion and within 5 minutes had detailed every member of the team to play a specific role in the murder attempt which had now become a reality. Incredibly, 15 minutes later the operation was underway, and it was only then that the team realised that they hadn't actually discussed a target. At this point it was decided to drive into a Catholic area and shoot the first male they encountered. Approximately 25 minutes after the first suggestion, the entire team had returned to the club and resumed their drinking, the celebration of the murder being led by Adair.'[1]

The ending of Mr Rafferty's life, the widowing of Mrs Rafferty and the orphaning of his five children was decided upon purely at random, by deranged killers, in cold blood, from start to finish in less than half an hour.

The very same day that the UFF had so callously killed an innocent Catholic, the Provisionals continued their economic warfare whilst poking fun at the Northern Ireland Minister, Richard Needham, for his comments which Adams had described as theatrical, following the incendiary attacks of earlier in the month. Two more firebomb attacks on the 27th destroyed shops in the outer centre of Belfast, although again there were no injuries. Richard Needham was later forced to announce that the NIO would pay £25,000,000 in compensation for the damage, but it would be redirected from other schemes which had been designed to relieve social and economic misery in the Province. Four days later, Mr Needham's boss met with Irish government ministers in Dublin for an Anglo-Irish Agreement (AIA) conference. Afterwards he – Peter Brooke – stated there was a real possibility of political talks in the future, but he emphasised 'possibility, not probability'.

The first month of 1991 ended with four deaths: a former policeman, two random and utterly pointless sectarian killings of innocent Catholics and the intriguing death of a PIRA man. The following month, the IRA's England team struck again in London.

1. David Lister and Hugh Jordan, *Mad Dog* (Mainstream Publishing, 2004), p. 101.

2
February

This was the month of the Victoria Station bombing and the consequent removal of litter bins from many public places; it witnessed two deaths, both of whom were civilians. One was a civil servant on his way to work and the other was a Catholic gunned down by mindless sectarian killers in North Belfast; although their deaths were several hundred miles apart, both men were entirely innocent. It was also the month in which the IRA 'welcomed' John Major into power, with a mortar bomb attack on 10 Downing Street. For the second month in a row, there were no military deaths.

On the 1st of the month, Sinn Féin President Gerry Adams, speaking to a Republican gathering, talked of British press speculation relating to a possible IRA ceasefire in 1991. Adams rejected comments from senior British political figures that the IRA's assault on the British way of life had failed, and would continue to claim in later years that 'the IRA was never defeated'. Instead, he told an adoring audience in Dublin that rumours of a possible IRA ceasefire were simply unfounded speculation. With a death toll by now approaching 3,500, and with more than 500 additional funerals still to come, and with most Catholic civil rights achieved, quite why Adams and his cronies continued to kill and encourage the Loyalists to continue killing is beyond the comprehension of most sane people.

On the 2nd, the Dublin newspaper the *Irish Independent* published an interview with former Taoiseach Garret Fitzgerald. In it he stated how close he had come to proposing a referendum on constitutional change to secure backing for the Anglo-Irish Agreement. He admitted that the section of the Irish Constitution which so upset Loyalists, asserting the Republic's sovereignty over the North, would need to be repealed. Six days later, the Irish government decided to honour their previously agreed arrangements for political talks on the future of the North. This gave Peter Brooke the right to decide at which point in the proceedings he could invite the leaders of the Irish Republic to participate in the talks. On the 14th, he was forced to admit to the House of Commons that there were still differences between the Northern Ireland political parties, the NIO and Irish ministers over the proposals for talks.

On the 3rd, following on from their controversial 'proxy bomb' attacks on British Army bases in October 1990 the Provisionals launched another similar attack, this time on the UDR base at Magherafelt, Co. Londonderry. Despite outrage even among some IRA supporters, who claimed it irreparably damaged the Republican movement, the tactic was used, albeit sparingly, until 1993. One of the Army's many civvie workers was abducted from his home close to the base, whilst his terrified wife was held at gunpoint by masked Republican terrorists. Warning him that, if he tried to escape, his young wife would be killed, the gunmen strapped him into his works' van, on top of a bomb weighing 500 lb (225 kg). The terrified man was forced to drive into the base, where he was able to get free and shout out a warning to the soldiers around the gates. The bomb exploded, causing massive damage to the base, severely damaging 50 nearby homes, but fortunately causing no casualties. Some of the damaged homes belonged to Catholics, although it is not recorded if they felt that their involuntary sacrifice was considered a worthwhile contribution to the Republican cause.

Later that same day, acting on a tip-off, the Garda Síochána in Dublin discovered six incendiary devices which had been placed in hotels around the city centre, although it was believed that there were as many as 20. It was only by good fortune that none of them exploded, but the Dublin Garda believed that there was an active UFF unit operating in the city. Ian S. Wood in his *Crimes of Loyalty* maintained that: 'The UFF were trying to put themselves in the same league as the Provos and were a more vicious group than the older crowd.' For those who remembered the Dublin–Monaghan bombings on 17 May 1974 it was a nightmarish scenario. The blitz of bombs that day had killed 33 civilians and a full-term unborn child, and injured almost 300. The Loyalist paramilitary rationale was that if the IRA could destroy northern cities, so they too could destroy the cities of the Irish Republic.

The 7th of February fell on a cold Thursday morning; in the Middle East, the Gulf War had passed its first significant stage; the Battle of Khafji had ended, the Iraqi incursion into Saudi territory was over and the campaign to liberate Kuwait was under way. In London, John Major was chairing the War Cabinet together with senior officials and top military men from the MoD. I was in central London on several business appointments that day, and whilst those attending the Cabinet meeting – including Hurd, King, Lamont, Mayhew, Mellor and others – were discussing how to bring about the downfall of Saddam Hussein, a member of the IRA's England team was parking a stolen van, just 200 yards away on Whitehall. The stolen van stopped at the corner of Whitehall and Horse Guards Avenue and the PIRA operative climbed into the back to prime three explosive charges which were sitting in a trio of home-made metal launching tubes. The white van had a section cut out of its roof, although as the snowfall began to get heavier, most people were too busy hurrying out of the whirling flakes to notice the hole.

After setting the charges, the driver was collected on a stolen motorcycle at around 10:05; three minutes later, as a police officer walked towards the van, deeply suspicious because of where it was parked, the electronic timer fired the three missiles, followed shortly afterwards by a pre-set explosive charge which destroyed the base-plate, setting the van on fire. The mortar bombs were a massive 4 ft long and were each filled with 40 lb (18 kg) of Semtex explosive; the three deadly missiles arced towards Downing Street, some 200 yards away, where the unsuspecting politicians plotted the downfall of a Middle Eastern dictator, blissfully unaware that it was their own demise which was rather more imminent. Two bombs hit a grassed area in front of the Foreign and Commonwealth Office and failed to detonate. The third landed in the gardens at the rear of 10 Downing Street, just 90 feet from the then non-armoured windows of the Cabinet Room. The windows, however, were bomb-netted and the explosion was partially muffled by this security measure. The people in the room threw themselves under the huge oak table, unaware that, had the mortar hit the building, they would have been wiped out, thus achieving what the IRA set out to do at the Grand Hotel in Brighton in 1984. The outside walls were scorched and the explosion left a huge crater in the ground. There were four minor injuries, including two of the police officers on duty. Major is said to have been phlegmatic and calmly remarked: 'I think we had better start again.' Charlie Brereton, a BBC employee, was standing at the rear of the building when the bomb landed and it was only by a miracle that he wasn't killed, as he was only 30 ft away from the blast. Newsreel at the time of the explosion records the sound of the blast and also shows the heavy, black wooden door of Number 10 actually bulging outwards with the concussion of the explosion.

Prime Minister Major told the House: 'I think it is clear from the timing of the attack this morning which suggests it was a deliberate attempt to both kill the Cabinet, and to do damage to our democratic system of government. It failed and could not in any circumstances have succeeded.' Douglas Hurd later told the assembled press: 'We were sitting in the Cabinet room when the windows caved in; that was the sum of my experience.' The Queen, visiting the Royal Brompton Hospital in London, spoke solemnly when she added: 'There are those who seek to undermine our democratic system and way of life. I would like to take this opportunity to remind them it will not succeed.'

In Whitehall, the van blazed and large swirling masses of black smoke poured from the burning wreckage. Passers-by in warm winter clothing rushed and slithered around in the snowy streets, as security men and police calmly but firmly shepherded the civilians away from the van, due to the unspoken potential for secondary explosive devices.

The *Daily Express* led with 'Only Feet from Death', and on page 2: 'Hundreds Thrown into Confusion as Terrorists Strike'. The newspaper reported: 'Eyewitnesses painted graphic pictures of the fear and confusion that followed yesterday's attack. Ministers and hundreds of shocked civil servants staggered from their offices overlooking Downing Street and the Houses of Parliament. They joined dazed tourists in the street as emergency services battled to seal off the area ... "I felt the building shake and everyone started screaming," said Versha Mulchs, 26, "then a man came running in and shouted: 'Everyone out; it's a bomb!'" [Another man said:] "I ... went through to Downing Street where I found a policeman had been hit on the back of the head by debris." Sound Engineer Nicholas Buckley said: "I saw a plume of smoke rising from the garden of number 10, and a cylinder was lying on the ground with yellow smoke billowing out of it. There was a nasty smell, so we all got away from it, fearing other explosions." Bus Driver Parvin Patel had driven his No. 24, packed with passengers, past the van moments before the explosion. "I looked in my mirror and saw missiles shoot out of the roof of the van," he said "they were shooting up in the air when the van suddenly exploded. I saw a man running away from the van but couldn't see any more because my attention had switched to the passengers. People were very frightened and some were screaming."'

The same newspaper interviewed two Irish-Americans in New York, one of them, predictably enough, in an 'Irish Tavern' on 45th Street, who said: 'It's despicable that they should start bombing London at a time like this. The Brits shouldn't have to fight a war on both fronts.' Another – Willie Donavan from Queens – showed that his heart was in the right place when he said: 'They should all be hanged, whether they're Irish or Iraqi. How can anybody condone terrorism when that's what we are fighting against in the Gulf?'

The IRA made two public statements. The first was by a Sinn Féin spokesman in Dublin who said: 'Let the British government understand that, while nationalist people in the six counties are forced to live under British rule, then the British Cabinet will be forced to meet in bunkers.' A few days later *An Phoblacht* – chosen by the IRA in a gesture of defiance following the RUC raid on its Andersonstown office – trumpeted: 'Like any colonialists, the members of the British establishment do not want the result of their occupation landing at their front or back doorstep . . . Are the members of the British cabinet prepared to give their lives to hold on to a colony? They should understand the cost will be great while Britain remains in Ireland.'

However, there was a guarded admiration for the professionalism of the PIRA unit that had planned and executed the attack. Peter Gurney of the Anti-Terrorist Squad told author Peter Taylor: 'It was a remarkably good aim if you consider that the bomb was fired 250 yards with no direct line of sight. Technically, it was quite brilliant and I'm sure that many army crews, if given a similar task, would be very pleased to drop a bomb that close. You've got to park the launch vehicle in an area which is guarded by armed men and you've got less than a minute to do it. I was very, very surprised at how good it was. If the angle of fire had been moved about five or ten degrees, then those bombs would actually have impacted on Number Ten.'[1]

On the 14th, the strategists amongst the Provisional IRA added a cynical and almost fatal twist to their particular brand of terror, killing through emotion and the lure of romance. Knowing how much people love the mystery and excitement of a Valentine's card, one of their bombing units packed a small but deadly charge in a brightly coloured envelope, delivered on the special day to a part-time UDR soldier in Killen, in the Strabane area of Co. Tyrone. The device exploded in his face, leaving him with severe facial and hand injuries. The very next day, a section from the Duke of Edinburgh's Royal Regiment (DERR) finished a border patrol in Co. Fermanagh. A helicopter had been summoned to extricate them from the area and return them to St Angelo Barracks, a former RAF base at Trory, close to Enniskillen. As the helicopter came in for 'a hot collection', PIRA units from across the border, using an assortment of automatic weapons, including at least one .50 calibre, opened fire on the aircraft and the waiting soldiers. The Garda Síochána later discovered over 360 empty casings inside the Republic; although the DERR soldiers returned fire, there were reportedly no casualties on either side of the porous border.

Despite the mortar attack on Downing Street, Londoners stoically went about their business, unconcerned about the threats of terror, or disguising it well if they did have any fears. After all, hadn't their grannies and granddads lived through the terror of the Blitz as Hitler's Luftwaffe had pounded most of London's East End into rubble and filled the temporary mortuaries to over-flowing? The Irish had been setting off explosions almost the entire length of the century, indeed as far back as the Clerkenwell bomb in 1867, and although they could not know it, sixteen years in the future, Islamic terrorists would take up the IRA's strategy and slaughter Londoners. The last major bomb targeting civilians in London had been well over seven years earlier, when a no-warning car bomb exploded outside Harrods, killing six people. After the negative publicity following the Royal Parks attacks, the Chelsea barracks bomb and Harrods, IRA leaders had seemingly called off the

1. Peter Taylor, *Provos: The IRA & Sinn Féin* (Bloomsbury Publishing, 1997).

campaign as being 'counterproductive'. The targets which they chose when they resumed their terror campaign on 18 February 1991 were railway stations, always vulnerable to attack and always difficult to defend.

The terror began at Paddington Station very early that morning, at 04:20 in fact when a small, but potentially lethal device, weighing around 5 lb (2 kg), exploded underneath the advertising hoardings where it had been placed some time on the Sunday evening. It damaged the station roof and smashed several windows, but disturbed no one, other than a few station rats – the furry rodent, not the IRA; no one was injured. Approximately 160 minutes later, at around 07:00, a man, said to have a strong Irish accent called the HQ of the London Tube and said: 'We are the Irish Republican Army. Bombs to go off at all mainline stations in 45 minutes.' Both the Metropolitan Police (Met) and the British Transport Police (BTP) immediately swung into action, but their orders were to search the stations, rather than evacuate them, as the rails carry upwards of 3,000,000 passengers into and around London every working day. At that time of the day alone, almost 500,000 commuters would have been en route for their offices and other places of work. In order to confuse the issue and cause more chaos, possibly lulling the police into a sense of false security, the same Irishman telephoned six more warnings through; all were hoaxes.

Victoria Station stands in the middle of London SW1; a busy, commercial area which combines the tacky with the modern – although sometimes the two are synonymous – the area is often quite shabby but at the same time SW1 is one of the most prestigious postcodes in London. After all, the area also contains Buckingham Palace and Harrods and a score of foreign embassies and delegations. The central London railway terminus and London Underground complex are named because of the proximity of Victoria Street, the latter being named after Queen Victoria. There are two stations; the underground which is on the Circle, District and Victoria Lines and the over-ground mainline station. The main concourse is a hub of activity with trains regularly going down to the Channel ports as well as all over the south of England.

On any given business day in London, Victoria Station is jammed with commuters, office workers and the like; the day on which the terrorists chose to strike was a Monday, the busiest of the week. It was a day on which strangers David Corner and Sue Hanisch found themselves standing, unknowingly, next to each other and, unwittingly, next to an IRA bomb. David Corner (36) would die, Sue Hanisch's life would be changed for ever, and over 40 other travellers would be injured, some badly, as Irish terror struck again at the very heart of the nation's capital.

At approximately 07:40, the moment which ended one life and ruined dozens of others, arrived with a suddenness, a flash of pure white and a violent shock, as a device weighing 5 lb (2 kg) – identical to the one at Paddington – exploded inside a litter bin on Victoria's main concourse. The blast smashed into the crowds of commuters, even as police were searching desperately for the suspected bomb, killing David Corner (36), father of a toddler child, tearing off Sue Hanisch's leg and Matthew Cyprus's foot, as well as injuring up to 40 people. Mr Corner was killed by a massive shrapnel wound to the chest, taking the brunt of the blast, and as Sue Hanisch writes in a moment, partially shielding her from the full effects. A senior policeman would later condemn the bombers who timed the outrage for when they knew that the station would be absolutely packed, in order to maximise the carnage. Looking back at how packed the area was, it is almost a miracle that only one person was killed. Nineteen people were kept in hospital overnight, of whom two were in a critical condition, another 'blow for Irish unity'.

Victoria Station
Sue Hanisch

I headed off earlier to Victoria and consequently ended up with 15 minutes to play with on the concourse. I decided to make a quick phone call to my Mum and Dad just to say 'Good Morning' to them before they headed off to their working days in Lancashire; where did the expression 'killing time' originate? I hadn't quite finished dialling when the explosion happened. The ceiling came down on my head and I was in the filth on the floor with both legs badly blown apart and my right foot hanging off. There were wires and blood everywhere, people screaming and legs running to and fro as travellers desperately sought a place of safety. My right hand was covered in blood and I could see exposed flesh. My hair was burned and the acrid smell which filled the air was nauseating. Several times I tried to get up, but onto what I ask myself now? Despite seeing the devastating damage to my legs I couldn't quite work out why I couldn't stand on them. Strange survival instincts kicked in without me even realising what I was doing, or that I even had such resources residing silently in my body for such an occasion as this.

The guy standing next to me, David Corner, took the main blow and died there and he probably saved my life. Even now I can sense the urgency as the paramedics tried to breathe life back into his body; but he was no longer there. I begged him to return to life out loud, but he probably didn't hear me. Goodbye David; you didn't know me in life, but I have certainly known you in your death and am sorry I never had the chance to meet you alive. I hope you had a good life.

Home Secretary Kenneth Baker visited the site of the bomb as soon as it was safe to do so. He told the waiting journalists and TV crews: 'The concourse of Victoria is covered in blood. This is the act of murderous criminals. All decent people will feel the deepest sympathy for those so tragically harmed. I am appalled and disgusted by this vicious attack on people innocently going to work.' Leader of the Opposition Neil Kinnock said that he regarded the attacks as 'a great horror, all the more so because they were clearly aimed to cause maximum harm to complete innocents'. Leader of the Liberal Democrats and former Royal Marine Paddy Ashdown said: 'The attacks are vain and futile.' Irish Taoiseach Charles Haughey was angered by the fellow Irish who had supposedly killed in his name, and spoke of his revulsion and shock. Finally, the Chairman of British Rail, Sir Bob Reid, who also visited the bombed stations, said: 'There are a number of evil forces operating in our country. What they want to do is to disrupt us. But this country has to go on operating because that's what we are made of.' The one dissenting voice belonged to that of gruff, belligerent Scotsman Jimmy Knapp. The National Union of Rail, Maritime and Transport Workers leader, who died in 2001, said: 'There was a three-hour time difference between the explosions at Paddington and Victoria. If there was a direct warning 40 minutes before the Victoria explosion, what were the police doing?' His words were almost certainly going to give comfort to the terrorists and appeared to show no sympathy for the family of the dead man, nor for the loved ones of the injured. I recall the anger which many around me felt at Knapp's outburst, as his ill-judged words must have been a 'gift from the Gods' for the men of violence.

The ever-cynical IRA immediately blamed the London police; their statement dripping with even more hypocrisy than usual, an apologist said: 'The cynical decision of senior personnel not to evacuate railway stations named in secondary warnings, even three hours after the warning device had exploded at Paddington in the early hours of this morning, was directly responsible for the casualties at Victoria. All future warnings should be acted upon.' Commander Churchill-Coleman of the Anti-Terrorist Squad responded: 'You will appreciate [that] the vagueness of the information, the manner in which it was passed, combined with the time lapse involved was quite deliberate. The bomb was quite deliberately intended to maim and kill.'

Police action was, of course, somewhat justified in that they did back in 1991, and even to this day, receive bogus warnings on a daily basis. In the several days before the Victoria bomb they had received 29 such warnings, all of them false, and they did indeed receive 19 on the day of the blast alone! The fact that six of these false alarms were deliberately started by the IRA adequately illustrates the truly perfidious nature and callousness of these 'Irish freedom fighters'. The leaders of the England team and their godfathers in the Army Council clearly wished to shed blood by their deception and subterfuge. They knew that there would be confusion amongst the searchers and a false relief at discovering that a threat was really a hoax as this would ensure that they were not at their psychological peaks when they undertook the next search. The anti-terrorist squad leader added: 'For the terrorists to blame the police for their own outrages is particularly galling and almost beggars belief.'

The following day, the British and world press led with the story of the bombing: The American media quoted several of the survivors: 'Matthew Cyprus, 22, who lost part of his right foot, described the Victoria Station explosion, saying: "There was a big blinding light, a wall of fire, followed by a noise which came toward me and then I fell over on to the floor." Jeremy Rose, who was inside the terminal when the bomb exploded, said he saw a man: "... with half his face missing. It was like he had gone through a car windshield at 100 mph."'

The *Daily Express* led the attacks against the terror group, emphasising the children who had been caught up in the blast: 'Frontline Innocents: Children Scarred by IRA Bomb Murderers'. Their three reporters combined to write: 'Innocent children this morning carry the scars of the IRA's renewed random bombing of the British mainland. David Corner, a civil servant, was killed when he was hit in the chest by shrapnel, leaving his 16-month-old son, Adam, fatherless. A boy of 12 had a four-inch piece of burning metal removed from his body. A teenage girl will be scarred for life and her 17-year-old brother faces a long battle to walk again. All were victims of yesterday's rush hour explosion at London's Victoria station. The 5 lb Semtex bomb was hidden in a metal litter bin between two platforms and next to phone boxes. Experts said it acted like a huge grenade, sending twisted metal fragments from the bin flying all around the station concourse. Passengers – many of them children

– were taken to hospital, some with horrific wounds. The innocents included people on their way to work, like Mr Corner from Thornton Heath, South London. Doctors said the injuries were worse than the 1983 Harrods' attack which killed six . . . The injured 12 year old boy from Hitchin, Herts, was recovering last night as his parents waited at his hospital bedside. His father said he and his son travelled to Victoria on a day out. "I had a cup of coffee in my hand," he said. "Suddenly the cup exploded out of my grasp and my son was knocked to the ground." Westminster Hospital surgeon Merion Thomas who removed shrapnel from the boy's body said: "He's in pain but very cheerful."'

There were further moving stories from survivors who had been using the public telephones and ended up with broken legs, others still who had simply been en route for work and suddenly found themselves facing months of painful skin grafts and other surgery. That these innocents were paying the price for the vanities and unrealistic dreams of Irish Republican terror groups is beyond debate. If Adolf Hitler and his chum Hermann Göring's Luftwaffe had tried and failed to pound London into submission with nightly air raids which killed thousands, why did Mr Adams, Mr McGuinness and their Republican cronies think that they would fare any better?

The *Daily Express* reporting team continued in the inside pages:

> A brave young victim of the Victoria bomb blast told of his terrifying ordeal yesterday as he was being wheeled into an operating theatre. Millions of TV viewers heard 22 year old Matthew Cyprus say: 'I've lost the best part of my foot, but I saw others with worse injuries than my own.' Calmly he added: 'I'm fine; maybe it will hit me later . . . All of a sudden there was a big blinding light, followed by a tremendous noise and a wall of fire which came towards me. There were lots of people on the floor and many more were running out of the station.' Despite his appalling injury, he picked up his bag and tried to hobble out of the station. A bus conductor pulled him from the rubble and carried him to safety. The ear-splitting explosion shattered the normal Monday morning bustle of commuters arriving from all over the southeast. The blast fired lethal shards of metal and glass at dozens of people, many of whom were hurled to the ground.
>
> The station filled up with a mushroom cloud of evil-smelling smoke. British Rail Inspector Granville Mayers said: 'One man must have been in agony. His leg was just a mass of blood. There was no skin left; it looked like it had been scorched off. A woman was lying near him with blood pouring from her head. She had a big cut running down her face. It looked like she was crying and only just conscious.'

The bombers were never caught and their identity remains known only to the godfathers of the IRA. There was understandable anger from the British, although none as extreme as that of Ivor Stanbrook, a Tory MP, who told the *Daily Express* that Irish Nationalists should be expelled from Ulster and that the Irish boundaries should be redrawn. That would of course have meant goodbye Rosslea and Crossmaglen!

On the 24th, the UVF killed an innocent Catholic in his own lounge in North Belfast. Peter McTasney (24) was a youth and community worker who lived in Bawnmore Park, Newtownabbey, close to the Loyalist Rathcoole, which was, given the interface nature of the area, a dangerous place to live. He was babysitting his three-year-old niece Lynette, when a

UVF gunman opened fire at the pair of them through the lounge window. He grabbed the child to take her to safety but a second man burst open the front door with a sledgehammer and he and another gunman rushed into the house, firing indiscriminately. The toddler was injured as Mr McTasney fell to the floor where he was shot a further five times; leaving the dying man in a pool of his own blood and the shocked and injured child amid unimaginable horror, the murder gang escaped in the direction of Rathcoole. The toddler had a bullet wound to the head but survived her ordeal. The leader of the UVF murder gang was alleged to be Mark Haddock, said to be an RUC informant with an extraordinarily long 'chain'. One of the gunmen was William Lindsay who was jailed for his part in the murder. While awaiting trial for murder in Crumlin Road jail, Lindsay held down a Republican inmate while part of his ear was bitten off; he received a further five years for this in May 1994. Also involved was Gary Haggerty, another RUC informant, who would go on to murder five more innocent Catholics between 1994 and 1997.

In January 2018 Haggerty was sentenced to six and a half years in prison for 202 terror offences. The former Ulster Volunteer Force chief, 46, pleaded guilty to five murders as his part of a controversial state deal that offered a significantly reduced prison term in return for giving evidence against other terrorist suspects. One individual is to be prosecuted over a murder using his evidence. Mr Justice Adrian Colton said Haggarty's was a case of 'exceptional gravity. The fact he was involved directly in multiple terrorist murders must be an aggravating factor.'[1]

Also on the 24th, a large PIRA active service unit (ASU) positioned inside the Irish Republic, opened fire on a British outpost in Silverbridge, Co. Armagh, with heavy machine guns. The firefight raged for over 15 minutes, without any casualties. There was some controversy as the British accused the Irish police of not taking any interest in the gun battle, despite the presence of *gardaí* in the area. A source told me, although the claim cannot be substantiated: 'The Micks were there and they couldn't have failed to see, let alone hear, what was going on. The truth is that they were yitten [scared] and just didn't wish to get involved or raise their heads above the parapet . . . Cowardly tossers, the bunch of them; they just wanted an easy life and turn a blind eye to their home-grown terrorists! They turned up soon enough after the shooting was all over.'

On the same day, PIRA bomb-maker Desmond 'Dessie' Ellis, a Dublin-born terrorist was in court in the UK to face terrorist charges. He had been arrested in 1981, but jumped bail, and managed to escape to the USA, seen by some as a terrorist haven across the Atlantic. In 1982, he was extradited from the USA to the Republic, despite the best efforts of the Kennedy clan and other leading Irish-American families and NORAID-provided legal teams. In April 1983, he was sentenced to ten years' imprisonment in Portlaoise Prison, before being warned that the British had applied for his extradition. In an effort to forestall this, he went on a 35-day hunger strike, which ended on 14 November 1990 when he became the first person extradited from the Republic of Ireland to the UK under the 1987 Extradition Act. On 24 February 1991, the Crown attempted to have new charges brought against him, which was contrary to the extradition agreement, and Dáil Éireann naturally objected. The British reversed the decision on 4 June, and the original charges

1. https://www.telegraph.co.uk/news/2018/01/29/loyalist-supergrass-garyhaggarty-gets-six-and-a-half-years-202.

were reinstated. Amongst the charges he faced were the manufacture of several bombs which caused loss of life and grievous injuries. Included were various bomb attacks: on Irish Guards returning to Chelsea barracks by coach, when two members of the public were killed and several injured; on the Commandant-General of the Royal Marines, Sir Steuart Pringle, whose right leg had to be amputated; and on the then Attorney General Lord Havers. Another bomb, at a Wimpy Bar in London's Oxford Street, blew up, killing a police explosives officer, Kenneth Howorth; all these incidents were in 1980/81. Ellis is now an Irish Sinn Féin politician, and a Teachta Dála (TD) for the Dublin North-West constituency; like many former Republican terrorists, he seems to have found a good life as a professional politician.

As described above, there were just two deaths this month, both civilian.

3
March

Following several months of relative calm in Northern Ireland, the killing broke out again, with soldiers being murdered once more on the streets of the Province, and more sectarian attacks, including two separate pub attacks by the UVF that left seven dead, including three members of the Provisional IRA. In all, 13 people died this month, almost as many as in the three previous months combined.

The 1st of the month fell on a Friday, the last day of the working week and traditional pay-day for many; for soldier Paul Sutcliffe it was to be his final day on earth. For the parents of his comrade Roger Love it was to be the start of a three-day vigil at their son's bedside before he succumbed to the wounds inflicted by a PIRA mortar. Sometime during that morning, a PIRA team backed by gunmen to keep locals away and to ensure their silence, had piled up a mound of dirt in a garden on the Mullaghcreevie Estate, to the west of Armagh City, and lined up an improvised mortar (known as a Mark XII by the Army) so that it was lying flat and pointing down the road towards where security forces (SF) mobile patrols passed by. The firing mechanism was linked to a command wire hidden in the same garden, behind a mechanical digger. Temporary traffic lights due to road works had been placed on Killyleagh Road, and it was hoped that an SF vehicle would pause here long enough in which to fire the mortar, horizontally: described by the IRA as a 'directional missile'.

In the early evening, a two-vehicle patrol from 2 UDR was halted by the lights, and after a short pause, the leading vehicle pulled off at the precise moment that the watching PIRA bombers pressed the remote detonator. They barely paused for breath before disappearing into the Nationalist estate and entering separate houses in order to lie low, and rid themselves of any incriminating forensics. At virtually point-blank range – used conventionally, the Mark XII had an effective range of 70 yards – the mortar bomb struck the leading vehicle, wrecking it and leaving it in a tangled heap on the road, killing Private Paul Sutcliffe (22) almost instantly. It fatally wounded Private Roger Love (20) and caused traumatic amputations to two other soldiers. Private Sutcliffe had previously served in the famous 'Duke of Boots' prior to joining the UDR and was from Lancashire. Private Love, who was from Richhill, Co. Armagh, was casevaced to the Royal Victoria Hospital (RVH) in Belfast where he was placed in intensive care. His parents raced to his bedside but he died three days later on the 4th, from his massive injuries. An RUC spokesman dismissed the IRA claims that it had a new guided weapon as 'laughable', and added: 'There is nothing new in what the IRA has to offer ... death and destruction.' Houses nearby were badly damaged and residents severely shaken as, once again, the Provisionals demonstrated that they had no qualms about turning heavily populated urban areas into battlefields, and no consideration was given to likely deaths or injuries to 'their' communities.

Eyewitnesses reported the vehicle as lying in a tangled heap, with the roof blown off and the doors torn away and flung 50 yards. A local man told the Belfast *News Letter*: 'My wife and I were watching TV when our windows and door were blown in and the force of the explosive lifted us up in the air . . . Moans and groans were coming from the shattered vehicle and other soldiers were frantically trying to get them out.' The same witness also spoke of seeing an injured soldier lying in the road, and nearby one of his boots which had been blown off. Alderman Sean Neeson of the Alliance Party also told the newspaper: 'Now that the Gulf War has ended, the Butcher of Baghdad has given way to the butchers of the IRA in an effort to grab world headlines.'

Private Love was buried at Seagoe Cemetery, near Portadown. A UDR party attended Paul Sutcliffe's funeral at his home town of Barrowford, Lancashire, the only UDR military funeral held outside Northern Ireland, although his ashes were later scattered in the Mourne Mountains. The *News Letter* reported: 'The small closely-knit community of Richhill is in mourning for the young UDR soldier murdered by the IRA. But in death 20-year-old Roger James Love, of Sleepy Valley Court in the picturesque Co. Armagh village, will help others as he did in life. For his heartbroken parents Jim and Lorna have donated his kidneys which will be used to give seriously ill patients a better future.' In 2011, on the 20th anniversary of the attack, the Craigavon Group published the following: 'Love, Roger, 2 UDR. In proud and loving memory of a beloved only son and brother murdered in the execution of his duty 4th March 1991 (aged 20 years) Roger you are not just a memory silently kept, you are part of our life and we will never forget. Always forever young, always and forever in my heart. Lovingly remembered by your mum Lorna, Keith, sisters Carolyn, Laura, Julie-Ann, brother-in-law Philip and niece Amy-Louise Richhill. Also, his comrade Pte. Paul Sutcliffe and Raymond Moore killed in Iraq 7th September 2007. At the going down of the sun and in the morning, we will remember them. Remembered with love and pride every day by his Daddy.'

During the writing of this book, I was told that former British soldier turned agent Kevin Fulton, who had infiltrated the Provisionals, used his expertise to develop the horizontal mortar. Fulton – not his real name – joined the Royal Irish Rangers, but was then persuaded by British Army Intelligence to fake a dishonourable discharge in order to gain entry into the IRA. He was 'green-booked' (inducted by the IRA) and worked on several operations in the Newry area of South Armagh. He admitted to taking part in operations which led to the death and injury of soldiers and policemen, but he also saved countless lives. I am merely reporting that there was and is a strong and credible rumour that he used his soldiering expertise to develop PIRA weapon technology and specifically invented the horizontal mortar. (*See also* Kevin Fulton, *Unsung Hero*, John Blake Books, 2006.)

On the same day as the deadly mortar attack, the European Court of Human Rights agreed to hear another complaint against the British government. The case involved the UK's derogation from the European Convention of Human Rights on the matter of the seven-day detention of suspects under the Prevention of Terrorism Act. Prime Minister John Major instructed the British legal team to stand firm against what one former soldier called 'the bleeding heart, PIRA-lovers in Brussels'.

Retaliation for the mortar attack followed, as surely as night follows day. It came in a bloody manner the next day, when a UVF murder gang opened fire on a Catholic-frequented pub in Cappagh, Co. Tyrone; their intention was to kill as many innocent Catholics as possible, but they ended up claiming credit for wiping out three PIRA gunmen. The pub – Boyle's – stands in Cappagh Road, near the junction with Lurgylea Road, close to the village's obligatory IRA memorial.

Cappagh is only six miles from the Irish border and the Irish culture is indomitable here, with Gaelic football the predominant sport. Boyle's was packed that Sunday night, the 3rd, following a local derby. In the late evening, two cars containing two separate UVF units from east Tyrone, recently purchased by a wealthy supporter, arrived in the small village; one of the units remained on the outskirts, whilst the other silently glided up to Boyle's. Just as they arrived, so too did another car, containing four local Provisionals: John Quinn (23), Malcolm Nugent (20) and Dwayne O'Donnell (17) and an unnamed man. Cusack and MacDonald (*UVF: The Endgame*, Poolbeg, 2008) state that it was the Loyalists' intention to ambush the PIRA men. However, in common with other students of the Troubles, I subscribe to the theory that they intended simply to kill any Catholic caught in their crosshairs and the killing of the IRA men was merely a 'bonus'. As the car stopped and the doors opened, the man who survived said that he realised that something was wrong as he saw a man illuminated in the headlights of another car; the man was clad in a balaclava and pointing a weapon straight at them. The driver of the car – Quinn – slammed the car into reverse, but was hit by the hail of bullets causing the car to crash as the men died there and then.

I wonder if the last thing which went through their minds was the sheer irony of it all. Did they see the balaclava – an IRA trademark – and the automatic weapon and the flash of 7.62 mm rounds being fired at them and think: 'This is what we have been doing to the people of this country for twenty plus years.' Stepping over their bloodied bodies, the UVF gang went into the bar and began firing indiscriminately at the drinkers. Several were hit and wounded, but Thomas Armstrong (52), an entirely innocent Catholic, was shot and killed. During the hail of fire, one local IRA man, Brian Arthurs – whose brother, Declan was killed in the Loughgall ambush in 1987 – managed to dodge behind the bar and lie low until the murder gang had raced outside and away from the bloodbath they had just created. One man, Malachy Rafferty, told a later inquest that he heard three shots, followed by a burst of gunfire; he added: 'I felt pain, a burning sensation in my arm. The shooting lasted for about 30 seconds and I lay for a while.' He explained that he then ran to the door of the pub but it was locked; he shouted his name and the door was opened. He added: 'I must have blacked out at this stage because I remember nothing more until I saw the ambulance.'

The following day, a spokesman for the UVF – the mythical 'Captain Black' – made the following statement: 'This was not a sectarian attack on the Catholic community, but was an operation directed at the very roots of the Provisional IRA command structure in the Armagh–Tyrone area. We conclude by saying that if the Provisional IRA were to cease its campaign of terror, the Ulster Volunteer Force would no longer deem it necessary to continue with its military operations.' Naturally they were cock-a-hoop with their 'success' claiming that it was a well-planned, well-executed raid, striking at the very heart of the IRA. This was nonsense, of course; it was a sectarian attack which brought them some much-needed political kudos and helped perpetuate the mythology of the organisation. What they overlooked was that the IRA men had decided that it was safe to drink in their stronghold and had only visited Boyle's on the spur of the moment, in what turned into a most fateful choice.

In America the *Philadelphia Enquirer* reported the subsequent funerals in its 7 March issue:

> Behind the four black hearses in the chill drizzle of a gray morning, they marched slowly, silently down the Galbally Road, 3,000 of them, faces grim, minds bitter. They had come yesterday to mourn four of their own, four Catholics, four men of County Tyrone. The four had been shot and killed Sunday night at Boyle's Pub in nearby Cappagh, killings for which a Protestant paramilitary group, the Ulster Volunteer Force (UVF), had claimed responsibility. The procession turned off the road and up the hill to St. John's Church, which had room for less than half of the mourners. The only sounds were the tolling of the church bell and the whir of a hovering police surveillance helicopter. After the four coffins had been carried inside, the Rev. Patrick McGuckin spoke to the throng about the deaths of the four, John Quinn, Thomas Armstrong, Malcolm Nugent and Dwayne O'Donnell. Three of them were accused by their killers of having been members or sympathizers of the Irish Republican Army.[1]
>
> 'Let others say what they will about them; harsh words will not affect them now,' Father McGuckin said, responding to the allegations, which are vigorously denied here. Outside, the drizzle was becoming a cold downpour, soaking the mourners who listened to a loudspeaker in the churchyard. The shootings in Cappagh, a hamlet 50 miles west of Belfast and just down the road from Galbally, were the deadliest act in what has been the province's most violent period so far, this year. On the street this week, the reaction to the shootings at Boyle's has been less one of grief than of anger and bitterness, a feeling that such acts are neither unusual nor accidental. Friday night, at Callanbridge, County Armagh, two soldiers of the Ulster Defence Regiment (UDR) were killed and two others seriously injured when their Land Rover was hit by a mortar fired by an IRA hit squad. On Monday night, a Catholic taxi driver, Michael Lenaghan, was shot and killed inside his vehicle after he picked up two men in the center of Belfast and took them to the Woodvale area, a Protestant stronghold in North Belfast. The UVF claimed responsibility for the killing, which police described as 'purely sectarian.'
>
> Early Tuesday morning, the IRA bombed the East Belfast headquarters of Shorts, an airplane manufacturing company and the largest private employer in Northern Ireland. No one was injured. But it was the shootings at Boyle's Pub here in rural County Tyrone that caused the greatest stir. The immediate area is a republican stronghold, while the larger region has been the scene of a rash of sectarian killings over the last two years. Cappagh is a drab, out-of-the-way village a few hundred yards long, with exactly four commercial establishments, the pub

1. Named in 'The Pensive Quill' as PIRA Volunteers. http://thepensivequill.am/2016/03/cappagh-martyrs-remembered-with-pride.html.

(which is next to a barn full of sheep), the post office, a fish-and-chips shop and a tiny, windowless grocery. None of these places has a sign outside; there is no need. Everybody in town knows where they are, and strangers rarely pass through. The community is more open about its politics. It has a memorial in the main street commemorating an IRA hunger striker who died in Belfast's H-block prison 10 years ago and eight IRA men shot dead in 1987. The talk in Cappagh this week has been about how it all could have happened, and the almost universally held theory is that the security forces – the government – had something to do with it. The reasoning, in its least conspiratorial form, goes like this: Day-to-day security is so heavy in and around Cappagh – the helicopters overhead, the constant patrols along the roadsides by uniformed soldiers, their faces marked by green-and-brown camouflage paint, their submachine guns drawn – that the killers could not have come and gone without some level of official collusion. Some residents are convinced that the security forces themselves carried out the killings, in which one of the victims was shot in a men's room.

On the 4th, the UVF were once again in action, this time 50 miles north-east of Cappagh, in North Belfast. Michael Lenaghan (40) was a Catholic father of four who lived in the Falls Road area, plying his trade as a taxi driver. By all accounts, he was a hard-working, industrious man, an innocent human being who had somehow come to the attention of men of evil. The Loyalist group had a short-wave radio and were able to monitor the driver's radio transmissions during that fateful night. Accordingly, they were able to engineer a pick-up from the city centre, with Mr Lenaghan as their driver. What probably swung the dispatcher's decision to send the Catholic was the stated destination: Malone Road in South Belfast was an affluent area that was considered safe for drivers. Two members of the UVF gang got into the car and told him that there had been a change of destination; telling him instead to drive to Heather Street, a dead-end in the heart of the Loyalist Shankill. As they arrived outside a house in Heather Street, they took out handguns and shot him several times in the head and back, killing him almost instantly. Leaving him inside the fume-filled, blood-soaked taxi, they calmly walked away. There are several streets, all residential, within earshot of the murder, but the RUC murder investigation discovered that everyone in Heather Street, Mossvale Street, Ottawa Street and Oregon Gardens was either out for the evening or suffered from acute deafness. It was only the 4th of the month, but already six people were dead.

Earlier in the day members of Belfast City Council voted by 21 to 19 to end the ban on visits by government ministers which they had imposed following the signing of the AIA. On the 25th, a ministerial delegation from John Major's new Cabinet flew into Belfast to commence the rebuilding of bridges with the Loyalist politicians.

On the 6th, five people – French and Irish nationals – were sentenced to jail terms for their part in the IRA arms-smuggling voyage of the MV *Eksund*. The ship had been carrying a Libyan consignment of arms and explosives to the IRA in 1987. Several members of the crew of the *Eksund* stood in the Paris dock.

On the 13th, Donald Kaberry (83), former Tory Chairman and friend of the recently deposed Prime Minister Margaret Thatcher, died following his injuries in an IRA attack in June 1990. Two IRA men had thrown a blast device through the window of the Carlton

Club in Mayfair, injuring several people. Lord Kaberry was one of the injured, and had spent the subsequent nine months in and out of hospital. He died in his home town of Leeds.

In *Sir, They're Taking The Kids Indoors*, I deal with one of the most heinous of all crimes carried out in the name of Irish Republicanism: the bombings of three pubs in Birmingham city centre on the night of 21 November 1974. Twenty-one people were killed and dozens maimed in a series of no-warning bombs. Bombs exploded in the Mulberry Bush and the Tavern in the Town. A third device planted in Yates' Wine Lodge nearby caused no casualties as the pub had already been evacuated. The death toll would have been around 40, had it not been for quick-thinking pub management and fast police action. Six Irishmen were convicted of the Birmingham attacks and sentenced to life in jail. The men – Hugh Callaghan, Paddy Hill, Gerry Hunter, Richard McIlkenny, Billy Power, and Johnny Walker – were disgracefully 'fitted up' for the crimes and sent to jail for life. This shameful miscarriage of justice, brought about by corrupt officers in the West Midlands Serious Crimes Squad, was only rectified on 14 March 1991 when the men – known as the 'Birmingham Six' – were freed by the Court of Appeal in London.

The forensic evidence was shown to be unreliable and there was further evidence that the police had forged notes of interviews, thus giving false testimony at the original trial, and had used violence and intimidation during the interrogation. In one instance, one of the six was hit in the face with a metal object, shattering his front teeth. I can accept that the police were under pressure to find the mass murderers, and that there are certain 'wartime exigencies', but the country wanted the real guilty men behind bars, not simply six Irishmen who 'fitted the bill'. Home Secretary Kenneth Baker accepted that this was the third case of a miscarriage of justice involving Irish people in the previous 18 months. The other two cases were the Guildford Four and the Maguire family, all framed by the same police force.

Peter Brooke announced on the same day that talks on the AIA were to involve the four main Northern Irish political parties (the Ulster Unionists – UUP; Social Democratic and Labour Party – SDLP; Democratic Unionists – DUP; and the Alliance Party) and were the first in a series which lasted from April 1991 to November 1992 and later became known as the Brooke/Mayhew Talks. (Patrick Mayhew took over from Brooke as Secretary of State before the talks were concluded.) This process was to include relationships within Northern Ireland and achieving a devolved government – this was 'strand one' of the talks; relations between Northern Ireland and the Republic of Ireland would be 'strand two'; and between the British and Irish Governments would be 'strand three'. In addition the three strands were to form a complete agreement – 'nothing is agreed until everything is agreed'. In what was seen as a show of unity, the four parties all agreed to talk about the future of Northern Ireland and the Irish Republic. The first talks began the following month, on 30 April.

On the 17th, a bout of fisticuffs in the ranks of the UDA/UFF in South Belfast led to the death of UFF member Stephen Audley (23) and proved the old maxim: 'Don't let children play with guns.' Two teenagers in the Ulster Young Militants (UYM) – motto: '*Terrae Filius*' ('Son of the Land'), a group of trainee Loyalist paramilitaries – had been issued with a pistol and dispatched into the Loyalist Village area of South Belfast in order to carry out a punishment shooting on a local mugger. They were unable to find their target and returned to their local area to explain. However, without surrendering the weapon, they later went to a party at Wauchope Court, where one of the UYM thugs started to argue with UFF member Audley. Another youth, in an act of bravado, pulled the weapon on the more senior UFF man. In the ensuing struggle, the pistol fired, mortally wounding Audley. Both of the young men went to jail for manslaughter.

Peter Taylor records that the UYM had its origins in the 'Tartan Gangs' of the early 1970s, unofficial Loyalist street gangs who gained their name from the tartan scarves and flash of tartan they wore on their denim jackets. It is also worth noting that Loyalist Milltown cemetery killer Michael Stone was a member of the UYM, another 'son of the land'.

The body of Francis Paul Taggart (17) was found near a leisure centre in Warren Park, a loyalist area of Lisburn, early on the 18th – a Monday – in a terribly mutilated condition. He had died from multiple stab wounds to the head, neck and stomach; it was simply another random act of sectarian violence. The young man was a Catholic and had called into a fish and chip shop on the Sunday evening. Reports state that he had become involved in an argument with Protestant youths over the result of that day's game in the Scottish Football League between Rangers and Celtic. The gang followed him out of the shop, and onto waste ground. The gang jumped him and kicked and stabbed him to death in a frenzied attack, full of sectarian hatred and spite. The Catholic boy was stabbed no fewer than 62 times. Some of the wounds were so deep that they could have only been delivered with absolutely venomous intent. A local man with UVF links was charged and convicted of his murder.

On the 19th, the DERR took part in a major operation – 'Mutilate' – in which a number of border crossings were closed and the vehicle control points at Derryard and Boa Island were removed.

On the 20th and 22nd, the Provisionals continued with their intimidation of companies which carried out contracting work for the Army/RUC. In the first incident, a Protestant man was shot and wounded in the arm as he drove to work at Locksley Engineering in Belfast. The IRA later said that it attacked him because he was employed by a firm which carried out work for the SF. Within 24 hours, Locksley Engineering, where the injured man worked as a manager, announced that it would cease working for the RUC and the Army. Just 48 hours later, a number of gunmen opened fire on a black Mazda sports car that had left the carpark of RUC Headquarters in Londonderry, and stopped at traffic lights. Six masked IRA gunmen had taken over the Strand Bar at the junction of Great James Street and Strand Road, where they had ordered staff and customers to lie on the floor. The driver – a civilian, Mrs Margaret Grant, a mother of three – was hit and seriously wounded. Their shots also hit a second car and caused terror to the passengers in a following bus. The would-be killers escaped out of the back door of the bar into a waiting stolen taxi, and were seen heading in the direction of the Bogside. The taxi was found burning in Oakfield Road just half a mile away from the murder bid. William McCrea, MP, said: 'How low can the terrorists get when an innocent and defenceless woman is their target?' Another local politician called them 'parasites' and demanded that Nationalists 'eject them from their midst'.

Mrs Grant was the widow of a police officer – Sergeant Tom Cooke – gunned down by the IRA, whilst he was off duty at Prehen Golf Club in Co. Londonderry, in April 1987. The point at where she was attacked was only half a mile away. This assault on Mrs Grant attracted the condemnation of community leaders, politicians and churchmen of all persuasions. The *Irish Emigrant* newspaper declared: 'It is some time since an IRA action generated so much distaste.' There can be no doubt that this woman was attacked quite deliberately, as her black Mazda was very distinctive and their scouts (or 'dickers' in Army slang) would have seen it many times and they would have known that she was the widow of a slain police officer. On the same day, the Provisionals were also in action in Newry where two RUC officers were injured when their vehicle was attacked by a rocket. In another incident on the same night, an off-duty UDR soldier was shot near Trillick, Co. Tyrone, but his wounds were not serious.

Worse was to follow on the 28th, as the UVF, not content with involvement in several of the deaths already this month, struck again with a violent attack on a mobile shop in Craigavon, Co. Armagh. I well remember the mobile shops which toured the vast council estates in the working class – and predominantly Catholic – east Leeds where I was raised. The 'Thrift Stores', as they were known at that time in the 1950s, were huge vans with removable steps, up which my late mother would struggle, grumbling all the while; they were crammed top to bottom, side to side with shelves with all manner of groceries. They were designed for those without cars and when the alternative was merely a corner shop or the local Co-Op.

One such mobile shop operated around the Nationalist Drumbeg Estate in Craigavon; the owner was popular with the locals, but had run foul of UDR patrols, as he refused to serve them, fearing the local IRA more than the soldiers. In the twisted logic of the UVF, this made him a Provie, or at least a sympathiser, and as such marked him for death. During the evening, Robin 'the Jackal' Jackson, the psychopathic leader of the UVF's mid-Ulster brigade, plus several other UVF gunmen, including Tom Harper, arrived at the location of the mobile shop and calmly walked over to it, in the manner of shoppers. They suddenly yelled: 'Provisional IRA, hit the floor!' Some customers managed to run away but three girls were trapped. The UVF men shot Eileen Duffy (19) in the head as she served at the counter. Another girl, Katrina Rennie (16), was also hit in the head as she perched herself on a crate, chatting to Eileen. Duffy had been suspicious at the approach of the men and warned 14-year-old Jaimie Smith to run away, just seconds before she herself was shot dead. The gunmen threw the 14-year-old out of the shop, calling her 'a Fenian bitch', and then turned to walk away. As they did so, another man turned up. He was Brian Frizzell (29). Like the two girls he was entirely innocent but Jackson made him lie on the ground before shooting him several times in the head from point-blank range. The attackers ran towards their stolen van and raced off in the direction of the Loyalist Mourneview where the vehicle was torched.

Eileen Duffy's brother Brendan lived close by and was quickly on the scene; he said later:

> Eileen was only 11 months younger than me, so we were very close; we started school the same day and made our First Communion and Confirmation together. I can still see us as kids sitting together under the Christmas tree opening our presents. She was the kindest hearted wee girl you'd ever meet. She'd give you her last penny. She was always laughing and wanting to make people happy. She saw bad in nobody. She played camogie for the local GAA club, Eire Og. She was proud to be Irish but she'd no interest in politics. Brian Frizzell was lying in a pool of blood. Katrina was still sitting on the crate. She was dead, but her blue eyes were

> wide open and there was a bullet wound on her neck. Eileen was slumped on the floor, shot in the head. Her face was badly swollen, and blood was pumping out of her head and ears. I tried to resuscitate her but, in my heart, I knew she was gone. I was so numb, I couldn't cry.

Their mother Olive Duffy ran to the shop; Brendan said:

> I didn't want my mother to look at that awful scene but she said she had to. She broke down when she saw Eileen lying dead.

The killing was claimed by the 'Protestant Action Force', a cover name for the UVF; one of the gang, Harper, was later jailed for life. According to the *Lurgan Mail*, Noel Clarke who was jailed for five years for his part in the killings, committed suicide in September 2012. Clarke originally faced three murder charges in relation to the killings. However, he was acquitted of involvement and went on to plead guilty, along with associate William Robert Abbot, then living at Down Royal, Maze, to hijacking a van used by the killers.

Newshound.com reported the following:

> The picture that broke a mother's heart – teenager Eileen Duffy lies in her coffin wearing the beautiful cream dress she'd bought to go to dances. But Eileen was brutally slain by loyalist paramilitaries weeks later so instead she was buried in her best dress. The 19-year-old was gunned down in a horrific triple murder as she worked in a mobile shop in Craigavon 20 years ago. Her killer, whose name is known to *Sunday World*, has never been charged. He freely walks the streets of Portadown. Eileen's family fear he'll never face justice because this week's admission that police files in Armagh's Gough barracks have been destroyed – allegedly because of contamination with asbestos – means any evidence linking him to the murder is gone. Grief-stricken Olive Duffy gave the never before published photo of her dead daughter to *Sunday World*. 'I want the world to see what I have to live with every day. My beautiful girl left the house laughing and smiling to go to work that night. She came home in a coffin,' Olive said, breaking down in tears. 'I can't get over it. I see friends she went to school with and they're grown up with children of their own. My Eileen was denied all that happiness. She's now dead longer than she was alive. I just want her back.' Eileen was known as 'Angel Eyes' because of her big brown eyes and loving personality. Her memorial card is always with her mother. 'A bouquet of beautiful memories sprayed with a million tears. Wishing God could have spared you if just for a few more years,' it says.[1]

There were 13 deaths this month. Of the seven civilians, Lord Kaberry was a Jew, a victim of the IRA, and six were Catholics, slaughtered in purely sectarian killings. The Loyalists were responsible for 10 of the deaths, with the blood of nine people on the hands of the UVF.

1. http://www.nuzhound.com/articles/breen/arts2011/sep18_Eileen_Duffy_murder_evidence_destroyed_SBreen_Sunday-World.php.

4

April

Seven people died this month, although for the third month in four, there were no military deaths. Two policemen were killed as were four civilians; additionally, an IRA man was killed by the RUC after he had carried out a mortar attack on a police station.

The first murder this month occurred when the UVF killed a former Protestant who had converted to Catholicism. Samuel Bell (54), father of five, was a taxi driver from Cliftonpark Avenue who had been born into the Protestant faith but changed his church when he married a Catholic woman. On the evening of the 3rd, Mr Bell answered the call for a taxi in Belfast's Broadway, on the edge of a Nationalist area; the three-man UVF gang knew that only a driver from a Nationalist area would answer such a call. A fourth passenger – a female student – was dropped off first, before the three men forced Mr Bell to drive to the Loyalist Glencairn area; once there, he was dragged out and shot dead. The gang propped his body up outside the vehicle, before setting fire to it and then melting off into the night. His badly burned body was found the following morning.

Mr Bell's daughter, Veronica Magee, who had heard on the radio that another taxi driver had been killed said: 'I would never have believed in a million years it was daddy.' She told the press that her father had removed the sign from his taxi in case it identified him as a Catholic. Sadly, it failed to save his life; he would not be the last.

In an edition the following month, the *Los Angeles Times* reported:

> 'In London your worst fear is someone sick in the cab, here it's a bullet in your head,' said a Belfast taxi driver who is thinking about quitting his job. Fear haunts Belfast's taxi fraternity because seven drivers have died at the hands of paramilitaries in the past 15 months, mostly in the bomb-scarred ghettos of the city. Other taxis have been hijacked [when] paramilitaries found out the driver's religion. 'We've all got a gut reaction there will be more killings,' said one taxi firm owner, adding, 'God knows, we're terrified.' He was unwilling to be identified for fear of losing his life. The 'Cabbie Killings' are the latest twist in Northern Ireland's bitter sectarian and political conflict which has pitted Protestant against Catholic communities.
>
> 'Dial-A-Catholic' is how Protestant paramilitaries have adapted the 'Dial-A-Cab' slogan. Killers have shot drivers in the back of their heads. In some cases drivers have been ambushed while walking from their vehicle to the pick-up address. At the depots callers are now questioned carefully about who they are, how many passengers there are and how old they are. 'But there's only so much you can do,' said another taxi firm manager. 'You see they're very vulnerable and for

> the gunmen they're soft [easy] targets,' he said. 'If you see three fellows in leather jackets you just don't bother,' said one driver who works the grim ghettos of this split city where Irish Republicans and those loyal to British rule mark out their territory with graffiti and flags.

On the 4th, having telephoned through a warning, the IRA detonated a massive bomb in the centre of Banbridge, Co. Down. The device was huge, estimated at 1,000 lb (450 kg); the damage was widespread and caused over £1 million worth of damage, destroying mainly Protestant businesses.

On the 5th, Manchester was hit by the first of three IRA bombings in a five-year period. On this occasion a number of incendiary devices were planted in the Arndale Shopping Centre. They were discovered and defused by police and Army bomb disposal experts. It was thought that the centre's profile and high revenue made it a prime economic target, as damage and disruption to business would force the owners to put pressure on the Major government for a British withdrawal. It was also attacked later in the year (covered in a further chapter) and of course, more famously in 1996, when the IRA targeted the centre of Manchester again.

On the 6th, a PIRA bombing unit planted a device underneath a car belonging to an RUC officer as he visited his elderly mother in Ballycastle, Co. Antrim. He had clearly been dicked by PIRA sympathisers over a period of several weeks, parking his car in the same spot each week after driving down from Limavady on the north Antrim coast. He chose the public car park in Castle Street in the small town. After Detective Constable John McGarry (46), father of three, had said goodbye to his mother, he started the car and began driving. The small but lethal device exploded, killing him almost instantly. The car continued moving and, on fire, it crashed into another vehicle, and that also burst into flames. Although severely shocked, that driver managed to escape with just cuts and bruises. Three PIRA operatives were later given jail sentences totalling 42 years; a local man, Gary Butler, was sentenced to life for planting the bomb. A policeman said later: 'It really is a moot point whether or not the IRA had been observing him for some time, or if a trusted neighbour of Mrs McGarry informed the terrorists that she received weekly visits from her policeman son. Someone in Ballycastle knew what they had done and I wonder if he or she could look that officer's grieving mother in the face when they passed her in the street.'

On the 9th, acting on flawed, or just hearsay evidence, a unit from the Provisionals' discredited Tyrone brigade killed a Protestant man in front of his young sons at Coagh. Derek Ferguson (30), a carpenter, was building a house at Aughaveagh Road, between Cookstown and Lough Neagh. Whilst the house was under construction, he and his family were living in a caravan on the site. PIRA intelligence had him marked as a UVF member, but his only Loyalist connections came through his family. He was a cousin of William McCrea, the DUP MP for the area and a leading Orangeman, but that was perhaps enough for the IRA to sentence him to death. In the early evening, shortly after he had put his two toddler sons to bed, two masked men burst into the caravan, where he was sitting with two of his other boys, aged six and seven. Ignoring the confused children, they pointed a gun at Mr Ferguson's head and asked if he was Derek. The older boy later told police that one of the men had simply said: 'Bye, bye, Derek,' before shooting his father several times. The killers then ran off to a waiting car, driving to Ardboe, before being collected in a second stolen vehicle. The older boy had the presence of mind to telephone his grandmother who dashed to the caravan and found the two children covered in their father's blood.

It was alleged that one of the killers was Lawrence McNally who was himself killed nearby, just 55 days later, when he and two other IRA men were ambushed by the SAS, on 3 June. If indeed McNally was the killer of Mr Ferguson, it was a pity that he wasn't stopped before the SAS caught up with him, as it is highly likely that he also killed an off-duty UDR soldier on 31 May (*see* next chapter).

Associated Press (AP) reported the murder in the following terms:

> The Irish Republican Army said today it killed the cousin of a Protestant legislator, a news agency reported. Gunmen shot and killed Derek Ferguson, 30, a Protestant builder, at Coagh 25 miles west of Belfast late Tuesday night, police said. Ferguson's cousin, the Rev. William McCrea, a member of Northern Ireland's Democratic Unionist Party, represents Mid-Ulster in the House of Commons in London. In calls to local news organizations, the IRA said it killed Ferguson because he was a loyalist terrorist involved in sectarian attacks, Press Association, the domestic British news agency, said. Loyalists support British rule in Northern Ireland. McCrea said Ferguson was a hard-working man 'who minded his own business and had one great goal in his young life – the building of a new home for his wife and four children'. Police said he was killed as he sat watching television with two of his four children in his temporary trailer home parked next to a house he was renovating in County Tyrone village. The gunmen fired through a window of the trailer. His other two children were asleep in the trailer. Police said first word of the attack was telephoned to relatives by Ferguson's 7-year-old son, who told them: 'Bad men have shot my daddy.' The building company for which Ferguson worked, Henry Brothers of Magherafelt nine miles north of Coagh, has had three other employees killed by IRA guerrillas because they did building work for the security forces. The IRA says it regards any civilian working for the security forces in any capacity as a legitimate target.

Four days later, the IRA also killed another Protestant based on yet more flawed intelligence.

Over the coming weeks, there was more evidence of 'big boys' rules', as PIRA terrorists found themselves bleating again about shoot-to-kill. In the first, a two-man mortar team set out to launch an attack on the RUC station at Downpatrick, Co. Down, some 20 miles south-east of Belfast. On the evening of the 10th, acting upon information received from a well-placed informant within the Down command of the IRA, RUC officers were placed in an area from where it was thought that a mortar attack would be launched. Officers watching a house in St Patrick's Avenue, observed two men, one of whom was PIRA man Colum Marks (29), working on what turned out to be a faulty mortar bomb that they were trying to fix. Warnings were shouted, and indeed police fired two rounds into the air, but both men ran off. Officers then opened fire, hitting Marks but missing the other man who escaped into the night. The Newry IRA man, who had joined after leaving the Irish National Liberation Army (INLA), was fatally injured and died after being rushed to hospital.

An Phoblacht, seemingly unaware of their own shoot-to-kill philosophy and clearly uninformed as to their own policy with regard to wounded enemies, then delivered what may justifiably be referred to as a pack of lies, designed to convince either their own terrorised supporters or the gullible Irish-Americans. Laura Friel wrote: 'No medical assistance was given. No ambulance was called. No one alerted the hospital that a seriously injured man was on his way. The hospital was just a minute's drive away but it was at least 30 minutes before the injured man arrived.' The Republican writer finished her article with: 'We are asking for recognition of Colum Marks' human rights.' I ask what about the human rights of the 2,000 people which your organisation slaughtered?

On the 13th, just four days after the mistaken killing of a man believed to be a Loyalist paramilitary, the IRA's Tyrone brigade killed another innocent Protestant. They were acting on Garda-supplied material, wrongly labelling Ian Sproule (23) as a UVF member. There is much complaining from the Republicans about RUC/Loyalist paramilitary collusion, but we hear little or nothing about Garda/IRA collusion. Mr Sproule's name and photograph were erroneously placed on an Irish police intelligence document, which was leaked to the IRA by one of the many sources within the Garda Síochána. The document stated that he was involved in a 1987 UVF operation, when in fact, the operation was carried out by the UDA/UFF, of which, equally, he had no part. On the fateful night, Mr Sproule was visiting his parents' home in Lisleen Road, Killen, close to Castlederg – an area where I have experienced the bitter hatred which the Republicans feel for the British. It was a regular visit, something about which the local Provisionals knew very well. Lisleen Road is in a very remote spot, with the road itself flanked by trees, fields and hedges, with long distances between houses and plenty of spaces for watching gunmen to hide. As he parked his car, masked men ran across to him and shot him dead. They quickly melted away into the Castlederg area, knowing that they had many safe houses there, or they also had a choice of the Irish border, which was but four miles away. Despite scouring the hate-filled archives of *An Phoblacht* in general and their writer Laura Friel specifically, there is no evidence that they or she complained about the violation of Mr Sproule's human rights, nor is there any condemnation of the IRA's shoot-to-kill policy.

UDR Soldier

Mr Sproule's pictures did indeed appear in local Garda stations, allegedly wanted for interview in connection with a fire bomb attack, and again he was arrested by the RUC on more than one occasion in the past. There is no doubt that PIRA obtained the information from Garda sources. This particular killing was carried out by Donegal PIRA with the assistance of local West Tyrone members from Castlederg – as would have been the case in many of the attacks carried out in the Castlederg area.

On the same day, the Provisionals targeted an off-duty police officer who lived in the town of Lisburn. Sergeant Ernest McCrum (61) had joined the RUC in 1955 and had served through the IRA's Border Campaign in the late 1950s and throughout the 22 years to that point of the Troubles. In the early part of 1991, he had announced that his retirement was imminent and that he was looking forward to helping out more frequently in the antiques shop which his wife ran in Antrim Street, Lisburn. On that spring Saturday, he was off duty and helping in the shop, which was empty at the time, when two PIRA gunmen walked in and calmly shot the policeman dead. He was shot at point-blank range, and then, just as calmly, the killers walked out. A later inquest was told by a detective that the killing was done 'without panic'. The killers locked the door after them and the keys were never found. A local radio station was called by the IRA who gave a coded message and officers were rushed to the shop where the sergeant's body lay in a pool of blood. His personal protection weapon was still in its holster when his body was found. His brother said: 'He had security measures but he never got the time to use them. They just walked in and shot him. That was it. The RUC was his life. He will be sadly missed.'

On Sunday 14th and on the following day, Bishop Desmond Tutu from South Africa was in Northern Ireland in order to mediate in the affairs of a foreign country, forgetting that his own reborn nation had problems enough of its own. At a church conference in Newcastle, Co. Down, he pontificated that Sinn Féin should be invited to attend the anticipated talks on the future of Northern Ireland. Quite what Peter Brooke at the NIO thought of that comment is not recorded; shortly afterwards he flew off with other NIO officials for a week-long visit to the USA to promote the forthcoming talks on the future of Northern Ireland.

As Mr Brooke was settling into his hotel in Washington, DC, and getting over his jet-lag, the Belfast Provisionals carried out a bomb attack on the Shorts aircraft factory in East Belfast on the 16th. There was some damage, but no casualties. At the time, Shorts was the largest private employer in Northern Ireland. It employed Catholics as well as Protestants, although given its location in Loyalist East Belfast, the daily journey into work, especially for those Catholics who lived in the Nationalist Short Strand, must have been a fairly stressful one.

On 17 April, a ceasefire was announced by the Combined Loyalist Military Command (CLMC) to commence at midnight on the 30th. The temporary ending of violence was to facilitate the proposed political talks between the Irish and British governments and would last as long as the talks. Attacks by all three organisations continued in the period immediately prior to the ceasefire. The wording of the statement declared: 'A universal suspension of aggressive operational hostilities.' The ceasefire which was supposed to be observed by the UFF, UVF and Red Hand Commandos was ended by the CLMC on 4 July 1991, although during this period there were at least two breaches that led to deaths. It was also a period when the Provisionals, the INLA and the Irish People's Liberation Organisation (IPLO) felt that they could kill in an unrestrained manner.

The next major attack on the Army was against the DERR; it took place on 20 April at the Gortmullan permanent vehicle control point (PVCP) in Co. Fermanagh; it was responded to with great vigour by the Army. For the first time in the Troubles a .50 Browning heavy machine gun was brought into action. Teams of soldiers came out from the base and skirmished towards the enemy, but by the time they got anywhere near their targets, the PIRA gang had retreated over the border. This was the battalion's last action in which fire was exchanged. They returned to Catterick in May.

Towards the end of the month, the Fair Employment Commission (FEC) published its first report on the religious composition of the workforce in Northern Ireland in those companies with more than 25 employees. The report showed that 65 per cent of the workforce was Protestant while Catholics accounted for 35 per cent. Although by now illegal, there was still a measure of discrimination against Catholics when jobs were being handed out. A Catholic worker was three times more likely to be unemployed than a Protestant of equal experience and qualifications. Although the days when employers could openly advertise 'Protestants only' or 'No Catholics need apply' were long gone, there were other, more subtle ways of ensuring that a workforce was either predominantly or wholly, Protestant. Someone living in the Ardoyne or the Falls Road in Belfast, was unlikely to be considered, especially if his competitor for the same job lived in the Shankill or Crumlin or Woodvale in the same city. Others might live in mixed areas, such as the Malone Road, but would fall foul when completing the 'Religion' section of an application form.

John Joseph Gerard O'Hara (41) lived in McAtemny Terrace on the Nationalist Short Strand. His wife Marie had been married before but her first husband had been murdered by Loyalists in 1975. Mr O'Hara, father and stepfather to five children, worked as a taxi driver and had gone to pick up a passenger at around 22:15. The man who called the taxi firm gave a Catholic name, thus lulling both dispatcher and driver into a false sense of security. As he drove along Dunluce Avenue, two masked UFF men stepped from the side of the road and opened fire, hitting him several times and mortally wounding him. The men then fled on foot down an entry between 124 and 126 Dunluce Avenue. Out of control, the taxi careered off down the road, smashing into several parked cars. A nurse who lived nearby ran over to the crashed car and saw what she at first took for a drunk driver who had lost control. However, when she examined him, she found blood from several bullet wounds and she tried desperately to stem the flow. She was then joined by a doctor and a student nurse, who also tried to save the dying man's life, but as the nurse said: 'I tried to keep the driver warm and stem the flow of blood, but he was slipping away fast.' Mr O'Hara died at the scene and a police officer was given the grim and unenviable task of informing Mrs O'Hara that she had become a widow for the second time, and telling two women that they had lost their stepfather and their three younger sisters that they, too, had lost a father. One of the killers was Stephen 'Inch' McFerran, the top UFF man in South Belfast, of whom I shall say more later. Despite his lofty position in the Loyalist terror group, he was knee-capped for his part in this murder as it was an unsanctioned attack.

A close relative of the distraught Mrs O'Hara said: 'It's bad enough going through it once but to see it happen a second time ...' AP reported: 'John O'Hara, 42, was killed in mid-April after the caller deliberately used a Catholic name to put the cab firm at ease.' The same man who had booked the taxi in a false name called back later and was laughing as he bragged to the dispatcher about the murder. The RUC later stated that the weapon used to kill the innocent Catholic was a South African Browning 9 mm; it was also used to kill Phillip Campbell at Moira in January 1992 (*see* Chapter 13).

The BBC reported on 21 September 2015 that the case of two men murdered by Loyalists was to be re-opened. 'Detectives from the Legacy Investigation Branch (LIB) said they had new information about the shootings.' The two men were John Benedict Devine [killed in 1989] and John Joseph Gerard O'Hara. 'Both these men were innocent Catholics who were murdered for no other reason than their religion,' a police spokesman said. Both victims were targeted by Loyalist gunmen in separate attacks. However, no one has ever been charged in connection with either murder.'

On Sunday 21 April, the Census – held at 10-year intervals – was conducted in Britain. In direct contrast to 1981, when there were widespread protests and civil disobedience, ordered by the Provisional IRA, there were no such protests this time. During the 1981 Census, Raymond Gilmour alleges that a Census worker, Joanne Mathers, was murdered by the IRA on the direct orders of Martin McGuinness. The results showed a total Northern Ireland population of 1,577,836. The total number of Catholics was calculated at 605,639; this was 38.38% of the actual population.

On the 28th, there was another mortar attack by the Co. Tyrone Provisionals. A two-man unit, undeterred by the death of Colum Marks at Downpatrick earlier in the month, opened fire at the RUC base at Carrickmore, again using a Mark XII. Damage was caused, but there were no injuries.

April ended with a Loyalist ceasefire, but heralded a relative Republican bloodbath in May. During the month of April, 7 people died: 2 policemen, 4 civilians and a 'combatant'. The civilians were 2 Catholics and 2 Protestants killed in sectarian attacks by the UVF and IRA respectively. Critics of my use of 'sectarian' in the murders of the Protestants by the Provisionals might prefer to emphasise 'flawed intelligence' instead. However, the IRA in my opinion, singled out the two men because they were Protestants.

5

May

Deaths rose again this month despite the CLMC ceasefire, with the Provisional IRA being responsible for the bulk of the killings. Four policemen, including a former RUCR man, killed because of past association, lost their lives in May. Four soldiers were killed as were two civilians; one of these deaths could be said to result from a mixture of political hatred and sectarianism.

On the first day of the month, the Provisionals launched a rocket attack on an RUC mobile patrol in the Beechmounts in Belfast; several officers from Grosvenor Road RUC station were injured, but one, Sergeant Stephen Gillespie (31), father of two, died in the RVH, the following day. An armed gang took over a house in Mica Street – which has now been redeveloped and is part of Mica Drive – which afforded a clear line of sight down Beechmount Street onto Beechmount Avenue. As soon as the RUC vehicle was due to pass into the sights of the RPG, young dickers signalled to the watching IRA gang and the missile was launched. One of the survivors later said: 'The vehicle shuddered and there was heat and a bright searing light. Sergeant Gillespie shouted: "We have been hit, we have been hit." I thought we were going to get through it when there was another really violent impact on the left-hand side, more violent than the first. This was accompanied by a bright, searing orange light, and I felt the heat on my face and forearms.'

Six youths from the Beechmounts were subsequently arrested and charged with being lookouts for the attack on the RUC vehicle. There were allegations that all six were 'tortured' at the Castlereagh Interrogation Centre and this became a *cause célèbre* amongst Republicans, with *An Phoblacht* and the *Irish News* claiming that they were guilty only of 'being Catholics'. I can totally understand the desire for the dead man's comrades to bring the guilty to justice quickly and will back them unconditionally in seeking legal retribution for the dead officer's family and other loved ones. It had become all too typical of Republican terrorists to attack and fatally injure a policeman and then skulk away to enjoy the adulation of their cronies in the 'Wild West' town of Dundalk in the Republic, whilst the young men they duped were left behind to face the music.

Almost 13 years later, a former British soldier, Tony Rodriguez, posted the following tribute to the murdered officer:

> I have remembered that day since I left N. Ireland and have always had a moment's silence on May 1st @ 11:00 for your father and the others injured. I was serving with the RCT [Royal Corps of Transport] attached to the Argylls based at North Howard Street Mill. I worked with your father and other members of the blues team for about 5 months. I wish to say your father was an inspirational man, who

> always brought a smile to my face and being only a young 19-year-old soldier at the time I felt safe in his company. Being a father myself now I have always thought about how much you and your family have sacrificed. I know my words will never take away the hurt your family has suffered along with the other RUC members on that patrol. But I hope you find some comfort in the fact that your dad's kindness and character has touched many people, some you know some you don't, like myself. I will never forget him or the sacrifice you have all made.'

Another RUC man wrote: 'Sergeant Stephen Gillespie is remembered as a good sergeant; even though he was based in Grosvenor Road and we were Springfield Road we worked together quite often. I was in the monitor room of Springfield Road RUC station that morning in 1991, on overtime with members of "B" section. I still remember that one of his favourite tracks was "Unchained Melody" and I still can't hear it to this day without remembering him and that morning.

On that day also, the Major government said that proposals for a Northern Ireland select committee at the Commons were worth considering. The concept was backed by Loyalists who were in favour of more integration with the UK in order to protect their position within the British framework. Loyalists have long been suspicious that the government is simply biding its time before walking away from Ulster and allowing it to become part of a 32-county Irish Republic.

On the 3rd, Robert Orr (56), father of two, was murdered by the IRA: his crime? He had been an active member of the RUCR until 1976, when he left for his family's sake and to concentrate on his accountancy career. The IRA's South Armagh brigade had erroneously identified him as a member of the UDR and accused him of harassing Catholics during house searches in the area. He was a senior partner in an accountancy firm and was involved with the Orange Order, but other than that, he had no links with either the SF or paramilitaries. A bombing unit had placed a 2 lb (1 kg) Semtex bomb underneath his car, with a mercury-tilt device. As his car reached the junction of Barrack Hill Road and the Mall in Armagh City, it detonated and he was killed instantly. A close friend of the murdered man said later: 'The greatest crime in the IRA's book is to be a Protestant who wishes to remain in the United Kingdom.' I spoke to a former UDR man who still lives in the Armagh area and was understandably nervous of being named. I agreed to publish his story, subject to verification, and agreed to respect his request for anonymity. I checked his story with a reliable source and am pleased to include the following:

Robert Orr
Soldier 'A' UDR

I have fuck-all love for the slime which calls itself the IRA; they are maggots and parasites and I wish the whole shite-bag of an organisation dead! I tell you this now, and I want you to write it down and tell the world, especially them Yankee fuckwits, that Robert Orr was not a member of the UDR and he was 15 or 16 years past being a serving peeler. He went to a Protestant church and he believed in the unity of the UK; if that is a fucking crime, then one million of us in this country are criminals too. Me, I can't stand the Romans, the Taigs, but he had no problem with them and just wanted to enjoy his life and his family. He was never outspoken and just wanted to enjoy winding down to retirement. To murder him as cruelly as the fuckers did was just terrible but for their Shinner gobshites to claim that he was UDR just underlines what cruel, murdering bastards the IRA are!

Danny Morrison, publicity director for Sinn Féin, appeared in court – he was later found guilty – on the 9th, along with seven other PIRA members and sympathisers, on charges of keeping an RUC informer captive, prior to interrogation, torture and likely execution. Morrison joined the IRA in the early 1970s and was interned in 1972. Known for his intellect and writing skills, he quickly rose within Sinn Féin as a publicist and mouthpiece for the terror organisation. This author has no time nor patience for Irish Republicanism, as I attempt to counter their attempt to rewrite the history of the Troubles; however, I will offer a begrudging word of congratulations to Morrison, who has condemned sectarian murder by the IRA of Protestants. As much as the Provisionals have also and will always claim that they were non-sectarian, there is little doubt that they practised the same overt hatred of Protestants as the Loyalists did of Catholics.

Morrison was charged with false imprisonment and conspiracy to murder Alexander 'Sandy' Lynch, a British double agent; he was sentenced to eight years in prison but was released in 1995. Lynch had been picked up by the West Belfast 'nutting squad' and taken to a house belonging to James Martin in the Nationalist Turf Lodge. Once there, he was interrogated by Freddie 'Stakeknife' Scappaticci who had informed him that he would: 'wake up upside down and it wouldn't matter about me screaming because no would be able to hear'. At one point, Morrison is said to have walked into the house. 'Stakeknife' was able to make a clandestine call to his handlers in the RUC's Special Branch, informing them that Morrison was present, and that if they wanted to save Lynch – one of their top agents – they had to move quickly. Armed RUC officers arrived and raided the house, although Morrison, who was alerted to their presence, had already fled into the house next door and pretended that he had been there for some time. This didn't wash with the police and he was arrested, at the same time that Lynch was being rescued and spirited away into the night to escape the 'nutting squad'. Morrison later said: 'On Sunday 7 January 1990, I was contacted by the IRA who said that one of their members who they had arrested and interrogated had admitted being an informer. This man, Sandy Lynch, had also confessed that his Special Branch handlers had been forcing him to set up for assassination two well-known North Belfast Republicans. They wanted these two men killed in revenge for an undercover operation that had gone wrong, resulting in the death of one of their colleagues.' However, Morrison was found guilty, along with Martin and five others, of false imprisonment and conspiracy.

The leaders of the main Unionist parties, meeting on the 15th, refused to accept the deadline imposed in the Brooke/Mayhew talks, and instead travelled to London for a meeting with John Major. Unionist representatives spoke to Major about the issue of the venue and nominations for the role of independent chairman of the talks. In particular, they voiced their objection to the nominee of the British government, Lord Carrington, as the independent chair for the 'Strand Two' negotiations, because of comments he had made concerning Northern Ireland politicians in his memoirs.

One police officer and a former officer were already dead, and as a consequence, RUC members were on high alert for further attacks; unknown to all but the men planning such atrocities, there would be two more Union Flag-draped coffins bearing the remains of policemen to be lowered into the ground before the month was over. On several recent trips to Northern Ireland, I have stayed in a small village near Enniskillen, amongst the few Protestant communities in that border area. Close by is the village of Lisbellaw, where I have taken an early morning stroll in order to buy newspapers; it is small and sleepy and very respectable. There are Union Flags around, but not the profusion of, say Rathcoole or Rathfern or the Shankill. It was a reasonably safe place to live, despite its proximity to the Republican hotbed of nearby Rosslea. At some stage on the 17th, Douglas Carrothers (51), father of three and a member of the RUCR since 1981, parked his car in a church car park at Tullygare Road. Guided by a local Catholic who had betrayed the policeman to the IRA, a bombing unit came over the border and planted an explosive device underneath the officer's car. Mr Carrothers drove home and later set off to report for work at his full-time job, and it was at this stage that the device exploded and he was killed instantly. IRA man Noel McHugh (32) was jailed for life in June 1993 for his part in the murder.

Douglas left a widow, Phyliss, as well as three children. She later became chairwoman of the RUC George Cross Widows Association and it was in this capacity that, in 2013, she welcomed Gerry Adam's apology to the family of a *garda* murdered by the IRA. She said that it was now time that the same man and the rest of the IRA apologised to the families of murdered RUC men as well. She told the BBC: 'It's very vague. I'd like clarification, does he mean families of the members of the RUC, UDR and army etc. that were murdered by Republicans. What's stopping him coming out and outrightly apologising and saying that, if that's what he means, otherwise he's just cloaking it.'

On the 19th of the month, the RUC lost another of its officers, when Constable Trevor Buchanan was found dead, along with a female friend, in an exhaust-fume-filled car in a garage in the 'Apostles', Castlerock. The two had apparently ended their lives in a joint suicide pact. In fact I believe in including suicides in the roll of honour of the Troubles for all security force personnel, but it would transpire, 19 years later, that the 'suicides' were actually murders, though not related to the Troubles.

On the 26th of the month, the IRA attacked a Protestant housing estate at Monrush, in the northern part of Cookstown in Co. Tyrone. A two-man team drove onto the estate and parked in Princess Avenue, leaving a car packed with explosives. The bombers casually sauntered away, knowing that their explosive handiwork could wreck lives as well as houses. Fortunately, they did telephone a warning through to the Samaritans, and RUC patrols rushed to the estate and began clearing the houses. The car eventually exploded, injuring 13 people, damaging 100 houses and destroying 26 in and around Princess Avenue.

Monrush Bomb
Ruth Forrest

It was Sunday evening and my husband, Adrian and I had arranged to go out for tea. With three young children, we never went out of Cookstown in case we needed to get home quickly, just a reminder of the times we lived in back then. That night we were home for 10 p.m. and our oldest boy, Aaron, who was six years old was still up. As I had to take the babysitter home, I took Aaron with me leaving my husband with our two younger boys who were three years and 18 months old.

Shortly after I left, my husband said there was continuous thumping on the door and he was reluctant to answer it, but as it persisted, he opened, and a worried looking police officer was pointing and shouting: 'There's a bomb in that car; get out now!' Adrian ran upstairs and lifted the two sleeping boys from their beds. He took them outside the house into the yard, which overlooked a large park and there he sat them on the wall to put their shoes on. He could see the car clearly parked with the bomb but thought it was probably a hoax. He had arranged for me to come and pick them up at the top of Princess Avenue where we lived.

I arrived within minutes and had literally just picked them up when there was a large explosion. The bomb had exploded! We drove on to my mother's house where we would spend the night. She was hysterical when we arrived as she thought we had been caught up in the explosion. Mum and I paid a visit to the bomb scene as soon as it broke daylight. Total carnage faced us. The house we lived in had no roof now, the concrete walls were splintered, with glass in every room and approximately 2 ft of the car that the bomb had been in was now in our baby son's cot, which he had been lifted out of just a few hours earlier. We were left homeless with three young children and with only the clothes we were standing in. The housing executive put caravans in the play park for the homeless, which is where we lived for three weeks. We were moved to temporary accommodation until we moved to the house we currently own.

Just four days after the murder of Douglas Carrothers, PIRA gunmen walked into Balmoral Market in Boucher Road, Belfast, and singled out Wallace McVeigh (45) from Glenmachan, in the east of the city. He ran the family business which had existed for some time in the Belfast area. The market is an easy run along Kennedy Way from the Nationalist Andersonstown Estate and a simple route in and out for the IRA murder gang sent to 'execute' Mr McVeigh as 'an agent of the Crown Forces'. Whatever twisted epithet the Provisionals applied to men and women who were simply trying to earn a living, he was marked for death. On the morning of the 21st, a car driven by Phillip Manning, containing at least two gunmen, arrived at the market; whilst Manning kept the engine running, the two gunmen, carrying weapons used in a previous murder, calmly walked up to Mr McVeigh and said: 'Are you Wallace McVeigh?' The unsuspecting businessman replied: 'Yes, how can I help you?' Without a further word, the two men shot him six times in the head and chest from point-blank range. Leaving him lifeless in a pool of blood, they ran outside to the waiting car. They drove at speed to a safe house where they disposed of the weapons and washed all forensics from their clothes and bodies. Phillip Manning received a life sentence in 1993 for aiding and abetting in the murder.

That same evening a former UDR soldier, Sammy Dillon, came close to death, but not as a consequence of his past association. Since leaving the regiment, he had taken employment as a bus driver, and one of his regular routes took him along the Crumlin Road. He had just dropped off his last two passengers at Carlisle Circus and was continuing up Crumlin Road. Unknown to him, a gang of yobs from the Shankill were lying in wait just ahead of him. Suddenly he noticed several men to his left and saw an object being thrown at him. His initial thought that it was a brick, but it was in fact a petrol bomb, followed by another, setting his cab alight; he began burning and struggled to kick open his door in order to escape. He forced open the door eventually and fell into the road on fire. Luckily for him a passer-by leapt to his help and beat out the flames. He was taken to the nearby Mater Hospital where he later recovered.

Samuel Dillon, Former UDR

When I was about level with the end of the railing round the wee park on the left hand side of the Crumlin Road I saw a young lad step out from behind the billboard a few yards further on. I saw him throw something which I thought was a brick. The next thing I knew a bottle hit me on the forehead and the front of the bus burst into flames. My hair and shirt went on fire and I got the bus stopped and tried to put the handbrake on. I put the flames out with my hands and tried to get the doors open. The security door stuck and suddenly the flames flared up again either from another petrol bomb or re-ignition of the petrol. I kicked the doors and got them open but by this time all my clothes at the front were burning. I beat at the flames with my hands and got them out. I remember screaming in agony. Some fellow in his late twenties came over and helped me to the Mater Hospital.

The plastic surgeon who saved the former UDR man's face told the subsequent court case: 'Mr Dillon was admitted to the Royal Victoria Hospital on 22 May 1991 having sustained severe burns allegedly in a petrol bomb attack. He had extensive injury to his face and limbs and chest as well as a smoke inhalation injury. The total body surface area of burn was approximately 55 per cent of which most was full thickness in depth. He required operations on three occasions. His operations were designed to remove the burn tissue and apply skin grafts from unburned areas of his body. He had a period of mechanical ventilation in the intensive care unit on account of his smoke inhalation injury. He now has very extensive scars as a result of this incident.'

Local teenagers Mark McAuley and Darren James McAllister were arrested by the RUC and eventually found guilty of the attack. Regular contributor M. C. told me: 'Sammy Dillon was a comrade of mine and "B. R." in 10 UDR; he was very badly burnt. I saw him afterwards and his face was and is very badly scarred, reminds me a lot of the injuries Simon Weston suffered in the Falklands. There was a real stink because it was Prod on Prod and the UVF caught up with McAuley and McAllister and they were kneecapped.'

On the 24th, Kevin Lynch, a member of the IRA's Fermanagh brigade attempted to murder a policeman at his home in a remote part of Fermanagh, close to the Irish border. Lynch, who was later jailed, was from Lisnaskea and should not be confused with the Kevin Lynch from Dungiven, Co. Londonderry, who was the seventh of the hunger strikers to die in 1981. An un-named chief inspector was off-duty and was working in his garden, when Lynch and another Provo arrived on a motorbike that had been stolen in the Irish Republic. Lynch shot the inspector several times, badly wounding him. As Lynch moved closer to fire more shots at the defenceless officer, the officer's son, a constable in the RUC, ran out of the house and opened fire on Lynch. Several rounds were exchanged, before the constable ran out of ammunition and had to duck back inside the house in order to re-load. The gunmen opened fire with a rifle, fortunately missing him, before racing off across the border. The wounded officer was rushed to hospital where he made a full recovery. One of the IRA men was hit, because blood splatters were found on the stolen motorbike when it was recovered from Maguiresbridge the following day.

Lynch was subsequently arrested and went on trial in Belfast two years later. The day after the murder attempt, the Belfast *News Letter* reported: 'An RUC man saved the life of his policeman father by taking on two men in a gun battle. The Constable had just come off duty when he heard gunshots outside his family home in Co. Fermanagh. He ran outside to find a man pointing a rifle at the head of his wounded father . . . "He was pointing the weapon at my father's head . . . At that stage, I opened fire with my own revolver."' Lynch was jailed but some years later having been released under the Good Friday Agreement, he made a complaint about being roughed up by the PSNI in his own home when they called to arrest him about non-payment of a fine. The complaint related to an incident in October 2002. One wonders if he remembered that he had previously tried to cold-bloodedly murder an unarmed man in *his* home before he repeated the Republican clarion call of 'police brutality'?

The final weekend in May opened up with a killing which owed much to the bitter rivalry of politics as well as sectarian hatred. It also included the murder of a soldier and a horrific injury to one of his comrades. Eddie Fullerton (56), father of six, was a councillor on Buncranna Council in Co. Donegal, in the Irish Republic. He was an exponent of a united Ireland but equally well respected by political allies and foes alike. On Saturday 25th, in the early hours of the morning, a murder squad from the UFF, having crossed the border and travelled some distance, smashed open the front door of the Fullerton house at Cockhill Cottages. The Sinn Féin man went to investigate the noise, and the paramilitaries shot him six times as he began to walk down the stairs. His horrified Birmingham-born wife Diana recalled afterwards that the silence was deafening. She walked out of the bedroom and found his body sprawled across the landing, eyes closed and blood streaming from his head onto the carpet; he died shortly afterwards. She ran barefoot out of the house to a neighbour's house, in a state of shock and bewilderment, covered in her husband's blood as she sought help. Later she would tell the press: 'It was all over in seconds.'

The Belfast *Sunday World* reported:

> The four-man murder squad was taken to Fullerton's home, at Cockhill Cottages in Buncranna, in the back of a trailer belonging to a local Protestant farmer, who, like many of his co-religionists in the county, loathed Sinn Féin and the IRA. Local Protestants had offered help and information through the UDA's north west 'brigade', some of whose members in Derry had family ties across the border in Donegal. Among the team hiding in hay bales, en-route to the Sinn Féin councillor's home, was one of the most senior UDA members in Northern Ireland, accompanied by another Lisburn man, 'the Gravedigger'. The UDA commander directed the killers into Fullerton's house with a series of hand signals.

The killing was claimed by the Protestant Action Front (PAF), the usual cover name for the UFF. This was during the period of a Loyalist ceasefire, but a spokesman for the CLMC stated that it did not apply to 'operations in the Republic of Ireland'. Fullerton was long suspected of being involved in the cross-border murder of a local Protestant man – Ian Sproule the previous month – but there is no evidence to link the dead councillor with the murder of Mr Sproule. There are two schools of thought as to how the operation was carried out. Many believe that the murder gang sailed across Lough Foyle in a dinghy and were taken to Fullerton's home in the back of a farm trailer, provided by Donegal Protestants who nursed a loathing of both the IRA and Sinn Féin. A second opinion is that they crossed the border close to the city of Londonderry and hijacked a car for the journey to Fullerton's house. The information was provided by a man now known to be an RUC agent who had infiltrated the UFF by the name of Ned Greer. Although he was not on the raid, led by the Gravedigger from the Northern side – whose name is not available for publication – he was certainly involved in the planning. The Gravedigger is thought to have been responsible for 6–10 murders carried out by the UFF's South Belfast brigade. Greer's career as a double agent inside the UDA came to an end late in December 1992, when he was whisked away by the RUC along with his family and taken to HQNI in Lisburn. The following morning, even before the milkmen commenced their rounds, a huge furniture van spirited away his family's belongings and furniture.

Later on that same day, the killing switched to North Howard Street Mill (NHSM), a former base of mine and the old 'Falls Forge'. The building had once been part of the Coombe-Barbour's Mill, or the 'Black Pad.' It was long abandoned when the British Army took over and fortified the site around 1969/70. It was ideally located, because of its position equidistant between the Catholic Falls/Springfield Road and Divis Street and the Protestant Shankill. If ever an Army base lived up to the epithet 'piggy in the middle', it was this one.

On that day – the 25th – a two-man PIRA unit sneaked into the adjoining derelict mill on Conway Street, and using the cover of the building threw a coffee jar, packed with as much Semtex as would fit it, together with a rudimentary detonator, into the base. The IRA will claim that their men heard voices behind the fortified metal walls and threw the grenade towards the sounds. The reality is somewhat more prosaic, though tragically so; it was simply, from their perspective, a fortunate shot, as several soldiers were underneath the point at which the device was lobbed. Army Dog Handler (ADU) Corporal Terence O'Neill (44), on his seventh tour of the Province, was hit at point-blank range by the blast and killed instantly. A comrade was also hit and horribly maimed, with both of his legs being torn off. I was told by a soldier who was there, but declined to be quoted directly, that the terribly wounded soldier was aware of his injuries and begged other troops to shoot him as he did not want to spend his life without legs. It is said that, as the bombers ran away towards the Springfield Road, they could have heard the man's agonising screams. He lost consciousness at this point and was rushed to the nearby RVH. Corporal O'Neill was originally with the Royal Regiment of Fusiliers (RRF), but at the time of his death was attached to the Light Infantry. I have been unable to contact the wounded soldier but would be honoured to include his story at a later date.

The ADU man was from Alnwick in the English north-east and the following is taken from the website 'A Galivant Aboot Alnwick'. 'War Memorial . . . One of the plaques is in dedication of Corporal Terence Gavin O'Neill, Royal Regiment of Fusiliers. Killed in Belfast, Northern Ireland, on 25th May 1991. Aged 44. Killed when a homemade IRA grenade was tossed over the wall at North Howard Street Army base in West Belfast. He was serving as dog handler and had just fed his Labrador.' His funeral was held at St Michael's in his native Alnwick, situated just off the picturesque Northumberland coast, looking out towards the North Sea. The Reverend Christopher Andrews told the congregation that the dead soldier, who was nearing the end of his career, was not bitter nor angry about anything he had witnessed on his many tours of Northern Ireland. He said: 'It is playing into the hands of the cowards who perpetrated this crime to go on in their hateful and bitter frame of mind.'

Later that same day, two IRA gunmen ambushed an RUC foot patrol in the Lisburn Road area near Queen's University and Belfast's Botanical Gardens. The four-man patrol was walking along Lower Crescent, although one officer had separated slightly from the group. Two PIRA gunmen had been in a car which drove past the officer before stopping; they ran back towards him, with their guns drawn. Eyewitnesses stated that they were both wearing suits in order to blend in with the people who generally populated the student/academic quarter. An eyewitness stated that the policeman's hands were hooked into his flak jacket and that one attacker grabbed both of the officer's hands and jammed them even more firmly into the body armour. Whilst he did this, the other gunman – allegedly Paul Holland who was then 22 – got close up behind him and shot him several times, one round hitting him in the neck. Constable Edward Spence (26), was hit five times; one of the bullets severed his carotid artery which led to his brain being deprived of oxygen; he was clinically dead when the vehicle in which he was placed reached the City Hospital on Lisburn Road. He was from Larne in Co. Antrim, close to the Larne–Stranraer ferry terminal, and left two very small children. A female colleague who was unarmed, passed out due to the shock; she was covered in the dying policeman's blood. Their colleagues saw the blood and assumed that she had been hit also; the two were placed in the back of a Land Rover, where their colleagues worked desperately on both of them until they realised that she was uninjured.[1]

Linzi told me: 'I have a daughter called —— who has my mother as a grandmother, but never met my dad, but she knows who he is and always kisses his picture.' The IRA men who killed this fine officer clearly felt no concerns for his family's feelings, describing him as a 'legitimate target'.

After the initial shooting, the gunmen fired several more shots at the defenceless policeman whilst his comrades and a passing UDR foot patrol fired back at them. The gunmen ran towards a waiting getaway car. One of them, Paul Holland, was not tried for the murder until some 12 years later, in 2003. At the inquest it was revealed that the gun used had also been used to kill two Special Branch detectives at Belfast Docks as well as being used in a total of seven IRA punishment attacks.

The day after the attack, Sunday the 26th, as congregations of both Protestants and their Catholic neighbours were pouring out of churches throughout Northern Ireland, Republican terrorists struck. A PIRA bombing squad, in a move that was both insensitive in its location – near a Protestant place of worship – as well as timing, detonated a huge bomb in Cookstown, close to a church. In the no-warning attack, 13 people including two

1. I wish to acknowledge the kind co-operation of Linzi Wilko, one of the dead officer's children, for additional information. I wish also to acknowledge the help of Maree Canavan who explained to me that she didn't think that all of the witness statements were accurate. I wish to thank her for her help.

RUC officers were injured, some seriously, and over 130 houses badly damaged. Retaliation was clearly going to follow closely behind, as we shall see.

On the final day of the month, the IRA killed three UDR soldiers, injured over 40 others and left nine children fatherless as they made another violent, but ultimately futile attack on the security forces. Glenanne is a small township in South Armagh, close to the Irish border. A UDR barracks was located there for strategic purposes, although by mid-1991 it was felt that it had outlived its usefulness and a decision had already been taken to close it down. Built in 1972, the barracks housed two companies of 2 UDR. It was purposely sited on the dividing line or interface between Catholic and Protestant areas.

At some stage during the previous day, a red Mercedes lorry had been hijacked in Kingscourt, Co. Cavan, in the Irish Republic and taken to a border farm where it was packed with 2,500 lb (1,140 kg) of explosives. Travelling in a convoy that included armed men inside a stolen van, the lorry was positioned at the top of a hill overlooking the barracks before being put into gear and sent rolling towards the base; the driver jumped clear once the momentum was set. It careered down the hill and smashed through the perimeter fence, and into buildings where it exploded, causing utter devastation. Three soldiers were killed in the blast with reports varying from 14–40 being injured; the blast was heard in Dublin which was some 60 miles away. The blast left a crater 20 ft deep with debris being hurled some 900 ft away; the base was destroyed in the blast and the subsequent fire, as petrol and oil stocks ignited and wooden buildings burned like tinder. Cows and sheep were killed in the fields round about.

The three murdered soldiers were Private Paul Blakely (30), father of four; Private Sydney Hamilton (44), father of three, and Lance Corporal Robert Crozier (46), father of two. Crozier and Blakely were alerted by gunfire and dashed out of the Recreation Room and were hit by the blast as they exited the building; Hamilton was already outside. All three soldiers were killed instantly.

The land from where the attack was launched belonged to a local farmer named Lowry, who was 80 at the time of the incident. He told the Belfast *News Letter* that he heard a terrible noise: 'like a big lorry emptying up an awful lot of heavy stones'. He also told the newspaper that the blast had blown in his windows and that he had cut his feet on the shattered glass as he walked out of his bedroom. He also mentioned the crying and groaning from wounded men in the shattered base. Nigel McCammond, who was wheelchair-bound, told the same journalist:

> 'I was just ready to go to bed, when the windows came in, and I was hurled to the floor.' He was forced to crawl along the floor to safety. Anne Cochrane who lived nearby was forced to throw herself on top of her baby son, who had been playing with his toys when the bomb exploded. In one local house a family had just removed their crying infant from her cot when the bomb exploded. They were covered in broken glass as their windows shattered and a giant lump of masonry crashed through the roof of their house, crushing the cot where moments before the baby had been sleeping.

Once again, the IRA must have known that a bomb as massive as the one they used was bound to cause damage to housing and possibly kill or maim innocent civilians. Among the survivors, a sergeant and his Greenfinch wife were in the bar on the base's first floor. He said later:

> I felt a thump at the back of my neck. It knocked me down to my knees. The next thing I remember, was someone shouting my name. 'Are you alive; are you there?' I stood up and saw that a reinforced wall had come down. The guard commander was lying there with reinforced concrete up on his chest, and he said: 'Fuck me, I thought I was going to lose my life.' I could see that the whole of his chest was trapped under this slab of concrete. The place was a mass of rubble. There was a big raging fire which was creeping towards him. It was only a matter of feet from him. The oil tank at the back of the building had ruptured and was just a big ball of fire. The ammunition in the back of the guard house was starting to explode in the heat . . . I put my arms under his armpits and pulled him clear . . . We went up the corridor . . . that's where we found the bodies of Paul Blakely and Bobby Crozier, They were lying face down. I turned them over. Their faces had gone, no eyes, no noses, just black holes.[1]

The Glenanne Bomb
J. B., Army bomb disposal officer

The weekend of 31 May 1991 I was in the detachment at South Armagh; the ATO [ammunition technical officer] office had a large backlit map of our patch with chinagraph markings showing out of bounds boxes, suspicious car sightings and previous tasks, the hall had display cases with examples of recent and noteworthy IEDs and racks with our kit ready to jump into if tasked, the whole Det had that feeling of a place ready to jump into action. You had the constant live feed of anything interesting going on around the province. Even so often the first notification of a task was, as happened tonight, the boss coming in and telling us: 'Job on.'

[An off-duty RUC man] spotted the men with balaclavas moving up the road towards his house, they had AK rifles in hand and as they approached his house he called to his wife: 'Get the baby and get down in the bedroom.' She hurried to the cot and lifted their infant cradling him in her arms, she crouched by the bed, he drew his personal protection weapon which all off-duty RUC had and crouched by the window waiting for them to make their move.

The terrorists moved forward past his house; the policeman saw them manoeuvring a large tipper truck into position, the type that the IRA had used for attacks before. He realised that they had not come for him and his relief for himself then became concern for those in the barracks. He phoned his station to alert the Glenanne barracks that the IRA were going to mount a mortar attack against them.

The equipment transfer was going full speed, the boss came down to get amongst it and informed us that the only helicopter available was a Wessex. This meant the kit needed to be broken into four loads rather than two, even more

1. John Potter, *A Testimony To Courage* (Pen & Sword, 2001), p. 352.

work to get done. We made it around to the [landing pad] in record time, under 15 minutes, and the boss jumped onto the first lift, the helicopter hovered above me in the dark in a whirl of noise and heat in the downdraft. The Royal Signals lad, called 'The Bleep', is with me and touches the earthing strop to hook on the helicopter which discharges the static, the bright electrical flash lighting up the darkness, before I slam the shackle onto the hook. He's an essential part of the plan as we had a member of the team sent home with a broken arm after being thrown off a load by the static discharge. The load is on and the helicopter disappears into the blackness.

The terrorists lined up the truck on the field with the barracks, the building is protected on two sides by lines of huge concrete blocks, the third protective line was removed after a complaint from the local farmer, who owns the field, saw them removed. The time and power unit is started, the vehicle is put in gear and drives on its way downhill towards the barracks. There is a function tonight, well known to the terrorists, fifty families are inside and unaware of what approaches. He jumps from the cab and the truck is sent on its way carrying two and a half thousand pounds of home-made explosives manufactured in safety in the Republic of Ireland. The vehicle rolls through the perimeter fence and down a slope crashing into the barracks wall; those inside having just been alerted by the warning from the police start their evacuation A characteristic burst of celebratory gunfire comes from the terrorists as they make their escape leaving the timer in the device to complete their cowardly work.

The crump of the explosion reaches us in Armagh, I know from the map I checked prior to leaving the Detachment that this was no mortar attack, the barracks is over 20 km away. The radio message reaches us soon after that the rest of the equipment will not be needed, just some forensic kit and the cameras. We leave the kit on the field and all deploy on the helicopter, spirits have already sunk in the team and the scene that greets us is worse than I could have imagined. The explosion has destroyed one end of the barracks, we circle once before landing and you can see debris spread across hundreds of metres of the surrounding fields. We land and I search the scene with the boss, the explosion has blown the walls completely off one end of the barracks, three soldiers have been killed Paul Blakely (30), Robert Crozier(46), and Sydney Hamilton (44). They were killed as they were evacuating the building, making a last sweep to ensure everyone was safe. I will not describe the worst of what I saw but the smell has never left me, there was a giant crater which, for scale, the boss had me stand in. The heat of the explosion was still there, there were broken pipes spraying water and an alarm beeping from inside what remained of the barracks.

The explosion blew out windows in houses for hundreds of metres, damaged buildings, and threw the structure of the barracks and the remains of the truck into the fields. We found an RSJ 400 m away and chunks of reinforced concrete all over; a giant piece of concrete struck the policeman's house, it smashed through the roof, through the ceiling and crushed the baby's cot, the child being safely held by his mother next to their bed. The husband saved lives with his warning.

I have seen claims by the IRA since that they fired the device by radio control or by firing a rifle at the bomb to detonate it. These claims are mere terrorist propaganda; the device was on a simple timer as they had no desire to be near such a large explosion and had already made their escape. Evidence from the scene, collected by the team wading through fields soaked in blood from a herd of cattle killed by the explosion prove the device to be nothing more than a timer set to a short delay. No warning was given as they knew the only people is the barracks were military and their families. The barracks was never rebuilt and there is a memorial to the lost soldiers at the location.

The lorry was blasted to tiny pieces and contemporary news reports of the time comment on the debris which was scattered over hundreds of yards. A spokesman for the Provisionals claimed that the blast was their handiwork and repeated calls for the 'British to get out of Ireland [*sic*].' What was particularly sad was that the area, although in the main Protestant, contained a number of Catholics and that hitherto, there had been no sectarian tensions.

Archbishop Daly said: 'I feel great sadness and weariness. It is absolutely morally repugnant; three young men are dead, and three families are plunged into grief.'

Sydney Hamilton was buried at St Luke's Parish Church in Newry; Paul Ronald Blakely was laid to rest at Kilmore Cemetery, in Kilmore, Co. Armagh, and Robert William Crozier at St John's Church, in Markethall, also in Co. Armagh. These deaths brought to 10 the number of UDR soldiers who had been killed by Republicans from this one base alone. It later emerged that one of the dead men, Paul Blakely, had survived an attempt to kill his family and himself, when PIRA bombed his house just before Christmas 1988

Ten people had been killed during this month; 6 of them during the final, bloody 6 days of May. Four soldiers, 4 policemen – including a former officer – and 2 civilians were killed, most of them at the hands of the IRA. One Protestant and a Catholic died, both of whom were sectarian victims in my opinion.

6
June

June was a month during which nine people died; two soldiers and a civilian were killed by the IRA, but six paramilitaries also died – five Republicans and a Loyalist – of whom two died at the hands of the respective 'nutting squads' of the Provisionals and the INLA.

The month was barely a day old, when in what the IRA would later admit was a 'mistake' a civil servant, Celia Gourley, was terribly injured as an IRA bomb, planted underneath her car, exploded and tore off both of her legs, outside her home in Co. Antrim. James F. Burns wrote in the *Orlando Sentinel* some years later whilst at the same time, bemoaning a bomb attack in Boston, Massachusetts:

> The Irish Republican Army, having a deep disdain for Northern Ireland civil servants, had earlier placed a booby-trap bomb under Celia's car. She got in the car and turned the ignition key. The blast blew her legs off. Yes, that's graphic and gruesome, a battlefield-type injury right there in your driveway. Terrorism's triad of kill, maim, scare can also trigger – after the initial revulsion – revenge, resolve, and a reaction that channels anger into a determination not to be beaten down by the bomb. In Celia's case, you might say she walked all over the IRA – by walking back into her Belfast office on artificial legs to tearful cheers from her co-workers just five months after losing her legs ... but not her heart ... to terrorism. Celia became a community activist and the leading board member of a charity that raises funds for victims of violence.

In 2005, Celia Gourley told Parliament: 'I am not bitter, but I am very angry. Anger was the driving motivation in my case, and I am still very angry.'

On the 3rd, in a major undercover operation in Co. Tyrone, the SAS took out three members of the Provisionals' Tyrone Brigade. The deaths of three terrorists produced the usual Republican complaints of 'shoot-to-kill' and 'state execution', but one wonders how much support they would have received from the nine fatherless children left orphaned by the PIRA lorry bomb at Glenanne barracks less than 72 hours earlier? Coagh in Co. Tyrone was the scene of the ambush by Britain's elite Special Forces' troops early on the morning of Monday 3 June. Coagh is located about eight miles from Cookstown. It was also home to several UDR soldiers, one of whom had been earmarked for murder by a three-man PIRA unit consisting of Tony Doris, Lawrence McNally and Michael Peter Ryan.

Off-duty UDR soldiers had long been prime targets for the IRA, and indeed, since 1988, in addition to several foiled attacks or near misses, over 10 men had been killed at their homes or work or en route between the two in the Coagh area alone. Edward Gibson, Leslie Dallas and Thomas Jamison were amongst those who had been killed by the Republican terror group in or around Coagh over the past three years. The British Army had at least one top-ranking informant within the Fermanagh/Tyrone IRA and it was information from this man about the intended murder of a UDR soldier that led to an eight-man undercover unit being placed in the village centre. A Vauxhall Cavalier car had been hijacked the previous day in Moneymore and its registration was known to the military. As the Cavalier drove along the main street, the undercover troops opened fire, causing the car to veer across Hanover Square and crash into a parked car, setting it alight. At least one of the IRA men returned fire and two of the occupants attempted to get out of the crashed vehicle. In an exchange said to have lasted 10 minutes, over 200 rounds were pumped into the car, killing all three terrorists and causing the vehicle to burst into flames; the bodies were so badly burned that dental records were used to identify Doris (21), McNally (38) and Ryan (37). Two rifles – AKM assault weapons – were later recovered from the burned-out wreckage of the Cavalier and later forensics showed that they had been used in the murder of Leslie Dallas in March 1989. The soldiers were all armed with Heckler & Koch G3K assault rifles firing 7.62 mm NATO-standard ammunition.

Peter Ryan had been on the run since his escape from Crumlin Road Gaol in 1981 and was wanted for a score of murders committed against the SF. He was regarded as the top IRA gunman in mid-Ulster; Laurence McNally's brother Phelim was shot dead by the UVF in 1988 in mistake for his brother Francis, who was a Sinn Féin councillor. Finally, Tony Doris was related to a Sinn Féin councillor in Dungannon.

Republican reaction was as predictable as it was bile-ridden; Sinn Féin councillor, Francie McNally, brother of one of the dead terrorists protested: 'The three men were good soldiers; executed by the British Crown forces.' On 5 June 2008, *An Phoblacht* reported: 'IRA Volunteers Tony Doris, Lawrence McNally and Pete Ryan died as a result of an SAS ambush in County Tyrone in 1991. This month is marked not only by the anniversary of their deaths but also the emergence of inconsistencies concerning the way in which they died which have sinister implications. It has always been known that the three Volunteers, who were on active service at the time of their deaths, died as a result of an SAS ambush. In classic shoot-to-kill style, presumably acting on information, the SAS established a killing zone and waited for the IRA ASU to enter the area.' The article was written by Laura Friel whose blinkered reporting I have previously questioned; she speaks blandly and predictably about 'shoot-to-kill', but can she deny that her 'heroes' were on their way to carry out a 'shoot-to-kill' on a likely unarmed and off-duty soldier?

My final words on the incident: 'Big boys' rules'.

It later emerged that the IRA team had already been chosen by the local Provisional commanders to attack a bus full of Protestant workmen in the Coagh area the following week. The murders would likely provoke a violent Loyalist backlash in which the IRA could then stand up and 'sell' itself to the Catholic communities as their defenders. It was cynical and murderous, but that was the Provisional IRA.

Just three days later the IRA's 'nutting squad', under the auspices of 'Stakeknife' Scappaticci, was in action again. On the 1st, they had abducted PIRA member Ruari Finnis (21) from the Waterside area of Londonderry, as he drank in a city centre pub. He was taken to a 'safe house' in Central Drive on the Nationalist Creggan Estate, where he was tortured for up to five days, before being taken out, late on the evening of the 6th, bound, gagged, with tape wrapped tightly around his eyes and shot in the back of the head. A later IRA statement claimed that he was a Special Branch informer and had been executed after having confessed his guilt. One can only imagine the unspeakable torture to which he was subjected with implements which could include sharpened screwdrivers, carpet knives, clubs studded with nails, angle-grinders and baths full of freezing water in order to partially drown their victim. Finger nails and teeth were often pulled out by pliers so that a confession was forthcoming, truthful or not! I simply cannot believe that the modern day, 'respectable' Sinn Féin leader and former 'butcher of the Creggan', the late Martin McGuinness, a Creggan resident, was not made aware of the 'interrogation' or even gave tacit approval for it to go ahead.

This savagely cruel behaviour was shamelessly followed by a message of 'sympathy' from the IRA to the Finnis family. 'To the family of Ruari Finnis we express our understanding of the suffering and the grief this death will inflict on them. We deeply regret the anguish and the pain that they are going through at this time and wholeheartedly hope that they understand or accept our need to protect our volunteers.' Their pious words were simply not credible, given the brutality and summary nature of the man's death. Even one of their own community, Archbishop Cahal Daly, was angered enough to ask: 'What kind of fair trial was offered to that poor man who was murdered. If this were to be done by others, to their organisation, there would be a terrible outcry from that same organisation.'

On the 9th, for the second month in a row, and again on a Sunday, the Provisionals planted a huge bomb on a Protestant housing estate, this time Clover Braes in Donaghcloney, Co. Down, about eight miles south west of Lisburn. The estate, off Donaghcloney Road on the Banbridge and Blackskull side of the village, was known for its sleepy image, which changed quite dramatically on that second Sunday in June. The device, weighing 600 lb (270 kg) exploded following a telephoned warning, and although there was much damage, there were no fatalities, as an Army unit had evacuated the area. The car bomb was left outside the home of Hilary Cairns, daughter of a local Unionist councillor. A spokesman for the RUC said: 'Only a quick response by the police prevented a major disaster. Those who carried out this attack put at jeopardy, the lives of men, women and children.'

The Belfast *News Letter* reported:

> More than a hundred people fled in terror minutes before a huge IRA bomb tore through the normally still streets of Clover Brae on the outskirts of Donaghcloney. Only the quick action of the RUC averted a possible massacre, with some residents dragged out of their beds to safety . . . A pregnant woman was too terrified to move and a child was blown out of bed and showered in glass and debris . . . The bomb left a crater measuring about 15 feet across and 5 feet deep.

The report said that at least five of the houses on the estate would need to be rebuilt. It is thought that a PIRA team from nearby Craigavon planted the device as a reminder of their presence to the 'Jackal' himself – UVF leader Robin Jackson lived on the estate.

On the 12th, there was an international development in relation to the Troubles, as the Mayor of New York City, David Dinkins – the first black mayor of the city – signed a law which would prevent any company in the state of New York from dealing with any Northern Irish firm which failed to recognise or comply with the 'MacBride principles'. This related to a demand for companies in Northern Ireland to stamp out religious intolerance in the workplace, ending discrimination in the granting of jobs and internal promotion. It also demanded adequate security for the protection of minority employees both at the workplace and whilst travelling to and from work, and the banning of provocative religious or political emblems at the workplace. Decent Protestant employers in Ulster had no reason to fear the US legislation, although many saw it as yet another example of Irish-American interference in the affairs of another country, given that the architects and champions of the principle were Seán McManus and the Irish National Caucus.

Private Brian Lawrence (34) lived in Imperial Street, Belfast, and when he wasn't being a part-time UDR soldier, he drove the three miles to work in Duncrue Street, taking him past the birthplace of the *Titanic*. Dependent upon traffic, the journey took at least 10 minutes. On the morning of the 17th, he made that journey for the last time. The night before, a PIRA unit from the New Lodge had hijacked a car, having taken over a house in Upper Meadow Street. The family were held at gun point whilst the murder gang used their car for the short journey to the industrial estate where the part-time soldier worked.

Because of his regular working hours, and only a finite number of possible routes, it was difficult to vary his routine, and it is thought that he had been dicked by an IRA sympathiser who had recognised him as a soldier. On the fateful morning, a two-man team arrived at the depot; the front-seat passenger got out of the car and walked directly towards where Brian Lawrence had just arrived in his vehicle. Without a word, the gunman fired 12 shots from a handgun, seven of which hit the part-time soldier as he tried to get out of his car; he died at the scene. The killer ran to the waiting car and the pair escaped towards the New Lodge where the vehicle was abandoned, but more importantly, where there was no shortage of safe houses and willing helpers. He left a young widow, Lorraine, who was inconsolable with grief at the death of her husband. His funeral was held at Hollywood Parish Church, where Bishop Gordon McMullan told the assembled mourners:

> In this statement I am also saying that political catch-lines and paramilitary slogans, from whatever quarter they come, do not cloud the reality that those who commit these crimes are murderers not patriots; are life-destroyers, not nation-builders; are wearers of the badge of shame, not the badge of nobility or pride, and have nothing positive or hopeful to offer any part of this community.

Also on the 17th, the four main political parties met at Stormont, Belfast, to begin talks on the future of Northern Ireland. The talks began with opening statements from each of the parties. Prospects of a breakthrough were thought slim, as a major AIA conference was scheduled to happen the following month. The significance of the planned inter-governmental meeting was that Loyalists had threatened to pull out if the July meeting went ahead. Interestingly enough, Sir Ninian Stephenson, a senior Australian High Court judge was named as an independent chairman for the June talks. Purely by coincidence, the following day, an extra 500 British soldiers were deployed in the Province, bringing the current number to 11,000. It had reached almost 30,000 at several points in the 1970s.

On the 19th, a murder gang from PIRA's Andersonstown unit, having been informed by dickers that an off-duty British soldier was visiting a house in East Belfast, hijacked a car and collected weapons from the Andytown quartermaster; one of the murder gang was Paul Lynch. Private Anthony 'Tony' Harrison (21), a London-born soldier from the Parachute Regiment, had become engaged to a young Protestant woman, Tracey Gouck, who lived in the Holywood area of East Belfast. He was visiting her in order to finalise their wedding plans, and had been at the house a few days. He had been taken to the house in Nevis Avenue by a taxi driver named Noel Thompson – later jailed for his part in the murder – on a number of occasions, and it was this man who betrayed the soldier to the IRA. Martin 'Marty' McGartland was selected by the PIRA ASU to be the getaway driver for the murder operation. Information had already been passed on to Special Branch, but for some bizarre reason, the warning was passed on to another soldier – in the UDR – whose life was also at risk from this operation.

The Murder of Tony Harrison
Martin McGartland[1]

On the morning of 19 June, I was contacted by one of the IRA couriers and told to attend a cell meeting that afternoon. As usual I went along, but there were only three people present instead of the usual eight or nine. Spud [Martin Murphy] said: 'This is not a meeting, Marty, we've got a job for you. You're to drive Stephen and Paul on an operation.' My heart sank and I feared the worst. I knew Paul Lynch to be one of the IRA's top assassins, a ruthless bastard who had a reputation for the most daring attacks and a ferocious hatred for anyone who opposed the cause. Even his mates believed he was a man without feeling. The other man I knew as Stephen [Savage], who was also a recognised IRA gunman.

Spud had decided that Paul should make his own way to the target, as all RUC patrols would be highly suspicious of three young men driving around Belfast together. 'Do you know East Belfast, Marty?' Stephen asked as we drove along. 'That's where we're heading,' he said, 'A house in Nevis Avenue, off Holywood Road.' I knew then that I was driving to the home of a soldier whom they intended to shoot in cold blood. I wondered what I should do; I wondered if there was anything I could do now to save the man's life . . . I debated whether I should try any trick, like stalling the car or crashing it into a vehicle, as if by accident. But Stephen, sitting by my side was armed with a hand-gun and I knew that if he suspected I was not playing straight, he would shoot me and walk away without a second thought . . . 'Stop here,' said Stephen who was sitting in the passenger seat, as we turned into Nevis Avenue, 'I'll be back soon.' A few minutes later, Paul arrived in a hijacked car and parked nearby. As Stephen got out of my car and walked away I prayed to God that the soldier had been spirited away, as most men had been when I discovered that the IRA had been targeting them. I knew that the Special Branch, and all the other security forces, did everything possible to save targeted men. I wound down the car window so that I would hear if any

1. Marty is a friend of mine and has given his permission for this extract from his first book to be used: *Fifty Dead Men Walking* (John Blake Books, 2009, pp. 250–2).

shots were fired. I prayed that I would hear nothing. I waited what seemed an age, but it was probably less than 60 seconds. Then I heard the shots – one, two, three, four, five – I counted them, and knew in my heart that some poor bastard had been murdered in cold blood.

The gunmen had entered the house after first knocking on the door, politely enough to lull Ms Gouck into a false sense of security, but one gunman pushed past her as she opened up, whilst the other held a gun at her head. Private Harrison, from 3 Para, was chatting to his future mother-in-law, Agnes Gouck, and a girl of 10, when Lynch and the other man burst into the lounge; without a word, they shot the soldier five times. The Londoner managed to stagger to the front door, despite wounds in his legs and back, before collapsing; he died at the scene. One of the killers laughed and joked about the murder, telling Marty McGartland that it was 'a piece of piss'!

Marty's days as an informer inside PIRA were coming to an end and his appointment with the 'nutting squad' was only a month and a half away (*see* Chapter 8). Incidentally, he also me that the taxi driver who dicked the young para had also tried to bring about the deaths of several other soldiers in Belfast, some months earlier. He had dropped them off at a pub in the centre and then reported their whereabouts to local PIRA commanders. A sweet-jar full of Semtex was hurriedly rushed into the vicinity of the soldiers with the intention of mass murder. For reasons known only to the IRA, the plan was aborted and the men whom Thompson had betrayed, lived to fight another day.

There was a mysterious death on or about the 21st of the month, one which initially appeared to have only a tenuous connection with the Troubles. It was one which would not come to light for 12 months and would then result in 'overtime' for the IRA's 'nutting squad' and the deaths of three Provisionals, as the IRA carried out some violent 'housekeeping'. Margaret Perry (26) from Portadown was taken to Co. Donegal in the Irish Republic and was killed by three IRA members, acting independently of their leadership, sometime between the 21st and the 30th of the month. Her battered body was buried in a field in Mullaghmore, Co. Sligo, not being found until 30 June 1992, a year later. The Garda had acted on a tip-off from the IRA. It would appear that she had been killed because she had discovered that her former partner, Gregory Burns, and two comrades were acting as informers and had been betraying IRA secrets to the British Army. The three Provos, including Burns, were killed probably in June 1992 for their involvement in her death and also for being informers. (*See* Chapter 19.)

On the 26th, in what was the third high-profile miscarriage of justice of the Troubles, following the quashing of convictions for the 'Guildford Four' and the 'Birmingham Six', the convictions of the 'Maguire Seven' were overturned by the Court of Appeal in London. The seven had been convicted of supplying the explosives which were used in the Guildford and Woolwich pub bombs in October and November 1974. Those cleared were Anne Maguire who was 40 at the time of the trial (she had served 14 years); her husband Patrick (42 and 14 years); their sons Patrick Jnr (14 and 4 years) and Vincent (17 and 5 years). Anne's brother Sean Smyth (37 and 12 years); family friend, Patrick O'Neill (35 and 12 years) The seventh member was Patrick 'Giuseppe' Conlon who was 52 at the time he was wrongly convicted, brother-in-law to Anne Maguire and father of Gerry Conlon who was also wrongly convicted as one of the 'Guildford Four'. To the eternal shame of British justice and the West Midlands Serious Crimes Squad, Giuseppe died in Wormwood Scrubs prison on 23 January 1980. Home Secretary William Whitelaw granted him parole on the day that the Belfast man passed away in a prison hospital wing.

On the same day that this miscarriage of justice was finally righted, a two-man PIRA unit planted two devices close to Queen Street RUC station in Belfast. The devices exploded as the men ran away, and two police officers received bad leg injuries; additionally, 18 civilians received some blast injuries. Two other officers raced after the bombers and rugby-tackled them to the ground, as it was too dangerous to open fire in the crowded streets. Detectives quickly arrived on the scene and wrapped the men's hands in plastic bags in order to preserve forensics and link them to the bombs. Eyewitnesses generally agreed that it was a miracle that no one was killed. After surveying the blast damage, Lord Mayor of Belfast Nigel Dodds said: 'Certainly the IRA fully intended to kill the policemen and they did not care how many civilians they killed with them. The street, a busy shopping centre, was filled with lunchtime crowds, including children, when the attack happened, not far from a toy store.' Six ambulances were called to the scene, as the injured were ferried to the RVH, with the injured RUC men under heavy police guard. The IRA tried on numerous occasions to 'finish the job' by attempting to kill wounded soldiers and policemen in hospital.

Surprisingly, there was some criticism, albeit diluted, from the Workers' Party, the political wing of the virtually defunct OIRA, of the men who had ordered the young bombers into the city centre to risk not only their own lives, but also those of innocent civilians.

On the 20th, the Londonderry brigade of the IRA demonstrated their scant regard for human life, with a lunchtime rocket attack in the city centre. A two-man team was tasked to fire the rocket from the west bank of the Foyle at the Army base at Ebrington Barracks, across the river. They set up a firing position at Union Hall Place. However, they were startled by the arrival of an Army mobile patrol close to Shipquay Street, and fired instead in the direction of the vehicles. Whether the shot was hurried, or just wildly inaccurate, it missed the target and smashed into a crowded office building, striking a first floor window. By some miracle, the warhead failed to explode. The luckiest man of the Troubles was insurance manager James O'Carroll, at whose feet the dud missile landed. He told the Belfast *News Letter*: 'I was making a few phone calls, when there was a crash, breaking glass and then a thud and this device just landed at my feet. I got up and left the office. I'm just glad to be alive.' Another eyewitness said: 'Had it gone off, there could have been dozens of dead and injured people here this afternoon.' A woman and a baby over whose heads the rocket flew were both treated later at Altnagelvin Hospital for severe shock; the IRA men disappeared into Magazine Street and were seen running towards the Nationalist Bogside. The RUC described it as: 'A reckless act by mindless terrorists.'

The IRA's England team showed that they could still be a nuisance, on the 28th, when a bombing unit left a device in a bin outside the Beck Theatre, in Hayes, Middlesex. It is suspected that it was the same unit which had left a similar device at Victoria Railway station in February. On this occasion, the bomb was defused by the Army and the theatre was evacuated.

On the 29th – a Saturday – the Provisionals carried out a high-profile assassination, when they shot and killed a senior UDA/UFF man, Cecil McKnight (32), father of two, at his home in the Loyalist Fountains area, close to the River Foyle. The top Loyalist lived in Melrose Terrace, alongside the main A2 road, against the side of the east bank of the Foyle. At one point in this street, it is possible to look through a gap towards the west bank and the Nationalist Bogside climbing away to its other equally nasty big sister estate, the Creggan.

A two-man murder gang, thought to be from the Gobnascale unit, arrived in McKnight's street. Tony Doherty and another man walked across to the house; they could see the Loyalist through his living room window, but there were also two uniformed RUC men sitting chatting with him. Despite their presence, with no hesitation, they fired several shots through the glass, hitting and mortally wounding McKnight before then fleeing on foot. The two officers chased after them, but Doherty and the other man fired at them and due to the presence of other civilians, the officers did not return fire. The gunmen then escaped in the direction of the Gobnascale.

One of the killers, Doherty, also known as Antaine O'Dochartaigh, was later jailed for life for this murder and the murder of another UDA man, Gary Lynch (*see* Chapter 8). However, under the GFA, he was released in 2000, having served only 9 years, for at least 2 murders and 72 other terrorist-related crimes.

Who Killed Cecil McKnight?
Undercover RUC officer

I was given the following information, in an interview with a former undercover policeman:

'The Provos were furious about the killing of a Sinn Féin man, Eddie Fullerton, in the May and they had been told that McKnight was the architect of the deed which involved UVF boys rowing across a lough to get to him. It was decided to take him out, and I can't believe that our friend Marty [McGuinness] as senior man in Derry, wasn't aware of the op and, in my opinion, must have actually sanctioned the hit. When the Provies arrived, there were two uniformed peelers in the house, but Tony Doherty and his crony must have had balls of steel, because they still shot the UFF man. More's the pity that the peelers didn't slot the two killers as they ran away. The boy, Doherty was then free to kill "Lofty" Lynch a couple of months later. My money is definitely on Marty giving his nod to this operation.'

On the final day of the month, INLA's own version of the 'nutting squad' went into action. Though not as experienced as Freddie Scappaticci's IRA unit, it was nevertheless, equally vicious. Gerard 'Skin' Burns (37) was an INLA member from the Ardoyne area of Belfast. He was picked up in a pub in the city centre and taken to a safe house in the New Barnsley area, close to the RUC station and just across the Springfield Road from the Springhill and Ballymurphy Estates. Whilst in the house, he was tortured and, according to a family member, 'brutalised' into admitting that he was an RUC informer. Finally after several hours of barbaric treatment, having been stripped of his clothes and re-dressed in a boiler suit, he was bound and gagged and his eyes covered with masking tape. The gang then took him outside into an alleyway behind a house on the same estate; he was shot three times and his body dumped where it had fallen. Neighbours thought that it was a PIRA attack on the nearby RUC station. One man found the body and at first assumed that it was a bag of dumped rubbish; shortly afterwards, police and soldiers arrived, but before it could be examined and removed, they had to check for booby-traps, a frequent but sick tactic of Republican paramilitaries.

'Skin' was a product of the Troubles and this man had led a colourful life, having been shot on no less than three different occasions since the early 1970s. He served in the Official IRA's wing in Long Kesh – later HMP The Maze – and joined the INLA in the wake of the bloody split and subsequent feud. During his funeral, a member of the INLA, to his family's clear displeasure, read a statement alleging that he had been killed as a paid RUC informer. His family have always fiercely denied the charge. Mary Burns, the dead man's sister, later demanded an explanation from the INLA as to why her brother had been tortured and murdered. She said:

> What I would really like to know is where the INLA got their information from, that Gerard was a police informer. I would like to know why he was shot, because within my own heart, I don't believe the accusations made against him. I would just like someone to come and tell me why my brother was shot three times; I want to know why they brought his body up an alleyway and shot him while he was lying on his back. I want the RUC to come and tell me if he was a police informer.

June ended with nine deaths, including two soldiers and a civilian. The other six deaths were all paramilitaries.

7
July

There were three Troubles-related deaths this month, of which there was just one military death when the ninth and final Royal Navy man was killed in the Province. Two civilians died, both of whom were Catholics: one was murdered in a sectarian attack; the other was killed by the IRA.

On Wednesday 3rd, in the face of continued Loyalist criticism and delaying tactics, Northern Ireland Secretary Peter Brooke, in a desperate effort to prevent the complete collapse of the Brooke/Mayhew talks, decided to end this particular 'phase' of the negotiations. The Loyalist representatives had informed Brooke that they were unwilling to extend the talks beyond the 9th of this month. However, worse news was just around the corner, when the CLMC announced the following day, that their ceasefire would end at midnight. There had been several breaches and sectarian attacks had continued. Northern Ireland was in its 23rd year of violent strife and the end seemed no nearer than it had been back in August 1969.

That particular week was only going to deteriorate for Brooke, as well as the people of Northern Ireland, when a court in Roermond, Holland, acquitted three members of the Provisional IRA of charges related to the murder of Australian tourists Nick Spanos and Steven Melrose in the Dutch town in May 1990. One of the four acquitted was Donna Maguire, who had been arrested in Belgium near the border with the Netherlands on 16 June 1990, after a farmer reported hearing gunshots in woods. A police search uncovered two handguns, a machine gun and explosives. A man who was with her managed to escape across fields and evaded arrest, but walked straight into a trap set by vigilant Dutch police. The other two PIRA members who were acquitted with Maguire were Paul Hughes, and Sean Hick; Gerard Harte, arrested with them in Belgium in June 1990, was found guilty and sentenced to 18 years, but he successfully appealed against the conviction and he was released. The three – excluding Harte – were then extradited to Germany in order to face charges of the murder of Royal Artillery officer Major Michael Dillon-Lee in Dortmund in June 1990. All three were acquitted of this murder as well, although Maguire was remanded and later convicted of taking part in bombing the British Army base in Osnabrück.

On Sunday, 7th, one can only imagine Brooke's reaction to more bad news, this time from south London. HMP Brixton is located in the London Borough of Lambeth, and was built in 1820 as the Surrey House of Correction. It was intended to house 175 prisoners, but at one stage held just over 800, and was renowned for its small cells and poor living conditions; not for nothing did it gain a reputation as one of the worst prisons in London. Amongst its former 'celebrity guests' were Mick Jagger, the Kray Twins, Lord Russell of

Liverpool and the DJ Simon Dee. It had also housed PIRA sisters Dolores and Marion Price, and another IRA man, Gerald Tuite, escaped from there in 1980. In 1991, it held two very dangerous IRA men: Nessan Quinlivan and Pearse McAuley. Both were on remand, awaiting trial on charges relating to a suspected plot to assassinate leading businessman Sir Charles Tidbury. Female members of the IRA's England team managed somehow to smuggle a gun into the prison – the governor of the jail was forced into early retirement and a senior official was sacked for appalling lapses in security – and the two terrorists were able to threaten their way out. Whilst it might be all too easy simply to brand the top officials there as incompetent and use them as scapegoats, there is evidence that the Metropolitan Police had warned the authorities as far back as January that a gun would be smuggled in to the prisoners.

Almost two years after the escape, Quinlivan was arrested in Ireland on firearms charges, and was sentenced to four years in prison, but released early, in November 1996, as part of an Irish government initiative. McAuley, on the other hand, had a slightly more colourful post-escape future. He made his way to the Republic, where, incredibly, a supine Irish judge granted him bail whilst extradition charges were prepared; naturally, he skipped bail and disappeared. He later emerged in 1999, when he was found guilty of the killing of Garda Jerry McCabe during a post office van robbery at Adare, Co. Limerick on 7 June 1996; he received a 14-year sentence. Released in 2009, he returned to his wife, a schoolteacher and former Sinn Féin councillor, Pauline Tully. The marriage broke up and, apparently in a fit of rage, he stabbed her to death at their home in Kilnaleck, Co. Cavan, on 24 December 2014; he is currently serving a 12-year sentence in the Irish Republic.

There is one other particular, shameful postscript to the Brixton escape. Alan Marshall, a former soldier who worked as a prison officer at Brixton uncovered the plot – later confirmed by the aforementioned police warning – by the two PIRA men to shoot their way out of prison. He warned authorities, but for some reason, beyond my understanding, Mr Marshall was forced out of Brixton and transferred to Sudbury Open Prison and then, once the escape had taken place, he was suspended on full pay in order to protect him from IRA revenge as his part in exposing the plot had been leaked to the press. He was suspended until March 2000, when he was eventually sacked for refusing, understandably, to return to prison work.

On the 12th, Ulster Marketing Surveys and Gallup published the results of an opinion poll into the public perceptions of the Brooke/Mayhew talks. There was a very high level of support for resumption of the talks in both countries: 73 per cent in the North and 87 per cent of those in the Republic. In mainland Britain, the supporters were also in the majority with 79 per cent of those polled wanting the politicians to sort themselves out. Four days later, the Anglo-Irish Intergovernmental Conference (AIIC) held a meeting in Dublin, for the first time in 11 weeks, to give some hope that peace was at least being discussed. The following day, ever mindful that the Provisionals had killed a previous British ambassador to Ireland and the ambassador to Holland, over the last decade, David Blatherwick replaced the incumbent British ambassador to Dublin, Nicholas Fenn, with some possible trepidation.

On the 18th, the IPLO made a further contribution to the 'fight for freedom' when they killed a member of the 'Crown Forces' at his DIY shop in Belfast city centre. Lieutenant

Commander John McMaster (47) was a member of the Royal Navy Reserve. He was there to be called up should the Royal Navy require his services in times of extreme national danger. He was not a Loyalist, nor was he, as the IPLO lamely claimed, a member of the Security Forces. At approximately 10:00, two PIRA gunmen walked into the shop in Church Lane and, without preamble, shot the RNR man once, causing him to collapse by the counter. Again, without a word, the gunman fired eight further shots into the helpless man's body as he lay on the floor. Mr McMaster's brother struggled with one of the gunmen, and a gun was held against his head, but it failed to fire; the killers then ran outside to a waiting car. The car had been hijacked in West Belfast and was later found abandoned on the Antrim Road in North Belfast.

Associated Press reported:

> Two men burst into a downtown shop on Thursday, shot and killed one man and injured another, police said. The Irish People's Liberation Organization claimed responsibility. The extremist group is a breakaway faction of the Irish National Liberation Army, itself a splinter of the outlawed Irish Republican Army. It said in a message to the British Broadcasting Corp. in Belfast that it 'executed' a member of the security forces in John McMaster's tool shop this morning. John McMaster, a 47-year-old navy reserve officer, and his brother Alan were working in their tool and hardware shop when two men burst in and one fired a pistol, the British news agency Press Association said. Police identified the dead man as John McMaster, but did not identify a man they said suffered facial and arm injuries while struggling with the intruders.

Then, on Friday 19th, there were three incidents in the Province, two of which led to deaths and the other could have easily led to many more. Kinawley, a small village in Co. Fermanagh, is some seven or eight miles from Enniskillen, but it sits less than two miles away from the Irish border. In terms of PIRA incursions, it is a short walk across fields, and they were able to trigger bombings and shootings from either just inside the Irish border, or where necessary, from a short distance inside the North and only a few minutes from sanctuary. They could also fire surface-to-air missiles from across the border, without fear of being arrested; on 19 July, they did just that. The RUC base at Kinawley housed both police and soldiers and, due to the danger of landmines and IRA ambushes, had become dependent upon airlifts for supplies, ammunition and for the ferrying in of fresh troops. On that day, two RAF Wessex helicopters were coming in to land, when a SAM-7 was launched from inside the Republic. A farmer who had just pulled up in his tractor near the base heard a loud bang, then saw a vapour trail shoot towards and then past the aircraft and then a further bang. Later reports showed that the missile had failed to lock on to either Wessex and exploded when it dived into the ground. It is likely that the IRA didn't have an operative well enough trained to fire them. Almost immediately, the PIRA unit opened fire from the border with what was possibly an M60 machine gun, but there were no reports of injuries from either of the two almost simultaneous attacks.

On that same day, the Co. Louth Provisionals moved against a Dundalk civilian whom they believed was an informer for the Garda Síochána. Thomas 'Tommy' Oliver (37), father of seven, was abducted by armed PIRA men from close to his home at Riverstown, and taken to a safe house near Dundalk. He was held for 24 hours and subjected to interrogation which included torture. On the morning of the 19th, he was taken outside and shot, his lifeless body being dumped at Belleek, on the Northern side. The Republic was very much half-hearted in its dealings, particularly in terms of its application of criminal law, with the Republican paramilitary groups. It was quick to mouth the mantra 'not in my name' at each successive IRA outrage, whilst secretly thinking, as long as they are killing and terrorising in the North, they are not doing it here. They were slow, to the point of inertia to extradite PIRA/INLA personnel either to the North or to the mainland part of the UK, because the Irish Constitution – later amended – gave the IRA a type of legitimacy in its activities as it called for the taking back of the Northern six counties and bringing them in line with the Southern 26. In short, the Irish government and their Supreme Court frequently displayed how pusillanimously they could behave when confronted with the IRA. Many British soldiers, as well as RUC officers have long deprecated the Irish attitude of laissez faire towards the IRA and the laid back nod and a wink which Garda and Irish Army personnel gave to terrorists as they re-crossed the border after a night of shootings and bombings in the North.

Mr Oliver had allegedly passed on information to the Garda which had resulted in several arrests – a great rarity in itself – of IRA men inside the Republic. It is alleged that Freddie Scappaticci crossed the border with members of his 'nutting squad' and carried out the beating, torture and eventual murder of the Riverstown farmer. The beating was so severe that a member of the family told the *Irish Times*: 'Whoever they were, they thumped him and thumped him to get him to say what they wanted him to say.' After the post-mortem a priest said: 'It looked like they'd dropped concrete blocks on every bone in his body.' *An Phoblacht*, in an attempt to deflect the massive wave of local anger at the brutal treatment of an innocent farmer, claimed he had been passing information to the Garda. They also claimed that Oliver had aided the IRA, providing sheds to store weapons and explosives, but that over a six-year period he had then given this information to the Garda, leading to several arrests. Under a headline of 'IRA executes Informer', the organ of the IRA wrote: 'The IRA has a duty to protect its organisation, its volunteers and the back-up provided by its supporters. Tom Oliver's death was due to his willingness to act as an agent for the Dublin Government's Special Branch.'

It later emerged that, unknown to Mr Oliver, the Republican terror group had hidden barrels of arms and ammunition on his land, and that, during drainage work, he had unearthed these barrels. However, he had not informed the RUC of their presence, although a top informer inside the IRA – allegedly 'Stakeknife' himself – had indeed passed on the information to the Irish police. It is entirely possible that Mr Oliver was killed in order to deflect suspicion away from the real informer, and that 'Scap' made the innocent farmer a scapegoat for what was a major blow to the Provisionals. There was worse to come, in that locals, aware of who the IRA personnel were and of their activities, and equally aware of the farmer's innocence, rebelled against the Republicans. Several villagers who were known to have assisted in the abduction and possibly in the torture of Mr Oliver, were ostracised by some members of their own families, and were refused service in pubs and shops in the area. It was very much a public relations disaster for the IRA, but it didn't return Mr Oliver to life. I will leave the final word of this sordid murder to the *Irish Times*: 'Tom Oliver has become a symbol of every family on this island whose lives have been shattered by the men of violence.'

That violent day finally ended with another death, and again it was a Catholic taxi driver, and yet again it was a sectarian murder by Loyalist paramilitaries. Thomas 'Toddler' Hughes (34), father of two, lived in Clonfadden Crescent, close to both the Divis Street flats and to the Army base in Albert Street Mill. On the evening of the 19th, he was en route to Divis Street and had just stopped at traffic lights. As he waited for the lights to change, a UVF murder gang drove by in a car stolen earlier from the Shankill. It is not known if it was a random sectarian murder, in that they had seen Mr Hughes driving out of a known Catholic area, or if they had called in the fare and knew that he would use the route that he took. They opened fire, killing 'Toddler' Hughes almost instantly. Whether the murder was random or planned mattered not a jot to his grieving family. The killing was later claimed by the UVF and they tried in their usual sickening manner to suggest that the dead man had Sinn Féin connections. The gang's car was later found abandoned in the Crumlin Road area.

On the 23rd, in news which would disappoint thousands of Loyalists, the Major government announced plans for the future of the Ulster Defence Regiment. In fairness, he had been in power only for eight months, and the origins for the White Paper were rooted during the administration of Margaret Thatcher. The plans included the merger of the Royal Irish Rangers (Royal Irish) and UDR into a new regiment which would be called the Royal Irish Regiment. Both the MoD and the NIO were quick to deny Unionist claims of political interference in the decision. The UDR had been the subject of sustained criticism by Nationalists since it was first formed, over claims of collusion, although these had seldom been upheld. Interestingly, the MoD claimed that whilst the UDR was 96 per cent Protestant, the Rangers were 30 per cent Catholic, with many Southern Irish in their ranks. However, they later had to retract this statement and revealed that in fact only 6 per cent of the Rangers were Catholic and only 5.87 per cent came from the Republic.

On the 25th, the case of the 'UDR Four' was referred to the Court of Appeal by Peter Brooke. They had been jailed for the murder of Adrian Carroll on 8 November 1983. Sinn Féin member Adrian Carroll was employed by Armagh Council and was on a city centre refurbishment job, painting railings near Abbey Street. Eyewitnesses – whose evidence was later questioned – stated that they saw a UDR Land Rover stop nearby and that one of the soldiers changed into civvies and was then marched away by two of his comrades, as though under arrest. The incident blurs at this stage, but a lone gunman – the killing was later claimed by the PAF, a cover-name for the UVF – walked up to Mr Carroll, and shot him several times. Carroll was mortally wounded and died in hospital a few hours later. It would appear that one of the UDR men, Neil Latimer, had donned civilian clothes and was dropped off close to where the killing would take place and then collected by the other three in the Land Rover. Three of the UDR soldiers were acquitted on appeal in 1992. However, Latimer had his conviction upheld and served 14 years in prison before being released under the Good Friday Agreement.

Although it was on a much tinier scale than 1974, on the 27th, the UDA/UFF demonstrated their capacity and willingness to strike inside the Republic. They planted over 50 incendiary devices in eight separate towns in the South, including three in Dublin, one at a Sligo supermarket, and separate bombs in a pub in Dunleer and another at a PIRA haunt in Dundalk. Other towns hit were Drogheda, Dun Laoghaire, Bundaron, Donegal and Ballyshannon. Fortunately there were no injuries, although damages were estimated at several thousand pounds. However, on the following Monday morning, Ian Paisley's daughter, Rhonda, a DUP councillor, demonstrated that she could be as insensitive and tactless as her father, when she justified the weekend's Loyalist attacks in the South as being 'perfectly understandable, given the betrayal of the British Government'. Twenty-two years into the Troubles, with six more long years to go, Ms Paisley's words did little to salve the agony of Ulster. A leading UDA man said: 'The bombs were . . . a wake-up call to the people of the Irish Republic, to remind them that there would be a price to pay if their government continued to interfere in Northern Ireland.'

Three people died this month; a former Royal Navy officer killed by the IPLO, as well as two innocent Catholics, killed by murder gangs from opposite sides of the sectarian chasm.

8

August

A total of 14 people were killed in this month, a month which was bloodier than of late; the dead included seven soldiers or former soldiers, killed because of past associations; two paramilitaries also died. The other deaths were a combination of sectarian murders or the IRA 'accidentally' killing one of their own community. It was the month in which British agent Martin McGartland cheated death and avoided an appointment with the 'nutting squad'.

In the first 11 days of August, four British soldiers died, all from different regiments and all from non-terrorist related causes. In many ways, this summed up what one soldier told me: 'In Northern Ireland, it was 95% boredom and 5% sheer naked terror.' The high number of deaths which were not caused by the IRA or the other paramilitaries demonstrates the danger contained within the 95% period of boredom.

On the 3rd, Sapper Dean Matthew Pitts (28), a soldier with the Royal Engineers from the Bristol area, died in an incident which can only be recorded as 'death by violent or unnatural causes'. His funeral was held at Bristol South Cemetery. Two days later, Lance Corporal Colin Michael Monteith (23) of the REME was killed in a road accident near Lisburn. He was from the Cranwell area of Surrey, where he is also laid to rest. Finally, in an incident which perfectly illustrates the boredom element of the Troubles, especially amongst young men who are cooped up in secure bases, with very little social relief, a soldier from the Royal Corps of Signals was killed. It was very often far too dangerous for off-duty soldiers to get out of their bases, with at least a dozen documented cases of soldiers being killed by the IRA, whilst relaxing, unarmed and away from their base. Sometimes the 'two cans of beer a day' were not enough to ease the tedium and young soldiers did silly things. On the 7th, Signalman William Thomas Dryden (22) was the victim of an accidental shooting at Palace Barracks in Belfast. He was from the Co. Durham area and is laid to rest at Thorpe Road Cemetery, Horden, near Peterlee. Finally, on the 11th, the UDR lost Lance Corporal Leslie David Wheeler (25) of their 7th Battalion. The young NCO's death was listed as 'death by violent or unnatural causes'; he was from North Belfast and is buried in Roselawn Cemetery. He was one of six UDR soldiers who were cleared by the Stevens' enquiry into charges of wrong-doing (*see* Chapter 27).

Four deaths, not one of which was caused in fighting terrorism, but had they not been in Northern Ireland, they probably would not have died; consequently all four are included on the Roll of Honour. As the November chapter will show, it wasn't just the IRA who caused the deaths of soldiers; roads, negligent discharges or just pure black depression also claimed lives.

On the 5th, the same day as Lance Corporal Monteith's car crash, the South Tyrone Provisionals killed a former UDR man at Finns Crossroads near Cappagh. The way that they killed him – 70 shots fired at his car – owed much to their desire for a 'meaningful retaliation' following the 200 shots fired at the three IRA members at Cappagh just eight weeks earlier. William Boyd (42), who lived in Cookstown, had been a member of the UDR in the 70s, but had left quite some time back, working full time at a sewage farm, filtering water. In the afternoon, he left his place of work on the Altmore Road, to drive home. As he reached Finns Crossroads, IRA gunmen who had lain in wait, opened fire with at least three automatic weapons, hitting his car 70 times, killing the former UDR man instantly. The three killers then ran to a parked car, in which they were driven away to safety. A later claim from the IRA that the dead man was a member of the UVF and had been involved in sectarian killings was as offensive as it was entirely without foundation. The killing of Mr Boyd by the IRA was either guilt through former association or simply sectarian; I will leave it up to the reader to decide. The dead man left a wife and two daughters, one aged 18 years and the other just 15 months.

On that same day, over on the mainland, the IRA's England team launched the first of three attacks in the London area which, whilst only having nuisance value, could have easily resulted in a series of conflagrations producing multiple deaths. In the first attack, a male and female team, posing as a couple so as not to arouse suspicion, planted several incendiary devices in and around the toilet area of the Cambridge public house in Charing Cross Road, close to the main-line station. A fire broke out and caused some damage, but there were no injuries. On the 29th, the team moved further west, this time out to Hammersmith, where they planted a further three incendiary devices at a London Underground depot. The devices were discovered under a seat and safely defused by the bomb squad. In the third attack, the IRA team moved back to the east and placed a firebomb inside the Bargain Bookshop on Charing Cross Road, close to the scene of the Cambridge pub fire; the device was defused safely.

On 29 June (*see* Chapter 6) an IRA gunman by the name of Anthony Doherty was part of a two-man IRA team who killed a leading Loyalist, Cecil McKnight, at his home in Londonderry. One of the pall-bearers at McKnight's funeral was Loyalist Gary Lynch (28); he had a full-time job but was also an election worker with the Ulster Democratic Party (UDP). It is unknown if the Londonderry Provisionals had already marked him down for death, or if he had increased his profile as a Loyalist by being seen in public carrying the coffin of a man whom the IRA had just killed. On the morning of the 9th, Lynch arrived for work at Lisahally, on the outskirts of Londonderry, where he was employed in a meat-processing firm: Foyle Meats. Doherty and another IRA man walked over to him and shot him dead as he parked his car. A later Loyalist statement – from the UDP – said: 'The cowardly gunmen waited for Gary to arrive for work at Foyle Meats, in the Lisahally area of Londonderry, and as he parked his car the PIRA/Sinn Féin terror gang opened fire, hitting Gary a number of times. It is widely believed that he was targeted simply because he had attended the funeral of his party colleague and friend Cecil McKnight.' Two years later, Doherty was given sentences totalling almost 750 years for the murders of Lynch and McKnight and also for his involvement in 74 terrorist crimes. At his trial the judge said that the IRA man had a 'profound and abiding commitment to terrorism'.

On the morning of the 7th, British agent Marty McGartland was contacted at his mother's house in Belfast and summoned to a meeting the following day with Pödraig Wilson at Sinn Féin headquarters at Connolly House on Andersonstown Road. Wilson was the 'Head of Discipline' throughout Belfast and, as such, liaised with Scappaticci. McGartland admits in his gripping book that he was very worried and knew that he should contact his handler in RUC Special Branch. He was able to do so via a secret radio, kept hidden at his house, and drove to a clandestine meeting, scouring the faces of everyone he saw en route, and checking any vehicles which he thought were following him, convinced that he was under 24-hour surveillance by the IRA. After the meeting he drove to Andersonstown Leisure Centre, parked, and walked into the Sinn Féin offices, to be told that Wilson wasn't there. At this stage, two men whom he states were well known members of the Punishment Squad – Paul 'Chico' Hamilton and James McCarthy – came up to him and 'offered' to take him to where Wilson was waiting. He willingly climbed into a car with them and they drove in the direction of the Nationalist Twinbrook Estate, where they parked outside a block of flats in Broom Park. He was taken inside where he met a third man and immediately McCarthy said to McGartland: 'Listen. Provisional IRA: you're under arrest,' and with that, a pistol was shoved roughly into his head.

They forcibly removed his trainers and emptied his pockets of money and car keys before forcing him to lie face down on the settee. At this point, his hands and feet were bound together with his own laces and a blanket was placed over his head, whilst one of the IRA men left the flat, it is thought to bring members of the 'nutting squad' to commence the torture and interrogation. After seven hours, he was desperate for the toilet and his captors allowed him to hop to the bathroom where, to his horror, he saw a bath full of water, knowing that drowning–reviving–drowning was one of the nutting squad's favourite methods of torture. McGartland takes up the story here: 'I poked my head out of the bathroom door and looked down the hallway at the sitting room window, wondering exactly how far I was from the ground. I tried to remember how many floors we had walked up that morning. I had no idea what was below that window – concrete, parked cars, trees, shrubs or grass.' Looking at the horizon, he realised that he was at least 40 feet in the air, but knew that if he didn't try, that he would be tortured and he knew that the nutting squad would take pleasure and take their time in violently extracting a confession from him. He was also aware that they would then bind masking tape tightly around his head, completely covering his eyes, make him kneel and then fire two shots into the back of his neck.

He hobbled towards the window and threw himself at the glass pane; as he writes: 'I don't even remember hitting the glass.' He was discovered by a passing Army patrol with his SB minder close behind, unconscious, covered in blood, and broken glass, suffering from a deep wound in his side. In addition, he had severe cuts to the head, a fractured jaw, several missing teeth and severe concussion. He was initially treated at the RVH, under armed guard, before being transferred to the Musgrave Park Hospital and then to protective custody at Palace Barracks. We shall hear from this remarkable man in a later book.

On Saturday 10th, both the UVF and the Red Hand Commandos were involved in the killing of a Catholic shop owner. Jim Carson (33), who was from the Andersonstown area, ran a small newsagent's business on the Falls Road. He was by all accounts, in a fine mood as he had had recently booked a holiday in Egypt with his girlfriend. He opened up early on the Saturday morning, where amongst newspapers such as the *Irish Times*, *Daily Mirror*, *Sun* and so on, he also sold *An Phoblacht*. It was this which cost him his life. Two men, one of whom was armed with a .38 Special, walked into his shop and shot him in the chest as he served behind the counter; as he fell, they leaned over the counter and shot him several more times in the back. A friend ran into the shop and found him dead; the killers had already made their escape. The murder was claimed by the 'Loyalist Retaliation and Defence Group' which was a pseudonym for the Commandos; quite why they were too shy to use their real title is not recorded. The previous day, the getaway car had been hijacked in the Shankill Road, with armed men using the name 'UVF'. It was abandoned in nearby Donegall Road, where the gunman then escaped in a second car.

On Sunday 11th, on the 20th anniversary of the start of Operation Demetrius – better known as internment – Sinn Féin held a major anti-British rally in West Belfast. Republican youths 'celebrated' the event by engaging police and Army in a day-long riot; there were many injuries on both sides and multiple arrests.

The following day, the UFF carried out what it termed as an 'assassination' of a Sinn Féin worker in Killen, Co. Tyrone; it was at first considered to be merely a euphemism for the senseless sectarian murder of a Catholic. However, Patrick Shanaghan (31), also known as Pádraig Ó Seanacháin, was a PIRA bomber and the brains behind countless under-vehicle booby-traps (UVBTs), one of which had killed a UDR soldier. Indeed, in 2003, the Provisionals acknowledged him as one of their own in a book which paid tribute to their 'active service dead'. The RUC had previously officially warned him that he was in imminent danger from Loyalist paramilitaries. Ó Seanacháin did not underestimate the threat that existed and took as many precautions as possible including installing security lighting at his home. At 08:00 on the morning of the 12th, as he drove along Learmore Road, several masked gunmen ambushed him at a point where they knew that he would be forced to slow for a bend. Using a South African AK-47, they sprayed his vehicle, hitting him multiple times in the head and chest; his van crashed and he died at the scene, the day after his birthday.

On the same day, it was announced that there would be a review of the case of Judith Ward, who had been convicted of the M62 coach bombing in February 1974. On 4 February 1974, a coach chartered for use by soldiers and their families set off from Manchester headed for North Yorkshire. A member or members of the IRA placed a large explosive device in the luggage hold. When the device detonated as the coach drove along the M62 close to Huddersfield, 11 people were killed and a twelfth died three days later. Nine of the dead were soldiers, and three civilians including two small children were also killed.

Judith Ward, or Mary Theresa Ward as she was sometimes known, was arrested in November 1974 and she readily confessed to having planted the bomb whilst the coach was parked in the centre of Manchester. She was born in Stockport, and worked for a time in Dundalk in the Irish Republic, before joining the Women's Royal Army Corps (WRAC) in 1971. After a brief period as a female soldier, she deserted and returned to the Irish Republic. Eventually she surrendered to military authorities and was later discharged. Prior to her arrest for the M62 bombing, she spent most of her time in an area under heavy IRA influence. On 12 August 1991, it was announced that her case would be reviewed, although it would be a further nine months before she was finally released, with her conviction deemed unsound; she had spent 18 years in jail. She had only confessed due to a mental illness that led her to attention-seeking behaviour and the making of false confessions.

On the 14th, in what might have proved a massacre, the UVF opened fire on a bus carrying the families of Republican paramilitary prisoners travelling back from Armagh Jail. The ambush took place just outside Markethill, North Armagh, on this Wednesday afternoon. The bus was carrying mainly women and children. UVF gunmen using automatic weapons sprayed the bus with gunfire, and it was only by a miracle, and the courage of the driver in driving out of the ambush, that just two women were injured.

The following day, the IRA killed Ronald 'Ronnie' Finlay (47), father of two, whose crime was that he had served 18 years in the UDR, but had resigned in 1988 in order to work on the family farm at Sion Mills in Co. Tyrone. (A year before Mr Finlay resigned from the UDR, his policeman brother, Winston had been shot by the Provisionals as he returned home from duty.) Sion Mills sits on the west bank of the Mourne River, just 2.5 miles from the Irish border, south of Strabane. On the morning of the 15th, Mr Finlay arrived for work, dropped off as usual by his wife, Kathleen, and their two children. As he got out of the car, a single shot was fired by one of several gunmen who had hidden in farm buildings, causing him to stagger and fall. This was immediately followed by a burst of automatic gunfire from another of the gunmen, at which point his distraught and shocked wife ran to his side. She was forced away by several masked men who levelled their weapons at her and her children. She had to flee across nearby fields whilst the IRA murder gang fired more rounds into the defenceless man's body. Leaving him dead, with a shocked and bleeding woman struggling across fields with two children, the killers made their escape into the Irish Republic. He became the second ex-UDR man to die at the hands of the Provisionals in just 10 days: another man judged guilty because of past associations.

Another brother, Leslie, spoke to the *Belfast Telegraph* in 2001:

> [He] gazes across the rain-sodden County Tyrone graveyard, softly counting the tombstones. As his eyes move from memorial to memorial, he whispers each name: every one is familiar. The first is that of his brother; the next, a nephew; two more are cousins, and another is his father's cousin. Listing their names, he says: 'Over there, by the wall, those are the graves of 17 of my friends.' Of the 24 people from Castlederg murdered by the IRA whose graves spread before him, Finlay knew 22. For each, he has a treasured memory, a hilarious anecdote, a tale to tell of trials shared, good deeds traded, friendships sealed. He knows, too, the identity of most of the men who slaughtered his friends and kinsfolk, even though there has not been a single conviction for any of the murders. In Northern Ireland, to know an IRA murderer's identity is not uncommon: proving it is the difficult part. IRA murderers are already walking free, released early from prison. He said: 'Now we are being told there may be an amnesty for these scum. What justice is there in that?'
>
> Finlay, a retired part-time sergeant in the Ulster Defence Regiment, does not believe in an eye for an eye: it is not, he says, the way of his community. He admits, however, 'Then again, I could not say, hand on heart, that if I knew for certain who gunned down Ronnie, that I would not go out with a gun and shoot him myself.' He adds: 'When you have to scrape up the remains of your family and friends and put them into black bin bags after an explosion, you don't easily forget.

This sounds so clinical, but it is a fact of life here: you never get all the remains. For days afterwards, you see the grey crows feasting on the bits you could not find. That is very, very hard for anyone to take.'

Mr Finlay's widow, Kathleen wrote a very poignant article in *Belfast Today* in which she spoke lovingly of her husband, cruelly murdered by IRA cowards who knew that he was unarmed and who carried out the murder in front of his children.[1]

Also on that fateful Thursday, even as Mr Finlay's body was lying in a mortuary in Co. Tyrone, the IRA killed again; this time it was one of their own community, a man who chose to walk across waste ground late at night. Around 22:00, James Woods (23) decided to visit an elderly relative in the Beechmounts, close to the Falls Road. He lived in Hawthorn Street, and his intended route took him between Oakman Street and Gortin Street, a journey which involved crossing waste ground in the dark. Hawthorn Street is in the maze of houses situated just off the Springfield Road and the trip ought to have taken around five minutes. Unknown to him a unit from the Falls Provisionals had made up a Semtex-filled coffee-jar bomb, similar to the one which had killed Corporal O'Neill on 25 May (*see* Chapter 5) and were lying in wait in the darkness for an expected Army foot patrol.

The IRA have always maintained that they mistook the lone Catholic civilian for a foot patrol – perhaps this was the IRA's Myopia Brigade? – but the device was thrown at Mr Woods, and the blast killed him instantly. He had worked for the St Vincent de Paul society, carrying out voluntary work in his own community and paid a nightly visit to his great-aunt as he was concerned for her safety. He was a well-respected man, known for his tireless work for the elderly and vulnerable in the Falls/Springfield Road area. An apologist for the Provisionals made a hollow and most insincere-sounding apology, but the fact remains that they killed far, far more of their own community, the very people they purported to defend, than did the British Army or RUC. And yet, Gerry Adams talks about the slaughter of Catholics by the Security Forces, when his own IRA slaughtered far more.

The following day – a Friday – two more people were killed by Loyalist paramilitaries in the continued upsurge of violence that followed the collapse of the CLMC ceasefire; one was an IRA man who also worked for Sinn Féin and the other killing was of an IPLO man, betrayed to the Loyalists by his own side. In the first killing, that of Thomas Donaghy (38), a UFF murder gang had lain in wait at the car park belonging to Portna Eel Fishery, by the River Bann, at Kilrea, Co. Londonderry, close to Garvagh. He was well known to the Loyalist paramilitaries who had marked him down for death over the previous three years. Jailed for 19 years in 1978 for conspiracy to murder SF members, and for possession of firearms and explosives, Donaghy was released after serving 10 years. Drawn to the 'Armalite and the ballot box' bandwagon, he moved to Sinn Féin, making his public profile even higher, and bringing him even more to the attention of the UDA/UFF.

On the morning of the 16th, as he drove into the works car park, at least two gunmen, dressed in Army combat jackets and balaclavas, moved from where they had been hiding and casually walked across to him; using a pump-action shotgun and a South African Browning revolver, they shot him several times in the head from close range. Gerry

1. I strongly recommend this article to the reader: http://www2.belfasttoday.net/orange/orange13.pdf.

Adams predictably whined about 'British death squads', conveniently forgetting the equally nefarious activities of his 'Irish death squads'. A spokesman for the UDA/UFF claimed the murder and stated: 'While the Protestant genocide continues, the Republican movement will pay a heavy price.'

Later that day, another Republican died at the hands of the Loyalists; this time the UVF was the paramilitary organisation involved. The victim was Martin 'Rook' O'Prey whom readers of previous books on the Troubles by this author will know well. He was OC of the loftily titled Belfast Brigade of the Irish Peoples' Liberation Organisation and he was based in the Divis Street area. A more violent, left-wing organisation, the IPLO emerged from the ranks of the IRSP/INLA (IRSP: Irish Republican Socialist Party). Gerard 'Dr Death' Steenson, Jimmy Brown and O'Prey himself were founder members, with Brown heading up the 'political wing' of the group, the RSC (Republican Socialist Collective). By 1991, it appeared to be more interested in the drugs trade, especially the manufacture and distribution of ecstasy and had even allied itself, along with elements of the UVF, with some English criminals making up an axis of drug dealers. There was a falling-out between the three ideologically opposed groups – do criminals have ideologies? – and the 'purer' more revolutionary socialist factions within the IPLO wanted O'Prey dead.

He had had a colourful career as a Republican terrorist, being involved in the OIRA, INLA and finally the IPLO, and was a leading player in the deadly feud with his former comrades in the INLA. He was involved along with Steenson in the murder of INLA man Emmanuel Gargan and the attempted murder of Kevin 'Bap' McQuillan and his brother Eamon, all in 1987. He then killed Loyalist leaders George Seawright and Billy Quee in 1987 and 1988.

On the evening of 16 August 1991, O'Prey was at home in Ardmoulin Terrace, close to the Divis Street tower; unknown to him, one of his associates had agreed with the UVF to set him up for death. This 'comrade' was in O'Prey's house and, on the pretext of getting a drink from the kitchen, had unlocked the back door. He then slipped away, going to a nearby hotel where he telephoned his UVF contacts who had a murder gang on stand-by. Under cover of darkness, they let themselves in via the unlocked back door before calmly walking into the lounge, where the IPLO man was sitting playing with his seven-year-old daughter on the settee. Without hesitation, they opened fire with Browning 9 mm handguns, hitting him around 20 times in the head and chest, slightly wounding his little girl. They dashed out of the house to a waiting car and sped away in the direction of the nearby Shankill. Jimmy Brown gave a graveside eulogy, but within 12 months, he too was dead, also gunned down by Loyalists. Quoted as it was written, the IPLO statement said: 'Shot at his home, Ardmoulin Terrace, Lower Falls, Belfast by loyalist gunmen. Martin was another fearless operator, and the O.C. of the IPLO at the time of his death. From an early age Martin regularly engaged the enemy. His fearless attitude brought him to the attention of the Brits and their Loyalist proxy's. Martins home was directly under the British army watchtower at Divis tower, yet no one stationed there seen or heard anything. Martin was another victim of the collusion that existed between the crown forces and the UVF.'

The dead IPLO man's sister later asked the Army for a copy of the surveillance video from one of the Divis tower rooftop cameras, but was told that the machine was not working at the time of O'Prey's death. I am unable to comment further.

On the 17th, the Coldstream Guards lost a popular NCO in a PIRA landmine explosion at Carrickovaddy Woods, near Crossmaglen. A patrol from their 2nd Battalion was tasked to search an area where documents, including photographs of PIRA personnel, were thought to have been lost. They were unsuccessful and were en route to rendezvous with a helicopter from Bessbrook Mill which was coming to extract them. At that stage of the Troubles, especially deep in 'Bandit Country', it was far too dangerous to travel by the roads. Lance Corporal Simon Ware (22) was walking past a mound of earth by the side of the track; unknown to him, it contained 300 lb (135 kg) of explosives. The landmine, planted by PIRA operatives from the South Armagh brigade, was detonated, and the young Londoner's body was shredded by the blast and he was killed instantaneously. He and his wife Carol had married in March, in the Guards Chapel in Wellington Barracks, London; sadly, his funeral was also held there.

The Incident
Darren Ware, Royal Green Jackets

At 08:00 hrs the patrol sergeant's team, with Simon being the third man, entered a fire break in the wood and followed it through to a distinctive bend. As Simon exited the left bend an explosion erupted only feet away killing him instantly and completely destroying his body. The patrol, having reacted to the attack, frantically searched the location for Simon. There was no hope of finding him. In the two-day follow-up search operation his body was never found, only parts of his body were found amongst the blood-stained trees. Only the barrel of his GPMG was located, mangled and bent; parts of blood-stained equipment and small parts of him that remained were found. The largest part that was found, his left lower arm, was located outside of the wood 330 feet away. His wedding ring was still intact; it was only five months old.

There was some controversy over the manner of Simon Ware's death, as the routes taken by patrolling soldiers through those woods must have been recce'd by PIRA dickers, observing from under cover. Their intelligence had also been aided by careless soldiers disposing of their ration-pack coverings, as well as discarded sweet wrappers and empty cigarette packets. This was PIRA territory; their families had either farmed or smuggled goods over the land for many years and their hatred of the British/English was legendary. It was seemingly programmed into their genes and fed to them at the same time that they drank milk from the breasts of their mothers. I accept that the lost documents had to be recovered, and that the troops had to re-trace the steps of the previous patrol, but this decision played into the hands of the bomb-makers. It robbed the Coldstreamers of a fine young soldier, Carol of a new husband, and Darren Ware –from the Royal Green Jackets – of his older brother. Darren at that stage was also deployed in Northern Ireland, in the Castlederg area of Co. Tyrone. Shortly after his brother was confirmed as having been killed, Darren was summoned to his base at Castlederg RUC station and told to report to his OC. I served in the same regiment as Darren and am proud to call him a friend, and a good friend at that.

The News about Simon
Darren Ware, Royal Green Jackets

The OC ushered me into his office and told me to sit down. There was something not right in his demeanour or his face and he said those immortal words that I will never forget: 'There's no easy way to say this, but your brother was killed by an IED in South Armagh this morning.' I said 'No.' Everything just fell apart; there was a pause of disbelief. I dropped to a sofa armchair and just burst out crying uncontrollably. The OC was emotional too and he had to leave the office. He was gutted too and he knew it would be a body blow that I did not deserve. He'd told me in a professional manner and didn't hesitate. His priority was to get me back to Rockwood and out of the Province pronto. I sat there still fully kitted up with my body armour, webbing and weapon and plenty of ammunition, just constantly crying to myself, in disbelief, not believing that Simon had been killed and I felt detached as I had lost a big part of my life; I no longer had the brother I looked up to, my only one. I looked up to Simon in many ways but most importantly because he was older and more experienced than me and I respected him for being older. I respected him for having joined the Army and giving me the influence, courage and support to do the same and follow in his footsteps.

Four days after the death of Simon Ware, the Provisionals attacked the RUC station at Kilrea, Co. Londonderry. A device weighing 500 lb (230 kg) was left outside the station, which was unmanned overnight; it caused extensive damage to the fortified base, as well as to over 100 surrounding homes and a Catholic church. Fortunately there were no deaths, although there were several light injuries amongst personnel and civilians. Later that day, conveniently forgetting that his comrades had just put the local community at such risk, Gerry Adams wrote to John Major as well as to the Irish Taoiseach and political and church leaders in Northern Ireland. In his letter, he demanded/suggested a series of 'open-ended discussions' to seek an end to the impasse which had plagued the country for a day or two over 22 years. The Northern Ireland office was quick to dismiss the offer as a gimmick.

On the same day as Lance Corporal Ware's death and the Adams letter, two Irishmen who had been warned to leave the island of Ireland by the IRA, entered Newry Cathedral in order to seek sanctuary. Alleged criminals Liam Kearns and David Madigan, who were 19 and 23 respectively, had been warned of 'direct military action' by the IRA who called them 'hoodlums who had terrorised their neighbourhood for years'. The two men were part of a gang of four who had been threatened by the IRA; one had left the country already, but one appealed to an IRA 'court' and had been reprieved. Jeff Maxwell of Families Against Terror and Intimidation said: 'Sanctuary wasn't a gimmick; it was the only place they felt confident their lives were secure.' An opposing view was espoused by a Sinn Féin councillor, Brendan Curran, a member of the district council: 'It would have been quite easy for the IRA to shoot them and be finished with it, but putting people out is an alternative to violence. Compromise is not possible now. It's like the Mounties. The IRA always gets its man.' However, the pair left the sanctuary on the 28th, after the IRA lifted the threats against the two men.

On the 24th, there was another sickening sectarian murder, this time in the HQNI town of Lisburn, Co. Antrim. Martin Watters (27) was another innocent Catholic who chose the wrong place and the wrong time to sleep off the effects of a drunken night out. He lived in Low Road and had been drinking heavily in the town centre; after he left the pub, he made his way home, but stopped to rest on a park bench beside the River Lagan, opposite the Queen's Road and promptly fell asleep. The spot where he was murdered is only a few hundred yards from his house. In the early hours of the morning, he was chanced upon by a Protestant gang, containing at least two members of the local unit of the UVF. They rifled through his pockets and upon discovering evidence that he was a Catholic, kicked and beat him very close to death. It is possible that he died from massive head injuries a short time later but, to make sure, they returned to the scene of the crime and threw his body into the river.

At the court case, all four gang members, including their leader James Beck and another UVF man, were given life sentences, with one of them given a jail tariff of 20 years. In court, one of the killers admitted that they had spoken to Mr Watters and that he had told them that his name was 'Seamus', usually a Catholic name, and that was what had prompted them to kill him.

On the 29th, Sinn Féin won a by-election for a seat on Belfast City Council. This victory brought the party's representation to nine members making it the second-largest party on the council.

On the 31st, the UFF targeted and murdered a Catholic man who not only had no Republican connections whatsoever, but was recovering from a heart bypass operation. Francis Crawford (57), father of five children, was off work following a long hospital stay and had volunteered to help friends make deliveries from a Chinese restaurant in the Antrim Road. In the late evening, a UFF gang took over a house in Vicarage Place and telephoned an order through for delivery to Corporation Street, close to the UDR barracks at Girdwood. Mr Crawford took the order but was unable to find the stated address; as he looked around for it, masked gunmen came out of the house where they had hidden, and shot the Catholic man at point-blank range, hitting him several times in the head. It was a classic 'dial-a-Catholic' murder, and Mr Crawford died instantly. The gun used was a .38 revolver that had been stolen in 1988 from an RUC base; it was also used in an attempted sectarian killing later in 1991. The men escaped in a taxi which had been stolen earlier from the Crumlin Road, finally dumping it in the Shankill area. To add further insult to the dead man's memory and taunt his five children and wife, from whom he was separated, the UFF falsely claimed that Mr Crawford used his meal delivery activities in order to ferry IRA arms around the city.

August had turned into a bloody month, with 14 people dead, including seven soldiers or former soldiers.

9

September

This was a month of 12 killings, which included the 2,000th civilian to be killed during the 22 years of the Troubles to date; four of the dead were soldiers, none of whom were killed in terrorist-related activities, and an RUC officer was also killed. There were six sectarian murders, including Sinn Féin personnel killed by Loyalists.

On the first of the month, a delegation of US politicians visited Northern Ireland, but for once it was not the usual gaggle of Irish-Americans interfering in the affairs of a foreign country on a pro-IRA 'fact-finding' mission, but desperately trying to pretend not to be. This was a delegation with a difference, led by Democratic member and Speaker of the House of Representatives Tom Foley. On his return to the USA, he urged Americans not to give financial assistance to NORAID, as the funds were, by and large, going to purchase arms and ammunition for the IRA. Somewhat refreshingly, he refused to meet Sinn Féin representatives until they were prepared to renounce violence. However, the goodwill gained during this visit was somewhat negated when a leading Unionist, John Taylor, whilst addressing a meeting of the Young Unionists, claimed that one-in-three Catholics, was 'either a supporter of murder or worse still, a murderer'.

His words were provocative and insensitive, given that later that day, a Catholic was murdered by a Loyalist paramilitary unit. Seamus Sullivan (24), son of a Sinn Féin councillor, was employed as a dustbin-collector by Belfast City Council. During the morning of the 3rd, two UFF gunmen, one of whom was Stephen 'Top Gun' McKeag, of the UFF's 'C' company, walked into the refuse depot at Springfield Avenue and opened fire on a bin lorry in which Mr Sullivan was a passenger. Although he tried to escape, the gunmen shot him several times through an open window; he still managed to crawl into the back of lorry, but McKeag then shot him in the head. He died instantly. The killers escaped in a stolen car in the direction of the Shankill. Mary MacMahon of the Catholic-dominated Workers Party, said she had known the young Sullivan for many years and that he had never been involved with any paramilitary groups. She said: 'He just wanted to do an honest day's work. He took a job as a road sweeper rather than be unemployed.'

He was the son of veteran Nationalist James 'Solo' Sullivan, who was closely aligned to the Irish Republican Army in the 1970s; indeed, he had commanded the OIRA's Lower Falls battalion. The elder Sullivan appealed for calm and said he did not want any retaliatory actions stating: 'I have been totally opposed to murder and violence from whatever source. I will not change my mind, even at this point. The killing must be stopped. I would not wish to have any other family to have to suffer the grief that my family are suffering tonight.' The UVF also tried to kill another Catholic that day, when they shot and wounded a man in the

York Road district in North Belfast about 5 p.m. The Catholic worked at a taxi depot in the area; he was hit in the neck by gunmen firing from a passing car, but later recovered from his wounds. Shortly after this attempted killing, the IRA tried to use another proxy bomb, this time in South Armagh, when they loaded explosives onto a tractor and forced the driver to head for an RUC/Army base. However, the driver jumped clear and the tractor and trailer slid off the road and into a ditch; the bomb failed to detonate.

Another man who survived a UFF attack was Dr Adrian Guelke, a South African academic who had fallen foul of the apartheid regime's BOSS (Bureau of State Security) and was living in exile in Belfast. To solve their problem, without getting their own hands dirty, BOSS agents had leaked information to the UDA/UFF that Guelke was a Republican who supported the IRA. Consequently, a two-man unit broke silently into his home in Fitzwilliam Street, South Belfast, and shot him several times as he lay in bed, but the victim survived the shooting. One of the UFF's favourite and oft-used expressions in relation to their murder campaign was 'put him down a hole'. In Dr Guelke's case, they singularly failed to do so.

On the 8th, Private Alan Craig McConnell (26), a UDR soldier, was killed in an RTA in Co. Down. I have very few details, other than that he was buried at Greyabbey on the Ards Peninsula by the shores of Strangford Lough. Nineteen days later, on the 27th, another UDR soldier, from 8 Battalion in Co. Tyrone, Sergeant George William Rollins (33), was killed on one of the Province's dangerous roads; regrettably, I have no further details.

On the evening of the 10th, the IRA killed a Protestant man at his home in South Belfast; they claimed that John Hanna (19) was a member of the UVF, and whilst there is some circumstantial evidence that he was a member of the paramilitary group, it is just that, purely circumstantial. Shortly after he returned home from work, Mr Hanna went upstairs to his bedroom in the house at Donegall Road, in the south of the city. Two masked gunmen burst into the house, brandishing guns and began searching for Mr Hanna; his sister bravely shouted out a warning to her brother and he leapt from his bedroom window, He must have landed awkwardly, as he was slow to recover, and one of the IRA men shot him from the open window, rendering him incapacitated. They then ran downstairs and shot him a further seven times, before running off to a stolen car and heading west in the direction of the Nationalist Andersonstown area. The RUC were quick to point out that the murdered man, despite a UVF tattoo and Loyalist posters in his room, was not a member and nor was he ever claimed by the UVF. This was a sectarian murder, pure and simple, carried out by the IRA – who always maintained that they were not sectarian. Later on, as if to add more mystery to the murder, a Loyalist mural supporting the UVF and Red Hand Commando, and containing a picture of Hanna, was unveiled in the Broadway in South Belfast.

On Friday 13th, both of the two main Loyalist paramilitary groups were in action in Belfast. In the first incident, the UFF planted two car bombs in the Nationalist Whiterock area, apparently in retaliation for two very recent attacks by the IRA in Protestant housing estates. An Army ATO was called in and soldiers defused both devices, after the RUC had evacuated the immediate areas. Quite what the Brit-hating, Army-hating local populace made of these courageous officers risking their lives to save the lives and homes of Nationalists and Catholics is not recorded.

The very same day, Kevin Flood (31), a Catholic father of two young children working as a taxi driver, was murdered by UVF gunmen who were simply roaming a Catholic area on the lookout for a random target. He had arrived home late from his shift as a cabbie and realised that there was something wrong with his car; innocently, he had opened his bonnet and was working on the engine. Unknown to him, the UVF men had been following a man several streets away with the intention of murdering him; however, he had managed to escape from them by jumping over a wall and running to the safety of his home. Undeterred, the gunmen got into their car and began cruising around the Ligoniel area in the hope of finding a lone Catholic returning home from the pub. At approximately 01:00, they drove along Ligoniel Road, where they spotted Mr Flood working on his car; they simply fired six shots into his neck, head and back; he fell to the ground and died just minutes later. They escaped in the direction of the Loyalist Shankill.

Cullyhanna Shooting
Lance Corporal Rob Hughes, Royal Green Jackets

It was Friday the 13th, just the day to head towards the 'pipe ranges' of Cullyhanna and Crossmaglen. During the brief prior to leaving, we were informed that the latest information was that there was a lot of Intel pointing towards a shoot with a secondary device in the area. There had been reports of automatic fire being heard in the border areas in the days leading up to this patrol, possibly weapons being zeroed.

We flew by Lynx helicopters to the drop-off points south of Newtownhamilton and we carried out our tasks as planned. I can remember glancing over my shoulder and being pleased with the way the brick was performing; perfect spacing and positioning and all looking switched on. It was an eerie dusk around Cullyhanna; as we moved south of the town towards the lakes I could see the smoke coming from the chimneys of this notorious village and scanned the likely firing points for any combat indicators.

I looked at the other bricks and noticed that they were dominating an area of high ground behind my position; so I moved towards a VCP on a road between Crossmaglen and Cullyhanna. As I scanned the area, I was suddenly thrown to the ground (with an 80 lb Bergen on) and felt immediate pain in my right leg and saw a blinding flash before my eyes. I say pain; it felt more like somebody had shoved a bloody red-hot poker through my right thigh!

To this day I can remember the noise as automatic fire rained down on us from three separate firing points. I was later to learn it was a GPMG and two AK-47s. I reached for my radio hand-piece which had become dislodged. When I moved, another long burst of automatic fire was aimed at me; I can remember watching the glow of green tracer rounds heading towards me and smashing into the ground around me. I admit to thinking that I was finished because there was no cover around me at all. I just looked up and watched the muzzle flashes of the PIRA gun team shooting at us, but what probably saved me and other casualties was the incredibly aggressive return fire from the blokes who hammered the rounds down back at the terrorist positions.

On the 16th, the UFF targeted a Sinn Féin councillor as he arrived at Magherafelt College of Further Education, where he was employed as a business studies lecturer. He was known to be hard-working, industrious and clearly cared for the lives of the people who had elected him to Magherafelt Council in Co. Londonderry. On the morning that he was killed, a UFF murder gang arrived at the campus and one man with a concealed weapon got out of the parked car and mingled with students near the college's main entrance. He saw Bernard O'Hagan (37), father of three, park his car and begin walking towards the entrance; the UFF man waited until Mr O'Hagan was level with him, then shot him several times in the head; he died instantly. The killer then ran through a crowd of shocked students, and into the waiting car which then raced away. The college closed down for the day as a mark of respect. At the precise moment that his body was being taken away, the funeral of Kevin Flood was taking place in Belfast. Fiona O' Hagan said of her dead husband: 'He was removed because he was successful and articulate.'

An Phoblacht was fast off the mark to allege collusion, and Laura Friel was quick to quote Oistin MacBride, a prominent Sinn Féin member: 'The killer, young and unmasked, fired eight shots and apparently walked out of the front gates of the college and wasn't seen by another witness. No getaway car was spotted or abandoned. No disguises or overalls dumped. No weapons ever recovered and no one ever charged with any aspect of the killing. Bernard's killer made it look easy and it probably was.' She then continued with her own, although highly unoriginal thoughts:

> In line with many other loyalist attacks, the killing of Bernard O'Hagan bore all the hallmarks of crown force collusion. The pattern is all too familiar in republican circles. Bernard became a target of heightened RUC and British army harassment. Then, three months before the shooting, the RUC informed Bernard that crown force intelligence files containing his personal details were in the hands of loyalists. The stage had been set. On the morning of the shooting, Bernard's brother noticed an unusual number of crown forces' checkpoints and patrols that a short time later, just prior to the killing, miraculously disappeared. Recent revelations exposing details of how the FRU [Force Research Unit, part of Army intelligence] operated in collusion with loyalist death squads have confirmed that the covert unit had the authority to order all other crown force personnel out of any area and routinely did prior to an operation. The demeanour of the gunman suggested he had been freed from the normal fear of capture. He made no effort to disguise his appearance and showed no particular haste to escape after the shooting. The killer displayed a confidence inappropriate to the crime – a confidence most easily understood within the mechanisms of collusion that ensured he'd never be brought to account.

There is, of course, no evidence to suggest that Friel is correct; the SF had very little interest in the Sinn Féin man; he was keen and articulate, and believed in a united Ireland, but he posed no threat to Northern Ireland's continued membership of the United Kingdom. There were far more sinister and dangerous types of Republicans who, if collusion existed on a large scale, would have been in greater danger from the 'crown forces' death squads'. The truth of the matter is that the Loyalist paramilitaries saw him as an enemy and chose him as a 'soft target'; paramilitaries on both sides considered just how easy a killing would be and chose as their targets people who would have little or no time to resist. It is entirely possible that the UFF unit who murdered Mr O'Hagan included a UDR member – as we have seen in previous incidents, that did happen – or had received information from a UDR soldier sympathetic to the Loyalist cause. It is entirely possible that the UFF murder gang had been briefed as to timings and routes of Army foot patrols in the area around Magherafelt College on that Monday morning. To allege such wide-scale collusion, however, as Friel does on every single occasion, is palpable nonsense. Had it existed on the scale that she rather tiredly suggests, can she explain why Gerry Adams, Martin Ferris, 'Slab' Murphy and Danny Morrison are still walking around? The theory which she alleges is of such epic proportions, that even a paranoid conspiracist such as Stalin himself would be embarrassed.

However, the IRA were quick to react and simply threw more broth into the boiling cauldron of sectarian hatred, by warning that they would target the Loyalists in their homes and that they would pay 'a high personal price' for their deeds.

The day after the murder of Mr O'Hagan, the Provisionals again tried out the horizontal mortar attack tactic on a joint Army/RUC patrol at Swatragh, Co. Londonderry. The attack took place a little under 10 miles north of the Magherafelt College murder, when a four-vehicle mobile patrol was under way in the southern part of the county. The Army contingent was from the King's Regiment, based at RAF Ballykelly, and had just driven across a bridge near Swatragh, when the IRA unit fired at the cluster of vehicles. The Mark XII mortar round smashed into one of the Land Rovers, containing an English RUC man, Erik Clarke (37), father of three, who had married a local girl and then joined the RUC. He was mortally wounded, and three of the King's were dreadfully injured. When Clarke died shortly afterwards of his wounds, he became the 288th RUC officer to be killed in the Troubles; 18 more names would follow his on the RUC's Roll of Honour before the Troubles ended. Just 24 hours later, the funeral of Bernard O'Hagan drove over the bridge at Swatragh, where Constable Clarke's lifeblood ebbed away; three deaths all linked by poignant moments in time.

On the 18th, the Royal Green Jackets lost one of their soldiers; Sergeant Thomas John Ross (39) was killed in a road accident in South Armagh; I am indebted to his former second in command, Kenneth Richardson, for this information. He was from Herefordshire and was buried at St Martin's Graveyard; I have no further details.

The Royal Military Police (RMP) lost 15 members during the course of Operation Banner. Their motto is *Exemplo Ducemus*: 'By example, shall we lead', and the sight of their red caps in garrison towns, such as Aldershot, Colchester, Catterick and Tidworth of a Saturday night, was enough to strike fear into the hearts of drink-fuelled squaddies, who could expect a night in the guardhouse and a sore head in more ways than one, the following morning. The day after Sergeant Ross died, Lance Corporal Duncan Mark Chappell (18) from Biggar in Lanarkshire was shot dead in the Province. Other than the fact that he was shot accidentally, little further has been revealed; I simply did not know if it was a negligent discharge or a 'blue on blue', until one of his comrades came forward (*see below*). He shares a grave in Symington Cemetery in Scotland with his father. The Elizabeth Cross is awarded to the next of kin of those who have died since 1 January 1948 while on operations or as a result of an act of terrorism. It was introduced on 1 August 2009 and was awarded to Mrs

Liz A. Chappell, mother of the dead Red Cap. He was the 14th RMP soldier to die during the Troubles; the 15th and final Red Cap died the following month.

The Night that Duncan Died
Soldier 'C', Royal Military Police

I was the patrol medic and was there when Duncan died. The team were packing up a VCP in Lisburn, ready to move on to another location. One of the patrol members, an RMP Corporal, decided to show off his new rifle and SUSAT sight system to a bunch of kids, but as he did so, he accidentally squeezed off a round, but it was more than just a negligent discharge, because it ended the life of a young soldier. The round entered his body about an inch below his rear ceramic plate, travelled through his body and hit his front ceramic plate; it then ricocheted through his body before exiting through his inner thigh. We were told that he died instantly, although the doctors at Lisburn hospital tried to save him. The lad who shot him was only charged with having an ND, given a monetary fine and posted out of the Province. Quite disgusting really which still makes me very angry to think about. This incident has been proven to have given me PTSD, as I had never lost a friend before. I thought we were invincible; hope this helps.

Following the deaths of the two soldiers in non-terrorist incidents, the IRA added to the bloodletting when they killed a local businessman whose company had been carrying out contracting work for the SF. John Haldane (34), father of four, ran a timber firm based in Belfast Docks which did repair work on SF bases; he was marked out by the IRA for murder on the 20th. During the morning, he was working in his office with a colleague when two men, dressed respectably, as though they were businessmen, walked into his office and fired several shots at him, hitting him in the head and chest. He was mortally wounded, dying shortly afterwards. His female colleague said that he tried to raise himself from the floor but was too badly wounded to do so. He managed to gasp out a final message to his wife before succumbing, the victim of a cowardly organisation who believed that they could reunite Ireland by wanton acts of murder. Mr Haldane's pointless death adequately illustrated the utter bankruptcy of Provisional IRA thinking and tactics. He was the 80th contractor to be murdered by the IRA for the 'crime' of doing business with the Army/RUC.

The following tribute to Mr Haldane is taken from Politics.ie:

> John Haldane was a decent sportsman, generous, and a family man. There wasn't a sectarian bone in his body. He was highly successful in business and employed people from across both main communities and his company was one that treated employees fairly and with respect. I have never heard a bad word about him. In one of his companies, McCue Dick, he was murdered for no reason other than doing his job. His crime was his company supplied the government with timber and construction services which involved work on police and army barracks. To have killed John Haldane there must have been information passed on to the IRA from within the company or people he had done business with. McCue Dick was sold by the family because of the painful memories it left them with. Haldane Fisher is

a legacy company, still run by the family, headquartered in Newry and it continues to employ people regardless of community background.[1]

Peter Brooke, the Secretary of State for Northern Ireland, never a politician to shy away from publicity, was in the news several times in the middle of the month. During 16–20 September, he held a series of meetings with the leaders of the main political parties in Northern Ireland in an effort to restart the stalled talks. However, with much speculation about the date of the next British general election – due in 1992 at the latest – no dates were set for a resumption of the talks. He then gave an interview to the *Sunday Times*, although it was not published for a further six days, the day after he had flown back from the USA following a five-day visit. He was reported as stating that Articles 2 and 3 of the Republic of Ireland's constitution were 'not helpful' in finding an agreement in Northern Ireland. He also warned that people should not seek to stretch the Anglo-Irish Agreement.

On the weekend of the 21st/22nd, Loyalist prisoners started a fire in the dining hall of Crumlin Road Jail, Belfast; this was followed by about 50 Republican prisoners also rioting in the 'Crum' and trying to barricade off part of the prison. The NIO said that the disturbances by Republican and Loyalist prisoners were part of a deliberate campaign to force the prison authorities to introduce segregation. Loyalists later threatened to kill prison officers to force the Major government to introduce segregation in the jail.

Then, on the 28th, the UFF killed a third Belfast newsagent for the spurious crime of (allegedly) selling *An Phoblacht*. If the IRA could do bankruptcy of thinking, so too could their Loyalist counterparts; equally if the IRA could take a human life for the most trivial of reasons, so too could their depraved counterparts. Lawrence Murchan (63), father of three grown-up children, ran a shop in St James Road in the Rodney's area of the Falls. The location is in the heart of Nationalist territory, and the murder gang would simply have had to approach from either the Falls Road or from the Donegall Road, the latter offering the best escape route. At around 08:50 on the Saturday morning, Mr Murchan was disposing of rubbish close to his shop, when a stolen car stopped immediately next to him and two masked men, without a word, shot him five times at point-blank range, in the head and chest, killing him almost immediately. The car, which had been stolen in Ballymena the previous night, then raced away, leaving an innocent Catholic lying in a pool of his own blood. Although a later message to the press claimed the killing on behalf of the Loyalist Defence and Retaliation Group, the killing was carried out by 'C' company, UFF. The unit was led by Johnny Adair, with this gang under the command of Stephen McKeag; it was the second sectarian slaying committed this month by these two men, following the murder of Seamus Sullivan on the 4th. Deaths attributed to the Troubles (including 400+ soldiers, ignored by both the MoD and the book *Lost Lives*[2]) were now approaching 4,000; Mr Murchan became the 2,000th civilian to die in these 22 years.

Mr Murchan's family later made a statement denying that he sold *An Phoblacht* in his shop and, indeed, stated that he had consistently refused to stock it. UPI reported:

1. http://www.politics.ie/forum/northern-ireland/179714-twenty-years-teebane-families-voice-frustration-11.html.
2. David McKittrick et al., *Lost Lives: The Stories of the Men, Women and Children Who Died as a Result of the Northern Ireland Troubles* (Mainstream Publishing, 1999).

> Protestant gunmen shot dead a Catholic shopkeeper in West Belfast Saturday, the 2,000th civilian slain in the sectarian violence that has torn Ulster for 22 years, the Royal Ulster Constabulary said. Laurence Patrick Murchan, 63, a father of three, was burning rubbish at the back of his store when two gunmen shot him, police said. Witnesses said six shots were fired point blank. The gunmen escaped with a third man in a stolen car later found abandoned in the Protestant Village area of Belfast. The Loyalist Retaliation and Defense Force claimed responsibility for the attack saying it was in revenge for the killing of a Protestant businessman by Irish Republican Army gunmen in Belfast 10 days ago. The group also claimed Murchan had been selling copies of the pro-Catholic 'Republican News'. This was the second killing carried out by the organization after last month's shooting of a Catholic newsagent in the same area of West Belfast.

As evidenced by the number of British Army, particularly UDR, deaths attributed to RTAs, accidents did happen in Northern Ireland, even during the Troubles. On the 29th of this month, a shooting accident took the life of an innocent man, killed by the RUC. A day later, a man was knocked down – he died the next month – by a car containing terrorists fleeing from the scene of a bomb attack. Both were accidents and both robbed families of loved ones; both were seen differently by the IRA and their Sinn Féin and *An Phoblacht* apologists.

In the first incident, student, Kevin McGovern (19), a Catholic from Co. Fermanagh, was in the wrong place at the wrong time, as he became civilian death number 2,001. On the evening of the 29th, he was with two friends and was observed to step out of the local graveyard and begin walking along Westland Road, Cookstown, in Co. Tyrone. They were heading towards a disco at the Greenvale Hotel in the town. An RUC unit – possibly from the Headquarters Mobile Support Unit (HMSU) – was attempting to ambush a PIRA team, known to be in the area and preparing a mortar attack on the police station there. They caught sight of the three men and warnings were shouted; it would appear that the three men were in a truculent mood and refused orders to stop. In the confusion and heightened tension of the situation, one of the undercover officers – PC Timothy Hanley – opened fire and the young man was hit in the back, dying at the scene. It must be stressed that Hanley only fired the fatal shot after first firing warning shots into the air. It was a tragic accident, which had occurred in the heat and tension of the moment; it was not the cold-blooded and calculated shot in the back of the head, so reminiscent of the bulk of the killings perpetuated by the Provisional IRA.

UPI reported the following day:

> British security forces said Monday they regretted killing a student on a Catholic housing project and acknowledged the dead man was not involved in terrorist activities. Kevin McGovern, an 18-year-old freshman at Loughry Agricultural College in Cookstown, 50 miles west of Belfast, was shot and killed late Sunday night by security forces. The Royal Ulster Constabulary initially reported the man was shot after throwing a 'device' and running away. In a later statement, the RUC said that 'As a result of its investigations the police now believe that the young man shot dead in Cookstown last night was not engaged in terrorist activity. The RUC

> deeply regrets the death of Kevin McGovern and has expressed its condolences to his family.' The RUC also said it would investigate the incident. Two other men with McGovern, also first year students at Loughry, were being questioned in the incident. The three had reportedly gathered in a cemetery, a well-known drinking place for young people in the area, according to a priest. 'The police know that perfectly well, that youngsters are inclined to go inside the wall of the graveyard to get a drink and therefore to see them coming out shouldn't have caused them any alarm or panic,' the Rev. Denis Faul told BBC Television. 'If they'd seen objects in their hands it obviously would have been . . . drinking material,' he said. Police said security forces were called to the area to investigate reports a mortar round had been placed in a taxi in the area and saw three men run from the housing estate. The RUC said only two of the men stopped when challenged. The third, McGovern, kept running, causing the officers to open fire. The shooting followed a warning by the RUC last week that anyone seen throwing a device at security forces could be shot. About 40 people have been wounded in the past month in attacks on security forces and bases by plastic explosives detonated in coffee jars.

A spokesman for the RUC openly and honestly admitted that they deeply regretted the killing and apologised for a terrible error. PC Hanley was charged with murder, but in a landmark decision, Belfast Crown Court cleared him of that charge in September 1994. Mr Justice Nicholson said PC Hanley had mistakenly but honestly acted in self-defence when he shot Mr McGovern. Reporting on the court case, the *Independent* commented: 'The three friends then passed near to a checkpoint "at the very moment when the police were afraid of being attacked". Police suspecting them of being part of the terrorist team, called on them to stop or they would open fire. After warning shots from PC Hanley, Mr McGovern's two friends "stopped dead", but he ran on followed by the policeman who fired a second burst before shooting the student as he turned to glance back.' I very much regret the innocent man's death and, should Kevin's family and friends read this account, would like to pass on my deepest and genuine sympathies.

On the last day of the month a PIRA unit made a bombing attack on the RUC station at Dunmurry in South Belfast. Afterwards, they raced off in a stolen car; part of their escape route included the Upper Dunmurry Lane; Roger Elwood (25) and his girlfriend,Amanda Stewart were hit by that car just before midnight. Ms Stewart suffered a broken leg, but Mr Elwood, a Protestant, was placed on a life-support machine after sustaining massive head injuries. The Provisional IRA later apologised for the incident, admitting that the car involved was used in an attack on the local RUC station. Mr Elwood died on 2 October; Ms Stewart was able to attend his funeral on Saturday 6 October, but had to use a wheelchair. The terrorists were driving a car but it was no less a lethal weapon than was the Ruger pistol which PC Hanley fired at Kevin McGovern the day before. Both killings were accidental, but I will leave it to the reader's imagination just how much political capital the Republicans made of the first of the two deaths.

September was over and 12 people had been killed, making it 26 in just nine weeks.

10
October

Deaths were down slightly this month, but for the families of the nine who died, there was little solace in that statistic. Sectarian attacks by Loyalist paramilitaries increased – if that were actually possible – and October saw the equal highest number of sectarian murders of the year, with six innocents dying, all Catholics. In total, civilian deaths were seven, as a Protestant who had been knocked down by a fleeing IRA gang the previous month died from his injuries. A Loyalist paramilitary was also killed and a soldier died in unknown circumstances.

On the 2nd, Roger Elwood's family took the incredibly painful decision to turn off the life-support machine which had been keeping him alive in hospital since his accident the previous Monday evening. With his injured girlfriend at his side, his parents made the agonising decision, once it became clear that he would not recover; his organs were donated to try and save the lives of others – a truly noble, but nonetheless heartbreaking decision, precipitated by the reckless actions of a terrorist organisation. Any apologies made by the IRA as a consequence were even more shallow and meaningless than normal.

On the same day that Mr Elwood died, Channel 4 Television added some unnecessary fuel to the fire when it jumped on the collusion bandwagon in order to sell its programmes. It showed a documentary called 'The Committee' in its weekly programme *Dispatches*. It claimed that there was an 'inner circle' in the RUC and UDR which was colluding with Loyalist paramilitaries in the killing of Catholics. Someone once rather famously said: 'Today's news is tomorrow's fish-and-chip paper,' and it is well known that 'Dog Bites Man' does not sell newspapers, but the converse does. For this reason I condemn Channel 4 for a programme which could only embarrass the SF and also give succour to the terror groups. A subsequent book on the controversy, also entitled *The Committee*, was not released in the UK by the American publishers who feared libel proceedings.

Later in the month, the BBC became involved, with their *Panorama* programme laying the blame for the recent collapse of the Mayhew/Brooke talks at the feet of recalcitrant Loyalists.

On the 3rd, in West Belfast, the Provisionals knee-capped four men for alleged involvement in distributing drugs. The four, plus twenty others, were ordered to leave both Northern Ireland and the Irish Republic. The RUC and the SDLP condemned the IRA for their hypocrisy and demanded that they allow the rapidly escalating drugs problem to be dealt with by the lawful authorities.

On the 5th, Loyalist paramilitaries attempted to kill a Catholic man, Pearce McKenna, as he went to work that Friday morning in South Belfast. He was shot in the back by a motorcycle passenger outside the Ormeau Bakery but his condition was not serious and he later recovered. Six fellow Catholics would not be so fortunate this month.

The Gaelic Athletic Association (GAA) is an Irish and international amateur sporting and cultural organisation focused primarily on promoting Gaelic games, which include the traditional Irish sports of hurling, camogie, Gaelic football, handball and rounders. The Association also promotes Irish music and dance, as well as the Irish language. At that time some of their halls were alleged to have been used as PIRA drill halls, whether voluntarily or not. On the 8th, the UDA/UFF made an arson attack on one of the organisation's halls in Kircubbin, Co. Down, and followed this up with a warning statement, declaring that all members of the GAA would be considered as 'legitimate targets'. This threat was roundly and correctly condemned by Protestant church leaders and Unionist politicians. The next day the UFF was forced to backpedal – a rarity in itself – and issued another statement which retracted the first, saying that it would only attack those members 'with strong Republican links'.

The following day, another Red Cap died in the Province, this time in circumstances unknown. Corporal Michael Alan Paul Heighton (27) is reported as having 'died whilst on duty'. Regrettably, all I know is that this may have been due to natural causes whilst performing his regular duties. The annual Conservative Party Conference was taking place at the same time; delegates praised the efforts of NI Secretary Peter Brooke to find an agreement over the conflict, and they also recognised the need for an 'Irish dimension' in any settlement. The conference also pledged support for Conservative candidates contesting elections in Northern Ireland.

On the 10th, the IPLO, known to some as 'ramshackle Republicans', burst back onto the front pages of the newspapers, when they went in search of a leading UFF man to assassinate, but settled for another instead. During the evening, having arrived in a car stolen in the Falls Road area, two armed IPLO men entered the Diamond Jubilee Bar, on the Lower Shankill and pointed their weapons at the assembled drinkers. They had specifically targeted John 'Bunter' Graham, a leading UVF man, as the IPLO considered that he was behind the killing of Martin 'Rook' O'Prey on 16 August. The IPLO had discovered that Graham often drank in this particular bar. In the bar at the time was Harry Ward (42), a long-time member of the paramilitary force. One of the IPLO men kept saying: 'Where's Bunter? Where's Bunter?' Ward panicked, perhaps thinking that the gunmen were looking for any Loyalist, and he tried to escape out of the back of the pub, running towards the off-sales counter. As he ran, the two IPLO men opened fire, hitting him in the back five times; he died at the scene. The gunmen escaped in their stolen car, which was later found abandoned in the Divis Street area.

In a slightly different version, author David Leslie in his very readable book *Lighting Candles* relays a conversation he had with IPLO Commander, 'Manny' McDonnell: 'The team was planning to kill him [Ward] one night and sat outside the Diamond Jubilee Bar on the Lower Shankill Road waiting for Ward to come out, but they were getting noticed. One of the guys eventually said "Oh, fuck this, I'm going in to get him." The two who went in didn't know what Harry Ward looked like and so decided to simply yell out his name ... the first IPLO guy went in and shouted: "Harry Ward here?" Somebody shouted: "No, but who are you?" The gunman shouted "It doesn't fucking matter who I am, I'm asking if

Harry Ward's here," but the customer said: "Well I'm asking who the fuck you are." At that, our guy said: "This is who I am," and shot him dead. It had been Harry Ward after all.'[1] Colin Breen in his excellent oral history of the RUC records an officer saying: 'The next thing, Johnny Adair, who was a well-known senior terrorist on the Loyalist side, arrived. He had with him his usual cronies. As others arrived on the scene, you could see them talking amongst themselves. It was soon obvious that a heated conversation was going on. I said to Tony Johnston: "We need to try to get surveillance on them. These boys are going to go out tonight and shoot somebody." I just knew the way they were talking that they were scheming.'[2]

As the officer states, news of the murder of Ward was quickly relayed to Johnny 'Mad Dog' Adair, leader of the UVF's 'C' company, which included Stephen 'Top Gun' McKeag. He was angered at the death of Ward, but also by the audacity of the IPLO in coming into the heart of the Shankill and dispatched a murder gang into the Ardoyne, Oldpark and New Lodge areas, with specific orders to kill any black-cab driver – in that area inevitably a Catholic – whom they met; the first one they saw would do. The first black cab which they came across that evening was being driven by Hugh Magee (52), an Ardoyne father of a grown-up son. He had just collected his last fare of the evening in Rosapenna Street and was taking them to the Ardoyne before returning home; as he turned out onto Oldpark Road, a stolen car which contained John McAuley and other gunmen drove towards him, having just approached from the Crumlin Road along Hillview Road. The gunmen sprayed the cab with automatic fire, killing Mr Magee, causing the taxi to career out of control into a nearby wall. At his funeral a few days later, the priest carrying out the service appealed to the gunmen to 'put away your guns'. What impact did this have on killers such as Adair, McKeag & Co? They gave their answer less than 72 hours later with the murder of another Catholic on the 13th.

Later on the 10th, on what was becoming a more than dramatic and eventful day, the IRA's Tyrone and Fermanagh brigade launched an attack on an Army checkpoint at Derryvollen, Co. Fermanagh, a mile or so north of the Republican village of Rosslea, and a mere 200 yards from the Irish border. The Republic juts salient-like into the North at this point, making Derryvollen to the west of the border. A 'flying column' of IRA gunmen opened fire on the base with automatic weapons, at first forcing the half dozen or so soldiers to take cover before their professionalism kicked in and they began to return fire. The gun battle lasted for at least 10 minutes, with several hundred rounds expended by both sides. Soldiers saw at least two of the gunmen fall and bloodstains were later found, but any IRA dead or wounded were dragged across the border. The wounded would have been patched up by an IRA-sympathising doctor on the Irish side of the border, or even secretly buried. PIRA often intimidated and bullied doctors into giving their men medical treatment with no Garda involvement; on occasion struck-off doctors were also used. There were no dead PIRA listed that day.

Over the course of the next four days, Loyalist paramilitaries orphaned 12 Catholic children as they continued their psychopathic tit for tat with the Republicans. In what the Belfast folk call the 'wee hors' of the morning of the 13th, Karl Hegney, one of the army of

1. David Leslie, *Lighting Candles* (Black & White Publishing, 2014), p.134.
2. Colin Breen, *A Force Like No Other* (Blackstaff Press, 2017), p. 50.

unemployed Catholics in Belfast, was returning home from a night out and a 'lock-in' at the Rose and Crown pub on the Ormeau Road. He had reached the point where the Ormeau Road meets Donegall Pass and was just half a mile or a 10 minute stagger from his home in Friendly Way in the Markets. Unfortunately, as he walked towards the Markets area, on what an RUC officer later called 'the wrong side of the road leading to the Markets and [he] was therefore seen as a Catholic', he was spotted by a Loyalist murder gang from the UFF, cruising the area looking for victims. The driver slowed to a crawl as he reached Mr Hegney, and one of the passengers fired both barrels of a shotgun into his body, mortally wounding him; he died very shortly afterwards.

He was aged 54, and was the father of four children. His worried wife had often tried to persuade him not to walk along the Ormeau Road because of the high number of sectarian attacks; sadly the effects of the alcohol he had consumed that evening had removed all his natural caution. It is thought that one of the killers was the UFF's South Belfast commander, Stephen 'Inch' McFerran. The gang almost certainly included Raymond Elder and Joe Bratty. These same men were involved in the murder of Harry Conlon on the 14th. It is thought that they were also part of the murder gang which carried out the later massacre at Sean Graham's bookmakers.

There was a reasonably spontaneous reaction to the murder of a man who was selected simply because he was identifiable as a Catholic, the sixth such killing in five days. Three hundred demonstrators walked in silence to Belfast City Hall in a candle-lit procession where they stood in silent vigil for the sectarian victims. One of the marchers told gathered journalists: 'I'm so disgusted with what's happened; if the gunmen were just shooting each other, well, that would be one way of getting them off the streets. But innocent people are being murdered. Somebody has to do something.'

Pauline Hegney, widow of the latest victim spoke to reporters in Belfast, saying: 'Karl was shot simply because he was a Catholic.'

Another 'unlucky' man was taxi driver Harry Conlon (54), father of four and a deeply religious and caring Catholic. Again it was the vile phenomenon of 'dial a Catholic', so characteristic of Northern Ireland and that violent turbulent part of its recent history. In the late evening of the 14th, a UFF member posing as an ordinary Catholic telephoned the taxi company for which Mr Conlon worked. The company was based in the Nationalist Andersonstown area, so that it was extremely likely that a Catholic driver would be dispatched. The pickup was to be at the Devenish Arms, which was to be the scene of another sectarian murder on 22 December (*see* Chapter 12). The pub is close to Finaghy Road North, on the outer fringes of the Andersonstown Estate. When Mr Conlon arrived, the passenger either forced him at gunpoint to take him to Finnis Drive, on the Protestant Taughmonagh Estate, or persuaded him that it was safe to do so; the former explanation is the more feasible of the two. Finnis Drive is just 1.4 miles, or a five-minute drive away, close to Priory Park. Once they reached the destination, a gunman, thought to be 'Inch' McFerran, shot him once in the head from point-blank range, fatally wounding him. He died very soon afterwards in Belfast's City Hospital and thus became the sixth Catholic taxi driver to be murdered in as many months.

McFerran, who as we have seen was involved in three of the sectarian murders covered in this book, and in others as well, was later unveiled as a top informant inside the UFF, working for the RUC's Special Branch. In his autobiographical work *Into The Dark*, Johnston Brown's description of the underhandedness, duplicity as well as borderline illegal, methods of the RUC's Special Branch, leaves me with the feeling that they didn't care how many people McFerran killed so long as he kept them supplied with information. It is rather a chilling indictment of that organisation that some at least within it were content to see the killers of innocent Catholics walk freely around the streets of Ulster

Also on the 14th, a West Belfast man, Brian McCabe (33), father of two, was shot and fatally wounded by UVF gunmen in Tamar Street in East Belfast. The location is very close to the Newtownards Road, a Loyalist area. He lived in Whiterock Road, between the Ballymurphy and the Turf Lodge estates, and worked for an organisation known as Extern. This organisation helped the care and resettlement of former Republican prisoners and former internees. This was his only link with Republicanism; he was not a member of the IRA. Part of his task was to help others out with mechanical repairs, and it is thought that he was lured to Tamar Street, almost within sight of the iconic 'Samson and Goliath' cranes at Harland and Wolff. Today the same street is liberally adorned with UDA/UFF graffiti and slogans such as 'Simply the Best' pay tribute to sectarian murderers and not to Tina Turner. Mr McCabe was sitting in his car when gunmen from the UVF, thought to be local men, walked over to him and shot him at close range in the head. He was left mortally wounded, with his blood pooling over his car seat and the driver's footwell. He died in hospital on the 16th. At this stage of the month, 12 children had been left fatherless thanks to the killers of the UVF and UFF.

The following day – the 15th – Loyalists murdered their fourth Catholic man in as many days, as they targeted John McGuigan (24), a Lenadoon, West Belfast boy who was forced either to take unemployment benefit or work in a potentially dangerous Protestant area. Fatally, he chose the latter and opted to work for a timber company in Ravenhill Road in East Belfast; very close to the Ormeau Road, a place where McFerran, Raymond Elder and Joe Bratty practised their dark art of sectarian slayings. His journey from Lenadoon Avenue, depending on traffic, took 15–17 minutes to cover the 6–7 miles; on the morning of the 15th, he made that journey for the final time. Whether or not his employers knew that he was a Catholic is a moot point, and so is the theory that he told his workmates. It is entirely possible that he may have inadvertently mentioned his former school, St Mary's Grammar School, which is clearly Catholic, or where his parents or siblings had married, thus accidentally revealing that he was a Catholic. The fact remains, however, that his workmates were Protestant and even though there were many decent Protestants, there were also many with sympathy for the Loyalist cause who might have passed this information on to a paramilitary godfather. It may even have been down to UFF dickers following him home one evening to a Catholic housing estate.

The job was to end in four weeks anyway, but the young Catholic lad was hoping that his soon-to-be-former employers would recommend him to a similar firm in Andersonstown, much nearer home and a safer place to work. Just after lunchtime on the 15th, as he worked in the timber yard, two men – one of whom was McFerran – walked over to where he was working and shot him several times in the head and chest from very close range. He died more or less instantly and his killers, knowing the area well, ran off down Ravenhill Road to disappear into Loyalist housing where they were afforded the same protection as were the IRA after a 'shoot and scoot' in a Catholic area. Mr McGuigan's brother Paul told the Belfast *News Letter*: 'My father warned John dozens of times that he was taking an awful risk by travelling to the Ravenhill Road to work. Over the four years that John worked there, he must have got a bit sick of us telling him about the danger ... but he wanted to work and he hated the thought of signing on.' The UFF claimed the killing but spuriously alleged that John was a member of the IRA; their claims were absolutely mendacious and simply added insult to injury for his grieving family.

Tragically, on the 16th, it became five murders in six days, when Brian McCabe's family took the decision, like Roger Elwood's family had earlier in the month, to switch off the life-support machine which had kept him alive since the UVF attack on the 14th.

On the 25th, the sixth sectarian murder of the month took place, when yet another Catholic was killed by Loyalists. In this case the victim had been an IRA member. Sean Anderson (32) was a plasterer by trade, but had been swept up in the pro-Republican resurgence of the late 60s and early 70s, and like many of his contemporaries had joined either the OIRA or the newly formed PIRA. He was jailed for 15 years in 1981 on firearms and explosives charges, and for the attempted murder of a British soldier; he served his time in the 'H' blocks in the Maze, before being released in 1988.

He lived at Loughbracken Road, Pomeroy, Co. Tyrone, in a very remote part of the county; he was known to visit his fiancée most nights, so the UFF decided to ambush him on the journey there from his house . In the early evening, under cover of the late autumn darkness, a three-man UVF team hid in the bushes which surrounded the lane to and from his home. At about 21:30, the gunmen opened fire with automatic weapons as his car drove past the ambush point. He was mortally wounded, dying shortly after his out-of-control car hit the side of the lane and came to a stop. The gunmen escaped in a stolen car which was hidden nearby. Mr Anderson's family have always denied that he was a current member of the IRA, and said that he had turned his back on the terror group after coming out of prison. There is a suggestion that he assisted in the 'Great Escape' from the Maze in 1983 but agreed to stay behind and finish his sentence. I have trawled many Republican websites but can find no evidence that he was a PIRA member at the time of his death. For this reason, his death is recorded as purely sectarian, the difference being that it wasn't random and, indeed, was carefully planned.

Also on the 25th, as if to demonstrate that they had 'teeth' and were not apologists or simply a political gesture, the Fair Employment Commission (FEC) announced that a Belfast company had been disqualified from receiving government contracts, because it had refused to comply with the fair employment legislation. It had failed to provide details of the religious composition of its staff. The following month, the FEC announced that the display of religious or political symbols at places of work might be considered as being intimidatory.

On Wednesday 30th, Desmond 'Dessie' Ellis was acquitted of conspiring to cause explosions, after a trial at the Old Bailey. Ellis had been involved in an extradition dispute between the Republic of Ireland and Britain earlier in the year. However, the next day, the 31st, the British Home Secretary signed an 'exclusion order' which banned Ellis from living in Britain. The court may not have ruled him a dangerous terrorist, but the Major government, judging by the exclusion order, was clearly sending a message of dissent.

The tenth month of the year ended and nine more people were dead. Most worryingly, six Catholics were killed in sectarian attacks by either the UVF or the UFF. So far this year, 33 people – the overwhelming majority Catholics – had been killed in sectarian attacks, compared with 21 in the whole of 1990. Sadly, in the final two months of 1991, a further 14 sectarian murders would be recorded.

11

'You Evil Cowards'

'Even the heavens wept as a shocked world witnessed the depths plumbed in the IRA's latest example of man's inhumanity to man.'

I have broken with m usual method of chapter titling because in this instance the headlines of contemporary press reports will more adequately convey the disgust with which many decent people reacted to the news of a hospital bombing.

This month was the bloodiest of the year, with a total of 22 deaths, including seven soldiers and a policeman. Additionally, five paramilitaries were killed – three Loyalists and two IRA – but, worryingly, nine civilians also died, the majority in sectarian attacks and most of them Catholics. Finally, as the title of this chapter suggests, the IRA bombed a hospital.

On the first weekend of the month, a physical location and a sporting event were about to collide and the two would, in the eyes of many soldiers and civilians in Northern Ireland, become synonymous. The sporting event was the 1991 Rugby World Cup, the second to be held but the first to be staged in the Northern Hemisphere. The final was scheduled to be played at Twickenham, London, on Saturday 2 November. The physical location was the Musgrave Park Hospital, or more specifically, the military wing of it. The MPH was located in south-West Belfast, separated from the Nationalist Andersonstown by the width of the M1 motorway.

The military wing was very well guarded, with armed soldiers – often UDR – manning all entrances, exits and approaches on a 24-hour basis. It housed wounded soldiers, policemen and even wounded IRA prisoners. In late October 1991, the West Belfast brigade discussed a plan to plant a bomb in the military wing at the MPH, specifically in the soldiers' rest area, designed to explode at a time of maximum opportunity. That time was to be when off-duty personnel were watching the Rugby World Cup final, particularly in view of the fact that England would be playing against bitter rivals Australia. The timing of the plan was decided by events on 26 October when England triumphed over Scotland in their semi-final. The England result in Edinburgh guaranteed that there would be standing room only in the soldiers' TV room the following Saturday at the MPH; that sealed the timing and date of the operation.

The military wing was separated only by a few feet from the Withers block, containing orthopaedic and children's wards, and the IRA planners would have known that a primed bomb would have to be carried past a ward full of ill and sleeping children. However, the reward – the deaths of a score or more soldiers – would make the risks worthwhile in their perverted logic. This was to be a colossally risky undertaking by the Provisionals; they knew the consequences of something going wrong – as frequently happened with their flawed intel and bodged operations. I cannot believe that senior men such as the then head of Northern Command, Martin McGuinness, were not aware of the potential consequences. Perhaps the Army Council also briefed Sinn Féin President Gerry Adams, or perhaps it was the other way around. I simply cannot believe that when news of the explosion filtered through at around 15:30, that either 'Marty' or Adams was in the slightest bit surprised.

During the evening of the 1st, hospital porter Liam Dougan, aged 24, from the Nationalist Poleglass area, carried a 20 lb (9 kg) Semtex bomb through the children's ward, past beds full of sleeping, innocent and poorly babies, toddlers and pre-teens. IRA men posing as workmen had previously sawn through security bars and a security door had been deliberately left open by a PIRA dicker, posing as a visitor. Dougan planted the device in an alcove in a service tunnel adjacent to the TV room, primed it and left. The bombers had timed the device for half-time, so that the Keller bar, for junior ranks, would be crowded with thirsty soldiers.

The game kicked off on a cold, rainy and windy day at Twickenham, in front of 56,000 fans and the soldiers crammed into the TV area, snug and away from the Belfast cold and well fuelled on beer, lager and pork scratchings. Half-time arrived with Australia 9–0 in the lead. The watching soldiers rushed to the bar to replenish their drinks before the restart. The second half started and there were two early scores, but Australia still held the lead. Then, at 15:53 hours, the bomb exploded, although only nine people were still in the bar, close to where the explosion took place. The blast killed two soldiers instantly and wounded virtually everyone in the bar. The dead soldiers were Royal Army Medical Corps CSM Philip Cross (33), father of two, from Manchester; and Driver Craig Pantry (20), Royal Corps of Transport, from the Gwent area of Wales. A total of 11 people were injured, including nine soldiers, a five-year-old girl and a baby of four months.

A Survivor's Story
Phil Winstanley, RAMC

Suddenly, there was a huge bang, louder than anything I have ever heard in my life and, for an absolute split-second 'What the hell' flashed through my mind. I was thrown onto the floor and all the air was instantly sucked out of me; it felt as though someone huge was sitting on my chest and I was unable to breathe; then very hot air was forced into my lungs; I was gasping for breath but all I could breathe was hot air. I started retching and coughing. The sound was a roar and then it all went black. Then, all I could see was sparks as the electrical wires which had been blasted, hung and crackled from the walls and ceilings. Then the silence hit me; it was deafening, if that makes any sense. There I was, lying on the floor, covered in the debris and afraid to move in case any more of the wall fell on top of me, and there was an incredible ringing in my ears. I'm not sure what the time frame was but it seemed like hours; perhaps people who have also been in blasts will understand what I mean. Eventually, I was able to get to my feet and began stumbling about, shouting out names and trying to make my way to where people had been before the explosion. I couldn't find anybody, even my mate Robbie, which was odd as he had been sitting right next to me! I tried to find the fire escapes, but these and every other exit were blocked by rubble. Later, I found out that the reason why no one was answering my calls was that they had all been knocked unconscious, but I really thought that they were all dead. What struck me was the vile smell; I can still smell it even now!'

I had the pleasure of meeting Phil on a cold, wet Saturday in 2008 in Huddersfield, pretty much like the day the IRA committed their depraved act. Phil cried as he related his story to me and I am not ashamed to admit that I cried too. We then met again on a summer evening in Leeds the following year; I am proud to know this survivor.

NIO Minister Richard Needham called the IRA 'fascist beasts who belong in Hell'. His words, however emotional, are impossible to argue with. He continued:

> In the second protocol to the Geneva convention of 1977, article 7 specifies: 'All the wounded, sick and shipwrecked, whether or not they have taken part in the armed conflict, shall be respected and protected.' Article 9 states: 'Medical and religious personnel shall be respected and protected and shall be granted all available help for the performance of their duties.' Clearly the IRA has cruelly and inhumanely violated those principles. The members of the IRA claim to be soldiers fighting a just war, but real soldiers are bound by the terms of the Geneva convention. The IRA has destroyed the credibility of its own claims. Members of the IRA are not soldiers, but assassins, carrying out a squalid murder campaign.'

The *Daily Mirror* raged:

> You Evil Cowards. Even the heavens wept as a shocked world witnessed the depths plumbed in the IRA's latest example of man's inhumanity to man. Rain has washed much of the blood and gore from the scene of yesterday's cowardly attack on the military wing at Belfast's Musgrave Park Hospital. A bomb blast left 2 soldiers dead, dozens hurt and 8 people seriously wounded including a 7 year old girl. But nothing can erase the stain caused by a nation's shame at a haven for the sick and dying being devastated by cold-hearted killers.

The *Los Angeles Times* reported:

> The Irish Republican Army blew up the military wing of a Belfast hospital Saturday, killing two British soldiers and injuring a 5-year-old girl and four other people. The blast devastated the hospital where British soldiers and police wounded in the warfare with the IRA are treated. The bomb erupted in the basement of the Musgrave Park Hospital directly beneath an operating theatre. The walls of the operating theatre collapsed. A children's ward adjoining the military wing was also badly damaged in the blast. Broken toys littered the ward. Fire crews rushed from all over Belfast to the scene of devastation, but rescuers working in torrential rain were forced back at one stage by fears of ruptured gas mains.

In a short statement, a triumphal spokesman for the Republican terror group told a Belfast radio station, incorrectly: 'We planted the bomb in a bunker in the officers' mess. We breached high security.'

One of the barmen – Kevin Conway – had taken his five-year-old daughter Susan to work with him that day, and she was discovered to be missing in the immediate aftermath of the blast.

The Little Girl
Phil Winstanley, RAMC

It was still difficult to breathe in all the smoke from the few small fires and my ears were still ringing; time just stood still. At that moment, Kev – the barman – shouted my name and I went to him. He told me that he been shouting my name for what seemed like ages; Kev had brought his daughter Sue, who was only 7 [*sic*] to help him behind the bar. He couldn't find her, so we both started looking frantically. The anguish on Kev's face is something I'll never forget. What we didn't realise was that the terrified kid had crawled into a cupboard under the bar to hide after the blast. It got to the point where we were struggling to breathe, both coughing and retching, the smoke was starting to sting our eyes. We started to look for a way out and found a small hole in the wall leading to the stairs, and crawled through helping each other get through the rubble. Then we heard voices and saw hands reaching through to help us.

Susan was later released from hospital after treatment for facial injuries

On the following Monday, Peter Brooke made a statement to a packed House of Commons:

> I regret to have to tell the House that a bomb planted by the Provisional IRA exploded in Musgrave Park hospital at 3.53 pm last Saturday, killing two soldiers and injuring 11 other people, among them a five-year-old girl and a baby of four months. The murdered soldiers were Warrant Officer Philip Cross of the Royal Army Medical Corps and Driver Craig Pantry of the Royal Corps of Transport. Two of those wounded have very grave injuries . . . The bomb which the IRA left in the hospital is estimated to have contained 20 lb of Semtex. It was part way along a service tunnel between two hospital buildings: first, the Withers block, containing orthopaedic and children's wards; and secondly, wards and other medical facilities administered by the RAMC for the benefit of service men and their families, and some civilians. I must stress the fact that this building is not, as the IRA has callously and cynically claimed, an operational military base. Rather, like the rest of the Musgrave Park complex, it is purely and simply a hospital dedicated to healing and the relief of suffering. The nearest security force base is more than a quarter of a mile away and was manifestly not the target of the attack. In addition to the deaths and injuries, the blast from the explosion caused severe damage to both buildings. In particular, a newly refurbished children's ward in the Withers block was damaged, with debris falling on a father who was nursing his baby daughter. Other children in that ward were immobilised in traction. So far, 97 operations due to have been performed early this week have been cancelled, 80 out of the 200 national health service beds in the hospital have been rendered unusable and damage totalling at least £250,000 has been caused. I am sure that

> the whole House will join me in utter condemnation of this appalling attack. But the cynical depravity of this outrage – placing a bomb that would inevitably cause massive damage to a national health service hospital and was intended to kill medical staff when it exploded and which, only by great good fortune, did not cause many more deaths and injuries – must surely mark one of the lowest points in the IRA's inglorious history.
>
> I reject all attempts to justify this attack. Let there be no doubt that it has shown the IRA in its true colours. It was an attack on the whole community – on sick children and their parents, on old people whose much-needed operations will have to be delayed, on the medical staff who devotedly care for them, and on the security forces who will continue to defend the community and bring terrorists to justice. Such attacks will not deflect the Government or the security forces from doing their duty in seeing off those evil men who want to destroy all that is best in our community. The horrible nature of the attack only underlines the fact that these are the sort of people whom all democrats oppose.

Dougan, the hospital porter who put all the children's lives at risk when he ferried a live bomb past their beds, received two life sentences at Belfast Crown Court. The men who planned and ordered the outrage, however, are still walking around free and busily re-writing history. Driver Pantry was buried at Lliswerry Baptist Church and CSM Cross was cremated in Salford, Manchester.

The following day, the death of another joyrider, shot by the RUC, seemed almost prosaic in comparison with the events at the MPH, only 24 hours previously. Despite the high profile and controversial nature of the deaths of joyriders at the hands of the SF during the Troubles, teenagers and other young men and women continued to steal cars and continued to taunt soldiers and policemen at VCPs. This was the Troubles, with violent death occurring virtually every single day, certainly every single week; people were shot and they were blown up; they were killed and they were maimed; but for these young people voluntarily to 'put their heads in the noose', so to speak, suggests that they had the spirits, if not the brains, of lemmings. During the Troubles, 11 joyriders were killed at or near VCPs in Northern Ireland, mostly in Belfast.

The 3rd of November was a Sunday, the scene was Lisburn; RUC officers spotted a car which had been listed as stolen on the Saturday – shortly after the MPH blast – from Donegall Road in West Belfast. Officers gave chase, and a high-speed pursuit then took place which raced from Lisburn to Poleglass in the south-western part of Belfast. I have been unable to ascertain the actual timing of the chase, but from the centre of Lisburn to Bell Street Road, Poleglass, where the incident took place, close to Stewartstown Road, is 4.3 miles. It was there that the RUC opened fire on the vehicle, hitting the 15-year-old driver and fatally wounding Gerald 'Gerry' Maginn (17), who was sitting in the back seat. The car managed to evade being stopped and was later abandoned, with the wounded driver running off, leaving his friend to die in the damaged car. Maginn's lifeless body was found by an SF patrol in the early hours of the Monday morning.

The RUC stated that the car was seen acting suspiciously in Lisburn and was followed out of town. A high-speed chase developed and a number of shots were fired at the vehicle in Poleglass. The statement went on to say that officers who opened fire at the stolen car believed a shot had been fired, prompting them to shoot back. At the inquest in 1993, a forensic scientist told the hearing there was no evidence of shots being fired from the car, and of the 13 shots fired by the three RUC officers, nine had hit the vehicle. Later it was suggested officers had been confused, thinking they were under attack after the car backfired. The dead boy's older brother is a singer with the Dutch band Moke and recently recorded a song titled 'The Song That You Sing' in memory of his dead brother. I have an enormous amount of sympathy with the loved ones of any 'innocent' person who was killed in the Troubles, but to take part in such a dangerous pastime as joyriding in a period of heightened tension was purely and simply suicidal.

There was near-tragedy on the 5th, just two days after the joyrider death, when two or more members of the UFF smuggled a Soviet-made grenade into a football match, already taught with sectarian tension. Linfield, a side supported in the main by Protestants, were at home to Cliftonville, a side more associated with Catholic support, in the Gold Cup. The match was played at Windsor Park, and the recent bombing at the nearby MPH had done little to reduce the tension between the two communities. During the course of the game, one of the UFF men threw the grenade into a part of the ground that was housing Cliftonville fans. There was a small explosion and there were some injuries, but fortunately the stand was half-empty.

The Royal Green Jackets, whose regimental motto is *Celer et Audax* – 'Swift and bold', can trace their lineage back to the American War of Independence, where their ancestors fought as the Royal Americans. All three of its battalions served in Northern Ireland throughout the Troubles and suffered 49 fatalities, the fourth highest in the Army, after the UDR, Royal Artillery and the Parachute Regiment. In 1991 tours of the Province, the regiment's battalions lost five soldiers: three in RTAs, one in a helicopter crash and one more whose death was attributed to 'violent or unnatural causes'.

On the 8th of this month, Lance Corporal Wayne John Harris (23), from Birmingham, and Rifleman Christopher Williams (18), from Eccles in Lancashire, were both killed and several other soldiers injured in a road accident whilst driving towards Aldergrove Airport. Wayne was cremated at Birmingham Crematorium in Perry Bar. Christopher's funeral was held in his home town of Eccles. A mere six days later, on the 14th, Corporal Matthew Christopher Maddocks (28), from Birmingham, was killed in a helicopter accident at Gortin Glen, Omagh, Co. Tyrone. The aircraft, a Lynx AH1, from 655 Squadron RAF, had just taken off, when it hit a flock of birds, clogging the engine intakes. The pilot tried to recover from the bird-strike, but lost control. The Lynx crashed to the ground, killing Corporal Maddocks (who was thrown out of the aircraft), badly injuring another soldier, who lost a leg, and wounding a further eight personnel. Some newspaper reports stated that another person died, but there is no evidence to suggest this. The crash took place at Jaspers Brush airfield.

The Bird Strike Europe Committee has cited gulls as being the likely culprits in the crash which killed the Green Jacket corporal. There was a half-hearted attempt by the Provisionals to claim that they had shot down the Lynx, but this was immediately discounted by the MoD. It was clearly an act of empty bravado by the Republican terror group in order to 'big up' its image amongst the Irish-Americans and swell NORAID coffers. It was a tragic accident: no more, no less.

Corporal Maddocks left a young widow, Marion; his funeral was held at Lodge Hill Cemetery in Selly Oaks, in his native Birmingham; he was the second 'Brummie' to lose his life in Northern Ireland in less than a week.

As if the IRA Wasn't Enough to Contend With
Dave Harding, Royal Green Jackets

On the 8th of November, Wayne and Christopher both died in an RTA, on the M1 whilst travelling to Aldergrove Airport, in order to fly home on leave. Both were in our Close Observation Platoon (COP). Two others in the car with them were badly injured after the car smashed into a bridge. No one knows what caused it, but it is so ironic that the IRA couldn't kill them, but a huge concrete structure did. It came just a couple of months after Thomas Ross was also killed in an RTA.

Just six days after Wayne and Chris were killed, Matthew Maddocks was killed when a helicopter in which he was travelling hit a swarm of birds which fouled up the rotor blades and sent the aircraft crashing into the ground at Gorton Glen, outside Omagh. Poor Steve Pendleton lost a leg in the accident and was also blinded by aviation fuel.

Pete Page, Royal Green Jackets

I am not able to add much to what you have already been told. The helicopter crash, following a bird-strike, happened at Gortin Glen on a damp, grey autumn morning. Rifleman Steve Pendleton suffered bad injuries to his leg and to his sight, but poor old Corporal Maddocks – 'Madds' as he was known – was thrown out of the aircraft and onto the still whirling rotor blade. There was a rumour at the time that the accident might have been survived, but there was far too much kit on board. The event was the final straw for Corporal Larry Wall who was scheduled to have been on that chopper, but 'Madds' took his place. Those few months in Omagh were a bad time for us.

The Green Jackets were based at St Lucia Barracks, Omagh, scene of a failed proxy bomb attack in October of the previous year. Corporal Maddocks lived in quarters there with his wife Marion and I am indebted to her for describing the awful realisation that the man she loved was dead.

A Day I'll Never Forget
Marion Mullin, Widow of Matthew Maddocks

It's coming up to Matt's 24th anniversary on 14 November, which is a day I'll never forget. It started in a quite ordinary way: me being upstairs, organising the children for school and Matt finishing his coffee in the kitchen. He called up to me saying: 'See you around six,' and I replied 'Yeah; OK.' I went about my chores and then popped into the community centre for a coffee and a gossip with some of the other wives before heading back over to St Lucia Barracks for my haircut. It was there I learned that there had been a helicopter crash from the local TV station. I just knew that Matt was somehow involved and went straight home. I recall pacing from one room to another, just waiting for the knock on the door. It wasn't long until Tony Manley our families' officer was standing there. As I opened the door, he just said: 'You know don't you?' I didn't know that when I said goodbye to him that morning, it would be the last time that I ever spoke to him.

On the 9th, three people lost their lives, as November was shaping up to be the worst month of the year for violent death. Only the day before this continued depressing news from the Province, some of the inequalities which were the precursors to Catholic grievances pre-Troubles, appeared to be on the brink of solution. The Equal Opportunities Unit of the Northern Ireland Civil Service produced a report on the religious composition of the Civil Service. The report showed that 57% of civil servants were Protestant, 36% Catholic, and the rest were born outside Northern Ireland; it also showed that 21% of senior positions were filled by Catholics.

However, the killing – courtesy of the Provisionals and their hated but equally psychopathic counterparts, the UVF – continued to orphan children and widow more women. A gang with close ties to the UVF decided to 'punish' Kathleen Lundy (40), mother of two, for her effrontery in converting from the Protestant faith to Catholicism. Mrs Lundy, a divorcée, lived in Glengormley, in the Newtownabbey area – predominantly Loyalist/Protestant, with a 56–44 sectarian split – in Belfast's far north. As she and her teenage sons, aged 16 and 19, slept, two local hoods – Richard McKay and Mark Whyte, both with UVF connections – poured petrol through the letterbox of Mrs Lundy's house in Harmin Crescent, with, as they later claimed in court, the intention of simply frightening or intimidating her. However, the fire quickly took hold and, given the time of the attack, at around 04:30, when the human body is at its lowest psychological and physiological ebb, Mrs Lundy and one of her sons – Colin (16) – had little time to react and died horribly in the blaze. The other son, Gerard, wakened by his mother's screams, tried to rescue her, but was beaten back by the flames and badly burned. He was forced to leap from an upstairs window and was seriously injured.

At their trial, in 1993, McKay and Whyte were found guilty and sentenced to 15 years each; the judge said he had a 'slight doubt' as to whether McKay and Whyte intended to kill, but concluded that it was the 'worst case of manslaughter short of murder and had been motivated by sectarian hatred'. The court was told McKay had remarked to a friend: 'Two less Fenians' after hearing of the deaths, and the judge said their remorse was hollow. The judge stated that young Gerard would be haunted for the rest of his life by the screams of his dying mother and brother.

Approximately 17 hours later, the IRA killed a UDR soldier, in yet another horizontal mortar attack, this time in Co. Londonderry. At 21:30, a two-vehicle 5 UDR mobile patrol, travelling between Portglenone and Bellaghy was ambushed by a PIRA ASU close to St Mary's Church on the Ballynease Road. The terrorists fired a Mark XII mortar at very close range, giving themselves just sufficient time to escape in the confusion, but giving the driver of the second Land Rover no time in which to avoid the missile. Two men were injured, Private Michael 'Micky' Boxall (27) fatally. He and another badly injured comrade were airlifted to the RVH in Belfast. Private Boxall died shortly after admission; his comrade later recovered, but lost an eye. Michael Boxall became the 196th UDR soldier to be killed by Republican terrorists. He was a full-time soldier and had been in the Regiment since July 1986. His funeral was held at Tamlaghfinlagan Parish Church, close to Ballykelly.

AP reported:

> A bomb hit a jeep during a joint police–army patrol in a village northwest of Belfast, killing an Ulster Defence Regiment soldier and wounding another, police reported Thursday. The Royal Ulster Constabulary identified the slain soldier as Pvt. Michael Boxall, 27, a full-time member of the Ulster Defence Regiment, a locally recruited unit of the British Army. A second soldier wounded in the attack remained in serious condition Thursday with leg and eye injuries. Police headquarters at Belfast said in a statement that the bomb hit one of four Land Rover jeeps comprising a joint police–army patrol traveling along the main street of the village.

On the 11th, Dublin City Council, normally supine and pusillanimous, for once showed spine, when it passed a resolution not to allow Sinn Féin to use the Mansion House for its annual Ard Fheis (party conference). The reason given was its failure to condemn Provisional IRA violence; this was somewhat confusing, as Sinn Féin had previously and consistently refused to condemn any of the many hundreds of dark deeds perpetrated by its 'military wing'.

On the 13th – a Wednesday – the Provisional IRA made three terror attacks in Belfast at points just five miles apart, killing two brothers, another man and his stepson, leaving four children fatherless. One of the deaths was a 'straightforward' assassination but the other three were either plain sectarian or simply the usual PIRA flawed intelligence. Inevitably this led, the following day, to a hurried but nonetheless bloody UVF retaliation. This response left three men dead – all innocent – and forced a further seven children to grow up without a father. Billy Kingsberry (35), father of one, and his stepson, Samuel MeHaffey (19) lived in Lecale Street, Belfast. In the house at the time were Mrs Kingsberry and her five-week-old granddaughter; the older man was playing with the baby on his knee, when, at 18:30, two or possibly three PIRA men burst into the house and opened fire with an AK-47 and a handgun, firing indiscriminately. Mr Kingsberry was hit five times in the head and chest and the younger man nine times; both died at the scene, with the gunmen fleeing in a stolen car towards the Falls Road. The baby girl was hit five times and survived only after seven and a half hours' intensive surgery. Fortunately, there were no other injuries, other than shock. On the same evening, a bomb was placed underneath the Orion car belonging to a neighbour and friend of Johnny Adair. The man – Gerry Drumgoole – had no connections with the UDA/UFF, but may have been singled out for attack as he occasionally drove around with his increasingly infamous neighbour. Mr Drumgoole lost a leg in the incident, and Adair vowed revenge; when that revenge came in April 1992, it was against an entirely innocent Catholic, Philomena Hanna (*see* Chapter 16).

Billy Kingsberry had been well-known in Loyalist paramilitary circles in the late 70s and very early 80s, but had severed his links, and whilst he may have maintained his support for Loyalist principles, he had not been active for many years. His stepson had no links whatsoever with the UFF or UVF, but a later PIRA statement justified his death, claiming that he had ties with the UVF gang which had murdered two Catholic shopkeepers for selling *An Phoblacht*. This accusation was arrant nonsense – and they knew it – and was simply another example of Republican mendacity. Samuel MeHaffey was another innocent sectarian victim.

An hour later, another PIRA murder gang stopped the stolen car in which they were travelling outside a house in the Upper Crumlin Road, at Ballysillian, just five miles away from the Kingsberry attack. Their target was an un-named UVF member who they thought still lived at the target house. The UVF man had moved out some time previously and what followed was yet another bungled IRA attack. The house was in fact the home of the Lynn family, and at the moment of the attack there were three brothers and two small children in the house, helping renovate the property, which they had just bought; none of them had Loyalist connections.

The PIRA murder gang opened fire at the men through the kitchen window with automatic weapons, firing several long bursts into the house, hitting two of the three brothers: Kenneth (28), father of a small child, and his brother Stephen Lynn (30), father of two equally small children. Both men were mortally wounded, dying at the scene, leaving a younger brother and two children shocked and covered in blood and broken glass. The IRA murder gang escaped in the direction of West Belfast.

Seven people had died violently at the hands of terror groups in the space of just four days; 11 children were fatherless and still the killing raged on, with three more people dying the following day as the number of fatherless children would rise to 18 in just five bloody days. Shortly before the next killings, almost unnoticed in the bloodshed, the United Nations Committee on Torture issued a report that criticised the British government's refusal to introduce a policy of using videotape to record interviews of paramilitary suspects while in police custody.

Following this recent upsurge in killings, especially the sectarian nature of the previous four weeks, the Major government announced on the 15th, that the RUC would be allowed to recruit an additional 440 officers and that 500 additional soldiers would be sent to Northern Ireland. At the same time, a battalion of soldiers was moved into Belfast from other areas of the region and 1,200 part-time UDR members were put on full-time duty.

The scene switched to Co. Armagh on the 14th, when the UVF attacked a car as it left the Hyster Fork Lift Truck premises in Craigavon, near Lurgan, knowing that it contained Catholics; when the smoke and cordite cleared, three men lay dead: two Catholics and a Protestant, united in death by their innocence, the sectarian divide no longer mattering. The UVF gang knew that the late evening shift ended at around 23:00 and accordingly set their ambush spot at the Carbet Road–Carn Road junction near Craigavon. They were aware that Catholic workers would travel along there, en route for their homes in nearby Lurgan. Two cars approached the ambush point, one of which contained Catholics Desmond 'Dessie' Rogers (43), father of three, and Fergus Magee (28), father of a baby son; the following car was being driven by Protestant, John Lavery (27), father of three very young boys, one of whom was a babe-in-arms. At a prepared signal, a stolen Ford Granada cut the two cars up, forcing them to slow down and then it stopped altogether, as men flashing red Army-like torches – of the type used at VCPs – signalled them to stop. As the cars containing the Hyster workers came to a halt, masked gunmen opened fire with several automatic weapons, killing the two Catholic men more or less instantly. John

Lavery slammed his car into reverse as he tried desperately to escape, but the UVF men opened fire on him, too, killing him and leaving the driverless car to crash into the side of the road.

The attack was carried out by the notorious 'Glenanne Gang', the UVF's mid-Ulster brigade, commanded by Robin 'the Jackal' Jackson. The attack, which the Loyalists claimed was in retaliation for the four men murdered by the IRA the previous evening, was not at all hurried; it was well prepared and well executed and clearly had been days, if not weeks, in the planning. Only one man was ever charged over the killings: Vicky Ahitty from Portadown, was charged with these and other murders and firearms' possession in 1992. The UVF later apologised, but only for killing the Protestant man; no mention was made of regret over the deaths of the two innocent Catholics. Shortly afterwards, UVF leader Billy 'King Rat' Wright reiterated the slogan 'You stop; we stop,' which the CLMC had issued to the Provisionals when the Loyalist ceasefire ended in July. When the UVF's so-called rationale was later revealed, it emerged that a Sinn Féin councillor worked at Hysters, and that he sometimes travelled in Dessie Rogers' car.

The next day, the 15th, the IRA's England team was denuded by two, as Patricia Black (18) and Frank Ryan (26) unwittingly removed themselves in an own goal explosion at a barracks near St Albans in Hertfordshire. Black, also known as Black-Donnelly, joined the Provisionals earlier in 1991. She was considered smart and suited to intelligence-gathering. However, after telling her parents that she was moving from Lenadoon in West Belfast to Dublin, she relocated to London where she was trained in the art of bomb-making. Ryan was English-born and bred and had spent much of his life in Harlow, Essex, later moving to the Nationalist Poleglass area of West Belfast. His Republican education commenced when he began selling *An Phoblacht* door-to-door, before joining the Provisionals in the late 1980s. Both volunteers were sent to London, where they adopted the roles of 'sleepers', keeping their heads down and refraining from talk of Nationalism or Irish unity, thus convincing their neighbours that they were simply two Irish people enjoying the London lifestyle. The *Independent* described this type of terrorist as: 'Teenagers who have been sent over to the mainland, obviously in the hope that their lack of open Republican links means they will escape the attention of the security forces. In yet another pattern, first or second generation Irish people in Britain have become involved. These are probably of particular value to the IRA, since they tend to have English accents and have an intimate knowledge of how to avoid drawing attention to themselves.'

On the night of the 15th, Black and Ryan arrived at their target, a theatre in St Albans: the Alban Arena where the band of the Blues & Royals were scheduled to give a concert. To kill more soldiers from the regiment which had suffered so grievously at Hyde Park nine years earlier, was seen by the Army Council in Dublin as a tremendous coup. Though the plan was to damage the Blues & Royals again, their band was replaced that night by the band of the Royal Marines, who had also suffered grievous loss at Deal in 1990.

Black and Ryan had a bag with them containing about 20 lb (9 kg) of explosives and were approaching a bus belonging to the band at the rear of the Alban Arena. They spotted police officers guarding the bus, and turned away. What happened next is unknown, but one of them may have been trying to prime the device when it exploded, shredding their bodies and killing them instantaneously. Alternatively, the bomb might have been on a timer which needed to be changed due to the aborting of the original plan; an attempt to change the timer could have been the trigger for the detonation.

A former soldier told me:

> As you know, Ken, a mate of mine was horribly injured in an IRA bomb in Belfast; he was in pieces with arms over there and legs in the opposite direction. But, the thing that chokes me up, geezer, is that he was still alive and in agony. I just cuddled him as best I could, but he was crying red tears and coughing up blood, trying to speak. I just prayed to God that he would die and when he did, I just felt guilty but relieved. That Irish bitch and the English boy died instantly; flash of white, no pain, nothing. I wish those two bastards could have died the same agonising way as my mate did.

Tony Swendell, who was a senior policeman in St Albans at the time, told the *Herts Advertiser*, 20 years after the blast:

> St Albans had a truly miraculous escape. I was sitting in my front room watching the television in Redbourn, when there was a huge thud and the patio doors vibrated. This was followed by car alarms going off outside. We thought that, as it was pretty near to Guy Fawkes night, that it was a late fireworks party. It was complicated by darkness. We made people leave their cars, which were parked closely in the city, in case something had been planted underneath them. Contrary to what people might think, the first 12 hours and maybe a little more of any operation of this nature is chaos with an element of organisation. And I was extremely lucky that I had experienced officers who did the job that they are trained to do. The area around the civic centre was one of devastation. The ground was littered with pieces of human tissue and bone, and there was a strong smell of Semtex, which smells like almonds. Pieces of bone and tissue were found a long, long way from the scene.

Somewhat chillingly, speaking at Ryan's funeral, a Sinn Féin leader said: 'Frankie and Patricia are not alone. They are representatives of a generation of Ireland's youth who have acquired the skills to remain hidden, who come forward when required to do so. How will the British defeat this invisible force?' A PIRA mural depicting a uniformed armed female Republican in uniform in the Lenadoon area of Belfast is jointly dedicated to Black as well as Laura Crawford, Bridie Quinn and Mairead Farrell. A memorial to Black and Ryan was erected in their honour at the Sally Gardens Centre in Belfast. West Belfast MLA Jennifer McCann has stated, both sickeningly and tellingly: 'They are our heroes and our inspiration. They are no longer with us, but let us take their vision forward.'

There then followed a period of nine days without any violent deaths, broken by an explosion at the Crumlin Road jail on the 24th which killed two Loyalist paramilitary prisoners, one of them dying on the 28th. On the 20th, the Anglo-Irish Intergovernmental Conference held a meeting in Dublin. Irish Minister for Justice Ray Burke confirmed that there would be changes to the laws on extradition. These laws, together with the wording of the Irish Constitution demanding the return of the North to their sovereignty, were the two biggest stumbling blocks between the respective governments.

The last several months had seen tension growing between unsegregated Loyalist and Republican prisoners on remand in the 'Crum', and there had been many injuries on both sides. On Sunday 24th, this erupted into a major violent scene, as an IRA bomb exploded, killing a UFF man and fatally injuring a UVF member who died four days later. Over the past few weeks, visitors to the jail had been smuggling in parts which, allied with other components found inside the prison, were fabricated into a bomb. Female visitors used their vaginas, rectums, mouths, babies' nappies and other ingenious hiding places, knowing that security was lax and that many prison officers (PO) could easily be intimidated into looking the other way. A whispered: 'The IRA know that you live at —— Street, Belfast, and that your kiddies, Mark and Jill, come home from school at 4 p.m. every day,' could drive fear into the heart of the bravest PO.

A tiny, but lethal device containing just 8 ounces (.25 kg) had been placed behind a radiator by an un-named PIRA remand prisoner, knowing that the area would be given over to Loyalists later on in the afternoon. At about 17:00, with Loyalists now in the area vacated by Republicans, the device exploded, showering the men with razor-sharp fragments from the radiator. UFF man Robert Skey (27) was killed instantly and eight others were injured; one of them, Ralph Caldwell (23), died on the 28th. Robert Skey's older brother, William, had been killed as an alleged informer in 1990. Thirteen months later, Loyalists retaliated by firing an RPG into the prison, aimed at several dozen Republicans who were eating in the canteen at the time (*see* Chapter 24).

The *Los Angeles Times* reported:

> The Protestant prisoners of Belfast's Crumlin Road Jail had just sat down together for their Sunday supper. For those unlucky few sitting too close to the bomb, it would be their last. A package hidden earlier by Irish Republican Army inmates blew apart the dining hall, killing two loyalists and wounding seven more in Northern Ireland's main prison for terrorist suspects awaiting trial. This Nov. 24 incident capped a bitter and bloody showdown taking place behind the bars of Crumlin Road, where the prison's warring Roman Catholic and Protestant factions, housed in the same wings, are stepping up efforts to bludgeon each other and the British authorities into segregating them. 'The IRA's ability to detonate a bomb in a high-security prison and kill people – obviously it is a major source of embarrassment for us,' said a senior prison official who, as a potential target for assassins, requires anonymity. Security sources believe that bomb-making materials were smuggled in by visitors. Killed in the blast was 27-year-old Robert Skey. A member of the Loyalist Ulster Defence Assn., Skey had been accused of severely beating and trying to abduct a Catholic pedestrian a year ago in the sectarian battleground of North Belfast. A second loyalist, Colin Caldwell, later died from his wounds. He was buried this week amid supporters of the outlawed Ulster Volunteer Force, a secret paramilitary group that kills Catholics in tit-for-tat retaliation for IRA killings. Caldwell had been awaiting trial on his alleged UVF membership and for an abortive murder attempt. When both deaths were announced within the 'Crum,' as locals call the overcrowded Victorian structure, republican prisoners are reported to have cheered their success. The coal-stained jail now houses more than 500 prisoners in three categories: Republicans who seek

> to force the British out of Northern Ireland at the point of a gun; Loyalists, who attack Catholics they deem 'Republicans' in the aim of maintaining the Protestant-majority state, and others charged with non-terrorist offenses, known universally as 'ordinary Decent Criminals.' The explosion marked the greatest outrage in two years of regular confrontations between the two sides, who share the goal of pushing the prison authorities into making their separation formal and complete. Their combined campaign has left about 80 guards and an unknown number of inmates injured this year.

The month was not quite over, and there were two more deaths to follow: on the 25th, the UFF killed an innocent Catholic in Belfast's Ormeau Road, in what was a second tragedy for the McCaffrey family. Mary McCaffrey had been killed by a PIRA bomb in 1978. Just over 13 years later, James McCaffrey (48) and a friend called in to the local Chinese restaurant on the Ormeau Road, to collect a meal for delivery to a customer. It is now known that the meal had been ordered for a bogus address, in order to lure the Catholic man into a trap. As he reversed his vehicle out of the restaurant's parking spaces, two masked gunmen from the UFF, thought to have been dispatched by Johnny 'Mad Dog' Adair, opened fire at him. He was hit in the head and chest, and died at the scene. One of the gunmen was 'Inch' McFerran, the other 'Top Gun' McKeag. This was the second attempt by the UFF to kill Mr McCaffrey; they had tried some months earlier to shoot him when he was making another meal delivery. This poor man was cursed by the murderous paramilitaries of both sides.

On the afternoon of Tuesday 27th, several PIRA gunmen who had been stalking a part-time UDR soldier, as he delivered 'pop' around the South Armagh area, seized as well a full-time soldier in the UDR who had volunteered to help his friend. Several armed men grabbed the two men as they stopped to make a delivery at a garage in Crossmaglen, near the border. The two were driven across into the Republic, where the abductors then separated Lance Corporal Kenneth 'Kenny' Newell (30) from the man they thought was his civvie workmate. The 'civvie', however, was a UDR soldier; he was later released close to the border, where he was found, in the early hours of the morning unharmed, by an RUC/Army patrol. Kenny Newell, however, was beaten and tortured in a terrible and barbaric fashion. Later the following morning his body was found, bound and gagged and shot in the back of the head, bearing the scars of IRA torture; he was dumped at the side of Creggandufff road at Cullyhanna. The survivor told a later inquest that they had both been taken to a shed, then separated, before being put through a mock execution, after which he could hear his comrade being questioned about members of the security forces. I have seen a photograph of the murdered soldier, lying face down in the grass, his arms trussed behind his back, a victim of IRA savagery. The Provisionals later admitted that they had 'seized and executed' the soldier.

Finally, on the 28th, four INLA gunmen were arrested in the Holywood home of leading Northern Ireland Conservative Dr Lawrence Kennedy. During the early part of the evening, his wife, Sarah, answered a knock at the door and was confronted by one of the gunmen. She was bundled into the house and three other men rushed inside. Mrs Kennedy, her two sons and a friend were put into an upstairs bathroom. Their intended murder victim, Dr Kennedy, was in London and due home later that night; however, he telephoned home. When the phone rang, Mrs Kennedy was allowed to answer it in a bedroom. This gave her the opportunity to press an alarm button which alerted the RUC. The house was soon surrounded but the men refused to surrender until they spoke to a local priest. They eventually left the house in the company of the priest. The four were charged with conspiracy to murder.

Having announced the deployment of extra troops earlier in the month, Minister of Defence Tom King informed the press that the troops were already in the Province. King announced the extra troops during a day-long tour of Army bases in Northern Ireland. He said the soldiers had been sent in after a request from Northern Ireland Secretary Peter Brooke. King, however, took the opportunity to berate the terrorists from both sides; he said that they were 'stuck in a time warp about 70 years out of date; the rest of the world has passed them by'.

The bloodiest month of the year, and indeed for several years had ended, with 22 deaths. The Provisionals killed or were responsible for 12 deaths, and between them the UFF and the UVF killed six. There was, however, a very worrying trend in that, in the recent upsurge in violence, 53 people had died in just 122 days; more worryingly, 26 of the deaths – virtually half – were clearly sectarian in nature.

12

December

This was a month of eight deaths, including just one soldier, but it included an infamous attack on a pub full of drinkers – enjoying a pint one minute, lying in a pool of blood the next; sadly, it would not be the last. It was a month in which the IRA's England team would blitz London and make bombing attacks in the north-west, hitting Blackpool for the first time.

Throughout December, the IRA's England team waged an almost non-stop assault on the London economy, which seems to have been their sick tribute to the dead St Albans bombers. A total of 75 incendiary devices were planted, of which 25 detonated and caused damage. This was their trail of havoc:

> 1 December: A number of incendiary devices ignited at the Discount Furniture Store, Habitat, World of Leather and the Reject Shop in Tottenham Court Road causing damage to property but no injuries.
>
> 2 December: An incendiary device ignited at Littlewoods, Oxford Street; again no injuries were caused.
>
> 14 December: Four devices were found in shops at the Brent Cross Shopping Centre; there were no injuries. The *Baltimore Sun* reported: 'The IRA is like the Grinch: It is trying to steal Britain's Christmas. And as it was with the infamous (although eventually rehabilitated) villain created by the late Dr. Seuss, nobody here thinks they'll succeed. "We're a pretty stubborn bunch in England," says Brian Hudspith, a spokesman for Marks & Spencer's department store. "We're going to conduct life as normal. We're determined that the terrorists won't win."'
>
> 15 December: An incendiary device partially ignited in the Sainsbury Wing of the National Gallery; yet again, there no injuries.
>
> 16 December: A bomb exploded on the railway line near Clapham Junction; surrounding areas were evacuated and there was only structural damage. The *Baltimore Sun* again:
>
> 'Yesterday, in probably the worst incident in England since last winter's IRA bombing campaign, an explosion ripped a track near British Rail's biggest junction, Clapham Junction station in southwest London. It happened at 6 a.m., 15 minutes after a telephoned warning from someone claiming to be with the Irish Republican Army, which is carrying out its threat to take its war against British rule of Northern Ireland to London. Hundreds of thousands of workers and shoppers

were unable to get into central London, or got there hours late. Margaret Hodge, spokeswoman for the Association of London Authorities, said the disruption of the commuter flow "will cost London's business and economy dear." About 40 percent of London's commuters travel into the city by rail, either directly or by connecting with the subway system, the massive London Underground subway. But the Clapham bombing wasn't all. Also yesterday, the Underground, in response to a warning, closed all 13 of its stations that intersect with British Rail from 6 a.m. to 9.30 a.m. Nearly a million people were inconvenienced. About 800,000 people pour through the Tube's 300 stations every weekday around those hours. Stations frequently have been closed in recent weeks as security agents investigate suspect parcels. Trains often fail to complete their journeys owing to bomb threats. 'Given the IRA involvement in London in recent weeks, we've been on a steady security alert,' said a spokesman for the Underground.

23 December: Several incendiary devices ignited at Ilford Underground Depot, Neasden Underground Deport and on a stationary train at Harrow on the Hill; there were no injuries, although an estimated 50,000 commuters were affected and the cost was reportedly around £45,000,000. Shortly after the latest blasts, the IRA announced that it would be observing a three-day ceasefire over the Christmas period.

Earlier in the month, on the 3rd, the Provisionals planted a stolen car, filled with 1,200 lb (550 kg) of explosives in Glengall Street, in the centre of Belfast. It was sited just outside the Grand Opera House, but close enough to the Ulster Unionist Party HQ for it to have been of significance to them. There were 16 civilian injuries, following an inadequate telephoned warning from the IRA to the Samaritans, but damage ran to over £5 million. A few days later, in what was the first visit to the Republic by a British Prime Minister since Thatcher's 1980 trip, John Major and Peter Brooke met Taoiseach Charles Haughey in Dublin, with a view to the holding all-party talks to bring a halt to the violent impasse which was making 1991 the third-worst year since 1981. The two leaders agreed to hold biannual meetings thereafter. Just a few days later, Peter Brooke was in the news in his own right, when he announced that there would be a freeze on spending on capital projects in Northern Ireland, due to the increased cost of repairing bomb damage as a consequence of PIRA's so-called 'economic warfare'. The decision was very widely criticised by all political parties. Tory MP Brian Mawhinney assumed responsibility for law and order at the NIO in order to reduce the pressure on Brooke, who appeared to be suffering under the weight of responsibility. Leading Provisional Brian Gillen one of their top men in Belfast, was once asked what he did for a living; with direct reference to the industrial and economic wasteland his bombs were creating, he replied sarcastically: 'I make car parks!' He was regarded as probably 'public enemy number three' by Adair's UFF, and several attempts were made on his life.

On the 7th and 8th, the IRA's England team, possibly a sleeper unit in Manchester, struck at two north-west targets. In the first attack, a Marks & Spencer store in Blackpool was damaged by a firebomb left amongst clothing racks. In total, 13 stores in the seaside town were attacked by the IRA, with one shopper having an incredibly lucky escape. The woman, from Crewe in Cheshire, purchased a suitcase from the Britannia store and then discovered an incendiary device inside when she got home; it was safely defused. Explosions took place at Food Giant, Tudor Car Sales, Express Discount, Blackpool Lighting Centre, Bargain Hunters and Leftons.

The following day, in an ominous dress rehearsal for the 1996 IRA attack on Manchester city centre, four stores in the iconic Arndale Centre were firebombed. After the 1991 bombings, Greater Manchester Police said: 'A number of items have been recovered and will be the subject of further examination. They are, however, in line with our previous statement of being consistent with incendiary devices.' However, somewhat prophetically, a Manchester fireman told the press: 'What bugs me is if there's a big one planted there's a lot of glass around here, and a lot of people will be killed.'

It was not until the 12th of the month that the first Troubles-related death occurred. A Green Jacket, Lance Corporal Lawrence Dean Wall (30), from Hemel Hempstead, known as 'Larry', died in circumstances which can only be described as 'violent or unnatural'. His funeral was held at St James's Church, Coundon, in the 'Land of the Prince Bishops', which is where he had lived since his wedding to Jill.

Dave Harding, Royal Green Jackets

Then Larry, who was an RP (Regimental Police) sadly committed suicide whilst on RP duty. He was in the Guard House, collecting and signing out PPWs [personal protection weapons]. He had suffered from cancer, but I think that he might have been in remission. However, because he was very depressed with everything, I am not sure that he should have been assigned to handling weapons; he left a wife and a young child. I think that there may have been other suicides on this tour, and some attempted ones, one of whom was a NIG in 'B' Company. This was a sprog, or New Intake Group; fresh out of training and placed in the Battalion.

Mick 'Doc' Hollowday, Royal Green Jackets

Wally Wall had cancer in the 80s and was cured, only for it to reappear during the Omagh tour. He kind of went off the rails a bit and lost the plot. I was told that he was taken off patrolling duties and put on the RP staff. He then got hold of a pistol and committed suicide in Omagh. I do know that people were very saddened by this and by how the senior officers dealt with it. I know that a few people left the Army as a result of this incident.

Between the 12th and the 18th, the Provisionals increased the tension inside Northern Ireland. On the 12th, their bombing units attacked two separate targets; first to be hit was the RUC station in Craigavon, Co. Armagh, close to the scene of the murder by the UVF of the two Catholics and a Protestant from Hyster's Fork Lift Truck depot. A stolen lorry filled with explosives, estimated at 2,000 lb (910 kg), was abandoned near the station. The explosion caused extensive damage to the base and many residential buildings were severely damaged, rendering the occupants homeless, further evidence of the Provisionals' irresponsible attitude in putting the lives of innocent civilians second to their terrorist aims. On the same day, a former Territorial Army base in Londonderry was blown up by an

IRA bomb; the building was derelict, so this action was seen as utterly pointless. Then, on the 16th, in a major breach of security in Belfast city centre, the IRA succeeded in planting a device weighing 500 lb (230 kg) outside the Law Courts. Despite the segment gates, draconian anti-parking measures and the 24-hour presence of RUC and UDR, the bombers still got through. The courts and other surrounding buildings were badly damaged.

On the 15th, a week of insanity commenced which involved the IPLO, INLA the Provisionals and the UFF, as the four terror groups ensured a miserable Christmas for the loved ones of the dead, and additionally made several children fatherless. The IPLO, who, like the INLA seemed to prefer killing their own, featured in four of the six remaining deaths in 1991. In the first incident, Christopher 'Crip' McWilliams, a notorious gunman, was involved in a fracas in the centre of Belfast which resulted in the death of Colin Mahon (39), father of three. On the night of the 15th, McWilliams's 28th birthday, he went to celebrate with other INLA and IPLO members in Frames Snooker Club in Little Donegall Street in Belfast. The manager, Colin Mahon, asked the group of men to leave after a drunken fight, but the INLA man and other IPLO men took exception to being 'dissed' and returned to the club with at least one of them armed, and, on encountering Mr Mahon again, shot him in the head from point-blank range; he died almost instantly. The Republican Socialist Collective, the so-called 'political wing' of the IPLO, claimed that the dead manager was a leading Loyalist, which was, of course, clearly untrue. They then back-pedalled furiously, and claimed that the pistol had been fired accidentally during a scuffle, which again they had to retract.

Colin Mahon, also known as Colm, was murdered just because he threw McWilliams out; he was not a Loyalist – he was a Catholic manager of a Catholic club – and he was doing his job: trying to protect other patrons of his club. In 1997, one of his daughters told the press: 'Since his death, I have felt alone and empty. One of the most important people in my life was gone. One wish I have is that no more people suffer the way my family and other families have suffered.' Mr Mahon left two other children to grow up without their father because of McWilliams's violent thuggery.

McWilliams had previously served nine years of a 14-year sentence for his involvement in two killings and now received a life sentence for Mahon's murder. It would appear that 'Crip' was universally despised by the PIRA, INLA and the IPLO for the senseless murder of the innocent bar manager. Shortly after the murder, the Provisional IRA issued a statement ordering the IPLO to disband, 'or face the consequences'. In late 1992, the IPLO formally surrendered to the Provisionals and units throughout the country were forcibly disbanded. McWilliams's stock was only lifted by his role in the killing in prison of leading Loyalist Billy 'King Rat' Wright in 1997. He died of cancer in 2008.

On 20 December, the IPLO was in the news again, when one of their gunmen, Patrick 'Teasy' McDonald (41), was shot by Dublin gangsters at the hairdressing salon he owned and ran in the Marino area. It is thought that he had fallen out with the 'ordinary' criminals of the Irish Republic. It is alleged that he was involved in a cannabis-smuggling operation that went wrong, forcing two of his 'associates' – former INLA men, Tommy Savage and Micky Weldon – to move the base of their illegal operations from Dublin to Amsterdam, a more drug-tolerant country. For reasons explained in Paul Williams's *Badfellas* (Penguin Books, 2011), McDonald was held accountable for this and it was decided by his erstwhile colleagues that he should die. On the afternoon of the 20th, it is alleged that Savage and Weldon walked into the salon in St Aidan's Road, and shot the IPLO man six times in the head and chest as he cut the hair of an elderly lady; he died in a pool of blood on the salon floor. The killers later fled the country. At McDonald's funeral, IPLO gunmen fired a volley of shots over the coffin of the terrorist turned criminal, but then again there are those of us who maintain that the two are synonymous. One of the former INLA men, Savage, also known as 'Zombie', was later jailed in Greece for five years on drug-smuggling charges. For further details of the seedy world of terrorism and drugs, I recommend Mr Williams's informative and well-researched book.

The following day, a young student, a purely innocent Protestant man, was gunned down whilst saving his father's life. The Co. Tyrone INLA had determined that a former RUCR man – Robert 'Bob' Farmer – several years retired, was an 'agent of Crown forces' and that killing him would be a step on the way to a reunited 32-county Irish Republic. Robin Farmer (19) had returned to the village of Moy, Co. Tyrone, after completing his first term at Stirling University and had volunteered to help out at his father's angling shop in Killyman Street. It was a brave thing to do, as just the previous month the INLA had left a car bomb outside the shop, but the Army had defused the device. This had apparently prompted Sinn Féin to assure Mr Farmer that there would be no further attacks; this, however, did not apply to the INLA. In mid-morning, a lone gunman, Anthony Cartmill, walked into the shop, openly holding a gun; Robin bravely shouted to his father to get down and then threw himself between the gunman and his retired RUCR father; the gunman fired four times and the young man was mortally wounded, dying shortly afterwards. The killer tried to escape but was trapped by the electrical locking system and was overpowered by the dead man's father, with a legally held handgun, and other shop staff. The cowardly killer had the effrontery to beg for mercy. The police were called and he was taken into custody. Cartmill, from Armagh, was jailed for murder in December 1992.

Worse was to follow that evening, as the IPLO struck at a Belfast pub frequented by Protestants. The Donegall Arms was, and still is, located on Roden Street, just off Donegall Road and close to Grosvenor Street. To reach this pub from the Nationalist Falls Road, Springfield Road, or more likely Divis Street is a simple enough matter; on the evening of the 21st it indeed proved easy. Today it is a no-through road and a mini peace-line separates the two communities, a sad reflection of post-Troubles Belfast. In 1991 it was different, and a stolen car containing three IPLO men parked outside the pub in Roden Street; the engine was left running after the driver had reversed, in order to face in the direction of Grosvenor Road. Two gunmen, armed with a handgun and a shotgun, walked into the pub and began firing indiscriminately at the drinkers. One blast hit Thomas Gorman (55) in the back, mortally wounding him, whilst Barry Watson (25) was hit in the head and died instantly. The wild shooting spree continued, with 10 other people being hit, three of whom were later rushed to hospital in critical condition; all three survived. One man was hit and fell to the floor, bleeding heavily, and remembers someone screaming 'Orange bastards; Orange bastards!' One of the gunmen held his pistol against the wounded man's head, but the firing-pin clicked on an empty chamber. The gunmen then dashed outside, jumped into the waiting car and raced up the street; however, just before Grosvenor Road, the car stopped and the two gunmen jumped out, racing on foot towards the RVH and the Falls Road. The car then drove on and was later found abandoned in Devonshire Place, near Albert Street.

That fateful evening, Mr Gorman, a retired binman who lived only a two-minute stroll away in Best Street, now demolished and replaced by Brassey Street, set off for the pub; it was to be his final walk. Mr Watson, who also worked on the 'dust', lived a little further away, in Ogilvie Street. The attack was sectarian, doing nothing to advance the cause of Irish Republicanism, and it inevitably invited retaliation from Loyalist paramilitaries. This retaliation followed within 24 hours, at the Catholic-owned and frequented Devenish Arms, as I shall explain shortly. The Donegall Arms attack was condemned by all parties, and even Sinn Féin were quick to distance themselves and the Provisional IRA from the outrage. Sean McKnight, Sinn Féin spokesman, hypocritically denounced the Donegall pub deaths as a 'sectarian outrage' and stated, albeit correctly, that the IRA was not responsible. Anglican Bishop of Connor Samuel Poynt said: 'The murders, four days before Christmas are yet another stark example of the sacrifice of people because of hatred and bigotry which has blinded individuals. I beg of them that there will be no further retaliations.' His words clearly fell on deaf ears.

Later that night, in fact just a couple of hours later, UFF gunmen kicked down the door of a house in Fortuna Street, just a few hundred yards from the scene of the IPLO attack on the Donegall Arms. It was far too close to the earlier scene of murder for the timing and location to be a coincidence. Shortly before midnight, two gunmen, one of whom was Stephen 'Inch' McFerran, burst into the home of William Johnston (28), a Catholic man who was living with a Protestant woman. Mr Johnston was aware that, living openly in a Loyalist area such as the Donegall Road, he was a marked man. He had lived in the house for only a few weeks and his presence had been brought to the attention of Johnny Adair and the thugs of 'C' Company in the Shankill. Clearly he had been marked for murder and the IPLO attack gave the UFF an opportunity to bring forward the date of his death.

Having kicked their way into the house, the two men rushed upstairs, pushing their way past the frightened woman before confronting her partner in the bedroom. Mr Johnston slept most nights fully dressed, hoping to effect a quick escape if the Loyalist thugs came calling. It is thought that McFerran was the one who shot the Catholic man in the side of the head and, as he lay mortally wounded on the bedroom floor, gasping for breath, the gunman forced his weapon into the barely conscious victim's open mouth before pulling the trigger. They then ran past the distraught woman, and, according to Lister and Jordan in their excellent *Mad Dog*, a grim exposé of Adair, shouted to her: 'You better go up there, your boyfriend is dead!'[1] McFerran was later jailed, but for other crimes, and not for the killing of 20 Catholic men over a period of only a few years.

Associated Press reported:

> A gunman killed a teenager in his father's sporting goods store near the Irish border Saturday. Hours later, two patrons were fatally shot in a crowded Belfast pub, police said. And in another incident in the latest spasm of violence in Northern Ireland, gunmen forced their way into a house near the pub just before midnight and fatally shot a man in his mid-20s, police said. No further details were available.

1. Lister and Jordan, *Mad Dog*, p. 105.

> The British national news agency Press Association said the Protestant Ulster Freedom Fighters, an outlawed paramilitary organization, claimed responsibility for the break-in shooting. No group immediately claimed responsibility for the earlier attacks. The first incident took place in Moy, 40 miles southwest of Belfast, in a store owned by a Protestant former reservist in the Royal Ulster Constabulary, news reports said. The constabulary is the police force of the British province.
>
> Police said there was a chance the youth, identified by the BBC as first-year college student Robin Farmer, was shot trying to protect his father. News reports said the father, a former police reservist, had been the target last month of an attack by the Irish Republican Army. The IRA allegedly planted a bomb under his van, but it was defused by the army, the reports said. Press Association said shop-workers managed to grab the gunman. Police said only that a man was arrested at the scene and a gun was recovered, and did not reveal the man's name. In the second incident, police said the gunman killed two men, one 20 and the other 60 years old, and injured three at the Donegall Arms pub, in a largely Protestant neighbourhood. Other details were unavailable. Elsewhere in the province, bombs exploded at two department stores early Saturday in a continuing campaign to disrupt pre-Christmas shopping. Police said there were no injuries, damage was slight, and both stores opened for business. More than 160 bombs have exploded in Northern Ireland stores this year, causing millions of dollars in damage, and about 100 others have been defused, officials say. The bombings have intensified both in Northern Ireland and on the British mainland in the busy shopping period before Christmas.

Further retaliation by Loyalists was only 13 days away (*see* Chapter 13).

The following day was a Sunday; at lunchtime, the Catholic-patronised Devenish Arms in Finaghy Road, West Belfast, was packed with men, women and children, enjoying a pre-Christmas drink. The long Christmas break had started, and despite the three murders of the night before there was a relaxed, if guarded, atmosphere in the pub. The pub is located at 33–37 Finaghy Road North, between the Upper Lisburn Road and Andersonstown Road, very close to Musgrave Park Hospital. It is described today as a: 'lively drinking and global dining venue, with beer garden, sport screenings and regular live music'. On this cold Sunday afternoon, a UFF gang, including Stephen McKeag, arrived outside, 9 mm handguns concealed under their coats. McKeag and another man walked into the bar and began firing indiscriminately at the customers, mostly, if not all, Catholics. Aiden Wallace (25) was playing snooker with his family, when he was hit twice in the head from very close range. A second man was also shot in the head and a third in the thigh. The worst horror of all was the calculated and cold-blooded shooting of eight-year-old Christopher Lawless who had crawled under a table to escape the carnage. One of the gunmen shot him through the left eye from very close range, before the pair ran outside to their waiting getaway car and disappeared in the direction of the Shankill. The shooting only stopped because both weapons, using Chinese-manufactured rounds supplied from the Lebanon, misfired.

The young boy was only in the pub as his father had to make a telephone call; he had left the boy with a packet of nuts and a soft drink. His life hung by a thread over the next few weeks, but he managed to survive such an appalling injury thanks to the skill of medical staff. One customer said: 'The gunman just stood there over the wee lad and fired. I just couldn't believe what was happening. Imagine? A young child? This was bound to happen, but I still couldn't believe it.'

A spokesman for the UFF claimed that: 'The sole responsibility for carrying out such attacks lay with the IRA and the Irish People's Liberation Organization, who over the last number of months have carried out a systematic murder campaign against loyalists.'

Some seven years later, Christopher Lawless, by then 15 years old, was awarded £200,000 for the trauma of the shooting and the loss of an eye.

December was over, and so too was 1991; if the optimists had thought that the 90s would herald a slowdown in the violence, they were clearly mistaken. True, December, with eight deaths, was not as bloody as previous months, but six of the deaths had occurred in a three-day period of insanity. Of the six civilian deaths, five were sectarian in nature.

1991 Deaths

Military	27
Police	8
Republican	14
Loyalist	5
Civilian	55
Catholic	40
Protestant	14

In all, 109 people had died this year, the fourth highest number of the decade; of the 55 civilians, 47 of the deaths were sectarian. Civilian deaths were the highest since 1976.

Part Two

1992

This was a year of 119 deaths, including 31 soldiers/airmen, 5 RUC officers and 67 civilians, the majority of whom were killed in sectarian attacks. This was higher than the previous year and the highest since 1976. It was a year in which the INLA ventured onto the streets of England for the first time since 1979 when they had killed Airey Neave, MP, at the House of Commons. It was also a year when the IRA decided to re-create the 1976 Kingsmills' massacre, this time at Teebane, Co. Tyrone, where they killed eight innocent Protestant workers. It was a year when the tiny hamlet of Teebane would mark another depraved low for the Provisional IRA.

13

January

The previous month had ended in bloody fashion with a glut of sectarian deaths; January was to prove no different, with 15 deaths in total, 13 of them sectarian. It included the infamous Teebane Massacre in which the IRA killed eight Protestant workmen, and yet another example of flawed intelligence by the Provisionals in which they killed an innocent Catholic. Loyalists killed four Catholics, as for once they were outdone in the sectarian slaughter business, by the 'non-sectarian' IRA.

The New Year – the 24th of the Troubles – began in dramatic fashion, when a large PIRA unit from the Tyrone and Fermanagh brigades attacked an Army outpost in Pomeroy close to the border. The firing lasted some time, but although soldiers claimed hits on at least one of the terrorists, there were no fatalities reported by the IRA. Several hundred rounds were expended.

Two days later, the sectarian slaughter commenced, with a 'reprisal' attack by the UVF on a butcher's shop in Moy, Co. Tyrone, close to where teenager Robin Farmer was gunned down by the INLA in his father's angling shop. At around 17:00, just before closing time on the 3rd, two UVF men from Robin Jackson's mid-Ulster brigade pulled up outside the McKearney butcher's shop. In the shop window was a huge cardboard cut-out of Santa Claus, proclaiming 'Merry Christmas'. They walked in, spotted their two targets, and immediately opened fire; Kevin McKearney (32), father of four, was hit in the head and face and died instantly, with his Uncle Jack also being hit and receiving fatal wounds. He died on 4 April. The shooting was indiscriminate, also hitting a young girl who was outside the shop. The gunmen escaped in a waiting car, which was found abandoned in a nearby Protestant area. The UVF were quick to claim the killing, alleging that the dead man was a member of the Provisional IRA. Their claim was, of course, wildly inaccurate; two of his brothers had been members, but both had been killed, in 1974 and 1987 respectively. A third brother, Tommy, was jailed for life in 1976, for the attempted murder of an off-duty UDR soldier. Two more family members were also killed by Loyalists in September 1992 (*see* Chapter 21). Loyalists also killed Carlie and Teresa Fox, relatives of the McKearneys, in 1993; shortly afterwards, the IRA connection was further reinforced, when their son, Patrick was jailed for being a member of the Provisionals, and for possession of explosives.

The McKearney family were well-known in Republican circles and felt they were particularly vulnerable to attack. In the late December 1990, Maura McKearney, mother of the murdered man, had received an anonymous phone call, stating that: 'three men in white coats will be killed in Moy Square', an obvious reference to the white coats worn in the family's shop. She reported the call to police through a local Sinn Féin councillor, Jim

Channing. A later report by the Historical Enquiries Team concluded: 'Kevin and Jack were not members of any paramilitary groups. They were both completely innocent victims.' It would certainly appear that the dead man and his dying uncle were not paramilitaries and that they had been deemed 'guilty through association'. It was a tactic used – and 'justified' – by terror groups on both sides.

Between the 1st and the 14th, the IRA attacked the Ulster economy and planted incendiary devices inside 20-plus stores: Budget DIY, Top Man, Sportsbowl at Glengormley, Suites Direct in Newtownards, Texstyle World, Belfast, and the Canon Cinema – where two devices exploded – to name just a handful of the attacks; extensive damage was caused.

The day after the Moy murder, the Provisionals planted a stolen car outside the Ulster Hall in Bedford Street in the centre of Belfast. Inside the vehicle was an explosive device weighing 800 lb (360 kg). A warning was telephoned through to the Samaritans and police and soldiers were able to evacuate the area. The device exploded shortly afterwards, causing extensive damage to the building and to surrounding property. The following day, the IRA again eluded security checks and planted a device in High Street, just a half mile away, close to the site of the old Grand Central Hotel, now Castlecourt Shopping Centre. Again, extensive damage was caused, but there were no injuries.

There are many mobile 'greasy spoon' fast-food outlets outside cities and towns in Britain. Philip Campbell (28) ran such an outlet from a caravan which he regularly parked at the Moira roundabout, close to Lisburn. He had sited the caravan there for some three years and was well known in the area, attracting customers who included soldiers travelling to and from Belfast; the Loyalists soon discovered that he was a Catholic. Drivers would park close by and amble over to the caravan for a bacon sarnie or a Belfast fry-up. It would therefore not have aroused any suspicions when a car containing gunmen from the UFF parked beside Mr Campbell's food stall. They walked across to an open side door, and one gunman, armed with a 9 mm Browning pistol, shot him as he served food, hitting him in his head and side; despite being rushed to Lagan Valley Hospital, he died within the hour.

On Friday 10th, several months after the mortar attack on Downing Street, the heart of the British government was again the target. This time, the attack was on a much less ambitious scale and was intended to have more of a nuisance effect. A 5 lb device (a little over 2 kg) concealed inside a briefcase was left in a public telephone box, close to Horseguards and just 300 yards from the Prime Minister's residence. There was no damage and no casualties; it was thought that the device was to have been placed closer to Downing Street, but the 'ring of steel' prevented this from happening. Prime Minister John Major was discussing security with Neil Kinnock, Paddy Ashdown and two other party leaders when the device exploded; the meeting continued despite the attack.

The following day, an innocent Protestant was fatally injured by Republican thugs, tasked by their IRA commanders to hijack a car in North Belfast. The plan was to seize a car, which would then be set on fire in the New Lodge in order to lure the RUC into the area, where concealed PIRA gunmen would open fire on them. Ivor McNabney (30), a Protestant lorry driver, was heading towards his home in Broughshane, some 35 miles north of Belfast. As he drove along the Westlink, close to North Queen Street, at around 03:30, five youths from the nearby New Lodge hurled a brick at the car, perhaps hoping to make it stop while the driver investigated the bump. However, the brick came through the windscreen and smashed into Mr McNabney's face. The car slewed across the roadway and smashed into a wall. Mr McNabney was fatally injured, dying in the RVH on the afternoon of the 13th. Five local men were charged with murder, but this was negotiated down to manslaughter and they received derisory sentences.

Also on the 13th, the IRA bungled yet another operation, based on poor intelligence, killing an entirely innocent Catholic joiner at his girlfriend's house in Coalisland, Co. Tyrone. The Tyrone Brigade decided to kill Michael Logue, because, according to information received from one of their army of dickers, he was employed as a labourer helping rebuild SF bases. Michael Martin Logue (21) was known to visit his girlfriend at her home in Glen Road, and generally not leave until the early hours of the morning. Sometime in the late hours of the 12th/early hours of the 13th, a PIRA bombing team placed a 1 lb (0.5 kg) device underneath his car. At around 01:15 hours, he kissed his girlfriend goodnight and got into his car. The device exploded, causing him terrible lower body damage. The shocked woman ran outside to investigate and found him fatally wounded in the wrecked car. He was pulled out of the wreckage, bleeding profusely and in great distress, by neighbours; an ambulance was summoned, but he died shortly afterwards. A spokesman for the IRA admitted that their information had been wrong, and made a half-hearted apology to the dead man's family. At Mr Logue's funeral, the Rev. Seamus O'Connell called the IRA apology 'the final insult'.

Gerry Adams and the late Martin McGuinness have often talked about the IRA's armed struggle and how the slaughtering of the Nationalist community by the British Army forced them into the actions which they took. Indeed, the rationale behind the rise of the Provisional IRA was, in part, to defend the Nationalist/Catholic communities from the Army and the RUC, as well as the stated aim of driving the British 'into the sea'. However, a study of the relevant statistics shows that, of the 1,696 people killed by the Republican terror group, 338 were Roman Catholics, that is the very people they claimed to protect. The British Army killed 299 people, of whom 258 were Catholics, and this figure includes many terrorists. Therefore, the question is begged: from whom were the Catholic communities most at risk? Clearly, the answer is the very people whose raison d'être was to protect them. The IRA talks about 'wholesale repression of our communities' when it is the very organisation which carried this out![1]

The next day, the UFF killed one of its own members in what was either part of an internal feud, or an amateurish attempt to copy Freddie Scappaticci's nutting squad. David Boyd (41), father of two, had long been suspected of being a Special Branch informer, and was known to be very nervous in the weeks leading up to his death. On the evening of the 14th, he left his home in Coronation Park, Dundonald, Co. Down, to get into an ordered taxi. There is some speculation as to why UFF gunmen were lying in wait there at the precise moment that he emerged. Were they tipped off by the taxi company, sympathetic to the Loyalists; were they simply aware that he was going out to a social event; or were they waiting on the off-chance that he would appear? Whatever the reason, as Boyd emerged through his security gates, he was blasted by a shotgun and then, as he lay injured on the ground, another blast from close range into his head finished him off. RUC Special Branch denied that he was an informant, but then again Johnston Brown's informative *Into The*

1. http://www.wesleyjohnston.com/users/ireland/past/troubles/troubles_stats.html.

Darkness shows what a truly Machiavellian organisation that they were and therefore, any comments from them are not necessarily to be believed. Ian S. Wood in his *Crimes of Loyalty* speculates that the killing of Boyd was more to do with 'score-settling' than any attempt to execute an informer.

On the 15th, Joe Doherty, a notorious Provisional wanted for the murder of SAS Captain Herbert Westmacott on 2 May 1980 learned his fate regarding his application to remain in the USA. The US Supreme Court ruled that Doherty, who had escaped from Crumlin Road jail, was not entitled to political asylum. He had fled in 1983 and had been feted, wined and dined and almost 'canonised' by his adoring Irish-American public. He was extradited to Ireland to face punishment for his crime just a few days after the Supreme Court ruling. Further information on the nine-year struggle to extradite Doherty can be found in Martin Dillon's excellent *Killer in Clowntown: Joe Doherty, The IRA and The Special Relationship* (Hutchinson, 1992). The book is a fascinating insight into both the public and the private scenes of the extradition of the killer of a soldier.

Teebane Crossroads

During the long and bloody history of the Troubles, there were many instances of multiple killings: Warrenpoint in 1979, where the IRA killed 18; they also killed 18 at the Droppin' Well in 1982. They killed 11 in Enniskillen in 1987; 11 at the La Mon Restaurant, 11 at Deal Barracks and 11 in the M62 coach bomb. They murdered 10 in the Kingsmills massacre and 8 in the Ballygawley coach bomb; the Real IRA killed 29 at Omagh. The British Army killed 13 on Bloody Sunday and the UVF killed 33 in Dublin/Monaghan and the UFF 8 at Greysteel. To this list of outrages can be added Teebane on 17 January 1992.

Karl Construction, a Protestant-owned company, was contracted to carry out bomb-damage repairs at Lisanelly barracks in Omagh. Formerly known as Blackbourne's, the company name had been changed to commemorate a murdered son, Karl who was killed by top Provo, 'Mooch' Blair in 1986. As part of the job routine, it used a minibus to transport its workforce to and from their homes in Cookstown; this was known to the Provisionals via its army of dickers in the area. They had observed the route for several days and knew that there were very few alternatives open to the driver ferrying the workers home. Some time, either during the afternoon of the 17th, or the previous evening, a double landmine was positioned along the route by the Provisionals. The explosives were packed into two plastic bins weighing 1,500 lb (680 kg); they were planted at the side of the busy A505 Omagh to Cookstown Road at the Teebane crossroads. The attack was said to be the brainchild of the IRA's South Londonderry unit, led by James Kelly, although there is evidence to the contrary, as it was also claimed by the East Tyrone brigade. The same unit also carried a massive bombing attack on the mainly Protestant town of Coleraine.

At Teebane, the PIRA ASU placed a command wire which led several hundred yards away into bushes close to a local quarry. The bombing unit concealed themselves there, ready for a signal from other members that the bus was almost at the target point. As darkness began to fall, the workmen in the minibus, probably tired after a long day's labour, and lulled by the vehicle's motion, likely wouldn't have noticed that a car ahead of them was maintaining 'a healthy' distance in front of their vehicle. Inside that car was a known PIRA female operative; when she passed a pre-arranged spot in the road, she flashed her lights several times to inform the bombing gang that the target minibus was approaching. At around 17:30, the van, driven by Oswald Gilchrist with 13 passengers, reached the crossroads. It was just seconds after an Ulsterbus, carrying 12 girls from a Catholic school in Dungannon had passed the same spot. Had the school bus passed exactly at the same moment as the Karl Construction vehicle, I have absolutely no doubt that the bombers would have still triggered the device, thus killing or injuring many of the girls. It would then have been the task of the IRA's department of hollow and meaningless apologies to talk about regret and sympathy before mentioning the insulting cliché 'collateral damage'.

However, the target vehicle was alone at the moment it reached the ambush spot, and the watching team detonated the bomb. The explosion wrecked the vehicle, hurling it into the air and causing it to crash onto its side, creating a crater 18 feet wide and 3 feet deep. Seven of the 14 men inside the van were killed instantly, and everyone else was badly hurt, with dead, dying and injured being hurled across the road. Bodies and body parts were thrown up to 30 feet away into the surrounding fields. The top part of the van was ripped off and the wreckage continued down the road for almost 100 feet further. Witnesses state that they heard the explosion from as far away as 10 miles.

Those killed at the scene were William Gary Bleeks (25); Cecil James Caldwell (37), father of one; Robert Dunseath (25); David Harkness (23); John Richard McConnell (38), father of three; Nigel McKee (22); and Robert Irons (61), father of a grown-up child. The driver, Oswald Gilchrist (44), was rushed to the RVH in Belfast where medical teams fought for almost four days to save him; he died on the 21st. Robert Dunseath was a Ranger (Private) in the Royal Irish Rangers, and is listed in the Military Roll of Honour as a member of the TA.

One of the survivors, Bobby O'Neill, later told the RUC that as he lay bleeding and injured in the road, he had seen a 'bearded man' appear at the scene of the bombing, walking dispassionately through the van's wreckage, showing no compassion or emotion, simply looking at the faces of the dead or dying. He made no attempt to help the wounded; O'Neill believed this man was one of the bombers. I often talk about evil, and this man who walked so calmly amongst the human carnage can only be described as evil or, at best, psychotic. No one was ever charged with this appalling crime, but it was an operation ordered by the very top of the IRA Command and I believe that Gerry Adams and the late Martin McGuinness, if not involved, must have been aware of the operation and the personnel who carried out the atrocity.

The following day, the *Daily Express* led with; '7 Workers Die In IRA Bombing', which relegated the news that Prime Minister, John Major was planning an April general election, to page 2. Their reporter wrote:

> Ambulance teams used floodlights in the search for bodies. A rescue worker said: 'They were blown to pieces and would not have known what hit them. It's sickening. I hope those who did this are proud of themselves.' Security chiefs were amazed that there were any survivors. Four badly hurt men were taken to Mid Ulster Hospital in Magherafelt. One was critical and another who lost an eye was transferred to Altnagelvin in Londonderry. A spokesman said: 'When word got around Magherafelt about the explosion, staff, from porters to top surgeons offered their services.'

The *Belfast Telegraph* interviewed one of the survivors just two days after the blast; reporter David Neely recorded the words of the injured man:

> We travelled 17 miles. We came down the road and myself and another fella were talking and I heard a wee dunt, just like our van had struck something. I was sitting two down on the passenger side. There were just two long seats on either side ... all on the driver's side were killed and one on our side was killed. I looked and all I could see was fire ... I was screeching and it was an experience I had never come through before ... fire was coming out of my eyes ... I just squealed for breath and I just seemed to be heading away ... I said a prayer: Lord, don't let me die, save me ... I was lying on the broad of my back and I couldn't see down to my legs and I couldn't feel them. I looked across the road and I saw a big sign – Omagh 17 miles. There were people lying on the ground. I couldn't tell you if there were two or three, or five lying there. Then a passer-by came across the road and he recognised me. I said: 'Are my legs on?' and he shook my legs but I couldn't feel them. I said: 'Get me up,' and part of my kneecap came off but I knew my leg was there and I thanked God that I was living.

On the 20th, Philip Derbyshire in the *Express* wrote of the suffering in just one of the eight homes that had been devastated by Republican terrorism:

> A little girl's heartache yesterday summed up the anguish of families devastated by the latest IRA atrocity. Two-year-old Grace Caldwell brought out her father's slippers and tearfully asked her mother Jean: 'When is daddy coming home?' She got no reply ... Mrs Caldwell said at her home in Cookstown: 'I am angry and bitter and filled only with hatred ... I just can't sit here and say that I forgive them. If I did, I would be telling a lie. I would hang them. Grace is her father's double. We were married 13 years before she came and he will never see her reach school age.'

The words 'honoured' and 'indebted' are much over-used and over-stated by some writers, including myself, but in the case of the following contributor, such words cannot adequately describe the debt I owe. Reading her words, prior to putting them into this book moved me to tears.

Teebane: My Tragedy
Ruth Forrest, sister of one of the murdered men

Friday 17 January 1992 was a dark, dreary day with a constant drizzle and six days after the 24th birthday of my darling only brother, David Harkness. David who was a joiner, was the youngest of six, having five older sisters: Heather, Doreen, Dorothea, Louise and Ruth (me). He had returned from Australia after a two-and-a-half-year period and only came home because mum was very ill. She had suffered a perforated bowel and pneumonia.

There was a scarcity of work for joiners and reluctantly he took a job with a firm called Karl Construction to make ends meet until he would return to Australia. This firm mainly worked for the security forces. David had been home approximately eight months. Mum, who had made a remarkable recovery, had travelled along with dad to London to visit her brother and family. David had come to visit me on the Wednesday, 15 January, and I had cut his hair and trimmed his beard; we had a great night together, but I wasn't to know that it would be our last together. I had been speaking to him on the phone on the following night, and he said that he was considering not going into work on the Friday, 17 January. He told me that if I was passing by the house and the blinds were up, I would know that he went to work. I was passing by the house on my way to style a neighbour's hair, and when I went past, the blinds were up.

Just after 5 p.m. that evening, I could hear sirens in the distance and I opened the front door. We were living in temporary accommodation as my husband and I and our children had lost our home and entire contents in another bomb, eight months earlier, which the IRA had been responsible for. When I opened the door, a neighbour was also outside and I asked him if he had heard anything. He said that he thought there was a large explosion from somewhere outside Cookstown. I knew it was in the direction of my home place, near the Omagh road, Cookstown. I had a gut instinct immediately that something terrible was wrong.

A news flash came on UTV around 5:45 p.m. and it was saying that three workmen were feared dead. I fell to my knees to the ground, crying to my husband that it was David. He told me to 'not jump to conclusions' but I just knew within myself that it was. I can't explain it, I just knew and I had the most sickening feeling. Immediately, I contacted my three other sisters who also had the exact same 'gut instinct'. None of us knew exactly who David worked for because it had never been discussed in our house. Meanwhile, mum and dad, being in London, also heard the news flash just as we had. Mum said: 'Cyril, phone home that's David!' Daddy phoned Cookstown Police Station, but there was so much confusion that they were not sure who owned the van. East Tyrone Brigade of the IRA had made a coded telephone call, claiming responsibility but stated that it was 'Henry Brother's Van' who were another construction firm who also worked for the security forces. Mum insisted that they get a flight home, but just before they boarded the flight, Cookstown Police confirmed to dad that 'David Samuel Harkness was on this van,' but they didn't know if he was dead or alive. Mum and dad flew home, not knowing, until they landed in Belfast International Airport, what had happened to their darling only son.

Back home, my sisters and I were ringing frantically trying to get in touch with David at home. There was no response; there were no mobile phones at that time. At approximately 8:30 p.m., my sister Louise phoned me; she said 'Ruth, I want you to prepare yourself for the worst; my husband has checked every hospital in Northern Ireland and no one has David.' I naively thought he could be helping someone at the roadside. She then stated 'The hospitals don't accept the dead.' I was praying that David would be alive, no matter how serious his injuries were. How selfish of me. At exactly 9 p.m., my sister Heather phoned; her exact words were 'Ruth, it's all over, David is dead.'

Meantime, Louise was at the airport waiting on mum and dad, along with a medical team to prepare them for the news. Louise said that she will never forget them coming off the flight and as mum and dad approached, Louise simply shook her head to confirm that David had been killed. Mum and dad arrived home to a packed house of mourners. David's body was released the following evening and we were the only family out of eight families to be blessed with an open coffin. He was buried on 20 January 1992, the day after my 26th birthday.

Life changed dramatically for us all after the death of David. He was a quiet, inoffensive, beautiful soul, who didn't deserve to be taken in such selfish and needless manner. He never got the opportunity to enjoy married life; have a family of his own; and has missed out on our children and grandchildren. Mum and dad did not get enough time with their beloved son. Dad passed away on 22 March 2006, aged 72 years; Mum passed away on 28 February 2012, aged 79 years. They never got justice for the murder of their son. 25 years later, we are no further forward, even though we were assured by the highest authorities that 'there would be no stone left unturned'.

The memorial stone which is placed at the scene of the atrocity has been vandalised numerous times, last year being the most recent. However, compared to the massive loss of life, no amount of damage to the monument will ever equate. It has been an extremely difficult journey for so many people, but for me, God has been my guide and refuge along with the support of my husband, Adrian, my children – Aaron, Clarke, Luke, and Stuart; my sisters, my father-in-law, Ted, my grandchildren and extended family and friends.

Teebane
Willie Frazer, founder of FAIR (Families Acting for Innocent Relatives), which seeks to help victims of the violence

Like many days in Northern Ireland for a great many people, today is yet another day of sad reflection, however that doesn't mean that my meme should exonerate those guilty of this crime by painting over the cracks in Stormont. We will remember and one way in which we do that is by making sure everyone knows who was responsible. This act of terrorism was carried out by Martin McGuinness and Gerry Adams Sinn Féin/IRA, yes the same people who today sit in government and call us extremists. They did this cowardly act and they will never be allowed to wash their hands of it. Lest We Forget.

The Provisionals were quick to claim the massacre as their handiwork, calling the dead and injured 'collaborators' and vowed that attacks such as this would continue. Their statement read: 'The IRA reiterates its long-standing call to those who continue to provide services or materials to the forces of occupation to desist immediately. Since 1985 the IRA has adopted a policy of taking military action aimed at ending Britain's cynical use of non-military personnel for the servicing and maintenance of British Crown Forces' bases and installations ... for our part, we in the IRA will not tolerate a situation where military personnel are freed from essential services and maintenance tasks and then deployed where they can carry out wholesale repression within our community.' Sinn Féin/IRA leader Gerry Adams was quick to blame the British for the indefensible actions of the terror organisation to which he belonged, describing the bombing as 'a horrific reminder of the failure of British policy in Ireland'.

On the Monday, Peter Brooke told the House:

I have to report to the House with deep sadness that, shortly after 5 o'clock on Friday afternoon, seven construction workers on their way home from work were killed and seven were injured, five very seriously, when their minibus was blown apart in a massive explosion at Teebane Cross, on the main Omagh to Cookstown road in County Tyrone. The police investigation is continuing, but it is believed that two plastic barrels containing some 300 pounds of home-made explosive were placed beside the roadside hedge and detonated by command wire from a vantage point overlooking the scene. The Provisional IRA has admitted that it carried out this mass murder. In addition, in the first three weeks of the year, five other people – all civilians – have been murdered by terrorists. I know that the House will join me in extending deepest sympathy to the families, friends and colleagues of all those killed or injured, and in utter condemnation of these attacks, which demonstrate the profound depravity and moral bankruptcy of terrorism. All those killed or injured were working men going peacefully about their lawful occasions, yet the terrorists did not hesitate to murder or maim them.

In the face of such unmitigated evil, the reaction of the community and the Government is one of grief and of righteous anger; but I and my colleagues are absolutely determined that it must also be one of resolute and vigorous action. No society which believes in democratic values can allow the ballot box to be overridden by the bomb and the bullet. Violence has not brought, and will not bring, the terrorists any advantage. The democratic path is the one that we shall tread, and we shall go where it leads, not where terrorists seek to direct. The first task for Government is to ensure that the security forces have the resources – legal and material – which they need. It is for the security force commanders to ensure that all the resources available to them are used with the maximum effectiveness. Both the level of available resources and their deployment are constantly adjusted as necessary to counter the foreseeable threat. When we judge that additional resources are needed, they are made available. My Honourable Friend the Minister of State announced on Saturday that extra troops would soon arrive. They are already on patrol. In addition, extra troops are also now in the Province in support of a specific operation to enhance the security and to improve the effectiveness of vehicle checkpoints in Fermanagh. We know that the terrorists can kill, but they cannot win. No democratic government or society can allow such people to prevail. Nor will we. The security forces will continue to prevent or deter, as they are now doing, by far the largest part of planned terrorist activity. They will also do everything practically possible to protect the public. With the assistance that is increasingly forthcoming from ordinary members of both sides of the community, they will resolutely and successfully pursue not just those who carry out terrorist attacks but also those who plan them. They will do so within the law; and they will continue to bring the criminals before the courts. That is the only way for a civilised democratic government to deal with terrorism.

Prime Minister John Major added: 'A policy of bombing is odious, contemptible and cowardly and will never change the government's policy in Northern Ireland.' Ulster MP Ken McGinnis said: 'The government must decide whether it is prepared to go on allowing people to die, and at the same time allowing the terrorist godfathers – and I mean those in the first division, the ringleaders – to have impunity to walk the streets.' The Catholic Bishop of Derry, Edward Daly, was angered by the atrocity and referred to the Provisional IRA as the real oppressors of the people and condemned the murders of innocent men. William McCrea, MP, said: 'The IRA have left a lot of broken homes and crushed families. The people of Northern Ireland are left to carry the burden of sorrow and tragedy.' Brian Mawhinney added to his colleague's comments: 'This was mass murder ... These were decent, honest workmen ... The softest possible target, going home to their families and friends.'

Twenty years later, the *Mid-Ulster Mail* ran a piece about the bombing, looking back on the events of two decades earlier:

> Almost 300 witness statements, 262 telephone records, 223 house-to-house enquiries and 18 suspects, but today, 20 years on from the Teebane massacre, no-one has ever been convicted of the murders of the eight Protestant workmen who lost their lives in the tragedy. But one photo-fit image, given to police by both a survivor of the tragedy and a witness who passed the spot where IRA killers planted the deadly bomb, could hold the key as to who one of the bombers was. In a chilling account given to police in the days after the atrocity, Teebane survivor Robert (Bobby) O'Neill described how a bearded man walked among the wreckage as the 14 Karl Construction workers lay dead or injured moments after the 500 lb land mine was detonated. This man showed no compassion, shock or emotion and never spoke or offered any assistance to any of the injured and he believed he was one of the bombers.
>
> Another man, known as 'Witness L', also told how he passed the spot where the killers laid in wait that morning, and witnessed a man of a similar description close to the scene of the bomb. Witness L stated he was a lorry driver who, about 10:35, on January 17, 1992, was driving on the A505 road towards Omagh. As he drove through the crossroads, he saw three men standing at a bus stop to his right and as he passed them, he thought the men seemed to take an unusual interest in him. He described the men, one of whom had a beard and said that he would recognise that man if he saw him again. He assisted police in compiling a photo-fit image of the bearded man.

Postscript

Karl Construction commissioned a black stone obelisk to be constructed at the site of the blast to pay tribute to the eight men murdered that day by the Provisional IRA. In common with many memorials placed to innocent civilians or soldiers, Republican supporters have attacked and defaced this memorial. Sites such as Ligoniel, which remembers the three Scottish soldiers murdered in a honey trap; Kingsmills, which remembers 10 Protestant workers killed in an IRA ambush; Warrenpoint, which commemorates the 18 soldiers killed by two IRA bomb blasts, are all fine examples of the nature of the Republican beast. The black stone which stands at Teebane crossroads has been attacked repeatedly since it was erected. It was destroyed in 1996 and replaced in 1997. This paragraph should be reprinted and handed to every single Irish-American who has put money into the collecting tins of NORAID.

In July 2016, I visited the scene of the outrage along with former UDR soldiers Trevor Loughlin and Mark 'C'. It was a rainy, windswept day and soon we were all soaked as we stood on the spot where the devices exploded, destroying the van and its human cargo. I looked at the road sign which the survivor had seen as he regained consciousness and at the staggered layout of the crossroads. I can only imagine the distress he had felt, injured, shocked, cold, and alone in the debris as his life appeared to be over. We saw that the memorial had been defaced yet again, with lumps of marble surrounding the structure and scattered around the ground. I wonder what excuse former NORAID leader Martin Galvin would make for this vile behaviour; it is likely that he wouldn't even try as he is every bit as odious as his supporters. The families of the dead have insisted on leaving the defaced memorial as it is, in the hope of showing just how vile and repugnant the followers of Irish Republicanism really are.

The following May, I returned to the scene with the same two comrades and we met up with Ruth Forrest, sister of one of the dead workmen, David Harkness. She is a striking woman and we greeted each other as though we were long-lost friends. She is brave and dignified, in direct contrast to the she-wolves who appear to dominate the female section of Sinn Féin. As we stood at the scene of the outrage, many cars stopped to see what we were up to and several risked crashing as their drivers concentrated on us, instead of the road ahead. In the entire Republican-dominated area, there is a heavy atmosphere of menace and it seemed that we were in an alien country, or trapped behind enemy lines. We were certainly trapped in a time-warp of hatred. As one vehicle slowed to eyeball me after I had crossed the road away from my party, the driver looked directly at me, menacingly drawing his hand across his throat. Memories die hard, very hard, as evidenced by the casual way these people desecrate our monuments, encouraged by the way that Sinn Féin only has to hint at a return to the Troubles, and the British government quickly backs down or makes yet another concession to their constant demands. It was an honour and privilege to meet this woman and I will remain impressed for the rest of my life at her courage, dignity and refusal to be intimidated by militant Republicanism.

As we shall see in the following chapter, retaliation was less than 19 days away. When it came, five Catholic families would be grieving, more children would be added to the growing legion of the fatherless, and a woman widowed by the Teebane atrocity would be sending her heartfelt sympathies to those Catholic families who would be sharing her grief.

Three days after the blast, John Major visited Northern Ireland, to show his face there in the light of the Teebane atrocity. The more cynical observers of the time, aware that a general election was coming soon – it was held on 9 April – and with Labour's Neil Kinnock ahead in the opinion polls, considered that it was Major's attempt to curry favour with the Unionist MPs whose support he would need in the event of a hung parliament. Under heavy RUC/Army guard, he did a walk-about in Belfast, before visiting the Industrial Development Board Offices, where he gave generous praise to the people of the city, despite some heckling from the crowd. He also met some victims of IRA bombs, including Celia Gourley, who lost her legs in an IRA attack in 1991. He also visited a school in Lurgan which was being re-built after the IRA wrecked the nearby RUC station.

PIRA's Londonderry unit was busy between the 22nd and the 24th of the month; they struck five times within this period. First of all, one bombing unit exploded two further devices outside the Allied Irish Bank and the Alliance & Leicester building, again without injuries. Then they detonated a bomb on the Londonderry–Belfast rail line, with train driver Brian Robinson narrowly escaping injury. Just a few hours later, close to the city centre, they wrecked the Ulsterbus depot, although there were no casualties. During this time, the Tyrone unit targeted the headmaster of Castlederg High School, John Dunbar. They tried to kill Mr Dunbar, simply because he had been an officer in the UDR several years previously. They fired several shots at him but he was uninjured.

On the 26th, another former soldier was killed; the question at the time was, had he been killed by Republicans, as had been the case with six other ex-military personnel because of their past association, or by Loyalists, because he was a Catholic? John 'Jock' McIver (36) had been a soldier in the Army Catering Corps (ACC). He was born in Glasgow, and after a short stint in the Army had moved to Northern Ireland. At the time of his death, he lived in Parker Street, in East Belfast, just off the Loyalist Newtownards Road. During the evening, he had gone to the Liverpool Supporters' Club on Templemore Avenue, a short four-minute stroll away near Albertbridge Avenue. Although he was not a devout Catholic, shortly before his death he had told friends that he was very worried, as others had apparently discovered his faith.

During the evening, he went into the club's toilets, where he was knifed to death in a brutal and cowardly manner by a Loyalist paramilitary. The killer followed the Catholic man into the toilet, before plunging his knife into Mr McIver's chest and twisting it around inside his body. An RUC officer described the murder as one of the most brutal he had ever seen, and a later coroner's court heard that it was 'a bloodbath in every sense of the word'. Although neither of the mainstream groups claimed the killing, it was thought at the time that, due to the proximity of UVF territory, it was they who carried out the attack. However, in 2001, the *Belfast Telegraph* reported that a new suspect had emerged, but that the man – by then murdered himself – was a member of the UFF. Geordie Legge was the new suspect; he died in 2001 and there is further speculation that expelled UDA man Jim 'Doris Day' Gray may also have clues as to the murderer or to the identity of the man who ordered the attack. The inquest heard that the RUC believed that a Loyalist paramilitary group had killed Mr McIver, but did not claim his death due to the fact that he was popular with his neighbours in the lower Newtownards Road area.

The day after the murder of Mr McIver, there was major controversy as an IRA bombing attack went wrong; they had placed a large amount of explosive in a car which was intended for Belfast city centre. It would appear that the device became unstable, and the car was abandoned at the bottom of Rockdale Street, without any warning being given to the residents. It was left close to the Falls Road, about midway between the Whiterock Road and the Beechmounts. The bomb exploded, causing major damage and injuring a resident. In attempting to deflect attention away from their recklessness and lack of thought in putting Catholic lives at risk, the IRA blamed the RUC. For their part the RUC denied that they had been contacted by the terror group. Once more the Provisionals demonstrated their callousness in allowing a residential area where children lived to be turned into a battleground.

The month was coming to an end, but there was still time for the paramilitaries to cause more death and destruction. On the 30th, the UFF killed a Catholic on his way to work. Paul Moran (33), father of a baby boy, lived and worked in Lisburn. The Loyalist group had observed that he worked at the Lisburn Hide Company in Dagger Road on the western outskirts of the town. It was noted that he stopped en route every morning to buy his daily newspaper at Longstone Street, some three miles from where he worked. On that fateful morning, he did what he always did; sadly, on this occasion, a killer from the UFF was waiting for him as he walked out of the shop, newspaper in hand. A lone gunman armed with a shotgun fired both barrels at very close range, blasting him in the chest and throat; he died on the spot, his lifeblood staining his newspaper and the pavement. The gunman dashed away, dodging traffic on the busy Moira Road, and disappeared down Manor Park Road.

Two women were united by separate terrorist activities, although they never met. Jean Caldwell, the mother of a young child, talked to the press about her feelings at being widowed by the Teebane bomb. On this day, she was joined by Paul Moran's wife, who said: 'My son is just one year old and he'll never know his daddy.' She also spoke of how upset her husband had been at the deaths of eight Protestants in the previous outrage and his spoken fears about how many Catholics would die in response. The UFF's intention was simply to murder a Catholic, any Catholic would do, but they sickeningly attempted to besmirch the dead man's memory as well as justify the murder by claiming that he was a member of the Republican movement. The RUC confirmed that Mr Moran had no paramilitary ties, and spoke warmly of him. A senior officer told the subsequent coroner's court that the dead man 'was very well thought of in the community and had never come under any adverse police attention'.

Later that day, the IRA's England team planted an incendiary device in a shop in the busy Elephant and Castle area in south London. Fortunately, the device was defused after the shop had been evacuated. Whilst this was happening, over in Dublin Charles Haughey announced his resignation as both Taoiseach and leader of Fianna Fáil, in order to spare his own reputation as well as that of his party. The Irish newspapers were about to commence a series of articles relating to Haughey's involvement in phone-tapping in the early 1980s. He was replaced the following week by Albert Reynolds.

Finally, on the 31st, PIRA gunmen hijacked a Post Office van on the outskirts of Dungannon in Co. Tyrone. The vehicle was driven to a remote farmhouse where a bombing team placed a 500 lb (225 kg) explosive device. It was then driven to a spot near the RUC station in the centre of the town and a warning telephoned through. It exploded 19 minutes later, injuring three RUC officers who were trying to clear the area. The base was severely damaged, as were many buildings surrounding it. Later that same day, the IRA planted a huge car bomb in Belfast city centre; when it exploded, it caused £1,000,000 worth of damage.

January was over and 15 people had died. The Provisional IRA was responsible for nine of the 15 deaths.

14

February

This month the Loyalists retaliated in bloody fashion for the Teebane atrocity, attacking a branch of Sean Graham's bookies in Belfast, killing five Catholics. Four Provisionals were killed in an SAS ambush, another was killed during the attempted murder of an off-duty UDR man, and an RUC officer killed three Sinn Féin employees, before shooting himself. In all, 20 people died, surpassing the 15 killed in January. It was a month of sectarian murder, committed in the main by Loyalists.

On the first Sunday of the month, Peter 'Babbling' Brooke (as he was known to many Loyalists) was interviewed by the BBC, with the discussion inevitably coming round to the forthcoming general election. John Major had 'sown the seeds' of coalition with the Unionists following his recent visit to the Province. Interestingly, Brooke refused to rule out the possibility of the Major government doing a post-election deal with Unionists, something which Margaret Thatcher had never had to contemplate. As the opinion polls had shown a huge surge in favour of Neil Kinnock's Labour Party, it seemed that it was something which Major might need to consider. Brooke stated that if talks were not successful, a solution might be imposed that was more integrationist than devolutionist. In the event, as we shall see in Chapter 16, Major won a working majority of 21 seats, and although this was considerably smaller than the landslide victories enjoyed by his predecessor, he had no need for Unionist support. However, by the 1997 election, that majority had shrunk to just 12, with Ulster Unionist support being required at times.

On that same Sunday, the killings commenced; it was now seemingly inevitable that they would, and it was no longer a case of 'if' but 'when'. This time, the UFF's 'C' company shot and killed a Catholic taxi driver because, they maintained, he was a member of the Provisionals. This was, of course, untrue and the target was chosen because he was a member of Conradh na Gaeilge, an Irish language group. It is very likely that he would have had Republican sympathies, but it is by no means certain. In the twisted logic of Adair, McKeag and McFerran, his cultural activities were enough to 'justify' his murder. On the evening of the 2nd, two UFF men riding a stolen motorbike pulled up outside the home of Paddy Clarke (53), father of four, in Rosemount Gardens in North Belfast. Unfortunately for the murder gang, the bike broke down and had to be pushed the final few yards. The house was located between the Cavehill Waterworks and Alexandra Park, close to the Antrim Road; the Antrim Road gave the killers an easy escape into Loyalist territory. At around 19:00, a helmeted gunman kicked open the front door of the Clarke house and stormed into the lounge, where the family – Mr and Mrs Clarke and their five-year-old son – were watching television. As Mr Clarke saw the gunman he bravely threw himself in front of his loved ones, screaming at them to get down. I have been told by an impeccable source that the gunman was 'Big Donald' Hodgen. He fired four times, hitting Mr Clarke in the head and chest, mortally wounding him. The killer then dashed outside to the waiting bike, by this time fixed and the pair drove to the Loyalist Ballysillian area. The bike was then disposed of by Sammy McKay who was later jailed for seven years for conspiracy. Mrs Clarke held her dying husband and it is thought that he tried to speak but was unable to do so, sadly passing away within minutes.

Lister and Jordan maintain that a female Protestant neighbour of Mr Clarke had complained about him to Adair, and that in return for a sexual favour from the woman, Adair agreed to have him killed.[1]

Between the 2nd and the 11th, the IRA beat security again, and managed to get two explosive devices – car bombs – into the centre of Belfast. In the first explosion, on Botanic Avenue, close to Queen's University and the railway station, there was widespread damage, estimated at well over £1 million, but no casualties. Then, just nine days later, they managed to get a car bomb into the same area; fortunately, it was defused by the Army after causing widespread traffic disruption.

On the 11th, an IRA bomb was defused on Parliament Street, in Exeter in England. The cathedral town itself is in the county of Devon, situated some 37 miles from the Royal Navy base in Plymouth and around 70 miles from Bristol. It was as unlikely a target for the IRA as it was thought to Have been for the German Luftwaffe, who raided the city 18 times between 1940 and 1942. Now the IRA attempted a repeat and left a car with around 200 lb (90 kg) of explosives in Parliament Street; Army bomb disposal were quickly on the scene and the device was rendered harmless. It is alleged that the man in charge of the IRA's England team was Owen Coogan and that it was his decision to bomb Exeter. He is alleged also to have been a member of the IRA's Revolutionary Council, and was one of the escapers from Long Kesh in 1974. The so-called 'great escape' of 1983, however, somewhat dwarfed Coogan's claim to fame.

The day after the murder of Mr Clarke, the IRA killed an innocent Protestant in what can be only described as a blatant sectarian attack, although they attempted to disguise their actions by claiming that Gordon Hammill (41), father of four, was a member of the UVF. It was utter nonsense as they knew and simply exposed them as a sectarian murder gang every bit as vile as the UVF and UFF. Mr Hammill was from Coagh, Co. Tyrone, and delivered bread around the area; he had been dicked by Republican sympathisers who relayed his daily routes to the local commanders. He didn't vary his journeys because he didn't need to; he wasn't a paramilitary, nor a part-time soldier or policeman and didn't consider that he was at risk from either side. At around 08:20 on the morning of the 3rd, he stopped at a supermarket in Newell Road, Dungannon, and started carrying a tray of bread into the shop. As he did so, masked PIRA men, who had followed his van, walked across to him and opened fire with an AK-47, blasting his body with round after round; he was hit a staggering 32 times and died almost immediately, his lifeblood draining away and staining his fresh bread an awful shade of red. The attackers drove off in a stolen Vauxhall Astra, abandoning it a couple of minutes away; it was set alight before they escaped in a second vehicle.

1. Lister and Jordan, *Mad Dog*, p. 129.

Associated Press reported the incident:

> Two masked men shot and killed a bread delivery man in a supermarket in Northern Ireland on Monday, and the IRA claimed responsibility. Gordon Hamill, 42, was the 16th person to die in political and sectarian violence in Northern Ireland this year. The Royal Ulster Constabulary spokesman said two masked men, one carrying an automatic rifle, followed Hamill into Cost Cutters supermarket in Dungannon, 40 miles west of Belfast. In a statement to news media in Belfast, the IRA claimed Hamill was a member of the outlawed Ulster Volunteer Force, a gang loyal to Britain with roots in the Protestant community. The IRA said the killing was in retaliation for the murders of Roman Catholics. On Sunday, a member of the Ulster Freedom Fighters, another outlawed group, killed Patrick Clarke, a 52-year-old Catholic. Police said two men were arrested. The Ulster Freedom Fighters described Clarke as a 'republican,' the customary term for an IRA supporter.

On Tuesday 4th, four people died, as a result of what *Lost Lives* terms the 'most bizarre killings of the troubles'. Constable Allen Moore (24) was a member of the RUC who had joined at the age of 18. In the six years that he had been a police officer, a total of 31 fellow officers had been killed on duty, mostly by the Provisionals. Two years earlier, he had been caught in an ambush during which his Land Rover had been attacked by Semtex-filled drogue bombs in Belfast. Although he was uninjured, the experience had been terrible, but for his part in apprehending one of the bombers he had received a Queen's Commendation. On Monday 3rd, he was arrested at a cemetery after he was found to be drunk whilst firing a volley of shots from his service Ruger over the grave of a fellow officer. The dead officer was called Norman Spratt; he had been murdered by his wife with his own service revolver. It is not thought, however, that Moore was particularly close to this officer. After psychiatric tests, and naturally the confiscation of the Ruger, he was released into the custody of a colleague, in order to sleep off his hangover; however, he left the house whilst the other man slept. Instead of returning home or to Newtownabbey RUC station, he disappeared. He had been based in the northern part of Belfast for some time, although he was living in Bangor, Co. Down, some 20 miles away. He made a series of very confusing telephone calls, in which he warned that he was going to kill some Republicans. Some colleagues had considered that he was mentally ill, based on his previous behaviour, but had not reported these suspicions as they feared that it would curtail his career as a police officer.

He drove his BMW car to the Sinn Féin offices in the Falls Road, collected a sports bag from the boot and walked towards the entrance, where he was admitted after stating that he was a journalist. Once inside, he began to fire a pump-action shotgun through the bag. First to be hit was Pat McBride (40), father of one, who slumped to the floor dead. He then opened fire on a further four people, critically injuring one man – Pat Wilson – slightly wounding a woman – Norah Larkin – but fatally wounding Paddy Loughran (61), father of eight children. He then shot and also fatally wounded Michael O'Dwyer (21), father of two very young children, one of whom was with him as he was shot, at point-blank range in the chest. McBride was a former IRA prisoner; Loughran was an employee of Sinn Féin, but Mr O'Dwyer, although an active Republican, was simply in the wrong place at the wrong time, having gone to the offices in order to complain about thugs and vandals in his area. Moore left the building and drove off. He then made a series of telephone calls before driving 15 miles to his birthplace of Ballinderry, and from there to Lough Neagh. Whilst there, he called Newtownabbey RUC station in order to confess to the killings. Shortly afterwards, he put the shotgun into his mouth, pulled the trigger and blew his own head off. Whatever the mental state of this officer – excluded by the RUC from their own Roll of Honour – he nevertheless left 11 children without a father and widowed three women. It was later revealed, that between 1978 and 1993, 57 police officers had committed suicide.

By coincidence, the President of the Irish Republic, Mary Robinson was on a visit to Northern Ireland. On hearing of the tragic killings, she told the press: 'This kind of violence and loss of life is a tragedy that seems all too common in Northern Ireland.' However, Gerry Adams was quick to claim that two gunmen were involved, for which, of course, there was absolutely no evidence.

Richard Latham, in his very informative *Deadly Beat*, explains how drink, stress, incredibly long hours in the fight against terrorism and a tolerance to violence brought on by the trauma of being so often a witness to it, could trigger the type of attack which Moore subjected the Sinn Féin workers to. Latham describes an incident at a mid-Ulster police station during an off-duty card game. 'Drink had been taken, and with emotions running high over comments made by one officer sitting opposite another, the aggrieved, extremely pissed-off policeman emptied the 6 rounds of his Ruger revolver into his colleague's groin area. The injured officer lived, but only by virtue of receiving prompt medical treatment. The attacking officer's career came to an abrupt end as he was charged with serious assault.'[1]

The inevitable Loyalist 'backlash' after Teebane was never going to be long in coming, and the Catholic community braced itself for the expected retaliation. When it came, on Wednesday February 5th, it came with a shocking suddenness and violence. The location was a bookmaker's shop, Sean Graham's, on Lower Ormeau Road, South Belfast. The branch was, and still is today, located at the crossroads of University Avenue and Hatfield Street; it has Queen's University to the west and the Lagan River to the east and is in a predominantly Catholic/Nationalist area. It was a likely target for Loyalist paramilitaries. At around 14:20, three men, possibly a combination of gunmen from Johnny Adair's 'C' company of the UFF and the local unit based in the Annadale flats, drove along University Avenue and parked just yards from the shop. Leaving the driver to keep the engine running, two UFF men exited the car. They are thought to have been local UDA/UFF men Raymond Elder and Joe Bratty (Bratty and Elder would be killed by the Provisionals in Kimberley Bar off the Ormeau Road on 31 July 1994). The two walked into the bookmaker's, which was packed with 15 punters. Armed with a VZ.58 Czechoslovakian semi-automatic rifle – similar to the AK-47 – and a 9 mm Browning, they gave no warning, and simply opened fire, hitting 12 of the people in the shop. In total 46 shots were fired in the attack, within the confined space. Because of the lack of room, the gunmen had to step over some victims to shoot others as they lay on the ground and then walk back across a floor already running with blood. McDonald and Cusack's excellent and informative *UDA: Inside the Heart of Loyalist Terror* captures in perfect and poignant detail the immediate aftermath of this appalling act: 'men

1. Richard Latham, *Deadly Beat* (Mainstream Publishing, 2001), p. 107.

groaning and screaming, blood splattered on the walls and the air filled with the sour reek of cordite. And while some of the victims lay dying, the horse race they had been watching at the time of the shooting, was coming to a finish on the television, the cries of the victims competing to be heard above the frenzied voice-over from the race meeting.'[1]

As it happened, gunmen from the UFF's rivals the UVF were only a short distance away, en route to kill a Sinn Féin Councillor – Jim Clinton – who lived on the Ormeau Road. The gang had just collected automatic weapons from an arms cache in Ormeau Park, when they heard the sustained gunfire from Sean Graham's. They immediately aborted the murder bid.

One eyewitness told the *Belfast Telegraph*:

> I was standing next to the door with a docket in my hand studying the form. At first I thought it was a hold-up but then the shooting started and somebody yelled, 'Hit the deck.' I just lay there and prayed that the shooting would stop. It seemed to go on for a lifetime. There wasn't a sound for a few seconds – everybody was so stunned, but then the screaming started. People were yelling out in agony. You could hardly see anything. The room was full of gun smoke and the smell would have choked you.

Four men were killed more or less instantly, with a fifth victim – a 15-year-old boy – dying shortly afterwards in hospital. The dead were Peter Magee (18); Christy Doherty (51); William McManus (54), father of four; and Jack Duffin (66), father of three grown-up children. Jack Duffin was found lying on top of another wounded man; his back was riddled with bullets, seemingly as a result of him trying to protect a friend. He clearly gave his own life in the selfless act of saving another.

The young victim was James Kennedy (15) who died in hospital despite the best efforts of the medical staff to save him. *Lost Lives* records that his final words were: 'Tell my mummy that I love her.' As the gunmen ran out of the shattered shop, spattered with blood and stinking of cordite, one of them shouted 'Remember Teebane' before jumping into the car which screeched off down the Lower Ormeau Road in the direction of the Annadale flats. The car used was a blue Ford Escort, registration RIJ 9090. This had been bought on 27 January at Carryduff Auctions for £370; a second getaway car was parked in nearby Bladon Drive. This was another blue Ford Escort, registration YIA 6097, also purchased at the same auction.

A relative of a survivor told the press that one victim was shot in the arms and legs, but that the gunman ran out of bullets before he could fire a fatal shot. James McManus was badly wounded, but stayed alert and conscious long enough to summon an ambulance.

On the following morning the *Daily Express* chose to lead with: 'My Secret Love Affair: Paddy confesses fling as wife stands by him', a lurid account of Liberal Democrat leader Paddy Ashdown's extra-marital affair; clearly the death of five Catholics at the hands of Loyalist terrorists was not as important – the story eventually ended up on page 7. That page began: 'Boy, 15 dies in terror massacre.' The report stated: 'A boy aged 15 was among five killed in a betting shop massacre yesterday. Members of the outlawed Ulster Freedom

1. Henry McDonald and Jim Cusack, *UDA: Inside the Heart of Loyalist Terror* (Penguin, Ireland, 2004), p. 223.

Fighters burst into the shop, in the heart of Catholic South Belfast and mowed down their victims with machine-guns. Nine other customers were wounded in the shop. "It's like a butchers" in there said an appalled survivor, "there is blood everywhere." "The place was crowded. Nobody stood a chance," said a wounded survivor. Another added: "It was a bloodbath. One minute everybody was chatting, smoking and studying form, the next it was a nightmare of bangs and moans and yells." A Catholic priest gave the last rites inside the shop. Four died at the scene and one later in hospital. The City Centre was on full alert last night as Belfast braced itself for an IRA backlash.'

Emergency medics described the scene as 'absolute and sheer carnage' as they battled to save lives. Harry Whan, Divisional Ambulance Officer for Belfast, who arrived within minutes of being alerted stated: 'The scene was horrific with bodies everywhere. In that confined space there was the smell of gunfire and all the bleeding and whatever that you couldn't describe ... for other ambulance men it was worse; they were knee deep in it, dealing with the dead and dying.' The Relatives for Justice website gives further details:

> There were chaotic and frantic scenes as people desperately sought to find out if their relatives were inside, with the atmosphere occasionally breaking back to calm and comfort as people found one another in the assembled crowd shedding their emotions in embraced relief. For others, who had either seen or were told that their loved ones were still alive and had been stretchered away, there was a sense of relief too on knowing that they were not dead. One woman comforted another telling her that her son, who was inside the Bookmaker's at the time of the attack, was still alive. This same woman did not know that her own 18-year-old son lay dead inside. Four bodies were brought out of the Bookmaker's shop. Word soon emerged that 15-year-old James Kennedy had died on arrival at hospital.[1]

When news of the attack reached HMP Maze, UFF prisoners cheered loudly on hearing of the deaths of five Catholics and began taunting Republican prisoners. Other Protestants saw things differently. Betty Gilchrist, widow of one of the Teebane victims, sent a letter expressing deep sympathy that was read out at the funeral later that week of one of the new victims, Jack Duffin; two widows were united in grief across the sectarian divide.

A pre-12 July Loyalist march later that year passed the scene of the murders, and it is reported that marchers taunted Catholic residents by holding up five fingers to indicate the number of those who had died at the hands of the UFF. A later UFF statement repeated the words: 'Remember Teebane!' They also claimed that the Lower Ormeau Road was a hotbed of IRA activity and this was the reason for the choice of the attack site. In February 2012 Jackie McDonald, one-time commander of the UDA South Belfast Brigade, admitted that the victims of the shooting had been innocent. However, he said that he could not apologise for the attack, saying that, as he was imprisoned at the time, he played no part in what had happened.

I will never – could never – seek to justify the actions of the Loyalist paramilitaries and as past readers of mine will be acutely aware, I do not reserve my opprobrium for Republicans; it is shared equally between them and the Loyalist paramilitaries. When I look at the Sean Graham massacre, I can only wonder if, had they stopped there and then and the IRA/

1. http://relativesforjustice.com/wp-content/uploads/2014/03/S.Graham-Full-Report-Web.pdf.

INLA/IPLO also stopped, would that have been the end of the matter. Could it have ended there and did a further 400 people have to perish before the so-called ceasefire?

The 6th started quietly enough, as to the south, Albert Reynolds was elected as leader of Fianna Fáil and also became Taoiseach, replacing Charles Haughey. However, the IRA as part of their border campaign against Fermanagh Protestants set out to kill a UDR man at Belleek. The man was a part-time soldier – Corporal Eric Glass of 4 UDR – who was also employed as a dog warden. A four-man murder gang which included Joseph McManus (21), James Hughes and Conor O'Neill, took over a house at Scardens Upper, right on the Co. Donegal border, where they held the family at gunpoint. A hoax call was made to the council dog department and, as expected, the IRA's target was dispatched to the remote farm to investigate. When he arrived at the gate of the farmhouse he was ambushed by the unit and ordered to get out of his van. The unit opened fire on Glass, who then reached for his handgun, which he always had ready, loaded and placed on the passenger seat of the van. A gun battle ensued in which Glass was badly injured but he managed to fight off his attackers, killing McManus in the process. The other three members, unaccustomed to soft targets actually fighting back, then ran away and crossed the border into the safety of the Republic. Corporal Glass later received both the Queen's Gallantry Medal and Distinguished Conduct Medal for bravery.

Eric Glass later told the Belfast *News Letter*:

> As I drove down the lane to the house I had my gun under a coat on the front seat. The minute I pulled up one guy came to the driver's door – he had a gun with binder twine on it slung round his neck – and the other one had a revolver. They came running out shouting and swearing 'Get out of the van – IRA.' The one with the revolver ran up to the passenger door. I cocked the gun and fired three shots out through the passenger side. I swung round quick and pushed the door into the other guy. He had the rifle round his neck on the string and was going to use his hands to get me out of the van but he ran off. They ran down firing on automatic and that's when I got the one I whacked on the legs. With the new magazine on I fired back and somebody roared 'Two, three and four run for it' and they disappeared into cover. When I shouted at the man in the house to phone for help he said he couldn't as the boys would come back and shoot him. I spent nine months in hospital because the bones in my left leg were shattered. Then when I eventually got out of hospital I found I didn't have a job to go back to with the council. That was hard to come to terms with after all those years working there.

Hughes and O'Neill were found on the Irish side of the border, hiding in a ditch by a Garda patrol; a rifle and a revolver were found with them. In October 1992, they were both sentenced to 12 years for the attempted murder of Corporal Glass. McManus, also known as 'Joe' was English-born, but had lived in an Irish area of London and became a Republican before he went to live in Ireland in 1976. He was the son of the then Sinn Féin chairman, Sean McManus. Gerry Adams attended the dead PIRA man's funeral, as an old family friend of the terrorist's parents. Adams gave the eulogy and had the brass neck to state – with a straight face as well: 'He had a secret life. I never guessed for a minute that he was a Volunteer.'

February was only six days old, and already 23 children had been left fatherless thanks to the paramilitaries of both sides. However, the bloodlust appeared to have been sated and there were no more deaths for 10 days, but when the killing re-started, after both sides had paused for breath, seven more people would die in the final 13 days of the month.

On the 10th and 11th, Prime Minister John Major was in the news. First of all, he announced that, in the light of the increasing violence in the Province, a further battalion of troops would be sent out to help. The following day, Major and Peter Brooke held meetings with the leaders of the main political parties in Northern Ireland to discuss the security situation. Later in the month, Brian Mawhinney, then Minister of State at the Northern Ireland Office, held a further meeting with the leaders of the four main political parties.

On Saturday 15th, the Provisionals managed to get past security checks and detonated a car bomb in Belfast city centre, again! The device, which weighed 250 lb (136 kg), was left In Adelaide Street, close to City Hall; it caused massive damage to buildings but there were no casualties; it was simply another day when shoppers were evacuated and shop owners lost yet more much-needed revenue. Damage was estimated at millions of pounds as the Provisionals continued their so-called economic war, seemingly bombing at will.

On the 16th, the Fermanagh Provisionals received a bloody nose, almost on the scale of Loughgall, when six of their gunmen were shot – four were killed – in an SAS ambush at Clonoe, near Coalisland. Acting on information received from a high-level informant inside the Provisional IRA, British intelligence learned that an attack would take place on the RUC base at Coalisland, using a very powerful DShK heavy machine gun mounted on the back of a stolen lorry. Such an operation would have had to be approved by the IRA's Army Council but would have been known to very few people so it had to be a top Provisional who leaked the information about the planned attack.

Hours before the operation, undercover soldiers had dug in around St Patrick's Church, Dernagh, to set up an ambush. So as not to give the game away, the soldiers simply observed and, in absolute silence, allowed the first part of the PIRA plan to be put into place. The unit – of seven members – drove across the border and parked several stolen cars in the church car park; they then took a stolen lorry on which they had already mounted the machine gun, plus another car, and drove into Coalisland, stopping close to the RUC station. It was now 22:30; PIRA member Kevin Barry O'Donnell was manning the heavy weapon and he opened fire at point-blank range, firing armour-piercing rounds into the metal security walls of the station. ITN footage later showed the incredible amount of damage caused.

The station was empty, however, as it had been clandestinely evacuated in anticipation of the attack. The lorry and the escorting car, flying a tricolour, then drove out of town towards the church to collect the escape vehicles. The two vehicles drove up Annagher Hill, deliberately passing the house of Tony Doris, a PIRA man killed on 3 June 1991 in an ambush in Coagh (*see* Chapter 6). As they did so, O'Donnell fired off the last of the DShK rounds, with several of the men shouting: 'Up the IRA; that's for Tony Doris,' as they clearly believed that they had left police officers dead back in Coalisland. Still elated, they arrived back at the church car park and leapt out of the vehicles to begin their escape. The SAS team saw the heavily armed gang and, after triggering a flare to illuminate the scene, opened fire, hitting six, possibly seven IRA men. The first to be killed were the two men in the lorry's cab. At least one, possibly two of the gang fired back, hitting a soldier, badly injuring him.

In the brief firefight, O'Donnell (21), Daniel Vincent (20), Peter Clancy (19) and Sean O'Farrell (23) were killed and Aidan McKeever was wounded. As the terrorists went down in a hail of bullets, one can only wonder what went through their minds at that moment of stark realisation that their lives were ending. As they died, did the irony of their situation strike them? Did they consider that this summary execution was the same instant justice which their cause had meted out to hundreds of others?

Three of the PIRA men died in the car park, a fourth was found entangled in the perimeter fence. Another of the terrorists was trying to get away in a car when he was hit; he managed to drive for half a mile before crashing; it is thought that he then made off on foot. Three men in all managed to escape, but they were caught and tried several years later. The roof of the church was accidentally set on fire by a stray round that hit a fuel storage tank, or possibly by the flare sent up by the SAS. Local people said that the shooting went on for quite some time, the sounds of the firing mingling with the screams of the dying terrorists. O'Donnell was known to the Army and RUC as a 'top IRA terrorist'. In addition to the partly dismantled heavy machine gun, two AK-47s were also recovered from the dead men.

Republicans immediately complained about 'shoot-to-kill' but what could they or their Irish-American apologists expect when the dead men had tried to kill police officers in cold blood just minutes before? IRA strategists called it the 'long war', but they didn't fight it in a conventional manner, and as the Musgrave Park Hospital bombing proved, did not adhere to the Geneva Convention either. Republican apologists also claimed that several of the dead men had tried to surrender.

Live by the Gun
Former RUC Officer (name withheld)

This, sadly was not one of the operations with which I was involved, but there were others which I can only mention in general and, naturally cannot mention names. One of the dead men at the church was known to me; an arrogant wee shite with a gob the size of a bucket. Sly, nasty, always wishing you well, but with that glint of evil in his eyes and you knew that he was plotting your demise. The rest of them had families but I can't bring myself to share their pain and grief because Ulster had enough of its own and I had my personal share. The mothers would look shocked and strained and they could not imagine that the man lying in a coffin in her living room, with an Irish flag covering it was the same wee baby she delivered after carrying it for 9 months, feeding it with her own milk, changing its shitty nappies and holding his hand for his first day of school. After her grief, wound up by her Sinn Féin friends, stirred with more hatred by the family priest, she would moan about injustice, murder, state execution and the like. But she didn't see the carnage her wee boy and the boyos had caused as they summarily executed innocents for the most spurious of reasons. She didn't see the young off-duty soldier I saw, when we were called to his house; she didn't see the body as he lay on his back, legs all over the place, eyes wide-open in shock, mouth open, as though screaming 'No!' palms frozen, facing outwards as he tried to prevent .45s or 9 mm bullets from tearing into his chest. Laying there, the blood stains turning his carpet a nasty shade of browney-red. The Republicans lived by the sword and they perished by the sword. Let the bastards reflect on that when they sang '*Amhrán na bhFiann*' [the Irish national anthem] at his wake!

Naturally, there was an internal IRA investigation which had four main criticisms of the botched operation. The DShK was employed at point-blank range even though it has armour-piercing qualities at up to 2,000 yards. The conduct of the gunmen after the shooting was unwise: they advertised their presence with hazard lights flashing, shouting and shooting and showed no discretion. The escape route was chosen so that they could 'showboat' outside the home of Tony Doris. The number of men deployed was also unwise, and had they had separate escape points, then fewer would have been killed.

The joint funeral of O'Donnell and O'Farrell was conducted in the expected paramilitary style, led by a bagpiper and their coffins draped in tricolours, complete with black berets and gloves. During the service in Coalisland, the officiating priest – Father MacLarnon – was predictably critical of the soldiers; no surprise there, but he did, in fairness, plead with IRA leaders – Adams and McGuinness were amongst the mourners – to replace the 'politics of confrontation' with the 'politics of cooperation', which caused local Sinn Féin councillor Francis Molloy to storm out of the church apparently in a sulk. O'Donnell's sister, Róisín Ui Mhuiri, with breathtaking hypocrisy raged: 'We demand the truth about the circumstances of the deaths of Peter, Patrick, Sean and Barry. We know the truth – our sons, brothers, were killed in a well-planned ambush.'

The *Daily Express* of Monday 17th, led with: 'Four Die as Troops Ambush IRA Gang'. Pat Mullarkey wrote:

> Four IRA gunmen were killed by the SAS late last night following an attack on a remote Ulster police station. The troops and police ambushed the heavily armed gang as they escaped after opening fire at Clonoe near Coalisland . . . Residents said there were large numbers of troops in the area before the terrorists' arrival – suggesting that security forces were tipped off about the operation. The raid mounted by the IRA's South Tyrone Brigade was intended to lure police from the station into a terrorist ambush. Early this morning, troops were combing the staunchly Republican area in search of booby-trap bombs intended for policemen pursuing the terrorists.

The same newspaper kept the story going the following day. John Twomey wrote:

> Exploding flares suddenly lit up the night sky and the IRA hit-squad led by Kevin O'Donnell realised that they had stumbled into a trap. Black-clad SAS men blasted them with automatic weapons and after a bloody 10-minute battle, six of the gang lay dead or wounded – betrayed by a tip-off . . . one IRA man fired indiscriminately around him, sending a hail of red tracer bullets close to nearby houses. Then, as a deathly silence fell, the SAS team emerged from their ambush cover. They took off their black balaclavas and put on peaked caps with the word 'Army' in fluorescent letters as they moved around the scene. One resident said: 'When the shooting started, the bullets flew up the lane past the houses. They seemed to be tracer bullets with a red glow. The next thing, I saw a blue light flashing at St Michael's church. The soldiers had a cordon up, but they let the priest and myself through.

> A man was lying in the driveway wounded, and the priest went over to him. But a policeman said it was all right – that the man had only a flesh wound. His shirt was pulled off him and there was a lot of blood.'

On the same page, John Twomey and Philip Derbyshire, under a headline of 'SAS Catches up with Baby-Faced Terrorist', discussed the recent acquittal of O'Donnell, who had managed to walk free from the Old Bailey despite being found in a car with two AK-47s and having traces of Semtex on his clothes. O'Donnell had made the following statement to the court: 'I do not support the IRA. I don't agree with killing and bombing. I come from a devout Catholic family. There's no way I support the taking of life.' The latest recruit to the IRA's England team was freed and deported back to Ireland, to keep on killing. A few months before their deaths, he and O'Farrell were arrested again; the *Express* takes up the story: 'He was found with an assault rifle, ammunition and a rocket warhead near his home in Coalisland. Caught with him was Sean O'Farrell, who also died in the SAS ambush, but both men were freed within two weeks when the charges against them were inexplicably withdrawn. O'Donnell was known locally as the "Kalashnikov Kid".' The newspaper also stated that he was sent to mainland Britain as a 'sleeper agent' enrolling as a student at Harper Adams Agricultural College.

On the 17th, Sinn Féin held their annual Ard Fheis in Ballyfermot, Dublin. A document, 'Towards a Lasting Peace in Ireland' (Sinn Féin, 1992), was launched during the conference. At the conference, a minute's silence was held for the four PIRA men killed at Dernagh. Five days later, Proinsias de Rossa, together with five other Workers' Party TDs, walked out of a party meeting in Dublin, later announcing that they were forming a new organisation called New Agenda (the name was later changed to Democratic Left). De Rossa had sought an assurance from party leaders that they had ended their association with the Official IRA; this was apparently not forthcoming.

Later that same day, the IPLO raised the sectarian stakes a notch higher, when it killed a 17-year-old youth who was helping out in a video shop in the Ballysillian area. Andrew Johnson was a young apprentice mechanic turned shop-worker, who was trying to earn a 'few bob' extra. One of the shop staff had been a member of the UVF and this was known to the Republican terror group. Just before closing time, as Andrew worked with a female colleague, two gunmen walked in; they were IPLO men, one of whom I know only as 'Charles' and the other was Conor Maguire. Just seconds before they walked in, the female worker had knelt below the counter in order to pack some shelves; the gunmen shot the innocent boy several times in the head and he died instantly. The dead lad was a church worker, and was about to become engaged to his girlfriend, Julie. The Republicans had gone out that evening to North Belfast with the sole intention of killing a Protestant; any Protestant would do.

In *Lighting Candles* David Leslie writes of the moment that the IPLO learned that the man they had killed that night was innocent. He quotes a gang member, Manny, as saying: 'What really sickened me was that when I went to see Charles, he was actually laughing.' The murder was claimed by the IPLO and naturally, they tried to claim that the dead man was UVF. The UVF however, was certain that they knew the identities of the killers, and from that moment, Maguire had just over two months to live (*see* Chapter 16).

There were two deaths on the 24th; one was prosaic – certainly by the standards of the Troubles – the other, horrific and brutal, but they caused grief in two households: one in Morecambe in north-west England, the other in Armagh. Earlier in the day, Private David Alexander Hatfield (19), a soldier in the King's Own Royal Borders, was killed in a car crash in the Londonderry area. He was one month short of his 20th birthday; his funeral was held at Lancaster and Morecambe Crematorium. Later, in East Belfast, a young Catholic mother, on her first visit to the capital city, fell into the bestial hands of the UVF. Anne-Marie Smyth (26) was the mother of two young children; she lived on the Catholic Longstone Estate in Armagh City and had taken the train to Belfast. No one will ever know why she strayed into Loyalist East Belfast, but it may have been a chance meeting with Loyalists in Belfast city centre who befriended her and lured her to the Ravenhill district. What is known is that her lifeless body was found in Ballarat Street, on the eastern side of the River Lagan. The spot where her body was found is close to Ormeau Embankment, deep in the heart of Loyalist territory, a place where the UVF and UFF vied for control.

Known as very pleasant and outgoing, but naïve about the outside world, she may have good-naturedly and innocently revealed that she was a Catholic to people she thought were new friends. After being lured to a house in Cregagh Street, she was taken to a bedroom where she was strangled, and beaten in a most vicious way by women as well as men. There was so much blood in the room that her killers were forced to take the carpets and bedding outside to be burned; later, they returned to repaint the entire room to eradicate any signs of the murder. Finally, she was carried or driven from Cregagh Street to Ballarat Street, a distance of 1.6 miles, by men who pretended to passers-by that the dying or possibly already dead woman was drunk. They finally reached waste ground overlooking the Lagan, where her throat was cut right back to the spine, in the manner of Lenny Murphy and the Shankill Butchers. Her body was dumped there; and two young children in Armagh would never see their mummy again. Political observers believe that the killers all had UVF connections and this savage murder was purely sectarian. In March 1997, the killers were finally brought to justice, with several men and women jailed for their part in this murder after a long and complex court case. Police sources say they believe that up to a dozen people were involved in the murder in various ways. One of the men who was jailed, said to be the ringleader, was described by the judge as 'a Catholic-hating UVF man' who headed the organisation in East Belfast; it was recommended that he serve 25 years. Anne-Marie Smyth's two young children were raised by their grandfather, Frank.

On the final two days of the month – the 28th and 29th in this leap year – the IRA's England team exploded two bombs in the centre of London. On Friday 28th, in echoes of Victoria station almost exactly one year earlier, they detonated a bomb at London Bridge station that injured 28 people. During the morning rush hour, a PIRA operative planted a medium-sized device in the men's toilets, timed to detonate at 08:30. When the blast occurred, 28 people were hit by debris and shards of glass. The *Los Angeles Times* reported:

> A bomb planted by the Irish Republican Army exploded in the men's room of a busy London rail station during the morning rush hour Friday, spraying glass shards for 40 feet and injuring 28 people, four of them seriously, authorities said. Less than nine minutes before the blast, a caller using a known IRA code word told Ulster Television's London bureau that a bomb had been planted in a central

> London rail station, police said. 'I am satisfied this was a typical, irresponsible, criminal and callous act carried out by the Provisional IRA,' said Cmdr. George Churchill-Coleman, chief of Scotland Yard's anti-terrorism unit. He said that the warning gave too little time for evacuation and that the bomb was designed to kill. The blast occurred at 8:30 a.m. in a platform restroom just as a crowded commuter train pulled into the London Bridge rail and subway station. The station is the fifth-busiest in the capital, handling 120,000 passengers a day. Police quickly shut all railway and subway stations in the capital to search for other possible bombs. None were found, but the shutdown snarled traffic, forcing many commuters to walk. 'I was knocked through the air like the man of the flying trapeze,' said Thomas Cranmer, 79, of Bexley, who was standing near the men's room when the blast occurred, smashing five large plate-glass windows near the roof of the room. 'They say I blacked out for about two minutes.' The 28 injured people were admitted to Guy's Hospital, most with shock, ringing ears and cuts.

Finally, just twenty-four hours later, they planted a device outside the Crown Prosecution Service building in High Holborn. A small 2 lb device (less than 1 kg) was left against an outside wall. The blast damaged the building and nearby parked cars, injuring two people. Later on the same day, another small device exploded outside a Burger King restaurant in the same area, close to Furnival Street.

February was finally over and another bloody month came to an end. Following the deaths of 15 people, February proved to be even worse, with 20 killed. The most damning statistics of the month were the deaths of 13 civilians, all in sectarian attacks, the worst equal monthly figures for several years. There had been 35 deaths in the first 60 days of the year, and 26 had been civilians. This was almost half of the previous year's total in just two months.

15
March

Deaths were down this month to 'only' four; these were a policeman and a soldier, and three Catholics, who were slain in sectarian killings.

On Sunday 1 March, early in the morning, a man walking his dog close to White Hart Lane in Tottenham, North London discovered a suspect device, close to Spurs' football ground. Later that day, 30,000 fans were due to watch Spurs play Nottingham Forest in the League Cup semi-final. The device was only 400 yards from the ground and placed on a route thousands of football fans would use. The bomb squad was called in and the device was safely defused. Nottingham Forest won the game 2–1 to book a Wembley appearance against Manchester United the following month.

On the 2nd, there was news which would have thrilled *An Phoblacht*'s IRA apologists, when an accusation of collusion was proven in a Belfast Court. Two UDR soldiers, Andrew David Smith, 29 years old, and Andrew Neville Browne, 25, were convicted, along with a third man, of 'aiding and abetting' the UFF in the killing of Loughlin Maginn on 25 August 1989. Republicans have almost always played the 'collusion' card whenever the Loyalists killed any Catholic and, sadly, they were shown to be correct on this rare occasion. In the overwhelming number of murders carried out by Loyalists, there was nothing which even closely resembled the faintest hint of collusion. *An Phoblacht* editorial staff conveniently overlook the instances when members of An Garda Síochána conspired with Republican terror groups to attack and kill members of the SF. There were numerous times when border *gardaí* telephoned PIRA units, especially the one commanded by Sean 'the Surgeon' Hughes, and warned them of SF activities. On two occasions, movements of British High Court judges were betrayed to Hughes and in both instances violent death resulted.

Also on the 2nd, Libyan President Muammar Gaddafi announced that he was breaking his country's links with the IRA, confirming that he would no longer be supplying them with arms or ammunition. This was a major blow to the Provisionals, but there were still the Irish-Americans, and the crumbling USSR to help maintain the killing and maiming.

On the 4th, the UVF killed a well-known lorry driver in the Armagh area, not because they suspected that he was a Republican and not just because he was a Catholic, although this alone could have been enough to seal his fate in their eyes. He was killed because he was a popular, hard-working Catholic who did not fit their cosy but paranoid view of how a Roman Catholic should behave. James Gray (39), father of five, delivered stone and other building materials to construction sites, using a very distinctive red and yellow lorry. On this day he had to deliver materials from his depot in Portadown to the town of Markethill, a distance of about 12 miles, which allowing for traffic would take around 20 minutes.

A three-man UVF murder gang lay in wait along his expected route, and as he reached countryside between Marlacoo Road and Cornascreeb, just five miles from his destination, he was attacked. Gunmen opened fire with automatic weapons, including an AK-47, hitting him around a dozen times, as they fired upwards of 20 rounds. He was killed almost instantly and his lorry crashed into the side of the road. The UVF claimed the murder, the 25th sectarian killing of the year so far.

On the 5th, a PIRA bombing unit drove a stolen car containing 1,000 lb (450 kg) of home-made explosives into the centre of Lurgan, parking as close as they could get to the RUC station. A warning was given and a bomb-disposal team was sent for, but they judged the device as too dangerous to attempt to defuse. The area was cleared and when the explosion came, it caused extensive damage to several commercial properties, including two banks, as well as some structural damage to the police station; there were no casualties. However, just 36 miles away across Co. Tyrone, between Augher and Clogher, an Army patrol was attacked by a PIRA gun team. The patrol was hit as a large landmine exploded, seriously injuring one of the soldiers, and gunmen also opened fire with automatic weapons. There were no reported hits on either side. As the border with the Republic was only three miles away, the PIRA team made it back to the South. The wounded soldier was picked up by helicopter and evacuated to hospital. Just four days later, the Tyrone Provisionals were in action again, when they planted a bomb at a petrol station on the Ballygawley to Dungannon road. They forced the staff out at gunpoint before destroying the premises; they justified this wanton destruction on the basis that the station had been supplying 'Crown Forces'.

On the 10th, John Major announced that the next general election was to be held on 9 April. On the same day, the IRA's London team was up to its usual deadly tricks. A small device exploded at one of London's suburban railway stations, although there were no injuries. Later on, a bomb was found in a trackside junction box near Wandsworth Common station, following a warning telephone call. Earlier, the Garda had uncovered a device, estimated at 3,500 lb (1,590 kg) together with a number of weapons at Drumkeen in Co. Donegal, 14 miles from the border with the North. Finally on that politically momentous day, London's Liverpool Street station was closed and all passengers evacuated following a warning from the IRA; however, after an extensive search, no bombs were discovered.

On the 12th, Army officer Captain Nigel Harold Edwin French (43) died on duty in the Province. The Northern Ireland Veterans' Association originally had him listed as UDR, but the National Memorial Arboretum Roll of Honour states that he was Royal Artillery. I have no further details, other than it may have been due to natural causes whilst on duty.

After a 'break' of eight days without a sectarian killing, the UFF's 'C' company was again in action, this time making the four-minute car journey from the Balaclava Road area to Alliance Avenue in the Ardoyne. A three-man murder gang – including two brothers from the Shankill – turned up at the house of Patrick McCartan (32). At around 19:30, Mr McCartan was about to go out when there was a knock at the door. As he opened it, one of the UFF gunmen shot him in the face, groin and arm. Without a word, the gunmen walked back to their waiting car and sped away. Mr McCartan's mother desperately tried to comfort her fatally wounded son, whispering a prayer into his ear. He was rushed to the nearby Mater Hospital, but died within an hour of the shooting. Meanwhile, the two brothers were taken to a safe house in order to remove any forensics, whilst the gun was cleaned and returned to Adair's armoury. The UFF claimed that the dead man was a member of the IPLO which was utter nonsense; they later claimed that he was a member of the IRA's 3rd battalion. The killing was sectarian; nothing more, nothing less. Lister and Jordan refer to the reason for their actions as 'dodgy intelligence'.[1]

On the 15th, a PIRA team situated just 100 yards inside the Irish Republic set up three heavy machine guns, thought to be two M-60s and a DShK similar to the one seized at Dernagh the previous month. The three fearsome weapons were mounted on tripods and opened fire on two Army helicopters as they were flying close to Rosslea, Co. Fermanagh, on the Northern side. Although well over 1,000 rounds were fired, the two aircraft continued flying and there was no reported damage.

On Tuesday 24th, a PIRA bombing team left a stolen car, packed with 1,100 lb (500 kg) of home-made explosives in Donegall Pass, Belfast, very close to the RUC station in Pakenham Street. The bomb caused extensive damage to property in the surrounding area, including commercial premises, as well as badly damaging the station. Additionally, over a hundred homes were also damaged. An innocent Catholic had a very lucky escape on the same day, when a UFF team attempted to murder him. Two UFF men, including Glen 'Titch' Cunningham, were attempting to get into his house, when they were confronted by the Catholic man. They opened fire, but fortunately missed him as he sought cover; they then ran off; Cunningham was later jailed for 25 years.

On the 27th, the IRA's South Down unit killed a female police officer, Colleen McMurray (34), in Newry, Co. Down; she became the first female RUC officer to die at the hands of terrorists since Tracey Doak in 1985. Constable McMurray was only recently married at the time of her murder. The IRA had set up a Mark XII mortar, to be fired in the horizontal position; the device had been placed in a car with a hole cut into the side to allow the missile to pass through. Ingeniously, they had covered the hole with flimsy cardboard, painted the same colour as the car's bodywork. However, their technology had also advanced in an unexpected manner. The device was triggered electronically by an ordinary camera flashbulb; all it took was someone posing as a photographer, using flash to illuminate their photo. At 23:30 on the 26th, an RUC mobile patrol passed into the killing zone in Merchants' Quay, alongside the Newry River. The IRA man – rumoured to be Patrick Joseph 'Mooch' Blair – pointed his camera at the car, pressed the shutter, the bulb flashed and the mortar tore towards its target. It later emerged that RUC Special Branch were aware of an impending attack, but rather than compromise informant Kevin Fulton – real name Peter Keeley – they allowed the attack to go ahead. A former RUC officer has told me that, in his and many people's opinion, South region SB were 'dirty'.

The device shattered the RUC vehicle, literally tearing it apart. Constable McMurray was mortally wounded, suffering terrible injuries; a male colleague had both legs torn off. Both were rushed to Daisy Hill Hospital in the town, where surgeons fought to save her life; she died in the early hours of the 27th. She was trapped in the wreckage for over 10 minutes, as rescuers fought to cut her out; it is thought that if she could have begun receiving medical treatment just 10 minutes earlier than she did, she might have survived. The injured male officer was Paul Slaine; inside Daisy Hill, doctors pumped 66 pints of blood into him, but

1. Lister and Jordan, *Mad Dog*, p. 130.

it was pouring out as fast as they put it in. In addition to the loss of his legs, his throat was slashed wide open and both of his hands were so badly mangled that doctors were forced to consider amputation.

It is alleged that former British soldier Kevin Fulton, who was encouraged to join the Provisionals and act as an informer, was involved in the development of this latest technology. Fulton travelled to the USA and helped develop light-sensitive triggers, activated by photographic flashes. This was to overcome the problem of IRA remote-control devices having their detonation signal jammed by Army radio units. 'Mooch' Blair was named by an MP in the House of Commons in 2002 as having 'helped to construct the Omagh bomb' and taken part in a series of other deadly attacks. 'Mooch' has always denied any involvement in the Omagh atrocity. He had been convicted in 1975 for the attempted murder of a constable but was released in 1982; he was convicted again of possession of ammunition in 2003.

The next day, the UVF killed a man in Co. Armagh, inside the 'murder triangle', simply because he was a Catholic, although they subsequently attempted to justify the murder on the spurious grounds that the victim was a member of the Provisionals. Craigavon hospital porter Terence McConville (43), father of three, lived in Bann Street in Portadown, close to the HQ of the UVF's mid-Ulster brigade. He and his wife Joan were in bed when three masked UVF gunmen – Laurence Maguire, Robin King and Ralph Phillips – broke into their house and began to make their way upstairs. Alerted by sounds, Mr McConville walked onto the landing and confronted them; their response was to shoot him several times in the chest and face. Leaving the dying man outside his bedroom door, the killers ran downstairs and out of the house. Joan McConville chased them down the street in her bare feet, but the men vanished. She told the *Belfast Telegraph*: 'I could have torn them to pieces with my bare hands. They have brought hate into a home which has only known loving.' Mark 'Swinger' Fulton was quizzed about the murder of Mr McConville, although he was never charged. Later, Joan McConville posted an obituary in the local newspapers, referring to her husband's killers as 'terrorist scum'. I find her words very difficult to argue with. Laurence Maguire from Moira was later jailed for five sectarian murders – he also killed Charles and Teresa Fox – and was subsequently found guilty of killing Mr McConville.

At the end of the month, the Fair Employment Commission published a report on the religious composition of the workforce, based on returns from over 1,700 employers in Northern Ireland. The report showed that Catholics made up 35% of those employed but 38% of those actually available for work. Progress had been made – something which the IRA never acknowledged – but there was still much to be done before there was complete equality in the Province. At around the same time, *The Times* published details of a MORI opinion poll, aimed at discovered British – but mainly English – attitudes towards Northern Ireland. Of those questioned, 31% said they were in favour of Northern Ireland becoming independent, 29% favoured the region remaining part of the UK, with 23% being in favour of a united Ireland.

As March came to an end, deaths were just five, considerably down on the first two months of the year.

16
April

Thirteen people died this month, including three soldiers, one of whom was killed in a mainland attack by the IRA; another Army civvie worker was killed and three civilians were killed by an IRA bomb in London. Three paramilitaries died but, worryingly, there were three more sectarian deaths, including the passing of a man wounded in January.

All Fools Day 1992 saw the UVF's own version of the 'nutting squad' in action in Co. Armagh, as they 'executed' Peter McClements (43), father of two, for 'treason'. He had been in the UDR some years previously, but had been asked to resign because of his UVF connections. He had been a member of the mid-Ulster brigade and may have had a disagreement with 'The Jackal' Robin Jackson or even 'King Rat' himself, Billy Wright.

McClements lived in Lower Toberhewney Lane, Lurgan, and late that evening, as he arrived home, a two-man murder gang was lying wait for him in the Loyalist Mourneview Estate. As he approached his house, the men stepped from the shadows and opened fire with automatic weapons, cutting him down and mortally wounding him. The killers ran off into the night, just as two local off-duty nurses, alerted by the sound of gunfire, came dashing across to help the stricken man, Despite their best efforts to save his life as he lay on his back lawn, he died at the scene. A later UVF statement would only admit that he had been shot because he had been 'informing on the organisation'.

In what was becoming a depressingly familiar incident, Loyalist paramilitaries killed an innocent Catholic on the 2nd of the month, in Co. Londonderry. Danny Cassidy (40) was the father of four children. He had done some electioneering work on behalf of Sinn Féin, but the UFF alleged that he was a member of the Provisional IRA. Unfortunately he had come in for some over-zealous attention from the RUC, a point which the Loyalists had noted. It must be remembered that police officers were being killed and maimed by the very persons whom Mr Cassidy supported and there was inevitably some resentment from them. He lived in Bladden Place, Kilrea, in Co. Londonderry. Driving home at around 15:00, as he was about to turn from Coleraine Street into Bladden Place, he spotted a neighbour and stopped for a chat. In what was clearly a well-planned ambush, two masked UFF gunmen walked over to his car and opened fire with automatic weapons, killing him almost instantly with shots to the face and chest. Naturally, there were accusations of collusion, especially when a montage of photos including the dead man was leaked to the press.

At face value, he was entirely innocent, however Cassidy is referred to as an *'oglach'* – the Irish word for soldier and thus a Provisional IRA volunteer in *Tirghrá*, a book recording fallen IRA volunteers and Republican activists.

There was a rather sick piece of graffiti scrawled on a wall outside Kilrea by Loyalists in the months following Mr Cassidy's murder. I feel the same contempt for both sets of paramilitaries, especially those who taunt loved ones and vandalise memorials. Billy Leonard of Sinn Féin said: 'This sick act is undoubtedly an attempt at annoying local people and raising tensions in the town. It is not the first time that loyalists have mocked Danny Cassidy. Everybody would think that they should have learned by now that such depraved nonsense has no place in this society. It is time that if there are a few people in local loyalism with sense to tell these people to catch on and stop letting everyone know that they have absolutely nothing to give to anyone [*sic*].' Perhaps Mr Leonard could also convey this message to his own party's supporters for their vandalism and desecration of memorials at Warrenpoint, Teebane, Kingsmill and Ligoniel?

On the 4th, Jack McKearney, wounded in an attack on a Catholic-owned shop in Moy in January, unfortunately died as a result of those wounds.

On the 6th, the IRA planted a small device close to London's iconic Eros statue in Piccadilly Circus; there were no injuries. However, this was merely a prelude to the Baltic Exchange blast just four days later.

1992 was a US Presidential Election year; the incumbent President, George Bush, ostensibly confident, knew that he was in a fight to the finish with the man dubbed 'the second John Kennedy', Governor of Arkansas William 'Bill' Clinton. The youthful Clinton was an opportunist politician and, despite the so-called 'special relationship' between the USA and Great Britain, saw the harvesting of Irish-American votes as crucial to his plans for victory and more important than maintaining this 'relationship'. On the 5th, he addressed the American-Irish Presidential Forum in New York City. To the surprise and disgust of the British, he promised to reverse the ban on Gerry Adams entering the USA; later, as President, he welcomed both Adams and McGuinness into the White House and shook their blood-stained hands, thus effectively legitimising the murder campaign of the Provisional IRA. As a further sop to the Irish vote, he agreed to continue the US support for the 'MacBride Principles' (*see* Chapter 6); he agreed to appoint a 'Peace Envoy' to Northern Ireland and, somewhat insultingly, raise the issue of human rights violations with the British government. Clinton was effectively promising continued US interference in the affairs of a foreign country, in order to ingratiate himself with the powerful Irish-American lobby.

Just four days after Presidential hopeful Clinton sucked up to the Irish, John Major had some good news at last. The 'grey man' stepped out of the long shadow of his predecessor, the displaced Margaret Thatcher, climbed on to his 'soap box' (literally) and led the Conservatives to their fourth consecutive general election victory. At the dissolution, Major's government had 376 seats, Kinnock's Labour held 229 and the Liberal Democrats had 22; the opinion polls forecast a slim Labour majority and if this proved correct, Kinnock, who had done so much to improve the party's fortunes, would be the next prime minister. In the event the Conservatives won a working majority of 21 and Kinnock was confirmed as 'yesterday's man'. Interestingly enough, Major, even when the polls were forecasting a Labour victory, told the BBC: 'I am stone cold sober and believe that we will win the election.' One bright spot for decent people, Labour or Tory, was the fact that Adams lost his seat in West Belfast to Joe Hendron of the SDLP, though he was to win it back again in 1997. Towards the end of this new parliament, as the Tories lost by-election after by-election and Major's majority was further reduced, the Unionists were able to increase their influence over matters related to Northern Ireland.

Tragedy struck the day after the election. The IRA's England team had been planting hundreds of devices, some big, some small, some high explosive, some incendiary, for many years now. People had been killed and maimed, but now the terror group were leading up to the 'big one'. Their target was the City of London, the financial heart not just of Britain but also of Europe, historically based in the 'square mile' which comprises Threadneedle Street, the Bank of England, Leadenhall Street, Lloyd's of London and of course, the Stock Exchange. Just half a mile from the Bank of England was the Baltic Exchange in St Mary Axe. Present-day visitors to London will recognise the iconic Gherkin building; the Baltic Exchange previously sat on the very same spot.

On the evening of the 10th, an IRA bombing team drove a white Bedford van, packed with a bomb containing a ton of fertiliser-based explosives, wrapped with a detonation cord made from 100 lb (45 kg) of Semtex into St Mary Axe. A warning of sorts had been telephoned through by the IRA, but at 21:22, with the area still being evacuated, the biggest bomb seen in Britain, let alone London, since Hitler's V-2 missiles of the Second World War, exploded. These weapons had a warhead only slightly larger than that IRA bomb.

The building was devastated – it had to be demolished later – by the enormous blast and tragically, because of the callously inadequate warning given by the Republican terrorists, three people were killed and 91 were injured. In addition to these casualties and the destruction of the Baltic Exchange building, the explosion caused considerable damage to the surrounding commercial properties, including the Commercial Union building. Casualties could have been much higher, but a company dinner planned by a group of ophthalmic surgeons was brought forward to the previous evening. Where they had planned to dine would have been directly in line with where the blast occurred. When the IRA had telephoned their warning through, they had either mistakenly, or perhaps more likely, deliberately, referred to the building as the Stock Exchange – which they had bombed a few years earlier. The Stock Exchange is a mile away from the Baltic Exchange, which gave the police very little chance of saving lives. I firmly believe that this was the IRA's intention. Those killed were Danielle Carter (15) who was sitting in the car which her father – a chauffeur – had driven to the underground carpark in the Commercial Union building. She was blown out of the vehicle, having taken the full force of the blast and was found by her father, lying face-down in a pool of her own blood. Her boyfriend, young sister and another family friend had come along for the trip and to see London; they were all injured and taken to hospital. An ambulance man gathered up Danielle's body and cradled her in his arms, but she was too badly injured to save and all he could do was to assure her that she wasn't alone. She died very shortly afterwards. Thomas Casey (49), father of four, was the doorman at the Baltic and was standing very close to the seat of the explosion; he was killed instantly. Baltic Exchange employee Paul Butt (29) was close to the entrance and he too died immediately.

Just three hours later another IRA bomb devastated shops at Staples Corner Commercial Park, next to the North Circular Road in London. It caused millions of pounds worth of damages, devastated the B&Q DIY building and created even more than the usual traffic chaos in that part of the capital. The Staples Corner bomb was placed in a white Bedford van that had changed hands seven times in ten days, making it very difficult for anti-terrorist police to ascertain the last owners before the explosion. The van was left underneath the flyover on the busy A406 and it was a miracle that no passing motorists were injured in the blast. The explosion causing serious damage to roads and nearby buildings and resulted in the closure of the junction. I was based at nearby Perivale at the time and recall seeing the damaged building many times over the course of the next few years, wondering if it would ever be rebuilt. It has often been speculated that the bomb was intended for the nearby Brent Cross Shopping Centre but that the bombers panicked and dumped the van.

Senior detectives believed that a unit of two or three IRA members had been ordered to carry out a 'one- off spectacular' timed for the day after the general election. The group was believed to have been on the British mainland for only a few days, during which it planned and executed the attack and left within hours; it is widely considered that they were not a part of the England team and in fact, the IRA men already there may have been unaware of their presence, so secretive was the operation. Police were convinced that the same people carried out both explosions because of similarities in the voice of the man who made the two warning calls, which used a recognised code word.

On the following Monday, it was 'business as usual' for a city and its workers, as it demonstrated a latter-day spirit of the Blitz. Contemporary photographs show streets knee-deep in litter, with eddies of shredded and blackened pieces of paper blowing around the rubble, which one bemused worker described as 'confetti.' Hundreds upon hundreds of torn window blinds hung down from the shattered frames and joined in the surreal movement of inanimate objects. Police in uniform as well as Scotland Yard detectives mingled with the crowds of workers, as well as the inevitable rubber-neckers, desperately seeking information which might help identify the bombers. Amongst the buildings damaged were a 13th-century Benedictine nunnery plus countless others of major historical importance. A fellow soldier told the author: 'That would have broken Samuel Pepys's heart.'

Not content with the financial and architectural damage that they had caused, the IRA's England team telephoned through a whole series of bomb hoaxes which caused major hold-ups for London's commuters, causing stations such as Clapham Common to be closed for several hours.

Michael Sangster, Royal Artillery

As the crow flies, I live about three miles from Bishopsgate and that one woke me out of a deep sleep, but the one at the Baltic Exchange was about ¼ mile from where I was working in my office. I remember a huge flash then the building shaking before the sound of the blast hit us. I was managing an executive car company in the City at that time and about a minute after the bomb went off, my telephone system lit up with frantic calls from various Japanese financial companies pleading for cars to take senior executives home . . . money no object. They took every car and driver I had.

Writer and banker Pieter Dorsman wrote:

> The next morning, the day off, I went to the area, camera in hand, and what I witnessed shocked and perplexed me completely. The area that had been damaged not only extended well beyond what anyone would have believed, knowing the location of the bomb; the damage done to that area, now cordoned off by police, was phenomenal. The impact of the explosion had covered the direct area with endless mountains of glass as nearly all of the windows of the adjoining Commercial Union skyscraper were knocked to smithereens. The force had also seriously damaged many other buildings, destroyed windows over a vast area, damaged cars and what amazed me and for some reason stuck in my mind: it left most traffic signs in a very wide area curved. The damage had thus also affected our building at the very end of St Mary Axe, although from the outside things did not look particularly bad. Apparently, there was significant damage and one of the greatest concerns was the structural damage not directly visible to the eye.[1]

A later memorial, remembering the three innocents, was incorporated into the edge of the open area around the Gherkin. Damage was later estimated at £800,000,000, which was more than the combined losses of the past 23 years in Northern Ireland.

The day after the explosion – Saturday 11th – Prime Minister John Major attempted to show the IRA that, as far as he was concerned, it was business as usual and announced the formation of the new Cabinet. Patrick Mayhew was chosen to replace Peter Brooke as Secretary of State for Northern Ireland. There were further changes at the NIO, with Michael Mates becoming deputy secretary of state and minister responsible for security.

Between the 11th and the 13th, the Provisionals stepped up their bombing campaign to keep up the momentum and the political pressure already placed on the new Major government. In those 72 hours, they badly damaged a Protestant-owned shop in Co. Tyrone and then placed a stolen car containing 500 lb (230 kg) of explosives near the RUC interrogation centre in Castlereagh, outside Belfast. The device was defused by ATO personnel and there were no casualties.

On the 13th, a male and a female soldier both lost their lives in the Province in non-terrorist incidents. Corporal John Neill (35) from Glasgow, a member of the Royal Army Medical Corps, died in circumstances I am permitted only to describe as 'death by violent or unnatural causes'. His funeral service was held at the Linn Crematorium in his home town of Glasgow. On the same day UDR 'Greenfinch' Private Heather Elizabeth Sloan (34) was killed in an RTA in the Ballymena area. She is buried in St Lurach's Cemetery in Maghera, Co. Londonderry.

The Irish National Liberation Army (INLA) – Arm Saoirse Náisiúnta na hÉireann – killed some 120 people during the course of its 24-year existence; these included 27 military personnel, 13 RUC members, 4 former police officers and 2 prison officers. Their most notorious murder was that of Airey Neave, MP, by an under-vehicle booby-trap in the House of Commons' car park in April 1979. They confined their killings mainly to Northern Ireland after that but on 14 April they struck again in mainland Britain. Sergeant Michael Newman (34), father of one, a soldier in the Royal Corps of Signals but then attached to

1. Source: http://www.pieterdorsman.com/blog/the-baltic-exchange-bomb.

the Careers' Office in Derby as a recruitment officer, had finished work for the day. He had been observed by the INLA to park his car in Derby city centre each day and this time gunmen lay in wait for him. The murder gang consisted of Michael Duffy, Anthony 'Fanta' Gorman and Joseph Magee. Two of the men stalked the soldier – he was dressed in civvies – as he walked to Liversage Street car park. One of the men then shot Sergeant Newman once in the head, from point-blank range, before they ran off to their getaway car. Only one of the men was ever convicted of the murder: Duffy in 2010. Gorman, the getaway driver, was a native of Co. Armagh.

The dead soldier had been in the Army for 18 years, although he had never served in Northern Ireland. A married man, he was seeking a divorce in order to marry Elizabeth Robinson who was a nurse. Some years later she told the press: 'I still can't rest 22 years after Michael's murder, and neither can his family. At least if [Gorman] was to surrender, I could get some closure. Michael was a lovely man, he was no harm to anyone, and was just a soft target for the gang that killed him.' Some weeks after the murder, the INLA wrote a mocking and sarcastic letter to Sergeant's Newman's parents to heap further grief on them.

At the time of the murder, the British government applied to the High Court in Dublin for the extradition of 'Fanta' Gorman, but this was refused on the flimsiest of grounds by the Irish judges. Gorman was eventually jailed for five years by a Dublin court in 1995, for having 26 weapons, including Kalashnikovs and machine guns, plus 2,500 rounds of ammunition. 'Fanta' is said to be still close to the INLA leadership; today he works as an artist in the town of Bailieborough, Co. Cavan, in the Republic.

Edward 'Ned' McCreery (46) was a former UFF commander who was alleged to be responsible for at least 20 sectarian murders and was known to take sadistic pleasure in the use of torture. He had 'graduated' from sectarian murder to racketeering and drug-dealing, rapidly being famed for his corruption and greed. In 1990, however, an internal UDA inquiry adjudged to him to be a informant for the RUC and to have also passed on information to the IRA. By April 1992, McCreery had stepped down from the UDA/UFF, concentrating on his East Belfast bar which he had financed, it is said, from his corrupt dealings and non-Loyalist activities. The bar was Avenue One on Templemore Avenue, some five miles from his home in Grahamsbridge Road, Dundonald, sandwiched between Comber Road and Upper Newtownards Road, in the heart of Loyalist territory.

On the night of the 15th, as McCreery returned home, UFF gunmen were waiting. When he stepped out of his car, they gunned him down and raced off, leaving the man who was once in the top six of the UDA dying in a pool of his own blood. The UDA/UFF later claimed the killing and stated grandiosely, that their Special Assignment Section had carried out the 'execution of an enemy of Ulster'. A year earlier, Ned McCreery's brother Thomas was forced to leave Northern Ireland after being shot and seriously wounded as he sat in a car outside a social club in the Shankill Road area. The shooting was the result of an internal dispute within the UDA/UFF. The UFF later stated: 'We wish to make it clear that no matter what happens, [Thomas] is still under sentence of death.'

On the 18th, the IRA's South Armagh brigade was responsible for the cold-blooded killing of an Army civvie worker at his home in Armagh City. It was another pointless death, which caused grief and heartbreak in the victim's family and devastated his two children. Brendan McWilliams (51) worked as a storeman at a UDR barracks in Drumadd, Co. Armagh. When the IRA killed him at his home in Killylea Road, he became the ninth and final Army civilian worker to be killed by terrorists.

Mr McWilliams, a Catholic, was a former TA soldier who had been employed by the Army since 1982; he lived with an elderly aunt in Niall's Crescent, a cul-de-sac of white-fronted houses just off Killylea Road in Armagh. Just before midnight, a PIRA murder gang approached his house, and seeing him through the front door's glass panel, opened fire with automatic weapons, hitting their fellow Catholic over a dozen times and mortally wounding him. They drove off into the night, likely in a westerly direction as the Irish border was less than eight miles away, leaving the dying man in his hallway, his distraught aunt trying desperately to comfort him as he breathed his last few gasps of air. I remember this murder with sickening clarity because, a day or two later, a PIRA spokesman made a despicable and mendacious statement 'justifying' the murder and asserting that the dead man had been 'an intelligence officer for the UDR'.

On the 23rd, two former moderators of the Presbyterian Church, sickened by the constant slaughter of the previous 23 years, revealed that they had held private talks with Sinn Féin president Gerry Adams, and leading Sinn Féin member Tom Hartley. This was the first signs of a willingness on the Protestant/Loyalist side to negotiate a way out of the morass of endless murder.

There were to be two more killings this month; one was a matter of karma for an IPLO gunman who had cold-bloodedly slaughtered a 17-year-old Protestant lad as he worked in a video shop; the second was the outrageous sectarian murder of a young Catholic woman as she worked at a pharmacy in Belfast's Springfield Road. Her death would lead to widespread condemnation.

Philomena Hanna (26) was the mother of two very young children; she lived in Dermott Hill, a small cluster of streets to the west of the Whiterock Road, and close to the New Barnsley area. She worked at the Springfield Pharmacy on the Springfield Road, just 1½ miles away. She was well-known and well-liked by both sides of the community and often volunteered to deliver prescriptions and other items across the 'peace line' into Loyalist territory. The shop no longer exists but stood at the bottom end of Lanark Way, a 500-yard-long road that connects the Loyalist Shankill Road to the Nationalist Springfield Road. It was a conduit down which Loyalist murder gangs drove to carry out sectarian murders and was occasionally sealed off by 'peace gates'. In the days before the murder, UFF commander Johnny Adair – whose face was well-known to many Catholics in the area – was spotted, brazenly carrying out what later transpired to be a scouting mission.

The 28th was a Tuesday morning and as Ms Hanna – mother of a six-year-old and a one year old – arrived at work, a Loyalist murder team was already preparing a stolen Suzuki motorcycle a few hundred yards away. Twenty minutes after the innocent Catholic – considered a 'saint' by Protestants and Catholics alike – arrived at work, a two-man UFF murder gang drove down Lanark Way, turned left onto Springfield Road, before turning and parking outside the shop. One man –Stephen 'Top Gun' McKeag – wearing a motorcycle helmet, walked inside and calmly shot Ms Hanna at very close range; as she slumped, mortally wounded, to the floor, he then fired several more rounds into her body; then, almost nonchalantly, re-joined his accomplice on the motorbike before returning along Lanark Way. He was known to refer to that route as the 'Yellow Brick Road' – and indeed eyewitnesses heard him singing 'Follow the Yellow Brick Road' as he headed towards the Shankill after the murder.

A later statement from the UFF was as deceitful as their attack had been violent and cowardly; the dead woman was accused of being an 'intelligence officer' for the Provisional IRA. They claimed to have based the attack on 'high-grade intelligence', a claim later dismissed by an RUC officer who said: 'If that was high grade intelligence, I wouldn't like to see their low-grade intelligence!' Hugh Jordan also wrote: 'The murder of Philomena Hanna set off something in Stevie McKeag. Over the next 18 months he waged an almost single-handed murder campaign that would write him into Loyalist mythology but also provoke more than a tinge of envy in Johnny Adair.'[1] The Loyalist terror group claimed, wrongly, that she was involved in the planting of a bomb under Gerry Drumgoole's car (*see* Chapter 11) and incorrectly labelled her as being the sister of a top Republican, Richard McAuley.

Ms Hanna was related to a McAuley – through her sister's marriage – but not the Republican cited by the UFF. Leontia McCauley said this of her sister: 'When Philomena died no police or police liaison officer came to our family to tell us that she had died. They fired bullets at her face and chest. When my father went to identify her body he fell on top of Philomena and cried. As he came home later we noticed that he had blood all over his shirt.'

The full UFF statement read:

> The UFF acting on top grade intelligence carried out this morning's assassination of female PIRA member Philomena Hanna, sister of Sinn Féin/PIRA member Richard McAuley. The UFF and the loyalist people have seen as recently as last week the central role females are playing within the republican war machine. The UFF wish to state once again that we make no distinction between male and female members of PIRA. The Government and the Northern Ireland Office should take note that no amount of failed security force policies will deter us from ridding Ulster of the cancer of republicanism once and for all.

I repeat: this was a vile mendacity!

The following day, the UVF shot and killed IPLO man Conor Maguire (26) as he worked in the Ligoniel Community Association Centre, just north-west of Belfast. Forty days earlier, he had been one of the men who had killed Andrew Johnson in Ballysillian. For 40 days, he had been a marked man and had taken to wearing a flak jacket, aware that Loyalists knew that he had killed the boy and would eventually be coming after him. Maguire, described as 'a real weasel-faced man, with brains of a newt' by an RUC acquaintance of mine, lived in the Ligoniel area, but must have hoped that he was safe in Nationalist territory. Earlier in the evening, a UVF gang had hijacked a taxi on the Shankill Road; gunmen, armed with 9 mm Brownings and an AK-47, drove towards Ligoniel. They parked close to Maguire's place of work on Conneywarren Lane, with two of them walking into the works, before singling out the IPLO man. They shot him six times in the chest;

1. Lister & Jordan, *Mad Dog*, pp. 130–1, 133.

several of the rounds penetrated the body armour but other shots to the head proved to be fatal. They ran out, leaving him lying in an ever-spreading pool of his own blood, just as he had left young Andrew Johnson.

Cusack and MacDonald in their excellent *UVF: The Endgame* highlight an incident a few days later when Maguire's funeral cortège passed through his home village; angry Loyalists threw eggs at the cortège. 'More lives were almost lost several days later at his funeral when crowds of Loyalists attacked mourners, including leading IPLO members such as Jimmy Brown, when the cortège passed by the Protestant part of Ligoniel.'[1]

April was over, and 13 more people lay dead. A total of 53 people had died in the first four months of 1992 alone.

1. Cusack and MacDonald, *UVF: The Endgame*, pp. 284–5.

17
May

Five people died this month, four soldiers and one civilian. There were just two terrorist-related deaths, but the month did witness another senseless sectarian attack on a bar, again involving the IPLO.

Cloughoge (sometimes spelled 'Cloghoge') is a tiny hamlet, located in a vital strategic area inside the North; situated between Newry and Killeen, it sits close to the main A1/M1 road, which links Dublin to Belfast, and to the Dublin–Belfast railway line. A permanent vehicle checkpoint – known as R15 – was built there, alongside the Forkhill/Drumintree Road, less than a mile from the Irish border. It was less than four miles away from the Three Steps Pub from where undercover soldier Robert Nairac was abducted in 1977, before being tortured and murdered. The Provisionals liked to use the many border crossings and unmarked roads to smuggle personnel, arms and explosives from their caches in the South to places such as Newry, Mayobridge and Warrenpoint. The Royal Engineers did try to make these roads impassable by blowing huge craters in them, but local farmers often filled in the craters or demolished blockades with their heavy agricultural equipment. Nonetheless, much traffic had to pass the PVCP, which played a vital role in curtailing IRA activity. PVCPs had been successfully attacked before and were recognised as very dangerous and exposed positions for the military/RUC personnel manning them.

In the very late hours of 30 April, a gang of four gunmen burst their way into a remote farmhouse at Killeen, a couple of miles from the PVCP. They took the keys for the farm's JCB excavator and drove it to the nearby main railway line where it was used to construct a temporary ramp up which to drive a Renault van which had been stolen from near Dundalk. The tyres had been removed and the metal rims modified so that they would run on the railway lines. Inside the van was 2,200 lb (1,000 kg) of home-made explosives with a Semtex detonator, similar to the one used the previous month at the Baltic Exchange. The digger was used to lift it onto the railway lines. It was ingenious, well-planned and very carefully thought out, showing that the Provisional IRA could be very clever, unconventional and resourceful.

At the time this work was being carried out, at least a dozen PIRA men, wearing stolen Garda Síochána uniforms – allegedly supplied by a sympathiser inside the Garda – set up fake VCPs on the Irish side of the border, in the Carrickcarnan/Dromad area. They also set up other VCPs on the Northern side to isolate the soldiers at the PVCP. At this stage, the van was driven about half a mile north along the tracks before a command wire – incredibly over a mile in length – was attached to the massive bomb. Around 02:00 on the 1st, the van was set in motion along the tracks, moving in the direction of the checkpoint, at that time being manned by the Royal Regiment of Fusiliers (RRF). The van's progress was monitored by a PIRA man equipped with binoculars and a radio; he spotted a soldier, who had been alerted by the noise of what he thought at first was a train; as the mobile bomb drew level with the base, the PIRA man radioed the command wire operative who immediately detonated the bomb.

The soldier was Fusilier Andrew James Grundy (22) from Ferryhill, Co. Durham; he had fired several shots from his SA-80 at the van in the vain hope of stopping it. He also had the presence of mind to press an intercom and shout: 'Proxy bomb. Back gate.' The explosion devastated the PVCP, killing the young soldier instantly and actually lifting a stone sangar off its foundations and hurling it 30 feet away, such was the force of the blast. Twenty-three soldiers were injured, some badly, but other military and RUC personnel survived inside a reinforced bunker, albeit with cuts and bruises. Gunmen on high ground opened fire, but there were no further casualties. One of the soldiers, Fusilier G. Colman, retrieved his dead comrade's body and for this action, as well as rescuing other wounded men, was later awarded a General Officer Commanding commendation (GOC) for his courage under fire. A subsequent report on the incident by senior British officers stated: 'This was a well-planned and well-executed attack indicative of the imaginative, innovative and capable nature of South Armagh PIRA.' The death of this soldier was a second tragedy for the Grundy family; they had lost Andrew's brother Philip in an RTA whilst he was serving with the Army in Germany. The dead soldier's father told the *Belfast Telegraph*: 'Now we hope to be able to bury Andrew alongside; we would like the boys to be together if that's possible.'

Fusilier Grundy was the 27th and penultimate soldier from his regiment to die in Northern Ireland. He is buried at Duncombe Cemetery in Co. Durham. One of the soldiers who survived the attack at Cloughoge that day was Lance Corporal Michael Beswick. Sadly this young NCO had only nine months left to live. On 9 February 1993, he died of wounds received in an IRA bomb blast in Armagh City (*see* Chapter 26).

The following morning's *Daily Express* clearly thought that the concurrent riots in Los Angeles eclipsed the anarchic violence of the IRA and relegated the story of the Cloughoge attack to page 13. Under the headline 'Soldier died to save his friends', Alan Qualtrough and Steve Crowther wrote:

> A hero soldier gave his own life to save troops and police in an IRA bomb blast yesterday. Fusilier Andrew Grundy stood his ground as 1,000 lb. [*sic*] of explosives came hurtling down a railway line towards a checkpoint. He screamed at his comrades to dive for cover but he had no time to save himself. The bomb devastated the fortified post near Newry . . . close to the Irish border. Last night, Northern Ireland Minister, Michael Mates paid tribute to Andrew's courage. 'Because of that, other soldiers who might have been wounded or killed were not, and that is a very commendable thing indeed,' he said. Andrew . . . told his mother, May he would be returning to England within weeks with his Irish girlfriend, Helen . . . His 46-year-old mother wept as she said: 'You couldn't print what I think about the bastards who did this.' His father Eric, 47, said: 'They are cowards. What I think about them is unprintable. Andrew phoned us at 7 p.m. on Thursday. He was very happy. He told us he was going out with a girl

> from Northern Ireland.' . . . Ten homes were reduced to rubble in the 2 a.m. blast which left a 20 ft crater.

The next morning, acting on a tip-off from an informer, Garda officers uncovered a large cache of arms, including 51 automatic rifles, in a concealed bunker at a farm near Newmarket, Co. Cork. This was 230 miles south of the partition with the North, belying the theory that the IRA only located caches close to the border.

On Tuesday 5th, an inquest looked at the deaths of PIRA men Eugene Toman, Sean Burns and Gervaise McKerr who were shot dead at Tullygally East Road, near Lurgan, Co. Armagh on 11 November 1982. As this took place, there was murder in the hearts of the IPLO. Billy Sargent (66), father of three grown-up children, lived on the Limestone Road; he was a regular drinker in the Mount Inn on North Queen Street, He was a Protestant and the bar was known to be frequented mainly by Protestants, plus the odd Catholic who certainly didn't advertise his faith. The pub was a short walk from Mr Sargent's home, but it was right on the sectarian interface between the Loyalist Tiger's Bay area and the Nationalist New Lodge. Mr Sargent was drinking at the bar when a lone gunman walked in and without speaking, unleashed several bursts of automatic fire, spraying bullets indiscriminately as the drinkers dived for cover. Mr Sargent was hit in the back of the head, dying instantly; another man was hit in the back and critically injured, with several others receiving minor wounds. The gunman ran outside to a waiting car and disappeared in the direction of the New Lodge. Two of Mr Sargent's sons went to the pub to identify their father, but police refused them access because of the horrific scenes inside. A friend of mine described it as 'like a butcher's shop, blood everywhere and a stench of cordite and that sickly metallic smell of blood'.

An SDLP spokesman referred to the IPLO as 'scum that floats on the surface, a criminal gang'. The organisation was as sectarian as any of its Loyalist paramilitary counterparts and it was around this time that it split itself again; two separate factions emerged: the IPLO Army Council and the IPLO Belfast Brigade. As Andrew Sanders writes in his *Inside the IRA*, 'It is significant that both groups were so keen to maintain the IPLO brand, the organisation having done more to divide Republicanism in its short existence than arguably any other group. Following the divide, the IPLO began to turn its guns on its own members; Jimmy Brown was killed by the IPLO-BB faction on 18 August 1992, with retaliatory killings taking place over the following months before the spiral of violence was finally cut short by the intervention of the Provisional IRA.' Mr Sanders then describes the 'night of the long knives attack' on 31 October[1] (*see* Chapter 22 of this book).

On the 8th, Home Secretary Kenneth Baker tried to allay public fears about the increasing violence employed by the IRA's England team by announcing a shake-up in intelligence-gathering. Henceforth, he stated, responsibility would pass from the Metropolitan Police's Special Branch to MI5. SB had failed to prevent terror raids on the mainland and the two recent 'welcome to government' bombs at the Baltic Exchange and Staples Corner had shown that the IRA considered themselves above counter-intelligence, clearly feeling that they could strike with impunity. Given that the IRA would go on to cause billions of pounds worth of damage in places such as Bishopsgate and Manchester,

1. Andrew Sanders, *Inside the IRA* (Edinburgh University Press, 2011), p. 196.

dwarfing previous losses, it might seem that MI5 was no more successful than SB. However, it is the attacks and bombs they prevented, which never came to the public attention, that are the mark of their success in the later years of the Troubles.

On the 9th of the month, the Staffordshires lost one of their men, Sergeant Dean Oliver, in the Fivemiletown area in Co. Fermanagh. Several days before, a PIRA bombing unit had placed a 1,000 lb (450 kg) device outside the RUC station, with the resultant explosion devastating the base. The Regiment's 1st Battalion was called in to protect the crews of workmen who were to demolish the ruins and help rebuild. A young soldier aged 18, whose name cannot be revealed, had a mental breakdown causing him to open fire with his SA-80, shooting Sergeant Dean Oliver (30). The NCO was hit seven times, dying in front of the shocked members of his platoon. The soldier was tried by a court in Enniskillen and charged with murder; he alleged that he had been provoked and somewhat surprisingly, was found not guilty. Sergeant Oliver was from Silverdale, Newcastle-under-Lyme, and is buried at the municipal cemetery there.

On the 11th, a UDR soldier, Private Stephen David Scanlon (24) of Newtownstewart, was killed in an RTA on one of Co. Tyrone's dangerous roads. He is buried at Ardstraw Parish Cemetery.

The Parachute Regiment is widely considered the elite of Britain's armed forces, serving with distinction through a world war, in the Suez Crisis and notably in the 1982 Falklands Conflict. It is axiomatic that they didn't exactly cover themselves in glory in Londonderry on 'Bloody Sunday', but they were being used in the wrong role there, and for that I blame both the Heath government and HQNI who allowed that most infamous of days to happen, as well as the IRA for provoking the violence. However, they can fight and are at their very best on the battlefield, but not in the streets and houses of Northern Ireland. In May 1992 the Regiment was based outside Coalisland in Co. Tyrone which was the area of responsibility of the King's Own Scottish Borderers (KOSB).

On or about the 11th, Private Alistair Hodgson, then 21, was on patrol in east Tyrone near the border when another patrol found weapons and ammunition; Private Hodgson's patrol was ordered to start searching also, but during the course of the search he triggered off a PIRA booby-trap, suffering appalling injuries which left him with no legs. He takes up the story in the *Belfast Telegraph*:

> I was walking along when I stood on a pressure pad and boom. That was that. It's funny as I have no memory of what happened before it but I remember every second of the explosion and afterwards. All I remember is excruciating pain. And death, thoughts of death. I just wanted to die. I looked down and one of my legs had been blown off and the other was just about held together by nerves and veins. I begged the other soldier to shoot me there and then, there was just so much pain. I just wanted death. But he refused. And I owe that man my life as well as the other doctors and nurses who helped put me back together. When I was lying there I knew my life had just changed dramatically and I promised myself I would get better. My left leg was blown off below the knee and the right was so badly damaged it later had to be amputated just under the hip. My belly was torn open, my arm broken, the tendons were severed in my left arm, and my pelvis was shattered in 18 places. I needed 52 pints of blood in total to be kept alive and had to have my

> gall bladder removed. I took a lot of putting back together! I was immobilised for three months and just refused to do anything, I even refused to eat. So I was like a skeleton. I was in so much pain physically and emotionally, my spirit was crushed and I felt as helpless as a baby.[1]

In 2000, I went up on two or three lifts at the British Parachute School at Langar near Nottingham with Alistair Hodgson. I chatted to this friendly young man about life and about his undoubted abilities as a skydiver. I still have a video of the jump, and recall watching, fascinated and admiringly, as he shuffled out of the door on his backside and launched himself out at 12,000 feet. He is now one of the world's top skydivers.

On Tuesday 12th, some of the wounded soldier's comrades, still incensed by the terrible injury to their fellow Para, made their way into two pubs in the village and allowed themselves to be provoked. It is unwise to upset a paratrooper and on this occasion, the locals who called sarcastic remarks at the soldiers came off worst. Five days later, there was another incident in the town, but on this occasion shots were fired and several civilians were injured. In this second incident, a four-man brick from the KOSB foolishly allowed itself to be taunted into an impromptu boxing match/fist fight with local yobs at Lineside Road. The soldiers set aside their weapons and engaged the youths, with injuries being reported on both sides, although none critical. The result of the fight is not recorded, but it is then alleged that a rifle was stolen. Although the rifle was discovered shortly afterwards, the patrol's radio was smashed up, and two soldiers were taken to hospital.

The Paras were sent in again as back-up. Shortly after they arrived, there were more taunts, with the soldiers fearing for their lives as this was an area of high PIRA presence, with a stolen SA-80 possibly in the wrong hands. At this stage, the growing crowd began attempting to drag individual soldiers away from their comrades. The Paras fired first into the air but, when this had no effect, they then fired several shots at the legs of some of the mob gathered outside the Rossmore pub in the town. Three civilians were rushed to hospital in Dungannon with gunshot wounds and four others were also hurt, whilst the soldiers returned to their barracks. An eyewitness told ITV: 'I seen this man and he jumped backwards and then the soldier fired in the air. It was like a cartoon; you didn't think it was really happening.' NIO Minister Michael Mates also said: 'They were not going out to control a riot, because there was no riot until the IRA organised one. The soldier concerned who fired the shots did it because it was in self-defence. He was one of those being dragged away by the crowd.' A spokesman for the Irish Republic said: 'We have been in touch with the Northern Ireland authorities. We have expressed our concern about the continuing presence of the Parachute Regiment in Coalisland, an extremely sensitive area. Effectively what we are doing is calling for the removal of the Parachute Regiment from Northern Ireland altogether.' However, in my opinion, just as it was wrong for the USA to interfere in the sovereign affairs of a foreign state as it did in Northern Ireland, so it was equally wrong for the Dublin government to do so. After all, they did have some measure of responsibility for the conduct and existence of the IRA; for them to

1. Source: http://www.belfasttelegraph.co.uk/life/features/at-21-paratrooper-alistair-hodgson-lost-both-legs-in-an-ira-booby-trap-bomb-today-17-years-later-he-is-one-of-the-worlds-best-skydivers-28511230.html.

be allowed to choose which regiments the British government deployed in another part of the UK was unacceptable.

The Army dismissed the senior officer in the area; the Paras were forbidden to carry out further patrols and the unit was ordered out of the Province, well before the scheduled end of the tour. One of the wounded civvies was the brother of PIRA man Kevin O'Donnell, who had been killed by the SAS at Dernagh earlier in the year (*see* Chapter 14).

On the 27th, Signalman Jonathan Lance Tear Edmonds (22) of the Royal Signals died from natural causes whilst on duty in the Province; he was from Holywell in North Wales, close to the River Dee. His buried at St Peter's, Rose Hill, Holywell.

May had been less bloody than of late, with deaths down to five in all; of the four soldiers who lost their lives only one did so at the hands of terrorists.

Pat Finucane was a Belfast solicitor who acted on behalf of the Nationalist community. He was shot by a UFF gunman on 12 February 1989 at his home in Belfast. Sinn Féin say that it is evidence of 'collusion' but findings to date have been inconclusive. (*Pacemaker Press*)

Sinn Féin's Gerry Adams and Martin McGuinness at the funeral of PIRA man Patrick Kelly in 1987. (*Pacemaker Press*)

Memorial to the UDR soldiers killed in the PIRA attack at Glenanne Barracks, 31 May 1991.

Evidence of the desecration of the memorial at Teebane.

Monument to the workmen murdered at Teebane crossroads on 17 January 1992.

Alleged site of the bomb's trigger point.

The approximate site of the Teebane blast.

The signpost which one of the Teebane survivors saw when he recovered consciousness.

David Harkness, one of the victims of the Teebane bomb blast.
(*Photo courtesy of Ruth Forrest, David's sister*)

Site of the UFF murder of five Catholics at a betting shop on the Lower Ormeau Road in Belfast, 5 February 1992, and the memorial that now stands nearby.

The scene outside the Brian Graham bookmaker's shop, North Queen Street, after a shooting when five men were injured, 29 April 1993. (*Belfast Telegraph*)

Michelle Baird (aged seven), murdered by the IRA in the Shankill bomb blast, 23 October 1993. (*Belfast Telegraph*)

Evelyn Baird (27), murdered by the IRA in the Shankill bomb blast. (*Belfast Telegraph*)

Sharon McBride (29), murdered by the IRA in the Shankill bomb blast. (*Belfast Telegraph*)

Leanne Murray (13), murdered by the IRA in the Shankill bomb blast. (*Belfast Telegraph*)

The scene of the UFF attack on Catholic workmen at the Andersonstown Cleansing Depot, October 1993.

The modern-day site of the Rising Sun pub at Greysteel where the UVF murdered eight drinkers on 30 October 1993.

A UDA mural in the Rathcoole/Rathfern area.

The 'temporary' peace lines still divide Belfast. This one is on Cupar Way, separating the Catholic Springfield Road and Falls Road from the Protestant Shankill.

18

June

The beginning of the British summer saw just three deaths, two soldiers and a policeman. It was a month in which IRA bombs continued on a regular – sometimes daily – basis.

On the 2nd, a PIRA unit from the Fermanagh Brigade, heartened by the 'success' of the Cloughoge van-bomb attack, fired several mortars at another Army PVCP. The attack at Mullan Bridge near Kinawley in Co. Fermanagh was carried out under cover of darkness; after firing the mortars at the base at the junction of Moher Road and Swanlinbar Road, around a half mile from the border, the men of the unit were able to escape into Co. Cavan on the Irish side. There was some structural damage, but no serious injuries among the Army/RUC personnel.

On the 3rd, at around 21:30, Loyalist gunmen attacked the home of a Catholic pensioner in Enid Street, Belfast. They fired rounds which smashed his front window and narrowly missed him as they embedded themselves in his living-room wall. He told the Belfast *News Letter*: 'I have lived in this house for 15 years but I will have to move now.' The street was very close to the Loyalist Newtownards Road; the un-named pensioner was lucky, but five weeks later a near-neighbour, Cyril Murray, would not be (*see* next chapter).

Tadcaster in North Yorkshire sits astride the busy A64 which takes traffic from Leeds to York, and then onwards to the east coast seaside town of Scarborough. Early on Sunday 7 June 1992, I was sound asleep at my cottage in Clifford, around four miles away. Unknown to me or the rest of the unsuspecting British public, Provisional IRA men Paul Magee and Michael O'Brien had driven up from London, en route for York. It was thought that they planned to carry out a bombing attack on either Strensall or Imphal Barracks in the city. Alternatively they may have planned to assassinate a prominent politician. There were several living in the area, including former Chancellor of the Exchequer Norman Lamont, and Sir Keith Joseph, once a Thatcher Cabinet member. In the early hours of the morning, they pulled off the A64 and drove into Tadcaster.

A police patrol car, manned by Special Constable Glenn Goodman and Constable Sandy Kelly, was in the town when the officers spotted a red Ford Sierra car parked in the market place. The occupants of the car noticed that they were being watched and drove off; the patrol car followed, stopping it just outside the town near the A64 slip road for Leeds. The patrol car, a Metro, pulled up on the hard shoulder, with both officers getting out. Glenn Goodman (37), who had been a police officer for only seven months, walked towards the stolen car, together with Kelly. They spoke to both men, noting their Irish accents, and were immediately suspicious of the men's explanations for their behaviour. Kelly walked across to the police vehicle to use the radio as Goodman remained close to the other car. At that point, Magee got out of the car, saying that he needed to urinate, but he pulled a pistol from his clothing and immediately opened fire on the unarmed police officer, hitting him in the chest. He then shot Sandy Kelly who staggered backwards, trying to take shelter behind the patrol car door, screaming for help into his radio as he did so. Magee fired again but the shot hit the policeman's radio, saving his life, although the force of the round knocked him into the car; more shots shattered the windscreen as he was hit a further four times. PC Kelly later said: 'The expression on his face was committed to my memory. I made eye contact with him, then the shooting began again. I will never forget his face.' Magee then fired another round into Glenn Goodman's defenceless body, fatally wounding him. He died shortly afterwards in St James's Hospital in Leeds.

The PIRA men's car then raced westwards towards Leeds, but another patrol car, – manned by PCs Mark Whitehouse and Susan Larkin – alerted by Kelly's distress calls began a pursuit. At one stage, speeds reached more than 100 mph; one of the terrorists – thought to be Magee – opened fire with a Kalashnikov hitting the police car nine times, causing it to crash. The IRA car braked violently to a stop, with both men jumping out and menacingly advancing on the helpless officers, who were trapped in the wreckage of their vehicle. Fortunately for the trapped officers, the terrorists were spooked by the sudden arrival of a civilian car; thinking that it contained police reinforcements, they raced back to their Sierra. They then drove in the direction of Leeds before making a left turn towards Towton, driving through Sherburn-in-Elmet – where Glenn Goodman lived, and then towards the picturesque village of Burton Salmon, around nine miles from the murder scene. They abandoned their car there and ran off across the fields. For the next four days, they roamed the farmland around Brotherton, Byram and Knottingley, sleeping in ditches and hedges, living off raw vegetables. Four days later, Magee, covered in filth and mud, with several days growth of beard, walked into nearby Pontefract and purchased two pairs of shoes, and two T-shirts. A shop assistant followed him out of the shop, spotting him dumping muddy shoes and clothes in a waste bin. He alerted the police who chased Magee on foot through the town, before overpowering him after a violent struggle. Some time later, O'Brien, desperate to find his fellow terrorist, also walked into the centre of Pontefract where he too was arrested.

Magee, also known as 'Dingle', was a member of the 'M60 gang', who had shot and killed SAS Captain Herbert Westmacott in Belfast in 1980. He, and another of the gang, escaped from the Crumlin Road jail in June 1981. Magee was sentenced to 30 years in 1993, but was released after only seven, under the terms of the Good Friday Agreement. O'Brien was 'clean' having no criminal record; he was also unknown to the RUC or mainland police.

Glenn Goodman was the first special constable to be murdered since 1942 and the first mainland police officer to die directly at the hands of the IRA since 1983. He was a lorry driver and father of an 11-month-old son. He had enlisted in the Specials the previous November, hoping that it would help his application to join the police on a full-time basis. Brian and Margaret Goodman, the murdered officer's parents spoke of their deep disgust that Magee, who had made their daughter-in-law a widow and left their grandson fatherless, was released after serving only seven years. In Tadcaster today, just outside one of the town's three major breweries, a brown marble plinth remembers the dead officer.

On the 10th anniversary of Glenn Goodman's murder, his 10-year-old son Tom left a message: 'To Daddy, for all the love I've missed,' at the memorial stone at the junction of Wetherby Road and Station Road in Tadcaster where SPC Goodman and PC Kelly first spotted what turned out to be the terrorists' car. There were also flowers from Glenn's parents Brian and Margaret Goodman, who lived at nearby Ulleskelf, and from his wife Fiona. The following piece is from a close friend of mine, a man I have known and respected for the past 18 years.

That Terrible Night
Graham Watson, Civilian

It's difficult to look back so far and recollect exactly what you were doing but I guess, as a 26-year-old, I was probably looking forward to my next night out. However, as a Tadcaster resident, something would happen that night which would shake this quiet town to its core.

The Troubles in Northern Ireland were something you saw on the TV, or read in the newspapers, not here in sleepy, rural Yorkshire, where a disaster was someone's cows escaping. We were awoken late at night to hear siren after siren after siren, and I remember getting up and, in those days of no social media or internet, you could only guess what was happening. Rumours abounded, with a fire at the big local brewery being the first guess. Slowly though, a story began to emerge of a policeman being shot by an IRA gunman. Here, in Tadcaster, unbelievable!

I remember the phone ringing and my dad answering. It was about my brother; he was a local gamekeeper and had been shooting rabbits at night. All of a sudden, he was surrounded by armed police. He said it was the scariest thing that had ever happened to him. He was taken to the local station where he was quickly cleared by the police but was told what was happening. As people rose for the early shifts, I can recall the shock in people's voices. I'm ashamed to say most thoughts, early on, were not with the policeman as they should have been. It was more a case of, are the IRA preparing another bombing campaign around here? Are buses and trains safe? As always happens in these cases the talk became laughably far-fetched. However, slowly, images of Glenn Goodman's wife came into the papers and reality struck home. He was a young man, with a young wife, and would never see his son start school, grow up, get married and have children himself. It was a solemn time, nothing like this, or anything even close, had happened here before. The town was full of police and security services for days. It was a stark reminder of what was happening all over the UK.

After the funeral, the police and media eventually left for other stories, other security scares and the town got back to normal. Twenty-four years later I took my 5-year-old grandson to school; as we passed the monument to PC Goodman, he asked what it was and I told him. It brought back the impact of what had happened and the effect it had for years on this small market town.

On the same day as the shooting in Tadcaster, 200 miles further south, the IRA's England team left a device in the Royal Festival Hall in London's SE1 area. The device exploded, causing damage to the building, but there were no injuries amongst staff or visitors.

This was the first of three incidents in and around London aimed at causing death or injury where possible, or simply economic and social disruption on the mainland. Three days later, and just a couple of miles away on the other side of the Thames, at Wilcox Place, another device was planted. The street has many commercial properties and is just around the corner from Westminster, the seat of the British government; perhaps the IRA's intention was that the blast might be heard by MPs sitting in the House. Five days later and a mile and a half north-east of Wilcox Place, an armed gang hijacked a taxi in London, forcing the driver to take it to St Albans Street, just behind Piccadilly, where a bomb detonated shortly after he had jumped clear. A later statement by the IRA said: 'We have thwarted highly increased security in Central London to detonate a bomb in the heart of the British capital. Our volunteers continue to serve notice on the British Government that there is a clear price to be paid for its continued occupancy of part of Ireland's national territory.' There were no serious injuries, but the vehicle was wrecked. The scene then switched to Coleman Street, very close to the Bank of England, but more notably a mere 500 yards from the wreckage of the Baltic Exchange which the IRA had devastated just 11 weeks earlier. In the Coleman Street incident a small but deadly amount of Semtex was left in a briefcase pushed underneath a car. The device caused serious damage to the vehicle and slightly injured a nearby policeman; he was later treated for shock.

On the 8th, several weeks after the jailing of British agent/Loyalist terrorist, Brian Nelson, the BBC aired a very controversial programme that must have caused considerable embarrassment in Downing Street. The programme-makers alleged that Nelson was a British spy who had been planted as an informant inside the UDA. It further alleged that he had been involved in the murders of 10 Catholics as well as several attempted murders. The programme claimed that many of the arms used in these sectarian killings were South African in origin, having been procured by Nelson. It also damned the Army for not passing on intelligence about planned murders to the RUC. The dirty war, if possible, was getting dirtier.

On the 17th, the IRA again managed to breach the high security in Belfast city centre. Linenhall Street is directly opposite City Hall and, as such, was well guarded. Somehow, a PIRA unit, thought possibly to have included women, left a car bomb outside Bulloch House – now demolished – before telephoning a very vague warning through to the RUC. They stated that the bomb was on Linenhall Street – 200 yards in length – but not the exact location. Police officers and local UDR units were in the process of clearing the area when the device exploded; five soldiers and two policemen were injured in the blast, which caused considerable damage. Minutes later, bombs exploded in a Littlewoods store in nearby Ann Street, and at Zeros Hardware in North Street and severe damage was caused by a bomb in Primark in Castle Street. Shortly afterwards, as a continuation of the IRA's 'nibble and bite' strategy, designed to keep the Army/RUC constantly occupied, more mayhem followed. Two bread-delivery vans were hijacked on the Whiterock Road and their drivers forced to drive to New Barnsley RUC station and Tennent Street RUC stations, with the implied threat that they were proxy bombs. Bomb disposal carried out controlled explosions, before declaring them hoaxes. Five car bombs were then discovered and made safe in York Street, Crumlin Road, Cliftonville Road, Shore Road and the Antrim Road. Hijacked vans were then left abandoned at Sprucefield near Lisburn and

Ballygomartin, Belfast. Bogus warnings were then called in, purporting to be from the IRA, relating to bombs placed on the railway lines between Belfast and Carrickfergus, and Dunmurry and Lisburn. Police closed down the network whilst a thorough search was made; it re-opened just before noon.

Helicopter Chase, 1992
Ian Manley, Light Infantry

We set off by Wessex from Newtownhamilton on a routine patrol with two RUC attached and were dropped off near Irwin's Crossroads. We had only been on the ground for a couple of minutes when suddenly, the helicopter came back in and 'Pilky' (Lance Corporal Pilkington) told us to get back on. I had no idea what was going as I had no radio and could just about see we were chasing a couple of cars; one of which split off from the other fairly quickly. I could not tell you how long that flight was, it could have been 10 minutes or half an hour but I have never experienced flying like it; the pilot was chucking that Wessex all over the sky, proper hedge-top flying. He was trying to land in order to set up a cut- off. The door gunner cocked his jimpy [General Purpose Machine Gun] but couldn't open fire, under rules of engagement. Pilky was the first to be sick; I thought a thermos of soup had exploded, but it was his breakfast exiting pretty sharpish; that set off a bit of a chain reaction as one of the lads plus one of the RUC guys went as well. The floor was swimming in vomit, but most of it left through the door when the pilot put it on its side.

We landed and Pilky, Kev and the RUC guys got out; me and Mark were held back by the loadmaster as the Wessex took off and landed again 30 seconds later. He shouted to us to secure the area around a Toyota Corolla parked at the end of a close, so we took up fire positions although we were unable to see any of the others. There was lots of shouting; the usual stuff: 'Brit bastards!' We knew that the others were in the thick of it, and then about 10 minutes later, the RUC lads came back, dragging a guy, with a woman slapping them and trying to free them, before they all ended in a heap on the floor! Just then, other troops began arriving and myself and Mark were ordered to escort them on a Lynx which had just landed.

The guy was shitting himself and we couldn't stop grinning at each other, because not only we had caught a player in the act, but we wouldn't have to freeze our arses off on a cordon on a bitterly cold night! We gave statements at Bessbrook Mill, before we were flown back to Newtownhamilton. When we got back, the place was almost deserted as most of the other lads were already deployed on the cordon by the PIRA car.

The next day, we got the info from the lads who had been out on the cordon on a freezing cold night. They'd managed to grab two of the bad guys but one had managed to get away, as they'd been surrounded by a crowd of 30 to 40 IRA supporters. The lads were trying to arrest them and at the same time, fend off the crowd; it had got very hairy and Kev had cocked his weapon ready to fire a warning shot but the round got jammed in the chamber! Then the QRF [quick reaction force] arrived and the crowd backed off. Job done!

On the 21st, a blast bomb containing a small but deadly amount of Semtex was hurled at an RUC patrol in Benburb, Co. Tyrone, whilst the officers were in the vicinity of a festival. Fortunately there were no injuries. The following day, as an Army patrol was passing through Cookstown, Co. Tyrone, an IRA gunman using a US-supplied Armalite fitted with a sniper scope opened fire on them. One soldier was wounded, but the gunman escaped. On the same day – a Sunday – Provisional Sinn Féin held its annual Wolfe Tone commemoration in Co. Kildare in the Irish Republic. At the 1992 event, leading activist Jim Gibney stated that if the British did withdraw (Gibney over optimistically used the term 'when') that the period before Ireland became reunited would need to witness negotiations between the warring parties of Nationalists and Loyalists. This was the first indication that the Republicans were considering either ending or scaling back their 'armed struggle'.

An Phoblacht published an interview with a PIRA insider who explained why their bombs could vary from the 'block-buster' such as the one which devastated the Baltic Exchange to the tiny briefcase bomb in nearby Coleman Street. He also told the interviewer why 'shoot and scoot' gun attacks on individual soldiers or policemen could differ from the mass murders such as that perpetrated at Teebane. 'The IRA's tactic is to chop and change guerrilla tactics. We will spread the Crown Forces into guarding as many areas as possible and stretch them to the utmost. We will nibble and bite them from every angle. We will not allow them to set the agenda or choose the field of battle. We will not let them contain the fighting.'[1]

On the 27th, 3 Para were on the last patrol of their tour of Co. Tyrone; they were in the 'cuds' as soldiers referred to the rural areas of Northern Ireland. Whilst crossing the River Blackwater near Blackwatertown, Lance Corporal Richard Coulson (25) sadly got into difficulties. His close friend Lance Corporal Peter Henry Sullivan (26) went into the water to rescue him. Tragically both soldiers were swept away and drowned, despite the brave efforts of their comrades to save them. Army Engineers later recovered their bodies. A civilian eyewitness later told the *Belfast Telegraph*: 'They were both heading back to the bank when they went under the water.' Peter Sullivan was from Billingham, Cleveland; he is buried in the cemetery there. Richard Coulson was from Tyne & Wear. Neither soldier is included in the MoD's official figures, and this exclusion speaks volumes about their efforts to reduce the significance of the Army's contribution towards the eventual peace.

Earlier that day, the Provisionals introduced a new – to the Troubles at least – and terrifying dimension to their bombing campaign; the limpet bomb. A lone bomber ran over to a police car with two officers inside, as it queued at traffic lights in High Street/Ann Street, Belfast city centre, and stuck the limpet bomb on the roof. The device exploded within seconds, causing the car to burst into flames; both officers were injured but managed to get clear, helped by shocked civilians, shoppers and office workers. The *Belfast Telegraph* reported the next day:

> One woman said: 'How anybody managed to survive that is a miracle. It's unbelievable what happened; we are numb with shock.' Another shopper said: 'One policeman seemed to be thrown out of the car and some people tried to get back

1. Quoted in Michael A. Innes, *Making Sense of Proxy Wars* (Angus & Robertson, 2012), pp. 53–4.

> to help him . . .' Two German tourists who arrived in Belfast on Friday told of the shopping street horror: 'We are very shaken; we did not expect anything like this.' A shop assistant ran to help the injured. She said: 'Everyone was in a state of shock and many were screaming. One young man had head and chest injuries caused by flying glass. I dealt with a couple of other younger men who were also bleeding badly.' A policeman said: 'We are lucky we don't have two dead colleagues.'

I have seen the aftermath photo, and it shows the jagged razor-sharp metal in the car roof; how the officers survived this attack with only cuts and bruises is simply beyond belief.

The bomb caused extensive damage and 21 people, mainly civilians, were injured, some seriously, by shrapnel. Martin Smyth, MP, said that the bombing 'was a dastardly piece of work in keeping with the IRA's brutality'. Others condemned the action as a 'scurrilous criminal act'. The Provisionals clearly gave no thought or consideration to the safety of others, particularly as the High Street was very busy with shoppers and office workers enjoying the summer sunshine. But then, a statement of 'regret' had probably already been prepared, blaming the RUC, the Army, the British government, anyone but themselves for this cowardly, irresponsible outrage.

On the final day of the month, acting on a tip-off from the IRA via a local priest, Margaret Perry's body was found not far from Mullaghmore in the Irish Republic. It would appear that the location of the shallow grave in which her strangled body was found was revealed by one of three IRA men who were in the not-so-delicate hands of the IRA's 'nutting squad'. Before they died (*see* next chapter), they admitted that they had strangled her and then beaten her in order to stop her revealing that they were informers. (*See also* Chapter 6.)

Three people died during June: two soldiers and a mainland police officer. The number of dead police, however, could so easily have been four, with officers Kelly, Whitehouse and Larkin all coming close to death during their brush with Magee and O'Brien.

19
July

There were perhaps six deaths this month: a soldier died in a non-terrorist incident; two Catholics were killed in sectarian attacks, and the bodies of three IRA men, killed by Scappaticci's 'nutting squad' were found in South Armagh, although it is highly likely that they had been killed earlier.

The three Provisionals whose bodies were discovered on the 1st were Johnny Dignam (32), Gregory Burns (34), and Aidan Starrs (29); all were from Portadown, Co. Armagh. All three men were abducted from their homes by Freddie Scappaticci's nutting squad and taken across the border to be interrogated, tortured and shot. The accusation was that all three had acted as informers for the RUC and MI5. One or more of the three Provos had murdered Margaret Perry, also from Portadown; she was abducted on 21 June 1991, and beaten to death. Her lifeless body was found buried in a field in Mullaghmore, Co. Sligo, on 30 June 1992 (*see* Chapter 18).

The South Armagh brigade had 'tried and executed them', torturing them horribly, before leaving their naked, hooded bodies in ditches at separate locations near the border in South Armagh. All three were dumped within 10 miles of each other at Newtownhamilton, Bessbrook and Crossmaglen. Their bodies bore evidence of beatings and each had bullet wounds to the back of the head. The men were experienced Provisionals who had been recruited either by MI5 or an undercover unit of the British Army to inform on IRA activities. They were interrogated by none other than 'Stakeknife' himself. After Dignam's funeral, a letter by him was given to his pregnant wife; it read: 'I have only a matter of hours to live. I only wish I could see you and the kids one last time, but as you know, this is not possible.' A confession had been extracted by torture from John Dignam; in this he said that he was an accessory after the fact and had helped Aidan Starrs to hide Margaret Perry's body.

All of the men were well-known Provisionals: Starrs and Dignam had both been convicted of serious terrorist offences; Burns had no terrorist convictions, but his brother, Sean, was an IRA member and had been shot dead by police near Lurgan, Co. Armagh, in 1982. The IRA claimed that Dignam had supplied information to the security services about his own brother.

Associated Press reported:

> The IRA claimed responsibility for the killing of three alleged informers whose naked, badly beaten bodies were left in plain view along a road. The killings sickened South Armagh, a Roman Catholic district of rolling pasture on the border with the Irish Republic. British troops recovered two of the bodies early

Thursday. A third hooded victim was left in the roadside grass until late in the day because Army bomb-disposal experts feared the body might be booby-trapped. The IRA's treatment of the men appeared intended to impress the community and deter future informing. One of the alleged informers was stuffed in a garbage bag with a milk crate resting on its chest. 'It was more something out of a butcher's shop than a human body,' said Seamus Mallon, the area's member of Parliament. He said the killings sent two messages – 'absolute vengeance and an unspoken threat to the entire community'.

Nearly Killed by Mistake!
Ian Manley, Light Infantry

My last tour in 1992 was probably the closest I came to getting killed; that said who knows how close any of us were? I was working airhead at [Bessbrook] and me and Corporal Butterfield – 'Butty' – had just hooked up an underslung with the ATO kit on its little wagon. I'd earthed the hook and attached the strop by the shackle and Butty had given the thumbs up; we'd started to walk away, when there was a God-Almighty bang and, suddenly, bits of razor-sharp metal were flying everywhere! I thought the Puma had taken an RPG or we had been mortared but it turned out be an electrical failure on the Puma's underslung hook which dropped the ATO kit about 50 feet onto the pad. It was a bit of a miracle that neither me, Butty or the ATO gut didn't get cut to shreds! I just remember the ATO guy going: 'Well that's fucked it! That's about a million quid in bits!'

Also on the 1st, the Royal Irish Regiment (RIR or Royal Irish for short) came into being; it was formed by the amalgamation of the UDR and the Royal Irish Rangers. The merger meant that the former UDR battalions, a total of approximately 6,000 soldiers, would continue to operate in Northern Ireland, whilst the two former Rangers battalions would be reduced to a single general service battalion, approximately 900 soldiers, who would serve abroad as well as in Northern Ireland. The UDR was a combination of full and part-time soldiers and sustained the highest number of casualties of all the British Army regiments who served in Northern Ireland. It had been the subject of sustained criticism from Nationalists since its formation in 1970, with constant sniping about their so-called collusion. These accusations had admittedly been proven in a very few instances, with rogue UDR elements who also belonged to the UFF, UVF and Red Hand Commando being identified. These were, however, in a minority and I am proud to associate myself with the regiment. For Republicans to accuse the UDR of being 'state-sponsored terrorists', or to claim that the soldiers who served were all involved in collusion, is as ridiculous as the accusation that every member of An Garda Síochána or the Irish Army was an IRA supporter. However, what is obvious is that elements of both the British and the Irish state's forces were involved with their 'own' terror groups, but in both cases, these were in a minority.

Between 1970 and May 1992, the UDR lost 360 soldiers, male and female; this compares with the highest fatalities from mainland Regiments: Royal Artillery 73, including Royal Horse Artillery; Parachute Regiment 57; Royal Green Jackets 49. Exactly

200 UDR soldiers were killed in terrorist-related incidents; a staggering 73 were killed in RTAs; 27 committed suicide; 26 were killed accidentally and there are a further 34 who died whilst on duty. Comrade and former UDR soldier 'M. C.' is taking great steps in tracking down the reasons behind those deaths.

'Natural Causes'
M. C., former UDR and Royal Artillery

In terms of 'natural causes', I was thinking more about this: many soldiers under 50 died from cancer. Research and testing have now proven that people close to bomb explosions may have got asbestos in their systems. This could well be the cause of cancer in some of the victims, especially those well under 50 years of age. In terms of the MoD and the way they have 'massaged' the actual death toll, look at Afghanistan for an example. Around 40 of the total deaths there were non-battlefield, but are still included on the Official Roll of Honour; why should Operation Banner be any different. If they hadn't have been there, would they have died anyway; I doubt it.

There was a lucky escape for soldiers on the 2nd of the month, near Coalisland in Co. Tyrone. A well-prepared trap, set by the IRA, designed to cause multiple loss of life, was thwarted by a stray wire. A UDR unit was patrolling in a quiet area between Washingbay Road and Annagher Road, around two miles away from Lough Neagh. The patrol was close to a small hamlet, when the point man noticed a command wire that had been hidden nearby, close to rocky ground. The area was sealed off and the local residents were evacuated; ATO then defused the device. Without the alertness of this soldier, the entire patrol might easily have been wiped out

Leeson Street is now a long row of modern townhouses in pleasant surroundings, linking the Falls Road/Divis Street with Servia Street; once upon a time, it linked directly into Grosvenor Road. It was immortalised by the artist Terence Cuneo in his 'Leeson Street Action' commemorating a successful engagement by the 3rd Battalion of the Green Jackets. Leeson Street had its share of other Troubles-related tragedies, however. In the late evening of 5 July 1992, Kieran Patrick Abram (35) left his house in Leeson Street and walked to the bottom of North Howard Street where it joins Cupar Way, now the site of one of Belfast's 'peace lines'. Earlier in the day, gangs of Catholic/Nationalists yobs had battled gangs of Protestant/Loyalist yobs from the nearby Shankill Road. From a few hundred yards away, soldiers based at North Howard Street Mill observed the bitter fighting as the respective mobs slugged it out. The Mill – once the Falls Forge – was strategically located at the Loyalist/Nationalist interface. I can remember patrolling up towards the Shankill and counting off the boringly repetitive streets: Fifth Street, Sixth Street, Seventh Street and then to no great surprise: Eighth Street.

After the RUC had dispersed the fighting elements, both sides retreated to their respective tribal areas, with the exception of a gang of six or seven thugs from the Shankill. They lay in wait behind the front sangar, in the hope that a lone Catholic might venture past. In the event, tragically for Mr Abram, he did walk by and several of the thugs, armed with pieces of timber with 6-inch nails embedded along the length, as well as hurley sticks and other cudgels, jumped out and beat the innocent Catholic to a pulp. He was kicked repeatedly as he lay helplessly on the pavement. The RUC arrived and arrested several of the men whilst two officers tried desperately to revive the mortally injured man; he died before he even reached the nearby RVH – another victim in Northern Ireland's senseless sectarian war. There was almost one more later that evening, when Loyalists attempted to kill a Catholic on the Ormeau Road. A murder gang, possibly the same ones who had killed five people in Sean Graham's, but certainly from the local unit on the Annadale, opened fire on a man standing outside a Chinese restaurant. He was hit and seriously wounded, but thankfully survived. The gang's car was found burned out on the Annadale Road the following day.

On the 8th, a Loyalist parade snaked its way down the Lower Ormeau Road in Belfast, just four days before the annual 'Twelfth' marches. When it passed Sean Graham's Bookmakers at the junction of Ormeau Road and University Avenue, several of the marchers began taunting watching Catholics, with many of them holding up five fingers to refer to the five dead in the February attack. Patrick Mayhew at the NIO angrily denounced the marchers, saying that their behaviour 'would have disgraced a tribe of cannibals'.

On that very same day, the UFF proved that the malaise of flawed intelligence was not restricted to the bunglers in the Provisional IRA as they killed yet another innocent Catholic in the mistaken belief that he had been part of a PIRA murder gang. Cyril Murray (51) had once been a teacher in the Nationalist Ardoyne, but was about to take up a new position in Randalstown, Co. Antrim. He had moved to Kerrsland Drive, just off the fiercely Loyalist Newtownards Road. The site is now occupied by a Tesco, a Spar, a Subway and a petrol station; in 1992, it was terraced housing. It was easy for a UFF murder gang to drive into the street, turn the car around and wait with their vehicle facing in the direction of Newtownards Road and a quick getaway. During the late evening, two masked men kicked Mr Murray's front door open, pushed their way past the teacher's sister and ran upstairs to blast the surprised man in the chest with a shotgun. As he fell, mortally wounded, the second barrel was fired into his body from very close range. It is likely that he didn't even hear the second, fatal shot. The real target was a Catholic civil servant who had allegedly supplied PIRA with personal information about RUC officers, judges and UDR soldiers.

The UDA/UFF later released a statement claiming that they had 'executed' Mr Murray because of his involvement in the murder of Protestant businessman Robert Metcalfe in 1988. However, after a wave of indignation from both churches, plus local Protestants who knew the teacher, and of course, the RUC, the terrorists were forced to admit that their claim was a complete lie.

On the 12th, the Welsh Guards lost Lance Corporal Mark Roger George Howells (22) in an RTA in the Province. He was a Welsh lad from Chepstow in South Wales; he was buried at Mathern Road Cemetery in Gwent.

As the month drew to an end, three of the four people known as the 'UDR Four' were released from prison following the quashing of their convictions. The court had heard that RUC notes of the confessions had been tampered with. However, as there was more substantial evidence against the fourth soldier, Neil Latimer, he was not released.

On the 30th, the Provisionals' England team struck with a small incendiary attack in Milton Keynes. Two devices exploded in stores; there was minimal damage but no injuries.

The evening of the 31st saw a Loyalist murder gang make the short journey from the Shankill to the Grosvenor Road in Belfast. Despite the proximity of the RUC/Army bases at Grosvenor Road, Albert Street Mill, NHSM and Castle Street RUC station, the gang opened fire on two Catholic homes in the area. Although there were no injuries, the UFF claimed that they had been targeting Republicans, one of whom was Sinn Féin member Pat Guinness. In the first attack, a sledgehammer was used to try to break down the front door of a Catholic home, but this failed to gain the gunmen entry. In the second attack, a grenade was thrown at another house. The UFF later claimed that their target had been an IPLO man.

Also on the final day of the month, Channel 4 and Box Productions were fined £75,000 in the High Court in London after they had refused to name the sources behind the information they received in the making of a sensationalist programme, 'The Committee', the previous October. The programme had claimed that there was an inner circle in the combined ranks of the UDR and the RUC. It claimed that collusion was institutional and that the UFF and UVF would warn the SF where a murder was going to take place, thus ensuring a withdrawal from the area of uniformed personnel in order to give the paramilitaries a free run. It also alleged that photo and documentary evidence was passed on to the Loyalists by the Army/RUC, also that weapons would 'disappear' from legitimate armouries. The programme further alleged that bogus VCPs would be manned by paramilitaries wearing police and Army uniforms. A book by the same title was planned, but eventually not published in the UK, as the American book company feared costly legal action brought about by the Major government.

Sean McPhilemy's banned book claims that the SF provided paramilitaries with money, arms and political direction. The Committee's alleged access to detailed official files and information, and the ability to provide 'hands on' involvement of RUC units, made certain that the sectarian murder forces were virtually untouchable. I have previously spoken about RUC/Army collusion with Loyalists and am equally condemnatory of Garda/Republican collusion. I firmly believe that neither existed on the grand scale which antagonists on both sides of the sectarian chasm appear to believe that they did. The following month, RUC Chief Constable Hugh Annesley issued a statement about Channel 4's 'The Committee' broadcast; he stated that there was no truth to the allegations.

July ended with six deaths.

20

August

Ten people died this month; six soldiers and an airman were killed, as was an innocent Catholic, accidentally caught in crossfire between the IRA and RUC officers, as the terror group once more turned a residential area into a battlefield. Additionally three Republican paramilitaries were killed as a result of the continued IPLO/INLA feud; the Provisionals' nutting squad were in action again. Also this month, the long-overdue banning of the UDA was announced by the Major government.

Bedford Street in Belfast connects the Dublin Road with the City Hall and, as such, was part of the so-called 'ring of steel'. However, just as they had struck at nearby Linenhall Street – which runs parallel to Bedford Street – on 17 June, the IRA attacked again with the same apparent immunity. This time, they left two large bombs which both exploded, causing extensive damage, although, other than shock, there were no injuries on this occasion. ITN news footage shows the panic on the faces of diners at a nearby restaurant as the bombs exploded; the timing was aimed at causing maximum destruction and maximum fear amongst the people whose money was keeping the Belfast economy afloat: barely. The worrying aspect from the perspective of both SF and the public was the apparent ease with which the terror group could penetrate security and plant their bombs.

On the same day, the IRA's south Tyrone brigade opened fire on an Army foot patrol in the Pomeroy area. Pomeroy is some 9 or 10 miles from the Irish border and lies between Lough Neagh and Omagh. In the early evening, gunmen opened fire on the soldiers, hitting one man, seriously wounding him. The patrol returned fire, but the PIRA men escaped in the direction of Cookstown.

On the evening of the 2nd – a Sunday– a Belfast PIRA team forced their way into a flat on the top floor of a block in Stratheden Street, at the top end of the New Lodge, where it joins the Antrim Road. The street is known to the locals as *Sraid Shraith édain*; like the remainder of the area, it is fiercely Nationalist. The gunmen forced the residents, who included two young children, into a back bedroom. They set up an automatic weapon on a tripod, positioning it to fire towards the junction of Duncairn Avenue and the Antrim Road. After they had waited for several hours, a Land Rover from the Scots Guards turned into the main road. Several bursts were fired at the vehicle from the rear, hitting the 'top cover' Guardsman in his back and neck, fatally wounding him. The troops were unable to return fire because of the proximity of civilians, a fact of which the IRA were aware, relying on the 'armour' of human bodies to protect them.

Whilst the gunmen made good their escape, melting away into safe houses, with an army of sympathisers ready to take the stripped-down weapons to the local armoury, the shocked soldiers saw to their badly wounded comrade, Damien John Shackleton (24), who was father of a small child. He was rushed to the nearby Mater Hospital which was only half a mile away; he died just minutes later. One of his comrades told the inquest: 'He smiled and said: "I can't feel anything." He was lying on his back and his eyes were rolling in his head.' The young soldier was from Blackburn in Lancashire; his funeral was held at Whalley & Wiswell Cemetery.

One of the standing jokes told by squaddies about the RAF is that, in battle situations, the soldier digs in, makes his 'slitter' and prepares to stand in icy water as the trench fills up; in the same situation the RAF man simply looks for the nearest four-star hotel. In fact the RAF, including the Royal Air Force Regiment, lost 20 personnel during the Troubles, including four directly at the hands of the IRA, four in helicopter crashes at Army bases and one airman deliberately mown down at a VCP at Aldergrove. On the 10th of this month, Flight Sergeant Malcolm Ernest Warnecke (37) died whilst on duty at RAF Aldergrove; he was from Hull and was the first member of the RAF to die in or as a consequence of the Troubles for almost three years. His funeral was held at Hull Crematorium, Chanterfields Avenue, in his home town of Kingston-upon-Hull.

On Monday 10th, Secretary of State for Northern Ireland Patrick Mayhew announced that the UDA was banned as an organisation from midnight that night. Naturally this was welcomed by Nationalists, with the SDLP stating that the move was long overdue. There had been an upsurge in Loyalist paramilitary violence in the last part of the previous year and in the first five months of 1992. It was noted that UFF/UVF killings had actually surpassed those carried out by the Republican paramilitaries. Did the banning order make any difference? In all, the UFF alone was responsible for around 300 deaths, the majority of which were innocent Catholics, killing in sectarian attacks. Their most high-profile attacks were the Sean Graham bookmaker's shooting, the Castlerock killings in March 1993 and the Greysteel massacre in October 1993 (*see* Chapters 27 and 34). Significantly, two of their biggest outrages were committed *after* the ban.

Also on the 10th, Rifleman Jamie Spencer Smith (24), a soldier in the Royal Green Jackets, was killed in an RTA in Co. Tyrone. The Merseyside-born boy was one of eight Green Jackets killed on the two-year posting. He is buried at St Nicholas Church, at Whiston near Prescott, Lancashire.

Whilst the politicians droned on and on and debated and debated, the killing continued. Ardmore Park is in the south-west of Coalisland in Co. Tyrone; Coalisland itself is pretty nondescript, although in 1992 it had recently been very much in the news. On 13 January, the IRA had killed a man as a consequence of bungled intelligence; on 16 February, four PIRA men had been shot and killed at Dernagh near the town; in the middle of May, the Paras went on a mini-rampage with a Nationalist mob, and on June 2nd, the IRA had come close to killing UDR soldiers patrolling near Washingbay Road.

Robin Hill (22) was a member of the Provisional IRA in the south Tyrone brigade; after a number of operations had failed or been aborted, suspicion fell upon him and on the 10th he was picked up from Moy Tir na nÓg Gaelic Athletic Club, close to his house. It is uncertain if he was abducted inside or outside the club, but what is certain is that members of Freddie Scappaticci's 'nutting squad' bundled him into their car and drove him the 42 miles to the Beechmounts in West Belfast, close to the Falls Road. What is not recorded, but easily speculated upon, is the panic, fear and apprehension of what he probably knew was going to happen, which went through the IRA man's mind on that terrible journey. That he was held and tortured for two days in a safe house is not in doubt; nor that he was forcibly dressed in a white boiler suit – to reduce forensic evidence – and finally bound, gagged, his eyes covered in thick masking tape, before he was taken outside and shot twice in the back of the head. An IRA statement claimed that he confessed to being an informant and was executed. What is in doubt is: *was he an informer?* Was it simply another of Scap's ploys to cover up his own role as an informer, as Joseph Fenton had also done until Scap caught up with him in February 1989, or was Hill's supposed confession true? No one other than RUC SB or Army Intelligence will ever know.

Soldier, Royal Artillery

The alleyway was between Beechmounts Gardens and Avenue; it was a typical dog-shit alley! We were on the scene at the same time as the RUC and I could see shit stains and other stains from bodily fluids and blood matting in his hair where the rounds had gone in. There was dog shit, old crisp packets, fag-ends and empty fag packets lying around. I remember that there was some white dog shit; you don't see that any more. The whole place stank of cats and it says a lot for the people of the Falls area when you think of their total lack of concern and pride in where their kids played. I looked at him and although I despised the Provos, I actually felt sorry for the lad; being dumped in such a cess-pit is something I wouldn't even wish on Gerry Adams; come to think about it though, I probably would.

American papers carried and Associated Press interview with the dead IRA man's father: 'They tortured him to confess to something he'd never had a part in. The IRA are corrupt murderin' scum!' The report concluded by printing a synopsis of the IRA statement in which they claimed that Robin Hill had confessed that he had been working for the RUC Special Branch (SB) for over a year.

On the 12th, London's Met Police uncovered approximately 12 tons of explosives when they seized three vans; the explosives had been brought into mainland England from caches inside the Irish Republic before being assembled at a West London 'bomb factory'. The police made several arrests, but all were released without charge.

On the 17th, Royal Army Ordnance Corps soldier Lance Corporal Andrew Dowell (23) from England's Lake District died in circumstances which I can only describe as 'death by violent or unnatural causes'. It is thought that he was based at HQNI; he is buried at St Mary's Church, Wigton, in Cumbria.

Jimmy Brown (26) had been a member of the OIRA, before leaving to join the IRSP and the INLA. He then moved on to the even more extreme IPLO, where he was declared the leader of the Republican Socialist Collective. In recent weeks, the IPLO had further split into the IPLO Belfast Brigade (IPLO-BB) and the IPLO Army Council (IPLO-AC). On the afternoon of the 18th, Brown met PIRA chiefs, hoping to negotiate the return of IPLO weapons the IRA had removed from a Falls Road arms cache. The meeting was held in the Clonard Monastery and was attended by a Sinn Féin councillor and two Catholic priests; it had been arranged in part to mediate in the dispute between the two warring

IPLO factions. The meeting broke up without resolution. Brown then drove from the monastery towards the Falls Road/Divis Street, only a matter of a few hundred yards, in the company of a fellow IPLO man.

As he reached the Michael Davitt GAA club, just off the Falls Road, he saw a man whom he recognised and called him over. It was at this point when things began to go badly wrong for Brown; the man he had called to was from the IPLO-BB and was armed. Brown was a known killer, so it isn't difficult to imagine what was in the other man's mind. The other man panicked, drew his pistol and fired several shots at Brown, hitting him five times in the head, shoulders and chest and mortally wounding him. The passenger jumped out of the car and fled up the Falls Road, only stopping when he reached the Divis Street flats, some 600 yards away. He told McDonald and Holland: 'I heard Jimmy shout: "No, No," and then there were shots. I remember turning around and seeing Jimmy get it in the head. I bolted from the car with my head down. My heart was beating real fast. I could still hear shots ringing out as I ran onto the Falls Road towards Divis Flats.'[1] It later emerged, that the man who had killed Brown was a former Provisional known as 'Huck', indeed he had been on the hit team which had gunned down the Shankill Butcher himself, Lenny Murphy, in December 1982.

In all my research for this book, I have only been able to identify 'Huck' as John 'M' and it is said that he gained his nickname through the DIY tattooing of the letters H.U.C.K on the knuckles of one hand. There is a possibly apocryphal story told about him that he was on an INLA operation to plant a bomb underneath the car of a known Loyalist, but the device exploded prematurely, removing all his fingers. Although he managed to escape the wrecked vehicle in which he had been travelling, he was later picked up by the RUC and questioned about the own-goal explosion. In the interview, so the legend goes, he asked what proof they had that he had been involved in an explosion; the officers produced a bag containing the severed fingers and asked him if he wanted them back.

I have written many times of the phenomenon of negligent discharge (ND) deaths amongst soldiers during the Troubles. I have identified 43 deaths by ND. This means that a minimum 3.14% of the 1,371 military deaths I record were caused by fellow soldiers negligently handling their weapons, through carelessness, fatigue or in some cases, 'horseplay'. On the 20th of this month, Private Michael Brand Lee (21) from Surrey, serving with 2nd Battalion Parachute Regiment, was shot dead by a friend and comrade, Lance Corporal Nicholas Wyatt. The pair were based at Springfield Road RUC station and had just returned from a foot patrol. Private Lee cleared his weapon, but in a state of exhaustion, Wyatt forgot to do so. The pair were fooling about and Lee waved his SA-80 at his friend, who jocularly responded, but a 5.56 mm round discharged and struck Michael Lee in the head, killing him instantly.

Generally, these types of ND deaths were swept under the carpet by the Army and dealt with in-house where possible. On this occasion, Corporal Wyatt was charged with manslaughter and the case went before the High Court in Belfast. I am very grateful to M. C. for sending me the Belfast *News Letter* which covered the trial. Under a headline of 'Victim's dad saves soldier from prison', Chris Thornton wrote:

1. Henry McDonald & Jack Holland, *INLA: Deadly Divisions* (Poolbeg Books, 2010), pp. 403–4.

> A father's emotional plea saved a soldier from jail yesterday. Grieving dad, John Lee told Belfast Court that the paratrooper who killed his soldier son had 'suffered enough'. Lance Corporal Nicholas Wyatt, 27, was sentenced after pleading guilty to the death of his friend and comrade, Michael Lee ... The court heard how Wyatt was horror-struck when he shot Lee on August 20 last year. The pair were fooling about after coming off a mobile patrol and Wyatt forgot he had put a round in his weapon while on the streets. The Crown said Lee brandished his weapon which had been cleared for safety, towards Wyatt and said something like: 'Do you trust me?' Wyatt waved his gun in a similar fashion, and it went off near Lee's mouth, killing the 21-year-old. A defence lawyer said the soldiers worked under stressful conditions – describing Wyatt's narrow escape from a coffee-jar bomb several days before the shooting. He added that some horseplay was natural, though there were tragic circumstances on this occasion. Lee's father, a sergeant in the Surrey police, was then called to the stand to testify on Wyatt's behalf ... The grieving dad met the corporal after the killing and found him a 'compassionate, thoughtful, meticulous young man who is suffering terrible guilt ... I think that it adds to our grief that he is suffering so much still,' said Sergeant Lee. [The judge said:] 'I have no doubt that this death will weigh on your conscience for the rest of your life.'

The judge later added that it would not be in the public interest to jail the contrite soldier and it was expected that the MoD would make a decision along with the Parachute Regiment as to whether or not he would rejoin his comrades and continue serving. I have been unable to ascertain if Nicholas Wyatt remained in the Parachute Regiment, but given the forgiveness of Michael Lee's parents, I hope that he was able to do so.

Negligent Discharges
Mark Ormston, Royal Artillery

One of the quirks of serving in R16 was the fact that we were ordered to have our weapons loaded (but not cocked) at all times, even indoors, which was quite unusual, but I believe was a result of the threat assessment which indicated that South Armagh PIRA might try an assault on the PVCP as it was relatively lightly manned. I think this along with the very limited sleep we were getting (about four hours in every 24 hours, but not in one go) contributed to the darkest moment of the tour for us. I was in the 'super Sangar' when I saw some of the boys coming in from a patrol in the pouring rain, they went indoors and several minutes later I heard a CASEVAC request on the radio for a gunshot wound and the NIPIN number[1] used began with a 'G'. There were only two lads with surnames beginning with 'G' in the troop, one of which was a fellow team commander and particularly good friend of mine. We felt utterly helpless in the sangar unable to leave our posts while we knew what must have been going on in the 'submarine' (the blast-proof accommodation/ops room). Eventually a helicopter came in from Bessbrook and took the casualty to hospital. It turned out to be one of the young members of the

1. Northern Ireland Personal Identification Number, used to avoid giving names over the radio in sensitive situations.

team and not my friend and what had happened was the patrol had come in and gone into the rest room and started cleaning their weapons and one of them had somehow had a negligent discharge and the bullet had passed through the stomach of the young soldier and lodged in his arm; he survived, but was medically discharged due to problems arising from his wounds. It just goes to show that the constant grind of operations in NI could lead to even experienced soldiers making mistakes and that it wasn't just PIRA that could lead to your death or injury.

On the same day that Michael Lee was killed, just several hundred yards away, the Provisional IRA was doing its best to kill more soldiers. As a mobile patrol drove along nearby Grosvenor Road, several gunmen opened fire from a nearby building. Shots were fired, resulting in the wounding of two soldiers; a typical IRA 'shoot and scoot'. The gunmen disappeared into the Balkans and Servia area, the sort of places where they were always assured of a safe house – whether through fear or just undying loyalty – a hot bath to wash the forensics from their clothes and an army of dickers to transport the dismantled weapons away. The soldiers were unable to return fire because of the proximity of civilians. Both wounded soldiers were hospitalised, later making full recoveries.

The following day, 21 August, at around 15:00, the IRA's alacrity in turning residential streets into battlefields had yet more fatal consequences in Flax Street, Ardoyne. Isobel Leyland (née Bradley, 41), mother of four, had been born in Belfast but moved to England in order to give her children a better life. Her brother Francis Bradley had been killed by a UVF bomb in 1975. She had come back to Northern Ireland to visit her sick mother, and planned to return home that evening. She was walking along Flax Street with a school friend, Jolene McAlister; Mrs McAlister had her four-year-old daughter with her, and her grandfather, Jimmy Clark, was there also. With civilians and school-age children in the streets – this was during the school summer holidays – the IRA embarked on a shoot-out with an Army mobile patrol at the very top of Flax Street. The gunmen were in nearby Jamaica Street and opened fire with high velocity weapons at the soldiers. Unfortunately, one of their shots hit Mrs Leyland in the back, throwing her to the ground, and another hit Mr Clark. All the dying woman could do was gasp: 'I'm hit,' before lapsing into unconsciousness and dying. The soldiers, seeing a number of innocent civilians about, did not return fire. Jolene later told the *Belfast Telegraph*: 'There were another two bangs. I had never heard shooting before so I didn't know what it was. Then I heard, "I'm hit, I'm hit," and a voice saying, "I'm hit too" and I looked up and there was blood coming out of Isabel's mouth.'

She had left Belfast in 1970 in order to escape the Troubles. Brian, her widowed husband, decided that she should be buried in Belfast where she had grown up in the days before the Provisional IRA turned her playground into a battlefield. Hundreds of local people turned out to express their sorrow and anger at the IRA, but many would not dare voice their fears once confronted by these men of evil with their US-supplied Armalites. After the funeral, the coffin was carried high on the shoulders of several local men, passing the still bloodstained spot in the street where an IRA bullet had left four children without a mother.

The next day, the IRA, sounding as insincere as only they could, made the following statement:

> The Belfast Brigade of the IRA deeply regret the tragic death of Mrs Isobel Leyland during an operation in Ardoyne yesterday. One of our volunteers fired four rounds at a British soldier standing in the back of a Land Rover. Tragically Mrs Leyland and Jimmy Clark were struck by a number of these rounds. The IRA extends its deepest sympathy to the Leyland and Bradley families and hopes for a speedy recovery for Mr Clark.

Eight women were killed in the Ardoyne between 1971 and 1992; Mrs Leyland's was the final female death in this area. The following chart demonstrates that the biggest killers of Catholic women in the Ardoyne were none other than the 'protectors' of that community, the Provisional IRA:

Name	*Date*	*Killed by*
Sarah Worthington	9 August 1971	IRA
Margaret Mcorry	20 December 1971	IRA
Elizabeth McGregor	12 January 1973	Army
Martha Lavery	5 August 1974	Army
Christine Hughes	21 December 1975	IRA
Geraldine McKeown	6 December 1976	UVF
Colette Meek	17 August 1980	IRA
Isobella Leyland	21 August 1992	IRA

Six days after the killing of Mrs Leyland, and nine days after the IPLO feud claimed the life of Jimmy Brown, the internecine killing kicked off again. Hugh McKibben (21) was a member of the perma-paranoid, perma-squabbling group, the Irish Peoples' Liberation Organisation; he had joined the IPLO-Army Council breakaway group that had been headed by Jimmy Brown. Indeed, he had been one of the IPLO 'guard of honour' at Brown's paramilitary funeral. On the afternoon of Thursday 27th, McKibben had played in a GAA game at the Lámh Dhearg ground at Hannahstown in West Belfast; he represented the Michael Dwyer team from the Lower Falls. Along with others, he was sitting in a minibus, waiting to leave the ground to travel back to the Falls Road/Divis Street area, when two men climbed on board and singled him out, before announcing that they were from the IPLO-BB. The gunmen opened fire in the confined space, hitting their rival six times and killing him almost instantly; two young girls sitting in front of the IPLO-AC man dived out of the way as stray rounds passed through their seats just where their heads had been. Two other men were wounded slightly and other stray rounds narrowly missed a baby. A club spokesman told the *Belfast Telegraph*: 'At first nobody seemed to know what was happening. Everybody was falling to the floor to protect themselves. Everybody is horrified; it could have been wholesale slaughter.'

If it wasn't for the death of the Republican and the near misses which almost cost the lives of two schoolchildren, this entire episode would be laughable. In an incident resembling a scene from Monty Python's *The Life of Brian* in which opposing revolutionary groups battle it out in a game of abbreviations, there were, as a UDR contact told me 'more acronyms and abbreviations flying around the Republican groups than there were bullets'. However, the days of the IPLO-BB and the IPLO-AC were rapidly coming to an end.

That same evening, the IRA's Bogside unit opened fire on the RUC/Army base in Bishop Street, Londonderry; there were no military casualties, but a civilian was treated for shock.

On the 25th, the IRA's England team was in action once again, this time 170 miles north-west of London, planting three devices in Shrewsbury. Incendiary devices were left in two high street chain stores and a third was planted in the Shropshire Regiment Museum in Shrewsbury Castle. Severe damage was caused in all three places, especially in the museum

The South Armagh Provisionals made two attempts on consecutive days to kill soldiers in Crossmaglen. On the 27th, as a Light Infantry foot patrol was in Carran Road in the centre of the market town, a lone PIRA gunman opened fire. Several aimed shots missed, and the gunman escaped. The road takes traffic north from the village and goes past St Patrick's Primary School. Just 24 hours later, at around 18:00, a unit from the Light Infantry was crossing the main square in the town, less than a mile or so from the attack the previous day. As the soldiers crossed the square – now renamed *Carnage an Chairdnéil O Fiaich,* or Cardinal O'Fiaich Square – a PIRA gunman waited in the town cemetery, around 250 yards away. He had set up a .50 calibre Barrett M82 rifle with a sniper scope, mounted on a wooden platform. He was using armour-piercing rounds which could cut through Northern Ireland Body Armour (NIBA) like a hot knife slicing through butter. The sniper was waiting for a soldier or RUC officer to appear in his crosshairs. As fate would decree, the man who did appear was Private Paul Turner (18) from the 2nd Light Infantry, a young man from Herefordshire on the English/Welsh border. Private Turner was on his haunches when he was hit by the high-powered round which struck him with such force, that he was blasted off his feet and killed instantly. A waiting car quickly drove the weapon away, as the killer melted into the hostile countryside around Crossmaglen, leaving Paul's grieving comrades to retrieve his lifeless body.

Toby Harnden in his excellent *Bandit Country*, quotes one of his sources on the Barrett M82: 'What's special about the Barrett is the huge kinetic energy . . . The bullet can just walk through a flak jacket. South Armagh was the prime place to use such a weapon because of the availability of Brits. They came to dread it and that was part of its effectiveness.' It was used with great accuracy by the IRA sniper, claiming several SF lives, including that of one of the final soldiers to be killed in Ulster – not *the* last – Stephen Restorick on 12 February 1997. In fact, nine members of the SF – seven soldiers and two RUC men – would die at the hands of 'one shot Willie', with one DERR man, Mark Overson, being wounded by the same sniper in 1993 and fortunately escaping with his life. There was much speculation about the PIRA sniper, known locally as 'Goldfinger', centred around NORAID's involvement in flying him to the USA and arranging for him to be trained in the use of the M82 by American soldiers at US Army facilities.

Private Turner became the 34th Light Infantryman to die in the Troubles but was the first to be killed since the eight deaths at Ballygawley almost four years before. His funeral was held at St Barthelmew's Church in Harpley, near Hereford. There is a plaque in his memory at his old school, Queen Elizabeth's, Bromyard; it reads: 'To the memory of Paul Turner, a former pupil and member of 2nd Battalion, Light Infantry, who was killed in Northern Ireland in August 1992, aged 18 years.'

Sandwiched between the two Crossmaglen shootings, the UFF attempted to kill a Sinn Féin member on the Bellaghy Road near Dunloy, Co. Antrim. Paddy McErlane, whose wife was a former Sinn Féin councillor, had known that he was under threat from Loyalists for some time. His brother-in-law was an IRA man – Henry Hogan – who had been killed in a shoot-out with the SAS in 1984. Mr McErlane and his brother were driving towards Glarryford when two masked gunmen opened fire on his car, hitting him several times; despite his injuries, he managed to drive for around a mile before losing control and crashing into a hedge Ironically, he crashed right outside the home of local Unionist mayor and former UDR soldier Joe Gaston. Mr Gaston had lost a leg following an IRA car bomb attack in the early 1970s; despite this, he had no hesitation in rushing to the aid of his political enemy. He told the *Belfast Telegraph*:

> I had a fair idea who he was right from the start, but I didn't care. All I wanted to do was whatever I could to help him. I got him a blanket, and reassured him that the ambulance was on its way. I stayed with him until the ambulance arrived. Both he and his brother were pretty shocked, and they were very scared that the boys that did this would come after them.

Despite this brave act of selflessness and putting sectarian and political differences to one side, *An Phoblacht* was deafening in its silence. To the best of my knowledge Laura Friel has not written any articles praising the former UDR man's actions that day.

August was over, and 10 people had lost their lives; including an innocent Catholic woman, killed by the IRA in a display of gross irresponsibility.

21
September

Another 10 people died this month, including two soldiers, a policeman and seven civilians; of the civilians, four were Catholics gunned down by Loyalist paramilitaries, another Catholic was killed by soldiers and two Protestants died. Following a slight lull, sectarian killings were back on the agenda.

On the 3rd, Glasgow-born Scots Guards soldier Andrew Wason (25) died in the Province in circumstances which may only be described as 'violent or unnatural'. I have received information from a former member of the 2nd Battalion and am led to understand that Andrew's death was as a result of a negligent discharge. He is buried at Lambhill Cemetery in Glasgow. He was the 23rd and final member of this famous regiment to die during the Troubles. Three days later, Lance Corporal Mitchell William Arthur Patterson (51) of the Royal Irish was killed in an RTA in the Province; the first Royal Irish soldier to die since inception. His funeral was held in Christ Church, Drumany, Co. Fermanagh.

On the 4th, there was one of those regrettable incidents, fortunately rare in the context of the Troubles, which gave IRA supporters ammunition for their assertion that the British Army was there simply to shoot Nationalists without pity. This was never the case, but when questionable incidents did occur, it gave *An Phoblacht* writers a field day and meant that donations from the IRA's foreign supporters would see an increase. During that early evening, a foot patrol of the Scots Guards had cause to stop and search Peter McBride (18), a father of two babies. Mr McBride was stopped in Upper Meadow Street, in the New Lodge, around 350 yards from Duncairn Avenue where, only a month previously, a Scots Guard soldier had been shot and killed by an IRA sniper. It is highly likely that tensions were running high, and that these soldiers would have been taunted, daily, by the local yobs with chants of 'One nil' and so on, no doubt orchestrated by the Provisional IRA. That said, there was no excuse for the lack of professional restraint shown by the soldiers in what happened next.

A young Catholic man, a known petty criminal, but certainly no Republican paramilitary, McBride was stopped by Lance-Sergeant Swift. He asked McBride his address and then told him that he would be requesting a radio check to see if he should be detained. The young Catholic pulled Swift's earpiece out and began to run. As he did so, two soldiers – Guardsman Mark Wright and Guardsman James Fisher – began chasing him. For several weeks the Scots Guards – the only Scottish regiment then serving in Belfast – had been the target of IRA attacks. Guardsman Fisher, 24, a veteran of the Gulf War who had only joined the Guards after sampling the military life in the Territorials, had been a pall-bearer at Paul Shackleton's recent funeral. As he chased after Peter McBride, he would have been acutely aware of the dangers he faced.

The two soldiers fired almost simultaneously at McBride with their SA-80 rifles, hitting him twice in the back with 5.56 mm rounds. He fell to the street, mortally wounded, dying shortly afterwards. They were later arrested and charged with murder; they subsequently claimed in court that they had thought that they were under threat from either Mr McBride or other persons in the vicinity, opening fire for that reason. The judge didn't believe them; they were found guilty and sentenced to life in prison. In his judgment, Lord Justice Kelly accused Fisher of having deliberately lied and was less than complimentary when speaking about Wright's evidence. He said he considered both men 'untruthful and evasive'. Kelly's judgment was later upheld when the men's appeal against conviction was dismissed and they were also refused the right to take their case to the House of Lords. The RUC officers who had dealt with him were saddened to hear of McBride's death, especially as he was known locally as a loveable rogue. His claim to fame, was that he had broken into 'Mad Dog' Adair's house, and stolen a video player, apparently 'for the thrill of it'. Adair was furious and was said to have threatened to skin McBride alive if he ever caught him.

The following day, the UVF killed a former member of their terror group, on the hypocritical grounds that he was a drug dealer; they also claimed that he had misappropriated UVF funds. Samuel Rice (30) had absconded to England in 1990 after pocketing money which he had been paid to carry out an arson attack on a Catholic-owned hotel. He had returned secretly from the mainland to Ulster, but he was spotted going into a house in Solway Street, just off the Newtownards Road in East Belfast on the evening of the 5th. Shortly afterwards, two UVF gunman walked in through an unlocked front door and found him sitting on the settee. According to Rice's girlfriend, neither man spoke, they just simply fired a total of 14 rounds at him, hitting him in the head and chest, killing him almost instantly. The following day 'Captain Black' stated that the Loyalists had killed Mr Rice because he failed to heed warnings about involvement in drug-dealing.

On the 6th, a member of the IRA's England team planted a small device inside the Hilton Hotel in Park Lane, London. The operative planted the bomb in the male toilets on the ground floor of the hotel, before fellow IRA members telephoned a warning through to the NSPCC (National Society for the Prevention of Cruelty to Children.) Police and security staff were searching the building when the device went off, causing slight damage. The warning was made an hour earlier. 'The call was not direct to us, I believe it went to the NSPCC,' Chief Inspector Robert Chidley of the Metropolitan Police said at the scene later. The actual warning used the terms: 'all the hotels in Park Lane', which is why staff in several hotels along the strip were searching when the Hilton bomb exploded. George Ashou, the Hilton duty manager, said that the bomb went off nearly 40 minutes after police began their search of the hotel. 'We hadn't evacuated the hotel because warnings of this kind are so normal now. The bomb went off in the gentlemen's toilets behind my desk. It went off with a bang but not a big bang. Fortunately nobody was in the toilet. Nobody was injured and there is no real damage at all.' The same team detonated a further five bombs in and around the central London area over the next 10 days; the bombs were a combination of high explosive and incendiary.

On the same day, tragedy re-visited the Fox/McKearney families in Moy, Co. Tyrone; earlier in the year, Kevin McKearney had been shot by men from Robin 'the Jackal' Jackson's UVF mid-Ulster brigade; in the same incident, his uncle was fatally wounded, dying later in the year (*see* Chapter 13). Charlie Fox (63) and his wife, Tess (53), parents of six children, were relaxing at their home in Listamlat Road, between Tamnamore and Moy. They were related to the McKearney family, who were known to have strong Republican links, which in itself was enough for the UVF to condemn them to death. However, the clinching factor was the jailing of their son, Patrick Fox, the previous week for possessing explosives and for being a member of the Dungannon Provisional IRA.

At around 23:00, masked UVF gunmen – including Laurence George Maguire – broke into the house where the Foxes lived. Mrs Fox defended herself with a sweeping brush, but one of the gunmen smashed her jaw with his pistol before shooting her dead. The other gunman then shot her husband dead and left the couple lying in pools of their own blood. The bodies were not found until the following morning, when their daughter, Bernadette, widow of Kevin, arrived at their house near Moy, with her four children. She walked in through the open door and into the kitchen where they lay. She told the *Belfast Telegraph*: 'Mammy and daddy had been shot the night before but I didn't find them until the next morning. Daddy was in his pyjamas. Most of his face had been blown away by the gunfire. Mammy had been shot several times and her jaw was broken. She'd taken the sweeping brush to one of the gunmen in a vain effort to protect herself. He broke her jaw with the gun before shooting her. Seeing them lying there was the worst moment of my life.' The weapon used was a Czech VZ.58 assault rifle. The couple were described by Tyrone priest Denis Faul as 'simple, decent, innocent people'. Even Unionist MP Ken Maginnis said the shootings were 'a blasphemy before God'. Five UVF members were later convicted for their parts in the double murder. In a later statement the UVF said that Mrs Fox was not a target and was killed in the 'confusion', which was scant consolation to her loved ones. In 1993, Maguire was found guilty of a total of 41 terrorist crimes and sentenced to five concurrent life sentences at Belfast Crown Court. His behaviour was described by the Judge as 'callous depravity'.

The following day, Mary Robinson, President of the Irish Republic paid a visit to the North. She went to Londonderry and was later taken to Enniskillen, where she paid homage to the dead of the Poppy Day massacre at the town's war memorial. Did she spare a moment's thought for the irony that she, as leader of a country rapidly gaining a reputation as a terrorist sanctuary, was paying tribute to the bloody handiwork of the very people which her country was known to harbour?

On the same evening, UFF gunmen tried to break into the home of a Catholic family on the Crumlin Road; after failing to get through the security measures, they opened fire with automatic weapons, indiscriminately spraying this as well as other houses. Inside the target house, a woman and her six children were forced to take cover on the floor as bullets swept around them; a 16-year-old girl was hit in the thigh, and a male neighbour was also injured.

The following day, in Markethill in Co. Armagh, an IRA murder gang attempted to kill the caretaker at the town's Presbyterian Church, claiming that he was a part-time soldier. He was hit in the chest and critically injured, recovering later in hospital.

Over the tortuous path of the Troubles – generally accepted as 1969–98 – there were many deaths which were not exactly 'straightforward'. Many of those which involved the tin pot psychopaths of the IPLO were anything but straightforward. A killing which they carried out on the 11th of this month is a case in point, involving Michael Macklin (31), father of three young children in Nationalist West Belfast. Macklin was thought to have been used by the IPLO-BB as the getaway driver following the murder of IPLO-AC man Hugh McKibben 15 days earlier. He wasn't a suspect in the eyes of the Army, RUC, Special Branch or anyone else, but the damning factor in the eyes of the mini terror group, was his association with their new rivals. Interestingly enough, the CAIN database, one of the accepted sources of Troubles knowledge, albeit Republican, gives Mr Macklin's status as 'paramilitary'.

Mr Macklin lived with his wife and young family in Whiterock Gardens, just off the Whiterock Road, near the Ballymurphy Estate. Late on in the evening of the 11th, a car containing at least three IPLO-AC men pulled up outside the Macklin home. Two of the occupants burst into the house; they pushed a boy, thought to have been around 13, out of the way and then fired five rounds into Macklin's chest and head, killing him more or less, instantly. They then escaped along the Whiterock Road, heading for the Divis Street area. A later statement by the terror group claimed that the dead man had been involved in at least two other deaths. Mrs Macklin told the *Sunday Tribune* that her husband was not involved with any paramilitary group, and that his greatest crime was that he was related through marriage to a man involved in the dispute.

On the 14th there was an attack by the UFF on a Republican club in Belfast. It is thought that Adair was displeased that the Annadale unit of the UFF had pulled off a 'spectacular' with the massacre at Sean Graham's in the Ormeau Road and was determined that his 'C' company would surpass that outrage with a strike against the Republican Dockers' Club in Pilot Street, Belfast. A murder gang comprising McKeag and others burst into the club, armed with automatic weapons – thought to include Kalashnikovs – firing at the drinkers quite indiscriminately. Customers John McCrystal, Gerry Cunningham and 'Johnny' Denver were all cut down and lay bleeding amidst the broken glass and shattered tables and chairs; all three men survived their wounds. Further bloodshed was prevented by the quick-thinking doorman who managed to help force the gunmen outside and get the doors closed and chained before they could shoot anyone else.

On Thursday 17th, whilst I was working only a few hundred yards away, the IRA's England team carried out a firebomb attack on Madame Tussaud's on London's Marylebone Road. Two members, one of whom was believed to have been a woman, plus very possibly the same the man who had planted the bomb in the toilet at the Park Lane Hilton only days earlier, left a device in the Chamber of Horrors in Tussaud's. The no-warning explosion caused a small fire, resulting in the evacuation of the exhibition and the calling of the fire brigade. Moments later an incendiary device exploded in the London Planetarium in the next-door building. There was no damage as it spluttered out immediately. The scene then switched to the Imperial War Museum in Lambeth Road. An explosion there started a small fire, but staff extinguished it before the fire brigade arrived.

As forensic science breakthroughs were made, such as the first use of DNA profiling in the 1980s, the IRA soon learned to do all they could to reduce detection via forensics. Their first crude technique of jumping fully clothed into a hot bath, to wash away evidence of cordite contamination and so on, soon gave way to more sophisticated methods. The Forensic Science Laboratory (FSL) in Newtownbreda in the south of Belfast represented a major problem to the IRA, as newer and newer methods were becoming a major threat to their liberty. On the 23rd, the Provisionals drove a huge lorry, packed with 3,500 lb (1,590 kg) of explosive to the FSL building there; it was one of the largest bombs ever detonated in Northern Ireland. The explosion demolished the building, and much invaluable evidence, much of it irreplaceable, was destroyed; over 1,000 homes in the area were damaged. The effects of the blast were felt over 12 miles away and the sound was heard even further away. Although there were no serious injuries, hundreds of residents were treated for shock. It was described as being as powerful as a 'mini-nuke'. An ATO friend of mine told me that all of the bomb disposal team in attendance lost their hearing, and several military vehicles were damaged; the cost of repairs was estimated at £6 million.

Following the deaths of Charlie and Tess Fox at the hands of the UVF, the same terror group killed another Catholic called Fox; Leonard 'Len' Fox was not related to the murdered couple, however. This particular Mr Fox lived in Lurgan, but was employed as a builder on a property in Loyalist East Belfast. The sinister paramilitaries had warned Mr Fox to leave the area, but he chose to ignore their warnings, sadly paying for this with his life. Early on in the Troubles, Len Fox (50), father of five, had been a member of the IRA; he had served time in the 'Kesh' for the possession of explosives but, by all accounts, he had turned his back on militant Republicanism and was trying to lead a decent life. He was working on a job for Belfast Housing Authority in the Loyalist Ballybeen Estate, sandwiched between the Coomber Road and the Upper Newtownards Road. He was helping renovate a house, along with one of his teenage sons, in Kilmuir Avenue, smack in the middle of the Loyalist heartland of East Belfast.

Sometime during the afternoon of the 24th, two gunmen from the UVF, one of whom was armed with a .38 handgun, walked into the room where Len was working, shot him several times in the head and chest, before calmly walking out and escaping into any one of a myriad number of safe houses. His teenage son was a shocked witness to the murder. Speculation was rife as to how the Loyalists were alerted to the victim's presence in the area, given that he was wasn't a high-profile Republican; it may have been that a former Loyalist 'guest' of HMP Maze recognised Fox from their days of past incarceration.

On the 25th, Prime Minister John Major held a meeting with the new Taoiseach, Albert Reynolds, in London. The two leaders set a date of 16 November 1992 for the next meeting of the Anglo-Irish Intergovernmental Conference. The Ulster Unionists were still boycotting the talks, which made the whole process somewhat meaningless. The following day, SDLP leader John Hume made a rather startling declaration when he stated that Northern Ireland was not 'a natural entity and therefore you cannot have a normal democracy'. He also went on to describe the SDLP's proposals, for the governance of Northern Ireland, which naturally involved a degree of control by the Irish Republic with major contributions from Sinn Féin.

On the 27th, a UFF murder gang was dispatched from the Loyalist Tiger's Bay area to a house in North Queen Street, on the eastern perimeter of the New Lodge. One of the top Loyalists in that area was James 'Jimbo' Simpson, also known as the 'Bacardi Brigadier'.

It is thought that UDA/UFF 'intelligence' had 'discovered' that Gerard 'Soggy' O'Hara (18), a schoolboy and part-time newspaper boy for the *Belfast Telegraph*, was actually a member of the IRA. It was arrant nonsense and I wonder if the UFF ever really believed the fabrications which it claimed about its enemies, real or imaginary. The gang had based itself at a house in Midland Close, just a hundred yards from the target house. Stephen McKeag and Norman Green had been watching the O'Hara house in North Queen Street and observed the schoolboy return home from the shops. They ran over, kicked in the front door, and found their victim as he watched TV with his mother Bridget, also known as Bridie. The boy was hit, but as he fell he managed to push the living room door closed; McKeag dropped to the ground and fired an incapacitating shot through a pane of glass at the bottom of the door. The two attackers then forced the door open, roughly pushing the defenceless boy's body out of the way. As she saw the handguns, Mrs O'Hara threw herself in front of her son and begged the gunmen: 'He's only a wee boy; shoot me, instead.' Her pleas cut no ice with the psychopaths, as they shot him in the head, and then again as he lay on the floor, killing him there and then. He was another victim of a sordid, squalid sectarian war. Henry McDonald and Jim Cusack, in their quite outstanding *UDA: Inside the Heart of Loyalist Terror*, condemn the UFF's intel as 'hopelessly wrong'.

The dead boy's father denied categorically that his son had been a member of any paramilitary association, telling the *Belfast Telegraph*: 'This is no IRA house; our door is open to Protestants and Catholics alike.' The family priest said: 'Gerard was a quiet, loveable, innocent little fella who loved nothing more than playing with his young nephews, listening to music and watching television. The nearest he got to the Troubles and violence was watching through a window.' It would appear that many others agreed with him, especially the Protestants from the sectarian interface with Tiger's Bay who sent flowers and messages of sympathy. Moreover, the UFF appeared sheepish in its claims that they had got the 'right man'. However, Loyalist thugs painted graffiti taunting the dead boy's family and threatening to kill other family members. Patrick Mayhew at the NIO made a statement the following day: 'I did not know Gerard O'Hara, but I am going to remember his name. For in the supreme act of hate that shot him down in his 19th year, had called forth from his mother the enormous act of love that offered her life for his [*sic*]. Let the scarlet act of wickedness of his murder never fade from memory in Northern Ireland.'

In another incident that night, a different UFF unit set out to kill an alleged IRA man; armed men burst into a house occupied by two nuns in Lever Street, Ligoniel, North Belfast. They kicked the front door open and forced their way into several rooms; fortunately the nuns were not harmed.

The final killing of the month took place on the 30th, a Wednesday evening, in South Belfast where friends were watching Glasgow Rangers playing the Danish team Linyi in a European match. Several Protestant men were in a flat in the Annadale block, at Ballynafeigh, close to the River Lagan. The blocks were the base of the UFF unit that had carried out the Sean Graham's massacre, although it must be pointed out that the men engrossed in the Rangers game had no connection with the murder gang. Earlier, a PIRA gang had hijacked a car on the Ormeau Road before driving to the ground-floor flat. The IRA men tried but failed to force their way into the dwelling, so contented themselves with firing over 20 rounds randomly through the windows. Several men were hit, but Harry

Black (27), father of three very young children, was hit four times in the upper chest and head; he was mortally wounded. Despite being rushed to the City Hospital on the Lisburn Road, he died within minutes.

The following night, an INLA gang attacked a nearby house in Sunnyside Street, where a UFF prisoner out on compassionate leave to attend his son's wake was known to be visiting. A Protestant woman was shot and badly wounded, but she survived. It must be stated clearly here that the dead man had only family connections with the UFF but was not thought to be a member. Several years later, however, his name appeared on a UDA 'Roll of Honour' in the Loyalist Sandy Row area, adding to the confusion of the incident.

September was over, with the death toll approaching 3,600 and the Troubles in their 279th month. This month 10 people had died with five of the deaths being clearly sectarian.

22

October

This month saw the deaths of nine people; four were military personnel, and a policeman was murdered by the IRA. Two civilians died, including a male nurse killed in a mainland IRA bombing, and a Sinn Féin politician was assassinated by Loyalists. Additionally an IPLO man was killed by the Provisionals. In a feud on the Loyalist side, a former member was killed. It was also the month that the Provisional IRA had their very own re-enactment of the Nazi 'Night of the Long Knives'.

On the 1st of the month, the IRA's South Armagh brigade staged a show of strength in the border area to demonstrate to watching journalists that they, and not the Security Forces, controlled the area. Meigh is located midway between the forest at Slieve Gullion and the hamlet of Cloughoge, approximately 1,000 yards from the border with the Republic. A 15-man unit armed with rifles and machine guns – almost certainly including men who had taken part in the attack on the PVCP at Cloughoge on 1 May which killed Fusilier Andrew Grundy – set up a series of illegal vehicle checkpoints (IVCPs) around Meigh. As FAIR's Willie Frazer stated: 'They tried to turn the place into a no-go area as they have been trying to do for the last thirty-odd years.' There were unsubstantiated claims that the PIRA men, armed with AK-47s and rocket-launchers, were actually taunting RUC officers and daring them to take them on. Willie Frazer has been very scathing about police inertia during this incident, and the IRA only withdrew after several hours. It was a significant embarrassment for the Major government.

From the 5th of the month onwards, the IRA's England team demonstrated their ability to regroup, plan and carry out a series of bomb raids – some admittedly merely 'pinprick' attacks – in and around the London area, in order to maintain the momentum of their mainland campaign. On the 5th, five people were hurt when a device exploded close to Piccadilly Circus. Moments later, another bomb exploded at Flitcroft Street, just half a mile away, with no injuries. The next day, a bomb was placed under a car parked close to the London Dungeon in Tooley Street; the explosion badly injured a passer-by; within minutes, another device exploded in Balcombe Street, close to the scene of the siege in December, 1975. Finally the scene switched to the carpark of the Royal British Legion building in Southgate, north London. These devices had been a combination of nuisance bombs and those intended to cause serious injuries; the next one would take the life of a nurse.

On the 9th, the Provisionals stepped up their so-called economic warfare, when they exploded two car bombs in the centre of Dungannon, Co. Tyrone, destroying several shops. It was clear that the Loyalist paramilitaries were increasingly angered by the IRA's bombing campaign; two more PIRA bombs at the end of the month would trigger a predictable response.

The Red Hand Commando (RHC) was a small, highly secretive Ulster Loyalist paramilitary group; it was nominally part of the UFF, certainly maintaining very close links with them, with their personnel and weapons often being interchangeable. On the 9th, the RHC killed a fellow Protestant in Parkgate Avenue, just off the Upper Newtownards Road in Loyalist East Belfast. There were the predictable claims of 'informer' with the associated nonsense which the paramilitary groups used to excuse their bloodlust, but the prosaic truth was that it was a simple case of score-settling. Michael Anderson (37), father of four with a fifth child expected, had been a Loyalist paramilitary. However, when he ended a six-year prison sentence for armed robbery – for stealing funds on behalf of the UDA/UFF – he had relinquished his ties with his former comrades. He had clearly made enemies, and on the pretext that he was an informer for RUC SB, a local unit from the Newtownards Road was sent to kill him. He was working in Parkgate Avenue, on rebuilding work in Mersey Street, when two men walked up to where he was chatting to workmates. The gunmen singled him out before shooting him with one barrel of a sawn-off shotgun; as he lay on the ground, the gunman fired another round into his head at point-blank range, which killed him instantly.

No one was ever charged with the murder. Score-settling also occurred in other paramilitary organisations, such as the Provisionals, with there being suggestions that some executed 'informants' were removed because it was expedient to do so. For example, there was a very strong rumour that a PIRA man who was having an affair with the wife of an on the run (OTR) volunteer decided that he wanted to make the relationship permanent. Consequently, he began spreading rumours that the other man was a 'tout'. His rival made a one-way visit to Freddie Scappaticci's 'nutting squad', being left hooded, with two bullet holes in the back of his head, at a roadside close to the border.

On the 9th exactly what the anti-terror police in London had feared following the build-up of bombs finally happened: an explosion took a life. A PIRA operative planted a device inside the Sussex pub, close to Covent Garden. It was a Friday lunchtime; the end of the working week was just hours away and the pubs were packed with workers, tourists and shoppers. A device was placed inside a toilet before a warning was telephoned to LBC Radio Station and relayed to the police. A spokesman for the Met Police described the warning as 'misleading and deliberately imprecise'. The caller stated that the bomb was: 'in the Leicester Square area' but the pub was in Long Acre, some distance away. David Heffer (30) was a psychiatric nurse from Luton; he was standing outside the pub when the bomb went off. Five people were injured in the blast, including Mr Heffer; he died the following day in University College Hospital. One man had been about to enter the pub just seconds before the blast, but was stopped by a tourist who asked for directions: the thin gossamer thread of fate, yet again.

The *Independent* reported:

> Commander George Churchill-Coleman, head of Scotland Yard's anti-terrorist branch, said the bomb was a small device, but big enough in the confined space to cause very serious injuries. 'This is now typical of the cynical disregard that the terrorist has for public safety and life, indeed people in general,' he said.

He appealed to the public to remain vigilant to help minimise the number of bombings, but added: 'Whatever you do, do not be deterred from going about your normal business – that's what the terrorists want you to do.' John Cracknell, 24, who was about 10 yards from the pub when the bomb went off, said: 'There was glass all over the pavement and some smoke coming out of the building. I ran in through the front door of the pub and downstairs to see if anybody was injured. The stairs were strewn with rubble.' An arts student, Sef Townsend, 44, said he had been about to enter the pub at 1.30, but had stopped to give a tourist directions. 'If I had been three seconds earlier, I would have been in there,' he said. 'I went in and saw the carnage. The bar was completely destroyed and there was a man lying there. He looked very ill.'

On the same day that Mr Heffer expired from the terrible injuries he had suffered at the Sussex pub, some 450 miles away in Belfast, Constable James Douglas (50), father of two children aged 12 and 17, became the 290th RUC officer to die in the Troubles and the first officer to be killed in a terror-related incident for seven months. The officer was known by the IRA to drink at the Monaco bar in Belfast on most Saturdays, duties permitting. The bar was on Lombard Street, close to the junction with Rosemary Street, some 500 yards from the Nationalist Markets area. An hour or so before his death, the officer went to a nearby bookies to place a bet and when he returned, he was a little shaken, telling his brother that he had seen a known player in the shop. He described the man to his brother as a 'bad bastard'. An hour or so later, at around 15:30, a black taxi which had been hijacked close to the Unity Flats, parked in Bridge Street, a two-minute walk from the bar. Leaving another man at the wheel of the taxi, two IRA gunmen made the short walk to the Monaco. Constable Douglas had just stood up to buy a round of drinks when the gunmen opened fire, one of them using a .357 Magnum; Douglas was cut down, which caused a major panic in the busy area. The police officer was hit in the face and body, dying instantly.

The *Independent* reported the incident as follows:

> Constable Jim Douglas, 50, was having a drink with his brother in the Monaco bar in Lombard Street when one of the gunmen singled him out and opened fire. He was shot twice in the body and once in the head. A lifeguard drinking in the pub tried to give first aid but Constable Douglas died almost at once. As the gunman opened fire, staff and customers flung themselves to the ground. The men, wearing baseball caps, fled into streets packed with Saturday shoppers. They left a suspected bomb in the front doorway of the pub, and the bar was evacuated amid fears that the device was about to explode. Army bomb-disposal experts carried out a controlled explosion on the package before declaring it a hoax. Police later found a black taxi that had been hijacked and abandoned about a mile from the pub in the west of the city. It is understood that it was used as a getaway vehicle by the terrorists. Police want to interview a person who is believed to have handed one of the terrorists, who was wearing smart casual clothes, his cap after he had dropped it getting into the cab during his escape. The taxi is thought to have been driven by a third terrorist. The IRA, in a telephone call to a Belfast radio station, claimed responsibility for the attack last night.

On the 16th, the UVF shot and killed a Sinn Féin activist, after stalking her as she walked from Queen's University to the York Hotel in Botanic Avenue. Sheena Campbell (29) was the mother of a son called Caolán, who was 11. She had been a member of Sinn Féin for a number of years; whilst not an active supporter of the IRA, she was nonetheless a committed Republican, which was enough in the eyes of the UVF to condemn her to death. She had been spotted eating a meal in the University refectory and was followed on the short stroll to the York Hotel – now called Madison's – on Botanic Avenue. At around 19:00, as she stood at the bar drinking with friends, a UVF gunman dressed in a baseball cap and head scarf walked across to her. Concealed in his jacket was a .357 Magnum which he drew, firing five times from very close range at Ms Campbell. The first round hit her in the heart and the gunman then stood over her, firing repeatedly into her upper torso. The bar was busy and people threw themselves to the floor in panic; in the confusion, the gunman was able to make his way out and escape on foot. Shortly afterwards, he was picked up by a stolen car which was later found burned out in the Loyalist Sandy Row.

Also on the 16th, the RAF lost the first of four personnel who would die in the Province in the space of 40 days. Squadron Leader Robert John Burge (35) – the most senior RAF officer to die during the Troubles – was killed in an RTA in the Aldergrove area. He was based at RAF Aldergrove; a native of Northern Ireland, he is buried at Roselawn Cemetery in Belfast.

The violence then switched back to the English mainland with a further five attacks between the 19th and the 30th. In the first attack, the IRA's England team targeted London's theatre land, with a device placed close to the Prince of Wales Theatre and the Comedy Pub in Oxenden Street. The explosion caused much damage as well as leaving two passers-by requiring hospital treatment for shock. Just two days later, five miles further west, the IRA detonated a bomb outside the Princess Louise TA Centre on Hammersmith Road. Three people were injured by flying glass, requiring hospital treatment. Hours later, another bomb exploded on the main rail line at Edmonton, injuring two people. The Provisionals were setting off bomb after bomb across London with apparent impunity. Over the next week or so there were three more explosions; on the 22nd, a sewage pipe was damaged by an IRA explosive device at Wick Lane, and three days later a car bomb close by injured several more people. Finally on the 30th, a black cab driver was forced to drive his taxi to the Downing Street area where it exploded, causing some damage to buildings near the Prime Minister's residence.

On the 20th, the IRA killed part-time soldier, Sergeant Robert Irvine (43), father of two, in Rasharkin, Co. Antrim; he became the first Royal Irish Regiment member to be killed by terrorists since the Royal Irish took over from the disbanded UDR. He was off duty at the time, and he and his wife and one of his daughters were visiting his sister at her home in Tamlaght Road, Rasharkin. The village is in north Antrim, midway between Coleraine and Ballymena; it was an area in which the Provisionals operated frequently. Sergeant Irvine had just stepped out of the bath wrapped in a bath towel, when gunmen who had hidden in the garden walked into the house, shooting him several times in front of his shocked family. They ran off leaving him in a pool of blood on the floor.

There was a sizeable Catholic population in the Rasharkin area; it is highly probable that the soldier, who joined the UDR in 1978, having previously been in the RUC, was dicked by one or more of these people. The last word should be left to Sergeant Irvine's sister: 'The neighbours began to appear then. They just stood there, staring at Robert's body, saying nothing. I felt that it had to be one of them who had done it, who had passed on the information. I've lived in the place all my life. We trusted these people. They were always in and out of my house and they were welcome to whatever we had. But I can't trust them now.'

Another Royal Irish soldier to die, Private Brian Daniel (21), lost his life on the same day in an RTA close to HMP Maze in Co. Antrim. He was from the Co. Antrim area and he is buried near the site of the former prison.

Earlier in the month, Loyalists had warned the IRA that if the indiscriminate bombing and destruction of the Ulster economy continued, they would step up their sectarian terror campaign. If that threat even registered with the Provisional IRA, there was little evidence as they carried out two major bombings, on the 21st and the 30th. In the first attack, a PIRA unit planted a 200 lb (90 kg) car bomb in the centre of Bangor, Co. Down. The device exploded in the main shopping area, causing extensive damage; there were no injuries. Nine days later, the scene switched to North Belfast, only this time there was no warning as a car bomb exploded outside Glengormley RUC station. The device weighed 250 lb (110 kg) with the resulting explosion injuring 13 people, some badly; most of the injured were police officers, and over 100 houses in the surrounding area were damaged. In the latter explosion, the British government would be forced to rebuild the station at enormous cost, but they would also have to contract the work out to civilian companies, thus increasing the chances of PIRA retaliation against innocent workmen

On the 29th, the Green Jackets lost another of their men, in what was turning into a bad year for the elite regiment. Rifleman Richard Andrew Davey (18) was killed inside his base in what may only be described as 'death by violent or unnatural causes'. He was from Milton Keynes and was cremated at Crown Hill Crematorium, Herts; he was the 47th Green Jacket to die in or as a consequence of the Troubles.

On the night of 30 June 1934, in what is known as the Night of the Long Knives, Hitler and his SS wiped out many hated rivals inside the Nazi Party. On the night of Saturday 31 October 1993, the Provisional IRA had its very own purge, as it pummelled the IPLO (both factions, IPLO-BB and IPLO-AC) into submission, destroying their power base, confiscating their weapons and forcing them to close down their movements.

In a display of gross hypocrisy, the Provisionals decided that the IPLO was 'destroying the credibility' of the Republican movement. This, surely, is what they themselves had done, having killed some 2,000 people with bullet and bomb, killed not only soldiers, policemen and prison officers, but also civilians, Catholic and Protestant, killed for the most spurious of reasons, massacred without pity. They had killed women and children without mercy, they had killed long after their own unrealistic dreams had long ceased to be attainable. According to Raymond Gilmour, a former agent who penetrated the INLA and IRA, they attracted cold-blooded, heartless men of evil: psychopaths, some of whom had unstoppable urges to masturbate after a killing, such was the sexual pleasure of death; the movement drew paedophiles, rapists, serial adulterers and the like to their cause. Men who needed the thrill of getting up close to their victims and who enjoyed looking into the eyes of those they killed, in order to achieve some sort of sadistic 'high'. This was the organisation which wiped out the IPLO because they gave Republicanism 'a bad name'.

On the Saturday evening, the IRA attacked both factions of the IPLO in Belfast, killing Sammy Ward, the leader of the IPLO-BB in the Catholic Short Strand area. In an extraordinary display of well-coordinated tactics, IRA gunmen raided IPLO haunts throughout the city. There were raids on pubs and clubs where IPLO members were taken outside and kneecapped; others were pistol-whipped, or beaten with sticks. Eight IPLO men were shot and wounded, but the Provisionals' main target was Ward (30), father of two, who lived in the Short Strand. On the evening that his organisation was wiped out, he went out for a drink in Sean Martin's, a club in Beechfield Street, little knowing that it would be his last. At around 17:30, armed PIRA men walked into the club and ordered everyone onto the floor, except for Ward; he was singled out and shot 10 times, including three times in the head. Top IPLO man Sean Caldwell received a message from the local PIRA commander, instructing him to report, accompanied by a priest, to a local Provo haunt, a social club in the Falls Road area. Immediately he entered, he was hooded and forced to sit down. It is alleged that he was told words to the effect of: 'Tomorrow morning, we want you and your fucking cronies to tell newspapers you no longer exist.'[1] With that, he was allowed to leave to report back to his fellow IPLO commanders, with the *fait accompli* handed to him by the Provisionals.

Just 48 hours later, on 2nd November, the IPLO-BB, following advice from their chastened second in command, surrendered to the Provisionals. Within days, all their arms and explosives caches had been turned over to local IRA commanders. Both IPLO factions simply ceased to exist.

Nine people died this month.

1. As reported by David Leslie, in *Lighting Candles* (Black & White Publishing, 2014).

23
November

This was a month which would witness 13 deaths: five of them being military personnel, four of whom were killed when two helicopters crashed at Bessbrook Mill. Six civilians would die, five of them in senseless sectarian attacks and the IRA's nutting squad would be in action once more, killing a suspected informer. The UFF would carry out another attack on a betting shop, with more carnage as a result.

On Tuesday 1st, the IRA planted two small bombs in the centre of Belfast allowing them to detonate without giving proper warnings. Their warnings were always deliberately vague, deliberately misleading in order to extract maximum deaths and maximum damage whilst presenting an image of 'Well, we tried to warn them, but they took no notice.' There was always the hinted suggestion to the press that the RUC/Army deliberately wanted a certain number of casualties in order to blacken the name of Republicanism. In the Belfast blasts, 27 police and civilians were injured. Almost simultaneously and several hundreds of miles away, the IRA planted a bomb near Tottenham Court Road Tube station which was safely defused by the bomb squad.

In the US presidential election this month Bill Clinton defeated the incumbent, George Bush, to become the 42nd President of the USA. Would he prove to be a friend of the British? We shall see, but his decision to invite blood-stained IRA men such as Adams and McGuinness into the White House, in defiance of the British, was seen by many as an act of insensitivity towards the British.

Michael Gilbride (36), father of three children, was known by the UFF to visit his parents' house in Fernwood Street, Belfast. Their house was just off the Ormeau Road, very close to the UFF Annadale Flats. He had been observed going to the house on several occasions; now, on the 4th, a murder gang which included Stephen 'Inch' McFerran, and possibly also Raymond Elder and Joe Bratty, arrived at the house where Mr Gilbride's parents lived. They lay in wait until their target turned up. The innocent Catholic had just got out of his car when the gunmen opened fire, hitting him three times in the head, killing him almost instantly. After the murder, they raced off in the direction of the Annadale. The following day, they announced that he was a member of the IRA, a claim which was dismissed by both his family and the RUC. It was just another senseless sectarian murder and the UDA/UFF were acutely aware that was the case.

One of the men likely responsible for this murder was, as previously mentioned, Joe 'Chinky' Bratty. He became head of the UDA in Ballynafeigh, leading his own unit from Annadale Flats and being one of the men who ordered the Sean Graham bookmaker's massacre in February 1992. It is said that his sadistic love of killing as well as his utter hatred of Catholics persuaded the IRA to reduce attacks on soldiers and RUC in the Belfast area and target leading Loyalists instead. On 31 July 1994, both he and Elder were killed by the Provisionals; McFerran was already in jail by this time.

Three days later, Bratty was again involved, this time at his own Annadale Flats. On the evening of the 7th, with the blood of Mr Gilbride not yet dry on Fernwood Street, Bratty decided that a Protestant woman, Donna Wilson (30), mother of three young children, should suffer a punishment beating; in the event, she was beaten to death. She had recently moved with her children from Tullycarnet in East Belfast, immediately alienating one of her neighbours, a 60-year-old man, who complained about her loud music. He took his grievances to Bratty as UDA commander in the flats. This then was the world of paramilitary rule, where instead of speaking to the police or local council, a complaint was taken to armed men, known to be murderers. In view of the man's demands that Mrs Wilson be taught a lesson, Bratty assembled a team of 10 men, armed with baseball bats, storming around to her flat. They kicked in the front door at around 19:30, before savagely beating her to death; she was hit time and time again, until her head was a bloodied pulp. They seriously injured three of her friends as well as completely wrecking the flat. An RUC source told me that: 'The flat looked as though a bomb had detonated and you couldn't see what colour her hair was, because if was absolutely caked in blood. The skull was completely caved-in.' It is very likely that 'Inch' McFerran – rumoured to be a Special Branch informant – was amongst the gang of thugs which carried out the savage murder. Ms Wilson, who was divorced, left three children under 10; they were taken into care by the local council.

Harry Robinson of FAIT (Families Against Intimidation and Terror) said this of Bratty's gang of thugs: 'These attacks give them something to do when they're not killing Catholics – they are a taster of things to come. It's a real macho thing: a band of young men go out and work themselves into a frenzy, like a pack of dogs, trying to outdo one another in brutality.'

On the 13th, in what was seen as their riposte to the UDA ultimatum about bombing Protestant areas, the Provisionals exploded a large van bomb in the centre of Coleraine, Co. Londonderry. The bomb caused extensive damage to the commercial heart of the town. Two days later, the IRA's England team attempted to pull off another Baltic Exchange-like spectacular, with a 1,000 lb (450 kg) car bomb at Canary Wharf. Built between 1988 and 1991, the 50-storey building was amongst the tallest in Europe at the time; in 1993, the *Daily Mirror* moved its HQ there. On Sunday 15th, the IRA drove the bomb to the iconic site, but the authorities, especially with the Baltic bomb still fresh in their memories, were alert to the threat.

The IRA had already worked out that to cause maximum damage, the bomb had to be placed under the Docklands Light Railway (DLR) bridge. The bomb was packed into a van which was driven to the designated place. Ironically, they parked on double-yellow lines and were spotted immediately by alert security guards. As the guards approached, two men, both armed, jumped out of the van, threatening the approaching men. One of the IRA men opened fire, but had a stoppage which undoubtedly saved the lives of the guards. The bombers ran off, abandoning the van, and escaped to where a waiting getaway car was parked, engine running. Police and the bomb squad were called, but as they were examining the device, the detonator fired. However, someone was watching over those men that day, as the main charge failed to detonate; it was swiftly made safe. The following day, a spokesman for the Provisional IRA stated that it was only ill-luck which prevented the bomb causing unimaginable financial damage in the area.

On the 14th, a week after the murder of Donna Wilson, the UFF were again involved, but this time it was their 'C' company on the Shankill, acting on the direct orders of Johnny Adair. Seemingly envious of Bratty's attack on Sean Graham's bookies in February, he ordered a similar attack on another bookmaker in the Nationalist Oldpark area, on the eastern side of the Ardoyne. The branch of James Murray's (part of the Sean Graham empire) was on the corner of the Oldpark Road and Rosapenna Street.

In the late afternoon of the 14th, a bitterly cold day, a stolen taxi containing several Loyalist gunmen, including 'Top Gun' himself, Stephen McKeag, pulled up on the Oldpark Road. Two of the men walked across to the bookies, frequented in the main by Catholics, although several Protestant punters were inside at the time. They had timed the attack to take place just as the 4 o'clock from Cheltenham was running, as they knew that the place would be packed. One kicked the door open – likely to have been McKeag – and opened fire with a Czech VZ.58 automatic weapon, whilst the other man – long suspected to have been Norman Truesdale – smashed the front window and threw a Soviet-manufactured hand grenade into the mass of people inside. The grenade-thrower shouted anti-Catholic insults whilst McKeag was busy firing at the helpless punters, some of his rounds passing through a first victim to hit a second with the same bullet. Francis Burns (62), father of four grown-up children, and Peter Orderly (47), also a father of four, were killed instantly. John Lovett (72) was also hit; he died in hospital the following day. A further 13 men were injured, some very seriously; they were rushed to the Mater Hospital. There were 16 people in the small shop, with 12 of them being injured; one man had his leg blown off by the grenade. Hugh Jordan described the premises as being a 'pathetically easy target'. One survivor was quoted as saying: 'I counted about six bodies on the floor. They were all moaning and only one man spoke. He said to me: "Will we be alright?"'

Apparently, the safe house where the killers went after the attack was only 100 yards away. Indeed, the killers would have heard the wailing ambulance sirens, as they scrubbed off the forensics and had their clothes taken away for burning and their weapons disassembled. When a fleet of ambulances arrived to begin taking the dead, the dying and the wounded, there were loud cheers from the Protestant side of the Oldpark Road. Indeed, shortly afterwards, there was a huge celebration on the Shankill with Adair buying drinks for the three attackers, slapping them all on the back, as he enjoyed the 'party atmosphere'. The following day, the UDA/UFF made a chilling statement: 'We again warn that the theatre of war will be full of casualties from the Republican community in the coming weeks.' This was a reiteration of the warning to the Provisionals from a few weeks back, after which the IRA stepped up their bombing campaign against Protestant targets, demonstrating that they were unwilling to back down. As neither side was willing to call a halt, the tit-for-tat slayings would continue and that was the nub of Ulster's tragedy: neither side would cede an inch.

The dead men each had his own life, his own story: Francis Burns lived in Manor Street, just a six-minute stroll away; he received six wounds, plus post-mortem shrapnel injuries from the grenade. He was already unable to speak having suffered from throat cancer. Peter

Orderly lived a little closer; he was hit in the lung and heart. John Lovett lived even closer – on Rosapenna Street – and was struck three times in the chest. He was a former British soldier, having been captured by the Japanese at the fall of Singapore, enduring sadistic torture at their hands in a POW camp. Of the killers, Truesdale was gunned down by the Provisionals at his grocer's shop on the Oldpark Road in March 1993, just four months later. McKeag died in September 2000 following an overdose of cocaine and pain-killers. The third man – the getaway driver – was never identified.

McDonald and Cusack wrote: 'The UDA on the Shankill justified the killings by pointing to the devastating IRA car bomb that tore through the commercial heart of Coleraine the same weekend. In its eyes, the nationalist population would have to pay the price for renewed IRA bombings of mainly Protestant towns across Northern Ireland.'[1]

Later that very same night, just before midnight in fact, a PIRA sniper – highly likely to have been the same US-trained gunman who shot Private Paul Turner in Crossmaglen on 28 August (*see* Chapter 20) – fatally wounded a policeman at the border. Constable Alan Corbett (25) was manning a VCP at Belcoo, Co. Fermanagh, along with soldiers, as they monitored traffic using the border crossing there. The village is sandwiched between Lough Macnean Lower and Macnean Upper, jutting into the Republic, on the main Enniskillen to Sligo Road.

The policeman was a member of the RUCR. Unknown to him, a PIRA gunman was setting up a firing point, just 300 yards across the border in Co. Donegal, just outside a hamlet called Blacklion. Using an AK-47 rifle with a night-vision sniper scope, he fired just one shot which tore into the young officer's chest. Unable to see where the shot had been fired from, the fatally wounded officer's comrades were unable to return fire. He was casevaced to hospital where surgeons fought for almost four hours to save his life; he died in the early hours of the following morning.

It is thought that the same unit – in many instances the same gunman – was responsible for the deaths of 11 members of the SF (10 soldiers as well as Constable Corbett) – carried out in a whole series of 'one shot' attacks between 1992 and 1994. They also used a Barrett .50-calibre and may also have had access to a Russian Dragunov. On several occasions they mounted the weapon in the rear of an improvised armour-plated saloon car, painted black, so making it difficult to spot at night. After an attack, the 'mobile gun platform' could be driven away, with all the forensics and empty shell casings contained within it for cleaning and later disposal.

On the 18th, Gerard Holmes (35), an unemployed salesman, was abducted from near his home in Londonderry, and taken to a safe house in the Creggan Estate, probably on Creggan Heights; four days later, he became the 30th victim of Freddie Scappaticci's nutting squad. He was held for around 96 hours, during which time he was tortured and brutalised by men purporting to be 'freedom fighters' and defenders of the Catholic community, using all manner of depraved barbarity. After constant torture, his arms were bound behind his back, he was hooded, taken out of the house in the dead of night, before being dragged into a filthy alleyway on Rinmore Drive. There he was forced to kneel, before two bullets in the back of his head, ended his life. No doubt, a tame Catholic priest had conducted a sham last rites, a discredited act of contrition, before Holmes was dragged away to be shot. At

1. McDonald and Cusack, *UDA: Inside the Heart of Loyalist Terror*, p. 238.

that time, the late Martin McGuinness was the top PIRA/Sinn Féin man in the North, let alone the Creggan; he must have been aware of the 'execution' but was strangely silent. The local IRA commanders delivered a tape-recording to the dead man's family. The tape was apparently two minutes long, but contained nothing of significance; indeed, it was said to be inconclusive by the family. The IRA said, however, that it was a 'confession' and that it was 'given willingly'. They further claimed that it proved that he was an informer for RUC Special Branch, which both the RUC and Mr Holmes's family vehemently denied. His body was found on the 22nd, shortly after he was shot. The torture and murder took place approximately 2,000 yards away from the Irish border.

IRA Torture Methods

In order to judge better what was happening to a victim during this torture, the following quotation from Martin Dillon's excellent *God and the Gun* might put things into more perspective. Dillon perfectly illustrates one such event when the squad had all but finished their dirty business and the bleeding and bruised man wished to make his peace. Dillon interviewed a priest known only as 'Father Pat' who had been summoned to a PIRA safe house and led upstairs to the bathroom, which had clearly been employed as a torture room: 'I froze when the bathroom door closed. I was suddenly dealing with evil and not just talking about it. The man in the chair was one of my parishioners. I remember looking at the bath filled with water wondering what they had done with him. He was stripped to a pair of wet underpants. His hair and body were wet so they'd obviously been holding him under the water . . . He was badly bruised and his eyes were so swollen he could hardly see me . . . The victim was incapable of walking. I put my arm around him . . . it seemed the only loving thing I could do. His lips were swollen and I heard him murmur: "Please help me, Father." I felt so helpless. Leaving that room was a nightmare I have to live with.'[1]

It is worth repeating at this stage, especially in the context of Mr Holmes's death, a description of what some observers have called 'the IRA's Spanish Inquisition'. In the first instance, the suspected informer might be summoned to a meeting with his (or her) cell or local commanders, ostensibly to discuss a pending operation or a debrief of a recent one. If it was felt that the suspect might be suspicious, or even resist, he would be abducted, from home or en route to the pub or wherever. He would be bundled into a car and immediately hooded, before being punched and kicked in order to soften him up. British agent Marty McGartland's 'summons' the previous August (*see* Chapter 8) was a case in point. The suspected informer – in many cases, the 'nutting squad' had already decided on a 'guilty' verdict – would be taken into a 'safe house' where he would be placed in a darkened room, that had been stripped of furniture, other than a single chair facing the wall, in front of a table and several chairs at his back. The curtains would be heavy material – like wartime blackout covers – with all things human (paintings, books, toys and so on) being removed. At this point, the questioning would commence: sometimes gentle, sometimes threatening. If the answers the 'nutting squad' wanted were not forthcoming, the suspect would be bound and the violence would begin.

1. Martin Dillon, *God and the Gun* (Routledge, 1999), pp. 99–100.

At first, a few choice blows from a wooden hurley stick or baseball bat would be rained down upon him, increasing in intensity. Next, he would be stripped and cigarettes would be stubbed out on his, or even her chest. One man told me that he was asked to clean up after an 'interrogation' and found a myriad number of tab ends, evidence either of chain-smoking torturers or the number of cigarettes that had been used to torture the suspect. If a confession was still not forthcoming, he would be dragged into the bathroom where a bath of cold water would be waiting. He would be forced into the bath and then live electric wires would be brushed agonisingly over his body. Alternatively, his head would be held under the water until he had to inhale and almost drown as water – by now bloodstained – rushed into his lungs. Next, it would be pre-heated pokers which would be pressed against bare skin, the stench of smouldering flesh assailing the suspect's nostrils. Sometimes, a red-hot poker would be inserted into the man's anus, causing excruciating pain. Then out would come sharpened screwdrivers and chisels which would be used to stab the victim; sometimes a rusty saw would be used to cut into his skin and bone. Another method was to douse his or her legs in paraffin and then set it alight.

One unnamed man, known to be a chief IRA executioner, even designed a medieval torture vault which he named 'Sing Sing' outside the village of Knockraha, near Glanmire in Co. Cork. I have been told of pliers being used to pull out fingernails and toenails. The same source quoted previously described how once, on a clean-up job, he saw several teeth lying around, having been pulled out by the roots along with several bloodied finger nails discarded on the specially prepared sheets of plastic. It is small wonder then, that following this mediaeval barbarism, a confession was made in virtually every instance. This then is NOT the image of the 'romantic freedom-fighter' which was sold to generations of Brit-hating, gullible Irish-Americans; one wonders if the drinkers in Boston's assortment of Irish bars would have kept their dollars in their wallets had they known the truth.

Portadown in Co. Armagh sits on the River Bann; it was brought to trade prominence with the advent of the Victorian railway age. It has a two-thirds Protestant majority; more importantly it was at the very heart of the operational area of the UVF's mid-Ulster brigade, responsible for at least a hundred sectarian murders. On the 19th, part-time Royal Irish soldier Lance Corporal Iain Warnock (28), father of a toddler son, drove, as he did many times, to Moy Park in order to collect his wife after work. He lived in Abercorn Park, in the south of Portadown, with his regular journey to Moy Park to the town's north-west taking only a few minutes. The area where his wife worked is very close to the Nationalist Craigavon district which was a stronghold of the Provisional IRA.

He arrived at around 17:00, with his three-year-old son strapped into a child seat in the rear of his car. As he stopped, two IRA men got out of a stolen taxi and immediately opened fire. Although wounded, he tried to get away from the car so that stray rounds would not hit his child. He managed to fire several shots back at his attackers, but fell, mortally wounded after a number of shots hit him in the head; in all he was hit 12 times. The little boy witnessed the terrible head injuries suffered by his daddy and it is difficult to see how this would not have affected him his entire life. The killers raced away, abandoning and burning the stolen taxi some 12 miles away. A former UDR soldier told me: 'It was obvious to me and it was obvious to everyone involved that he was dicked, but not just by some Republican sleazebag hanging around, but by someone who knew Iain's wife and knew that he picked her up at the factory after work. It was someone who worked with her, maybe knew her well or just nodded to her, but was a Provo sympathiser and he or she passed the information to IRA commanders in Craigavon. I wonder if he was able to look her in the eyes later.'

On the 25th, IRA gunman Pearse Jordan (25), from the Ballymurphy Estate, was shot dead by the RUC in West Belfast. *Lost Lives* yet again refers to the circumstances of his death as 'disputed'. During the early part of the evening, Jordan – a known player – was spotted by four uniformed RUC officers in an unmarked car; he was driving a stolen car along the Falls Road. As it was suspected that he was carrying arms and possibly explosives, the patrol car put on its sirens and signalled to Jordan to stop. The IRA volunteer refused, accelerating quickly away, causing the RUC men to give chase. Eventually they rammed his car, forcing him to stop; he jumped out of the car and began running away. As he did so, another patrol car arrived on the scene, containing Headquarters Mobile Support Unit (HMSU) officers, including a sergeant who yelled at him to stop. Jordan turned towards the sergeant in an aggressive manner, and his arms were down with his hands out of sight; the sergeant's vision was obscured, although he feared that the IRA man was armed and posing a threat to the officers' lives. In his statement he said that he felt that he had no option but to fire. He fired three shots at Jordan, who fell mortally wounded to the ground. I would ask those who think that I should be more impartial to consider the murder of Lance Corporal Iain Warnock, shot dead in front of his three-year-old son, just six days earlier.

There were the usual accusations from Sinn Féin of 'shoot to kill', and the incident provided more colourful propaganda for the Provisionals and their multitude of supporters all over the world. Senior politicians often insensitively refer to times when it is a good day in which to bury bad news; for the IRA who had just tortured and murdered Gerard Holmes three days previously it was a good day of this sort. They could brush aside accusations of barbaric behaviour, diverting attention instead to their brave, dead volunteer, 'gunned down by Crown Forces'. At the IRA man's funeral, attended by hundreds of mourners, Gerry Adams ensured even more prominence, as he helped carry Pearse's coffin.

Alan Barker in his very readable *Shadows: Inside Northern Ireland's Special Branch* writes: 'This propaganda which has been promoted by Adams, McGuinness and their supporters, both inside and outside the Republican movement, is a figment of their imagination. The truth is, and they all well know it . . . those members of the INLA and PIRA who were shot by members of the security forces while out to commit murder were killed justifiably. They (the IRA) claimed to be fighting in a war and in a war soldiers get killed. So why the hypocritical hue and cry when the security forces engaged in fire-fights with the terrorists and came off best?'[1]

Finally, on the 26th, a double helicopter crash at the SF base in Bessbrook Mill, Co. Armagh, cost the lives of three RAF pilots and an officer in the Price of Wales Royal Regiment (PWRR), injuring a dozen more men. In the late evening, two helicopters – an Army Air Corps Gazelle and an RAF Puma – were coming in to land at the huge heliport – the biggest in Europe at the time. The two helicopters had been out on operations over 'bandit country'. Suddenly the Gazelle's rotors hit the cockpit area of the Puma. The Puma crashed to the ground, killing all four men on board. The Gazelle, out of control, hovered

1. Alan Barker, *Shadows: Inside Northern Ireland's Special Branch* (Mainstream, 2004), p. 198.

for a few more seconds, before plunging into a perimeter fence and bursting into flames, seriously injuring several men on board. The men killed were Squadron Leader Michael Haverson (39), Flight Lieutenant Simon Marcus John Roberts (26), Flight Sergeant Jan Robert Pewtress (33), all from RAF Aldergrove, and Major John Barr (36), a soldier with the PWRR. Major Barr was the first and only soldier from the Regiment to be killed in Northern Ireland. Michael Haverson was from Belfast; Simon Roberts was from Lincoln; Jan Pewtress was from Peterborough, and John Barr was from Liphook, Hampshire.

A later investigation showed that the accident was caused by both crews failing to see the other helicopter and being unable to take evasive action in time; also by inadequate use of the correct radio procedures as well as a breakdown in the passage of information between the RAF and the AAC.

Major Dan McBride, Army Air Corps

From talking with the investigators months after the crash, the Puma collided with our aircraft from about our 11 o'clock position which shredded 2–3 feet off our rotor blades. Effectively this would have cut the control runs in the starboard side of the Puma meaning the 4 personnel (3 x RAF and 1 x Army) on board the aircraft had little chance of survival. It should also have meant that our rotor blades should have been ripped off. However, they managed to stay on. At this point I believe that I was hit by flying debris as my helmet was cleaved into two pieces and I was knocked unconscious. Obviously a helicopter without rotor blades is, by definition, not a helicopter and a fall from such a height should have been the end for us. However, our fall was broken by a little metal bridge over a V-shaped ditch. The co-pilot was thrown clear in his armoured chair, breaking his left arm and fracturing his right hand. As I was in the right seat I was not quite so lucky and ended up trapped in the wreckage between what was left of the bridge, the Gazelle and the ditch. It is worth noting at this point that if we had still had our rotor blades they could have cut the bulk fuel pipeline which was directly next to the ditch. The ditch ran down towards the Puma which was now on fire. A breach in this pipeline could have had catastrophic consequences for many people that night. The troops in Bessbrook and crews at rest in the heli-ops rooms came rushing out in order to try and make sense of what had happened; I believe that at first it was felt to be terrorist action. All attentions were rightly turned to the burning Puma and the four poor souls on board. Bearing in mind it was very dark and the majority of the Gazelle wreckage was folded into a ditch on top of me, it was the co-pilot who, approximately 15 minutes after the crash, went to raise the alarm. Covered in mud and my blood he must have looked a sight as apparently the first thing he was asked was 'Bloody hell, are you from the Puma?' to which he answered: 'No I'm from the Gazelle,' with the obvious comment of 'What Gazelle?'[1]

November was over, with 13 people dead, including five military personnel and a policeman. Six civilians had died.

1. From *Air Clues: The RAF Safety Magazine* (2013).

24

December

In 1984, when Band Aid sang their – seemingly omnipresent – hit single 'Feed The World,' it contained the words: 'Do they know it's Christmas time at all?' This question could easily be asked of the Ulster Volunteer Force, as they gave a Catholic family in the Upper Crumlin Road the type of Christmas present which would ruin their lives forever. In all, four people would die in this month: two Catholics killed in sectarian attacks, a soldier whilst on leave and another Catholic killed by his 'defenders', the Provisional IRA.

On the 1st of the month, the IRA, as part of its pre-Christmas bombing campaign, designed to terrify people out of London's shopping areas, planted a stolen van, packed with explosives, on Tottenham Court Road. British Army ATO were called out in order to tackle the bomb. After several hours' work, they carried out a controlled explosion; the potentially lethal bomb was made safe. The IRA responded the following morning, when a spokesman in Dublin made it quite clear that, despite being thwarted on three separate occasions with massive London bombs that failed to go off, it still had enough men and explosives in place for a pre- Christmas bombing blitz. On the same day, the IRA exploded three devices in Central Belfast. In one incident, a bag containing a large amount of Semtex was left inside an office in the Castle Court Shopping Centre. It detonated within a few minutes of a telephoned warning, leaving dozens of workers in danger from the subsequent fire. Staff on upper floors threw chairs through windows to allow smoke to escape, allowing them to breathe some fresh air. There was only one serious injury, with most of those hurt being allowed to go home after treatment for cuts, bruises and shock in the Mater hospital. A total of 27 people were injured, including one man who received serious burns after being engulfed in flames by the blast. The day ended with an RPG-7 attack on an Army outpost on the top of one of the four tower blocks in the Nationalist New Lodge area. There were no injuries, but the possibility of the missile falling short and smashing into the residential flats hardly bears thinking about.

On the 4th, the IRA's England team struck again, this time at the capital of the north-west, Manchester, exploding two bombs to try and wreck the city's economy by intimidating Northern folk, making them too nervous to spend their money. The Provisionals were using a double-edged sword: terror and economic ruin. The bombs were timed to go off at the height of rush hour; when they did, it caused traffic chaos and pandemonium amongst city centre workers and shoppers alike. The first bomb exploded in the city's Parsonage commercial district near a tax office. Sixty-four people were injured by flying glass as they sought refuge near the Anglican Cathedral after the first blast; the second bomb was designed to catch those who were escaping from the first.

It was the IRA at its most cynical, with one man being seriously wounded when the second explosion sent debris cascading onto a street to which he had been evacuated after the first blast. The Acting Bishop of Manchester, Colin Scott, told the press: 'They were pretty shaken. Having already experienced one explosion, they thought they were safe in the cathedral.' The IRA had deliberately misled police by telephoning in vague warnings about location and the number of devices. National Anti-Terrorist Co-ordinator, Commander David Tucker, stated that the warnings, from callers using recognised IRA code words, had given imprecise or wrong information about the location of the bombs. He said: 'That is by design and not by accident.'

A former Manchester Police Officer and friend of mine has said:

> What Tucker said is correct; they wanted to kill people, because for all their mealy-mouthed hypocrisy about not wanting to hurt civilians, they worked on the principle that one bomb in England was worth five in Northern Ireland. If they killed or maimed people in England – they never attacked Wales or Scotland – they knew that people would start to put pressure on the government to pull out of Ulster. Secondly, and more importantly, they knew that if they destroyed enough commercial property, they knew that they could destroy businesses, as well as terrifying people from spending their wages in places where they thought bombs might go off. These businesses would put pressure then on their insurance companies who in turn would put pressure on the government. It was a very vicious circle, but it was a very clever vicious circle! Adams and McGuinness might have been heartless, but they were also very clever!

A survivor – Colin Cookney – told me:

> Basically, I had gone to work that day, but for a change, I didn't drive, I took the tram. Normally, if I had driven, after parking, I would have walked past Parsonage Gardens which is where the first bomb went off. I was in the office when the fire alarms started to go off, and we evacuated the building; the police pushed us towards the Cathedral. I don't blame the police whatsoever; anyone who blames the police for the subsequent injuries is barking up the wrong tree. We were standing chatting and laughing and joking about the waste of our time. People's attentions then turned towards the first explosion which we had heard. Then the second explosion occurred, and it is amazing just how small a human being can make themselves. I crouched down, and my backside was touching the floor. Then the glass started to fall to the ground; you feel the glass, which fell like hail, touching you. The first instinct was to run, and I shouted: 'Don't run!' There was only myself, a man I now know was called Neil Tattersall and a woman; he was clearly hurt with a large piece of glass in his back. I then did a stupid thing, as I pulled the glass out of his back which caused the blood to spurt out. There was a rush of blood, so I was forced to use my tie to try and stem the flow. A couple of police officers came over, telling us to get away, and that they would take care of Neil. We got to Albert Square, where we drifted apart from each other; I jumped on the tram and got away. Mr Tattersall later recalled that it was two women who helped him; I would love him to know that it was me.

On the same day as the Manchester bombs, Sir John May published the report of his investigation into the miscarriage of justice involving the Maguire family. The May Report called for the establishment of a review tribunal to look at alleged miscarriages of justice.

Just a week after the Castle Court bomb in Belfast, on the site of the former Army base at the Grand Central Hotel, IRA units detonated two car-bombs on King Street, just 400 yards away from the earlier blast. Several people were injured as crowds fled in panic and a large part of the street was devastated. King Street which was in sight of Belfast City Hall, contained bars, restaurants and offices.

On the 7th, the Provisional IRA used the first of what were to become known as its 'barrack buster' devices, a play on words alluding to RAF Bomber Command's 'block buster' bombs, dropped on German cities in World War II. The IRA version used a Mark XV mortar which could fire an explosive charge weighing 122–260 lb (55–120 kg) up to a maximum range of 275 yards. One weapons expert described it as having 'the effect of a flying car bomb'. Their target on the 7th, was the RUC base at Ballygawley, Co. Tyrone, not far from the scene of the 1988 coach massacre where eight soldiers from the Light Infantry were killed by a PIRA landmine.

The attack was carried out by PIRA's East Tyrone brigade, on the seventh anniversary of a previous attack on the same base. On that occasion, two RUC officers were shot dead and the base was completely destroyed by a bomb. In this fresh attack, several police officers were injured in the explosion, some very seriously. However, fortune was on the side of the RUC that day, as the huge missile hit a tree and the branches deflected the device which in this case was estimated at 250–500 lb (110–220 kg) There were no fatalities. Just six days later, a similar device was fired at the joint Army/RUC base in Annaghmartin, Co. Fermanagh; a number of soldiers were slightly injured, but none seriously. On the same day as the Annaghmartin attack, one of the Golf observation towers just outside Crossmaglen in South Armagh was attacked and damaged by a PIRA mortar, but again there were no injuries. The 13th ended with a gun attack on the RUC station in the Oldpark area of North Belfast; there were only slight injuries. Five days later, on the 18th, the IRA launched a third mortar attack of the month, this time in Markethill, Co. Armagh. A PIRA team launched a mortar at the RUC station there, badly damaging the base, but thankfully causing no serious injuries. The above list may appear to be simply a litany of PIRA aggression, but it shows that PIRA actions, sometimes minor, sometimes not, were a constant threat.

The IRA's research and development of mortars was designed with four main objectives: increasing range, increasing payload, increasing lethality and increasing reliability. The Mk 15 was not the IRA's longest-range mortar but it did become its standard large-calibre weapon of choice. It was used over 80 times during the Troubles, but this was as big as they could make them; anything bigger was beyond their manufacturing abilities and, when used, invariably failed. Though never as successful as they would have wished, their development of such a system compelled the British government to provide enormous financial resources in order to add substantial armour to security bases. The installation of costly protection schemes, however, singularly failed to deter the IRA. They were intent on killing as many of those sent to protect the Northern Irish population as possible; that the British had to bear huge financial costs to counter the 'flying car bombs' would undoubtedly have given satisfaction to Adams, McGuiness and the IRA army council who never missed an opportunity to strike at Westminster in any form.

On the 8th – a Tuesday – the pious IRA crossed swords with a convicted paedophile and one-time Republican paramilitary named John Collett (36), father of three, on the Shantallow Estate in Londonderry; the 'defenders of the Catholic community' had received a number of complaints from worried families in the neighbouring Carnhill Estate, approximately a mile from where he lived. The former INLA man was separated from his wife, who had accused him of sexually assaulting his own children. The *Independent* reported that most of his victims had been girls, at least one as young as seven. On one occasion Collett raped a girl whilst a 13-year-old boy was forced to watch; the boy was then urged to rape her as well.

At around 20:00, several PIRA gunmen turned up at Collett's house where they used a sledgehammer to smash their way in. They seized him, forced him to lie down in his own lounge and then shot him behind both knees with a .38 handgun. It is not known if the self-appointed 'Catholic police' intended simply to kneecap him or if they intended to wound him fatally. With the bones, tendons, muscles, and more importantly the arteries of both legs shattered, he must have been in some agony, but managed to crawl to his front door and part way into his garden. He screamed for help, hammering against the front door to attract attention. His neighbours, knowing of his paedophilia and that the IRA were involved, wisely kept their distance. By the time an ambulance was summoned, he had almost bled out, quickly losing consciousness; he was taken to Altnagelvin Hospital. A neighbour quipped: 'I accidentally dialled 9-9-8; no wonder I couldn't get an ambulance.' The IRA admitted that they had killed the convicted paedophile. Collett's heart had stopped beating on the way to hospital, leaving his brain severely starved of oxygen. During the treatment to save his life, both of his legs were amputated; he remained in a coma until he died on the 13th.

On Thursday 10th, the UFF – this time it was their mid-Ulster brigade – crossed the border into the South to take the incendiary war into Dublin. I try to treat the Loyalist paramilitaries with the same contempt as their Republican counterparts, but can understand the indignation of Loyalists at seeing the IRA slowly destroying Northern Ireland's economy and seeing a need to fight back. One UFF unit drove into Dublin, planting several incendiary devices in seven city centre shops in the Irish capital, whilst a second unit attacked commercial premises in other Irish towns close to the border. Several of the devices failed to explode, although there was some damage; fortunately, there were no serious injuries. A later statement by the UFF warned: 'Sheer luck prevented our operatives from bringing you a fiery Christmas. You will not be lucky in 1993. We will bring 1993 in with a bang.'

That same day on the British mainland, the IRA's England team stepped up their pre-Christmas bombing blitz. A bombing unit exploded two devices at the Wood Green Shopping Centre in north London. Due to the usual imprecise misleading nature of the warnings, 11 people – police and shoppers – were injured in the two blasts. Hours later, just half a mile away, the same team of bombers placed explosives into a hijacked lorry before parking it at Woodside Park; the detonator fired, but it failed to ignite the main charge. Lives and property were saved thanks to the bomb-makers' lack of expertise.

On the 12th, the UFF struck in the mainly Loyalist town of Ballymoney in North-West Co. Antrim, when they fatally wounded a former IRA bomber and Sinn Féin party member. They were aware that a former IRA prisoner, Malachy Carey (36), visited his girlfriend who lived close to the centre of the town. As he walked along Victoria Street, a stolen car glided to a halt behind him, and a UFF gunman got out, before casually walking up to Carey. A struggle ensued as Carey fought for his life, but he was shot four or five times. The gunmen raced off – the driver was later jailed for conspiracy to murder – as the former IRA man lay badly wounded in the street, close to St James's Presbyterian Church. He was rushed to hospital, where it was thought that he would make a full recovery, but his condition deteriorated overnight. The following morning, with his girlfriend at his side, he died from his gunshot wounds. On the same day that Mr Carey died, an unidentified Loyalist paramilitary group –thought to be Johnny Adair's UFF 'C' company – launched a rocket attack at a part of the Crumlin Road Prison believed to be occupied by Republican prisoners; there were no injuries. This was clearly the long-expected retaliation for the IRA attack which killed UFF man Robert Skey and UVF member Colin Caldwell in the 'Crum' in November 1991 (*see* Chapter 11).

On the 16th, Northern Ireland Secretary Patrick Mayhew gave a speech in Coleraine. Speaking at the campus of the University of Ulster, he said that the British government had no 'pre-selected constitutional outcome' in political talks. He was adamant however, that Sinn Féin could only be included in future talks if the IRA ended its violent campaign. Within 24 hours, Adams proposed a joint initiative, involving both the United Nations (UN) and European Community (EU) having a role in finding a political solution. He also said that Sinn Féin's exclusion from political talks was undemocratic. The IRA were quick to scream 'undemocratic' and 'human rights' but never did they consider the democratic or human rights of their victims.

On the 20th, the UVF killed an innocent Catholic whose only crime was to be related to a Sinn Féin councillor, Bobby Lavery; their hopelessly flawed intelligence had 'discovered' that Martin Lavery (40), father of four was an IRA volunteer. The sad truth is that he was no more a member of the IRA than I am. He lived with his family in the Upper Crumlin Road in Belfast, close to the Nationalist Ardoyne but equally close to the Loyalist Ballysillian. On that Sunday evening, as Belfast shivered in winter temperatures, Martin Lavery and his wife, with their five-year-old daughter sitting on his knee, sat in a cosy house, wrapping Christmas presents. Suddenly, the door burst open and masked gunmen ran into the lounge. Without sparing a thought for the little girl, they fired four shots at her father, hitting him the chest, killing him almost instantly. The gunmen ran off, but Mrs Lavery bravely chased after them, her little girl in hysterics at the bloodied sight of her daddy. One of the gunmen – thought to be the same killer in a baseball cap who had shot and killed Sheena Campbell in the York Hotel on 16 October – turned and fired a round at her from his 9 mm Browning; the round missed, but it caused her to stop the pursuit; she ran back to the scene of horror she had left just moments before.

The following afternoon, several hundred miles away across the Irish Sea, just as the rush-hour was warming up, the IRA attacked North London commuters in the upmarket Hampstead area. At 16:32, a caller claiming to be from the IRA, telephoned a warning through to both the Press Association and the Samaritans. He warned of bombs at both

Hampstead and Archway stations but did not specify times or locations. As London Transport Police were evacuating the Hampstead Tube station, the bomb, which had been left on a staircase, exploded, just 16 minutes after the first warning. No one was badly hurt in the blast, but it threw dozens into panic, leaving several people requiring treatment for shock and ear problems. Confusion in the station had almost led to disaster as some passengers were actually ushered towards the staircase where the bomb was located. A misinformed train driver had urged his passengers to get off and go upstairs; responsibility for what might have resulted can only be laid at the door of the Provisional IRA.

The *Independent* quoted Chief Superintendent Tony Buchanan as saying:

> Clearly, it is murderous behaviour. There could have been a large number of casualties. There was not enough warning given. Lives were put at risk and we are very fortunate there were no deaths or injuries.' The same newspaper also quoted a survivor, Ruth Clarkson, who told of her ordeal: 'We were still standing in the lift with the doors open when the bomb went off. It was very close. I've never heard anything like it. There were young girls in there screaming their heads off but no one did anything to help. Two trains went through after the bomb exploded and at least one must have stopped because people were still coming towards the lift. When we got to the top someone said: "If you're feeling woozy, walk down to the Royal Free Hospital." There were people near to collapsing.'

The callous attitude of the IRA came very much to the fore in Cookstown, Co. Armagh, the day after the Hampstead bomb. At a VCP just outside the town, a young soldier waved down a car and spoke to the female driver. Instead of the usual abuse, the woman smiled and said that she was a Protestant and appreciated what the soldiers were doing for them. As a token of that appreciation, she gave the soldier a tin of Quality Street chocolates, apparently still sealed, asking him to share them with his comrades back at Cookstown RUC station. However, suspicions were aroused when on closer examination, it was seen that the sealing tape had been tampered with. On the instructions of the soldier's alert and vigilant CO, ATO was called in. The tin was opened safely, to reveal a 1 lb (0.45 kg) Semtex device inside. There was sufficient power in this bomb to kill or maim many soldiers or policemen in the close confines of their base. The IRA's intention was to catch a young soldier, probably missing his home and family, probably spending his first Christmas away from England, with his guard down.

Interestingly enough, there was a postscript to this incident. Johnny Adair's 'C' company set out to kill a leading PIRA female, a member of Cuman na Mban, who lived in Andersonstown in West Belfast. A two-man UFF team drove to the woman's house before leaving an incendiary bomb by the front door, somewhat mockingly inside a tin of Quality Street chocolates.

On Christmas Eve, the Provisional IRA declared a 72-hour ceasefire, which would end at midnight on the 27th. There some reported breaches on the Republican side, with soldiers and police still having to maintain their security patrols. Had they cut them back, the IRA no doubt would have taken full advantage to move arms and ammunition around between Nationalist districts as well as conduct illegal VCPs in apparent shows of strength. Some soldiers painted 'Merry Xmas' on the side of their Humber Pigs whilst others wrapped their SA-80 assault rifles with holly and tinsel. Quite what affect this had on the sullen Republican supporters on the Ballymurphy, Whiterock, Turf Lodge, Andersonstown, Ardoyne and New Lodge estates in Belfast or the Creggan, the Bogside or the Gobnascale estates in Londonderry, is not recorded.

Thomas Begley was an IRA gunman from the Nationalist Ardoyne area; he would later achieve infamy – and the obligatory song performed by an Irish band – when he killed himself and nine others in Frizzell's Fishmongers' shop in the Shankill on 23 October 1993 (*see* Chapter 34). He and two other gunmen driving in a stolen Ford Sierra, covered the one-mile journey from the Ardoyne to the Old Westland Road around dinner time on the evening of the 30th. They parked very close to the house of Private Steven Archibald Waller (23), a young full-time soldier from the Royal Irish, home on leave from Dhekelia in Cyprus. He was relaxing at his home between Cavehill Road and Cliftonpark Golf Club. As he watched TV with his wife of just eight months and family, there was a knock at the door. Mrs Waller recalled hearing someone ask for her sister-in-law who house-sat for her whilst they were in Cyprus. Mrs Waller walked towards the hallway, but a man she described as 'smirking', a man she would later recognise as Thomas Begley, burst past her and fired 14 rounds from an AK-47 into her helpless husband. He was mortally wounded and left unconscious on the lounge floor. The gunmen escaped, although they were observed driving back towards the Ardoyne; one of the passengers was a woman. The young soldier died within hours despite medical treatment at the Mater Hospital. His funeral was held at Roselawn Cemetery in Crossnacreevy, Belfast.

Close to midnight on New Year's Eve, the UDA/UFF issued an ominous statement and a warning that 1993 would not see the end of the Troubles. A spokesman said chillingly that the UFF would increase its 'campaign of violence to a ferocity never imagined'.

December – and 1992 – was over; only four people died this month.

1992 Deaths

Military	31
Police	5
Civilian	67*
Republicans	11
Loyalists	5
Total	119

* 38 of the killings were sectarian in nature.

Part Three

1993

During this year, 'only' 18 serving soldiers were killed, the lowest number since 1985, and the second-lowest since 1970. Services' losses were, however, swollen by the deaths of three former UDR soldiers who were killed by terrorists using the perverted justification of past association. Six policemen were killed and civilian deaths rose again. In all, 111 people died as the Troubles lumbered bloodily into a 24th year. It was also the year when a fish shop on the Shankill Road would soon be on the lips of the world. Within eight days of Frizzell's, another massacre, this time at the Rising Sun pub in Greysteel would join it in the litany of violence, as 17 people died in the worst period of sectarian murder of the Troubles.

25

January

Eight people were killed this month. Although there were no military deaths, an RUC officer was murdered in Londonderry by an IRA gunman. Seven civilians were killed, six of whom were victims of sectarian murderers.

On the first day of the New Year, two Catholic men had a very lucky escape, when a stolen car containing three members of the Red Hand Commando fired at them in a drive-by shooting. The two men were washing a car on Manor Street, North Belfast, close to the sectarian interface with the Oldpark Road. Both were wounded, but survived the random attack. It was close to the scene of the UFF massacre at James Murray's bookies in November. A spokesman for the Loyalist terror group claimed that the attack was in retaliation for the murder of the Royal Irish soldier two days earlier.

The Provisionals ensured that Christopher Donnelley, a 22-year-old Belfast man, was not so lucky. A punishment squad burst into his home in North Belfast, forced him to the floor in front of his horrified mother, before shooting him in both legs. His injuries were so severe that one of his legs was subsequently amputated; even as he recovered in hospital, local PIRA commanders issued a death threat to him, ordering him to leave Northern Ireland immediately. Five months earlier, another Belfast man found 'guilty' of anti-social behaviour, Micky Sherlock, who was 20, was kneecapped by a PIRA punishment squad; he, too, had to have one of his legs amputated. The local PIRA leader 'graciously' waited until he came out of hospital before he was ordered to leave the country; the banishment order was later lifted by more senior commanders.

On the same day, the grandiosely titled Irish National Congress (INC) took direct action to attempt the reopening of several border roads, which had been blocked by the Army to impede the supply of IRA arms and explosives flooding into the North. These 'unapproved' roads had been closed during the early part of the conflict to secure the porous, undefended border with the Republic. The action to reopen the roads coincided with the end of European Community internal boundaries, enabling free movement across the EC.

On the 3rd of the month, the UVF murder gangs were in action again; this time it was the 'Jackal's' mid-Ulster brigade who made the 20-mile trip to a Catholic-owned shop at Lisnagleer, two miles from Dungannon in Co. Tyrone. Patrick Shields (51), father of four, and his sons Diarmuid (20) and Davog were working in the family-run village shop. None of the three had any Republican connections. The two brothers were members of a GAA club, which was hardly enough, other than in the perverted logic of the UVF, to warrant a death sentence. UVF gunmen – including Laurence Maguire – burst into the shop, immediately opening fire with automatic weapons. Pat and Diarmuid were both killed more or less instantly, whilst 24-year-old, Davog was seriously injured. Not content with what they thought were three more dead Catholics, the gunmen attempted to kill the remainder of the family. Mrs Brid Shields and two more of her children saved themselves by barricading themselves into the lounge. Davog was rushed to hospital and, thanks to prompt medical treatment, his life was saved. Loyalist paramilitaries always claimed that the GAA was merely a 'front' for the Provisionals, but the truth was simpler: all three men were innocent Catholics, just attempting to make a living in order to maintain a decent standard of life. Just 27 days later, Julie Statham, fiancée of Diarmuid Shields, took her own life as she was unable to live with the tragedy: another victim for Loyalist terrorists. She and the dead man had been due to marry in March 1993. The *Irish Times* later wrote: 'The pain goes on for all those left behind to grieve for them. Every time the killers invade someone's home to visit death upon a family, they inflict more agony on a people who have already had their fill.'

On Monday 4th, somewhat ironically in the light of the flag dispute that has been raging in Belfast over the last several years, there was a proposal to introduce power-sharing on Belfast City Council. This was rejected by the Social Democratic and Labour Party (SDLP), a pivotal part of Sinn Féin's current – as I write – dominance in Belfast City Hall. The balance of power in Belfast is currently held by a Republican coalition of SDLP, Sinn Féin and Alliance Party councillors. This alliance is maintaining the proposition which bans the Union Flag from being flown above the City hall, other than under the conditions under which it is flown on government buildings in the rest of the UK. The current (2019) composition is Unionists: 22; Sinn Féin/Alliance/SDLP coalition: 31; others: 7.

The following day, PIRA's England team struck again in the heart of London, when they targeted the iconic shopping area of Oxford Street. Terrorists, passing themselves off as New Year Sales' customers, planted four incendiary devices in shops along the famous street. Warnings were telephoned through and the area was evacuated, shortly before fires started; there were no injuries. Two days later, a firebomb planted in a bookshop in Charing Cross Road was defused.

Meanwhile, back in Belfast, the Provisionals stepped up their 'economic warfare'. On the 5th three soldiers were injured by a blast, whilst evacuating City Hall in Belfast after yet another inadequate warning from the Republican terror group. The IRA did call before the bomb exploded, stating that the bomb was actually inside the building, when in fact it was in a nearby street; damage was slight. The following day, a 25 lb (11 kg) bomb was detonated in the centre of Dungannon; damage was again slight without injuries. On the 7th, the IRA attempted to detonate a bomb at an oil and gas storage depot in East Belfast. On the 8th, a large PIRA unit attacked the joint RUC/Army base at Kinawley, Co. Fermanagh, with mortars and heavy machine guns, damaging the base and a helicopter on the ground. There were no serious injuries, but it demonstrated once again that the Provisionals were still very capable of carrying out effective military-style operations when so motivated.

On the 11th, Republican paramilitaries demonstrated that they could be as blinkered as their Loyalist terrorist counterparts when it came to 'connections' or 'legitimate' targets. Just as Loyalists interpreted GAA participation as being tantamount to IRA membership, so did the Provisionals see Orange Order membership as being proof that someone was a Loyalist paramilitary. Dairy worker Matthew Boyd (60), father of four, was just that:

a member of the Pomeroy Faith Defenders Orange Order, but in the eyes of the IRA's south Tyrone brigade, he was a 'gunman in a Loyalist death squad'. He had been stalked by a PIRA gunman who followed him that day as he drove towards Dungannon, until Mr Boyd stopped at Donaghmore Road to the west of the town centre. As the Orangeman remained in his car, close to McAleer's bar, two PIRA gunmen walked over to him and shot him several times in the head. He was fatally wounded, dying five hours later in hospital. The same men also planted a 90 lb (14 kg) bomb in a bag, hidden just behind a wall near where the victim lay, half in and half out of his car. Fortunately, when the Army arrived, they were suspicious, and an ATO man was sent for to examine the device; it was defused safely.

The Provisionals issued a statement the following day, continuing the pretence that the killing was anything but a sordid and senseless sectarian murder: 'Boyd had a long involvement in the UVF dating back to the 1970s. His increasingly crucial role in UVF sectarian murders became clear and IRA intelligence had him under surveillance along with several other UVF personnel. The IRA will not get involved in a sectarian campaign, but, as on Monday afternoon, we will execute those involved in sectarian killings.' However, this was just that: sectarian. It was an attack based on a combination of flawed – or non-existent – intelligence, or it was a case of 'Any Protestant will do.' Murders by both sets of paramilitaries paid scant attention to 'facts' or accuracy; murders were simply and inexcusably justified just as long as they got the 'right' religion. PIRA spokesmen appeared to believe that if they claimed enough times to be a non-sectarian organisation, people would accept that. The only difference was that, based on the evidence of the entire period of the Troubles, Republicans believed their own propaganda, whereas Loyalists didn't, nor did they appear even to put on a pretence.

Also on the 11th, Secretary of State for Northern Ireland Patrick Mayhew gave an interview to the BBC in which he stated that Articles 2 and 3 of the Irish Constitution were 'unhelpful' and would need to be a central element of any future talks. Despite this comment, Dick Spring, the Tánaiste – deputy Irish Prime Minister and Minister for Foreign Affairs – promised that there would be 'openness and flexibility' in any future political talks. Later in the month, Mayhew met Spring in Dublin where they agreed to hold informal discussions between the British and Irish governments, in advance of any new political talks in Northern Ireland.

That same day, a punishment unit from the Tyrone brigade of the IRA confronted a man in Dungannon, whom they considered a persistent anti-social offender. He was dragged out of his house, screaming in terror, before being pushed to the ground. Very thoughtfully, the punishment gang pulled the man's jeans down in order to prevent the planned kneecapping from being infected by bacteria. However, his struggles caused the shots to miss the spot behind the patella, and instead tear into tendons and arteries, in pretty much the same way as in the bungled punishment shooting of John Collett the previous month. In this instance, despite the prompt arrival of an ambulance, the un-named victim lost one of his legs. On the same day, the RUC base at Woodbourne in South Belfast came under attack from a PIRA unit firing an RPG-7, which fortunately caused no serious injuries. Three days later, there were virtually simultaneous attacks using mortars and rockets at the RUC bases in Andersonstown and New Barnsley in Belfast.

The Times reported on the 12th, that the UDA/UFF was planning to target all those Catholics/Nationalists who were considered to be part of the 'Pan-Nationalist front'. This was interpreted as meaning all those who were members of the SDLP, Sinn Féin, the Irish government, the Gaelic Athletic Association (GAA), and naturally the IRA or INLA; in fact, almost anyone who attended a Catholic church, was called 'Paddy', or had a rural Irish accent.

Retaliation for the Boyd murder was not far away; on the 14th, the Annadale Flats UFF killed another Catholic. Anthony 'Tony' Butler (40), father of one, lived in Agra Street, close to the Ormeau Road in Belfast. He had been a member of the INLA, but, seduced by the get-rich-quick lure of the booming illegal drugs trade, he had turned his back on violent Republicanism, beginning instead a new 'career' as a drugs dealer. 'Chinky' Bratty was aware of the ex-INLA man's presence and dispatched a three-man murder squad, including Stephen 'Inch' McFerran, from the Annadale Flats to where they knew that Butler was meeting two other men. It was a brief car journey, going via Candahar Street, Delhi Parade and Delhi Street, less than 150 yards by a more direct route on foot. When I drove down this street on a recent trip to Belfast, I was struck by the smartly painted terraced houses, resplendent in uniform white. The gunmen burst into the house, just after 23:00, and shot Butler several times in the head. Leaving him mortally wounded but ignoring the other two men in the house, they ran outside, probably being back in the Annadale Flats just minutes later. Butler died in the ambulance, en route for hospital. Later, a spokesman for the UDA claimed that the dead man was a member of the INLA, declaring that the killing was in retaliation for an earlier aborted INLA attack on a leading UVF man in the Shankill.

On the 15th, the IRA detonated two car bombs close to Belfast city centre, which destroyed a car showroom, wiping out its entire stock; whilst no one was injured, it was yet another drain on the financial resources of the sorely pressed insurance companies. It also meant that the showroom's staff would be made jobless and there would be further depleting of Social Security funds; the IRA was costing the British government a small fortune, as it was clearly winning the 'economic war'. On the same day, the South Tyrone brigade left a booby-trapped device along a well-used foot patrol route in Carrickmore's main street. The blast injured several soldiers and policemen, some seriously. Almost unnoticed in all of this, a PIRA unit from the Bogside was involved in a short fire-fight with an Army foot patrol in Londonderry.

On the 17th, yet more flawed PIRA intelligence almost led to the deaths of one or more members of a Catholic family named Coachman, who lived in one of Belfast's Protestant areas. There can be doubt, in my opinion, that had the incident caused any Catholic deaths, the operation would have gone unclaimed, being blamed conveniently on Loyalists! PIRA gunmen burst into a house in Tavanagh Street in the overwhelmingly Loyalist Village area, indiscriminately firing several rounds. It would appear that they had gone in search of a leading UFF gunman who, they believed, lived in the house. The target concerned was known to possess photomontages of Republican suspects which he had stolen from a police station. The man had left the area, and the Coachman family had moved in afterwards. Fortunately, the terrified family managed to convince the IRA gunmen that they had made a mistake; at this, the terror gang left the house. The following day, a spokesman for the Republicans asserted that the Catholic family had nothing to fear. But by doing so they had, deliberately or otherwise, highlighted the presence of a Catholic family to extremist Loyalist elements in the area.

On the same day that one Catholic family narrowly cheated death at the hands of the IRA, just five miles away at Shore Road, another Catholic was not so lucky. Sharon McKenna (27) was a taxi-driver living in Arthur Avenue, Newtownabbey. In addition to being a hard-working woman, she also cared for an elderly female friend who lived in the Loyalist Mount Vernon area, close to the Shore Road. In the early evening of the 17th, being aware of her routine, two UVF men – one of whom was reputed to be Mark Haddock – had followed her to the house. They kicked in the door, pointing a shotgun at her, demanding the keys to her taxi. Clearly in fear of her life, she turned to get them from the fireplace, but was instantly blasted in the back from close range. Even though she was clearly mortally wounded, the gunman stood over her, firing another blast into her body, killing her. Leaving Ms McKenna's elderly friend in a state of shock and great distress, they ran out of the house to their getaway car – they didn't take the taxi although they had the keys – before escaping along the Shore Road.

A later statement from the UVF's 'Captain Black' contained an astonishing claim which totally lacked credibility; they stated that Sharon McKenna was an INLA spy who regularly used the mercy trips to her friend's house as cover for her espionage activities. This was, of course, palpable nonsense used to cover an overtly sectarian slaying. This was quite naturally denied vehemently by the RUC, the dead woman's family and of course by the INLA. The simple facts were that it was a sectarian murder; it was also an easy kill, carried out in an attempt to redress the balance between rival Loyalist gangs. Quite simply, the UVF were being out-killed by the UFF.

At Ms McKenna's funeral, the officiating bishop told the mourners: 'She dared to cross ... barriers, barriers erected by those who wanted a particular area to be a no-go area for those who differed from them in religious belief.' One of the suspected gunmen was Mark Haddock, described as an 'unsavoury character [and] drug-dealer'. He is also said to have been an informer for RUC SB. He was subsequently interviewed about the murder on several occasions – once, rather farcically by one of his own handlers – but released without charge. He is believed to have been involved in 10 killings, all of them of innocent Catholics such as Ms McKenna. Former RUC man Johnston Brown said recently of Haddock: 'of course there were elements within Special Branch who knew what he was doing but they chose to ignore it.'[1]

On the 20th, the Provisionals used a new type of mortar, recently perfected by their 'engineers', which fired an explosive charge weighing 300 lb (135 kg) over an effective range of 100 yards. A unit from the Tyrone brigade launched an attack on the RUC base at Clogher during the late evening. The mortar bomb cleared the perimeter's protective blast walls and exploded inside the barracks; several police officers were injured and the blast caused some structural damage. By all accounts, the explosion was heard 20 miles away.

On the 21st, John Major wrote to SDLP leader John Hume, rejecting calls for a new inquest into the events of 'Bloody Sunday'. Nine days later, there was a rally in Londonderry to commemorate the 21st anniversary of the January 1972 shootings; it was largely trouble-free, but several out-of-control thugs were arrested by the RUC.

1. Johnston Brown, *Into The Dark: 30 Years in the RUC* (Gill & MacMillan, 2005).

Later that same day, just to show that flawed INTEL and blatant sectarianism were not the sole province of the Provisionals or UVF/ UFF, the INLA killed a Protestant man close to Crumlin Road in Belfast. Samuel Rock (30), father of a young child, lived with his partner in Rosewood Street. It was a Protestant enclave sandwiched between the Ardoyne and the Catholic side of the Oldpark Road. In December, Mr Rock had bought a car from a leading Loyalist paramilitary. The INLA knew the number plate of the Loyalist's car, but didn't know it had changed hands. When one of their dickers spotted the car in Rosewood Street, they put two and two together and came up with five. Friends of the innocent Protestant, equally aware of the connotations, begged him to sell the car or at least change the number plate. Mr Rock fatally neglected to do so. On the evening of the 21st, INLA gunmen burst into his house and shot him dead in front of his shocked partner, firing eight rounds into his body. Mr Rock's sister said afterwards: 'I still want to know why my brother was killed . . . He was completely innocent. Sam was never involved in anything. We know a lot of Catholics. Sam's best friend was a Catholic. They shot him eight times; that was hate.'

In this life, there are facts and there are interpretations; some of the latter are coloured, some biased and some are altered in such a way as to make them appear as 'fact'. One such incident occurred on the 23rd in Londonderry when an RUC officer, Michael Ferguson, was shot dead. The facts as seen by eyewitnesses, and neutral observers: the RUC officer was walking along Shipquay Street on patrol, when a PIRA gunman – from the Bogside – came up behind him, and shot him twice in the back of the head; killing him instantly. That is fact.

The following travesty is taken from the New York edition of *An Phoblacht* (28 January 1993): 'The attack was launched at 2.15 pm on Saturday afternoon with a Volunteer, armed with a handgun taking up a position in the Diamond area. Other IRA Volunteers were also in the area and watched as the RUC patrol arrived. One RUC member, armed with an automatic rifle and a handgun took up a covering position outside one of the centre's doorways. At this point the Volunteer approached the RUC member, and shot him dead. Despite the rapid movements of crown forces into Shipquay Street, the Volunteer evaded both these and others in the vicinity'

Constable Michael Ferguson (21), formerly from Omagh, Co. Tyrone, was on foot patrol in Shipquay Street, close to the Nationalist Bogside. As he passed the Richmond Centre, a PIRA gunman walked up behind him and, from very close range, shot him twice in the back of the head with a .38 handgun; the shots killed him instantly. As he fell, lifeless, to the ground, panic set in amongst the shoppers as the shots echoed around the narrow streets in deafening fashion. The killer ran off but was clipped by a passing car as he crossed the road. He stumbled but recovered and headed in the direction of Butcher Street where he disappeared. The dead man's comrades were unable to fire as there were too many civilians around. Ferguson was the first RUC officer to be killed in the city of Londonderry since 1988. The killer has never been identified, but in 2014, a Londonderry man – Christopher O'Kane – was charged with several crimes relating to the murder. The *Ulster Herald* reported: 'In total, the 41 year old was charged with 18 offences linked to terrorist activity over a 6 year period between January 1988 and August 1994 – including impeding the apprehension of Michael Ferguson's killer, by wiping finger or palm prints from a car that

O'Kane knew the shooter had used immediately after the killing.'[1] He was found guilty of assisting offenders in relation to Ferguson's murder and also of firing a mortar bomb at a police vehicle in the Fanad Drive area of Londonderry in October 1993; causing an explosion with intent to endanger life near Ebrington Barracks in December 1993; placing a bomb on a windowsill at the home of a senior police officer in February 1994 – on that occasion, O'Kane telephoned a bomb warning to the Samaritans. He was also found guilty of being part of an IRA gang who placed a bomb at the Fort George jetty in Londonderry on 23 May 1994. He was jailed for 10 years but released early under the terms of the GFA.

On the 23rd, there were two major incidents in the Province: in the first, the IRA planted a stolen car containing 600 lb (270 kg) of explosive close to the centre of Cappagh, Co. Tyrone. The bomb failed to go off, forcing a very sheepish IRA caller to inform the RUC who called in Army ATO to detonate the device safely. That same day, the IRA sent a gunman to kill an off-duty Royal Irish soldier – who does not wish to be named – at his home in Newtownstewart. The plan went terribly awry for the gunman who thought that he was going to be attacking an unarmed or unsuspecting victim. Although the gunman managed to wound the Royal Irish man, the soldier fired back, incapacitating the would-be assassin. The RUC were called and the IRA man was arrested.

On the 24th, in a second attack at the British Army PVCP at Derryard/Killyvilly near Rosslea in Co. Fermanagh, over 200 heavy machine gun rounds were fired by a PIRA unit but there were no injuries; the Army reported that they did not return fire as most of the rounds passed harmlessly over the soldiers' heads. A similar attack was carried out at the joint RUC/Army PVCP at Newtownbutler, but again there were no injuries. On the same day, an off-duty RUC member who lived in Lisnaskea found a bomb under his car. ATO later defused the potentially lethal device.

The Army Council of the Provisional IRA always believed that one bomb in London was worth far more in terms of its impact and publicity than a dozen in Northern Ireland. The fact that there are large Irish emigré populations in London, and that the British media was largely London-based, meant that bombers could find sanctuary in Irish areas such as Kilburn, and correspondents were on hand to observe and report on attacks, giving them the oxygen of publicity. There have been many such high-profile attacks from the siege of Balcombe Street in 1975 up to Bishopsgate in 1993, and others covered earlier in this book. One of the nastiest was the 1983 bombing of the Harrods store in Kensington and on 28 January 1993, the IRA's England team – using English far-left activists – attacked Harrods for a second time.

Around 09:15 that Thursday, the BBC received warnings that two devices had been left inside and outside the store, which was due to open around 45 minutes later. The Met Police and bomb squads were quickly on the scene where they immediately began clearing the area. However, a few idiots decided to ignore the cordons, foolishly congregating close to Harrods, despite repeated warnings from the officers. A device, made of around 2 lb (1 kg) of Semtex had been placed in a litter bin outside the shop, packed underneath rubbish. At 09:40, it exploded, injuring four people, one of them seriously, and also damaging the front of the building on Kensington High Street. Damage was estimated at over £1 million.

1. http://ulsterherald.com/2014/10/13/derry-man-to-face-trial-in-connection-with-omagh-policemans-murder.

The IRA's England team were conscious that, even in areas of high Irish settlement, their active service personnel still stood out, with Special Branch, MI5 and anti-terrorist police quick to spot new faces. In this latest campaign, they decided to use English activists, albeit with IRA connections. The men concerned were Jan Taylor, a former Royal Corps of Signals soldier, and Patrick Hayes who worked as a computer programmer; both had joined a far-left group, 'Red Action'. The group had formed as recently as 1981 and generally operated as a 'rent-a-mob', confronting far-right organisations such as the National Front and Combat 18. The two men were arrested in March in a swoop by armed police in the Stoke Newington area of London. Both men were sentenced to 30 years for the Harrods' attack and for the bombing of a train in February.

Later that same evening, several hundred miles away in Co. Tyrone, the UVF killed again, when a bomb intended for a Catholic with only tenuous at most Republican connections, instead killed a young man leaving two tiny children denied a life with their father. There can be no debate that the killers who stained the streets and fields with mainly innocent blood were ruthless assassins, but there was something more than this: it is almost axiomatic that they were also inept and incompetent. Two plumbers, Martin McNamee (25), father of two from Swatragh, in Co. Londonderry, and an older colleague, were sent to fit water pipes at a partially constructed house at Drum Road, Kildress, to the west of Cookstown. In the early hours of that morning, a UVF team was dispatched by the 'Jackal' himself to booby-trap the house under construction. The stated intention was to kill or maim the Catholic man on whose behalf the work was being done. Under cover of darkness, the UVF gang removed the pin on a hand grenade and wedged it in place over a door. The man concerned had no strong links with Irish Republicanism; he was known to the police but had only ever been charged with very minor offences.

The older plumber pushed the door open, causing the primed hand grenade to fall to the ground; Mr McNamee bore the full brunt of the blast and was killed instantly. The UVF, taking a leaf from the IRA's very own book of hollow apologies, stated that the man was killed 'in error'. The important point is that the murder gang who placed the grenade had no idea who would be the next person to push open the booby-trapped door; it could have been a workman delivering items for the building work; it could have been a curious young child, or as indeed transpired, two innocent plumbers going about their lawful profession.

The month ended with a UVF gun attack on a Catholic taxi company in North Belfast. The gang's intention was to burst into their office and kill as many Catholics as possible. However, new security locks and a toughened door saved the lives of the staff inside, forcing the UVF gang to skulk back to their holes.

In all, nine people were killed this month, including one policeman. All eight murdered civilians died in sectarian attacks.

26
February

During this month, a total of eight people were killed; three soldiers, two policemen and two Catholic civilians, murdered in sectarian attacks. Additionally, the IRA's 'nutting squad' executed another alleged informer. There were three more bombing attacks in London and the IRA struck at Warrington for the first time; the next time that they did so, there would be utter devastation for two families.

On the first day of the month, the UDA made bomb attacks on the Belfast residences of two separate SDLP politicians, following up their 12 January threats against anything even vaguely 'Republican'. The homes of SDLP councillors Dorita Field and Alasdair McDonnell were attacked, which was somewhat ironic as both were vehemently opposed to Republican paramilitary violence. As if by clockwork, PIRA's England team exploded two small devices in London, close to where the British and Irish government representatives were meeting to discuss bilateral talks relating to the much-discredited Anglo-Irish agreement (AIA).

On the 2nd, trying as always, to bloodily outdo its UFF rivals, the UVF carried out the first of two sectarian murders in the space of nine days. Eugene Martin (30) was a taxidermist who lived in the Ballyronan area of Co. Londonderry; each day he would drive alongside the picturesque Lough Neagh with his uncle, crossing into Co. Antrim, where he had a workshop in Toome on the other side of the lough. No amount of research into this man's life has revealed the slightest Republican sympathy or leaning, nor any vague connection with the paramilitaries. However, this was not enough for the UVF who decided that he must die because their INTEL 'confirmed' that he was a Republican. The estimable *Lost Lives* states that he was killed at his workshop in Tomé, but the *Independent* states that he died at his home in Gaussen Villas, Ballyronan. Both agree on the time of day – 20:00 – and both state that he went to answer a knock at his window. As he did so, one of two masked gunmen shot him four times in the head and chest; he died almost instantly. The gang fled in a car they had stolen in Belfast the previous day. The following day, they made a statement claiming that he had been killed because of his 'active Republican connections'. The RUC later said Mr Martin was not known to them as a member of a paramilitary organisation. Barry McElduff, a local representative of Sinn Féin, which denied Mr Martin belonged to the party, said: 'This is part of the escalating campaign of murder and intimidation being waged against the nationalist community by loyalists.' In the statement, the equal condemnation of the Republican intimidation is conspicuously absent.

The IRA's England team was back in action on the 3rd when they exploded two small devices in the London area. The first caused damage at South Kensington underground station, when a bomb in an underground passageway detonated, and the other did the same at Kent House railway station, near Bromley, when a bomb left on a train exploded; there were no injuries in either blast. On the 5th, Lieutenant General John Wilsey gave up the 'hot seat' in HQNI, when he stood down as General Officer Commanding of the Army in Northern Ireland; he was replaced by Lieutenant General Roger Wheeler. Three days later, the leaders of the Catholic, Methodist, Church of Ireland and Presbyterian churches flew to the USA to see American political and business chiefs to sell the case for investment in Northern Ireland. With the Provisionals intent, despite the bankruptcy of their campaign, on destroying the country's economy, this was no easy task.

On the 6th, an Army foot patrol in the Falls/Divis Street area of Belfast were lucky to suffer no serious casualties after a PIRA attack. Ross Street runs parallel with the Falls Road and joins Albert Street before running into the now demolished Divis Complex, known to generations of soldiers as the 'Zanussi'. During the morning, despite the proximity of civilians, an IRA unit set up a firing point close to where they expected soldiers to pass. As the Army personnel appeared, the ASU fired a Mark XVI grenade, which exploded harmlessly; the terrorists disappeared into the rabbit warren of terraced housing around the Balkans, Sultans, Plevnas and Raglans. Just a week later, a similar attack in Cookstown also came to nothing, as the grenade failed to explode.

On the same day, Freddie Scappaticci and his 'nutting squad' were called into action again, this time close to their own West Belfast turf. IRA volunteer Christopher Harte (24), father of a toddler, was a community worker, employed at the Turf Lodge Enterprise Centre. He lived in Dermot Hill Parade, close to the Whiterock Road and the Nationalist New Barnsley area. Some time on the 5th or 6th, he was abducted, bundled into a car, where he was likely hooded and his hands tied behind his back, before being driven off. He was then taken on a terrifying 86-mile journey, passing Lough Neagh and Omagh before crossing into the Irish Republic. It is probable that he was taken to a remote farmhouse somewhere between Cronalaghey and Meenagolan. PIRA commanders in West Belfast suspected that he was an informant, owing to a large number of operations linked with him which had gone wrong. More importantly, however, having been charged with terrorism offences by the RUC, he was then mysteriously released. It was a war which *Irish News* journalist, Allison Morris described thus: 'It was such a dirty war, you start to wonder who was really fighting who.' In such a 'dirty war', it is not beyond the realms of probability, that RUC SB released Harte in order to sow the seeds of suspicion about him and divert attention away from a real informant inside the cell to which Harte belonged. It is very likely that he wasn't an informant, but was sacrificed on the altar of intelligence expediency.

Following five or six days of interrogation, his agony ended when he was taken across the border and killed; his lifeless body was found dumped by the side of the rural Laghtmorris Road and Garvaghblane Road, just inside the Northern Ireland border, close to Castlederg, Co. Tyrone, in the early hours of the 12th. A forestry worker on timber-felling duties discovered the corpse; Harte had been hooded, his hands trussed behind his back before the trademark two shots were fired into the back of the head. His body bore the usual signs of IRA savagery and he had clearly been severely tortured and beaten before being shot.

On Wednesday 10 February 1993, the new Irish Taoiseach, Albert Reynolds, nominated Gordon Wilson to become a member of Seanad Éireann, the Irish Senate. Mr

Wilson's daughter Mary had been killed in the IRA's 'Poppy Day Massacre' in Enniskillen. His famous words shortly after the bombing echoed around the world, and outshone the brutality of the IRA's actions that day: 'I bear no ill will. I bear no grudge.' He served in Seanad Éireann until his death in 1995, but his words of forgiveness which dwarfed the evil actions of the Provisional IRA will in some but not all people's opinion, long outlive what they did.

Lance Corporal Michael Joseph Beswick (21) was a soldier in the Royal Regiment of Fusiliers from Heywood near Rochdale in Lancashire. In May of the previous year, he had survived the PIRA van bomb on the PVCP at Cloughoge, which killed Fusilier Grundy (*see* Chapter 17). He had just arrived in Armagh on the 8th and, in the early hours of the 9th, was leading a foot patrol in Armagh city centre. PIRA's South Armagh unit had placed three explosive devices, each weighing 44 lb (20 kg) along Cathedral Road, two on one side and one on the other. The positioning was to guarantee casualties, so that no matter where soldiers set up an incident control point (ICP) or wherever they took shelter, some would die or be maimed. At around 02:00, the joint Army/RUC patrol was returning to base at the RUC station at Friary Road and had just reached Cathedral Road, close to where it joins Upper English Street; at that point, the first device exploded. In the first blast, Michael Beswick was fatally hurt, with others receiving injuries. As the soldiers collected their thoughts, saw to their wounded and tried to set up an ICP, the other two bombs exploded, seriously injuring three more soldiers, with shrapnel wounds to their legs and body; another two soldiers and a policeman were treated for shock. Ambulances began to arrive fairly quickly, but so too did civilians who gathered to watch and jeer at the plight of the wounded men. The crowd – little more than ghouls – began to mock as the critically injured soldier called out to his mother, clearly in terrible agony. As his stunned comrades continued to behave in a professional manner, they had to make sure that their wounded comrades received fast treatment, all the time, ensuring defence against any further attacks. Whilst they conducted themselves with a dignified urgency, the locals behaved in a way unexpected of civilised people.

Around midday, Michael Beswick died of his wounds. The young soldier was cremated at Heywood. UPI later reported:

> Suspected IRA bomb blasts killed one British soldier and wounded seven others Tuesday near the residences of the Catholic and Anglican church leaders in Armagh, 45 miles west of Belfast. No group immediately took responsibility for the bombings, but the blasts were believed to be an attempt by the Irish Republican Army to embarrass Catholic Cardinal Cahal Daly and the Anglican primate, Archbishop Robin Eames, who are currently on a joint goodwill visit to the United States. Lance Cpl Michael Beswick, 21, died ten hours after the explosions from the multiple injuries suffered in the blasts, an army spokesman said. The unmarried Lancashire-born soldier, from the 2nd Battalion of Royal Fusiliers, had joined the army in March 1989. The bombs exploded less than half a mile from the residences of the Catholic and Anglican church leaders, who are with a group of other leaders attempting to persuade U.S. businessmen to invest in Ireland. Beswick was the most seriously injured soldier. The injuries of the four soldiers remaining in hospital were not thought to be life threatening, the army spokesman said. 'The first one to

be detonated had been placed behind a wall on Cathedral Road. The other two were placed in the pillars of a gate on the other side of the road. These two were detonated simultaneously,' he said. Windows and doors in surrounding buildings in the road, most of them houses, were shattered by the explosions, which police believe were caused by the IRA. St Patrick's Roman Catholic Cathedral, less than 200 yards from the main blast, escaped damage.

On the 10th, IRA personnel left a small device outside a block of flats close to Victoria station in London SW1. The bomb exploded, but there were no injuries. However, just 17 days later, a device placed in a rubbish bin in Camden High Street, north London, exploded without any warning; this time, 18 people were injured, two very seriously.

The day after the Victoria bomb, the UVF killed another Catholic, also in Co. Armagh, only 12 miles away from the IRA bomb that had killed Lance Corporal Beswick. The rationale this time was that the UVF's mid-Ulster brigade thought, repeat 'thought', that the Molloy whom they killed was actually a different Molloy, a Sinn Féin councillor. The man they wanted to kill was Francie Molloy; the innocent Catholic they did in fact kill was Thomas Molloy (32), father of four young children. He lived in Derrymagown Road, between Loughgall, and Moy; on the evening of the 11th, as he watched TV with his family, a murder gang drove along his street. They slowed to a crawl directly opposite the living room of the house and began firing automatic weapons through the open car windows. Mr Molloy was hit four times in the head and chest; he died instantly. One of the rounds also hit his year-old son, slightly injuring him.

Mrs Molloy bravely threw her children to the floor, covering them with her own body. As the car raced away, she was able to crawl over to where her dead husband lay. She later told the press: 'I took the children into the hallway and then went back. When I looked at Thomas's head, I knew he was dead, so I said a prayer.' The UVF quickly claimed that the dead man was a Sinn Féin activist, a part of what Loyalists were calling the 'Pan Nationalist Front', and as such was a 'legitimate target'. However, they had killed the wrong Molloy, but metaphorically shrugged their shoulders, chanting their sickening mantra: 'Yabba dabba doo; any old Taig will do!'

Another Royal Irish soldier died on the 15th, as a result of being dicked by PIRA sympathisers. Lance Corporal Mervyn Johnson (38), father of two teenagers, was a part-time soldier. He lived in Highfern Gardens, part of a Loyalist/Protestant area to the south of the Ballygomartin Road in West Belfast. The houses have a fellow Loyalist estate at Woodvale to the north, but their immediate neighbours were the Nationalist New Barnsley and Ballymurphy estates. Its precarious location made the potential of an IRA incursion very high. A two-man unit from the Ardoyne IRA, thought to have been dispatched by 'Bubbles' Copeland, drove into the estate of neat, red-brick townhouses from either the West Circular or Ballygomartin Roads; whichever route they took in or out, the 'Murph and New Barnsley were only a short journey away. They spotted the part-time soldier, as he was wheeling a bicycle belonging to one of his children up the street. They stopped opposite, immediately opening fire with a Russian-manufactured AKM, a more modern version of the AK-47. The soldier was hit four times, collapsing mortally wounded to the ground; one of the gunmen got out of the car, stood close to the wounded man and fired three more shots into his head from point-blank range. As the car screeched off, Mrs Edith Johnson, alerted by the gunfire, dashed into the street, only to see her husband lying dead in a pool of his ever-spreading blood.

Corporal Johnson had joined the UDR in October 1986 and was now serving in 'D' Company, 7 Royal Irish; he was the fourth member of the regiment to be killed by terrorists. In total, between 1992 (inception) and 1998, 36 members of the new regiment were killed in or as a consequence of the Troubles. Seven were killed by the Provisional IRA; nine took their own lives; four were killed in a fire at an RUC station; 12 were killed in the seemingly ubiquitous RTAs which claimed so many UDR lives, with a further four dying on duty. Mervyn Johnson's funeral was held at Roselawn Cemetery in Belfast. His daughter, Alison, and son, Jason, carried a simple wreath which read: 'Dad'. The following piece is a posthumous contribution from the late Rab McGough who died in hospital in Glasgow in January 2016; it relates indirectly to the manner of Lance Corporal Johnson's death.

Rab McGough

It is when I read of deaths like this, of off-duty soldiers, killed wheeling his bairn's bike or shot with a wee 'un on his knee, that I think of all the greetin' [crying] when a Provie was shot by the SAS boys. Now, when I read about the Harte brothers, Brian Mullen, the Grews and Lynagh and all these scum shot at Loughgall, I have no twinge of conscience, none whatsoever.

On the 16th, 'Teflon Man' himself, Gerry Adams, was in the news again, as the *Irish News* published an interview with the Sinn Féin President. In the interview, Adams called for 'inclusive dialogue' towards a new Anglo-Irish agreement. He was keen to insert the word 'partition' into his comments, a word over which Irish Republicans have obsessed since 1921. It wasn't 'partition' Mr Adams; it was simply that the majority of the population of the north of the island didn't wish to be part of your 'Thirty-Two County Small Farmers and Workers Republic'. It was simply that two-thirds or more of the population of the North didn't wish to be part of a system where your 'volunteers' killed, maimed and destroyed in a hopelessly vain attempt to achieve an impossible and unrealistic dream. Even today, Adams's fellow 'Shinners' cannot bring themselves to refer to Northern Ireland by its legitimate and lawful name, referring to it only as the 'north of Ireland'.

On the 17th, Rifleman David Terance Fenley of the Royal Green Jackets (20), from Morpeth in Northumberland, was killed at his unit's base at RUC Strabane in Co. Tyrone. I have done much research into this young soldier's demise, finding it initially very difficult to ascertain the cause of death, other than that it was an accidental shooting. I was certain that he didn't take his own life, narrowing it down to an accidental discharge whilst cleaning his weapon, or possibly barrack-room horseplay. However, prior to publication, one of his comrades came forward with the facts. On what another Rifleman called 'a dark day amongst others on that tour' as Rifleman Fenley dismounted from a Land Rover, to help set up a VCP in Strabane, his troop commander's SA-80 accidentally discharged, the round striking Rifleman Fenley and sadly killing him instantly. The Geordie lad's funeral was held in his native Northumberland. The same source informed me that the dead soldier was planning to get married in the near future.

On Wednesday 24th, there was more discord in the so-called 'special relationship' between the USA and the United Kingdom. Prime Minister John Major met President Clinton to discuss – amongst other weighty matters of state – the Northern Ireland situation. Clinton had only been in office for a little over a month at the time, but seized the opportunity to ingratiate himself with the Irish vote both inside and outside the United States government. He suggested to Major that a US-appointed 'peace envoy' be sent to the troubled Province to report on the situation and act as an influence to both sides. Clearly Major did not appreciate yet more American interference in the affairs of a British province, and later told the British and international press that he found Clinton's suggestion to be 'unhelpful'. Major did, however, agree that the American President was welcome to send a representative on a fact-finding visit to Northern Ireland, though he probably hoped that the person sent would be less anti-British and less geographically challenged than Senator Edward Kennedy, who famously told two Belfast soldiers in the UDR to 'get back to your own country'.

On the 24th and 25th, the Provisionals killed two more policemen. RUCR Constable Reginald 'Reg' Williamson (46), father of two, and Constable Jonathan Reid (30) became the 293rd and 294th RUC officers to die in the Troubles in less than 24 years. This makes for grim reading, when compared with say, the UK mainland, where in the same period 50 officers were killed from a population some 30 times greater, or Australia, where in a population 15 times greater, the figures were but a fraction of those of Northern Ireland, per capita or otherwise.

In the first incident, on the evening of the 24th, Reg Williamson had been for a quiet night out with his girlfriend in the village of Moy, Co. Tyrone. There is some speculation that the part-time policeman had been recognised by local dickers and reported to the local PIRA unit – Moy is a Nationalist area with Loughgall nearby. It is entirely possible too that the operation was not as a result of reports by dickers in Moy, simply that PIRA had picked up on the fact that the RUCR man and his girlfriend had regular nights out in the village. Whilst the couple were enjoying what would prove to be their last drink together, a bombing team placed a lethal amount of Semtex under the policeman's car. The couple set off for one of their homes in Armagh, albeit in separate cars. Their mini convoy had travelled less than three miles along the Aughanlig Road when the device exploded. The car was hurled into the air, finishing on its roof in a ditch, the explosion tearing off Williamson's legs. His distraught girlfriend ran to the shattered man's side, cradling his head in her arms. He died before the ambulance arrived, leaving a young woman covered in the blood of the man she loved; yet another 'Ulster widow'. It was the second tragedy to visit the Williamson family; his brother Freddie, a soldier in the UDR, was killed by INLA gunmen near Moy on 7 October 1982.

The following day, in an incident which had echoes of the IRA sniper-killing of Constable Alan Corbett the previous November, another sniper shot and killed Constable Jonathan Reid in Crossmaglen, in the very black heart of 'bandit country'. At 10:00, a joint RUC/Army patrol had set up a VCP on the Blaney to Castleblaney Road to the north-west of the town, just a few miles away from the Irish border. The unit contained 14 personnel; Constable Reid was lying in the long grass at the side of the road on 'cut-off' duty. He stood up in order to speak to a colleague, when suddenly a 7.62 mm bullet fired from a tripod-mounted AK-47 smashed into his back, exiting through his chest. At the point where he was shot, the road is flanked by trees and hedges, with the border less than two miles away, both to the west and north-west. In other words, there is plenty of cover, providing a lot of advantage for a man with a powerful rifle fitted with a sniper scope. Despite the best efforts of an RUC colleague who tried to revive him, the police officer died at the scene; he wasn't wearing a flak jacket although it is still quite likely that the round would have still torn through him.

Ulster Unionist MP Jim Wilson spoke about the murder of the policeman the following day. He made direct reference to a recent Irish-American conference in the USA which had pledged support – financial and moral – for the IRA. Several delegates had made spoken of the human rights of terrorists who had been shot by the Army or RUC. He said: 'It is ironic that Irish-Americans express concerns over human rights in Ulster on the same day that the IRA slaughter members of law and order [*sic*].' Seamus Mallon, MP for Newry and Armagh, speaking in the House of Commons, referred to the killers of the two police officers as 'petty little Hitlers who use the name Republican'. He also went on to condemn Loyalist paramilitaries.

On the 20th, an Army mobile patrol was in the process of returning to their base at Woodbourne RUC station in South Belfast, when a carefully arranged PIRA ambush took place. A missile from an RPG-7 fired from residential housing smashed into the vehicle, injuring four soldiers, some very seriously. The terrorists escaped, and unfortunately there were no arrests. On the same day a three-man PIRA team attacked a Protestant-owned bar in central Belfast, wounding three Protestants, including an off-duty Royal Irish soldier. The following day, Dunnes Department store in Belfast's Park Centre was hit by a series of incendiary devices planted by an IRA team; there was considerable damage, but no injuries. Two days later, two police officers were badly injured when Rosemount RUC station was rocked by a bomb blast in Londonderry; the IRA's Creggan unit was responsible.

Warrington in Cheshire was the next mainland British town to be hit; the events of the 26th of this month, were merely a portent of tragedy to come. In the late evening, a police officer pulled over a van he had become suspicious about. As he approached the driver's side, a passenger fired a handgun, badly wounding him. The gunman's car sped away although the injured officer was able to radio for assistance.

The men were part of a bombing unit, in the process of escaping after planting bombs at the gas storage facility in Winwick Road. At approximately 04:00, their bombs detonated, causing major destruction, cutting off the town's gas supply. The blast caused a jet of flame which reached over 1,000 ft into the night sky; over 100 homes were evacuated.

Following a high-speed chase on the M62, two of the bombers were caught, but only after they had hijacked a car in nearby Lymm, forcing the owner into the boot. As they were being pursued along the motorway, they opened fire on the pursuing police cars. The IRA men who were arrested were Páidric Mac Fhloinn and Denis Kinsella; a third man, Michael Timmins, managed to escape. In 1994, Mac Fhloinn was sentenced to 35 years in prison and Kinsella to 25 years for their part in the bombing.

On Sunday, 28th, Dick Spring, the Irish Deputy Prime Minister, was interviewed by the BBC. Inevitably, the discussion came around to Articles 2 and 3 of the Irish Constitution, written in 1922, and replaced in 1937. Articles 2 and 3 referred to the claim to the six northern counties of Ulster by the Republic. It demanded their return and effectively legitimised the IRA's campaign of violence. Rather surprisingly, Spring, when pressed over the thorny issue of the claim, stated that the articles were 'not cast in bronze' and were in fact open to negotiation. Ever since the AIA, these had been major – actually insurmountable – stumbling blocks in the negotiations over the future of Northern Ireland.

February came to an end, with eight more deaths.

27
March

March was bloodier than of late and 14 people died this month; three soldiers and seven civilians, four of whom were Catholics killed in sectarian attacks. The dead included two young children in an IRA blast in Warrington. Additionally, a paramilitary from either side died, one of whom was an IRA man killed by the 'nutting squad'. There might have been four military deaths, on the 8th, but sometimes miracles do happen.

On the 1st of the month, a unit from the IRA's South Armagh brigade launched two mortar bombs at the joint Army/RUC base at Bessbrook Mill – at that stage the largest heliport in Europe. There were no fatalities, but over 30 houses were badly damaged as the missiles fell short; three civilians were injured. With 50 or 60 families bombed out, a nearby community centre was turned into emergency sleeping accommodation on a night when temperatures dipped below freezing. One wonders if at the time, there were any PIRA sympathisers, clad in their pyjamas, wrapped in Army-issue blankets from Bessbrook Mill's QM stores, their night's sleep rudely interrupted. Seven days later, another unit launched an identical attack at Keady (*see below*).

On Wednesday 3rd, six serving soldiers in the UDR were awarded undisclosed damages by a Belfast court, in addition to an apology. The court demanded that RUC Chief Constable Hugh Annesley apologise for their arrest on 8 October 1989, following the Stevens inquiry. The Stevens inquiry looked into allegations of collusion between the security forces and Loyalist paramilitary groups. One of those soldiers, Lance Corporal Leslie Wheeler, was only cleared posthumously as he had taken his own life on 11 August 1991 (*see* Chapter 8).

On the 5th, Dick Spring, gave a speech at a meeting of the Irish Association in which he further acknowledged that changes to the Irish Constitution would be required in any future settlement of the Northern Ireland problem. Three days later, Patrick Mayhew welcomed the speech made by Spring, stating that he thought that the Tánaiste was 'someone I could do business with'. Mayhew had given a speech in Bangor, Co. Down, earlier in the week, in which he stressed that the union between Britain and Northern Ireland would only be changed if a majority of the population voted for some new constitutional arrangement.

On the 6th, a three-man unit from the Ardoyne, thought to include Eddie 'Bubbles' Copeland, PIRA commander for the area – a man of whom we shall hear more later – set up an ambush on Shankill Road. The location, in the very heart of Loyalist country, whilst considered militarily daring was only a short distance away from his own power base in the nearby Ardoyne. The attack was allegedly in direct retaliation for Loyalist attacks on Sinn

Féin members over the preceding few weeks. Copeland's team parked in Berlin Street, close to where it joins the Shankill Road, the same location where Thomas Begley and Sean Kelly would park their car on 23 October 1993, before the fateful walk to Frizzell's. Waiting in their parked car, weapons cocked, Copeland and another gunman watched a car driven by known Loyalists approach them. At the optimum moment, the PIRA members opened fire with AK-47s, spraying the Loyalist vehicle, hitting and seriously wounding the driver. Copeland's unit made the short journey back into the safety of the Ardoyne.

'Bubbles' himself was an interesting character; his father was shot by a soldier in 1971, which probably motivated him to join the Provisionals and he rose through the ranks to command the Ardoyne unit. He was the architect of the Frizzell's bombing (*see* Chapter 35) and was later wounded at the funeral of the man who placed the bomb in the crowded shop that day. He hated Adair with the same passion with which Adair hated him and the two terrorists swore to kill the other. In 1996, a UFF bombing team, led by Red Hand Commando Frankie Curry, placed a device under Copeland's car, which seriously injured the IRA man. Quite unbelievably, this man who had terrorised the area and was responsible for violence and bloodshed, was awarded £60,000 in compensation!

'Bubbles'
RUC Officer, now retired

I had occasion to speak to this sleazebag on a number of occasions, between the late 70s and early 90s. His da' was shot by a soldier in Ladbroke Drive in October of 1971. If I recall correctly, a foot patrol came under fire from a sniper and they shot back, killing Mr Copeland who was standing nearby. Eddie, who became known as 'the Godfather' on the Ardoyne, got involved and turned into one nasty, vicious bugger. He was a bully who always looked as though butter wouldn't melt in his gob! The Ardoyne area was always under threat from Loyalists on the Shankill and Crumlin, but the Catholics were just as terrified of Copeland and his thugs as they were of the UDA. He was always staring at us and watching us and mentally noting our tactics and our behaviour; you could see it in his eyes that he was constantly analysing and planning ways to bring about our demise. That man was pure evil: bitter, angry and with a massive chip on both shoulders. After he was shot in '93 – and I wish that the wee bastard had been killed – he had to wear some sort of shit or piss bag, and we all just loved giving it a squeeze when we saw him in the street. He was given a lot of money after he was shot and then even more when a 'freelance bomber' blew him up. I was retired by the second award and I nearly chocked on my fucking cornflakes when I seen that!

On the 7th, in open defiance of the UDA/UFF threat to create 'rivers of Catholic blood' if the bombing of Ulster's cities did not cease, the Provisionals planted a huge car bomb weighing 200 lb (90 kg) in the centre of Bangor, Co. Down, close to the RUC station. The bomb was timed to detonate in the early hours of the morning, with the intention of causing massive destruction and killing any officers entering or leaving the base. Just before 03:00, the device exploded, seriously injuring four RUC officers, including a female PC, as they walked towards the station. Thirty buildings, mainly banks, shops and offices, were destroyed as the blast devastated the centre of the town, which had been attacked in a similar way only six months earlier. Bangor was a popular seaside resort, well-loved by a mainly Protestant clientele, something of which the IRA bombers were only too aware. The officers were treated for fractured bones, cuts and shrapnel wounds; the policewoman who was a mother of two, was the most badly injured, having part of her leg amputated some 10 days later. The cost of the damage was later estimated at £2 million. Just five days before Patrick Mayhew had made a speech of encouragement to businesses in the town.

The following day two more RUC officers were injured, along with three civilians, when the IRA detonated a no-warning car bomb in the centre of Belfast. On this occasion, damage was estimated at £2,000,000; whereas the IRA knew that they couldn't kill the British in sufficient quantities to drive them into the sea, they understood that the next best thing was to bomb Northern Ireland back into the stone age to try and achieve their hopeless dream.

Shortly afterwards, a few miles away in West Belfast, a PIRA gunman opened fire on an RUC VCP close to Andersonstown. Several gunmen had taken over a house, holding the occupants at gunpoint whilst they set up a firing point in a bedroom window. A policeman was hit by a single round and badly injured; he was rushed to the nearby Musgrave Park Hospital. The PIRA gang escaped, in the full knowledge that the police and soldiers would not fire back because of the proximity of innocent civilians.

On the 8th, the Provisionals launched a Mark IV mortar attack on the RUC base at Keady in Co. Armagh. Keady sits some four miles from the Irish border, not far from the site of the infamous INLA attack on the Pentecostal Church at Darkly in 1983; it is of strategic importance to the IRA. On the morning of the 8th, just after 10:00, one of their units drove a lorry, hijacked the previous day in Belleek and since then modified as a mobile baseplate, to a point about 80 yards away on the Castleblaney side of the Davis Street base. They fired three 'barrack busters' at the joint RUC/Army base. When the missiles rained down without warning, a civilian worker, Nigel Thomas James McCollum (25), a contractor on the base, was caught in one of the blasts. He was working on a crane, lifting portacabins into place, when the explosions took place. Five other civilians – all Protestants – were injured, three of them seriously, but Mr McCollum, from Sandholes at Cookstown, was killed more or less instantly. The blast which killed him caused the crane he was working on to topple over, crushing him as it hit the ground. The dead man's grandmother, Lily, had been killed by a PIRA booby-trap bomb in 1983 (intended for her brother who was a soldier in 8 UDR) and Mr McCollum's brother Reginald, a soldier in 8 Royal Irish, would be murdered by the same terror group in 1994.

Mr McCollum worked for Henry Brothers, a Magherafelt building company who had four of their staff killed by Republican terrorists over the course of the Troubles. NI Secretary Mayhew said the attack was 'disgusting, but the time would come when this period of great blackness and evil would be brought to an end. It would be the people of Northern Ireland who defeated violence.' Fine words indeed, but the IRA on one side and the UFF/UVF on the other were killing with apparent impunity. Peace, if it may be described in such terms, was still several years away. On the same day, evil went a-knocking, once more. Former UDR and Royal Irish soldier Phillip Martin lived in Donaghmore, Co. Tyrone, a married man with two children then aged four and nine. Mr Martin had survived several previous attempts by the IRA to kill him. On the evening of the 8th, the terror group targeted him again, expecting him as a civilian to be less prepared than he would have been in his military days, but they were in for a surprise. He was prepared for an attack should it come by being permanently armed. At the time of the attack, he was standing in the back garden with his two children and his grandfather, playing with the family's Alsatian puppy. Several IRA gunmen approached him simultaneously from opposite sides of the house. In the past, they had demonstrated a total lack of regard for the proximity of family members in their indecent haste to kill off-duty SF members. Certainly, they would have been unmoved by the fact that a nine-year-old boy and a four-year-old girl were directly in the line of fire as they unleashed a volley of shots. They were not going to be deterred by the prospect of spilling the blood of children.

Mr Martin takes up the story, as he told Ric Clark of the Belfast *News Letter* at the time: 'We were very exposed, but I had talked to the children about what to do if anything happened. We have been living in fear of attack for some weeks and I had told the children that if people started shooting, they should get on the ground immediately and keep moving around if they had nowhere to hide. There were four of them and we were easy targets. Everybody did exactly as they had been told. We were under heavy attack. About 20 shots were fired before I could get off a single shot. Wee Maxine managed to find cover behind a bus in the yard. She was very lucky as shots missed her by only two inches. Leigh and his grandfather were both down and moving.' Then, as the gunfire intensified, Mr Martin didn't see a gunman running at him from behind. 'It was then that Leigh shouted "Daddy! Daddy!" The shooting was very heavy but he ran across and knocked me over. It was only then that I saw the other gunman behind me and I then fired a number of shots at him. Leigh was totally defenceless, yet he was just great. If it wasn't for him, that gunman would have killed me.' Thanks to this shouted warning, the lives of Phillip Martin and his family were saved; the gunmen ran off to their getaway car and vanished into the border area.

Five days later, the IRA employed another 'barrack-buster' in an attack on a British Army observation post at Glasdrumman, Co. Armagh; on this occasion, there were no casualties. ITV News covered the attack; their reporter stated that, as the SF built stronger defences, so the IRA built more powerful weapons. The area's Unionist MP said: 'The use of this type of weapon is simply going to result in mass slaughter some day.'

The Belfast *News Letter* reported: 'Windows were broken in business premises and at some houses in St Matthew's Estate at Lir Gardens about 200 yards away. A woman in St Matthew's said: "I was going out to close the gate when the first explosion happened. I was so frightened I ran back to the house. I am still shaking." Police denied an IRA claim that residents were warned to get out before the attack. Michael McMullan, whose home is next to the base, had moved from watching TV into another room to put coal on the fire when he heard two massive thuds. "If I had been standing at the window, my head would have been cut off with the glass coming in." He told of how the coal blew up in his face and the windows smashed. "There was no warning," he emphasised.'

The IRA's dual strategy of terror and intimidation ensured that they attacked and killed anyone, under their umbrella phrase of 'legitimate targets'. Just as the UFF/UVF had their 'Pan-Nationalist front' range of targets, considering not just the IRA, but anything remotely Irish as worthy of death, so too did their Republican counterparts. In the eyes of

Republican paramilitaries and the others, serving and former military and police personnel were legitimate targets as were prison officers, judiciary, army civvie workers, and anyone who was employed by the 'Crown forces'.

Minutes after the triple blast at Glasdrumman, a little over 24 miles away two RUC officers and a civilian were injured by an IRA bomb in the centre of Lurgan, as they locked the town's security gates. The device went off without warning close to their vehicle; afterwards, because of the possibility of additional devices, 50 houses were evacuated. Thanks to the constant supply of money and weapons from the USA, the Provisional IRA had an apparently bottomless pit of arms and explosives in order to continue their war of terror.

On the 9th, the IRA made its second attack in the south-west of Belfast in the space of a few weeks, when it attacked an Army foot patrol in the Woodbourne area. On this occasion, IRA gunmen took over two houses close to the RUC station, holding two families at gunpoint whilst they set up an RPG-7 firing point. As the soldiers walked back to the base, the rocket was fired, but it exploded harmlessly, with no injuries.

Later on the same night as the RPG attack, the IRA shot and wounded a soldier on foot patrol in the Catholic enclave of Short Strand. Before that night was over, another PIRA unit had lain in wait outside the RUC station on Grosvenor Road, close to the Falls/Springfield Roads. A gunman opened fire on an RUC officer at the front sangar, badly wounding him. The gunman escaped, managing to lose his pursuers in the grounds of the Royal Victoria Hospital. The officer was hit in the leg and taken to the RVH, probably along the very same route that his assailant had taken; he made a full recovery.

On Wednesday 10th, the House of Commons decided by 329 to 202 votes to renew the Prevention of Terrorism Act. John Smith's Labour Party voted against the motion, whereas in previous years the party had abstained. Also on the 10th, the South Tyrone Provisionals tried to kill a former UDR soldier, whose name is withheld at his request. In this attack in Dungannon, shots were fired at the former soldier, but they missed, although his nine-year-old son was hit and wounded in the hip. He made a full recovery. The violence for that day was not yet complete: Norman Truesdale (39), father of four, was shot dead by the Provisionals in his shop at the junction of the Oldpark Road and Century Street, Belfast, close to the local public library. IRA commander Eddie Copeland dispatched a three-man unit to the sectarian interface with the Oldpark Road to kill Truesdale. The Provisionals considered that he was the grenade thrower who helped kill three Catholics on 23 November the previous year, in the attack on James Martins' Bookmakers. One of the IRA killers sent to exact revenge for the sectarian attack, was Thomas 'Ta' McWilliams; he and one other man walked into Truesdale's sweet shop, which was just 200 yards from where the slaughter of November had taken place; they were intent on revenge. As they walked in, their target was serving a twelve-year-old boy with a packet of sweets; this clearly was no deterrent. One of the men shot Truesdale twice in the chest from very close range; as he slumped to the floor, the second gunman stood over him, shooting him with an AK-47, killing him almost immediately.

Their mission complete, the gunmen ran to their waiting car, speeding back into the safety of the Ardoyne, where McWilliams had his girlfriend wash all the clothes he had worn in the attack, thus erasing the forensic evidence. He was jailed in 1995, but released early under the GFA, only to be returned to jail after he was convicted of handling weapons used in another IRA shooting. At his original trial, McWilliams shouted 'Up the IRA' as he was led away after the verdict. He was identified by security camera but the other killer was masked by a black balaclava. The IRA later claimed the killing, stating that the dead man was a UFF member; this was denied by his family, although the UDA/UFF later claimed him as one of theirs. A UDA mural in his memory was later painted on a gable wall in the area.

Some years later, there was an interesting development in the case, when the dead man's brother, Dessie Truesdale, spoke to the *Belfast Telegraph*. He said: 'The bookies was "done" and the IRA tried to get Johnny Adair. But they missed Johnny and then the following fortnight they got Norman. I tried to ask Johnny about that situation. I know Johnny, I know when I am spooking him. And when I mentioned that, he got angry. Now, I'm led to believe that Norman was involved in those murders. Norman was arrested for the bookies and the police kept him in for three days. The IRA found that out and that's why he was shot in the shop.' Quite clearly, Dessie Truesdale believed that his brother was killed in revenge for his part in the betting shop massacre. It is clear also that he blamed Johnny Adair for his brother's death, because it was 'Mad Dog' himself who ordered the attack.

On the 15th the North Belfast UFF shot and killed a Catholic whose only crime was to volunteer a few hours of his time to helping Sinn Féin during elections. Robert Shaw (56), father of four grown-up children, had driven from the ferry port of Larne across to Belfast Lough at Whiteabbey. He had driven over to the lough to buy fishing equipment; as he parked outside the shop, two UFF gunmen walked over to the driver's side of his Ford Transit and shot him several times in the head and chest. The UFF's Rathcoole unit were aware that he made regular trips to the fishing shop, having staked it out on a number of occasions. On this particular day, a murder gang was waiting for him, shooting him dead by the shop entrance. Later claims of PIRA membership were so far-fetched, as to be little more than wild fabrication. He had survived several heart attacks, open heart surgery and the removal of a lung, but he was unable to survive this attack by cowardly Loyalist gunmen intent on killing a soft-target Catholic.

Local Unionist Party MP Roy Beggs stated later that he was very happy to confirm that the murdered man had no paramilitary ties, acting only as an occasional volunteer for Sinn Féin. He was described by friends as 'a deep thinker and a man of deep sincerity who had no time for evil-doing or conflict'. This was not enough to satisfy the Loyalist killers; the death toll ticked on towards the next milestone: 4,000.

Forkhill is located in an area that was of strategic importance to both the SF and the Republican terror groups. It is less than a thousand yards from the border with the South, and only five or six miles from Crossmaglen. It truly is in the heart of what former NI Secretary Merlyn Rees labelled 'bandit country'. On the 17th, an Army patrol from the Royal Scots was lured into an ambush in what transpired to be a classic IRA 'come on'. The soldiers were patrolling through fields when they spotted a man acting in a suspicious manner; naturally, they followed him. However, the man deliberately led them into an open area which the ambush-setters had designated as the 'killing ground' for an IRA sniper, hidden in a red Jeep, close to trees. The first soldier into his sights was Lance Corporal Lawrence Kivlin Dickson (26); the Edinburgh-born soldier was hit in the side and collapsed, fatally wounded. His comrades returned fire, but were unable to hit the sniper who escaped in the Jeep, hidden near the Shean Road, very close to the border. The wounded man was casevaced to Daisy Hill Hospital in Newry, but died within hours; his funeral was held at Leith's Eastern Road cemetery, close to Hibernian football ground and a short distance from the Firth of Forth. He left a widow and an 18-month-old daughter.

The sniper's round entered a gap in his NIBA (Northern Ireland Body Armour); a notorious weak point and one deliberately targeted by the IRA man, thought to have been trained by a weapons' expert in the US Army. The (Glasgow) *Herald* provided the following technical information: 'There has been no official confirmation but a high-powered long-range rifle is thought to have been used yesterday, possibly an American-made Barrett (Light Fifty) which has a killing range of up to 1,800 metres and which fires half-inch rounds. Anyone hit in the upper part of the body or head would have almost no chance of survival.'

Earlier, that day, the Provisionals, despite the global opprobrium their cowardly attack at Teebane had provoked, attempted another atrocity at Aghadowey, Co. Antrim. In the early hours of the morning, a two-man bombing team planted a small but potentially lethal device underneath a bus that they knew would be carrying Protestant workmen. The men were employed by a local construction firm, working on an SF base near Coleraine. Their bus – driven by a known Loyalist – had just delivered the men at the base, following a journey of around four miles. The driver and passengers had just got off when the device exploded; although shocked and cut by flying glass and shrapnel, all of the men miraculously survived.

Before the day was over, a Loyalist mob attacked an undercover RUC officer in York Road, North Belfast, close to the Loyalist stronghold of Tiger's Bay. The undercover officer was reporting on UFF activity when he was spotted and attacked. He was badly beaten and left for dead by the mob; his Ruger pistol was also stolen. Four local men were later arrested for the attack. Before midnight, a UFF team driving from the Shankill Road, down McKeag's famed 'yellow brick road' – Lanark Way – entered Springfield Road in West Belfast. Their car stopped outside the Orient Bar on the corner of Cupar Street. The men planted an incendiary device outside the bar. However, an alert doorman had seen the Loyalist paramilitaries plant the device before roaring away in their stolen car. The quick-thinking and courageous man kicked the device away, but it exploded the second his foot made contact, badly burning him; he was taken to the nearby RVH.

Although it had a history dating back to Roman times, Warrington had no noticeable international reputation before 1993. However, on the 20th of this month, the IRA put the town's name on the map with a cowardly and unprovoked attack which left a small child dead and another fighting ultimately unsuccessfully for his young life.

The 20th fell on a Saturday, very much the main shopping day of the week back in those days when there was little Sunday trading. The IRA knew this, and some time during the late morning, blending in with the throngs of shoppers, planted two devices in rubbish bins along Bridge Street. It was a cool day, a typical early spring day with temperatures around 9 °C (49 °F); the main shopping centre was busy, especially so in the Golden Square Shopping Mall/Bridge Street area. The first bomb exploded at 12:25 just outside the British Gas showroom; this blast injured many and the red-hot metal shrapnel cut into little Jonathan Ball (aged three) who was shopping for a Mothers' Day present for his mum.

Mothers' Day that year was the 21st, the following day. The toddler never stood a chance and despite an off-duty nurse being on the scene within seconds, fighting desperately to save him, he died in her arms.

After the first explosion, just as the bombers had planned that they would, terrified shoppers ran in all directions. Less than a minute later, the second device exploded in a cast-iron rubbish bin outside Argos. The blast injured over 50 people, tearing the limbs off several; it fatally injured Timothy Parry (12) who was in the centre, shopping for a pair of Everton Football Club shorts. He suffered massive head injuries, sadly dying five days later in Liverpool's Walton Centre for Neurology. Like many others, he was caught in the second blast as he tried to escape. In 2007, I had the honour, albeit only briefly, of meeting Tim Parry's parents at a Northern Ireland Veterans' Association memorial at the National Arboretum in Staffordshire.

Police said later that a coded warning was made to the Samaritans at 11:58 about a bomb outside a Boots' chemist shop in Liverpool. There was no time to evacuate the area after Merseyside police informed the Cheshire force of the deliberately misleading warning. The IRA's intention was simple: to kill and maim; it was of no consequence to them if women and children were the victims. Emergency services worked tirelessly and selflessly to rescue, comfort and treat the victims of an atrocity, which I steadfastly refuse to believe that McGuinness, Adams, Morrison and the 'respectable' leaders in Sinn Féin were unaware of. Buses were being organised to ferry people away from the scene with 20 paramedics, some on motorcycles, sent in to administer on the spot treatment. Seventeen ambulances were required to transport casualties to Warrington General Hospital. Specialists from the regional burns unit at Whiston hospital in Knowsley were also sent to aid those maimed and burned by the blasts.

Jonathan Ball's father told the press: 'He is what made me live. He was great. My life is just shattered now, absolutely shattered. A child of 3 years and 10 months and they took his life. He has done nothing to anybody. In my heart I don't think that I can ever forgive them.' Just over a week later, I watched the funeral of Tim Parry, learning that he had been buried in his beloved Everton's team kit. At my then home, in Clifford, West Yorkshire, I watched through tear-stained eyes, with a growing contempt for Irish Republicanism. Even today, I have to restrain my temper when I see Sinn Féin politicians attempting to re-write history, pretending that La Mon, Darkley, Droppin' Well and Warrington never happened. I have often been questioned about my well-publicised loathing for the Irish-Americans, Irish-Australians and Irish-Canadians who funded the IRA's war of terror; peruse again what I have just written and that should answer the question. I am informed by the Labour Left, that I shouldn't be angry, because these people were 'worthwhile sacrifices for the cause of Irish liberty'. The hackneyed clichés are trotted out with an apparent conviction, as well as an eagerness to blame the British 'establishment' for the deeds committed by Irish republicanism; Labour supporters forget only too easily that the bulk of the population of Northern Ireland expressed a desire and an intention to remain part of the United Kingdom.

The bombing received extensive coverage in the world's media and caused widespread anger, even leading to mass protests against the IRA in Dublin. Loyalist paramilitaries inevitably carried out several revenge sectarian attacks in Northern Ireland over the coming weeks. The bomb was vindictive, murderous and counter-productive and the IRA commanders who had ordered the attack knew that it would lead to even more global condemnation of their organisation. They knew equally that it would lead to even more Catholic bloodshed; still, the roots of Irish Republicanism have to be refreshed by the occasional blood of the innocents. Criticism of the bombing was made in the US, Australian, South African and Canadian press.

The *Independent* wrote of: 'Screaming and bleeding children and adults fleeing the devastation of the first blast in the Golden Square market area at the heart of Warrington, Cheshire, were caught in the second explosion 100 yards away. The area was sealed off by police and firemen were pulled out as Army bomb disposal officers investigated a number of other suspected bombs and carried out one controlled explosion. Fears about other possible bombs, and the desire to preserve forensic evidence, meant that the body of the boy, described by a witness as angelic-looking with blond hair, lay in a shop doorway for four hours.'

Incredibly, the IRA claimed that they had issued adequate warnings, then had the brass balls to attempt to switch responsibility for this blatant act of terror when they declared: 'Responsibility for the tragic and deeply regrettable death and injuries caused in Warrington yesterday lies squarely at the door of those in the British authorities who deliberately failed to act on precise and adequate warnings.' The police responded by saying: 'Yes, a warning was given half-an-hour before, but no mention was made of Warrington. If the IRA think they can pass on their responsibility for this terrible act by issuing such a nonsensical statement, they have sadly underestimated the understanding of the British public.' Home Secretary Kenneth Baker said to a war-weary British public: 'I am horrified by this brutal attack in a crowded shopping centre. Even by the standards of the IRA, this was a deliberate attempt to murder people simply in an attempt to shock.'

That very night, in several parts of Northern Ireland, units of the UVF and the UFF sat together in a blacker than usual mood; some undoubtedly would have shed crocodile tears others may well have shed genuine tears, but only one thing was absolutely certain: innocent Catholics would soon die across the Province. Some 38 miles south of Warrington, members of the IRA stole an Iveco lorry in Newcastle-under-Lyme, and quickly drove it towards London, stopping en route only to switch number plates. That vehicle would be packed with explosives and a month later would detonate in Bishopsgate in the heart of the City.

Retaliation for Warrington was swift. On the 23rd, the UFF's Stephen McKeag attempted to kill Sinn Féin councillor Gerard McGuigan at his North Belfast home. The gunman fired several shots into the Sinn Féin man's house but he was uninjured; in the confusion, the UFF gang escaped towards Tiger's Bay. It was the second attack on McGuigan's home in just over 12 months; on the previous occasion, two hand grenades exploded against an outside wall. Before the chimes of midnight struck that night, the IRA had exploded a large device in Magherafelt, devastating the commercial centre of the Co. Londonderry town. One of the men responsible for planting the 400 lb (180 kg) device was 25-year-old Damien Mullholland from nearby Maghera; he was quickly arrested and tried the following month.

The first of the 'retaliation' victims to die was another Sinn Féin member, Peter Gallagher (44), father of six children, who lived at Toomebridge in Co. Antrim. He was a full-time building worker with the Antrim Housing Executive, employed at that time on a project near Grosvenor Road in Belfast. He was very likely a marked man because of his Sinn Féin activities, but it is also entirely possible that Protestant workmates at the Distillery Street site leaked information regarding his presence to Johnny Adair and his UFF 'C' company cronies.

Each day, Peter Gallagher travelled the 30 miles to work, making his final trip on the morning of the 24th, even as Tim Parry lay dying with Wendy and Colin, his distraught parents, at his bedside. Mr Gallagher had just parked at the building site and was opening up storage units on the Enterprise Centre premises, at around 08:00. The site is only 70 yards from the nearby A12 Westlink expressway – it connects the M1 and M2 motorways – and is shielded by trees, hedges and a metal railing. Hidden behind this cover, was 'Top Gun' himself, Stephen McKeag; as soon as the Sinn Féin man arrived, McKeag opened fire with a 9 mm Browning, the same one which he had used in the attack on Mr McGuigan the day before. He fired several shots through the railings, fatally wounding his target and causing other workers who had just arrived to dive for cover. He then calmly cycled down the Westlink on the bicycle on which he had arrived. Mr Gallagher died a short while later in the RVH. McKeag covered the couple of miles back to 'C' company's HQ where he was feted by the other sectarian killers. He dumped both bike and gun at designated spots before being taken back to Adair's HQ by car. Gallagher's main 'crime' was that of pasting up Sinn Féin posters, handing out leaflets and so on at election time. His death was one of several sectarian murders in a short period; the following day, the scene switched to the seaside town of Castlerock in Co. Londonderry.

Castlerock is a popular resort for caravanners and golfers alike; situated on the northern coast of Ulster, it is 27 miles east of Londonderry city and eight miles north-west of Coleraine. It was considered perhaps the last place in the country where a mass sectarian slaughter might take place. However, on the 25th, five Catholic workmen turned up to continue renovation work on a housing estate at Gortree Park, a Housing Executive site in the seaside town's south-west; they had been employed on the site for some time, as the UFF's North Antrim unit had become aware. When the men arrived for work, the doors of a waiting van – bought days earlier in Ballymena and now containing at least three gunmen – opened up to reveal men armed with AK-47s. Two of the paramilitaries, one of whom was Torrens Knight – later involved in the sectarian slaughter at Greysteel in October – opened fire on the men who were still inside or in the process of exiting their vehicle. The first to be struck was James McKenna (52), father of four; he fell, fatally injured; the others were all hit, with James Kelly (25), who was a member of the Provisional IRA, dying instantly from shots to the head. Noel Kane (21) was also hit in the head and fatally wounded; he died later in hospital. Gerard Dalrymple (58), father of six, was also fatally wounded, and he too, died in hospital. A fifth, unnamed man was wounded, but he recovered after medical treatment. Ten children were left fatherless. While the Loyalist terror group could claim that they had actually killed a Republican, three other innocents were slain for them to 'achieve' this.

There is no doubt that three of the men were simply Catholic workmen who died randomly because of blind, sectarian hatred; there is a suggestion that the PIRA man, Kelly, was deliberately targeted by Knight and his UFF team. Immediately after the shooting, the murderers jumped back into their stolen van and drove north towards the centre of Castlerock, before turning around and heading towards Downhill, one and a half miles away. Somewhat bizarrely, certainly inexplicably, the gang re-traced their escape route, passing the bodies of the dead and dying as they did so. The van was found burned out at nearby Springbank. As the gang split up to clean off the forensics, the weapons used were taken away by another UFF member and hidden in a ditch alongside the Agivey River, some 16 miles south of the murders. A party of anglers subsequently stumbled across the weapons and told the RUC. However, at this point the plot thickens; the rifles were removed by undercover RUC officers – likely to be Special Branch – but never made public. There have been allegations the RUC knew of the Castlerock and Greysteel massacres in advance, but did not stop them to protect an un-named informer. Knight, Jeffrey Deeney, Robert Glasgow and Stephen Irwin were all later convicted for the murder of eight men at a pub at Greysteel; it is conceivable that two of these same men took part in the Castlerock murders along with Knight.

The dead IRA man – James Kelly – was commander of the South Derry brigade. The UFF wrongly considered him the man behind the Teebane massacre in January 1992 (*see* Chapter 13). He was also wanted for a string of SF killings in the south Londonderry area. Kelly lived in Maghera, Co. Londonderry, and was afforded a traditional IRA funeral, with a black glove and beret atop a tricolour-shrouded coffin at St Patrick's Church in Glen; McGuinness himself was in attendance. The dead terrorist's parents had earlier indicated that they would not stand in the way of a full-blown paramilitary funeral.

The killing was still not over and again the UFF was involved, this time a different unit to the Castlerock killings although one no less deadly; Adair dispatched several 'C' company members, including McKeag himself, to the Twinbrook area of south-West Belfast. It is thought that they simply intended to kill a random Catholic or Catholics when they set off for the Dairy Farm Shopping Centre. As they arrived they noticed Damien 'Didi' Walsh (17) locking up a fuel supplies shop where he worked. McKeag walked up to him and held a gun just inches from the young man's head; twice he pulled the trigger and twice it failed to fire. The boy made a break for it once the initial shock wore off, but before he had gone a dozen paces, McKeag fired again, hitting him several times, fatally wounding him. Another member of the gang then fired at one of Damien's friends, but, incredibly, his weapon, too, failed to fire, even though the trigger was pulled five times. The surviving boy told the inquest that the badly wounded Damien tried to get up, but fell over as his friend tried to drag him to safety. He died later in hospital.

The murdered teen's mother described him as 'an innocent child, a typical wee lad. All he wanted to do was enjoy himself. He had no interest in politics.' One of the gunmen was interviewed by David Lister and Hugh Jordan who have stated that the gunmen were told – probably by Adair – that 'Didi' Walsh was an IRA member. The young man was of course no such thing; he was simply an innocent Catholic in the wrong place at the wrong time who was killed by sectarian murderers. The driver of the UFF getaway vehicle told the same authors that they were all elated and that McKeag was singing as they drove back to the Shankill Road. The weapons were returned to the armourer as the killers each went to separate safe houses to destroy any forensics. 'You would get changed and scrubbed down as quick as you could and then go down to a bar and make yourself seen.

Sometimes the bath was already run for you and there'd be a girl waiting to take your clothes. Sometimes you used lemon juice on cotton buds to wash out your ears and nose properly.'[1]

The 25th of the month witnessed a large PIRA unit from Co. Monaghan, including several wanted men from the South Armagh brigade, make an attack outside Crossmaglen. The target was one of the large Army 'Golf' towers in the town once described as 'the most dangerous place in the world to be a British soldier'. In a well-planned and well co-ordinated attack, the unit used heavy machine guns, lighter automatics and RPG-7s against the tower. The attack left structural damage, but there were no casualties; soldiers returned fire, but the terrorists sneaked back across the border into the Republic.

On the 26th, an RUC search unit, acting on a tip-off from an informer, raided premises on the western outskirts of Nationalist West Belfast. They discovered over five tons of fertiliser of a type used in the manufacture of home-made bombs. Where this information came from is known only to former RUC commanders, but the incident illustrates the types of problems which the Provisionals had, in terms of SF infiltration. This was why the 'nutting squad' was kept occupied so frequently.

On the 27th and 28th, the Royal Irish lost two of its soldiers. Private William Gordon Samuel Harkness (50) and Private Robert Watson Gardner (24) were involved in a road accident at Omagh, Co. Tyrone. Private Harkness died on the 27th and his critically injured comrade the following day. The older man's funeral was held at Dublin Road, Omagh.

Finally, on the 30th, the Irish state broadcasting organisation, Radio Telefis Éireann (RTE), the Irish equivalent to the BBC, appeared in court in Dublin to hear the results of an appeal. The British government had banned TV and radio companies from interviewing terrorists or terrorist spokespersons, although some media organisations had managed to circumvent the restrictions by employing actors with Northern Irish accents to do voice-overs. RTE had also banned interviews with members of either Sinn Féin or the IRA. However, the Irish courts had informed them that they had misinterpreted the Broadcasting Act and were compelled to lift their ban immediately. RTE argued that the purpose of the order was to prevent its broadcasting system being used for the purpose of subverting or undermining the authority of the state. As with many legal and governmental decisions made in the Republic, the latest incident showed the deep-rooted sympathy and support which the Republican terror groups enjoyed amongst judicial and political leaders in Ireland. The words pusillanimous and supine are often applied to the leaders of Ireland; not without considerable justification.

March was over and 14 more people had been killed as a consequence of the Troubles.

1. Lister and Jordan, *Mad Dog*, pp.149–51.

28
April

The previous month of March had been bloodier than of late. April was not as violent: three people died and although no serving soldiers were killed, one of the deaths was that of a former UDR soldier, killed because of past association. In this month, the IRA's England team exploded the first 'billion-pound bomb' in the world, when they caused damage of unheard of financial proportions in the City of London, also killing a photographer who got too close.

On Thursday 1st, Taoiseach Albert Reynolds gave a speech in the Daíl concerning the prospects for peace in Northern Ireland. Reynolds defended the Irish Constitution – especially in relation to the controversial clauses demanding the 'return' of the North – and called for a new framework to help take the gun out of politics on the entire island. On the same day, the Belfast *News Letter* published a poll of its readers which showed that, of those who took part, 42% supported the use of violence by Loyalist paramilitaries against the IRA; sadly, however, most of the Loyalist violence was against innocent Catholic civilians.

Later in the month, Patrick Mayhew made a major speech on Northern Ireland to an audience at the Institute of Irish Studies in Liverpool. He stated that the British government was against the notion of 'joint sovereignty' but did want to see a devolved government with wide powers.

Whilst on the subject of talks, James Molyneaux, leader of the Ulster Unionist Party (UUP), made it very clear that he was unwilling to enter into a new round of political talks about the country's future if the SDLP were involved. He was clearly less than enamoured with John Hume's cosy fireside chats with Gerry Adams or the fact that Hume's party was in open discussions with IRA/Sinn Féin. He clearly saw no distinction between either the terror group or its 'political wing', and he was certainly not alone in his thought processes. It would appear that the only people who believed that there was any separation between the IRA and Sinn Féin were themselves. DUP leader Ian Paisley made it known that he would not enter new political talks: full stop!

Between the 3rd and the 7th, the IRA's South Armagh brigade made two attacks on soldiers in and around Crossmaglen. On the 3rd, Lance Corporal Mark Overson of the DERR, a personal friend of mine, was shot and wounded on the Creggan Road, just outside Crossmaglen. He and his company sergeant-major and two other members of his brick were manning a snap VCP on the rural road, close to Cullyhanna. Lance Corporal Overson had been chatting to a motorist who, having been checked out, drove away; suddenly a shot rang out, and the Reading-born soldier collapsed to the ground having been hit by a sniper round. He takes up the story himself, but I am relieved to say that the tall Berkshire boy made a full recovery and even earned a rebuke from his mother back home in Reading who refused to believe that he had been shot.

'I Got Fucking Shot!'
Mark Overson, Duke of Edinburgh's Royal Regiment

My brick was on the road and we were all under cover; I remember that 'Sticks', the brick medic, was on 'cut off' and my chat-up man was the CSM. That day he was just acting like an ordinary private and I think that he just wanted to stretch his legs and get out of the base. We saw a white 4 × 4 which might have been a Toyota Isuzu, but I can't be absolutely certain and, when it got close, we jumped up and indicated to the driver that we wanted him to stop. I then conducted a plate check over the radio whilst the CSM checked the driver and chatted to him and kept him distracted. The plate check came back as clear and I asked the CSM if he was happy and he nodded yes and I remember saying to the drivers' mate: 'On your way.' The driver then said to me – jovially, I think: 'You might want to keep your heads down today, lads,' and I laughed and waved him through. The vehicle drove up the hill towards a dip in the road and had only gone about 100 metres when I turned to get down under cover again.

I heard a terrifically loud crack and my first thought was that the CSM had had an ND and I just called out 'Was that you?' 'Fuck off, Ovie – it wasn't me – was it you?' Looking back, I don't know why I said that as I knew that I had been shot! I felt an awful pain, as though someone had punched me in the back and then felt a burning sensation. I shouted 'Fuck me, I think I've been shot!' and the CSM just looked at me and replied 'Fuck me, you have!' Then, my knees buckled and I went down like a sack of shit! Even though the CSM was, compared to me, only a little guy, bless him, he dragged me under cover at the side of the road. Both my arms had terrible pins and needles and, in the shock and confusion, I forgot my basic training and didn't immediately radio in 'Contact'. Despite going into shock, it should have been the first thing I did. Anyway, I got on the radio and called in 'Contact – Wait – Out' and, as was SOP, the net went silent. Then the multiple commander on the hillside broke the silence. 'What's happening Any casualties?' Before I could reply, the CSM called out to 'Sticks': 'Get your arse down here; Ovie's been hit.' He started to patch me up and I began to flap, imagining the worst. I asked him how bad it was, and I remember him saying 'It's pissing with blood, but I think it's only a scratch.' His hands were shaking so much that I remember the CSM having to help him with the bandages. Suddenly, my training kicked in and I got back on to the multiple commander and informed him that we had one times casualty and that the potential firing point was about 300 metres to the north.

Just four days later, Mark's unit was again in action when the IRA launched three Mark XV mortar attacks on their Golf tower, causing some damage, but fortunately no injuries. They were in action a further 13 times before the year ended, losing two members of the Regiment (*see* Chapters 30 and 31).

The first death of the month occurred on the 4th, when the UFF killed one of its former members in Portavogie on the Ards Peninsula, Co. Down. The tiny but picturesque coastal town is sandwiched between the cold and often turbulent waters of the Irish Sea and the calmer waters of Strangford Lough. William Killen (36), father of two, was a former UDA man who was jailed in 1982 for conspiracy to pervert the course of justice. He had played a role in the attempted cover-up of the murder of Terence McSkimmon on 8 August 1974. On Killen's release in 1987 the UFF decided that he had breached their 'code of honour' and ordered him killed. In December of that year, he escaped a gunman's bullets, but the Loyalist paramilitaries have elephant-like memories and bided their time until the moment was right.

That moment and that opportunity arrived on the evening of the 4th, when a murder gang from the mid-Ulster UFF hijacked a taxi close to Portavogie and stuffed the driver into the boot of his own vehicle whilst they drove to their target's flat in Westlea Gardens in the village. On arrival, they burst down the door and charged into the house, guns drawn; to anyone within earshot of the flat, it must have sounded like the infamous Western gunfight at the OK Corral, as almost 30 shots were fired by the murder gang. Mr Killen was chased from room to room, as he desperately sought to save his life, throwing anything in the way in a vain attempt to barricade himself in. Eventually he crawled underneath his bed, but the gunmen simply fired through the bed. Leaving him close to death, the gunmen fled in the stolen taxi, later releasing the driver unharmed. The *Independent* reported: 'Killen's personal history gives a glimpse of a squalid loyalist paramilitary underworld of violence and disorder. He joined the paramilitary Ulster Defence Association in his teens and in 1974, aged 18, was involved in the murder of a Protestant ex-prisoner shot in the head in North Belfast. The man had been given a UDA "trial" and sentenced to death because he had "run around with Taigs [Catholics]" while in jail. In 1982, Killen was charged with murder, but the charges were reduced. He was tried that year and sentenced to six years' imprisonment for his part in the killing. The court was told he had left the UDA in 1976. More recently he gained a reputation as a nuisance and trouble-maker in Portavogie, a village which has been almost entirely untouched by the Troubles. He was well known to the police, who received complaints about wild parties and his misbehaviour. Locals said that he was always in trouble and "always up in court". On Saturday night police were called to a noisy and drunken party at his home. While the exact reason for the murder has yet to emerge, it is not inconceivable that he may have been killed because of the trouble he caused.'

On 8 November 1987, Gordon Wilson's daughter Marie was one of those murdered in the atrocity at Enniskillen, sacrificed on the altar of the IRA's unrealistic and unachievable dream of Irish unity. Five years and five months later, on 7 April 1993, the leadership of the Provisional IRA agreed to meet Mr Wilson. In a move which was seen as brave in some quarters, foolhardy and irresponsible in others – I sit firmly in the latter category – he met the terrorists face to face and tried to persuade them to discontinue their terrorist campaign. He would later state that he was 'saddened' by the outcome. It is very likely that it was the two bombs at Warrington on 20 March which prompted him to request the meeting with the terror group.

It is thought that the meeting was held in the Republic – probably in a safe house in Dublin – but, despite his pleas, all the IRA gave in return was a hollow, shallow and meaningless, ultimately belated statement, offering 'sincerest condolences and apologies' for the death of Marie. Shortly before his death in 1995, Mr Wilson admitted that the meeting had been 'quite pointless' and said that many Protestants never forgave him for speaking to the IRA leadership. He died on 27 June 1995, aged 69; many felt that he died of a broken heart. Ten years to the day after the Enniskillen massacre, Gerry Adams formally and, in my opinion, half-heartedly, apologised for the outrage.

Whilst the IRA's leadership were meeting Mr Wilson, their foot-soldiers on the mainland were in action again. The England team were busy trying to take lives and destroy property, moving this time to London's WC1, close to King's Cross railway station, where there were two separate attacks. First a small device exploded in nearby Argyle Street, just off Euston Road. The device was placed inside a builders' skip but there were no injuries. Shortly afterwards, in Judd Street, close to St Pancras station, a taxi was hijacked and a small device exploded after the driver was able to jump clear; the cab was destroyed, but there were only minor injuries. Just hours later, some four miles away, another taxi was hijacked and a small device placed on board. It exploded outside Manor House Underground station, close to Seven Sisters Road; again there were no injuries.

Three days after the IRA's rebuff of Mr Wilson, there was another controversial meeting when Gerry Adams was seen visiting the home of SDLP leader John Hume in Londonderry. Later, they told the press that they had met for extensive discussions in order to look at the prospects for peace. The two were forced into a public statement, after a leading Irish newspaper, the *Sunday Tribune*, revealed the 'secret' discussions. They were to meet again on the 23rd. I wonders if Mr Hume mentioned the Warrington outrage to 'Teflon man'.

A few days later, Irish Tánaiste Dick Spring visited Oxford University to address the British–Irish Association. He stated that a possible solution to the conflict in Northern Ireland lay in a 'Europe of the regions'. The day after, British Foreign Secretary Douglas Hurd continued the theme when he said that '[The] Republic's willingness to consider changes to the Irish Constitution provided a positive context.' On the 19th, in what was rapidly becoming a month overflowing with meetings, NI Secretary Patrick Mayhew met with John Alderdice, then leader of the Alliance Party of Northern Ireland (APNI), at the start of a new round of bilateral talks with the main political parties. The day after, the number of meetings reached almost epidemic proportions when Ulster Unionist Party leader James Molyneaux presented a set of proposals entitled 'Blueprint for Stability' to John Major in Downing Street. Finally, on the 21st, Albert Reynolds flew to the USA to address Irish-Americans and dampened their hopes when he said the recent suggestion by President Clinton of a 'peace envoy' was not appropriate at the present moment.

Belleek: 1993

Corporal Paul Hughes, Royal Welch Fusiliers

We were in the Co. Fermanagh area and we were out sussing out the territory and got lost. Naïvely, we asked a local for directions and followed them to the letter. All was going well until we realised that the paving stones, lampposts and murals were becoming a colour known as 'hint of Tricolour'. We soon realised that we were now on our very own little sightseeing tour of a Republican heartland! Then, Jase pointed out that I was in fact wearing a Northern Ireland football shirt, which really did not compliment the Celtic shirts which covered the area. Nervous laughter began to give way to serious thoughts of needing to get out of the area rather rapidly, and all I could think about was those poor corporals who drove into an IRA funeral in the late eighties.

With our pistols between our legs, for security, we decided to drive 'normally' so as not to attract any more attention than my football shirt was already doing. Finally, we found our bearings; slightly embarrassed and very relieved we got back to Fermanagh. The OC was happy to see his car in one piece. We didn't have the heart, or the bottle to tell him it could have been so different; lesson learned.

On the 22nd, the Provisionals staged another of their, fortunately rare 'shows of strength', on this occasion in Cullaville, South Armagh. It was partially to intimidate any wavering support for their iron rule in 'bandit country' but also to send a huge propaganda message to their supporters in the USA.

At some stage during this morning, 12 armed PIRA members set up an IVCP at the main crossroads of Cullaville, thus isolating the small village for a two-hour period. An Army 'Golf Tower' was only a few hundred metres away, but the soldiers manning the OP were unable to see the IRA men in action; consequently there was no military response. The gunmen began to stop drivers, demanding identification; heavily armed IRA men showed off their apparent invulnerability to admiring residents and also to invited members of the world's press. They displayed the usual assortment of US-supplied AK-47s as well as one of their deadly M60 machine guns. However, their *pièce de resistance* was a Soviet-issue DShK heavy machine gun. Naturally, *An Phoblacht* claimed the whole performance as a great 'victory' although the truth was somewhat more prosaic. Eventually tiring of portraying themselves as brave urban guerrillas, the terrorists withdrew, before the Army realised that they were there. The NIO played down the incident, but Fine Gael politician Bill Cotter, forgetting rather conveniently that his party had tacitly sanctioned PIRA operations in the North by turning a blind eye to their border activities, stated: 'It is clear that private armies have the ability to take over any of our towns whenever they choose, but worse than that they have displayed their ability to wreak carnage of huge proportions. It is also clear that there is a hardening of attitudes in the North at this time.'

On Friday 23rd, the IRA's England team, possibly containing the same team who were responsible for the deaths of Jonathan Ball and Tim Parry at Warrington the previous month, turned their attention to 'Geordieland'. There was a giant Shell Oil terminal in North Shields and it was there that a PIRA bomb exploded, damaging a large oil storage tank. There were no injuries, but the IRA, having attacked the north-east for the first time in the campaign, would return in June, hitting the same depot again as well as targets in Gateshead.

The following day, Saturday 24th, an Iveco lorry – stolen in Newcastle-under-Lyme on the day after the Warrington blasts – was parked, packed with explosives, on Bishopsgate, the busy A10 which cuts through the 'Square Mile' of the City. The stolen vehicle was left around 350 yards from the scene of the Baltic Exchange blast of the previous year, just outside the HSBC building close to Wormwood Street. The vehicle had been re-sprayed a different colour before being loaded with around a ton of explosives.

The lorry was parked around 09:00; shortly afterwards, a spokesman for the South Armagh brigade of the Provisional IRA telephoned a warning through to the Met Police, but as usual it was misleading and loss of life as well as huge financial damage was bound to follow. The message stated baldly: 'There's a massive bomb . . . clear a wide area.' At 10:27, as the area was being searched, the bomb exploded. At the moment of detonation, a press photographer from the *News of the World*, Edward Henty (34), walked past the lorry. He was killed instantly as the massive explosion ripped the heart out of the area.

It is worth noting that 50 years earlier the German Luftwaffe, bombing the same area, used bombs which weighed on average 250 kg. Mr Henty, who was from Putney, was en route to take some photographs of the incident for inclusion in the Sunday newspaper. The blast caused a huge crater and the unfortunate man's shredded body was found in the rubble of the HSBC building; death was mercifully instantaneous.

A further 44 people were injured, some very seriously, the blast causing damage estimated of at least £300 million with top estimates of £1 billion. As a result of the attack the anti-terror police were forced to erect a 'ring of steel' around the City and many firms were forced to prepare disaster recovery plans in case of further attacks.

A very close friend and comrade of mine, who has asked not to be named, kindly supplied me with a statement from his elderly mother who had lived nearby during the Blitz of 1940/41; she was close enough to Bishopsgate when the IRA bomb exploded for it to trigger horrific nightmares of Hitler's attempts to crush us in our island home.

Terry 'F' Former Soldier

Ken, I asked her about the Bishopsgate bomb which she remembered so clearly as it took her back to the dark days when the Germans tried to blast London back into the Stone Age. These are her words: 'They used to come over nightly and often through the day but our boys gave them what's what! It was a terrifying time but as a little girl, I didn't mind as we got off school an awful lot. There was a huge bomb which the Jerries dropped which we called a 'blockbuster' because it weighed over 2,000 lb and used to take out entire streets. We could hear that awful catterwauling of the sirens and then there would be a huge thunderclap and you would feel everything shake and the air would be sucked out of your lungs. You could hear them go off even when you were underground and I remember when the Irish bombed that bank in Bishopsgate, the sound and the way the ground shook took me back to when I was a little girl.'

Buildings up to 500 yards away from the IRA bomb were badly damaged, affecting over 1.5 million square feet of office space and smashing every pane of glass for hundreds of yards around. The iconic Natwest Tower, then London's tallest structure, was very badly damaged with thousands of windows smashed. The 52-storey building resembled the mouth of a street fighter with huge gaps in his teeth; Liverpool Street station was badly damaged and the ancient St Ethelburga's church, built in 1250 and a survivor of the Great Fire of 1666, simply collapsed, such was the force of the IRA bomb. It was a miracle that only 44 people were injured, in addition to the death of Mr Henty; it was a Saturday morning, however, with the area being occupied by only a small number of residents, security guards, builders, and maintenance staff.

Gerry Adams later issued a joint statement along with John Hume of the SDLP; the statement ran: 'We accept that the Irish people as a whole have a right to national self-determination. This is a view shared by a majority of the people of this island, though not by all its people. The exercise of self-determination is a matter for agreement between the people of Ireland.' The IRA's mouthpiece, *An Phoblacht* was even more blunt, with a melodramatic announcement, clearly designed for its adoring North American audience, which would ensure the continued rattle of NORAID collecting tins in Philadelphia, Boston and Chicago: 'Our bombers exploited a security loophole after having spotted a breach in the usually tight security around the City. No one should be misled into underestimating the IRA's intention to mount future planned attacks into the political and financial heart of the British state. In the context of present political realities, further attacks on the City of London and elsewhere are inevitable. This we feel we are bound to convey to you directly, to allow you to make fully informed decision.'

The subsequent pay-outs by insurance companies resulted in staggeringly heavy losses, causing a crisis in the industry, including the near-collapse of the Lloyd's of London market. It was to be the penultimate major IRA explosion in London and it almost certainly caused Prime Minister John Major to consider the possibility of talking to the leaders of the terror group.

The following day, there was a further example of 'guilt by past association' as the Tyrone brigade killed a former UDR soldier as he returned home following a night out with friends and family. David Martin (33), father of three young children – daughters aged 13 and five and an eight-year-old son, had parked his car overnight in Tulnacross Road, following a social evening in the village's Braeside Inn. At some time during the early hours of the morning, alerted by dickers, a PIRA bombing team had placed a device underneath his red Audi. He retrieved his car in the morning, setting off for his home in Pomeroy; however, around 07:15, as he reached Flo Road in Kildress, the device exploded, killing him instantly. The Provisionals, as equally skilled at propaganda as they were at senseless murder and maiming, tried to claim that the dead man had left the UDR in order to become a Loyalist paramilitary. A PIRA spokesman made the outrageous claim that he was a member of the UVF. This groundless accusation was denied by both the RUC and the man's grieving family. It was simply another pointless and vindictive murder by the IRA, every bit as sectarian as other killings by the Loyalists.

On the final Thursday of the month – the 29th – the UFF, carried out yet another gun attack on a bookmaker's shop in Belfast; during the Troubles, betting shops were fast becoming the most dangerous places to frequent. Five Catholic men were wounded in this attack. The gang, believed to have been dispatched on the orders of Johnny Adair, hijacked a car on the Shankill Road, driving the short distance to the Catholic New Lodge, where they parked, engine still running, close to a branch of Brian Graham's bookmakers, in North Queen Street. Leaving the driver sitting at the wheel, at least two masked gunmen ran into the crowded shop as punters gathered around the TV to watch the 3 p.m. race. The gunmen immediately opened fire with automatic weapons, firing around 15 shots, seriously wounding an elderly man, hitting him several times in the chest; four more customers were wounded as the panicked men threw themselves to the floor. Good fortune then stepped in, as one of the attackers' weapons jammed, forcing them to beat a hasty retreat. They dashed back to the waiting car, but still managed to fire off several more shots as they escaped towards the Shankill. The car was abandoned at a pre-arranged spot before they escaped to safe houses in another vehicle.

AP reported: 'Witnesses said lives were saved when an automatic rifle used by one of a number of gunmen jammed, but they claimed up to 15 shots were fired in the small premises in the New Lodge district. The most seriously injured was an elderly man hit in the chest.' The *Independent* reported: 'Local people said the RUC and Army should do more to prevent such shootings, pointing out that the attack took place about 100 yards from a police station. The area, one of Northern Ireland's most violent, is generally heavily patrolled by troops and police.' The attack was clearly an attempt to emulate two previous bloody attacks on Catholic-frequented branches of Sean Graham's. A local priest, Father Francis McAllister, was quoted as saying: 'It's just terrible. There's no way you can guard against something like this. It was the time when schoolchildren were coming home so they could quite easily have been injured as well. People here are living in fear and terror. They're just totally shattered. It's very easy for anyone to come in and do a shooting and then make a quick escape.' A relative of one of the survivors said: 'When I got to the bookies there was pandemonium ... Everybody was squealing. Somebody says to me, 'Mairead, it's your father, it's your father,' just as they brought him out on a stretcher.'[1]

This month a former UDR soldier was killed by the IRA and Loyalists killed a Protestant and a Catholic. The latter was a member of the IRA.

1. http://www.independent.co.uk/news/uk/five-hurt-as-gunmen-attack-betting-shop-in-belfast-jammed-rifle-averts-massacre-as-loyalists-try-to-1458185.html.

29

May

Three soldiers died this month and two innocent Catholics were killed by Loyalists in obviously sectarian attacks. Gerry Adams was refused an entry visa for the USA, an act which must have had which had the Irish lobby in the US Senate spitting blood. PIRA proved that it had no shortage of explosives as it stepped up its bombing campaign around UK local election time.

On 1 May, Loyalist paramilitaries killed a Catholic father of five in the Nationalist Andersonstown district of West Belfast, when the UFF carried out the murder of Alan Lundy (39), visiting from the Ardoyne. Johnny Adair sent a murder gang which included 'Top Gun' himself, Stephen McKeag, to kill Sinn Féin councillor Alex Maskey, who lived in Gartree Place. Maskey was a key ally of Gerry Adams having joined the Provisionals around the time of the Official/Provisional split. He was interned in the 1970s and later, although retaining his ties with the terror group, he became the embodiment of the Armalite and ballot box strategy. He won a by-election for a seat on Belfast City Council in the Upper Falls, becoming the first member of Sinn Féin to be elected since the start of the Troubles. Maskey had survived a previous murder bid by the UFF in 1987, when he was blasted at close range by a man wielding a shotgun but was saved by prompt medical treatment. Somewhat belatedly, he had realised the need for enhanced security at his Andersonstown home. A local PIRA member, Lundy was also something of a handyman and as a consequence he was sent to help install Maskey's security equipment.

Little is known about Lundy, other than that he was arrested in possession of explosives, as he was about to plant a bomb in a restaurant in Victoria Street, Belfast, in 1971. He served 10 years for the attempted bombing and returned to the Provisional fold on release from the Maze. He is considered by many to be the victim of a sectarian attack, but his son made the following statement in 2012: 'My father was a lifelong member of the Republican Movement, as both an IRA Volunteer and Sinn Féin activist.'[1]

Lundy was working on a security screen at the front of Maskey's house when McKeag and his gang arrived in a stolen Ford Orion; Maskey was in the house but was upstairs playing with his children. 'Top Gun' himself, having dashed towards the house, fired several shots at Lundy – it is not known if he recognised the PIRA man or if he worked on the basis that any Catholic would do. McKeag and another man chased after Lundy, who had run into the house, mortally wounding him with several shots to the back. Alerted by the gunfire, Maskey grabbed his children before barricading them all in the bathroom. The Loyalist gunmen were unable to gain deeper access and roared away along Ramoan

1. http://thepensivequill.am/2012/09/airbrushing-out-alan-lundy-would-be.html.

Gardens before disappearing in the direction of North Belfast. Alan Lundy died shortly afterwards.

On the 5th, Gerry Adams, President of Sinn Féin and former PIRA commander, had planned to fly to the USA for a lecture tour that would include meetings with NORAID and a series of fund-raising dinners with influential Americans. Despite heavy pressure by the powerful Irish-American lobby, the US State Department refused to issue him an entry visa. On the same day that the Irish lobby was complaining about conspiracies, a Royal Irish Rangers' soldier was found dead. Corporal Robert Newell (22) died from gunshot wounds at his home in North Belfast. I am permitted only to state that his death was by violent or unnatural causes. The news was dominated that day by the inconveniences suffered by a former terrorist leader. His organisation's campaign to 'drive the British into the sea' was derailed, pro-tem. That decision was overturned, much to the apparent fury of Prime Minister John Major, by President Clinton some eight months later. On 31 January 1994 the Clinton administration issued a 48-hour US entry visa to Adams, the granting of which, in the words of the Dublin-based Royal Irish Academy 'disturbed a 70-year-old diplomatic equilibrium between the United States and Great Britain over Northern Ireland'.

There was a near tragedy on the 6th, when an un-named Loyalist paramilitary group – thought most likely to have been the UFF – made an attack on a Catholic family in a house close to Springfield Road. Entering through a pedestrian gate in the 'peace line', a gang of five thugs, armed with iron bars, crashed open the front door and attacked a man, his wife and his elderly mother. Even though the man held a young baby in his arms, they threatened to kill them both with the bars they carried. Alerted by the screams of the family, several neighbours attacked the gang, who escaped back through the pedestrian gate before there were any serious injuries.

Perhaps inspired by hatred or just wound up by the fact that Adams was dominating the world's media that month, the UVF issued a death threat against all politicians in the Irish Republic. In the end, it was mere gesture politics and resulted in another surge in the support for this paramilitary group in its own heartlands but nowhere else. It is worth noting that the IRA or INLA killed five MPs/MPAs during the Troubles: Airey Neave (allegedly INLA, 1979), Robert Bradford (PIRA, 1981), Edgar Graham (PIRA, 1983), Anthony Berry (PIRA, 1984), Ian Gow (PIRA, 1990); on the other side Senator Paddy Wilson was murdered by the UFF in 1973.

On the 9th, there was a further attempt to kill and maim on the English mainland as either the IRA's England team, or what may possibly have been a rogue INLA group, planted an explosive device in the west country city of Bristol. The police were given a brief warning but managed to evacuate the city centre, before the small bomb exploded in the Galleries shopping area. Just three days later, on the 12th, it was the turn of the ancient university city of Oxford. An incendiary device was placed inside a stolen van and driven close to the Cornmarket area, but damage was minimised and there were only light injuries.

Sandwiched between these two mainland attacks, Patrick Mayhew, Secretary of State for Northern Ireland, promised proposals for new political talks, encouraging Republicans who felt that their costly attacks on the City of London's economy were now forcing Major and his Cabinet to the negotiating table. Conversely, this angered and distressed the Loyalist side who saw this as further evidence of them being 'sold down the river' by the

Westminster elite. One Loyalist told me in 2008: 'We had seen the English Prime Minister fly to Munich in 1938 and fuck the Czechs; now another one was doing the same to the Loyalists!'

On the 13th, there was an accidental death of a British soldier at Palace Barracks in Holywood, Belfast. The 1st Battalion, Parachute Regiment, was in occupation there on a two-year residential tour, working alongside 7th Royal Irish Regiment. They were responsible for, amongst others, the Republican Short Strand and the hard line Loyalist Newtownards Road. During that evening, Private Peter Franz Joseph Gross (20), from the Ipswich area, was shot and killed inside the barracks. He is buried at Waldringfield Church Cemetery, near Ipswich, close to the River Deben. I have been given a confidential version of the events which led up to Gross's death, but have been cautioned against putting it into print. It must remain sufficient to write that his death was as a result of 'violent or unnatural causes'. I have been told that a fellow paratrooper was charged with Private Gross's death.

Four days after Mayhew's apparently appeasing remarks towards the Nationalists, the Combined Loyalist Military Command (CLMC) stated that it would take a close look at the results of the local government elections, due just 48 hours later. It stated that it would be analysing the results to see if there was any unusual co-operation between what it termed 'pan-Nationalist candidates'. Their main targets were not just Sinn Féin and the SDLP but also the Alliance Party, Democratic Left, Independence Party and naturally, the so-called 'political wing' of the OIRA: the Workers' Party.

Sinn Féin have allegedly long used the illegal practice of 'personation' which, as I have explained before, is the practice of voting using false papers, including the papers of dead people and also of registering fake addresses and intimidating postal workers to deliver voting papers to said fake addresses, under threat of violence or death. For this reason, many observers have been quick to question certain results, raising possible chicanery as a factor in certain electoral outcomes. The following Friday, the Loyalists (UUP, DUP, Independent Unionist, PUP and Ulster Popular Unionist) won 50.7% of the vote and Nationalists (Sinn Féin, SDLP, Alliance, Labour) 44%. Worryingly, the Republicans were narrowing the gap with those who were fighting to remain within the Union.

On the day of the election, the Provisionals managed to park a rubbish lorry containing 1,000 lb (450 kg) of explosive outside the Grand Opera House in Glengall Street in Belfast. The location was significant, designed not only to terrorise shoppers and theatre-goers away from the city centre, but in locating the bomb close to the most-bombed hotel in the world, the Europa, it reduced the credibility of the SF and their ability to make Belfast's commercial heart impregnable. It was also very close to the headquarters of the Ulster Unionist Party, thus sending a message to PIRA's enemies. Twenty people, including several RUC officers, were injured in the blast, with damage estimated at £6.5 million in 1993 values. In view of a later PIRA statement, it is unclear as to which of the three damaged buildings was the actual target. A PIRA spokesman claimed responsibility for the blast, telling journalists: 'Despite an unprecedented level of crown forces' activity in Nationalist areas and the so-called ring of steel around Belfast city centre, our volunteers this morning successfully detonated a 1,000-pound bomb at the Europa.'

This turned out to be the first of four explosions in a five-day period, as a car bomb exploded in Portadown, Co. Armagh, on the Saturday, injuring six people. The device was identical to the earlier Belfast device – 1,000 lb (450 kg) – but caused an estimated £8 million worth of damage. The following day, they detonated an even larger device, 1,500 lb (680 kg) in Magherafelt, Co. Londonderry. On this occasion, it was placed in a stolen van which they parked close to the bus station in the town's square, right outside the Ulster Bank in Broad Street. A warning was telephoned through to the RUC, but the bomb exploded a mere 20 minutes later, injuring several officers as they attempted to clear the area. A spokesman for the police described the warning as 'totally inadequate. It was a miracle that no-one was seriously hurt.' The blast damaged or destroyed two-thirds of the small businesses located there. The town lost over a thousand jobs in 1993 alone as a consequence of the IRA's so-called 'economic war'. However, the latest blast wasn't enough to deter the townspeople from holding their annual 'bash' in the devastated town square. Indeed, the *Guardian* of 27 May reported: 'About 150 stalls were crammed into side roads around the Market Square. Traders were denied the best pitches, in Broad Street, devastated three days earlier by a van bomb, but the fair went ahead. Bertie Montgomery, vice-chairman of the district council, said: "It would have been a disgrace otherwise."'

The following day, it was Belfast's turn again, as a PIRA bombing unit from either the Andersonstown or Poleglass area parked a hijacked car containing 200 lb (90 kg) of explosives in a car park outside the Drumkeen Hotel on the Ormeau Road. The bombing unit drove off in a second hijacked vehicle. A warning was telephoned through; having evacuated the hotel, the RUC were in the process of clearing nearby streets when the device exploded. There were no significant injuries, but the explosion shattered virtually every window in the building and the blast was heard 10 miles away. William Ross, MP, told UPI: 'This proves that since the IRA political wing won increased support in the elections, the IRA believes that it now has a mandate to step up its bombing campaign in Northern Ireland and Britain.' The UPI report continued: 'In Belfast, more than 400 guests and disco revellers in the Drumkeen Hotel, 4 miles from the city center escaped to safety only five minutes before a massive car bomb exploded at 1:30 a.m. Sunday, the police said. The blast demolished half of the hotel and blew the roofs off surrounding homes as families slept in their beds, police said. Windows and doors were blown in and hunks of twisted metal from the bomb punched holes in walls and wrecked scores of cars. "Six people were treated for shock following the bomb blast, which is heartening considering the hotel was extensively damaged and around 50 homes suffered blast damage such as broken windows," an RUC spokesman said.'[1]

Thus, in the space of just five days, the Provisionals demonstrated that they clearly had no shortage whatsoever of explosives and other bomb-making components as they exploded four bombs weighing a combined total of 3,700 lb (1,680 kg). The organisation irrevocably destroyed many businesses and injured a score of people, as well as costing the Ulster economy *c.* £35 million. The war had been running almost 24 years with a death toll approaching 4,000. Tragically, the end was still over three years away, three very long years. On the same day as the Drumkeen bomb, there was a small item of encouraging news for the ailing Major government – racked by scandals and resignations, in addition to daily sleaze accusations – as the European Court of Human Rights, for once, ruled in

1. https://www.upi.com/Archives/1993/05/23/Bombs-damage-homes-shops-in-Northern-Ireland/5050738129600/.

their favour. Having considered an appeal against the use by the UK of a seven-day period of detention under the Prevention of Terrorism Act, the Court rejected the appeal on the grounds that the situation in Northern Ireland justified the detention of suspects for longer than four days. On the following Thursday, the President of the Republic, Mary Robinson, flew to London to attend a meeting with the Queen at Buckingham Palace. This was historic as it was the first official contact between an Irish president and a British monarch. Over at the NIO, Michael Ancram replaced Jeremy Hanley to become Political Development Minister. 'So what?' muttered several hundred thousand Loyalists and over a million Northern Ireland residents.

The Red Hand Commando (RHC) is or was a highly secretive Loyalist organisation, perhaps only able to remain so because of its narrow base and small membership; unlike its bigger brothers the UVF and the UFF it has not had a single supergrass. Moreover, I understand that there have been very few attempts to infiltrate it with Special Branch or Army agents. It was formed in the Shankill Road area by John McKeague and other members of the Shankill Defence Association. Although always a smaller, more tightly-knit group than the other Loyalist paramilitaries, it has drawn recruits from East Belfast, Newtownabbey, Sandy Row and from as far afield as Co. Down. Nominally independent, it allies itself closely with the UVF often sharing both weapons and personnel; consequently, the UVF has often credited operations to the RHC as a 'flag of convenience'. On the 30th, the RHC made a rare foray into the Dundonald area of Co. Down to carry out the sectarian murder of a Catholic grandfather: Edward McHugh (55), who lived at Canberra Park.

'Eddie' McHugh was a retired painter and decorator, well known in the Canberra Park area where he had lived and worked for over 20 years. On that fateful evening, close to 23:00, two men riding a stolen motorcycle stopped outside Mr McHugh's house; the driver kept the engine running whilst his armed colleague, head covered in a white motorcycle helmet barged into the unlocked house, pausing only to push Mrs McHugh roughly to the floor. The gunman, fired several shots from a 9 mm Browning into the helpless man's head and chest before rushing out of the house, leaving Eddie lying mortally wounded on the living room floor; he died shortly afterwards. He had no Republican associations whatsoever, a fact later confirmed by the RUC. The same weapon would be used later that year, on 13 September, to kill a Red Hand Commando, Vernon Baillie (*see* Chapter 33).

There was to be one more killing this month; the Provisionals murdered an off-duty soldier at Moneymore, Co. Londonderry. Private Charles Christopher James Wren (34), father of one, had originally served with the UDR but had transferred to the Royal Irish. Moneymore is approximately five miles south-west of Magherafelt, where the Provisionals had devastated the town centre with a massive car bomb only a few days earlier. Private Wren lived in Northland Road, working full-time and combining his employment with his military duties. A few days before his death, he had been forced to take time off both roles with an illness; it is known that his car had been unused in his back garden for several days. Using information passed on to them by their 'army' of dickers, the local IRA commanders decided to booby-trap the vehicle, knowing that there was little chance of discovery. It is not possible to pinpoint the exact day on which the bombing team interfered with Private Wren's car. At around 14:00 on the 31st, he set off to drive towards Cookstown; shortly after starting the journey, he spotted a neighbour, naturally offering her a lift. She innocently declined, thus unknowingly saving her own life. As Wren drove alone along Carrydonagh Road, the device exploded, dreadfully injuring him; he died in the ambulance en route to hospital. He is buried at St John's Church in his home village of Moneymore. A former UDR soldier (who asked not to be named) told me: '[PIRA] knew that they had a nice easy target because he was off sick and therefore they knew that his car would likely be unattended. They knew where he lived as he had either been dicked by a local Taig, or they had followed him home after he had finished duty on a VCP somewhere one night. I can't say to you that it was a neighbour or even a Taig with any certainty, but he was very careful to make sure that he wasn't followed. Either way, they did it the cowards' way because he was a soft target. It was also a miracle that the wee lassie from his street didn't accept a lift from him that afternoon. Otherwise we would have been burying two of them at St John's.'

So, May was over and five more people were dead; three soldiers and two civilians were victims of the Troubles in different ways.

30

June

Two of the deaths this month graphically illustrated the moral bankruptcy of the IRA's campaign. A former soldier and a former policeman died because of that utterly immoral excuse of 'guilt by past association'. A serving soldier also died as did a Catholic man killed by the INLA; PIRA's nutting squad were in action again and a Loyalist paramilitary died in a classic 'own goal' explosion. During this month, the Irish President shook the hand of Gerry Adams, thus provoking further outrage from Unionists. In this month also, a member of the IRA's biggest fan club in the USA – the Kennedy family – was appointed Ambassador to the Irish Republic.

On the 1st there was an announcement by the Ministry of Defence that from October 1993, women soldiers would be armed with the SA-80 rifle. The SA-80 had replaced the SLR 7.62 mm ('Paddy whacker') some years previously, the 5.56 mm calibre not proving popular with soldiers who had previously used the SLR, with its greater stopping power.

On the same day, Ranger Morris Irvine (22) of the Royal Irish depot died of those seemingly ubiquitous 'violent or unnatural causes'; regrettably, I have no further information. Also on that day, the UFF murdered a Catholic man in Comber, Co. Down, based on yet more flawed intel. They claimed that he was a member of the IRA, but the reality was that he was just another easy target, a Catholic who had turned his back on the IRA and was working away unsuspectingly in his daily job. Brendan McKenna (29) was a lorry driver; his everyday routine involved moving materials from a quarry at Hillhead Road, Comber. At some stage on 1 June a UFF murder gang, thought to be from south-East Belfast, hijacked a car and drove to a position with a good view of the quarry where their target would be the following day. When Mr McKenna arrived, they drove off, stopping along the Ballystockyart Road, aware that he would eventually drive past them. As he drew level, they blasted the cab of his vehicle with automatic weapons, mortally wounding him. The wounded man managed to drag himself out of the ruined cab, falling to the ground, from where he managed to crawl just a few yards before collapsing. An ambulance quickly arrived but there was little that they could do for him; he died shortly after, covered in the glass of his shattered windscreen and his own blood.

The killers sped off in the direction of Dundonald, some seven miles away, leaving the stolen car burned out in the area close to Ballybean Square. There was some confusion the following day when the UDA/UFF claimed responsibility for shooting a PIRA member by the name of Brendan McKinley. This was compounded when their spokesman amended the dead man's name to Brian McKinley. More doubt was cast upon their claims when the RUC stated that there was neither a Brian nor a Brendan McKinley in the IRA and that the

RUC believed the dead man was killed merely because he had served a prison sentence for Republican activities (but had had no subsequent contact). Just as I condemn Republican terrorists for killing former soldiers and policeman for past associations, I do the same for their Loyalist paramilitary counterparts.

On the 10th, it was confirmed that Jean Kennedy Smith, sister of the late President John F. Kennedy, would be the next American Ambassador to the Republic of Ireland. A frequently repeated criticism of this author has been my use of 'repetitive vitriol' when discussing the biased and immoral support given to Irish Republican terrorism by the USA. Whether or not this was from mainstream politicians, such as Edward Kennedy, Hugh Carey, Daniel Moynihan and 'Tip' O'Neill (the so-called 'Four Horsemen'), or simply Irish-Americans who hated the British because of some basic, inherent instinct, there was a very public backing in the USA for the IRA. I maintain that it is necessary to the narrative that this major support is constantly re-stated as one should never lose sight of the fact that Britain's self-proclaimed special allies did much to prolong the war of terror, either through naivety or through malice aforethought.

The day after the appointment, Queen Elizabeth paid a visit to Northern Ireland. At the same time, SDLP leader John Hume held another meeting with Gerry Adams; ostensibly they discussed electoral strategies, strategic voting and so on amongst other weighty topics. It may well have been entirely innocent and above board, but it further served to deepen Loyalist suspicions about the anti-Union coalition. Although back in 1993 the 'Nationalist coalition' was in its infancy, it would ultimately result in the present-day flag protests, and lead to more division, further exacerbating Unionist antipathies. My stance on this is firm, resolute and entirely consistent: Northern Ireland is part of the Union and should remain so, just as long as it is the majority will in that country.

Five days later, John Major met Irish Taoiseach Albert Reynolds in London; they called for talks between the Northern Ireland political parties to be resumed. A weak and vacillating leader, Major did play a significant role in paving the way to the Good Friday Agreement (GFA), although his successor, Labour Prime Minister Tony Blair, and Blair's enthusiastic, dedicated Northern Ireland Secretary, Mo Mowlam, have gained more credit for this. In other political news, on the 15th, the Standing Advisory Commission on Human Rights (SACHR) argued for changes to the way in which the House of Commons dealt with legislation on Northern Ireland matters. Following the re-introduction of direct rule in the mid-eighties the province was governed under a Temporary Provisions Act, and Northern Ireland legislation was introduced by way of Orders in Council. The main criticism of this procedure was that the legislation could not be amended in the House of Commons.

Some time on the 12th, acting on the orders of Freddie 'Stakeknife' Scappaticci, several members of the 'nutting squad' picked up John Joseph Mulhern (23) on Nansen Street, close to the Falls Road and Broadway in Belfast. He was driven around 90 miles to the Irish border close to Castlederg on the Northern side. It is unknown if he was lulled into a false sense of security by being reassured that he was being 'collected' for a 'meeting' or if he was simply bundled into a car and roughly held down in the back seat, his cries and vision stifled by a thick blanket. If it was the latter, it must have been a truly terrifying journey for the former PIRA volunteer. He had been 'green booked' but had only served for a few months as a low-level operator. PIRA command had suspected that he was an informer for the RUC and gave orders to Scappaticci to 'investigate'. It is thought that he was held for around 11 days in a safe house in Co. Donegal, during which time he was subjected to hideous medieval methods of torture. After this period of interrogation he was forcibly dressed in a boiler suit before being taken to a spot close to the border. He was bound and gagged before being blindfolded and forced to his knees. The 'sentence' would have been read to him as though it gave a semblance of respectability to his tormentor. It is also highly likely that a 'tame' local Catholic priest was brought to listen to Mulhern's confession; in the IRA's eyes this also helped confirm the civilised status of their murderous brutality. Mulhern was shot twice in the back of the head in classic IRA execution style; his body was dumped on a lonely rural road, close to Lough Derg on the Northern Ireland side of the border with Co. Donegal. He was found on the 23rd, indicating that he died during 21–23 June. The dead man's father spoke to the BBC in April 2016 on the news of an enquiry into Freddie Scappaticci's links with British Intelligence: 'The thing that I feel is really strange is that everyone is talking about Scappaticci, but ultimately what about the people who actually pulled the triggers? It just seems like they are getting a free pass. So, to me, the whole thing just smacks of being almost this inquiry to use as a political football to beat the British government with.'[1]

On the 17th, the INLA, then commanded by Hugh 'Cueball' Torney, killed a Catholic man in a hotel on Botanic Avenue, Belfast, simply because he had been a former RUC officer. John Murphy (38) joined the RUC in 1976 and served until 1992, resigning at the start of the year. The INLA had marked him down for death and were aware that he liked to drink at the York Hotel in the Queen's University quarter, close to the Botanic Railway station. During the middle part of the evening, two men, both armed, pushed their way past drinkers in the crowded bar, singled out Mr Murphy, who was alone, and shot him three times in the chest. As the panicked drinkers dived for cover, the two gunmen walked out of the pub, before disappearing into the night. The former policeman died at the scene, on almost the same spot as Sinn Féin's Sheena Campbell was gunned down by UVF gunmen on 16 October the previous year (*see* Chapter 22). Despite the killing, the INLA was in a very much weakened state following the feud with the IPLO – ended by PIRA on the infamous 'night of the long knives' on 31 October 1992 (again, *see* Chapter 22). Mr Murphy was only the second person Torney's men had killed in 1993, following the murder of Samuel Rock in January. However, in 1994, they would kill six, as they became increasingly active in the countdown to the Good Friday Agreement.

The following day, Irish President Mary Robinson, following her very recent meeting with the Queen, now paid an unofficial visit to community (in other words Nationalist) groups in Belfast. The visit went ahead against the wishes of both the Major government and the NIO. During the visit she met Sinn Féin President Gerry Adams, publicly shaking his hand. This gesture provoked a wave of entirely predictable Loyalist anger. The Loyalists saw it as further indication that their southern neighbours were little more than 'mouthpieces' and advocates for the Provisional IRA. A few days later, in an incident which may or may not have been connected with NIO anger at Robinson's visit, Michael Mates resigned, being replaced at the NIO by John Wheeler. The following week Prime Minister John Major, in

1. http://www.bbc.co.uk/news/uk-northern-ireland-36010970.

what was the latest of a long round of visits this month, began a two-day trip to Northern Ireland. It turned out to be largely a non-event, during which he did little more than call for a resumption of political talks between the constitutional parties.

The day after the discovery of ex-PIRA volunteer Mulhern's body, his former bosses killed a man who had once been a UDR soldier, in Lurgan. John Lyness (57) had joined the UDR in 1972, serving until 1992, finally quitting to work full-time for Craigavon Borough Council as a maintenance worker. Even though it had been a year since he left the service, he knew that he was still a target; having been warned by the RUC that his life was in danger he always carried a personal protection weapon. On the evening of the 24th, he arrived outside his home in Lime Grove, Lurgan, where he was approached by two men who had been hiding in an entry way; one of the men was thought at the time to have been PIRA member Colin Duffy.[1] Mr Lyness was hit several times before he was able to draw his weapon; badly wounded, he slumped to the ground, dying at the scene. The two killers used stolen cycles to escape through a nearby park, less than a mile away.

The Duke of Edinburgh's Royal Regiment was formed on 9 June 1959 by the amalgamation of the Royal Berkshire Regiment (Princess Charlotte of Wales's) and the Wiltshire Regiment (Duke of Edinburgh's). Known as 'the farmer's boys', it saw service throughout the Troubles, losing seven soldiers in all during Operation Banner, but up to 26 June it had not suffered any fatalities since Private Brian Allen was killed by a PIRA gunman in Crossmaglen in 1974. Almost 19 years to the day later, the Regiment lost Private John Randall (19) from Langley, Berkshire. A DERR section was patrolling across fields in South Armagh, close to the Irish border with Co. Louth, when a shot was fired from a Barrett .50 calibre rifle, mounted on a tripod in the back of a van. Private Randall was hit in the stomach, and fell to the ground mortally wounded. He wasn't immediately noticed by the others as the sound of the single shot was heavily muffled by drum and band music coming from the nearby town; his comrades only realised that he had been hit when they were alerted by his agonised moans. He died of his wounds at Daisy Hill Hospital in Newry. The 'Cullyhanna Gun Crew' had struck again. Having gone 19 years without a fatality, the regiment was to lose another soldier just three weeks later.

John Randall
Mark Overson, DERR

The lads in the forward of the two sections were desperately trying to ascertain the firing point and a platoon commander, Lieutenant Telfer, radioed to see if his team members were OK. All replied with one exception and it was realised that John Randall had not replied and the officer dashed from cover in order to search for him. Lieutenant Telfer searched for him amongst the reeds of a nearby stream, near which the team had taken cover. Private Randall was found, lying wounded on the ground, clearly having taken the single round which had

1. Duffy was found guilty of the murder and sentenced to life imprisonment but was freed on appeal as one of the eyewitnesses had been discredited and his evidence was discounted. In 1997, Duffy was also charged with the murders of two policemen, but the charges were later dropped. See further *Lost Lives*, p. 1321.

been fired; he had been mortally injured, as the round had hit him in the kidney area.

At this point, the lads in Corporal Travers's team had seen three civilians running towards a car, into which they climbed and drove off; the position was identified afterwards as the exact firing point. Despite incredible efforts by the team medic to save Randall's life, he later died of his wounds in Newry. His funeral service at Langley was well attended by members of the Regimental family, and in particular by his comrades from the 1st Battalion.

On the same day, an Orange Order march was proceeding along a planned route which would take it close to the Springfield Road 'peace line' in West Belfast. The RUC were under instructions to prevent this, which resulted in a violent and bloody confrontation, eventually leading to the death of a Loyalist paramilitary. UVF member Brian 'Herbie' McCallum (26) was involved in the rioting which followed the confrontation. The trouble was sparked off close to Workman Avenue and Lanark Way, which were routes favoured by UFF and UVF death squads, making hit and run sectarian attacks on the Catholic side of the peace line. Indeed UFF 'C' company gunman, Stephen 'Top Gun' McKeag, referred to Lanark Way as the 'Yellow Brick Road'. On the day of the confrontation, McCallum was in possession of a home-made hand grenade. It was alleged that he was positioning himself to throw it at RUC officers, close to Ainsworth Avenue. However, as he reached into his pocket, it exploded prematurely, fatally wounding him as well as badly injuring 18–30 people. A handgun discovered near his body was found to have been used in the murder of a Catholic. McCallum was rushed to the nearby RVH but he died on the 29th; his funeral the following month led to major rioting. His family later stated that 'Herbie' had not intended to throw the grenade but was instead trying to make it safe. There is a memorial to him in the Woodvale area.

On the 27th a former Royal Navy sailor died from wounds which he had sustained exactly 23 years earlier. Petty Officer Frederick MacLaughlin (who was awarded the George Medal) was severely wounded during the vicious rioting in the Crumlin/Ardoyne on 27 June 1970. He was shot in the spine, almost certainly by an OIRA sniper, whilst driving an ambulance, refusing medical treatment until he had completed the evacuation of another gunshot victim.

On Monday 28 June, the Labour Party, then under the leadership of John Smith, revealed that it had produced a discussion document in 1992 on the future of Northern Ireland, apparently without consulting or advising Unionist politicians. The document contained a proposal that, in the absence of agreement between the major political parties, there should be joint authority between Britain and the Republic of Ireland, over Northern Ireland for a period of 20 years. Suffice to say, the proposals were welcomed by Nationalists but were overwhelmingly rejected by Unionists.

June ended with seven deaths; three soldiers, including a former UDR member, were killed, as was a former RUC officer. The paramilitaries lost two men: a former PIRA member and a UVF man.

31
July

This month would see only one death; that of a serving soldier in the 'bandit country' of South Armagh. It was the month also in which Yorkshire Television claimed that the UVF had received outside help in the 1974 Dublin/Monaghan bombings.

On the 1st of the month, the Standing Advisory Commission on Human Rights (SACHR) published its annual report. SACHR called for a review of the legislation that covered the use of lethal force by the security forces. The report also supported the use of video recording of RUC interviews with those suspected of paramilitary-related offences. The report found favour in tricolour-dominated areas but much less so in those where the Union flag adorned most houses. Videoing of police interviews in the UK is now usual.

The following day, there was serious rioting in Belfast, Bangor and Lurgan, after the highly charged atmosphere of 'Herbie' McCallum's funeral. Over that same weekend, Sinn Féin President Gerry Adams was interviewed by the *Sunday Tribune* in Dublin and appeared to be making some concessions in his plans to 'end partition'. He was reported as stating that Republicans might accept joint authority as 'part of the process towards an end to partition'. On the 2nd, in keeping with the spirit of conciliation, the Provisionals detonated a huge device in the centre of Newtownards, a predominantly Protestant town south-east of Belfast. The bomb, weighing 1,500 lb (680 kg), was planted in a stolen vehicle before this was abandoned in Regent Street. The RUC later said that a 20-minute warning had been telephoned through to a local radio station but the area was still being evacuated when the bomb went off; seven people were injured, one seriously. Associated Press reported: 'BELFAST, Northern Ireland – An IRA bomb exploded Monday near Belfast, damaging about 20 businesses and injuring 17 people, including five police officers. The bomb, placed inside a van, went off outside a pub in the town of Newtownards as police were evacuating the area following a coded warning from the Irish Republican Army. Virtually every window within a quarter of a mile was blown out.'

On the 3rd, a PIRA bombing unit managed to leave a car packed with explosives close to the court house in Strabane, Co. Tyrone. A warning was given, but three people were still badly injured when the device exploded. There was some suggestion of Garda Síochána involvement and Allison Morris in the *Irish Times* reported an alleged plot by a Garda informer who she claimed had smuggled the device across the border and left the car close to the Court House. This has never been substantiated.[1]

On Tuesday 6th, Yorkshire Television broadcast a documentary entitled 'Hidden Hand – The Forgotten Massacre' made as part of its *First Tuesday* series. The programme

1. http://www.irishtimes.com/news/informer-let-bomb-strabane-says-witness-1.351946.

dealt with the Dublin and Monaghan bombings of May 1974 in which 33 people were killed and over 300 injured.

The programme claimed that the UVF would have required assistance to carry out the bomb attacks, and speculated where such assistance might have come from; whilst no firm conclusions were drawn, there was the clear suggestion that the British Army might have played a role. Republicans, notably Sinn Féin, have always claimed that the terrible deeds of that day were at the hands of 'Crown forces'. The programme made allegations concerning the existence of a covert British Army unit based at Castledillon. The makers further claimed that, as well as links between that unit and Loyalist paramilitaries, the then Secretary of State for Northern Ireland, Merlyn Rees, had known of the unit's existence. I watched the programme when it was first shown and it is my opinion, then as well as now, that it was intended to be mischievous, at a time when it had become fashionable to blame the British government for anything and everything.[1]

Nine days later the UVF released a statement in which it claimed sole responsibility for the Dublin and Monaghan bombs. I have always believed that the outrages – seen as a both a retaliation, and demonstration of the 'Protestant backlash' for the almost daily carnage on the streets of Belfast and Londonderry by the Provisionals – were conceived and executed by Loyalist paramilitaries and that the British government of Harold Wilson played no role in them. The suggestion is simply scurrilous and symptomatic of Irish Republican re-writing of history; it may well serve an admiring Irish-American and UK left-wing audience, but I reject absolutely the programme's allegations.

Jeanne Griffin, Irish-American Historian
My views on the Yorkshire Television Programme: *The Hidden Hand*

I am the author of numerous Wikipedia articles about the Troubles, in particularly [concerning] Loyalist paramilitaries. My most ambitious were [on] Robin Jackson, Billy Hanna and the UVF Mid-Ulster Brigade, the main perpetrators of the Dublin and Monaghan outrages which slaughtered innocent Irish people going about their daily business. I am Irish-American. In order to carry out the extensive research required to write the pieces I examined both the judicial 2003 Barron Report and the 'Hidden Hand' programme. I found both sources to be invaluable. However, the implication that the UVF were incapable of carrying out these attacks [because of] the expert construction of the three Dublin bombs in my opinion is erroneous as it minimises the fact that the mastermind of the operation was Mid-Ulster leader Billy Hanna, a decorated Korean War veteran who was also weapons instructor in the UDR. He gave the instructions for the construction of the bombs, which were so well put together that it gave rise to persistent rumours that the car bombings were the nefarious machinations of British Intelligence, fully sanctioned by the British Government led at the time by Harold Wilson, a man who displayed scant sympathy towards Ulster Loyalists during the Ulster Workers' Council strike which was in its third day when the terrorist attacks took place on 17 May 1974. The programme's main researcher was Joe Tiernan, a probing journalist

1. The programme is available at: https://www.youtube.com/watch?v=wNvZHDafi38 so readers may form their own views.

to whom I owe a great deal in providing a detailed account of how the bombs were brought by Hanna and Jackson in the latter's poultry lorry to Dublin which certainly enhanced the integrity of my articles. That acknowledged I think he and subsequently the YTV programme concentrated too much on the fact that Billy Hanna had contacts with British Intelligence in Lisburn. He doubtless did as he was later shot by Jackson (identified in the programme by his soubriquet The Jackal), for having been an informer. But it is a big step to suggest they ordered him to bomb Dublin and Monaghan. The decision came from the UVF Brigade Staff on the Shankill of which Hanna was a member. In fact the bombing teams for Dublin were made up of both Belfast and Mid-Ulster units. The UVF Chief of Staff at the time was Ken Gibson who nevertheless allowed Hanna and his Mid-Ulster Brigade a considerable degree of autonomy. Gibson, who was leader of the unionist Volunteer Political Party was alleged by Tiernan to have been part of the UVF team that bombed Dublin in late 1972 and again in early1973, killing three [public transport workers].

If anything, the suspicion should fall on the Irish Military Intelligence. The Garda Síochána team set up to investigate the bombings, and headed by John Joy, was obstructed at every turn by the government which was led by the anti-IRA Liam Cosgrave, whose recent death went noticeably un-mourned by Sinn Féin. The Garda had identified David Mulholland, driver of the first car bomb which exploded in Parnell Street, yet he was never extradited to Ireland from Northern Ireland. Why? Eyewitnesses picked his photo out early in the investigation. Additionally all the files pertaining to the bombings were later destroyed, key forensic evidence as well. Even on the day of the explosions, there were no roadblocks set up even after the RUC had alerted Dublin Castle after the car that would end up in Talbot Street, was stolen in Belfast Docks that same morning!!! And the three cars were parked for about fifteen minutes in their designated streets with their original plates yet the *gardaí* walking their beats paid little heed nor were they instructed to keep an eye out for the stolen vehicle. Despite it being the third day of the UWC strike, which was in violent protest against the Sunningdale Agreement and the resulting power-sharing Executive that would have allowed Dublin input in Northern Ireland, this attack was unexpected. Finally I wish to recognise that the relatives of the 33 victims of the bombings are rightly angry at the Irish Government for having ignored them all these years and [never seeking] to obtain any convictions. It is now too late as all the bombers and their associates are dead. However, their disappointment at the negligence of the Irish Government remains palpable even today.

The UVF statement denying the claims made in the programme ran as follows:

Following the sinister allegations of collusion mischievously constructed by presenters of the recent *First Tuesday* programme which supposedly investigated the 1974 Dublin and Monaghan bombings, the UVF avails itself of this opportunity to state clearly and without reservation that the entire operation was from its conception to its successful conclusion, planned and carried out by our volunteers aided by no outside bodies. In contrast to the scenario painted by the programme, it would have been unnecessary and indeed undesirable to compromise our

> volunteers by using clandestine Security Force personnel, British or otherwise, to achieve [an] objective well within our capabilities. The operation whilst requiring a fair degree of preparation and not a little courage did not as was suggested by the so called experts require a great deal of technical expertise.
>
> The comments made by some of those interviewed were at best naive if not deliberately misleading. Given the backdrop of what was taking place in Northern Ireland when the UVF [were] bombing republican targets at will, either the researchers decided to take poetic licence to the limit or the truth was being twisted by knaves to make [a] trap for the fools . . . The minimum of scrutiny should have revealed that the structure of the bombs placed in Dublin and Monaghan were similar if not identical to those being placed in Northern Ireland on an almost daily basis. The type of explosives, timing and detonating methods all bore the hallmark of the UVF. It is incredulous [*sic*] that these points were lost on the Walter Mittys who conjured up this programme. To suggest that the UVF were not, or are not, capable of operating in the manner outlined in the programme is tempting fate to a dangerous degree.

Irish Tánaiste Dick Spring spoke to the *Guardian* on the 8th, suggesting that the British and Irish governments would benefit from talks about a settlement for the North, which once agreed, could be put to the electorates of the North and South in the form of a referendum. However, the problems which had existed since before 1921 still prevailed and were effectively insoluble: Protestants wished to remain in the Union and loyal to the Crown; Catholics still cleaved to the breast of mother Ireland and never the twain would meet. Protestants wanted no part of what they saw as a 'Papal State' and Catholics – despite not being averse to benefitting from the UK's financial largesse – did not wish to be ruled by the English. At around the same time, a meeting of the Anglo-Irish Intergovernmental Conference (AIIC) took place: posh names, posh titles, lots of hot air and rhetoric and the outcome was the same – stalemate.

A few days after Spring's interview, UUP leader James Molyneaux made a startling accusation against the NIO, virtually accusing it of holding military talks with the Provisional IRA. He claimed that towards the end of 1992, a year in which 119 people had died, almost 70 at the hands of the Provisional IRA, the NIO, in all likelihood acting on behalf of John Major, had presented PIRA with peace proposals. My understanding of Loyalist attitudes, their 'siege mentality' so to speak, both during the Troubles and even today, is that they are deeply entrenched. There were periods of calm during which Ulster Loyalists might trust the British government, but these were few and far between; those in the North who wish to remain part of the Union have felt forced to examine every word and syllable uttered by Whitehall, searching for signs of betrayal.During the Troubles there was never a shortage of violence and mistrust and who could blame either set of interests for their mistrust? The Loyalists had seen almost 4,000 deaths, the vast majority at the hands of Irish Republicans and they had seen their country being dismantled brick by brick by IRA explosives. The British on the other hand were equally war-weary; they had seen their young men and women blown to pieces in pubs and buses, from Ulster to Manchester to Leeds to London to Deal and on the European mainland. They had seen soldiers cut down in civilian clothes at railway stations and now the IRA were exploding bombs causing billions of pounds worth of damage. It is indeed a major tribute to both the Ulster people and the British government that, almost 50 years on, there is still much co-operation between the two sides, however strained it is at times. However, Molyneaux's fears have always haunted proceedings. The GFA is seen by many people in Northern Ireland to be a necessary evil, but that is not to detract from Major's efforts to get the ball rolling.

Back on the mainland, John Major was in trouble in the Commons – his majority was shrinking with each by-election setback – and under incessant attack from the very skilled Labour Leader John Smith. Major was forced to tell the House of Commons that there was no truth in the rumour that he had entered into a deal with the UUP in return for support during the debate on the 'Social Chapter' of the Maastricht Treaty. UUP MP the Rev. Martin Smyth demanded that a select committee on Northern Ireland be established in the near future.

It was business as usual on the 10th, as the Tyrone unit of the Provisional IRA set up a mortar attack on the RUC station at Cookstown. Prior to the onset of the attack, a gang of masked gunmen took over a house in the area, holding a family hostage before seizing their two vehicles, both of which were later abandoned. The mortar unit set up the base plate in the van, but unfortunately for them a charge exploded prematurely, badly injuring the IRA operative and damaging a nearby barn. Other IRA men tried to help the wounded man across the border in a commandeered taxi but they were arrested at a snap VCP close to Newtownstewart and the wounded terrorist taken to Tyrone County Hospital, Omagh, then to Altnagelvin, Londonderry, before finally being transferred to a hospital in Belfast. He was kept under armed guard there before he was pronounced fit enough to appear in court.

On the 17th, the Cullyhanna Gun Crew/Crossmaglen sniper struck again when he/she shot and fatally wounded Lance Corporal Kevin John Pullin (28) as he patrolled in Carron Road, near St Patrick's Primary School. Kevin Pullin was from Kingsthorpe in Northamptonshire and had been in the Army for several years. At around 13:30, firing from an elevated position around 800 yards away, a PIRA gunman using a Barrett Light .50 mounted on bales of hay fired a single shot at the Northamptonshire boy, striking him in the chest. The blow was so powerful, it knocked him off his feet, fatally wounding him. As his comrades rushed to his aid and set up all-round defence, the gunman was able to sneak over the border into the Irish Republic just over a mile away. The dying soldier was airlifted to Daisy Hill Hospital in Newry; sadly, he was dead on arrival. His funeral was held at Kingsthorpe.

Kev Pullin
Martin Blackmore, 1 DERR

I was the Company Clerk during the Mar.–Sep. '93 tour at XMG [Crossmaglen], and at times I heard about/saw certain pieces of intelligence that the rest of the lads never. I think that I was well liked amongst all ranks because I wasn't the usual rear echelon type! I was always a real soldier first and foremost, always out on patrol – nearly every day. The CSM & OC wanted me to be the Coy clerk because I had half a brain, knew my way around a computer and could spell better than their previous clerk.

Around the 3rd, some two weeks before Kev was killed, the RUC received an anonymous phone call – which they recorded – in the early hours of the morning. The caller was a female and she started giving hints as to when and where the next sniper attack would take place. One of the RUC came over and passed on the details to the OC . . . just after breakfast. All parties thought it was just somebody who'd had too much to drink and was on a wind-up, although the RUC said they'd trace the call and would let us know if they received another similar call. Then about two or three days before the 17th the RUC received another call in the early hours from the same female caller. So they came across and got the OC and CSM to listen to the recording. During her call she kept referring to a shooting taking place very soon in XMG on a long road from a fast firing point and she also kept mentioning the number seven.

They all laughed it off and nicknamed her the 'cryptic caller'. Then on the day Kev was killed, he was shot whilst knelt down in between two cars outside of number 7 Carran Road! From memory, Carran Road is a long road and the firing point was a car. I'll never forget the look on the OC's & CSM's face after we'd lifted Kev on to the helicopter to be casevaced to Musgrave park Hospital. They were both ashen-faced when they realised he'd been killed outside number 7. Was it pure coincidence? I truly don't think so, and the burning question for me is why would a member of the IRA taunt us with cryptic clues? If indeed she had anything to do with the IRA. I'm certain you'll be able to verify the above by using your former RUC contacts. The RUC told us that the female had made the calls to the station from a public pay phone just across the border. Ken, this will probably seem very trivial or of no use to you at all but it's something that I think of often. More so than remembering seeing Kev lying in the road lifeless. I've never spoken to any of the lads about the above and probably never will.

Kevin Pullin

Lieutenant Paul Muspratt, Duke of Edinburgh's Royal Regiment

My team proceeded to the road to where we were going to set up our snap VCP. The town was busy, it was Saturday, and the bars were full. Having turned down the road we walked on for another 50–100 metres away from the junction. Ptes Mead and Price, a Kiwi, were in front and L/Cpl Kevin Pullin and I were at the back. Kevin was, prior to the tour, the company's PTI and was therefore known and liked by all. He wasn't an ego-inflated PTI, just a very fit, happy go lucky guy. He wasn't a regular as such either, he'd been in the TA and had volunteered for a stint in the regulars . . .

I remember him telling me he was looking forward to going for a run during our R&R that was coming up shortly; exercise was a bit limited for a squaddie in XMG. As we walked down the road I pointed for Kevin to go over to the right-hand side of the road, I went to the left. We went firm and then I signalled to Kevin to start stopping the traffic, we usually took it in turns and as Kevin was a lance jack he was really in charge of the brick, whilst I concentrated on the multiple. The first car that came through, was a known player, this was probably the first time we'd had a good look at this bloke so Kevin called in the plates and had a chat, after that we went firm again, taking up squatting position on either side of the street behind whatever cover was available. Next thing there was a tremendous whizzing noise, not like a rifle shot at all. I looked across and could see Kevin was down, I stood up, looking down the road, but couldn't see anything, as the road dropped into dead ground, and ran over to Kevin. The first thing I noticed were his eyes; they had a vacant quality to them, and I shouted the other two over and we started to give him first aid.

He wouldn't respond to his name, and I remember shouting at him 'Corporal Pullin, Corporal Pullin' and one of the lads – Mead – very gently said to me: 'His name's Kevin.' The entry wound appeared small and wasn't bleeding; I suppose I was getting pretty agitated now, and we couldn't find a pulse or put the drip in. Looking up the road I could see the bar had emptied and the drinkers had moved onto the street; we obviously provided better entertainment than the TV at that point. I called in the contact report and probably broke with SOPs by telling them his name rather than his number. They were to send the Pig out as an ambulance and I gave a casevac location in the field at the bottom of the road, it seemed closer at the time. After an age the Pig arrived, but someone had put the wrong fuel type in and they couldn't get it going. Of the three of us only Price thought he'd seen something, a car partly obscured, but that was it (it later turned out they were using a car with a hatch back and the seats removed on one side as a firing platform for their Barrett light 50). We'd been giving Kevin first aid for about 10 mins by now, it felt much longer, as soon as the Pig stopped we put Kevin on a stretcher and placed it in the vehicle. One of the medics from the camp was in there and he took over from us. It then drove down the road and we all ran down after it. I believe Kevin died on the spot, maybe shortly after we got to him. The 50 calibre armour-piercing round, entered about his navel, through his dog tags and below his flak jacket, the tip was later found in his water bottle. We maintained the cordon whilst the RUC went to work; I remember Patrick, the OC, coming up to me whilst still on the road and I cried whilst he spoke to me.

The murder of Kevin Pullin, Crossmaglen
By a former DERR soldier

L/Cpl Pullin was serving in 'C' Company based at Crossmaglen and was killed by a terrorist using a new large sniper rifle, the Barrett Light .50. The local IRA ASU had launched several mortar attacks on SF bases in the area and they were clearly keen to continue this tactic and thus the chance of further attacks was very high . . . several anti-mortar searches were organised. The idea was to discover potential launching sites in order to prevent further attacks. At least two companies were involved and in mid-July we set up VCPs on the roads which led to the areas in which we were operating Nothing particularly helpful was found, but the local civilian populace appeared quite surprised at the timing and scale of our efforts. Despite this, we immediately began to attract the attention of known players and their helpers who were observing our troops . . . There was a feeling that we were vulnerable to attack and our instincts were sadly proven correct, although the skills we had learned over the years stood us in good stead and we never gave them the opportunity to attack us on that first day.

The next day, we patrolled again, but with greatly reduced numbers. We had intended to change over the personnel in an observation tower just south of Crossmaglen but this had been delayed due to the activities of the previous day. Whenever this changeover was effected, we were exposing ourselves to attacks from the town and so a patrol was actually put onto the streets to provide cover for the operation. One of the platoon commanders, Lieutenant [Muspratt] with three teams went into the town and we set up what we called a 'snap VCP' but no sooner had we done this, when a round was fired from the north. One of the lads, Lance Corporal Kevin Pullin was hit as he positioned himself in a doorway and very seriously wounded. Two of the lads, Private Mead and Private Price, both fought desperately to save him, but, sadly, after he was casevaced by chopper, he died of the internal injuries caused by this dreadful wound.

The following day the IRA again targeted the centre of the town of Banbridge, Co. Down. A stolen car containing several hundred pounds of explosives was left close to houses before the bombers ran off. It is thought that their intention was to drive into the commercial heart of the town, but that the car may have developed a fault. A warning was telephoned through, and Army bomb disposal were called in to make a very dangerous device safe. One particular ploy of the IRA was to booby-trap devices to kill ATO personnel as they worked on bombs which had apparently been 'abandoned'. The RUC were forced to evacuate 50 nearby homes whilst the bomb disposal crew carried out their dangerous task, declaring it safe after some five hours.

On the 23rd, the UFF sent a bombing team to attack the Sinn Féin offices in the Nationalist New Lodge; the order was given by Adair himself. A device was placed outside the front door where it exploded shortly afterwards; however, it was faulty and only detonated partially, causing slight damage. Four days later, Adair sent a different team to the Twinbrook area of south-West Belfast; their target was the home of Sinn Féin councillor Annie Armstrong. The gunmen arrived in a stolen car, before two of them advanced cautiously towards the house. On seeing lights on, they fired several shots through a downstairs window, narrowly missing Mrs Armstrong's daughter but wrecking the television. The councillor had just arrived home from a Lisburn Borough meeting in Hillsborough. Speaking shortly after the attack, she described the events: 'When the firing started I threw Frances and myself to the ground. The worst thing was not knowing if my other children were okay. I could hear them screaming upstairs and I shouted up to them but I couldn't get up the stairs until the firing stopped.' The gunmen escaped back to the Shankill, clearly frustrated at the lack of a kill, but they would be more successful just 12 days later.

Finally, on the last day of the month, very close to the spot where DERR soldier John Randall was shot and killed in June, a PIRA sniper opened fire on a mobile VCP which had been set up by soldiers from the same unit. It was again the handiwork of the Cullyhanna Gun Crew, who had already killed six and wounded one in the previous 12 months. This time an Army mobile VCP had been set up on the Newry Road close to Newtownhamilton; a single shot, likely from the same Barrett .50 Calibre was fired at around 22:00, narrowly missing members of the patrol. The soldiers fired back, but no hits were reported and the gunmen and weapon melted back over the border into the sanctuary of the Irish Republic.

The *Independent* reported:

> Security forces in Northern Ireland yesterday mounted a major search operation after a shot was fired at a mobile army checkpoint on a border road, near the scene of a sniper attack which killed a soldier. The intense level of activity by the Royal Ulster Constabulary and the Army over the incident on Saturday night, in which no one was hurt, reflects the concern that an IRA sniper team is at work along the border. Six members of the security forces have been killed in single-shot attacks in the border area over the past year, five in the area of South Armagh known as 'bandit country', and the other in south Fermanagh. It emerged at the weekend that Lt-Gen Sir Roger Wheeler, General Officer Commanding Northern Ireland, sees the sniping threat as a major challenge, and has made it a priority to catch the IRA team. When the latest attack occurred, at 10 pm, the soldiers were stopping cars on the Newry Road, near Newtownhamilton, Co. Armagh . . . Police and army patrols are regularly fired on without injury in the ghettos around Belfast and Londonderry, but the fear is that a sniping team has been trained and is using the Barrett 'Light Fifty' Rifle, among other weapons. The 0.5 in calibre weapon, 5 ft long and weighing more than 30 lb, has a range of more than a mile and is capable of piercing body armour with bullets that leave the muzzle at 1,907 mph. A man who was nearby on 17 July, when the last victim, L/Cpl Kevin Pullin, also of the Duke of Edinburgh's Regiment, was killed, is convinced that a high-powered weapon was used. He said the bang was so loud many thought a bomb had exploded. The same witness heard the shot that killed Police Constable Jonathan Reid on 25 February 1993, one of three to die in Crossmaglen, and said it was fired from a different weapon, probably an AK-47. One close observer of the scene in South Armagh said the IRA's change of tactics to sniping is a response to the army's decision to build high watch-towers which overlook most of the hilly countryside and make it difficult for the terrorists to use bombs with command wires to attack patrols. The apparent success of the switch in tactics and the security forces' determination to catch the team was reflected in the aftermath of the last attack, he said: 'The soldiers were very, very scared. Really nervous. When an attack happens they don't know where the shot has come from. That was the second soldier from the same battalion to die.'[1]

July was over and whilst there had been only one death, that of a soldier; as always, there had been numerous near misses as well as many injuries. The war was about to start its 24th year; almost 4,000 were dead but the British were no nearer being driven into the sea as they had been in the early moments of the Provisionals' painful and ugly birth, from the womb of the Official IRA. Moreover, most or all of the Catholic civil rights demands had been met, Sinn Féin had been declared a legitimate political party, but the killings were continuing in the same old, depressing way; they would continue to do so for many more years to come.

1. www.independent.co.uk/news/uk/sniper-attack-leads-to-security-search-police-fear-armed-ira-team-at-work-on-border-1458676.html.

32

August

There were three deaths this month; all were Catholic civilians and all were killed in sickening sectarian attacks. There were more attacks on the mainland, as the IRA's England team penetrated the 'impenetrable ring of steel' in the City of London; there was the shortest-lived death threat in history and another British politician waved a red rag at the Provisionals. The same terror group exploded bomb after bomb, seemingly at will, in several Northern Ireland towns.

Adrian Loughlin joined the UDR around 1986, serving both as a full-time and part-time soldier, before leaving around 1990. Although he was now a civilian, in the eyes of the IRA he was still a 'legitimate target' who warranted a 'death sentence'. In the early hours of 4 August, a PIRA bombing unit, including Peter Galen, under cover of darkness placed an explosive device underneath his car as it was parked outside his home. A friend and comrade of mine takes up the story.

My Brother, Adrian
Trevor Loughlin, UDR

On the morning of 4 August 1993, my late brother Adrian got up as usual for work; he worked in Killen about five miles from our home in Castlederg. Around 08:45, he set off and on arrival, he parked his car, a red Nissan Sunny, in the yard outside the workshop. At lunchtime, he drove home again, where he met his girlfriend. Later, he set off for petrol and she accompanied him.

However, as Adrian went around a left-hand bend in the road, he heard a rattle from the underside of the car; he pulled over and, leaving her in the car, went to investigate. Initially he had thought that it was the exhaust which had fallen off. He suddenly realised it was in fact an UVBT that had fallen off the car. Suddenly, a Mini Metro came around the bend, and despite his best efforts to warn them, they drove straight over the top of it, but again it failed to explode! The RUC were informed and soldiers from the nearby Rockwood base, including bomb disposal were called to the scene. In the meantime, word had reached our sister Lucinda back at home, so she went to investigate where the car had been parked; a quick search found a dowel rod which had been used to hold the bomb in place!

Adrian had served in the UDR for approximately 3–4 years both in a full-time and a part-time capacity, but when the incident happened he had left the Regiment for some 3 years. After the incident, Adrian became very withdrawn and into himself. He was a totally different person. He would not go out of the house – he wouldn't even go to the shop if he needed anything like fags or personal items such as shower gel toothpaste soap etc. He would send someone to the shop for him, just wouldn't go out himself. On numerous occasions he spoke of ending his own life, but no one was aware that it was him displaying signs of PTSD. Some three years later, a local man, Peter Galen, from Scraghy Road outside Castlederg, was convicted of the attempted murder of Adrian and the same man was also convicted of the murder of a contract worker, Andrew Bogle, on the 18th of August 1990 in the yard where he was about to load a JCB onto a trailer, Adrian continued to suffer PTSD although he was getting some counselling, and it was as I could see starting to help him a little. Unfortunately he began drinking heavily and lost all faith in life. Our late mother told me she had found him sitting out in the back yard in the rain with only a pair of tracksuit trousers on and looking up to the sky, asking 'Why God did they do this to me?' Adrian was not a religious person but I guess it was the PTSD and his way of dealing with his demons. Unfortunately Adrian passed away on 17 June 2004 at the age of 36, it is my belief that had he not got the bomb under his car he would still be with us today. The coroner's report put it down as a massive heart attack due to the medication he was subsequently on for depression and various other medications all related to that terrible day . . . And it is now so hard for the family knowing that Galen is walking a free man due to the farce of the Good Friday agreement, I do not use the word FARCE lightly as that is exactly what it was.

On the 8th, Johnny Adair's 'C' company was in action again, this time on the nearby Antrim Road, as they failed in an attempt to kill a leading Sinn Féin councillor, but murdered his son instead. Sean Lavery (21) was a student who lived at home with his parents, one of whom was Bobby Lavery, a well-known Sinn Féin member from the New Lodge Road, whom the UFF had tried to kill before. An armed UFF gang, including 'Top Gun' himself, Stephen McKeag,[1] hijacked a vehicle in the Shankill area. The gang left Adair's HQ, driving onto the Antrim Road. At approx. 21:30 that Sunday evening, the car pulled up outside the Sinn Féin man's house, the gunmen fully expecting Bobby Lavery to be at home. McKeag jumped out, barely wasting a second, before blindly opening fire through the downstairs window. He raked the room with automatic fire, with at least 21 rounds hitting the people and furniture inside. Sean Lavery was hit twice in his side, fatally wounding him. Despite his wounds, he managed to stagger into his father's arms where he collapsed. He was rushed to the nearby Mater Hospital, but died shortly after arrival. The previous Christmas, the boy's uncle, Martin Lavery, had been shot and killed by the UVF (*see* Chapter 24). Just three weeks before the death of his son, Councillor Lavery had survived another Loyalist attack when a bomb that had been thrown into Sinn Féin's advice centre on the New Lodge Road failed to detonate fully.

UPI reported: 'The Ulster Freedom Fighters, an outlawed Protestant paramilitary group, claimed responsibility for the attack, which killed Lavery's 21-year-old son Sean as he was watching television at the family home in the New Lodge district of Belfast. "The

1. Identified by McDonald and Cusack in *UDA: Inside the Heart of Loyalist Terror*, p. 244.

attack last night on my family could have resulted in the slaughter of my whole family if they had been in that room at the time," Lavery told a news conference Monday. "The back wall of the house was totally raked with gunfire. Anyone who was in that room would not have survived. This was a blatant attempt at mass murder." BELFAST, Northern Ireland – Leaders of the political wing of the outlawed Irish Republican Army demanded the right to carry weapons for self-protection Monday after loyalist gunmen shot dead the son of a Belfast City Council member. The leaders of Sinn Féin, the IRA's political wing, said the drive-by shooting at the home of Councillor Bobby Lavery Sunday evening was part of a growing trend and justified permitting members of the political group to carry weapons for self-defense.'[1]

The tragic and utterly unnecessary death of Seamus Hopkins (24), between the 6th and 11th in the Shankill Road area became something of a high-water mark in the gruesome history of sectarian killings during the Troubles. The murder was senseless and evil at best, bestial and cowardly at worst. Back in 1987, when he was only 18, Mr Hopkins had been confronted and attacked by so-called Loyalists – thugs would be a better description – after the young Catholic had strayed into a Protestant area. After he was beaten, a heavy breeze-block was dropped on his head as he lay unconscious on the ground and he was left for dead. He never really recovered; now suffering from epilepsy and violent headaches for the remainder of his short life, he lived with his parents on the New Lodge Road. He was attending the Mater Hospital on the Crumlin Road, as an out-patient. During the first or second week in August, he was walking in the vicinity of the hospital as he regularly did, when he was abducted by a known UVF paramilitary. He was taken the short distance to waste ground by Sherbrook Way, just off North Boundary Street. He was then systematically kicked to death: smashed around the head, neck, throat and torso. *Lost Lives* describes his injuries thus: 'His voicebox was shattered. He also had a fractured skull and broken ribs.'[2] The beating was so savage and ferocious, even allowing for the anarchic violence and the appalling sectarian hatred of those violent times, it is my (admittedly unqualified) opinion that the killer or killers were either completely depraved or violently insane. In 1994, a man was charged with the murder but he was acquitted after the judge refused to accept certain evidence. I am not able to name the man in these pages. The *Sunday Herald* reported the funeral of the Catholic boy: 'Father Aidan Brankin told hundreds of mourners at the funeral service for Seamus Hopkins, 24, that after a sectarian attack six years ago, when Mr Hopkins was battered over the head with breeze blocks, he had: "the mentality of a child and often behaved like a child. It's hard to imagine a softer or easier target than Seamus Hopkins." Mr Hopkins's body was found on waste ground off the Shankill Road by a six-year-old boy. Police believe it had lain undiscovered for several days.'

The day after Seamus Hopkins's body was discovered, the Provisionals attempted to transport a bomb into the centre of Portadown, Co. Armagh. Only three months previously, another huge PIRA bomb had wrecked the centre of this town; this time, they tried to plant a 3,000 lb (1,350 kg) device, presumably to devastate the centre further, although thanks to them it was already lying in ruins. However, the RUC, acting on a tip-off, managed to

1. https://www.upi.com/Archives/1993/08/09/Son-of-City-Council-member-shot-dead-in-Northern-Ireland/6879744868800.
2. *Lost Lives*, p. 1323.

intercept the vehicle en route for the target area and made several arrests, with Army ATO men defusing the deadly device.

The day after, PIRA's England team again turned their attention to the genteel holiday town of Eastbourne on England's southern coast. Back in 1990, they had killed Conservative Party MP Ian Gow with a car bomb outside his house on the outskirts of the town. During that Friday – the 13th – PIRA operatives planted eight bombs around the town-centre shopping area. There were five immediate explosions, one of which was in a Maples furniture shop and three other nearby shops were also damaged. As the day wore on, it was assumed that all of the devices had either been found or had exploded, but there was a sudden, unexpected explosion on the pier which caused some structural damage; several people were cut by flying debris and broken glass. The bombers had telephoned Brighton police earlier in the day, warning of attacks on Bournemouth, Brighton and Torquay.

The *Independent* reported: 'Officers recovered a "substantial" explosive device from beneath Bournemouth pier. The bomb may have been in place while 800 people watched a show in the pier theatre on Thursday night. Before the discovery, the pier and four shops in the town centre were damaged in incendiary explosions early yesterday morning, which Dorset police said bore "all the hallmarks of the Provisional IRA". The most serious damage occurred at Maples furniture store, where two firebombs went off in the basement. Incendiary devices also ignited at Waterstone's bookshop and two clothes stores in the town centre. The sixth device damaged the west side of Bournemouth pier.'

Being a Soldier in England

Corporal, Royal Green Jackets

Roughly during the period that you are writing about, I was based in Dover after a spell at Osnabrück in what was then West Germany. I had a girlfriend up in [London] and used to get the train from Priory Station to Victoria every free weekend that I had. I remember that we were advised not to hitchhike because there was no telling who might be driving the car and we were also advised not to travel in uniform. The IRA had shot three lads going home on leave in Staffordshire and killed one of them, so that was out of the question, in any case.

One time, I did hitch a ride in Dover, but it wasn't until we had gone for a couple of miles or so, that I realised that the driver had a Northern Ireland accent. Well, I near shit myself and asked him to stop and claimed that I was going to be sick; he did so and he then roared off whilst I walked back to the nearest train station. He might have been innocent, but with IRA men and women all over England and West Germany, I was taking no chances. In any case, you get in a car with a civvie and when they find out that you're a squaddie, they inevitably ask one of two very offensive and insensitive questions. It is either: 'What's it like to kill someone?' or equally as tactless: 'Have you ever killed anyone?'

Even on the trains, I was so obviously a soldier and I get would get friendly smiles from people, like the old lady whose son was over in Northern Ireland. I had to pretend that it was OK over there, and that the press exaggerated everything to sell papers. I didn't let on how scared I had been on my two tours in the 80s. The worst type were the studenty ones, with long hair and Uni scarves and copies of left-wing newspapers, like the 'Militant.' If there was only one of them, it was

OK, but if there were 2 or 3, once they found out that I was a squaddie, they would start on me. 'Baby-killers, kiddie-killers, Nazi bullies, fascist Army' were just the mild ones. One of the pricks had a Bobby Sands t-shirt on and he was full of slavver about how we were occupying 'Ireland' and we had forced them to kill themselves on hunger strike because we were shooting them and imprisoning them for nothing. I was outnumbered that day, but one weekend, some time later, as we got off in a crowd of people at Victoria, I noticed one of them on his own and he had been giving it large in front of his mates when we were on the train. I waited until there was lots of people around and covering my actions; well, I just loosed my size 9s into his Achilles area and down he went and he was in agony. I enjoyed that, but if they would have listened instead of repeating 'Militant' and 'Red Mole' parrot-fashion, I could have explained to them that the IRA were not freedom-fighters, they were cold-blooded murderers, just barbaric and evil.

On Saturday 14th, in what was seen as a very significant diplomatic error by the Major government, further damaging Anglo-Spanish relations, a group of supporters of ETA (Euskadi Ta Askatasuna) from the Basque region were allowed into the UK. To compound this error further, the Basque separatists paid a visit to Belfast where, naturally, they expressed support for Sinn Féin/PIRA. ETA ran a terror campaign against the Spanish government during 1958–2017, killing approximately 820 people.

Two days later, Ambassador Jean Kennedy Smith paid another unofficial visit to Northern Ireland, speaking to Nationalist groups in Londonderry and Co. Fermanagh. It is easy to speculate that she took back with her to President Clinton harrowing tales of British occupation, state terror groups, collusion and destruction of civil rights.

On the 14th, the IRA attacked the centre of Strabane, Co. Tyrone, in a bid to terrorise civilians and force more economic pressure on Protestant businesses in the town. It was the second such attack in the previous six weeks, following the earlier bombing of the court house. There was major damage but no deaths. It was the first of seven PIRA bombs in the space of just nine days, with an eighth exploding on the 31st. On the same day as the second Strabane attack, a 21 lb (9.5 kg) device exploded outside a restaurant in Londonderry, followed shortly afterwards by an attempt to kill marching Loyalists on an Apprentice Boys' parade close by. They struck again in Strabane on the 16th, demonstrating an easy ability – as well as a seemingly bottomless pit of explosive materiel – to defeat security measures. On the 18th, they penetrated Belfast city centre again and left a car packed with explosives on the Dublin Road; the explosion caused almost £1 million worth of damages, devastating businesses including hotels there. There were no serious injuries thanks to prompt RUC action in clearing the area.

On the 20th, the IRA launched a mortar attack on the still-ruined court house in Newry, Co. Down, which they had wrecked as long ago as 1985. In this latest attack, a PIRA team, suspected to have been from the town's fervently Republican Derrybeg Estate, fired three rockets at the ruins. They had set up a base plate on the back of a stolen lorry close to the centre from where they launched all three missiles. Two of them were duds, but the third landed within yards of its target, detonating in a tree. Ten people were injured, including a young child and two policemen, a miraculously small number, as the

Provisionals demonstrated a repeated callousness for the lives of the innocents in the area at the time.

Associated Press reported the story:

> The IRA said its members fired three mortar bombs Friday, and 10 people including a 10-year-old boy, were injured. The bombs were fired in an attack on a courthouse already closed by previous bombings. Only one projectile exploded of the three fired from a nearby abandoned truck in central Newry, a mostly Catholic border town 35 miles southwest of Belfast, a Royal Ulster Constabulary spokesman said. That shell hit a tree and exploded, breaking windows, damaging cars and a courthouse wall and knocking flat eight civilians and two police officers, he added, speaking on condition of anonymity. Injuries were reportedly minor. The Newry courthouse has been closed since an Irish Republican Army attack in 1985. The IRA frequently has used makeshift mortars – huge, unwieldy projectiles made from 4-foot-tall gas cylinders and timer-fired from the backs of parked trucks – in its 23-year campaign against British rule of Northern Ireland.

On the 22nd, there were two more PIRA bombs in Belfast; the first caused considerable damage to premises on Gloucester Street. Two German tourists had a very lucky escape as jagged pieces of shrapnel from the bomb passed close by their heads. Kerstin Schrottke and Doerte Jahnk told the Belfast *News Letter*: 'We were just walking down the road and we heard an explosion . . . we saw a bit of dust coming up and then these huge metal pieces flew past us in the air . . . I thought there was more danger from an IRA bomb in London . . . I cannot understand why the IRA bombs its own country. It's unbelievable.' The following morning, another car bomb, outside a bank on the Ormeau Road, caused extensive damage. Belfast centre was being dismantled, brick by brick, business by business. On the same day, there was a lucky escape for an RUC mobile patrol when an IRA ASU fired a rocket-propelled grenade at their armoured vehicle. The gang had held residents and staff hostage in a West Belfast nursing home, before using the roof of the home to fire their missile from. Thankfully it missed but it blasted a massive hole in the roadway.

A few days earlier, the NIO and sources within Sinn Féin issued separate rebuttals to an article in the British *Sunday Times*. Both parties denied a report which claimed that the British government and the Army had drawn up a secret peace strategy towards the end of 1992 involving contacts and eventual talks with the IRA. This followed claims earlier in the month by UUP leader James Molyneaux. The essence of the article was that both warring sides had discussed a 'blueprint for reducing violence' that ran to 60 separate points. The NIO reiterated the British government's position that 'there cannot be talks or negotiations with people who use or threaten violence to advance their arguments'. This was later shown to be misleading, when details of a series of secret talks were revealed in November.

On the 25th, the Red Hand Commando reported via its usual political sources (the UDA), that it would attack bars or hotels where Irish folk music was played. They stated that Irish folk music was part of the 'pan-nationalist front'. It is a moot point, in that songs such 'Fields of Athenry' have been long considered as IRA marching songs, but millions of others, not so immersed in the Troubles or their precursors, see them as little more than pleasant examples of Irish culture. It became the shortest-lived threat in history when, following widespread criticism, they withdrew the threat the following day! On the same day, there was a classic 'red rag to a bull' moment when NIO Minister Sir John Wheeler was interviewed by the BBC and said 'The IRA is already defeated.' A spokesman for Sinn Féin/PIRA issued a statement in reply the following morning. Amongst the usual anti-British rhetoric was the comment: 'We will meet head-on any British persistence with the failed policies of the past.' Over the following four days, they demonstrated that they still had the capability to do so.

On the 27th, a mortar crew attacked the RUC barracks at Lisnaskea in Co. Fermanagh; several rounds landed short, resulting in over 60 nearby homes being damaged in the attack. Later on in the day, one of PIRA's Belfast units planted an explosive device close to Cromac Square, to kill and maim soldiers on foot patrol in the area; injuries were thankfully light. Within 24 hours, the England team managed to penetrate the 'ring of steel' again in the City, by transporting a huge device through the security barriers put in place since the Bishopsgate bombing earlier this same year (*see* Chapter 28). Adequate warnings were given, however, and London police managed to evacuate the area before the bomb squad successfully defused the massive device.

Following the split in the IRA in 1969/70 the Officials (OIRA, sometimes derisively known as the 'Stickies') largely ceased their 'military' campaign, accepting that the more militant Provisionals (PIRA) were stronger, and better equipped. The OIRA later split into another faction, the Irish National Liberation Army (INLA) which then further split. From this division, the Irish People's Liberation Organisation (IPLO) emerged, forming an independent unit. Over the years there was constant animosity between the OIRA and PIRA with occasional violence, although harsh words and contempt were usually as far as things went. However, on 29 August, firing broke out between the two organisations in the Nationalist Markets area of Belfast. Dozens of shots were fired as the war of words for once turned violent. A few 'Stickies' were wounded, but there were no deaths, with the OIRA being forced to retreat once again, in the face of their bitter and much more powerful rivals.

On the 30th, Adair's 'C' company of the UFF was again in murderous action. Their target was a Peruvian Catholic who had lived much of his life in the Belfast area, notably around the Oldpark and Fortwilliam Park. Adair wanted to kill Republicans, but the reality was that any Catholic would do. Maximo de Mogollon had very tenuous links to the Nationalist movement. In 1972 he was working at a garage/petrol station on the Oldpark Road, at a time when it was known to the IRA that an off-duty RUC officer, Raymond Carroll, worked on his car there in his spare time. A murder gang from the Ardoyne parked close by, before simply walking in and shooting the officer dead. There was nothing whatsoever to link Maximo with the killing of the policeman, but despite the lack of evidence and the passage of 21 years, Adair nevertheless instructed 'Top Gun' McKeag to kill him. A gang arrived at the semi-detached home of the family at Fortwilliam Park, McKeag boldly marched up to the front door. He noticed a shape behind a glass window, and fired blindly through the glass, hitting Marie Teresa Dowds de Mogollon (48), mother of four, in the face and neck. She died at the scene as the UFF members escaped back into the Shankill. Lister and Jordan argue that by this stage of the killings, Adair was becoming careless, as indeed was McKeag: for the second attack in a row he had fired blindly into a house, uncaring as to who his bullets struck. The UDA/UFF later apologised for the killing of the innocent woman, although their words were as hollow and insincere as those of the Provisionals, when they made statements of regret about killing the 'wrong' person.

On the final day of the month, the Provisionals made two separate attacks in Belfast. A car bomb planted near a shopping centre in South Belfast devastated several businesses, causing over £1 million worth of damage, but there were no serious injuries. In the afternoon, as soldiers were patrolling through the Ardoyne, an explosive device was thrown at them from behind the cover of a high wall in Etna Drive. It wounded two men, one badly, in the legs; a civilian was also treated for shock.

August had ended – the 25th since the commencement of the Troubles – and three people had died; all three were Catholics, killed in sectarian circumstances, all by Loyalist paramilitaries.

33
September

For the second month running, no soldiers were killed, although four civilians died in sectarian attacks, three at the hands of Loyalists and one – a Catholic contractor who worked for the Army – who was murdered by the Provisional IRA. The Red Hand Commandos executed one of their own towards the middle of the month. The US Ambassador to Ireland visited the North as did another Irish-American politician, Bruce Morrison, prompting a week-long ceasefire by PIRA.

During the Troubles, all members of the military were under constant threat, as were RUC officers, on as well as off-duty. Innocent civilians were in fear of sectarian attack or simply being in the wrong spot at the wrong time. Also under threat were prison officers (POs) although, it had been some time since the last murder of a PO by the IRA. That was to change on the 1st of the month, although the death wouldn't be at the hands of the IRA. Jim Bell (49), a Catholic prison officer, was killed but there was a major question as to whether or not it was simply the politically motivated murder of a PO by a Loyalist, or whether they considered that they were killing another Catholic. Mr Bell lived at Chemical Street in the Catholic Short Strand district, working at Crumlin Road jail. On the day in question, he was helping friends out at the Riada ice cream plant in the Short Strand, close to the UVF base on the Newtownards Road. He was loading ice cream into the back of a van when several UVF gunmen approached him from behind. Without warning, they fired a total of 11 shots into his back, his head and both arms. The gunmen ran off, their escape route taking them past an RUC car with an armed officer sitting inside. He failed to react, stating that he had not heard the gunshots – 11 of them – and was not overly concerned by the sight of several men running past his car.

Mr Bell had only the vaguest of connections with the Republican movement: his late brother, Gerard Bell, had died in 1972 in an IRA 'own goal' explosion. However, the UVF failed to mention this tenuous connection when they admitted killing Mr Bell; it is almost certain that they would have done so as means of justification if they had been aware of it. They did later warn that any POs found to have abused Loyalist prisoners would be placed on a death list, but it is unknown if this was merely a double bluff to cover their tracks. They withdrew the threat on the 10th of this month.

The same day, the Unionist-controlled Belfast City Council, finally reacted to the interference of the newly elected, very proactive Irish President, Mary Robinson, by voting to ban her from entering any council-owned building. This included the City Hall, which back in 1993 proudly flew the Union flag. The next day, a PIRA bombing team exploded a 1,000 lb (450 kg) device in the centre of the town of Armagh, which killed no one but caused considerable damage to the mainly Protestant-owned businesses in the area, against whom it was targeted.

On Saturday 4th, Sinn Féin/PIRA announced a suspension of 'military' attacks for a period of seven days until the following Saturday. It was a very cynical and self-serving move on their part, in order to impress a visiting party of Irish-Americans on a fact-finding mission to Northern Ireland and the Irish Republic. The group was led by former United States Democratic congressman Bruce Morrison. The group spent time with Sinn Féin over a three-day period, both in Belfast and in Dublin. Whilst in In Belfast, they were also received by Loyalist figure Gusty Spence, David Ervine of the Progressive Unionist Party and Gary Mitchell of the Ulster Defence Association. The Irish-American delegation believed that Sinn Féin's inclusion in the peace process was essential to bring about an end to violence. This was the second temporary ceasefire during 1993; the first in May had coincided with the visit of the then co-chairman of the Irish group, a former mayor of Boston. However, according to Republican sources, this fizzled out when his expected meeting with Sinn Féin/PIRA failed to take place. It should be pointed out that Morrison was anything but neutral, coming with a clear agenda: the reunification of Ireland. During his time in office, in the USA, he put together the Morrison Visa programme which allowed 40,000 permanent residence visas for people from the Irish Republic. Together with the publisher of *The Irish Voice*, Niall O'Dowd, Morrison acted as a key intermediary between Gerry Adams, the White House, and the Irish government led by Albert Reynolds. Along with Bill Lenahan of the Irish American Labor Coalition these men were crucial in paving the way for Adams's controversial entry into the USA in February 1994.

During this somewhat artificial ceasefire, executed to prevent a public relations disaster – irreparable harm would be done to the IRA's public image if an Irish-American visitor stumbled into the path of one of their car bombs – the UFF and the Red Hand Commandos launched a five-day period of attacks in which they killed three separate Catholics on purely sectarian grounds. On the 7th, Adair dispatched another murder gang that included 'Top Gun' McKeag and another man whom Lister and Jordan refer to only as 'Pete' to a hairdresser's on the corner of the Falls Road and Donegall Road. Their target was apparently Frankie 'Studs' Lanigan, a leading INLA gunman who ran another hairdresser's in West Belfast. Just before 16:00, McKeag and another gunman walked into the wrong salon and calmly shot Sean Hughes (40), father of three, as he stood with his back to them. Mr Hughes fell to the floor, face down, unmoving. McKeag stood over him, pausing for a second or two, before quickly firing six more rounds into his helpless body with an automatic weapon. The innocent hairdresser died very quickly afterwards. The clearly psychopathic McKeag fired a further shot at one of the female members of staff, who ducked down for cover behind the shop counter. 'Pete' ran outside, into what had now become a fairly crowded street, and dived into the car, but McKeag simply sauntered after him, holding the gun high above his head, grabbing a terrified woman. Whilst the gang were urging him to hurry, he sang in what was described as a 'maniacal voice' the first few lines of 'Follow the Yellow Brick Road' to the by now hysterical woman. The killers eventually raced away in the direction of the Shankill, leaving chaos and terror in their wake. The RUC estimated that McKeag personally killed 12 innocent Catholics, but many of his paramilitary associates suggest that the figure was much much higher.[1] A figure in excess of 20 has been mentioned in some quarters.

The world didn't have to wait long for further evidence of McKeag's obsessional sectarian hatred, less than 24 hours in fact. Michael Edwards (39), a father of six, who lived at Finaghy Park Central, owned a newsagent's on Glen Road in the Andersonstown area. Just three weeks earlier, two UFF men had gone into his shop to ask for a copy of *An Phoblacht* but the newsagent truthfully told them that he didn't stock it. That didn't prevent a visit to his home on 8 September. A little after midnight, a four-man UFF team arrived at Mr Edwards's house, which he shared with his wife, Marie; the gang entered silently, making their way upstairs to the couple's bedroom. Without saying a word, McKeag fired two shots at the sleeping man, hitting him once in the stomach, missing with the other. The gang left the house, speeding off in their stolen car. Despite her shock, Mrs Edwards managed to summon an ambulance for her badly wounded husband. He was rushed to the nearby Musgrave Park Hospital, where, surrounded by his family, he fought for his life. Sadly, his condition deteriorated and he died soon afterwards, with Marie and his children keeping vigil. Stephen 'Top Gun' McKeag, 'Stevie' to his mates, had killed two innocents in the space of 24 hours and left nine more children fatherless.

The *Sunday Herald* wrote:

> The new hardline leaders of loyalist terror groups have left many people in Northern Ireland walking and sleeping in fear, a leading churchman said yesterday. The loyalist killers aped the organisation, activities, and methods of the IRA, and aped them very successfully, said Roman Catholic Primate Cardinal Cahal Daly. The Ulster Freedom Fighters and Ulster Volunteer Force have committed four murders in five days and more than 20 murders this year. Cardinal Daly said they were 'under a new kind of leadership which is much more hardline, much more ruthless and, alas, much better organised and better equipped'. He added: 'The new escalation of loyalist violence, the new signs of their "professionalism" are highly disturbing. I know that many people are walking and sleeping in fear.' Catholics, especially those living alone in predominantly Protestant areas, were particularly fearful of being targeted over the weekend. Some stocked up with food and drink yesterday and prepared to batten down the hatches and not emerge until next week. But the loyalist killers have struck in private homes three times this week. Their latest victim was West Belfast newsagent Michael Edwards, shot dead in his home in the south of the city in the early hours. UFF gunmen smashed down his front door, ran upstairs, and shot him a number of times as he slept alongside his wife Marie. Mr Edwards, 39, had six children who rushed to the room after the gunmen fled, crying 'Daddy don't die, daddy don't die.'

Five days later, US Ambassador to Ireland Jean Kennedy Smith began a week-long fact-finding visit to Northern Ireland, acting as the eyes and ears of President Clinton. The new US President was seemingly forging links with Prime Minister John Major, although, judging by the evidence of television and newsreels, the relationship appeared forced and lacklustre, certainly on the President's part. It would be four more years, and the election

1. McDonald & Cusack, *UDA: Inside the Heart of Loyalist Terror*, *passim*.

of a Labour government under Tony Blair, before the 42nd US President formed a close friendship with a British PM, the first since the Thatcher–Regan days.

'Bollards!'
Mark Ormston, Royal Artillery

We were based at R16, at Cloughoge, whose predecessor had been blown up by a modified van full of explosives being rolled down the main Belfast to Dublin railway line before being detonated (see Chapter 17). The replacement was a fairly modern PVCP and among the defensive features designed to prevent a vehicle-borne IED getting into the base were some very substantial hydraulic steel bollards which were recessed into the road when the search bay was in use, and raised when not to prevent a vehicle driving in; they could also be raised instantly in an emergency.

We had two incidents involving them during our tour; one funny the other not. The funny one involved some RUC officers in a brand new armoured Ford Sierra Cosworth, who had been visiting the base for some reason and when they came to leave the driver decided to show off and hammer down the access road onto the Forkhill Road. However, in his haste, he decided to drive over the bollards while they were still lowering. Of course, he misjudged it and they were still too high for the vehicle to clear; result one written off brand new Ford Sierra Cosworth and some very embarrassed RUC officers. The other incident involved a coach from Southern Ireland carrying a hurley team and supporters travelling north for a game, when the brakes failed; the driver saw the A1 search bay and tried to take his bus off the main road and onto the search bay slip road. Unfortunately for him, the bollards did their job and the coach, minus its axles and wheels came to rest just outside the search bay! We rushed down the hillside covered walkway to assist casualties and call for ambulances etc. After the incident we thought we had done a good job, however in the Republican press the following day there were claims – fabricated, of course – of how we had refused first aid and refused to call ambulances etc. Bloody typical!

On the 13th, there was some 'in-house cleaning' by the Red Hand Commandos as they executed one of their own. Vernon Baillie (49), whose girlfriend was pregnant at the time of his death, had been a Loyalist paramilitary for a number of years, having served at least one jail sentence for crimes committed on their behalf. The Loyalists claimed at the time that he had been executed for 'touting' but of this they produced no evidence. It was further suggested that the killing was as a result of an internal drugs deal gone wrong. Whatever the reason, it meant that another child would be born into Northern Ireland society never having known its father. Mr Baillie lived in the Carrowdore area, on the Ards Peninsula, around seven miles from Newtownards. He had just arrived home when he was approached by several men, one of whom was armed with a 9 mm Browning; some words were spoken before one of the men shot him nine times; he died very quickly afterwards outside his front door, in a pool of his own blood.

UPI reported: 'Two gunmen ambushed and killed a man late Monday who had recently been released from prison after serving a sentence for extortion connected to Protestant paramilitary groups, the Royal Ulster Constabulary said Tuesday. Vernon Baillie, 49, was shot at point blank range by two gunmen who ambushed him on the doorstep of his Carrowdore home in County Down, 20 miles (32 km) southeast of Belfast, shortly before midnight Monday. Police said Baillie had recently ended a lengthy prison sentence for organised extortion by Protestant paramilitary groups. One police source said Baillie had been responsible for terrorising businessmen and organising rackets for the Ulster Defence Association, an outlawed Protestant paramilitary group, for more than 10 years. Police said they did not believe the killing, the sixth in two weeks, was sectarian, and may be linked to Baillie's association with extortion.'

On the 16th, SDLP leader John Hume travelled to Downing Street for a further meeting with the Prime Minister. Following the meeting, the Ulster man stated that he did not 'give two balls of roasted snow' for those who criticised his continuing talks with Gerry Adams, and the IRA. As if that was not sufficient hot air for Major, the next day, UUP leader Ian Paisley arrived in Downing Street for talks also. Little of any significance came from either meeting, but Paisley had a not entirely unexpected sound-bite for the press, when he condemned Hume as 'the voice of pan-Nationalism'. Added to this dizzying round of meetings, representatives from the SDLP held a meeting with Michael Ancram at the NIO, to discuss the possibility of future political talks; meetings about meetings as the satirists of the time were quick to point out. The Campaign for Labour Representation in Northern Ireland (CLRNI), which was established in 1977 to try to persuade the British Labour Party to stand for elections in Northern Ireland, was dissolved without achieving its central aim.

On the 16th, the IRA's England team brought further proof to the residents of London that they could export their brand of terror to the capital, seemingly at will. They planted two incendiary devices in the Curzon Phoenix Cinema in Charing Cross Road – I had seen a film there only five days previously – but both fortunately malfunctioned. Later the same day, another incendiary device was planted in the MGM Cinema at Shaftesbury Avenue; it too malfunctioned, without significant damage. The chilling words of the IRA after the Brighton bombing would haunt Londoners for many years: 'Today we were unlucky, but remember we only have to be lucky once. You have to be lucky always.'

Back in Northern Ireland, the IRA did what they were very good at: murdering innocent and defenceless civilians. Adrian McGovern (34), father of four, lived in Lisburn, the town chosen by the British Army as HQNI. Mr McGovern was a building contractor who had done some work in the rebuilding of several RUC stations which had been damaged in PIRA attacks. In the early evening of the 16th, whilst he was putting his young children to bed, he noticed a lorry pull up outside. He would have been immediately cautious, but, having recognised it as a friend's vehicle, he went downstairs to let him in. Unknown to him, a PIRA team had hijacked the lorry, knowing that he would be lulled into a false sense of security by the sight of a familiar vehicle. Mr McGovern was looking after his four children, the eldest being just eight, whilst his pregnant wife was visiting relatives. When he opened the door, waiting gunmen opened fire on him, hitting him in the head, torso and upper leg. The gang raced off in a second stolen vehicle as neighbours, alerted by the shooting, rushed to help. The children, all pyjama-clad were crying over the body of their dying father; the eldest boy, Tony, had telephoned 999; Mr McGovern died at the scene.

The Belfast *News Letter* wrote: 'Two youngsters played in the garden of their home yesterday – the latest child victims of the violence which blights Ulster. Around them, police officers continued the hunt for the clues for the killer gang which murdered their father, Adrian McGovern, as his four kids huddled indoors. Yesterday the haulier's youngest children blotted from their minds the true horror . . . Neighbour Eleanor Calvert said: "Their little eyes pierced my heart. They were all alone for those minutes. It will be many a long night and day before that episode will go out of their minds."'

Mrs Calvert's words sum up the absolute moral bankruptcy of Irish Republicanism. She speaks of the children screaming that their daddy had been shot, and of their confusion and despair. It is the images of those pyjama-clad children, kneeling over their dying father who has been cut down, not because he was a murderer himself, or a robber, or a paedophile or any sort of criminal. He was shot only because he had commercial dealings with the legitimate security forces of his country. The philosophy of PIRA/Sinn Féin is so devoid of decency, compassion and humanity that it is difficult to understand Irish-American support, why the top echelon of the Labour Party gave their moral backing and why a newly arrived Irish emigrant to Australia could describe the IRA as her heroes. IRA killers can sing songs about their 'martyred dead' with such emotion and compassion, yet can shoot a man dead in front of his young children with utter ruthlessness.

Associated Press reported:

> The IRA has claimed responsibility for killing a Roman Catholic trucker, saying he supplied building materials to the police and army. Sean Adrian McGovern, 34, was gunned down when he answered a knock at the door of his home near the village of Stoneyford, 7 miles west of Belfast, a police spokesman said. Police said the gunmen approached the house in a hijacked truck after dark Wednesday and apparently presented themselves to McGovern as truckers. Then they shot him several times at close range and sped off in a stolen car, which was later found burned out in the outskirts of West Belfast. The outlawed Irish Republican Army said in a statement to Belfast media Thursday that McGovern was killed because he delivered supplies to police and military barracks. The IRA, waging a 23-year campaign against British rule in Northern Ireland, has frequently killed civilians with business links to the security forces. In January 1992 the paramilitary group blew up a work van after it left an army base, killing eight Protestant construction workers.

Over the course of the Troubles, several leading Labour Party MPs – notably Jeremy Corbyn and Ken Livingstone – have invited alleged terrorists to visit the House of Commons. Now may I invite the reader to imagine a scenario in which members of the 1939–45 British parliament could have invited Luftwaffe commanders to survey the damage which their Heinkels and Dorniers had wreaked upon the East End; would that not have been an act of treason? If treason means giving succour and support to the enemy, should we not interpret as treason the conduct of hard-left Labour MPs in inviting alleged terrorists to London in the 80s and 90s?

On the 18th the RUC issued a statement in reply to Sinn Féin claims that members of the IRA's political wing had been refused licences to carry firearms for personal protection. The

RUC denied that there was any such policy, pointing out that five Sinn Féin councillors had been issued with firearms certificates. Three days later, several UFF teams placed explosive devices at the homes of four SDLP members in order to 'send their message of disapproval' over their party's recent talks with the IRA. Leading UUP MP David Trimble criticised the Hume–Adams Initiative as 'misconceived and bound to fail'. Shortly afterwards, Hume and Adams stated that they had sent a joint message to the Irish government, aimed at the creation of a peace process; the full text has never been published. Shortly afterwards, the talks were suspended whilst a report from them was being considered by the British and Irish governments. A report in the *Irish Times* claimed that the Hume–Adams Initiative required the British government to state that it had no long-term interest in Northern Ireland and that it would use its influence to persuade Unionists that their best interests lay in a united Ireland. Whilst this has never been substantiated, it is likely that the report was reasonably accurate.

Later in the month, in an effort both to allay Loyalist fears and to answer the likely essence of the Hume–Adams proposals, Secretary of State for Northern Ireland Patrick Mayhew asserted the right of 'self-determination of the people living in Northern Ireland'. He also stated that Sinn Féin would only be welcomed at peace talks when it could prove definitively that the IRA had ended the violence for real.

On Thursday 23rd, there was a major gun battle on the Newry Road, just east of Crossmaglen in South Armagh between the Army – possibly a unit from the DERR – and a large PIRA unit firing from lorries fitted with improvised armour. The ASU was attempting to destroy three British helicopters as they were lifting off from Crossmaglen RUC station, opening fire with at least one .50-calibre heavy machine gun. Several hundred rounds were exchanged, before the IRA unit was forced to flee in their vehicles over the nearby border; many of their weapons were abandoned, demonstrating either a panicked flight or just a glut of weapons available to them, making the loss less significant than once would have been the case.

The battle commenced at around 14:00, when the IRA's South Armagh brigade, placed five lorries around the RUC base, and close to St Patrick's Church. According to Toby Harnden, their primary targets were an RAF Puma carrying troops out on patrol and two British Army Lynx escorts. They opened fire with two Russian-manufactured DShK heavy machine guns as well as two or three LMGs. According to later statements from the IRA, several of their weapons jammed and they were forced to withdraw after some initial success, having hit the Puma with almost the first round they fired. They also hit the two other helicopters from weapons located near the Community Centre. Two of the lorries and a smaller vehicle raced away along the Newry Road, chased over a 12-mile route by the helicopters, during which there was a continuing and fierce exchange of gunfire, with the British aircraft firing several thousand rounds. As the chase continued one lorry turned into a farm and the smaller vehicle disappeared from view.

The fortunes of war then played their hand, with fate decreeing that the terrorists would escape; one of the Lynxes had the lorry smack in their sights but the machine gun jammed. Just moments later, as the second Lynx came in to destroy the PIRA vehicle, the first Lynx flew straight into their line of fire. The IRA gang abandoned the vehicle and fled across the border in a stolen Transit van. The engagement was assessed by the British Army as the most intense gun battle ever in South Armagh. Security forces personnel later recovered a DShK, two light machine guns and an AK-47. On 26 April 1994, Staff Sergeant Shaun Wyatt, commander of Lynx 2, was awarded the DFC for his courage during the battle. Damage to Army property was light, and no lives were lost. I recommend Toby Harnden's excellent *Bandit Country* for more in-depth details.

On the 28th, a PIRA bombing unit from the Falls Road area planted a large bomb close to a shopping centre at Boucher Crescent, a retail area sandwiched between the Falls Road and Lisburn Road. Immediately adjacent was Gulliver's Kingdom where children played on innocently, unaware of the drama and potential death which uncaring terrorists from their own community had planned for the area in which they frolicked. The children were from the Nationalist Turf Lodge, members of the Holy Trinity Club. They were Catholics, just like the bombers who set off to kill and maim their enemies in continuance of their so-called 'economic warfare'.

The following day, the *Belfast Star*'s headline was 'Shamed: Kids caught in bombers' shops terror'. Alongside a photo of terrified children, Joe Gorrod wrote:

> These are the innocent terrified victims of the IRA – photographed as a bomb turned their play area into an arena of fear. Their youth club's night out became a terror target when Provo bombers blew up a block of shops next to the Gulliver's Kingdom adventure centre where 124 children were playing. Troops and police were desperately trying to clear the area when the blast swept through the pleasure dome's bouncy castles and whirly-gig slides, shuddering walls decorated with giant cartoon characters. The only warning they got was a soldier who burst through the door screaming: 'Hit the deck!' Some children were still in their socks when they were led to the sanctuary of a nearby newspaper office. Mark McGarrity, 10, said: 'There was a bang and I was blown up. Everybody started screaming, so I knew that I wasn't dead.' Office worker, Marian Henderson added: 'It was heart-breaking to see the horror on the youngster's faces. One girl couldn't stop screaming at all no matter how close we cuddled her.' Youth club leader, Jim Valente said: 'There was a flash of light and the whole place shook. It was the younger ones who came off worse.' The day after, Turf Lodge Headmistress Mary Muldoon angrily denounced the bombers: 'It was despicable; it will scar their young lives forever.'

There were fortunately no deaths or injuries, thanks to the bravery of a Royal Artillery soldier who writes below.

The IRA Didn't Care
Ron Gwyer, Royal Artillery

At the time, I was a young gunner and part of the first brick to respond to a bomb warning in Boucher Crescent Retail Park, in Belfast. We set up cordons around the area of the suspected car bomb and waited for Felix to turn up and sort it out. However, with just minutes before the telephoned warning from the IRA had announced that it was due to explode, I saw a man inside the cordoned off area. I ran over and told him to 'Fuck off; quickly!' but as I did so, I noticed a light on in one of the nearby industrial units, inside the cordoned-off area, in a direct line of sight of the bomb. I went inside and found dozens of children playing in a kiddies' activity centre; the type of place that had slides going into plastic ball pits etc.

They were very close to the bomb and hadn't a clue what was going on, and as I was the Brick's driver/gunner, I had no comms, so couldn't radio for back-up. As the bomb was only seconds away from detonating, I just quickly gathered all the kids and adults together and explained what was happening to the grown-ups. However, they went into panic mode and were no use at all. I made the children gather in the far corner of the room and then made them all lie flat. Just as I did that, Boom! the bomb went off. It seemed like every child in the building tried to climb up my body, seeking comfort. Fortunately nobody was hurt. It had damaged the back wall of the building and all the ceiling tiles were falling into the room on top of us, but apart from that everyone was unhurt, although they were all screaming hysterically.

The next thing I knew, an RUC policewoman runs into the building and tells me that there is a secondary outside the front door and then she runs off again and leaves me to it. I couldn't stay in the building because the second bomb would wipe us out, so I organised the adults amongst the children and started to evacuate the building. They could see where to go, because of all the blue flashing lights and lots of TV crews watching from outside; I was last man in the building. I remembered that all the children had gone out bare foot, as being in an activity centre they had to remove their shoes to play, and so I upturned a dustbin and filled it with their shoes. It was a wet and cold September night, and I couldn't leave the young ones in bare foot. I had to hurry, because the secondary device was only some 30 feet away from me.

What really pissed me off was the policewoman was given 12 weeks off on the sick for this incident, yet I barely saw her. Also the children sent her flowers and chocolates for her help, but I received nothing as I was still serving in the Province; when I went to see the doctor after the event, he gave me two hours' rest time for shock. It hardly seemed fair when she got 12 weeks and my two hours was ruined by other soldiers coming in with bits of corrugated steel in their webbing pretending to be hit taking the piss out of me. It also turned out that the secondary was a hoax, as Felix blew it up in order to confirm and the explosion set the children off screaming again! The next day, the paper reported that I shouted: 'Hit the deck!' Just for the record, that is bollocks! I didn't shout that.

September ended with the deaths of five people; three Catholics were murdered in sectarian attacks, another was killed by the IRA for assisting the RUC and the Loyalists killed one of their own in an internal squabble. The last three months had been quiet with 'only' nine deaths, but it remained to be seen if October would follow that pattern.

34

October

Bloody October. The Troubles were by now in their 291st month; was there any more which could sicken the decent, the impartial, or the neutral? After countless and endless atrocities could anything else seriously outrage us? As Britain moved into its cold autumn season, the Provisional IRA clearly had something up their sleeves which would raise the stakes substantially. The UFF and UVF would also up the ante as they retaliated with another outrage in response. Attacks on a fish shop in Belfast and a pub in Greysteel, Co. Londonderry, would leave 18 dead, in a seven-day period of violence. Two entirely different places of commerce would soon resemble slaughterhouses; more blood and more broken glass. A staggering 29 people died this month, and whilst there were no military deaths, a former UDR soldier was killed by the UFF. It was the highest death toll for any month since 1976.

The month was only a few days old when the IRA's England team struck at the heart of what is sometimes called 'London's poshland'. Hampstead is where many wealthy people and celebrities live. Now the IRA began by planting five bombs in the area; three exploded, injuring six people and damaging several shops and flats. Two days later, more bombs injured four more people in the same area.

On the 5th, there was an incredible escape for the crew of an RUC armoured vehicle as it passed along Fanad Drive in Londonderry's Creggan estate. A PIRA unit containing Christopher Paul O'Kane – later jailed for 10 years for his part in this crime and others[1] – fired a horizontal mortar bomb at their vehicle. The team had taken up position with a clear view of Fanad Drive, setting up what they christened their 'doodlebug' mortar. Instead of detonating on impact and probably killing all the officers, the missile ricocheted away into the nearby residents' gardens. That no one was hurt was pure luck on the part of these terrorists, who clearly had no consideration for the innocent civilians in very close proximity. Given the very short distance between the target and Holy Child Primary School as well as a nearby sports field, it is very difficult to accept that the IRA were confident that the operation was entirely risk-free; did the late PIRA commander Martin McGuinness have any comment to make at the time in relation to this irresponsible action?.

The first death of the month occurred on the same day; a UFF unit containing at least one man from the Derriaghy area of Lisburn as well as others from Belfast attempted a mass murder at the Catholic-frequented Derby Bar on Stewartstown Road in the Poleglass estate. The murder team had only a two-mile drive to the pub, which had already been the subject

1. http://www.belfasttelegraph.co.uk/news/northern-ireland/derry-man-handed-10year-jail-sentence-for-ira-terrorist-offences-34304971.html.

of several reconnaissance trips. They were aware that it had no security staff, and timed the attack for just on closing time when there would be maximum noise and maximum confusion as drinkers downed the final dregs of the evening before rushing home as quickly as possible. These were, after all, dangerous times and sectarian killers were on the prowl, seemingly on a nightly basis. For one of the drinkers, Jason McFarlane (20), father of a small baby, it was to be his last night on this earth, cut down by violent sectarian psychopaths; another child would be left to grow up without a father, another widow without a man. Mr McFarlane had only gone to the bar that night in order to celebrate his engagement to the mother of his small child.

It was a cold, grey October night at around 22:30 when the UFF murder team dashed into the pub, armed with two pistols and a shotgun, immediately opening fire into the mass of people around the bar or playing pool. Mr McFarlane was hit almost immediately, dropping to the floor fatally injured, whilst several others were wounded as they tried to escape the insanity of that moment. Fortunately one of the handguns jammed; almost immediately, so did the shotgun. Leaving behind a metallic stench of blood, the smell of cordite and shards of broken beer glasses littering the floor, the murder team made good their escape. They abandoned their stolen car at Milltown Village before driving in a second vehicle towards the Lisburn area. Mr McFarlane was rushed to the RVH, where he died in the early hours of the morning. The UFF claimed the killing, and in a sickening comment that could have been taken straight from PIRA's handbook attempted to justify the attempted massacre, blaming the ongoing Hume–Adams talks for their murderous actions, citing an IRA statement that had welcomed the dialogue.

Two days later John Hume travelled to Dublin to meet Albert Reynolds and Dick Spring, to give them a report on the meetings he had held with Gerry Adams. Adams was also in Dublin and said that a declaration by the British government on the right of Irish self-determination would lead to an end of the campaign of violence by the IRA. Another interpretation of his remarks could be: 'Talk to us or we will continue bombing and shooting security forces and innocent civilians and even people who have dared to have a business relationship with the legitimate police force of the country.'

On the 8th, during the annual Conservative Party Conference in Blackpool, John Major delivered a vibrant speech stating that he had heard lots of statements from the IRA, but the only message he wanted from them was one indicating that the organisation was finished with its campaign of violence for good. I remember saying at the time that such an expectation was highly optimistic. At a fringe meeting at the same conference, UUP leader James Molyneaux opined that the Hume–Adams Initiative had wrecked any prospect of future inter-party talks. DUP leader Ian Paisley wrote a letter to Major in which he claimed that the Hume–Adams Initiative was 'aimed at Ulster's destruction'. Taoiseach Albert Reynolds, speaking at the same time, offered a small olive branch to Loyalists when he said that, if there was an overall political settlement, then Articles 2 and 3 of the Irish Constitution could be changed by a referendum.

Between the 8th and 14th, UFF gunmen made two separate machine-gun attacks on taxis known to be carrying Catholic passengers. In the first, a unit thought to include McKeag opened fire on a black cab on the Falls Road, wounding all six occupants; thankfully all of the wounded survived after being rushed to the nearby RVH. Later, the same unit opened fire on another taxi, this time on the Oldpark Road; fortunately for the passengers, the automatic weapon jammed, and no one was hurt. The sheer wanton rampage of the killing sprees, particularly by Adair's 'C' unit and mainly by McKeag himself, was beginning to unsettle the UDA godfathers. Indeed, more than one Troubles' author hints at comments and complaints from senior men being made to Adair. However, on the evidence of the continued killings, he took little notice. On the 14th, a third taxi was shot up by the UFF, slightly wounding a Catholic woman. On the same evening, in search of a 'Republican', the same unit fired shots blindly into a house at Mountpottinger in East Belfast.

On the 9th, a PIRA team mortared a British Army base in Kilkeel, Co. Down, using a 12-tube Mark 15 multiple mortar; not all the rounds exploded, and injuries were very light. It did, however, demonstrate the ease with which the IRA could launch attacks in remote areas, and how little defence soldiers had in those rural areas against such attacks. On the same day, the increasing number of sectarian murders carried out in recent months by the UFF, the UVF and the Red Hand Commando forced several Protestant leaders to comment publicly about the insane bloodbath which was destroying the local communities.

Church of Ireland Primate Robin Eames was the first to speak out, condemning the UFF threat to the Catholic community, noting that ten Catholic civilians had been killed since 8 August, by both the UFF and the UVF. Within 24 hours, a leading UUP MP, John Taylor, called on Loyalist paramilitaries to end their campaign of violence. Two weeks after those Protestant leaders made their impassioned pleas on anti-Catholic violence, Protestants would also be slaughtered in a fishmonger's on the Shankill Road.

At the same time as the churchmen were expressing their fears and concerns, UUP MP and Grand Master of the Orange Lodge Martin Smyth gave an interview to the BBC in which he stated that Sinn Féin might be included in talks on Northern Ireland's future within the UK: 'if they ended their support for the Irish Republican Army'. He was criticised by some of his fellow UUP members and other Unionists for his comments. The Irish *Sunday Independent* published the results of an opinion poll held in the Republic, which showed that, of those questioned, 72% supported the underlying principles behind the Hume–Adams Initiative. On the same day, in Dublin, Albert Reynolds met the recently elected President of South Africa, Nelson Mandela, who was on a state visit to several European countries; Mandela gave his endorsement to the Hume–Adams Initiative.

There were more incendiary devices planted in businesses in central Belfast and in Lisburn on the 11th, which caused considerable damage and continued the financial agony for the mainly Protestant-owned companies, each attempting to remain solvent throughout the worst excesses of the IRA's 'economic campaign'. An IRA attack a few days later also caused blast damage at the Court House in Cookstown in Co. Tyrone.

In January 1992, a PIRA landmine placed at Teebane Crossroads close to Omagh had killed eight workmen. The massacre was yet another low point in the IRA's vicious campaign. Loyalists, however, were eager and more than willing to emulate them, and they too targeted innocent workmen. On the 12th, the UVF tried to kill a van-load of mainly Catholic workers as they travelled in a company-owned vehicle to Shorts Aircraft in Belfast. The UVF gang, armed with automatic weapons, and dressed in blue boiler suits, had followed the Shorts van along Sydenham Road, close to Harland & Wolff and what is now the Titanic Experience. As the two vehicles stopped at traffic lights, several masked men jumped out of the UVF car, immediately opening fire on the helpless men inside the van. Five were hit; one of them, Joseph Reynolds (40), a Catholic father of five from Andersonstown, was killed instantly. The UVF gang abandoned their vehicle and escaped across nearby railway lines in the direction of the Loyalist Newtownards Road. Later, in a gesture of solidarity, workers at the Shorts factory – thousands of Protestants as well as Catholics – staged a temporary walk-out to protest at the Loyalist attack and also to pay tribute to their slain workmate. Men of both denominations from the affected factory, and also Harland & Wolff, made the short walk from their respective workplaces to the scene of the shooting.

In the Irish parliament, Albert Reynolds declined opposition requests for a debate on Northern Ireland, stating that the matter was at a delicate stage, no doubt holding out some hope at this point of something tangible coming out of the Hume–Adams talks. Adams himself stated that peace in Northern Ireland would come about as a result of 'total demilitarisation, but [demilitarisation] was not a prerequisite for a peace process'.

The month was half-way through when Paddy McMahon (23), father of a small child, became the third person to die. Mr McMahon was a Catholic from Spamount Street in the New Lodge and, together with his girlfriend and baby, had just arrived at a friend's house in Newington Avenue, a short four-minute drive away; it was approximately 19:30. Unfortunately for them, waiting just across the street in a derelict house was 'Top Gun' McKeag. As the young family got out of their car, McKeag stepped into the street, immediately firing a hail of shots at them. Mr McMahon was hit several times, falling to the ground, as his partner bravely threw herself on top of her child, using her body to protect the infant from McKeag's bullets. Leaving the dying man and the distraught woman, 'Stevie' ran along an alley and climbed down a drainpipe before running the short distance to the Loyalist Tiger's Bay area, where he was guaranteed any number of safe houses. Mr McMahon, a promising boxer, died at the scene.

Much about the attack remains a mystery: was this was a planned operation, sanctioned by Adair – if so, why was there no back-up? Was it a lone, freelance and unauthorised attack by McKeag? Even if it was not agreed by Adair, he would surely have congratulated McKeag on the death of another Catholic. I asked a leading Belfast journalist for his opinion, in relation to the targeting or otherwise of the young Catholic. He told me: 'I don't know; McKeag was Adair's robot. Highly unlikely he would do it on his own. But the whole neighbourhood is Catholic, so it might have just been McKeag hanging around for an opportunity.' Another top writer and an expert on the UDA told me: 'Why "Top Gun" was there, on his own, has always been a mystery to me too. He most certainly had psychopathic tendencies, and he did take a lot of risks, but why would he have gone into a Nationalist area, alone and just on the off-chance that he would be able to shoot Paddy McMahon: seems a bit risky and with no guaranteed outcome. Even if it was to shoot ANY Catholic who walked into his gunsights, well even that was taking an enormous risk as well!'

An IRA murder gang targeted a man whom they thought was an off-duty RUC officer at his home in Dunmurry on the same evening; this man's name has never been made public. Several men barged their way past the man's elderly mother and restrained her as they awaited his return from work. As he walked in, the gunmen shot him several times in the chest before escaping from the house, leaving the badly wounded man and his hysterical mother; he survived the attack. Earlier that day, the Equal Opportunities Unit of the NIO reported that Catholics were fairly represented in most levels of the Northern Ireland Civil Service, the exception being in those posts at a senior level. This was further indication that the civil rights grievances which Republicans claim lent moral weight to their campaign of violence had been resolved.

On the 18th, a PIRA bombing team exploded a device close to shops and homes in Castlederg, leading indirectly to the death of an elderly civilian. Annie Bogle (74) lived in the Derg Fold retirement home in Castlederg. The town itself is a hotbed of Nationalism, there is a PIRA memorial and there is still much bitterness and hatred held in the hearts of the Catholic population, which I have personally witnessed as recently as 2016.

On that fateful evening, the local PIRA unit planted a 15 lb (7 kg) bomb outside a Chinese restaurant, just a few yards away from Derg Fold on Lower Strabane Road. The RUC had received information about the device and were in the process of evacuating the area, when it exploded at 21:35. Mrs Bogle collapsed just over two hours later and died despite the best efforts of medical staff to save her. Canon Walter Gill of the Church of Ireland said: 'She was dead in a very short space of time. I'm not a doctor but I am convinced that there is a definite link between the explosion and Mrs Bogle's death.' Her son was a UDR soldier – William Bogle – shot dead by the IRA in 1972 as he waited in his car with his three small children, outside shops in Killeter, Co. Tyrone.

Earlier in the month, the IRA had issued threats against the staff of five named firms which were undertaking building work on behalf of the security forces. Now they targeted John Gibson (51), father of a university student, on the 21st. He was a director of Henry Brothers, a construction and civil engineering company in Co. Antrim. His company had previously lost three other employees to IRA bullets and one in a mortar attack on a base, murdered simply because their company did work for the SF. Mr Gibson lived in Carnvue Road, Newtownabbey, north of Belfast. At around 20:00, shortly after he arrived home and drove down his driveway and got out of his car, two men ambushed him, coming out from behind his garage to shoot him three times, without warning, in his back; he died shortly afterwards, another victim of sectarianism, as senseless and pointless and as illogical and unjustified as any Loyalist killing. There can be, and should not be, any distinction between the sectarianism of either set of paramilitaries.

John Gibson was highly regarded for his charity work, notably for the diabetic community in NI and beyond. At his interment at Drumcoo Cemetery, Dungannon, children with diabetes from the surrounding area, who had benefited from Diabetic Holidays which John had run, placed flowers on his coffin as it was lowered into the grave.

A Belfast man called Robert Duffy was convicted of Mr Gibson's murder but was freed on appeal four years later. He was subsequently sentenced to life for attempting to murder Colin O'Neill in the Emerald Bar in Dundalk in March 2007. There was further turmoil brought on by Duffy's alleged role in the 1993 murder, when a family relative, Brian Duffy was shot dead, apparently in retaliation, by the UFF on 5 December this year (*see* Chapter 36).[1]

1. http://www.belfasttelegraph.co.uk/sunday-life/news/video-nasty-28407636.html.

Whenever the loved ones of those who died in Ulster during this turbulent period agree to write for me, I am always, without exception, deeply honoured. I am indebted to the following contributor, John Gibson's son, who agreed to put his emotions into writing.

My Dad
Peter Gibson

I will remember until the day I die, the evening when a young PC and WPC called at my mother's door to inform us my father had been shot dead. Also, a couple of days later, I had to attend Forster Green Hospital, to identify my father's body. I still see the look of shock and horror on his face. Since his murder, I have been let down repeatedly, time and again, by the so-called forces of law and order. The system is so tilted in the direction of perpetrators, rather than victims, that the United Kingdom is becoming a world-wide joke, showing that violence and terrorism ultimately pays, and wins.

On the 19th, James Molyneaux was back in London to meet John Major in Downing Street, where he repeated the Northern Irish government's opposition to the Hume–Adams Initiative. Major had previously told the House of Commons that he 'knew nothing' of the details of the Hume-Adams Initiative. Home Secretary Michael Howard signed an 'exclusion order' which banned Gerry Adams from entering mainland Britain. Adams had been invited by left-wing Labour MP Tony Benn to address a meeting at Westminster. On the topic of the much-vaunted Hume–Adams Initiative, John Alderdice of Northern Ireland's Alliance party said that it had cast a shadow over efforts to get political talks re-started. Somewhat immodestly, Hume told the House of Commons that he thought his talks with Adams were the best chance of achieving peace that he had seen in 20 years. This was only 24 hours away from the name of Frizzell's being on the front pages of the world's media, for all the wrong reasons.

Frizzell's Bombing

Ulster, by now in the 24th year of the Troubles, had been thought hitherto unshockable, but two events in the space of a mere seven days would prove otherwise. Attacks at Frizzell's and the Rising Sun pub at Greysteel cost the lives of 18 people and left 30 children fatherless, as the UFF and Provisional IRA demonstrated that there were no limits to their shared 'qualities' of depravity and vicious revenge.

On the sunny morning of Saturday 23 October 1993, an innocent trip to a fish shop cost the lives of nine innocents plus a PIRA bomber. On the 30th, UVF gunmen killed eight innocent Catholics at a pub in Greysteel in the far north of Ulster, in the infamous 'trick or treat' massacre. Sandwiched in between the two atrocities, a further six Catholics were murdered by Loyalists, leaving another 10 children without a mother or a father.

Frizzell's had been a fishmonger's on the Shankill Road since the 1960s. Shankill historian Bobby Foster wrote in the *Belfast Telegraph*: 'It was part of a tight-knit ribbon shopping area; next door was a doctor's surgery, to the other side was a dry cleaner's and Jackie Phillips' fruit and veg shop. It was one of those basic essential shops, it had everything and prices in it to suit everyone. They brought their fish up from places like Ardglass, Kilkeel and Portavogie, and had mussels, cockles, whelks – any fish you could think of. I remember the Frizzell family being very fair to their customers, they would never have turned anyone away empty-handed. It was more community than purely retail-focused which is why I think the bomb had such an enormous impact and was seen as an attack on the people, an attack on their community.'

As that Saturday morning dawned, nine Protestants were still alive and well, uncomprehending that this was to be their final day on earth. All nine were living their lives as best they could under the awful and violent conditions that had been visited upon Ulster. Their names were John Desmond Frizzell (63), father of three, eponymous fishmonger from Kilcoole Park, close to the Loyalist Ballysillian area of North Belfast; his daughter, Sharon McBride (29),who served in her dad's shop, the mother of a small child; George Williamson (63) and his wife, Gillian (49), parents of two, from Drumard Park, Lisburn, who were in Belfast shopping for curtains for their new house; Michael 'Minnie' Morrison (27) and his partner, Evelyn Baird (27), parents of three, and their little girl Michelle Baird (7), from the Forthriver area. They were on the Shankill for two specific reasons: to buy a wreath as Michael's father had died two days earlier, and to buy some crabsticks, their favourite delicacy. Leanne Murray (13) from the Shankill was in Frizzell's to buy whelks, which were her favourites; her mother and stepfather were next door in the greengrocer's. Finally, in Westway Gardens, just over a mile away from the shop, Wilma McKee (38), mother of two, woke up in anticipation of a bus trip to the Shankill for a Saturday afternoon's shopping. For all but one of these victims, this Saturday would be the last day of their lives; Wilma McKee would die the following day from her terrible injuries.

On the nearby Ardoyne, three other men also woke up, possibly even earlier than the other actors in the grim drama which was about to unfold on that Saturday morning. The difference was that they had murder and hatred in their hearts; perhaps they were a little nervous as they would be carrying a bomb. However, they knew that they might soon be hailed as Republican 'heroes' once they had wiped out the leading lights of the UFF's 'C' company, which included McKeag and Adair. This final category of Saturday-morning risers were PIRA men Thomas 'Bootsey' Begley (23) and Sean Kelly, who was 21 at the time, and a third, unidentified volunteer. The architect of the bombing was Eddie 'Bubbles' Copeland, IRA commander on the Ardoyne, but the order came directly from the IRA's Army Council; the late Martin McGuinness had a major hand in the decision. Begley was already 'of interest' to the police, thought to have been the gunman who shot and killed Royal Irish soldier Stephen Waller on 30 December 1992 (*see* Chapter 24).

Begley and Kelly set off for the target dressed in white overalls to pass themselves off as fish deliverymen. It was common knowledge in IRA circles, that a known UDA/UFF haunt was situated above the shop. It was believed that Johnny Adair would be meeting members of his 'C' company there to discuss tactics and target areas. Moreover, the Provisionals knew that Saturday mornings were when the UDA/UFF paid 'hardship' money to the families of Loyalists imprisoned for paramilitary crimes; they also were aware that in addition to high-ranking UFF officials, there would also be family members in the building. What they didn't know was that Adair and the others had already been there earlier than usual but, with the meeting over, quietly left by a rear entrance. There was a later (unconfirmed) claim in Loyalist circles that at least two of the target men were sitting in a pub across the street from the shop when the bombing team arrived.

The three PIRA bombers drove from the Ardoyne along the back streets of the Shankill, before finally parking in Berlin Street. I have been told that the car was parked between Riga Street and Pernau Street, leaving the bombers a walk of perhaps 50 yards to Frizzell's.

Two men clad in white carried the device towards the shop, whilst the getaway driver remained with the car, facing north along Berlin Street to be able to drive away from the scene of the blast, rather than into the chaos which the Shankill Road would shortly become. The bomb – weighing 5 lb (2.3 kg), fitted with an 11-second fuse – was placed inside a holdall slung nonchalantly across Begley's shoulder. The pair arrived at the crowded shop, packed with women and children, at a little after 13:00, pausing at the door. Begley then pushed his way through the throng of shoppers to place the bomb on a refrigerated counter, whilst Kelly waited at the entrance. Begley reached inside the holdall to activate the timer, but the device exploded instantaneously, killing the IRA man; nine others were killed or mortally injured; Kelly, at the door, was also hurt, losing an eye and badly damaging his arm; he may have been cushioned from the blast by the packed humanity inside the shop. In addition to the nine dead innocents and the IRA bomber, a further 57 people were hurt. Tons of rubble crushed the dead, dying and injured; the two-storey building was wrecked. The upper floor came down on top of those inside the shop, trapping the survivors under the rubble, where they remained until rescued some hours later by volunteers and emergency services. Many people in the street were injured by flying bricks and glass, as the blast hurled debris well into the road and beyond.

After the deafening explosion, all that could be seen was dust, clouds of blue-tinged smoke, and the hazy, blurred shapes of shocked survivors staggering around; there was the smell of fresh fish, mingled with the metallic tang of blood and the choking odour of cordite. After the first few seconds of shocked silence came the screams of those alive, but in a state of fear and shock; this was followed by the low moans of the injured and deafened, unable to hear their own pleas for help and pity, but worst of all, there were no sounds at all from those already dead, dying or unconscious. Those people, who had once been loving human beings, with laughter and tears, hopes and fears, plans for a Saturday or for a full life, were now just bloody piles of rags, torn and crushed beyond recognition. Their life-clocks had stopped suddenly and irrevocably, because men on the IRA's Army Council had decided to sanction the planting of a bomb, inside a shop which sold fish and other seafood.

Scores of people were quickly on the scene, including fire and ambulance services, soldiers and police officers as well as ordinary civilians, desperately trying to free those trapped inside the wrecked shop. Gradually, the bodies were pulled out one by one, limp and lifeless and some already beyond help. The saddest sights according to one RUC officer were the bodies of the two children Michelle Baird and Leanne Murray; as they were gently lifted out grown men turned their faces away to hide the tears which streaked down their blackened faces, marking channels of sorrow which they wiped away with grimy hands.

Wilma McKee was found in the middle of the road, dreadfully injured by flying masonry; she was rushed to the nearby Mater Hospital, but she died the following day. Rescuer Raymond Elliott told the *Belfast Telegraph*'s Suzanne Breen: 'There were body parts stuck to the wall, blood and guts. People's insides were lying there. I saw somebody's scalp. Adrenalin kept me going. I was no hero. Everybody that day did all they could to help. The terror on one victim's face haunts me. There is nothing from a horror movie that comes close to that expression. People have tried to tell me it was like a light switching off for those killed and they didn't suffer. If you saw the look on that face, you wouldn't believe it. The IRA destroyed my life and I lost no one in the bomb. I can't even begin to imagine what the bereaved families have been through.' In the same interview, Ms Breen – a journalist for whom I have much admiration – spoke to Michelle Williamson who lost her parents that day: 'I waved them goodbye and the next time I saw my father he was lying dead in hospital with his head bandaged and blood seeping onto the pillow. I held his hand and kissed him on the cheek. I never got to say goodbye to mummy. She was in such a bad state that relatives thought it would be too distressing for me see her in the morgue. I'll regret that for the rest of my life. I should have gone in and told her how much I loved her.'

On That Day
Spike Millican, Royal Irish Rangers

I personally remember the day as it was a terrorist attack on the road that played such a large part of my life as a boy. The first thing I thought of was my mum as she always goes on to the road to do her shopping for the weekend. When I couldn't reach her on the phone my heart and mind went into overdrive. Watching the images on the telly was gut-wrenching, seeing some faces that I knew from my childhood in the crowds of people ripping rubble away with their bare hands. I finally got hold of my mum and dad later that day, that was emotional as they were both fine. Later when they were reading the names of the victims out, I found out that Michael, Evelyn and their young daughter had been killed; I was really angry inside myself, just not knowing how the republican bastards had had the audacity to walk into a fish shop in the heartland of the Shankill Road and deliver a bomb. I know that the West Belfast UDA used the flats above as their HQ and that Saturdays were a busy time for them as they usually had all the families from UDA prisoners collecting their prison visit passes and getting transport to the Maze prison. It's ironic that Johnny Adair was sat in a cafe across the road when the bomb went off, he was their target. An hour or so earlier no doubt he would have been killed. That day it etched its way into my brain as did the Four Step Inn and the Mountainview Tavern.

Several leading Loyalist paramilitaries were quickly on the scene, including Adair and Billy McQuiston who, as noted, may have been drinking in a pub just around the corner. Whilst neither man needed any motivation for revenge, it is not difficult to conjecture what plans were being formulated in their heads as they surveyed the gruesome scene. In his excellent book *Loyalists* Peter Taylor actually quotes McQuiston as saying: 'Anybody on the Shankill Road that day, from a Boy Scout to a granny, if you'd given them a gun they would have gone out and retaliated.'[1] Somewhat ominously, the UFF made a statement shortly afterwards: 'John Hume, Gerry Adams and the nationalist electorate will pay a heavy, heavy price for today's atrocity.'

1. Peter Taylor, *Loyalists* (Bloomsbury, 1999), p. 224.

The main bomber, Begley, was in tiny shredded pieces of bloody human tissue, but amongst the rubble on the footpath was a badly injured Kelly; his hands were shrouded in plastic gloves, which caused the rescuers a little puzzlement. He was carried across the Shankill Road by three men and laid outside Hogg's chemists until the ambulance arrived. At the time, it was unknown that he was one of the two perpetrators. The third PIRA man abandoned the stolen Escort in Berlin Street, and made good his escape on foot, no doubt looking for all the world like just another shocked and bewildered survivor, as huge numbers of people raced towards the blast in order to help.

One of the three men who carried the wounded Kelly across the road was Jimmy Verner, then a 36-year-old from the Shankill Road and now a friend of mine. To this day, as he has admitted to me, he has never got over how he innocently and inadvertently helped the man who had helped destroy the shop and blasted nine lives out of existence, in the process ruining dozens of others. Anyone who knows Mr Verner will tell him that he has nothing to reproach himself for, and that we all would have done exactly the same as he did that day.

Jimmy Verner
Shankill Road Man

It is a day that I have never forgotten and never will; if only I had known the person that I carried to safety was Sean Kelly, I think I would have killed him, instead of having to suffer a life of depression for unknowingly helping to save a murderer. I saw the man lying there close to the shop, badly injured and I knew that I had to help him as I thought that he was one of the shoppers who had been hurt. I was 36 at the time and lived all my life on the Shankill. I knew Leanne Murray's dad and, sadly, he had passed away some time before. As a young boy growing not a hundred yards from Frizzell's shop, I would go there with friends to get whelks in the summer. I also knew many of the others killed and injured that day. Myself and two lads called Sammy and Alfie picked the injured Kelly up and carried him over to Hogg's chemist where he would be safer, especially as there were bricks and timber which could still fall from the wrecked shop. Then the ambulances began arriving and I flagged the first one down and directed the ambulance to Kelly and I think there was another injured person put in too.

What really upsets me even more is that my wife and mother-in law and other family members were usually on the Shankill that time of day, out shopping, and frequently went to Frizzell's and could so easily have been caught up in that IRA bomb. I still feel guilty and depressed about my actions that day, and had I known that the injured man that I was helping was Kelly and that he was the one who had just bombed Frizzell's, then I would have walked away and helped someone else.

Everyone tells me that I did the right thing and that I had no idea that I was helping a Provo terrorist. I know I was doing my best for my people, but I knew most of the people killed and it saddens me to see his face these days and know that not one bit of remorse has passed his lips. He has never apologised for his crimes and is still an active rebel scum.

The world's press was outraged, with the bulk of the British reports appearing in the Monday editions. The *Daily Express* relegated the story to page 2 under 'Premier Condemns Bombers As Families Grieve', followed by 'They Went Out To Kill Mad Dog, Instead Nine Innocent Victims Died' on pages 12 and 13, with the subheading: 'Why Us, Ask Angry People of Shankill'. Their reporter spoke of the tragedy:

> These are the innocent victims of the IRA's plot to kill a Loyalist leader known as 'Mad Dog'. In redbrick houses the length of Belfast's Shankill Road yesterday, the full horror of the fish shop bombing was being felt. Families mourned an 'angelic' child who was killed as she went about an errand, a wife who died in the rubble and a husband who was murdered as he minded the shop. Saturday's attack came as the shopping street at the heart of loyalist West Belfast was packed. Horrified bystanders who seconds before had been window shopping, scrabbled amongst the debris. Some wept as they worked, others cursed the IRA. One stunned survivor said: 'I went over to try and help but there was nothing I could do. There were people lying dead in the middle of the street. It was horrific: women and children ... what did they do to deserve this?' Among those killed instantly was Leanne Murray, 13, whose mother, Glen, had sent her to buy some seafood while she was in another store nearby. [She] was one of the first on the scene searching even before the dust had settled. Yesterday the mother wept as she told of the moment she realised that her daughter would not be coming home. 'I couldn't find her, she was under the rubble, it was horrible,' she said. 'Leanne was our little angel, a beautiful little girl.' She said: 'I hate the IRA! People say that you should forgive and forget, but they have destroyed innocent people's lives'

The reporter also spoke to Michelle Williamson – whose parents, George and Gillian, were killed – who said: 'My feelings are of hatred. I knew that I had lost my father and we did not know where my mother was. Then I got a phone call to come to the hospital and I found my mother dead. I will never forgive them for what they have done. My life has been devastated.'

Some of the victims were taken to the RVH on the Falls Road, where a Catholic nurse called Cameron, who lived at Conor Rise in the Lenadoon area, worked tirelessly to help ease the suffering of those injured that day, along with her other nursing and medical colleagues. Her husband was called James and he worked at the Council Cleansing Depot in Lower Kennedy Way; sadly, we shall hear more of this man shortly.

The following contribution from one of the first police officers on the scene is published in an abridged form; I intend to publish his full interview in due course in my forthcoming book *50 Years of Pain*.

The Shankill Bomb
Detective Constable Ian Millar, RUC

I was at the edge of the rubble pile on the footpath and nearest the shop front. Next to me was another member of my section, then a paramedic, then a fireman. As we lifted individual bits of rubble, we passed them to the members of the public who were behind us in a human chain. After some time (time had stopped for me) I uncovered what was obviously the foot of a child who was wearing a white-coloured boot. Eventually, we uncovered her full body; as we were doing so, the fireman also uncovered the head of a lady next to the young girl. He said that he thought he could still detect a pulse in the woman and so, because the young girl was obviously dead, we had to concentrate on getting to the woman. What happened next will haunt me to the day I die. To lift the rubble off the woman, I had to stand on the body of the child. I had no choice. This was not done out of callousness, but I had to get the rubble off the woman. Because of the crush injuries to the child, she had no bones left and it felt like I was standing on a bag of jelly. I will never forget that, and my heart is breaking even now whilst I am writing about it. The fireman said that the woman had died.

I don't know how, when or by whom, but the body of the child had been removed from the scene. As we worked forward in our line along the footpath, we fully uncovered the body of the woman and she too was removed. The next body we recovered, who was lying next to the woman, was another young girl and again obviously dead; her body was removed. Lying next to her was the body of a man, again obviously dead. He was uncovered and removed. I have no idea of the period this all took, a few hours at any rate. You must remember that there were literally tons of rubble lying about 2 or 3 feet thick on these poor people. During the clearing, I found a handgun (that was obviously from the area of the explosion). I lifted it and handed this to one of our scenes of crime officers who was present nearby.'

The Shankill Bomb
Chris Hill, Devon & Dorsets

For me, this was one of the of the hardest days of all my five tours in Northern Ireland. I was on top cover that day, and actually went past the fish shop a few minutes before the bomb went off. We turned off the Shankill Road, towards North Howard Street, where we were based at the old mill there, known to generations of squaddies as NHSM. It was less than half a mile as the crow flies, and just as we pulled through the massive security gates, we heard the sound of an explosion. I just thought: 'What the hell was that?' By that stage of our experiences over there, of course, we all KNEW what it was, but we had to wait for orders.

Shortly afterwards, the report came in that a bomb had gone off on the Shankill Road, with news of civilian casualties, and we were sent back out, probably about an hour or so after the blast. The scene was horrendous: people everywhere, wandering about, smoke filled the air, the smell of cordite and blood in the air, which never goes away. We felt so helpless because we couldn't do a thing to help those poor people,

The days that followed were very busy for us as well as the RUC, with tit for tat killings going on all the time, especially the Council Yard killings in West Belfast. We were told that the UFF gunmen actually chased their victims, shooting at them as they ran. That was followed by the funeral of the IRA bomber, Begley; the Falls Road was packed, and we even had Adams there! During this time, a Protestant – not sure if was UVF or UFF – lad tried to throw a grenade across the peace line but it exploded and took his hand off.[1] This was near the end of my very eventful year in Belfast and I was looking forward to leaving and going home. I have to confess that, to this day, I still feel guilty about the Shankill bombing.

One of the youngest victims that day was a tiny 22-month-old toddler, Marcus Lowe, injured by the blast whilst riding in a taxi along the Shankill Road. He was hit in the head by shrapnel, sustaining cuts that required several stitches; his mother was also treated for facial wounds. One survivor, Walter Harris, on the way to watch a football match with his 13-year-old, called the IRA: 'yellow cowards. They did not care about who was going to be blown up. I do not often pray, but I am praying for my son and for all those families who have lost loved ones. It is terrible for them all.' Michael O'Flahery, writing in the *Daily Express*, cannot possibly have realised just how prophetic his closing words would prove: 'As night fell, the people of the Shankill suffered their own darkness. Anger rose from it like the smoke from a smouldering volcano. Tomorrow, you felt it would erupt.'

United Press was amongst the first of the US agencies to report:

> Prime Minister John Major, speaking in the wake of a bomb blast in Belfast that killed 10 people and injured at least 61 others, said Sunday the Irish Republican Army would never win its violent campaign to end British rule in Northern Ireland. His comments came as police in Northern Ireland said one member of the IRA was among the dead. A second suspected bomber was seriously wounded when the IRA bomb exploded prematurely in a fish shop in the heart of the staunchly Shankill Road district. 'What on earth do the IRA think this sort of atrocity is going to do,' the Prime Minister told the BBC's *Breakfast with Frost* programme from Cyprus, where he is attending a Commonwealth conference. 'There is only one message that I want to hear from the IRA and that message is that they have given up violence for good. Yesterday they sent a different message,' Major said. Police said two men walked into a fishmonger's shop on Shankill Road, put down a box and left, shortly before the blast. The explosion demolished an entire building, leaving a gaping hole in a row of terraced brick buildings fronting onto the road. Parts of adjoining shops also collapsed, trapping many people. The IRA said its target was the former headquarters of the outlawed Ulster Defense Association, a Protestant paramilitary group, which had a room directly above the West Belfast fish shop. The IRA released statements Saturday saying the attack had gone 'tragically wrong' and that the men who planted the bomb were unaccounted for. Among the dead were two girls, aged 13 and 7, five women and three men. The injured included 27 men, 32 women and two 2-year-old boys. A number of them are seriously ill in hospital Sunday, some without limbs that were blown off in the blast. Police said they had identified all but one of the victims. They named the IRA bomber as Thomas Begley, 23, from West Belfast. Another man who was seriously injured is under armed police guard in hospital, but police did not say if he was the second member of an IRA active service unit. Prime Minister Major said the IRA could not achieve their aims in Northern Ireland by using the bomb

1. In fact a reference to Herbie McCallum, a Loyalist who had been killed on 29 June 1993.

as a political weapon. 'There's no way they can bomb and kill their way to their own aims,' he said. 'It can't be done. The sort of atrocity we saw yesterday will isolate and marginalize the IRA increasingly. I believe they will come to understand that.'

In 2016, the *Belfast Telegraph* interviewed one of the rescuers, Alfie McCrory, who told Ivan Little:

> It was pure pandemonium. We never thought about any dangers, we were just hell-bent on getting the injured out. There were people lying everywhere, inside and outside the shop. Some were moaning, and some were obviously dead. One man had virtually no face left. One policeman was hit on the head by falling bricks, but he just wiped the blood away and went on trying to save people. The fire service brought in a sniffer dog and heat-seeking equipment and told us to get out because we could be sitting on top of injured people. Every so often there would be calls for quiet as someone heard a cry for help. The silence was eerie with hundreds in the area and yet you could have heard a mouse scrambling in the wreckage. [At the Mater Hospital] I saw the name Sean Kelly on a list of the injured; I knew there were no Sean Kellys on the Shankill and I then realised that he must have been a bomber and he must have been one of those helped into an ambulance. I remembered that after I lifted him his hands fell by his side and he had on surgical gloves. If I had known who he was, I would have killed him for what he had done to our people.

Mr McCrory later helped to carry the coffin of the second-youngest victim, 13-year-old Leanne Murray; 'I later discovered that as I was bringing her down Silvio Street, Gerry Adams was carrying the coffin of the bomber Thomas Begley in the Ardoyne. That was very upsetting.'

Ivan Little's 2016 article continued:

> Marty Marchant reflects on the painful memories of the nightmarish hours on the Shankill after the blast and the funerals of three members of the Baird family in the week following the appalling atrocity. He says: 'I would defy anyone – even members of Sinn Féin – not to cry if they could see pictures of those coffins coming over the brow of the hill at Glencairn that day.' For Marty Marchant it had been a Saturday that kicked off with the usual tingle of excitement as he readied himself to go to watch his favourite football team, Linfield. As he waited for a lift on the Shankill not far from Frizzell's shop, he heard the unmistakable sound of an explosion. 'The whole place was black with dust rising and falling. I ran down and one of the first things I saw was a pram sticking out of the rubble. We immediately started to dig among the wreckage, but we didn't know what we were doing. We got a chain going to pass bricks and stuff out of the shop. Tiles, bricks and pieces of wood were falling down from what remained of the building, but nobody cared. There were girls trapped in a hair salon above the shop next door, but we didn't know whether to get them out first or help people on the ground until the emergency services arrived. I remember one body was stuck to tiles with hard blood and there were bricks with flesh on them which the ambulance men

were telling us to keep. They were also bringing out limbs in plastic bags. I will never forget any of it.'

The Belfast *News Letter* interviewed one of the survivors, John Foster from Wheatfield Drive, close to the Republican heartland of the Ardoyne. He was well known for his solo preaching of the Gospels in and around the Crumlin Road area. He was labelled the 'living miracle' for surviving the blast, suffering a large shrapnel wound in his back as well as severe kidney damage. When the bomb exploded, he was in the adjoining decorator's shop, buying wallpaper. He told the newspaper that he felt a dull thud, before building debris began piling up around and on top of him. He explained how he was pulled from the rubble, feeling tremendous pain, but refused offers of assistance as he wished to help the others, despite his own pain. He said: 'I saw all the people pulling at the rubble, and I knew that there had to be people trapped so, when the ambulance came for me, I said get the worst people first, the ones who had lost their limbs. They started bringing the stretchers in and the dead out and again I said that I wouldn't go to the hospital because I knew there had to be people worse than me. Then the pain got so bad that I cried for help. Every time I see it on the news, every time I think about it, I hear the mortar falling. I don't know how I was saved. I'm a living miracle.'

At Begley's funeral, Gerry Adams provoked outrage by carrying the IRA killer's coffin and then, in act of gross insensitivity, provoked further anger in praising the bomber as 'a volunteer who made the ultimate sacrifice for his belief'. The Provisionals still insisted that they had been trying to kill Adair, McKeag and others, who, they believed, would be meeting on the floor above Frizzell's. They have always maintained that they had no intention of killing or hurting Protestant civilians. I strongly believe that the IRA itself knew – but arrogantly refused to admit it – that their intelligence was poor. Copeland, Begley and the others who planned and executed the bungled bombing were aware, through their own dickers' reports along with their recces on the Shankill, that on a Saturday lunchtime, the area would be heaving with shoppers. Even had the 11-second fuse worked, the blast would have caught those too slow, or shocked to exit the shop after a shouted warning, especially John Frizzell and his daughter Sharon McBride who were behind the serving counter and would have stood no chance of escape. Moreover, there were also scores of shoppers innocently walking past, who would have had little chance to avoid the blast, especially as a dozen or more people were simultaneously scrambling to get out of the narrow door, in mortal fear of their lives.

This view is supported by one of my friends from Belfast, as follows:

Isobel Braiden Coe

One misconception which many people hold is that Frizzell's was a fish n' chip shop but this wasn't the case as they sold, mainly, fresh fish. The only cooked food on the premises were potted herrings (cooked in the shop). Leanne had called in for a cup of fresh-cooked 'willicks' – known as periwinkles to anyone not from Northern Ireland – which I understand she loved. The IRA bombers would have known how busy the shop was on any given day and would have known that people came from the Falls and Ardoyne and other Nationalist areas to shop on the Shankill. It was a really small shop, and once inside, it was only a couple of steps and you were at the counter, so no one inside would have stood a chance of surviving or escaping. I will never forgive, and I also feel sad that other innocent people lost their lives in revenge for this act.

If Adams and McGuinness were involved in sanctioning this operation, they could hardly fail to have considered the Loyalist reaction; they knew that the Loyalists would exact a bloody revenge – which they did – and that even more innocent Catholic blood would be spilled. Only a blind and deaf and dumb man was not aware that the 'tit for tat' killings would inevitably follow. As we shall see shortly, more than a dozen Catholics would die in bloody revenge for the fish shop outrage.

It didn't take long for the rumours to begin about the identity of one of the survivors, as it soon began to emerge that one of the injured was one of the bombers. Sources say that Loyalists quickly cobbled together a plan to shoot Kelly, once it was known that he had been among the injured taken to the Mater hospital in Belfast.

Inside the hospital, word had also quickly spread and, with anger rising among the injured and their relatives that the bomber had been brought to the Mater, the RUC were aware that they needed to act. Hospital staff became increasingly concerned that Kelly could be targeted, and it was agreed that he should be transferred immediately to the RVH on the Falls Road. He was rushed the short distance between the two hospitals under guard. It later emerged, that a Shankill Road man had, ironically, tried to comfort Kelly in the ambulance that was taking an injured relative, as well as the bomber, to the Mater.

In 2013, what I have called the Adams–McGuinness–[Danny] Morrison axis was in action again as part of their attempt to re-write the history of the Troubles. In what can only be described as a campaign of insensitivity, they unveiled a plaque paying tribute to the weasel-faced Begley. The plaque, placed at the entrance to the Ardoyne on Crumlin Road reads: 'Belfast Brigade: Oglach Thomas "Bootsey" Begley: Died on Active Service 23rd October 1993: Always remembered by his many comrades and friends.' Protestants were rightly outraged by this crass display. Amongst those present was his fellow bomber Kelly, who was pictured embracing Begley's father. In fairness to Mr Begley senior I should record that he said: 'As you well know, this is not a celebration or a glorification of that tragic day that happened. It's also [not to] degrade the innocent people on the Shankill Road.' Michelle Williamson, orphaned in the blast, sent a letter to Begley's parents, stating that she had no problem in acknowledging their loss, but said the unveiling of the plaque to a bomber was: 'a sick and cruel insult to the memory of our loved ones'.

Frizzell Controversy

The Troubles were a time of violence and of controversy; it was a dirty war and must rank amongst the dirtiest wars of all. An RUC source very close to me has suggested several theories as to why the bomb exploded so prematurely and so disastrously. As he pointed out, this was the 24th year of the Troubles; the Provisionals' bomb-makers had developed an expertise and a professionalism in the construction, transportation and detonation of all types of explosive devices. They had progressed from the early days of the 1970s, when it appeared that they had an amateurish approach to bomb-making with many of their 'experts' removing themselves in a series of catastrophic, careless incidents, to become the deadly professionals of the late 80s and early 90s. Given their wealth of expertise and experience, how or why did the Frizzells bombing go so badly wrong?

The first theory, and possibly the most feasible, was that Begley and Kelly were informers, either for the RUC's Special Branch or British Army Intelligence, and that this had become known to their IRA bosses. If this was the case, then the Belfast brigade could kill several birds with one stone; they could – as they claimed they intended – wipe out the top echelon of the UFF's 'C' company, including possibly Adair and McKeag, whilst also ridding themselves of two 'touts'. It would have avoided the use of their 'nutting squad' and they would have been spared the embarrassment of admitting that two of their top men were informants. Of course, if this was the case, Copeland and the rest of the PIRA commanders knew that their bomb wouldn't just kill Adair and company, it would also massacre many innocent Protestants.

A second theory was the truly chilling prospect– but given the nature of the dirty war, not entirely beyond the realms of possibility – that British Intelligence or RUC Special Branch had an informant or informers inside either Copeland's unit or in the Short Strand unit where the device was assembled. The device may have been interfered with to ensure an instantaneous explosion, with resulting mass deaths discrediting the Provisionals, along with their exposure as sectarian murderers, something which they have always denied. If this was the case, then innocent lives were sacrificed to weaken the Provisionals' image on the island of Ireland, and particularly in the USA. Although this is not entirely implausible, I don't believe that this explanation has over-much credibility.

The final possibility is again that it was intended that the bomb would detonate the very second that Begley pressed the detonator; the intention was that people would die, with Begley and Kelly and the innocent shoppers being merely collateral damage. Some of my contacts, and my own research, suggest that the Provisionals were aware that they could not win what their tacticians had dubbed 'the long war', and that defeating the British was no longer militarily possible. Successive British governments had played a long game, and had kept the Republican paramilitaries largely tied down, with only the occasional 'spectaculars' possible. If that was the case, there could have been a movement inside the Provisionals' Army Council which wanted the war to end and would have been only too happy to allow the Belfast units to be severely discredited by the atrocity which would inevitably unfold at Frizzell's. It would be another nail in the coffin of the hawks who wished to continue the fight to drive the British into the sea. Of the three theories, I find this the least plausible.

What was lost in the aftermath of this maelstrom of violence and murder was a spate of actions by the IRA's England team; between the 24th and 29th they exploded three separate devices in the south of England. The first was on a railway line in Berkshire; two further devices were defused at Reading and Basingstoke stations. This was followed by a detonation on a bridge above a railway line in Buckinghamshire, before an IRA bomb then exploded in Edwards Square, London.

Whilst any Troubles-related news is naturally germane in this account, in all the bloodletting of this period of gross turmoil, chronicling any of the contemporary political meetings seems tame in comparison. However, it was announced that the Anglo-Irish Intergovernmental Conference (AIIC) meeting planned for 27 October would be postponed as a mark of respect after the Shankill Road bombing. The UUP members on Belfast City

Council decided not to engage with the SDLP, until the Hume–Adams Initiative had ended. Meanwhile, the promised and expected tidal wave of Loyalist paramilitary revenge was about to roll forward; 12 more Catholics were about to die.

The scene switched then to Glengormley in North Belfast; to the west of the Antrim Road, close to the picturesque Belfast Lough, there is a small Catholic enclave. In that enclave, a GAA member, Sean Fox (72), father of four grown-up children, lived on his own, having done so for several years since his wife had passed away. He had the most tenuous of associations with Republicanism, in that a relative of his was convicted of the 1974 murder of RUCR officer John Rodgers in the nearby Glen Inn. It was enough for the UVF, especially in the blood-charged atmosphere that had blanketed all of Northern Ireland like a London smog since Saturday afternoon's carnage on the Shankill. At some stage late that afternoon, several armed UVF members had forced their way into Mr Fox's home where he was 'interrogated' and tortured, before being shot several times. Later that evening, alerted by neighbours, the RUC entered the house and found the one-eyed pensioner, battered and dead on his living room floor. Quite why the Loyalist murder gang needed to 'interrogate' the man will probably never be known. It was simply another senseless sectarian murder.

That same evening, as the minutes ticked towards midnight, that most repugnant of Loyalist paramilitary tactics – 'dial a Catholic' – once more came into play: This obscenity involved a Loyalist telephoning a taxi or food delivery company in a Catholic area, highly likely to employ only Catholics. A real address in any of the Catholic areas – with a good means of escape – would be used to place an order. The gunmen would hide nearby, under cover of darkness, waiting for the arrival of their victim. On arrival, he would be seized and driven off to be murdered or simply shot dead and left lying in a pool of blood. Around 23:00, with the smell of smoke still hanging over the ruins of Frizzell's less than three miles away, UFF gunmen phoned a Chinese restaurant and ordered a meal to be delivered to Vernon Court, close to Donegall Pass, a wholly Catholic area. The delivery driver was Martin Moran (22), father of a tiny baby; he arrived at the given address and stopped. As he turned to get the meal from his front seat, gunmen stepped from the shadows and shot him twice in the head, fatally wounding the young man, who died on the 25th. At home, his partner Lorraine waited his return; their five-week-old baby girl Amanda was in her cot, sleeping; she would never know her daddy.

In 2013, both women spoke to the *Belfast Telegraph*:

> 'The people of the Shankill were devastated as were those in the aftermath, the lives taken of those innocent people [*sic*]. What gutted me even more was the plaque [erected to Begley]. What is he? A "hero"? What is he a hero of? Murdering innocent people? It hurts you more when you see things like that. If those two [Begley and Kelly] hadn't gone out that day and caused that horrific Shankill bombing my Martin wouldn't have been shot that night in the first retaliation. We would still have him here,' she said. 'My child would be sitting here at 20 with her father, knowing him. I could have had more children, who knows?' She said 20 years on she still struggled on a daily basis to cope with the loss of her partner and best friend. 'You're empty, you're lost . . . Your life is empty, stolen from you. He was a gentle, loving person, very kind and a fella who would do anything for anybody. He had the most lovely big smile. You don't know what your life would

have brought you. Instead you're crushed, but you have to try and be strong. We were robbed and for what? It's still going on today. What was it all for? What was all the innocent life taken for? You put a brave face on and a pretend smile, pretend you're coping and just try to get through your day.' Amanda said: 'You feel lost in a way. I would love to know what it feels like to have my daddy around, but I never will . . . I know I am not the only person in Northern Ireland that feels robbed because many people have lost family members, but he was my daddy and I was only five weeks. That is my daddy. My daddy should be here.'

It was now Tuesday morning – the 26th – Adair felt that he too had to make a statement about the Shankill bomb, but it wouldn't be of the verbal kind. He dispatched a carload of gunmen over to the Council Cleansing Depot on Lower Kennedy Way in West Belfast. Adair planned the attack for around 07:45, when he knew that the workers there – Catholics in the main – would still be relaxing, having a morning cuppa before the day's work commenced. Late arrivers might still be coming in, which meant that the heavy security gates would be constantly opening and closing. It is alleged that the team included Gary 'Smickers' Smyth and Robert 'Rab' Bradshaw from the UFF's 'C' company, along with Thomas Beggs driving a Citroen stolen from a Shankill taxi company.[1] All of the gang members wore hi-viz jackets and other working clothing which might help them blend in with the types of men who would be expected to be seen there at that time of day. James Cameron (54), father of three from Lenadoon (wife of the nurse mentioned earlier), was just closing the gates when the UFF gunmen burst in, immediately opening fire on the two dozen or so employees in the yard. Using a pistol and an automatic weapon, they began shouting: 'Take that, you bastards!' spraying rounds indiscriminately. Mr Cameron was hit as he tried to take cover behind a skip, dying almost immediately. Seconds afterwards, Mark Rodgers (28), father of two, also from Lenadoon, was hit in the chest and collapsed to the ground mortally wounded. He was covered in leaking diesel, after a nearby tanker was hit several times by automatic fire. Five others were hit and fell wounded, at which point one of the gunmen ran over to a bleeding victim and fired again, but his gun jammed; an eyewitness saw him stand with his foot on the back of the wounded man, holding him down as he feverishly and callously worked at clearing the weapon, so that he could fire at the man again. With the stench of cordite and the seemingly ubiquitous scent of blood hanging in the air, now mingled with the smell of diesel, the gunmen ran back to the waiting Citroen and screamed off in the direction of Lisburn Road where they later abandoned the car, before escaping in another stolen vehicle. Mr Cameron's 12-year-old son Colum simply could not understand the tragedy which had hammered its way into his young life; he was later observed in a distraught state outside the depot, crying for his lost father. A woman living opposite who called the RUC stated a little over a year later, in court, that the two killers returned to the stolen Citroen looking 'calm and collected'. A man who lived nearby ran into the yard, and later told the media: 'They were lying there like slabs of beef.' Only the day before, Adair had boasted to police officers at an RUC VCP: 'I'm away to plan a mass murder!'[2]

1. Lister & Jordan, *Mad Dog*, pp. 164, 166.
2. Belfast *News Letter*, 6 December 1994.

Colum Cameron told the BBC some years later: 'Nothing was gained through the massacre. I don't feel bitterness against the people that done it but I do hope for justice someday, as these people still walk the streets ... Twenty years ago our life changed dramatically. They just didn't take a person that morning, they took my father, a husband, a brother and a son. Also, with the Rodgers family the same thing. Our family will never be the same. There was a hole left when my father was killed that can never be replaced.'

The *Daily Express* was far more concerned with the state of a relationship between actress Jenny Seagrove and film director Michael Winner than an attempted mass killing, relegating the Lower Kennedy Way shooting to page 2. Even on that inner page, the shooting of a mourner at Begley's funeral took precedence over the deaths of the two Catholics, with the attack subheaded: 'My daddy's dead shouts boy after revenge attack on workmen'. Even at this very late stage of the Troubles with sickening precedent set after sickening precedent, it was incredibly naive of the press to talk about 'revenge' attacks. Of course, Loyalist outrage was at a maximum following the terrible slaughter at Frizzell's, but the Loyalist paramilitaries, like their Republican counterparts did not need any excuse for bloodletting.

The getaway driver, UFF member Thomas Edward Beggs, was found guilty at Belfast Crown Court in December 1994 of the murder of the two workmen and the attempted murder of five others. Lord Justice Kelly told Beggs:' You were the driver who drove the gunmen responsible, knowing full well their mission was to murder as many Catholic workmen as they could.' Beggs was given concurrent life terms of 144 years, but he was released early under the GFA. Also jailed was Wendy Ann Davies, who received four years for conspiracy. She had allowed her home in Moltke Street, Belfast to be used by the gunmen before and after the attack. In her defence, it was said that she was 'mentally retarded' and the UFF gunmen used her to full advantage. Justice Kelly said of her: 'It appears quite clear that she was a girl who was used and abused by people for their own ends – evil ends.'

On that same day as the Council Depot shooting, PIRA bomber Thomas Begley was buried with full Republican honours, with masked gunmen firing a volley of shots over a tricolour-draped coffin, complete with black beret and matching gloves. To the disgust of the watching world, Sinn Féin president Gerry Adams helped carry the body of the mass-murderer; he did this surely in the knowledge that three of the Frizzell's funerals were taking place very close by. Michael Morrison, Evelyn Baird and their daughter Michelle's coffins were driven side by side along the Shankill Road as they were taken to be buried together, as a family. Few photographs of funeral processions in the Troubles have encapsulated the grief of death as clearly as the sight of the three hearses driving line-abreast over the brow of the Shankill Road.

The dead bomber was buried in the Republican plot at Milltown Cemetery, where a soldier in the ADU (Army Dog Handlers Unit) had earlier seen his dog defecate in the as yet empty grave of Begley. The soldier concerned wrote to me and confirmed that it had happened, and felt it 'an appropriate way to send Begley to Hell'. Back at the dead terrorist's house in the Brompton Park area of the Ardoyne, family friends called around to pay their respects. SF were in attendance, including an armoured Land Rover containing RUC officers and soldiers. Eddie 'Bubbles' Copeland, IRA leader in the Ardoyne, was outside the house, vetting visitors, in order to ensure no Loyalist revenge attack took place. The security forces also feared a Loyalist attack, deploying soldiers whose task was to give cover to mourners, about 30 of whom were gathered in the garden at Begley's house. In the back of the SF vehicle was Trooper Andrew Clarke, who was 27 at the time. He saw Copeland appear, then, without warning, fired two rounds from his SA-80 5.56 mm rifle, hitting him in the neck and stomach.

The *Guardian* takes up the story:

> Trooper Lee Potter, one of Clarke's colleagues in the Land Rover, told the High Court that shortly before the incident, soldiers, including Clarke, had been shown a montage of suspected IRA terrorists. They included Eddie Copeland, named in the Commons in 1995 by David Trimble, now Ulster Unionist leader, as the likely mastermind of the Shankill Road bomb. Trooper Potter said that the soldiers were advised to 'sit tight and take the flak' if they recognised any of the IRA suspects. At one point, as they passed the house, Clarke made a joke about shooting some of them and cocked his rifle about the same time. When they next drew close to the mourners, Clarke suddenly opened fire from his SA 80 rifle. He fired two single shots, then switched to automatic, and emptied his magazine of 20 bullets in three or four bursts. He was trying to reload when his colleagues wrestled the weapon from him. He was shouting: 'You fucking bastards.' Copeland, now 28, was hit in the back. The bullet went through his bowel and came out his abdomen. He was in hospital for 16 days and needed to wear a colostomy bag. He told the High Court he still suffered hernia problems and required further surgery. Loyalists later tried to assassinate Copeland, who suffered relatively minor injuries in a car bomb attack in December 1996. Clarke, dismissed from the army, was sentenced to 10 years for attempted murder. He apologised at his trial, telling the court: 'I am sorry that even Mr Copeland was hit, actually.'[1]

Whilst by no means condoning the actions of the soldier, it must be stated that he had witnessed the carnage at Frizzells and was now close to the bomber's house. Also living there was the man named in the Commons as the man behind the attack, Eddie Copeland. 'Bubbles' was parading himself about, and it is no surprise to me that Clarke snapped and succumbed to the hatred to which he had been subjected since the commencement of his tour from these people. I will make no further comment.

It was now Friday 29th and almost six days had passed since the Shankill Road bomb; already four Catholics had been killed in revenge attacks by the UFF and the UVF. On this day, the UVF would kill two Catholic brothers. Gerard Cairns (22) and his younger brother Rory (18) lived in Bleary, in Co. Armagh. The place itself is a small township, south of Lough Neagh, and some 12 miles east of Portadown. The area was part of the notorious 'Murder Triangle' and home to the Glenanne gang, a violent, sectarian organisation, part of the UVF's mid-Ulster brigade. Gerard and Rory lived with their parents and a younger brother aged 15, as well as a sister, Róisín, who had just celebrated her 11th birthday and was being allowed to stay up late. At around 20:00, a car containing several UVF gunmen parked outside the house, before they entered through the back door which was unlocked. They barged past the young girl in the kitchen, rushing into the living room and taking the

1. https://www.theguardian.com/world/1999/jan/26/law.theguardian.

brothers completely by surprise as they watched television. No words were spoken as they shot both boys in the head and chest at close range, before running out, leaving the 11-year-old girl stunned and terrified. The two young men had posed for a family photograph to celebrate Róisín's birthday less than an hour before the murder gang arrived. Neither boy, nor indeed any family member, had any real Republican associations, other than a murdered cousin who was a member of Sinn Féin (Sheena Campbell, shot and killed by UVF gunmen in October 1992; *see* Chapter 22). The killing of the two young brothers was senseless and clearly sectarian, but to the Loyalist paramilitaries the events at Frizzell's were all the justification that they needed.

On the same day as the murders of the Cairns boys, John Major, and Albert Reynolds were meeting in Brussels. At the conclusion, they issued a joint statement containing six points outlining their determination that there would be no secret deals with the paramilitary groups. However, the statement also made clear that, if there were an end to violence, then both the British and the Irish would respond imaginatively. They stated that they would not adopt or endorse the proposals contained in the Hume–Adams Initiative. However, as they uttered these grandiose words and made clear their 'bold' intentions, someone was not listening; the UVF and UFF weren't listening, and neither was the Provisional IRA.

Greysteel Massacre

On the previous Saturday, 10 people woke up on what was to be their final day on this earth. This Saturday – the 30th – was, tragically going to be similar, in terms of both weather and outcome. Greysteel sits on Lough Foyle, astride the main coastal A2 road to Londonderry, close to Limavady, and the site of the 1982 Droppin' Well massacre. Just set back a little from the busy A2 is the quieter Killylane Road; here facing the lough is a long, grey, one-storey building, the Rising Sun pub. It is closed now; when I visited in 2015, it was open, albeit devoid of customers; the landlord, I understand now sadly deceased, allowed me and my companions to take photographs of the interior. Jim Moore owned and ran the pub in 1993; he may have been the man that I met, and I wish that I had known, because I would have liked to have put my arms around him. I cannot imagine that it was wholly different, 22 years earlier, on the evening of 30 October 1993. The Rising Sun was a Catholic-frequented pub in a Catholic community, although several Protestants were drinking there that fateful night. There were two separate bars open that evening, with around 200 customers present.

When I visited, it was silent and lifeless and whilst not unfriendly, it felt haunted; unsurprisingly, given the events of Halloween Night 1993. Back in 1993, the exterior was a cheerful red brick, with a bright plastic sign which read: 'Rising Sun. Bar. Lounge. Restaurant'. Inside were pink curtains, patterned wallpaper and Formica-style table tops. Very soon, the colour of blood would be added to the polished wooden floor. In another bar, there was a small counter, with bottles and optics and plastic-padded bar stools, and the same polished wooden floor; soon, it too would be drenched with the blood of dozens of people.

That morning eight people, two of them Protestants, woke up with the promise of a pleasant Saturday and a weekend away from work. Karen Thompson (19) from Limavady and her fiancé, Steven Mullan (20), had a wedding to plan and to dream about, as they intended to be engaged at Christmas. James Moore (81) was the father of five grown-up children including the Rising Sun's owner. There was Moira Duddy (59), mother of six, also from Greysteel; John Moyne (50) and John Burns (54), father of three. Mr Burns was a Protestant and former UDR soldier from Eglinton; he had three teenage children. There was also Samuel Montgomery, a former officer in the 'B' Specials who lived alone; he was 76 at the time of the attack. Finally, there was another Greysteel resident Joseph 'Joe' McDermott (60).

The evening began in good spirits – literally – with a Hallowe'en party, many guests were wearing fancy dress; the place was rocking on its foundations, because even in the Troubles, people had a right to be happy. Outside a stolen Opel Kadett pulled up; it held three UFF gunmen, Stephen Irwin, Geoffrey Deeney and Torrens Knight, all from North Antrim. They took up their weapons and donned balaclavas before entering the noisy, packed pub. Because many people were wearing fancy dress, not much notice was taken of them initially. Irwin was carrying a Czech-manufactured VZ.58, a similar-looking weapon to the AK-47, firing the same 7.62 mm round, with a terrifying rate of fire of 13 rounds a second. He shouted the words: 'Trick or treat', to which a nearby female drinker – Karen Thompson – responded: 'That's not funny!' He turned in her direction, levelling the VZ towards her head and immediately opening fire, hitting her in the face and mortally wounding her. The plan was that he would empty the 30-round magazine before the others commenced firing. He then turned his attention to a party of women on a hen night, spraying them and anyone close by, turning the dance floor bloody. It was later said that the screams of terror drowned out the harsh rattle of the Czech-made weapon.

Then it was Deeney's turn. He opened fire with his 9 mm Browning automatic, but it jammed after just one shot. He couldn't clear the stoppage and could only watch as Irwin loaded a second magazine. One of the revellers, John Moyne, threw his wife to the floor but he was fatally hit, protecting his wife from Irwin's bullets. John Burns, the former soldier, was on his way to the toilet when the shooting started, causing him to turn to face the gunmen; for his trouble, he was hit in the stomach and mortally wounded, dying shortly afterwards. His wife was also shot and badly wounded. James Moore was hit four times, dying where he fell. Moira Duddy was blasted in the legs before being killed with shots to her heart.

Knight, meanwhile was standing at the front door with a double-barrelled shotgun which he was unable to use, indeed, had no need to use. Almost as soon as the firing had started, it suddenly stopped; as the echoes of the gunshots died down, the three killers ran outside, laughing and joking before speeding away in the stolen Opel.

A fourth gang member, Brian McNeill, had driven to nearby Eglington where he met the others; together they torched the Opel before escaping in the car driven by McNeill. They left behind seven dead innocent civilians; Mr Montgomery was fatally wounded and died on 14 April the following year. All the dead and dying were Catholics apart from Mr Montgomery and Mr Burns who were both Protestants. One of the wounded women, Lorraine Murray, who was shot and injured along with her mother, Mary McKeever, in the massacre was still being treated for her injuries at the time of writing, in 2017, some 24 years after the attack. I wish them peace and comfort.

On the Monday morning, the *Daily Express* front page had a poignant photograph of Karen Thompson and Steven Mullan, with the caption: 'Couple who planned to marry will now be buried together after massacre at pub'. The headline also included the words of a young woman who had left a card amongst the floral tributes outside the pub: 'God Might Forgive. We Cannot.' The report read: 'They were a devoted young couple with everything to live for. Now they are set to be buried together. [They] were among the seven victims of Ulster's Hallowe'en massacre. Karen's father found her bullet-riddled body when he stopped to help in the carnage of the Rising Sun pub at Greysteel, Co. Londonderry. Her weeping mother is a Protestant like the killers. The tragic sweethearts had planned to marry next April.'

Inside the newspaper the words were sterner, quoting the comment of a leading RUC officer; 'They are the scum of the earth!' The inner headlines roared: 'Killers will be hunted like rats!' The article continued: 'Karen Thompson's father found her dead in the pub after he stopped on the way home from visiting a friend in hospital. He was driving past when he saw the crowd and pulled up to see if he could help. He went into the bar, stepped over four corpses and saw Karen dead on the floor.' A friend of the murdered girl – who was shot in the face – told the newspaper: 'Karen was a lovely, lively ordinary wee girl; how could they shoot her?' RUC Chief Constable Hugh Annesley told the *Express*: 'They have a bloodlust and appear to be psychotic killers.'

It later emerged that two of the nurses in Londonderry's Altnagelvin Hospital were forced to hide their own grief and help with the catalogue of injuries from the attack, as the victims were rushed the short 10 miles from the scene of the murders. Nurses Jackie O'Doherty and Katrina Moore worked desperately, helping dress wounds and comfort survivors, despite knowing that Jackie's mother (Moira Duddy) and Katrina's stepfather-in-law (James Moore) were amongst the dead. Gillian Burns, daughter of the former soldier, John Burns, told the Belfast *News Letter*: 'I feel ashamed of my religion.' One survivor also told the newspaper: 'It was pandemonium, everybody was screaming. It was all over in two minutes, just two minutes, four bursts of machine-gun fire, all over, seven people dead, two minutes is all it took.' Jim Moore, the bar's owner, said: 'I thought it was a few bangers being let off because it was Hallowe'en. It was carnage and panic. People were lying dead all over the place. I saw my father first, then a young girl then all the others. I know my father is dead but I want no revenge for it. I am not bitter. I was never a bitter person.'

Prime Minister John Major said afterwards: 'Last night we saw yet another evil act of butchery in which members of both communities were mown down. I appeal to all the people of Northern Ireland to show no tolerance to the gunmen and the bombers. If they are known, they should be identified to the police and brought to justice. Revenge breeds revenge. They are acting against humanity.' The Loyalist reaction to Major's weak but well-intentioned words was fast and it was predictable. The UDA/UFF swiftly made a statement about the handiwork of Irwin, Knight and Deeney: 'This is the continuation of our threats against the Nationalist electorate that they would pay a heavy price for last Saturday's slaughter of nine Protestants.'

The killers were caught, but sadly, not the UDA godfathers who ordered the massacre: Torrens Knight was convicted – along with three others – for the killings; he served seven years in the Maze Prison before his release in 2000 under the terms of the GFA. Stephen

Irwin pleaded guilty to the killings and was given eight life sentences but was also later released under the GFA; in 2005 he was jailed for four years for knifing a football fan. Jeffrey Deeney also received a life sentence for his part in the shootings, but he too was released from prison under the same terms. Deeney has since publicly stated that he 'felt dejected that his gun had jammed' during the shootings. Deeney said he did not believe the attack was right but that it 'had to be done' in retaliation for the Shankill fish shop a week earlier.[1]

The 31st fell on a Sunday, but without even a pause for breath, the violence was off and running again, this time in Newry, Co. Down. The town's RUC had set up a snap VCP in Upper Edward Street, close to Monaghan Row and the Royal Mail depot. It was also close to the overworked Daisy Hill Hospital but, equally, only a short 10-minute walk away from the belligerent and fiercely Nationalist Derrybeg Estate. As the final remnants of an interdenominational service for peace in Market Square were fading away, a PIRA gunman, lying full stretch in a hatchback car, fired a single shot with a high-velocity rifle which hit RUCR Constable Brian Woods (30) in his neck, whilst he was on traffic duty. He fell, fatally wounded, as his comrades tried to return fire at the gunman; Constable Woods sadly died from his injuries on 2 November.

Bloody October was finally over, with a truly awful 29 people dead, of whom all but one were civilians; 27 of the killings were obviously sectarian. Ulster was on the precipice, facing a crisis as bad as 1972; the responsibility lay with the paramilitaries of BOTH sides.

1. http://www.belfasttelegraph.co.uk/news/northern-ireland/greysteel-gunman-speaks-of-regret-that-more-didnt-die-28332020.html.

35
November

After virtually a death per day the previous month, it was almost as though the whole of Ulster had paused for collective breath, to take some sort of stock; whilst violence continued, there was more talking this month than previously, albeit much of it hot air. A policeman and a soldier died, and an innocent Catholic was killed by the UFF in East Belfast.

During the first week of the month, Prime Minister Major invited John Hume to a meeting to discuss the SDLP leader's recent proposals; Major told Hume that his initiative in tandem with Adams 'was not the right way to proceed'. Hume countered by claiming that there could be peace in a week, if his proposals were listened to. Later, in a reply during Prime Minister's Questions, Major said: 'to sit down and talk with Mr Adams and the Provisional IRA … would turn my stomach!' To feel this way was entirely correct on Major's part, but given that his government had been in regular communication with the Provisional IRA since February – this was revealed on the 28th of this month – actually to say it to the Commons was a catastrophic error. It made the Prime Minister out to be a liar, enabling Sinn Féin simply to bide their time, before deeply embarrassing the British government. Major then tried to make amends by proposing a series of bilateral meetings with the leaders of the four main (constitutional) political parties to initiate a talks process. However, the main Unionist parties represented in the House of Commons – the DUP and UUP – announced that neither of them would talk to the SDLP until the Hume–Adams Initiative was ended.

On the 2nd, RUCR Constable Brian Woods (30), father of one, died in the Daisy Hill Hospital in Newry, following his wounding by a PIRA sniper in Upper Edward Street, just two days earlier, whilst he manned a VCP. He lived with his wife and child at Begney Road, Dromara, and had been a policeman for less than eight months. One of his colleagues, who was standing with Woods when he was hit, described the sensation as the high-velocity round passed him as being akin to a smack in the face with a cricket bat. Constable Woods became the 100th RUCR officer to be killed in the Troubles.

On the 4th, Gordon Wilson, father of Marie Wilson who was killed at Enniskillen on the Poppy Day Massacre in 1987, revealed that he and two others had held a meeting with three leaders of Loyalist paramilitaries earlier in the week. He had talked to the leaders of the Provisional IRA some time after the Enniskillen bomb and whilst many admired his courage and forgiveness others, myself included, felt that he had played into the terrorists' hands and effectively legitimised them in the eyes of the world. The previous month, Irish Taoiseach Albert Reynolds and his deputy Dick Spring had announced at their party's annual conference that they had put forward proposals to Gerry Adams which, if accepted, meant that 'peace could begin by the end of the year'. On the 6th, Adams, having discussed the Irish government's suggestion with the IRA's Army Council, firmly rejected the Reynolds/Spring proposal.

Romeo-16
Mark Ormston, Royal Artillery

I was serving as Team Commander with a troop from 20 Commando Battery RA who were attached to 22 Regt RA for the tour. Operating in Warrenpoint, Portadown, Rathfriland and surrounding areas conducting urban, rural and boat patrols as well as manning a PVCP, known as Romeo-16.

While we were operating out of R16 we sometimes used to get visits from members of a special unit tasked with gathering intelligence. On one visit I was briefed by a guy that he would be taking the place of one of my team. He would act as the 'chat up' man, and we were to patrol in the area to the west of R16 toward the village of Meigh and carry out VCPs at pre-arranged locations and that he would indicate for me to stop a particular car at some point. Off we went and carried out several VCPs stopping random cars and carrying out searches and plate checks etc. and then during one of the VCPs he asked me to stop a certain car, and while I was carrying out the plate check on the radio he went over and spoke to the driver. Once he had finished he told me we could call it a day and head back to base, he was dressed the same as us except for a slight modification to his SA80 and something inset in his helmet, which I assumed was either a camera or microphone, or both. [I thought that] the patrol was just a ruse for an agent handler to meet his agent and get information in such a way that even in the area of South Armagh where we were patrolling it would not raise suspicion if anyone was watching.

On Sunday 7th, a little over a week since the Greysteel massacre, approximately 3,000 people attended a peace rally outside the still-closed and shuttered Rising Sun bar. The *Independent* reported: 'The Greysteel walk was organised jointly by residents of the mainly Catholic village and the people of the mainly Protestant neighbouring village of Eglinton. Among those present at the prayer meeting outside the Rising Sun after the walk were relatives of those killed and injured in the atrocity. Mary McGuigan, one of the organisers, described the turnout as fantastic. She added: "I am really touched. I think it is just brilliant. I did not expect anything less but I am still delighted. The message we are sending out is that we as a community are even closer than we were when this happened last week."'

Much further south, a PIRA sniper in the New Lodge shot and wounded a soldier on patrol from North Queen Street RUC station, as his team walked along Spamount Street. The slightly wounded soldier was taken to hospital, but his comrades were unable to return fire, as the gunman was 'swallowed up' in the plethora of side streets and taken to a safe house. The weapon was disassembled and returned, piece by piece to the New Lodge quartermaster, even under the eyes of searching soldiers. On the same day a large PIRA unit armed with machine guns and mortars attacked the tiny RUC base at Caledon, Co. Tyrone. Caledon is very close to the Irish border – less than three miles – meaning that escape for the terrorists was very easy. The mortar shell used was a 'barrack-buster' approximately 200 lb (90 kg) in weight, which detonated outside the base. The explosion was followed up by an indiscriminate burst of heavy-machine-gun fire.

The *Independent* reported: 'Meanwhile, more than 50 people were evacuated from their homes early yesterday after an RUC station close to the border with the republic came under a gun and bomb attack. A church and several buildings, including houses at Caledon, Co. Tyrone, were damaged but no one was hurt. The mortar landed in the grounds of the local Presbyterian church prompting an RUC spokesman to say that it "could have very easily resulted in a mass murder atrocity".'

The following day, there was a most regrettable incident which led to the court-martialing of a young soldier, following an incident at a VCP close to Omagh in Co. Tyrone. A woman driver with four children in her car approached the VCP when inexplicably one of the soldiers from the Royal Irish Regiment shot her. Fortunately she survived the incident. I have no further information, other than to say that from Army sources, it appears this was nothing more than a tragic accident. Naturally Sinn Féin claimed that it was deliberate.

On the 11th, Michael Ancram and colleagues from the NIO met representatives from the UUP in London to discuss their attitudes towards, and help with, the peace process. On the same day, the DUP published its proposals for the future of Northern Ireland in a document entitled 'Breaking the Log-Jam'.

The 12th witnessed another of the IRA's operations to attack and wipe out a small Army base (similar to the 'Derryard action' of December 1989) when one of the 'Golf' observation towers at the combined RUC/Army barracks was hit by an improvised flame-thrower. The towers – 10 in all and mostly in South Armagh – were designed both to protect the soldiers and to dominate the land around, observing virtually everywhere. The *Sunday Times* described them thus: 'The towers are high-tech fortresses with rooms buried beneath, where soldiers can live for months at a time. Computer terminals are linked to the main military intelligence databases, Vengeful and Crucible, and video enhancing equipment allows soldiers to see for miles, even across the border to the Irish Republic.'

This particular tower was being manned by four soldiers from the Grenadier Guards. At 18:28 they noticed a tractor which had been working on the farmland behind the base, suddenly stop and then reverse towards the tower. It came to a halt at the foot of the tower, before spraying fuel everywhere. The driver then ignited the fuel and the tower burst into flames, which Toby Harnden in his excellent *Bandit Country* describes as: 'A 30 foot fireball fuelled by an estimated 1,100 gallons of petrol engulfed the tower for a full 7 minutes, sending the temperature inside soaring.'[1] The men inside realised that they were very likely to die, but calmly took it in turns to cool themselves by standing inside a cold shower, as their quarters quickly heated up like an oven. Fortunately, their plight was spotted by Sergeant David Adkins and the Grenadiers' CO, Lt-Col Oliver Lindsay. The two soldiers and other troops dashed across to the burning tower but were beaten back by the intense heat. Adkins then ordered the driver of a Saxon armoured personnel carrier to drive towards the cause of the conflagration – the burning muck-spreader – as he stood in the turret directing the rescue. The APC rammed the burning vehicle out of the way, and the troops were then able to rescue the slightly 'well-done' soldiers. Adkins later received a

1. Toby Harnden, *Bandit Country*, p. 123–4.

well-deserved 'mention in dispatches'. The incident once again proved the callous ingenuity of the South Armagh Provisionals.

How Big is the Bomb?
Mark Ormston, Royal Artillery

While [we were] operating out of R16 PVCP on Cloughoge mountain (more like a hill,) intelligence indicated that South Armagh PIRA were planning to attack using a vehicle-borne IED of up to 1000 lb, and as a result we found ourselves on standing patrols watching the main A1 road every night for a week or so. Our intention was to engage the vehicle when given the nod, and to ensure we stopped it we had been issued rifle-launched grenades (RLG). Off we went south down towards the border and got into a good over watch position off the road and got settled in for the evening. After a while, one of the younger members of the team asked: 'What is the range of the RLG?' I replied that it was about 120 metres. He responded: 'How big is the IED meant to be?' When I told him that it would be around 1,000 lb, the penny suddenly dropped! We would be a little too close if the RLG hit the vehicle and the bomb detonated. I quickly suggested that we relocate somewhere with a bit more hard cover; sharpish!

On Monday 15th, the first stage of what would soon turn into a period of severe embarrassment for John Major began, following his 'slight untruth' to the Commons about not speaking with the IRA. The *Belfast Telegraph* carried a report that Sinn Féin had held face-to-face meetings with senior British government officials and exchanged documents about how to end IRA violence. One source described the talks as 'protracted' but that they had been concluded in June. A spokesman for the Republican group refused to deny the claims, but the British government flatly rejected them. On the same day, Major caused a little confusion when he made a keynote speech about Northern Ireland. He spoke to a selected audience at London's Guildhall and told them that 'The opportunity for peace in Northern Ireland was better than at any time for many years.' This flatly contradicted the gloomy assessment which he had presented the country only days earlier.

Late in the evening of the 21st, a unit from PIRA's Tyrone brigade attacked the home of a former UDR soldier whom I have agreed not to name. The man had served with the UDR but had resigned some time earlier, though that wasn't enough for the Republican terror group. Shots were fired, but there were no injuries and the unit slunk back across the border. However, a soldier did die that day, when the Royal Irish lost Corporal Robert Armstrong (31) in an RTA in Co. Armagh. He is buried at Randrageet cemetery in Armagh.

On the 20th/21st, Hume and Adams met again and issued a joint statement calling for the adoption of their initiative. A rally in support was held on the Falls Road in West Belfast. Approximately 2,000 attended the event. The following day, not to be outdone, Patrick Mayhew gave a speech at Queen's University Belfast in which he stated that the British government would never talk with IRA/Sinn Féin until they ended their campaign of violence. At the same time, the Combined Loyalist Military Command stated that they were earnestly seeking peace. However, they also warned that the Loyalist paramilitary groups were preparing for war in case peace was 'bought at any price', which they were not prepared to accept.

On the 24th, there was a major blow for the UVF when British police received a tip-off from a 'high-ranking' informer that a large supply of arms and ammunition was being landed at Middlesbrough. The police raided Teesport dockside and made several arrests, seizing 300 assault rifles, thousands of bullets, two tonnes of explosives, and detonators, all of which had originated in Poland.

Throughout the later part of the month, there was a whole series of smaller PIRA devices going off over much of London. These were effectively nuisance bombs; some were potentially lethal but others were just designed to tie the emergency services in complete knots. Devices exploded at Staples Corner on the North Circular, at Highgate Hill, and in many other places including some as far out as stations in Berkshire.

On the 27th, at Cookstown, Co. Tyrone, John Hume addressed the annual conference of the SDLP. In his speech, he highlighted John Major as holding the key to peace. Hume cannot have felt confident, given that Major, had said that talking to the IRA would make him 'sick to the stomach' and the Provisionals had told the *Irish Times* that there would be 'no unilateral cessation of violence'. Meanwhile, approximately 40 miles away, on the other side of Lough Neagh, in Castlereagh, the DUP was also holding its annual conference. In his keynote speech, leader Ian Paisley told delegates that Northern Ireland faced 'the greatest threat to the Union since the Home Rule Crisis'.

The 27th fell on a Saturday and it must have been a most apprehensive Prime Minister who sipped his evening cocoa with his wife Norma, no doubt already alerted to the main story in the following morning's *Observer.* There is no record of how well he did or didn't sleep, but the paper quickly sold out at newsagents the length and breadth of the UK, as it revealed that John Major had been economical with the truth in relation to his government's dealings with PIRA.

The full nature and extent of a series of secret talks between the government and the Provisionals was revealed in the newspaper, which claimed that a secret channel of communication existed between the British and the IRA, and had done so since February of this year. The newspaper claimed that a Catholic priest called Denis Bradley had been an intermediary and that he had worked with the apparent blessings of the IRA's Army Council.

The *Observer* report stated:

> A secret communication chain has been running between the Government and the IRA with the Prime Minister's approval, an authoritative British source has told *The Observer.* The contacts have been in place for many months. Confirming that there had been contacts, the Northern Ireland Office said in a statement to *The Observer* last night: 'The IRA have not delivered the ending of violence envisaged in their original approach. They have continued to inflict untold misery and grief upon the public. It is for them to explain this. There can be no excuse for such terrorism. Their duty is to end it at once.' Later, in an attempt to limit the impact of today's exclusive *Observer* report . . . Whitehall said the IRA leadership had sent a message to the Government in February, to the effect that '"conflict was over, but they needed our advice as to the means of bringing it to a close". The

> Government obviously had to take that message seriously, though we recognised that actions, not words, would be the real test.' The communication link was said by the source to be a message-delivery service run by unofficial intermediaries; deniable 'heroes' who began operating after British Ministers' public overtures – going back as far as 1989 – brought a positive reaction from the IRA. The process, so secret that it was not even disclosed by John Major to Albert Reynolds, the Irish Prime Minister, was described as an essential response to the terrorists' 'peace feelers'. The go-betweens included clergymen, professionals and businessmen. The *Observer* source said that messengers often put their own lives at risk. Although the source emphatically denied direct government involvement, Sinn Féin chief of staff Martin McGuinness and others have said that a civil servant was used.[1]

The following day, the confusion deepened when Sinn Féin publicly released a number of documents that provided details of the secret talks. Martin McGuinness stated that the message of 22 February 1993 was a fake and he accused the British of 'counterfeiting their own documents to meet their current needs'. Patrick Mayhew then addressed the House of Commons in order to give the British version. He presented a series of documents which 'proved' that the government was being accurate in its claims and denials. However, just 48 hours later, he was forced to admit to a staggering 22 errors in the documents he had presented. A furious Ian Paisley, apoplectic even when calm, was livid with rage and screamed at Mayhew that he was a 'liar'. It is of course, contrary to Parliamentary practice to use such a word about another member, which left the distinctly unimpressed Speaker of the House, Betty Boothroyd, to eject Mr Paisley from the Commons. Prime Minister Major's dealings – or not – could be brushed under the carpet for the time being, but there was more to come back and haunt him in later years.

On the 29th, clearly fed up with talking instead of killing, a PIRA unit carried out a gun and bomb attack on the home of an off-duty officer in Armagh City. The officer was only slightly hurt; the murder gang escaped before reinforcements could arrive. It is possible that the same gang left a massive bomb some two miles away outside the town, but it was fortunately defused by the Army.

On the 30th, just over a month since the last sectarian murder, the UFF struck in Dundonald in East Belfast, killing a Catholic man who had absolutely no Republican connections and was thus no threat to the Loyalist paramilitaries. Sean Hagan (47), father of five, lived in the Nationalist Lenadoon area, although he worked at a car components company in Dundonald on the outskirts of Belfast, making a daily 26-mile round trip. It is thought that a Protestant workmate with links to the UDA told someone who informed someone else in the UFF that Mr Hagan was a Catholic and would be in the company car park every day at the same time; the rest was simply a matter of timing. Adair had been quiet for a while, owing to some time spent in police custody and the fact that he was also under constant surveillance. On his release, he briefed 'C' company members, ordering them to make the nine-mile journey to the factory on the Upper Newtownards Road to kill their target in the early hours of the morning as he finished his night shift. At round 00:30, the gang, thought to include McKeag, saw Mr Hagan reversing out of his parking

1. https://www.theguardian.com/uk/1993/nov/28/northernireland.

space; they ran over to the car and shot him several times through the car window; he died at the scene. His son told the *Irish News*: 'With the upturn in sectarian killings he was a bit worried about it, but [it] didn't deter him. He had a job to do, money to make, a family and he just looked at that. He was doing it to keep us.'

November was over and fortunately, there had been more talk than killing this month. For, as Winston Churchill famously once said, 'meeting jaw to jaw is better than war'. Three people had died: a soldier and a policeman and a Catholic civilian who was killed in a clearly sectarian attack.

36

December

There had been extraordinary levels of violent deaths in October, but just three in November so as Northern Ireland entered in the build-up to the 25th Christmas of the Troubles what would December bring? In fact there would be 14 deaths, including six soldiers and two police officers. Three Catholics were killed in sectarian attacks, and three other civilians – two Protestants and a Catholic – at the hands of PIRA and the UFF. It was also the month of the 'Downing Street Declaration' which gave fresh hopes of peace, but still over 70 people would be killed in 1994, with both sets of paramilitaries seemingly reluctant to end the violence.

The first death of the month occurred very early on, but neither *Lost Lives* nor a search of death records in Belfast gives the exact date of Alexander Scott's death. At an unknown date in 1972, Mr Scott (then aged 39), a Protestant, was chatting to soldiers in Donegall Road, when he was hit by a round fired by an OIRA sniper. He survived the shot but spent the following 21 years in chronic pain, which required repeated pain-killing injections. He died this month, a belated but no less real victim of Republican violence.

On the 2nd, the Royal Artillery suffered their first fatality in nine months, their 66th overall, when Lance Bombardier Paul Andrew Garrett (23) was shot and mortally wounded in Keady, Co. Armagh. The Royal Artillery and the Royal Horse Artillery, both used in the standard infantry role, lost a total of 73 soldiers in and as a consequence of the Troubles during the period 1969–98. Only the UDR had a higher number of killed and injured.

Lance Bombardier Garrett, a South London boy, was on foot patrol in Victoria Gardens, Keady. Just as he passed a gap in the houses at Lir Gardens, a PIRA sniper firing from Granemore Road, across a large grassed area, hit him with a single round which tore into his stomach. A comrade ran to his side, but could not initially see any signs of injury; young Garrett was in shock and was unable to provide vital information as to the location of the wound. Within seconds a local doctor and a nurse, despite threats to their own lives, raced over to help him and desperately tried to save him. He died within six minutes of the shot. His father, who was a former soldier himself, told the press: 'They shot my boy like a dog, but I just hope that his death serves some purpose. I hope that he is the last soldier to be killed there. I just hope.' The family were from British Guyana; heartbroken at the loss of their son they eventually returned to the Caribbean. He has a CWGC headstone which stands defiantly over his grave at London Road, Mitcham; the headstone reads: 'To the world he was a soldier, to us he was the World. Goodbye, Paul. Rest in Peace.'

On Thursday 2nd, Sinn Féin released more information on the secret talks between the Major government and the Republican movement. Martin McGuinness claimed that the

British government had begun the contacts as far back as 1990. It was more embarrassment for Major, but the reality was that talks with the British government had started initially as far back as 1972, when Prime Minister Edward Heath had arranged for several members of the Provisionals to be flown in for a secret meeting at Paul Channon MP's private house in Chelsea, along with the then Secretary of State for Northern Ireland, William Whitelaw. The 1972 IRA party included Gerry Adams – who publicly claims that he was never a member of the IRA – who was specially released from the Maze where he was detained at the time for terrorist activities. The talks came to naught, because the Republicans simply wanted a timetable for withdrawal of the British Army and didn't wish to discuss peace. The 1972 talks broke down around 7–12 July and it is no coincidence that, according to Brendan Hughes – a PIRA comrade of Adams – an Adams-ordered blitz of Belfast City Centre took place shortly afterwards. The series of multiple bombings over an hour or so killed nine people on 21 July; a date known as 'Bloody Friday'. Ten days later, there was the bombing blitz which devastated the village of Claudy, Co. Londonderry, killing nine, which I and many others believe was ordered by Martin McGuinness.

On the 5th, there were two more sectarian murders, both of Catholics, in North Belfast, yet again on the orders of Adair. Fresh from killing Sean Hagan six days earlier, 'C' company gunmen including McKeag drove towards a Catholic taxi office in Ligoniel, simply to see if any likely targets were in the vicinity. The UFF gunmen arrived in Ligoniel Road and saw a taxi with its engine running, a passenger ready in the front of the car. The driver was Robert John Todd (31), who was now working for a local company, having previously worked at Shorts. He had been persuaded to join his friend Kevin Flood in the taxi trade, though Flood himself had been killed by UVF gunmen in September 1991 (*see* Chapter 9). The passenger this evening was Brian Duffy (15) who was in voluntary care at a children's' home; the taxi had been arranged to take him there. Once the UFF car had stopped, one of the passengers got out and, using a parked bus as cover, approached the taxi. He was armed with what witnesses described as an 'elephant gun'. Without warning, the gunman blasted the two people inside the taxi, with lethal 'big game' pellets smashing into their heads and chests, causing 'terrible injuries'. The killer ran back to the stolen car which did a U-turn, hitting a car belonging, coincidentally, to Kevin Flood's widow; another taxi driver who had seen what was happening, bravely tried to ram the UVF men, just failing to stop them. They drove off in the direction of the Shankill, later abandoning the car before collecting a second vehicle. The young Brian Duffy was related to Robert Duffy who was jailed in July 1996 for the October 1993 murder of John Gibson (*see* Chapter 34). Brian Duffy died almost instantly with Mr Todd dying en route for the Mater Hospital. The older man was engaged to be married and was shortly to leave for a new job and new life in England. There is no evidence to link the murder of the boy with any paramilitary crimes committed by his uncle.

Between the 3rd and 7th, there were two major attempts by PIRA units to kill soldiers and police officers; on the 3rd, a massive PIRA device was abandoned in the Poleglass area of south-West Belfast. Thanks to the efforts of ATO, the area was made safe. Despite the bravery and professionalism of the Army bomb disposal staff in saving Nationalist housing and Nationalist civilians, the locals came out to show their 'gratitude'. Bricks and bottles were thrown by local thugs as the soldiers were taunted throughout. Four days later, a PIRA unit mortared the RUC base at Newtownbutler in Co. Fermanagh; there was some damage but injuries were light.

On the day of the Newtownbutler attack, there was another odd death amongst the SF, and the second of this nature: Corporal Terence Heffy (43) of the Royal Logistic Corps was killed in a railway accident. In 1972, the Argyll & Sutherland Highlanders had lost Private David Harper who was killed by a passing train whilst patrolling near a railway track. Corporal Heffy was from the St Helens area and his funeral was held at St Helens Crematorium; I have no details of the accident, other than it involved a train.

Adair's murder gang still had their dirty work to do, as sectarian attacks continued. Their target on the 7th, was Robert McClay (37), father of four, who lived in the middle-class East Belfast suburb of Ballyhackamore. His house was on Hillview Avenue, just over four miles from Adair's house in the Shankill, a journey time of around 11 minutes. That evening, at around 21:30, Mr McClay was sitting in his living room, watching television. He got up to answer a knock at the front door, but the second that he opened it, one of the gunmen, armed with a handgun, shot him at point-blank range in the stomach. Mortally wounded, he slumped to the ground, dying seconds later on his own front doorstep. The murder gang raced back to the Shankill, with another dead Catholic to their 'credit'. The UDA later claimed that the dead man was a member of the IRA, a claim dismissed by the Belfast Coroner as 'quite scandalous'.

That weekend, the *Irish Times* reported the results of a poll which it had conducted in the Republic on Anglo-Irish relations. Of those questioned, 59% were in favour of talks between the British and Irish governments. The figure for Catholic respondents was 88% in favour whilst the figure for Protestants was much lower, at 37%. This followed an earlier poll for the newspaper which had asked questions about a political settlement in Northern Ireland. Among Catholic respondents 33% favoured the option of joint authority while a surprisingly low 32% wanted to see a united Ireland.

On the 12th, two RUC officers were killed in Fivemiletown, Co. Tyrone, by gunmen from the Provisional IRA, an attack which left five more children fatherless. Fivemiletown is around 70 miles west of Belfast, roughly six miles from the nearest border crossing into the Republic. Around 01:30, RUC Constable Andrew 'Drew' Beacom (46), father of three, and RUCR Constable Ernest Smyth (49), father of two, were patrolling in an unmarked Renault 21 along Main Street between Clabby Road and Coneen Road. The two officers had a combined total of 43 years' service between them. They drove straight into a well-prepared ambush, as two PIRA gunmen opened fire from opposite sides of Main Street with automatic weapons, hitting the car at least 20 times. Both men were fatally wounded, dying shortly afterwards. One of the first on the scene was Constable Beacom's wife who ran a nearby restaurant. Alerted by the gunfire, she dashed from the house to find her husband close to death in the shot-up car. Army helicopters were quickly on the scene, but the PIRA operatives had a .50 calibre heavy machine gun ready, with which they opened fire and hit one of the helicopters several times. The pair were the fifth and sixth police officers killed this year with the RUC's toll of dead now standing at 290.

The two officers, both based at Clogher RUC station, were buried the following week; a senior Orange Order leader said of their murders: 'Such senseless acts of barbarity were the dastardly deeds of faceless criminals – intent on causing nothing other than death and destruction on the streets of our beloved Province.' RUC Chief Constable Hugh Annesley went further: 'This senseless act of barbarity, carried out in such a cowardly fashion by faceless criminals is in sharp contrast to the dedicated and caring attitude exemplified by these two officers.'

On the 13th/14th, PIRA's England team again brought the war back to the commuters in the south of England, by reminding them that the IRA, whom John Major had claimed were defeated, hadn't quite gone away. On the morning of the 13th, a coded message was received from Republican sources in Dublin, just before the morning rush hour. Shortly afterwards a bomb exploded on the Woking–London Waterloo line, between West Byfleet and Woking; it left a crater one foot deep and two feet wide, severely damaging one rail. No one was hurt, and a British Rail maintenance train later travelled over the crater without being damaged. British anti-terrorist squad officers, British Transport Police and local police sealed off the area before carrying out a thorough examination. Meanwhile City, clerical and other types of workers fumed in packed but train-less stations, or stalled trains, as the IRA again damaged the British economy on the mainland. Over the next 48 hours, there were further explosions and continued disruption to passenger traffic near Brookwood and Farnborough stations in Surrey.

Also on the 13th, the UFF killed a man aged 26, who had a mental age of only 12 according to family and the local authorities. Noel Cardwell (26) was very tall (6 ft 4 in) but had learning difficulties. He made a living collecting glasses in the Diamond Jubilee Bar on St Peter's Hill, just off the Shankill Road. He was somewhat over-impressed by the UFF 'C' company men who drank there, hero-worshipping the paramilitary thugs who killed for Adair. In early December, some of the 'boys' thought that it would be a 'laugh' to spike his beer with ecstasy. As a consequence he was taken very ill and was rushed to the Mater Hospital. Whilst he was there, RUC detectives routinely questioned him; in his childish innocence, he named two of the UFF gang. They were arrested, but later released without charge. There the matter might have rested, but there was an informer within the UFF – not Mr Cardwell I hasten to add – who notified his handlers of a UFF arms cache in a flat on the Lower Shankill. Consequently, the RUC were able to raid the location, seizing arms and ammunition. Adair is said to have been enraged, with immediate suspicion falling on Mr Cardwell; he ordered a 'court martial' on the disabled man.[1]

Noel was released from hospital on the 13th, but later, on his way to his sister's house in Tennant Street, he was seized by UFF thugs, punched and kicked, before being taken to his own home in Boundary Walk. There he was badly beaten and then taken to an empty flat on the floor above. He was again beaten and 'interrogated' but couldn't admit to being an informer. At the end of the questioning, Adair himself appeared, demanding to know if Cardwell had confessed. On being told 'no', he left the room, to return minutes later, wearing paramilitary gear and armed with a silenced pistol. Mr Cardwell was bound and hooded before being dragged to a corner of the seedy flat. Adair ordered him to kneel before he personally put the pistol against his victim's head and fired one round. Lister and Jordan allege that was the one and only time that Adair personally killed anyone.[2] The man's body was left where he slumped when 'Mad Dog' Adair and crew went off, presumably to

1. McDonald & Cusack, *UDA: Inside the Heart of Loyalist Terror*, p. 253.
2. Lister & Jordan, *Mad Dog*, pp. 193–4, 338.

celebrate. The media were informed, immediately passing on the information to the RUC who were unable to find a body, alive or dead, in the location given. At about 09:00 the following morning, a local man was walking to a shop when he noticed that the door of flat 34C Boundary Walk was open. On his return he noticed it was still open and went in to investigate. He found Noel Cardwell lying in the corner of the living room in a large pool of blood and saw that he was still breathing. He phoned immediately for an ambulance, which arrived at approximately 09:31. The RUC also arrived just as the victim was being removed to the ambulance. He was brought to the RVH where a doctor found his blood pressure unrecordable and that he was very cold to the touch, as if he had been lying for some time before he was found. He was pronounced dead at 10:20. The temperature in the room had been below freezing which had prevented massive blood loss and kept the young man from dying. One of the men present was Gary Witty McMaster, who was arrested the following day and later convicted of his role in the murder.[1] He received an 18-year jail sentence.

Also on the 14th, the Provisional IRA again caused the death of an elderly woman. It was the second such death, following that of Annie Bogle in October. The leader of the PIRA unit in the Markets area of Belfast – who I am legally unable to name – decided on an attack to kill and maim members of an Army foot patrol in Cromac Square. A device was hidden behind billboards between Friendly Way and Cromac Street, intended to explode when the soldiers passed by. The device was discovered and while it was being dealt with the RUC decided on an evacuation, and began waking up residents, including Mrs Bridie Glennon (78) and her daughter, also called Bridie. As they left the house, the 1,000 lb (450 kg) device exploded, causing massive damage to property, but the resultant shock brought on an instant and fatal heart attack for Mrs Glennon, Sr. Her grieving daughter was interviewed later that day; she told the Belfast *News Letter*: 'All I can say is thanks to the brave boys on both sides, the Nationalist and Loyalist paramilitaries, thanks very much fellas for giving me a happy Christmas with no mother ... thanks brave men – for what? For murdering my mother. I'll never forgive you for what you have done ... never, never!'

The following day, the 15th, for sheer brass neck, Sinn Féin proved that they had no equals, when one of their spokesmen, Sean McKnight, was interviewed by the *News Letter*. He expressed his 'deep regret and sadness' at the death of his neighbour. He went on to say: 'I heard of Bridie's death in Mayfield Leisure centre ... and [her] death came as a terrible shock to me.' I have scoured the article and at no time does the Sinn Féin man condemn his comrades in PIRA for planting the bomb. The article goes on to say that the dead woman's family were 'sickened' by the actions which caused her death and also by the shallow regrets voiced by the Sinn Féin spokesman.[2]

Later during that fateful day of the 15th, the Provisionals turned their attention to Ebrington Barracks in Londonderry; the barracks, now closed, was situated in the Waterside area on the eastern bank of the Foyle. Back in 1993, there was a railway line running close by. This was targeted by the IRA who placed a trip wire bomb designed to kill or maim soldiers as they patrolled the area. In the very late evening, as a patrol returned to the barracks, one of the soldiers stumbled over the wire. The explosion injured two soldiers,

1. http://www.courtsni.gov.uk/en-gb/judicial%20decisions/publishedbyyear/documents/2011/[2011]%20nilst%201/j_j_mor8116final.htm.
2. Belfast *News Letter*, Wednesday 15 December 1993.

one of whom suffered perforated eardrums. In 2015, a PIRA member, Christopher Paul O'Kane, was sentenced to 10 years in prison for his involvement in that attack and for his part in the murder of RUC officer Michael Ferguson in January 1993 (*see* Chapter 25).[1]

Also on the 15th, a soldier from the Royal Army Pay Corps died in circumstances which are best described as 'violent or unnatural'. Private M. A. McLeod is on Northern Ireland Veterans' Association roll of honour, but I have been unable to find any further information. Twenty-four hours later, the Royal Welch Fusiliers lost Corporal David Wright (27), who was killed in an RTA whilst on duty. He was from the Clwyd area and his funeral was held at Wrexham Crematorium.

On the 15th, following an earlier meeting between the two at a European Community summit in Brussels, John Major and Albert Reynolds issued a joint Declaration from 10 Downing Street, henceforth to became known, rather unimaginatively, as the 'Downing Street Declaration'. The stated aim of the two leaders was 'to foster agreement and reconciliation, leading to a new political framework founded on consent and encompassing arrangements within Northern Ireland, for the whole island, and between these islands'. Speaking in the House of Commons, Major tried to allay Unionist concerns about the Declaration by drawing attention to the matters which were not in the document, which had the effect of further confusing the Unionist MPs. He said: 'What is not in the Declaration is any suggestion that the British government should join the ranks of the persuaders of the value or legitimacy of a united Ireland.' It would appear that Reynolds and Spring, when addressing the Dáil had a much easier ride, informing the TDs that paramilitary groups would have to hand over their weapons following the end of violence. In London, Ian Paisley's first reaction was to inform the press that he would organise a series of rallies against the Downing Street Declaration.[2]

If reaction from the Unionists was an anticipated combination of suspicion and anger, there was almost certainly much guarded gloating from Hume and Adams. John Hume met Adams again on the 20th, arranging a follow-up once Adams had reported back on Sinn Féin's response. In essence, however, once Adams had agreed, it was expected that the IRA's Army Council would rubber-stamp the decision. Adams called for clarification of certain points of the document, possibly not understanding why there was no timetable for the reunification of Ireland. Somewhat surprisingly, certainly unpredictably, UUP leader James Molyneaux, speaking to BBC Radio, argued that the Downing Street Declaration was not 'a sell-out' of Unionists. Ulster Marketing Surveys carried out a poll in Northern Ireland on behalf of Independent Television News; 56% of those questioned said that they were in favour of the declaration.

On the 19th, PIRA's Creggan unit left a large landmine in an area which the Army were known to patrol, detonating the device by command wire, despite the proximity of civilians to the intended seat of the blast. Several soldiers were injured, but six civilians, including two children, were hospitalised. I can find no record of apologies from the Provisionals, despite a thorough scouring of *An Phoblacht* back issues. There was damage to property

1. http://www.belfasttelegraph.co.uk/news/northern-ireland/derry-man-handed-10year-jail-sentence-for-ira-terrorist-offences-34304971.html.
2. The full text of the declaration is available at https://www.britannica.com/place/Northern-Ireland/Cultural-life#ref715980.

valued at £450,000. On the same day, a large device was left to kill and maim a rural patrol at a derelict farm at Pomeroy, Co. Tyrone; the Army managed to defuse the bomb.

The following day, a PIRA bombing unit left a 110 lb (50 kg) device in a residential area on the Suffolk Estate in West Belfast; the device exploded, injuring a soldier and a Catholic civilian; no apologies have been recorded. On the mainland, a number of IRA firebombs exploded in stores, and a letter bomb in a post office in East London caused minor damage. Seven incendiary devices were also made safe . The IRA were determined to make Christmas as miserable as possible, and their tactics ensured that the police and bomb disposal teams were spread very thinly with a whole series of attacks. They left a holdall containing six incendiary devices in the Travellers' Tavern, Elizabeth Street, Victoria, London, one of which ignited, causing minor damage. Another letter bomb was discovered and made safe at Mount Pleasant Sorting Office, London; shortly afterwards, a small device ignited inside one of the few remaining litter bins on railway property, this one at Northfields Tube Station, London W13.

Just two days before Christmas, two Royal Marines were acquitted by a court in Belfast of the murder of Fergal Caraher on 30 December 1990. Caraher was a Sinn member at the time he was killed; he was shot dead while travelling in a car in Cullyhanna, Co. Armagh.

Also on 23 December, the IRA announced a three-day Christmas ceasefire. It was observed, with minor infringements, but came to an end on the 27th, when a car bomb exploded at the RUC station on Springfield Road, Belfast; there was some damage but no injuries. Shots were fired at a Territorial Army base in Portadown, Co. Armagh, but again, there were no injuries. Before the day had ended, a PIRA unit launched a mortar attack on the RUC base at Fintona, Co. Tyrone, not far from Ballygawley. The missile fell short and exploded, injuring a civilian in addition to causing much damage to surrounding businesses. There were two final mortar attacks of the year. The first was on an Army patrol in West Belfast on the 28th; one soldier was injured by a round from a horizontal mortar. The following day, an IRA unit fired a missile at a British patrol on Upper Library Street in Belfast; the device missed and there were no injuries. The Provisionals claimed that this was a new armour-piercing mortar projectile.

December wasn't quite finished; two more soldiers died before the New Year bells could chime in 1994. On the 29th, the Royal Logistic Corps lost another soldier. Private Matthew Edwards (20), a Somerset boy, died in circumstances best described as 'violent and unnatural causes'. He is buried at Ebdon Road Cemetery, Weston-super-Mare.

On the 30th, the Provisionals killed another soldier, again deep in the heart of 'bandit country' in the Republican town of Crossmaglen. The Grenadier Guards were in occupation at the joint RUC/Army base in Crossmaglen; it was only days since the 'flame-thrower' attack by the Provisionals. Guardsman Daniel Blinco (22) was a Derbyshire lad, living in Melbourne; he had been in the Army for several years, being due to leave in 1994. Only days after the Downing Street Declaration, there was a feeling that it might be all over, or at least calming down, with a possible reluctance on the part of the Republicans to initiate any violence. How wrong could people be.

As the Grenadiers moved out of their Crossmaglen base on a routine patrol Guardsman Blinco walked along Newry Street close to the Murtagh Bar. A single shot rang out and the 6 ft 6 in tall soldier slumped to the ground and died shortly afterward in hospital. ITV News reported: 'The Christmas ceasefire has only just ended, but the IRA's campaign continues without let up. This afternoon in the heart of Crossmaglen, the personal effects of their latest victim were being collected as a soldier was shot in the arm and shoulder as his patrol moved through the town. He was taken to hospital but died later. There are thought to be several snipers operating in the area probably trained originally by one of the older IRA men in the area. They use high-velocity rifles that are deadly accurate from great distances.'

The death, coming at a time of guarded optimism, prompted this break from the ranks, when a local SDLP Councillor said: 'Many supporters of Sinn Féin have locally and publicly said: let's give this a chance. I think that they'll be asking questions of the Provisional IRA why this man had to die, and why this action had to be taken today.' The great difficulty which both soldiers and police faced in the Crossmaglen area in particular was that they were forbidden to cross the border, whereas terrorists could cross at their ease and convenience; as one senior officer stated: 'We are up against an enemy who are not even in Northern Ireland.'

On 9 November 2013, there was a memorial march to honour the memory of this young soldier. The BBC reported: 'A British infantry regiment has marched through a Derbyshire village to honour a soldier killed in Northern Ireland almost 20 years ago. Daniel Blinco, 22, died in a sniper attack during a patrol in South Armagh in December 1993. The Grenadier Guards marched in Melbourne to mark his death on the day before Remembrance Sunday. A bench at Melbourne Hall was also rededicated to him as part of the ceremony . . . Joanna Swain, Guardsman Blinco's sister, said: "It is absolutely wonderful that Daniel has not been forgotten – it is beyond belief, to be honest." She said the original bench would be taken back to her home and placed in her garden. His mother Nina Blinco said: "We are overwhelmed – it is a wonderful thing that the people of Melbourne have turned out. Daniel would have loved every minute of it."'

The final act of 1993 was a statement by the UVF that it did not feel threatened by the Downing Street Declaration. Displaying for once a hint of responsible behaviour, it declared that it would not support another of Ian Paisley's 'publicity stunts'.

December was over, and in the month of so many supposedly earnest desires for peace, 14 people had died. Of the 14 deaths, six were at the hands of the IRA and four at the hands of Loyalists.

In the year, despite the terrible outrages at Frizzell's and Greysteel, overall deaths fell slightly to 99.

1993 Deaths

Military/former military	21
Police	7
Republican paramilitary	5
Loyalist paramilitary	3
Civilian	63
Catholic	41*
Protestant	22*

* Sectarian deaths were 53 (Catholics 40, Protestants 13).

The Killing of Soldiers and RUC by Loyalist Paramilitaries
Mark 'C', UDR and Royal Artillery

Firstly let me say, I do not condone Loyalist killing in any way, in fact my own family suffered at their hands; as Maggie Thatcher once famously said: 'Murder is murder, is murder.'

I often read in soldiers' accounts in NI, that they got it equally from both sides during the conflict . . . the casualty rates do not bear it out, as the vast majority of Security Force killing was done at the hands of Republicans. Of course there were times when the Security Forces came into conflict with Loyalists, I am thinking of the early days of 1969/70 on the Shankill, the rise of the UDA in East Belfast in 1973/74, the 1977 Loyalist Strike and of course at Drumcree and Holy Cross at the end of Op. Banner. But there was never an orchestrated campaign by Loyalists against the Security Forces apart from some of those and others already mentioned.

1,228 members of the Security Forces, i.e. Regular Army, UDR, Royal Irish, RUC, PSNI, NIPS, NIFB, Garda, IDF, former members of above, family members of above caught up in attacks on their loved ones and civilian staff of above, were murdered in terrorist attacks, 1969–present, if we take in the now dissident Republican attacks. Out of this total of 1,228, Republican terrorists of the OIRA, PIRA, INLA, IPLO, SAOR EIRE and the dissidents murdered 1.209 and Loyalist groups like UVF, PAF, UDA, UFF, RHD murdered 19. Viewing these 19 killings by Loyalists dispassionately, very few were planned or premeditated; most were SF in the wrong place at the wrong time. For example, R/Cons Mildred Harrison had only been in the RUCR for 2 months, when she just happened to be passing a Catholic-owned bar in Bangor Co. Down; a bomb placed on a window ledge there by the UVF exploded, killing her instantly, or Cpl John Geddis of 10 UDR drove into a petrol station on the Crumlin Road, unaware the UVF had planted a bomb there because it had refused to shut down during the 1977 Loyalist strike; again he was killed instantly and his wife injured when the bomb exploded, ironically his father was one of the strike leaders.

Other cases like Pte Henry Russell of 9 UDR, and Pte Terence Maguire of 10 UDR, murdered by the UDA, were believed to be killed because simply they were Catholics living in Loyalist areas and nothing to do with their UDR membership or Captain Tim Armstrong of 8 UDR who was shot by a UFF gunman because he was walking down what would be classed as a Catholic street in Belfast. Of course some were planned, examples being the murder of RUC Constable Michael Logue, when a joint UVF/UDA operation lured SF into the Highfield area of North Belfast, to attack them after the Army had shot and killed a Loyalist on the Shankill, or the UVF shooting of Private Raymond Hall of the Green Howards, killed during rioting in a Loyalist area of East Belfast because other Loyalists had been arrested and interned in the area by the Army, others like the murder of Prison Officers William Burns and James Peacock by the UVF were in supposed retaliation for ill treatment of Loyalist prisoners in Crumlin Road and Maze Prisons and one of the last RUC officers to be murdered, Constable Frank O'Reilly, was killed by a Loyalist blast bomb in Portadown that was claimed by a group called the Red Hand Defenders saying it was because of the RUC action in stopping an Orange parade along the Garvaghy Road.

So to finish: no right-thinking person could condone these awful murders, but I don't think you can say soldiers or police were in the same danger patrolling Loyalist streets as they were in Republican streets; the facts just don't bear this out and again I say every terrorist murder was wrong and those responsible should be punished. However, there was never an orchestrated campaign of killing against the SF by Loyalists, whilst Republicans actively planned and carried out premeditated murder on a grand scale.

A Letter to a Politician

You weren't there; you don't know; I signed up and was prepared to go.
I took the shilling and fell in line, then off to Ulster; it was our time.

You weren't there; you don't know; amidst the bullets, bombs, snipers and so.
You didn't know how hard we tried, but still you sent us and you lied.

You weren't there; you don't know; now you reap what you did sow.
You turned us out onto the street, and now some are wrecked in quivering heaps.

You weren't there; you don't know; now I hate that you didn't go.
You kiss babies and you shake hands; your words are like drifting sands.

You weren't there; you don't know; you never saw the blood that flowed.
I still can't see what it was for, but unlike you, I know it was a war.

You weren't there; you don't know; you in Blighty, lying low.
You never had to run and weave, the gunman's bullet to deceive.

You weren't there; you don't know; you never felt the terrorist blow.
You never heard the noise like thunder, which blew soldiers asunder.

You weren't there; you don't know; what it was like to let a comrade go.
But I was there with hope and truth, as others died in their youth.

You weren't there; you don't know; of the pain we feel whilst you're on show.
You sweep the veterans under carpet, but we had the spirit to stand on the parapet.

Jim Coyle[1]

1. Jim Coyle served with the British Army in Northern Ireland in the 1980s.

Select Bibliography

James Adams, Robin Morgan & Anthony Bambridge, *Ambush: The War between the SAS and the IRA* (Pan, 1988)

Alan Barker, *Shadows: Inside Northern Ireland's Special Branch* (Mainstream, 2004)
David Barzilay, *The British Army in Ulster*, Vol. 1 (Century, 1973)
———, *The British Army in Ulster*, Vol. II (Century, 1975)
David Beresford, *Ten Men Dead* (Harper Collins, 1994)
Colin Breen, *A Force Like No Other* (Blackstaff Press, 2017)
Johnston Brown, *Into the Dark: 30 Years in the RUC* (Gill & MacMillan, 2005)
Jonathan Burgess, *The Exodus* (Causeway Press, 2011)
Michael Burleigh, *Blood and Rage: A Cultural History of Terrorism* (HarperCollins, 2009)

Anne Cadwallader, *Lethal Allies* (Mercier Press, 2013)
John Campbell, *The Iron Lady* (Vintage, 2012)
A. F. N. Clarke, *Contact* (Secker & Warburg, 1983)
George Clarke, *Border Crossing* (Gill & MacMillan, 2009)
Liam Clarke & Kathryn Johnston, *Martin McGuinness: From Guns to Government* (Mainstream, 2001)
Eamon Collins, *Killing Rage* (Granta Books, 1997)
Kieran Conway, *Southside Provisional* (Orpen Press, 2014)
Jim Cusack & Henry McDonald, *UVF: The Endgame* (Poolbeg Press, 2008)

Nicholas Davies, *Dead Men Talking: Collusion, Cover-Up and Murder in Northern Ireland's Dirty War* (Random House, 2011)
Martin Dillon, *Political Murder in Northern Ireland* (Penguin, 1973)
———, *The Dirty War* (Arrow, 1990)
———, *The Shankill Butchers* (Arrow, 1991)
———, *Killer in Clowntown* (Arrow, 1992)
———, *Stone Cold* (Hutchinson, 1992)
———, *25 Years of Terror* (Bantam, 1994)
———, *God and the Gun* (Routledge, 1999)
———, *The Trigger Men* (Mainstream, 2003)
Richard Doherty, *The Thin Green Line; History of the RUC* (Pen & Sword, 2004)

Aaron Edwards, *UVF: Behind the Mask* (Merrion Press, 2017)

Brian Feeney & Gerry Bradley, *Insider: Gerry Bradley's Life in the IRA* (O'Brien, 2009)
Kevin Fulton, *Unsung Hero*, John Blake Books, 2006)

Tony Geraghty, *The Irish War* (Harper Collins, 1998)
Raymond Gilmour, *Dead Ground: Infiltrating the IRA* (Little, Brown)

Desmond Hamill, *Pig in the Middle* (Methuen, 1985)
Toby Harnden, *Bandit Country* (Hodder & Stoughton, 1999)
Jack Holland & Susan Phoenix, *Phoenix: Policing The Shadows* (Hodder & Stoughton, 1996)

Michael A. Innes, *Making Sense of Proxy Wars* (Angus & Robertson, 2012)

Hugh Jordan, *Milestones in Murder* (Mainstream, 2002)

George Larmour, *They Killed the Ice Cream Man* (Colourpoint, 2016)
Richard Latham, *Deadly Beat* (Mainstream, 2001)
David Leslie, *Lighting Candles* (Black & White Publishing, 2014)
David Lister and Hugh Jordan, *Mad Dog* (Mainstream Publishing, 2004)

Denzil McDaniel, *Enniskillen: The Remembrance Day Bombing* (Wolfhound Press, 1997)
Henry McDonald and Jim Cusack, *UDA: Inside the Heart of Loyalist Terror* (Penguin, Ireland, 2004)
Henry McDonald & Jack Holland, *INLA: Deadly Divisions* (Poolbeg, 2010)
Marty McGartland, *Fifty Dead Men Walking* (John Blake, 2009)
David McKittrick et al., *Lost Lives* (Mainstream, 1999)
Ed Moloney, *Voices from the Grave* (Faber & Faber, 2010)
Kevin Myers, *Watching the Door: Cheating Death in 70s Belfast* (Atlantic, 2008)

Sean O'Callaghan, *The Informer* (Corgi, 1999)

John Parker, *Secret Hero* (John Blake, 2004)
Phoenix Project, *Stories of Sacrifice* (2015)
John Potter, *A Testimony to Courage* (Pen & Sword, 2001)

Andrew Sanders, *Inside the IRA* (Edinburgh UP, 2011)
Andrew Sanders & Ian S. Wood, *Times of Troubles* (Edinburgh UP, 2012)
South East Fermanagh Foundation, *I'll Never Forget* (SEFF, 2011)
——, *For God and Ulster* (SEFF, 2015)
Alan Simpson *Murder Madness* (GM Books, 1997)
Michael Stone, *None Shall Divide Us* (John Blake, 2003)

Peter Taylor, *Provos: The IRA & Sinn Féin* (Bloomsbury, 1997)
——, *Loyalists* (Bloomsbury, 1999)

Mark Urban, *Big Boys' Rules* (Faber & Faber, 1993)

Nick Van der Bilj, *Operation Banner* (Pen & Sword, 2009)

Andrew Walsh, *From Hope to Hatred* (History Press, 2013)

Ken Wharton, *A Long Long War: Voices from the British Army in Northern Ireland, 1969–98* (Helion Books, 2008)

———, *Bullets, Bombs and Cups of Tea: Further Voices of the British Army in Northern Ireland* (Helion Books, 2009)

———, *Bloody Belfast: An Oral History of the British Army's War against the IRA* (History Press, 2010)

———, *'Sir, They're Taking The Kids Indoors'* (Helion Books, 2011)

———, *The Bloodiest Year: Northern Ireland 1972* (History Press, 2011)

———, *Wasted Years, Wasted Lives*, Vol. 1 (Helion Books 2013)

———, *Wasted Years, Wasted Lives*, Vol. II (Helion Books 2014)

———, *An Agony Continued: Northern Ireland 1980–83* (Helion Books, 2015)

———, *Another Bloody Chapter in an Endless Civil War*: Volume 1: *Northern Ireland and the Troubles 1984–87* (Helion Books, 2016)

———, *Another Bloody Chapter in an Endless Civil War*: Volume 2: *Northern Ireland and the Troubles 1988–90* (Helion Books, 2017)

Paul Williams, *Badfellas* (Penguin, 2011)

Barbara N. Wilson, *A Quiet Courage; UDR Greenfinch* (Shanway Press, 2011)

Ian S. Wood, *Crimes of Loyalty*, Edinburgh UP (2006)

Index

Adair, Johnnie ('Mad Dog) 24–25, 56, 101, 114, 119, 122, 126, 144–145, 147, 159, 167–168, 198, 200, 212, 222–224, 244, 248, 252–253, 261, 263, 281, 284, 289, 292, 302–303, 306, 308, 314, 316, 318, 330, 333–335

Adams, Gerry 21–22, 24–26, 33, 85–86, 88, 94, 107, 133, 135, 138, 147, 150, 153, 162, 167, 190, 210, 216, 219, 221–222, 239, 250, 255, 258, 261, 263–264, 269–271, 274, 292, 295, 297, 301–303, 305, 308, 311, 313–315, 317, 319, 321, 325–326, 328, 333, 337

Altnagelvin Hospital, Londonderry 71, 135, 221, 278, 323

An Phoblacht 23, 29, 48, 52, 66, 77, 83, 93, 96–97, 115–116, 157, 181, 196–197, 232, 259, 261, 337

Andersonstown 23, 29, 56, 69, 82, 91, 102–103, 106, 127, 223–224, 229, 245, 263, 266, 293, 303

Andersonstown Cleansing Depot 310, 318

Anglo-Irish Agreement (AIA) 22, 25, 40–41, 68, 235, 242

Anglo-Irish Intergovernmental Conference (AIIC) 75, 277, 316

Ardboe 47

Ardoyne 24, 50, 72, 101, 158, 186, 193–194, 212, 222, 224, 232, 238, 243–244, 247, 263, 273, 289–290, 306–307, 313–315, 319

Armagh (*see also* Co. Armagh) 22, 34, 36–39, 43–44, 53, 61–64, 78, 84, 87–91, 94, 115, 119, 123, 125, 155, 157, 160–161, 166, 171–172, 183, 192, 195, 199, 204, 215–216, 220, 223, 237–238, 240–241, 243, 245–246, 254–255, 259–260, 265, 272, 274, 282, 285, 291, 297–298, 320, 326–328, 330, 338–339

Army Dog Handler's Unit (ADU) 59, 319

Ashdown, Paddy, MP, Liberal Democrats 31, 132, 148

Associated Press 47, 76, 126, 146, 183, 190, 274, 288, 296

Baker, Kenneth, Home Secretary 31, 41, 172, 251

Ball, Jonathan 249–250, 259

Ballymurphy estate 72, 103, 200, 216, 224, 238

Baltic Exchange bombing 163–164, 170, 172, 179, 211, 259

Beechmounts, Belfast 52, 85, 142, 189–190

Begley, Thomas, PIRA 224, 244, 312–313, 319

Belfast City Council 21, 40, 89, 90, 228, 263, 285, 291, 316–317

Belfast Sunday World 58

Belfast Telegraph 84, 136, 142, 148, 160, 171, 173, 181, 193–194, 196, 199, 202, 248, 305, 307, 313, 317, 328

Bessbrook Mill 87, 180, 216, 243

'Birmingham Six' 41

'Black, Captain' 38, 198, 231

Blair, Joseph 'Mooch', PIRA 134, 159–160

Bogside 13, 42, 72–3, 198, 227, 234, 236

Bratty, Joe 'Chinky' (UFF) 210, 230

Brixton, HMP 74–75

Brooke, Peter (NIO) 22, 25–26, 41, 49, 74, 96, 100, 109, 122, 138, 151, 165

Brooke/Mayhew Talks 41, 54, 74–75

Cappagh, Co. Tyrone 38–40, 81, 233
Castlederg 48, 84 , 87, 142, 236, 270, 283–284, 304
Castlerock 55, 189, 252–253
Churchill-Coleman, Commander Anti-Terror Police 32, 156, 205
Clinton, William, US President 162, 210, 240, 258, 264, 287, 293
Coagh 46–47, 65–66, 145, 151
Combined Loyalist Military Command (CLMC) 49, 52, 58, 74, 85, 116, 265
Cookstown, Co. Tyrone 46, 55, 60, 65, 81, 97, 134, 136–137, 139, 181, 188, 234, 236, 245, 267, 278, 302, 329
Copeland, Eddie 'Bubbles', PIRA 238, 243–244, 306, 319, 320
Corbyn, Jeremy, MP 296
Corner, David 30–2
Craigavon, Co. Armagh 37, 43–44, 67, 115, 123, 160, 215–216, 272
Creggan Estate 67, 72, 119, 213–214, 241, 255, 300, 337
Crossmaglen 33, 87, 92, 119, 183, 195–196, 213, 220, 240, 248, 254–255, 272, 278, 280–282, 297, 338–339
Crumlin Road, Belfast 34, 56–57, 66, 78, 89, 96, 101, 115, 117–118, 134, 177, 179, 188, 218, 222, 232, 285, 291, 314, 340
Cullaville, South Armagh 259
Cullyhanna, Co. Armagh 92, 119, 255, 272, 278, 281, 338

Daily Express 28, 32–33, 135, 148, 153, 171, 310, 319, 323
Daily Mirror 108, 211
Deal Barracks, Kent 21
Dernagh, SAS ambush 151, 154, 159, 175, 189
Derrybeg Estate 287, 324
'Dial a Catholic' 102, 317
Divis Street, Belfast 59, 78, 86, 100, 125, 185, 191, 194, 200, 236
Doherty, Anthony, PIRA 72, 81
Doherty, Joe, PIRA 134
Doris, Tony, PIRA 65–66, 151, 153
Downing Street 26–9, 132, 179, 207, 258, 295, 337
Downing Street Declaration 332, 337
Downpatrick, Co. Down 47, 51
Drumbeg estate, Craigavon 43
Dublin 25–27, 29, 34–35, 61, 75, 77–78, 114, 116–117, 122, 124, 134, 143, 154, 166, 170, 174, 188, 218, 221, 229, 250, 254, 257, 264, 274–277, 287, 292, 294, 301–302, 335
Duffy, Eileen 43–4
Dundalk, Ireland 52, 76, 79, 83, 170, 304
Dungannon 66, 135, 143, 145–146, 158, 174, 199, 204, 227–229, 247, 304

Elder, Raymond, UFF 102–103, 147, 210, 289
Ellis, Desmond 'Dessie', PIRA 34, 104
'England team' 25, 27, 32, 71, 75, 81, 116, 121–122, 143, 145, 154–155, 163–164, 172, 178, 186, 195, 198, 200, 204, 207, 211, 218, 221, 218, 233–235, 255, 259, 264, 283, 286, 289, 295, 300, 316, 335
Enniskillen 24, 29, 55, 76, 134, 173, 199, 213, 237, 257–258, 325

Falls Road 40, 50, 82, 85, 96, 100, 114, 125–126, 142, 146, 185, 189–191, 194, 209, 206, 236, 270, 292, 298, 301, 310, 315, 328
Fitzgerald, Garrett 26
Fivemiletown 22–23, 173, 334
Foley, Tom, US politician 90
Forkhill, Co. Armagh 170, 248, 294
Forrest, Ruth 55, 136, 141
'Four Horsemen' 270
Friel, Laura, *An Phoblacht* 48, 66, 93–94, 196
Frizzell's 224–225, 244, 395–307, 309, 313–314, 316–317, 319–321, 339
Fulton, Kevin 37, 159–160

Gaelic Athletic Association (GAA) 43, 100, 191, 194, 227–228, 230, 317
Galvin, Martin, NORAID 141
Garda Síochána 26, 29, 48, 76, 157, 170, 184, 274
Gillespie, Sergeant Stephen 52, 53
Gilmour, Raymond 51, 208
Glasdrumman, Co. Armagh 246–247
Glenanne 61–62, 65,
Glenanne Gang 116, 320
Gobnascale, Londonderry 72, 224
Good Friday Agreement (GFA) 58, 72, 78, 177, 233, 248, 270–271, 278, 284, 319, 323–324
Goodman, Police Constable Glenn 176–178
Gortmullan PVCP 49
Graham, John 'Bunter', UVF 100
Greysteel 134, 189, 225, 252–253, 300, 305, 321–323, 326, 339
Grosvenor Road, Belfast 52–3, 125, 185, 187, 193, 247, 252
Guardian newspaper 266, 277, 320

Hanisch, Sue 30–1
Hanna, John 91
Hanna, Philomena 114, 167–168
Harte, Gerard, PIRA 74
Haughey, Charles 31, 122, 143, 150
Headquarters Mobile Support Unit (HMSU) 97, 216
Headquarters Northern Ireland (HQNI) 59, 88, 173, 190, 236, 295
Holland, Paul 60, 191
Hughes , Sean 'The Surgeon' 157
Hume, John, MP, SDLP 22, 201, 231, 255, 258, 261, 270, 295, 301, 308, 325, 329, 337

Independent newspaper 98, 116, 205–206, 221, 223, 235, 251, 257, 262, 282, 286, 326, 327
Irish National Liberation Army (INLA) 47, 49, 65, 72–73, 77, 86, 119, 124–125, 129, 131, 150, 165–166, 188, 190–191, 203, 208, 216, 221, 230–231, 240, 245, 264, 269, 271, 289, 292, 340
Irish Peoples' Liberation Organisation (IPLO) 49, 77, 80, 86–7, 101–2, 125–7, 152, 157, 162, 171–3, 175, 190–1, 193–4, 197, 203, 207, 211–212, 269, 276, 292, 294, 346
Irish Republican Socialist Party (IRSP) 86, 190
Irish Times 77, 83, 228, 274, 297, 329, 334

Jackson, Robin 'the Jackal' 22, 43, 67, 116, 161, 199, 227, 234, 276

Karl Construction 134–136, 140
Kelly, Sean, PIRA 244, 306, 309, 313
Kennedy, Senator Edward 240, 270
Kinawley, Co. Fermanagh 76, 176, 228
King, Tom, Secretary of State 120
Kinnock, Neil 31, 132, 141, 144
Knight, Torrens, UVF 252, 322–323

Lamont, Norman, MP 27, 176
Light Infantry 59, 180, 184, 195, 220
Lisbellaw, Co. Fermanagh 55
Lisburn 42, 48, 58–60, 67, 80, 88, 95, 110, 127, 132, 143, 179–180, 203, 276, 281, 295, 298, 300–302, 306, 318
Lisburn Road, Belfast 60, 127, 203, 298, 318
Los Angeles Times 45, 108, 118, 155
Loughgall 38, 151, 238–240
'Loyalist Retaliation and Defence Group' 24, 83
Lurgan 22, 44, 115, 141, 158, 161, 172, 183, 201, 247, 272, 274
Lynch, Kevin, PIRA 57
Lynch, Paul, PIRA 69

Magee, Paul, PIRA 176–177, 182
Magherafelt, Co. Londonderry 26, 251, 266–267
Major, John, Prime Minister 22, 26–27, 37, 40, 54, 88, 122, 132, 135, 139, 141, 144, 151, 158, 162, 165, 201, 231, 240, 258, 261, 264, 270–271, 277–278, 293, 301,

305, 312, 321, 323, 328–330, 335, 337
Mallon, Seamus, MP 184, 241
Manchester 46, 83, 107, 110, 122–123, 172, 218–220, 227
Marks, Colum, PIRA 47–48, 51
Mater Hospital 57, 158, 189, 212, 218, 224, 284–285, 307, 313, 315, 333, 335
Mathers, Joanne 51
Mayhew, Patrick 41, 54, 165, 186, 189, 202, 222, 229, 243, 245, 255, 258, 264, 298, 328, 330
Maze, HMP 73, 104, 149, 201, 208
McCrea, Rev. William, MP 42, 46–47, 140
McCurtain, Coireall 21
McFerran, Stephen 'Inch' 50, 102, 119, 126, 210–211, 230
McGartland, Martin 'Marty' 69–70, 82, 214
McGinnis, Ken, MP 139
McGuinness, Martin 33, 51, 67, 72, 107, 133, 135, 138, 153, 162, 210, 214, 219, 250, 253, 300, 306, 315, 330, 331–333
McKeag, Stephen 'Top Gun' 24, 90, 101, 119, 167, 212, 252, 263, 273, 284, 289, 292–293, 303
McNally, Lawrence, PIRA 47, 65–66
Melrose, Steven 74
Morrison, Danny, PIRA/Sinn Féin 54, 94, 250, 315
'Murder Triangle', Co. Armagh 160, 320
Murphy, 'Slab' 94
Musgrave Park Hospital (MPH) 82, 106, 108–111, 127, 152, 245, 279, 293

Needham, Richard (NIO) 21, 25, 108
Negligent Discharge (ND) 80, 94–95, 191–193, 197
New Barnsley, Belfast 72, 167, 179, 229, 236, 238
New Lodge 68, 101, 132, 172, 188, 197, 201, 218, 224, 261–262, 281, 284–285, 303, 326
Newry 37, 43, 47, 64, 88, 96, 159, 170–171, 241, 249, 272–273, 278, 281–282, 287–288, 297, 324–325, 338
Newtownards Road, Belfast 103, 132, 142, 166, 172, 186, 198, 201, 205, 265, 274, 291, 294, 303, 330
'Night of the long knives' 172, 204, 208, 271
NORAID 34, 90, 111, 141, 195, 261, 264
North Howard Street Mill (NHSM) 59, 187, 311
Northern Ireland Office (NIO) 22, 25–26, 49, 78, 96, 108, 122, 165, 174, 186, 202, 259, 267, 271, 277, 288–289, 295, 304, 327
'Nutting squad' 54, 65–66, 70, 72, 77, 80, 82, 133, 161, 182–183, 188, 205, 210, 213–214, 235–236, 243, 254, 269–270, 316

O'Hara, Gerard 'Soggy' 202
O'Hara, John Joseph Gerard 50
Omagh, Co. Tyrone 111–113, 123, 134, 136–137, 139–140, 160, 188, 232, 236, 254, 278, 302, 307
Ormeau Road, Belfast 102–103, 119, 147–149, 186, 200, 202, 210, 230, 266, 288
Osnabrück, West Germany 74, 286

'Pan-Nationalist front' 230, 246, 288
Parry, Tim 250, 252, 259
Philadelphia Enquirer 39, 261
Protestant Action Force 44
Proxy bombs 26, 86, 91, 112, 171, 179

Queens' University, Belfast 60, 145, 147, 207, 271, 328

Radio Telefis Éireann (RTE) 254
Rathcoole, Belfast 33–34, 55, 248
Rathfern, Belfast 55
Red Hand Commando 49, 82, 91, 184, 205, 227, 244, 267, 288, 291–292, 294, 302, 348
Republican Socialist Collective 86, 124, 190
Reynolds, Albert 143, 150, 201, 236, 255, 258, 270, 292, 301–303, 321, 325, 330, 337
Rising Sun pub 225, 305, 321, 323

Robinson, Mary, President of the Irish Republic 21, 147, 199, 267, 271, 291
Rosslea 23–24, 33, 55, 101, 159, 233
Royal Artillery 24, 74, 111, 158, 164, 184–185, 190, 192, 294, 298, 326, 328, 332, 340
Royal Green Jackets 19, 86–88, 92, 94, 111–112, 123, 184–185, 189, 208, 239, 286
Royal Irish Rangers (RIR) 184
Royal Military Police (RMP) 94–95
Royal Regiment of Fusiliers (RRF) 59, 171
Royal Victoria Hospital (RVH) 36, 52, 59, 71, 82, 113, 125, 133, 135, 186, 247, 249, 252, 273
Royal Welch Fusiliers 258, 337
Ryan, Michael Peter, PIRA 65–66

Sandy Row, Belfast 203, 207, 267
Sangster, Michael 164
Scappaticci, Freddie 'Stakeknife' 54, 66, 77, 183, 270
Scots Guards 188, 197
SDLP 22, 41, 99, 162, 172, 189, 201, 228, 230–231, 235, 255, 258, 261, 265, 270, 295, 297, 317, 325, 329, 339
Sean Graham's Bookmakers 102, 144, 147–148, 186, 200, 201, 212, 262
Shankill 24, 40, 50, 55–56, 59, 78, 83, 86, 89–90, 92, 100–101, 126–127, 155, 158, 166–168, 185, 187, 191, 212–213, 224–225, 230, 243–244, 249, 253, 261–262, 267, 276, 281, 284–285, 289, 292, 302, 305–320, 324, 333–335, 340
Short Strand, Belfast 49–50, 209, 247, 265, 291, 316
'shoot-to-kill' 47–48, 65–66, 152
Silverbridge, Co. Armagh 34
Sinn Féin 21–22, 26, 29, 35, 49, 54, 58–59, 66–67, 72, 75, 78, 81–83, 85, 88–90, 93, 97, 107, 114, 116–117, 125–126, 131, 138, 141, 144, 146–148, 150, 152–154, 161, 162, 167–168, 181, 187, 190, 196, 201, 204, 207, 214, 216, 222, 228, 230, 235, 238–239, 248, 250–252, 254–255, 263–265, 271, 274–276, 281–282, 284–285, 287–289, 292, 296–297, 302, 313, 319, 321, 325, 327–328, 330, 332, 336–337, 339
Smith, John, Labour leader 247, 273, 278
Spanos, Nick 74
Spring, Dick, Irish Deputy Prime Minister 229, 241, 243, 258, 277, 301, 325
Springfield Road, Belfast 53, 59, 72, 85, 125, 167, 191, 247, 249, 264, 273, 338
Strabane 29, 84, 239, 274, 287, 304

Tadcaster 176–178
Taoiseach 26, 31, 88, 122, 143, 150, 201, 236, 255, 270, 301, 325
Teebane 129, 131, 134, 136, 138–141, 143–144, 147–149, 162, 181, 249, 253, 302
Thatcher, Margaret 21, 40, 78, 122, 144, 162, 176, 294, 340
The Times newspaper 160, 230
Turf Lodge 54, 105103, 224, 236, 298
Twinbrook, Belfast 8382, 253, 281

Ulster Defence Regiment (UDR) 19, 22, 24, 26, 29, 36–37, 39, 43, 47–48, 53–57, 60–61, 64–66, 68–69, 78–81, 83–84, 89, 91, 94, 97, 99, 106, 111, 113, 115, 119, 124, 131, 141–142, 144, 150, 157–158, 161, 165, 167, 173, 179, 184–187, 189, 194, 196, 207, 215, 225, 239–240, 243, 245, 247, 255, 261–262, 267–268, 272–273, 275, 283, 300, 304, 322, 328, 332, 340
Ulster Freedom Fighters (UFF) 24–25, 27, 41–42, 48–50, 58–59, 71–72, 83, 85–86, 89–91, 93–94, 96, 100, 102–105, 111, 114, 118–120, 122, 124, 126–128, 132–134, 142–145, 147–149, 155, 15–159, 161, 166–168, 184, 196, 189, 196, 100–203, 205, 210, 212, 221–224, 227, 230–232, 235, 244–246, 248–249, 251–253, 257, 261, 263–264, 267, 269, 273, 281, 284, 289, 292–293, 297, 300–302, 304–306, 308, 311, 316–323, 330, 332–333, 335, 340
Ulster Volunteer Force (UVF) 21–22, 33–34,

36, 38–40, 42–46, 48–51, 57, 66–67, 72, 78, 81–84, 86, 89–92, 100–101, 103–105, 113–116, 118, 120, 123, 131, 134, 142, 145, 148, 154–155, 157–158, 160–161, 168–169, 184, 187, 189, 193–194, 198–199, 201, 207, 215, 222, 227, 229–232, 234–235, 238, 245–246, 251, 261, 264, 267, 271, 273–277, 284–285, 291–300, 302–303, 305, 311, 317, 320–321, 329, 333, 339–340
Ulster Young Militants 41–42

Victoria Station 26, 30–2, 155, 238

Ward, Harry, Loyalist 100–101
Ward, Judith 83
Ward, Sammy, IPLO 209
Ware, Darren 87–88
Ware, 87–88
Warrington 235, 241, 243, 249–251, 257–259
Whiterock, Belfast 91, 103, 142, 167, 179, 200, 224, 236
Wilko, Linzi 60
Winstanley, Phil, RAMC 107, 109
Woodbourne, Belfast 229, 241, 247
Woodvale, Belfast 39, 50, 238, 273

'Yellow Brick Road' (Lanark Way, Belfast) 167–168, 249, 273, 292